KNIVES
2016

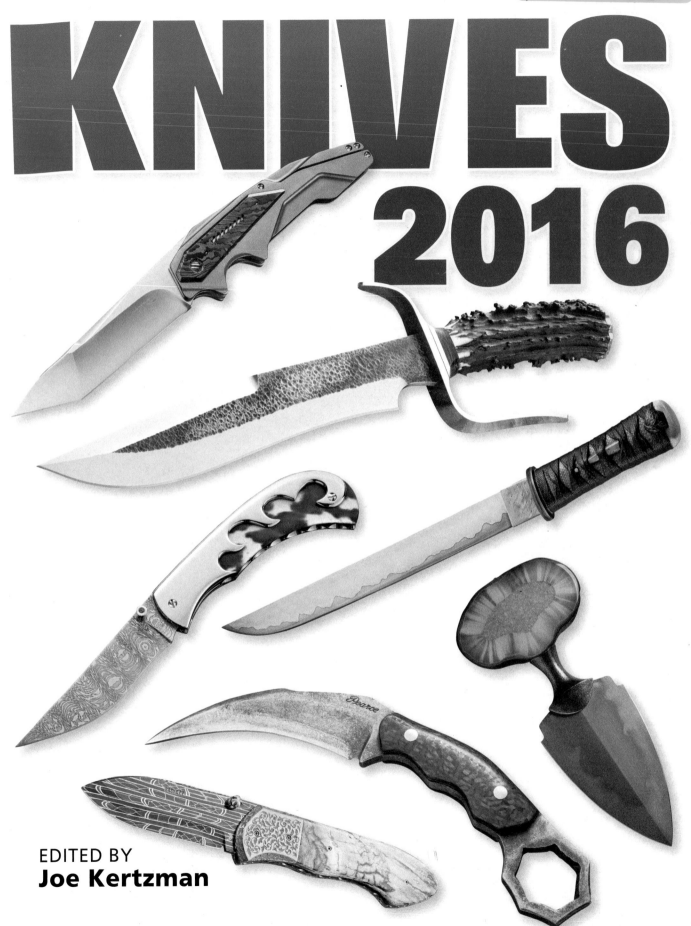

EDITED BY
Joe Kertzman

Published by

Krause Publications a division of F+W Media, Inc.
700 East State Street • Iola, WI 54990-0001
715-445-2214 • 888-457-2873
www.krausebooks.com

To order books or other products call toll-free 1-800-258-0929
or visit us online at www.shopblade.com

ISSN: 0277-0725
ISBN-13: 978-1-4402-4442-1
ISBN-10: 1-4402-4442-1

Design by Dane Royer
Edited by Corrina Peterson

Printed in the United States of America

10 9 8 7 6 5 4 3 2 1

Dedication and Acknowledgments

The knife industry is much like a grass-roots movement in that individuals at all levels, but particularly those who buy, make, collect, use and preserve basic cutting tools, keep the industry, and thus the movement, alive. Knifemakers fashion edged objects one at a time or in small batches, and then take them to gun or knife shows, post pictures of them on the Internet, send out eNewsletters, create websites and package the knives, sending them to dealers who promote them, all in an attempt to reach an end user or collector. Small clubs and organizations of like-minded people with common interests form to promote the craft. Often the associations are formed by people who collect or make knives, use knives on a daily basis, want to learn more about knives, wish to meet fellow collectors or makers, promote knives or trade knives. It is the basic level of organizing for a common interest.

The "State/Regional Associations" Directory section in the back of the book lists these organizations: the Arizona Knife collectors Association; Australian Knifemakers Guild Inc.; California Knifemakers Association; Canadian Knifemakers Guild; Finnish Knifemaker's Guidl; Florida Knifemaker's Association; Georgia Custom Knifemakers' Guild; Kansas Custom Knifemakers Association; Knife Group Association of Oklahoma; Knifemakers' Guild of Southern Africa; Montana Knifemaker's Association; New England Bladesmiths Guild; North Carolina Custom Knifemakers' Guild; Ohio Knifemakers Association; Saskatchewan Knifemakers Guild; and the South Carolina Association Of Knifemakers. I'd like to acknowledge and dedicate the *KNIVES 2016* book to the members of each association, recognizing their efforts in joining together with other people who view knives favorably and wish to share their love of edged utilitarian art with their peers.

A typical mission statement for such an association reads similar to that of the Arizona Knife Collectors Association, which is, "Act as a business league; promote education/public awareness in use, handling and safety of edged implements; to assist in development of information regarding every aspect of knives; coordinator and sponsor of trade shows." The Montana Knifemakers Association, which formed 1994, is a "non-profit educational organization created to further the art of knifemaking through seminars at the annual knife show in Missoula, Mont., hammer-ins and sponsored two-day, one-on-one learning experiences with other members." Its website notes, "Recently, organization members have been involved in teaching knifemaking to high school seniors working on their senior projects."

Many people in the knife industry are familiar with other, larger organizations, such as The Knifemakers' Guild, the American Bladesmith Society and the Porfessional Knifemaker's Association, a powerhouse trio of knifemaker's guilds that aim to preserve the art of knifemaking for generations to come. Whether large, well-known organizations or small, regional groups, each of the associations has similar goals and aspirations, and every one of them furthers and promotes knifemaking, knife collecting and responsible knife use. They are there to teach, learn, share knowledge and exchange ideas, all of which is good for the knife industry. It is my pleasure to recognize their efforts.

As Editor of the *KNIVES* book, it's been my pleasure to work with some of the most talented books acquisitions editors (Corrina Peterson), magazine editors (Steve Shackleford) and publishers (Jim Schlender). On a more personal level, I often feel like the luckiest man alive, married to my wife of 20 years (Tricia) who becomes more beautiful the older she gets, and having two smart, good-looking and nice kids (Danny and Cora) of whom I'm so, so proud. I also have a tight family, one who made every attempt to raise me right and keep me in line. Thanks, Mom, Dad, Pete, Chris, Pat and Tim. I love you all and dedicate this book to you.

Joe Kertzman

Contents

On The Cover

The styles of knives may vary, but the workmanship is ultimately rewarding on each and every one of the four edged examples that grace the front cover of *KNIVES 2016*. Standing at attention on the far left is a Kevin Casey hunter sashaying a 6-inch, feather-pattern damascus blade the maker forged himself, including a full, extended tang, as well as a blackwood handle and some creative Konstantin Pushkarev silver wire, mother-of-pearl and ruby inlays that further enliven the piece. Only partially folded to its immediate right is a pearl-handle William Tuch beauty that definitely does not disappoint. It displays engraved and 24k-gold-inlaid bolsters in a dragon motif from the masterful hand of Rick Simmons, as well as a 3 1/8-inch 440C stainless steel blade and a 416 stainless handle frame. And how about the flipper folder below it? A Brian Nadeau flipper, it features a 3D-machine-textured, blue- and gold-anodized 6AL-4V-titanium handle frame, and a 4-inch "aspirated" CPM S35VN blade. Finally, it's on to the big boy. Tilted slightly toward its edge at far right is a Peter Mason fighting knife, not that you'd ever use the gorgeous piece for such, parading a blued and sculpted damascus blade, a spalted maple handle and hand-carved bronze fittings, including a creatively stippled double guard and stippled pommel nut. Thank you, makers and knife embellishers, for sharing your work with the *KNIVES* readers, and particularly this duly impressed book editor. (Cover photo by Kris Kandler)

Introduction

So much in life relates to knife. Living on the edge means taking risks, thinking outside the box, putting yourself out there, living precariously or dangerously, basically enjoying life to its fullest. So let's think about that. A guy comes home from work, and says, "Honey, I'm quitting my job and going into knifemaking full time, no health care or benefits, no 401K, paid vacations or holidays. I'm going it on my own, making a living with my own hands, building bladed objects, marketing them and selling my wares. I'm taking pictures of the finished knives, uploading them onto the Internet and traveling to knife shows. I'll buy materials, build and purchase machinery, toil in the shop and ship the knives out. And with the profits, we'll pay the bills, buy groceries, make the house payment and send the kids to college."

Now that's living on the edge!

And how about keeping your nose to the grindstone? It doesn't sound like that knifemaker will have a lot of free time for golf, lying on the beach, playing poker or going to the theater. In order to succeed as a craftsman, one works all hours of the day and night, suffers over profits and losses, accounts payable, income and debts due. The work can seem overwhelming, and the payback negligible. Until one sees the glimmer in the eye of a customer who just purchased a handmade knife, then the fruits of one's labor are worthwhile.

Could you cut it? There's something about knifemaking that's ultimately alluring to a certain few, those who wish to combine handcraft, utility and art into useful objects—man's oldest tools—knives. Call it primitive, modern or a mixture of the two, there's a calling and it's strong enough to attract the 2,000-plus makers listed in the Custom Knifemaker Directory section, starting on page 193, of the *KNIVES 2016* book. In the Directory, makers list their specialties, patterns, technical information, remarks, prices and maker's marks, along with their names, addresses, phone numbers, email addresses and websites. Once collectors and knife enthusiasts see the gorgeous examples of the cutler's art in *KNIVES 2016*, many will look up a knifemaker, inquire as to the status of a particular blade or two, and possibly even have a nice chat, talk about the weather and life in general.

And what a slice of life it is. Not many folks fashion items for a living, as true craftsmen and women, as entrepreneurs and innovators. They have to innovate. Make no mistake about it, knives that look and work like those that came before don't cut it in this industry. Looking at the "Trends" section of *KNIVES 2016*, beginning on page 57, you'll become acutely aware that many of the flipper folders, push button automatics, frame-lock folders, and even hunters, daggers and bowies are modern renditions, with high-tech materials, mechanisms, textures, bevels, grinds and grooves. These aren't your daddy's pocketknives.

In the "State Of The Art" half of the book, in full living, breathing color, are art pieces and highly embellished works of art with "Sculpted Bods," "Slack-Jaw Scrimshaw" and "Filigree & Filework," as well as "Stacked and Secure" models featuring stacked handle material, those with "Golden Touches" and still more tagged "A Life Savings of Engravings." If silver wire inlays, carving, precious jewels and damascus are on your knife radar, then your appetite for all things sharp will be satisfied as you turn page after page, drinking up all that has been prepared for your own private viewing.

They've honed their skills. The knives are piercingly beautiful, sharp dressed and edgy. Not a stone was left unturned as knifemakers sought out natural and synthetic materials, pointed patterns, the latest gadgets, locks, pivots and propulsions. These puppies are honed and ready, so forge ahead, and keep a sharp eye out for what might just trip your trigger.

Joe Kertzman

2016 WOODEN SWORD AWARD

Quite a departure from the goblin folders featuring carved stag, bone or ivory goblin heads as the pommels of folding knives, these two beauties by American Bladesmith Society master smith Larry Fuegen take the genre to a whole new level. Fuegen's "Roman Centurion 'MAX'" friction folder (below), for example, showcases a carved fossil walrus ivory handle ending in the carved mammoth ivory face of a Roman infantryman, complete with walrus ivory eyes and wearing armor of Argentium sterling silver. The centurion's helmet is trimmed in 14-karat gold and topped with a brush-like plume or crest holder. The 6.25-inch multi-bar damascus blade was inspired by the Pugio daggers carried by Roman soldiers, and the tang is a carved eagle with a gold eye. In similar fashion, the "Cabeza de Vaca" folder (above, right) includes the face of a Spanish conquistador, with hematite eyes, no less, carved in mammoth ivory. Like the centurion, the conquistador also wears 14k-gold armor and a helmet trimmed in gold. The plume that adorns his helmet is 14-karat rose gold, and the accompanying handle is carved black buffalo horn with 14k-gold bolsters. The 5.5-inch ladder-pattern Damasteel damascus blade is creatively carved and sculpted, and all work on both knives is by the maker. You could call these sole-authorship pieces, and for that, the editor of the *KNIVES 2016* book waves his wooden sword, lavishing praise and the 2016 Wooden Sword Award upon Larry Fuegen for his incredible artistry. If I'd had a Roman gladius or Spanish belduque, I would have waved one of those.

Joe Kertzman

Buy What You Like... That You Can Afford

Understand the market so you can buy custom knives as collectibles, investments or just for fun

By Les Robertson

buy what I like. This, of course, is the mantra of custom knife buyers around the world. In 1984, while serving as an infantry rifle platoon leader in the 101st Airborne, I bought my first custom knife. I bought "what I liked" with the caveat "that I could afford." What I wanted was the Sly II knife by Jimmy Lile. I ended up with a hollow-handle fighter by Robert Parrish, an excellent knife in its own right.

I bought my first custom knife to be used. The idea of the Robert Parrish knife being a collectible or an investment was not something I even considered. As many knife enthusiasts know, buying that first custom knife leads to a second custom knife. A fellow lieutenant and knife collector asked if I had ever been to the BLADE Show. After responding that I hadn't, plans started for our "assault" on Knoxville, Tenn., for the 1985 BLADE Show. Then, as now, it was three days of heaven for knife aficionados, and it was at that show that the hook was set deep. Over the next two years, as a collector, I bought, resold and traded over $10,000 worth of custom knives.

I was purchasing custom knives utilizing the mantra of buying what I liked and that I could afford. Part of the joy of buying any collectible is that spontaneous rush you feel when you purchase or trade for that object of desire. However, it did sting a little every time I sold one of my knives and lost money on it. Something had to change. I had to attain a better working knowledge of the custom knife market and aftermarket. I needed to do some homework.

In 1986 I went to the best source for information at the time—*KNIVES 1986*—the very edition of this book that was published 30 years ago. As it is today, the book was an invaluable resource, and utilizing

Winner of the Best Tactical Folder and Best New Maker Awards at the 2014 BLADE Show, Brian Nadeau fashions sleek, slim, light and strong knives like these "Typhoon" models in CPM S35VN blade steel and 3D-machined titanium frames. *(SharpByCoop image)*

the different Trends and State of the Art categories, as well as the numerous photos, helped me to focus my search. Using the Custom Knifemaker Directory, I was able to get in touch with those whose work I was interested in. Information was gathered as to what materials certain makers used, their delivery times and pricing. This allowed me to compare each knife to others in a particular category, gaining what I thought to be a substantial level of knowledge regarding the custom knives market. In September of that year I took the next step and became a custom knife dealer, and nine years later, in 1995, a full-time dealer.

In 1993, while working on my MBA, I was fortunate enough to be able to use my business model for many of my course assignments. It was during this time that I created my custom knifemaker matrix. Utilizing the Custom Knifemaker Directory in the back of *KNIVES '93*, each maker's name was entered into each category of knives they made. Then pricing for comparable knives was added to the matrix. What became obvious was that pricing was all over the map. To make some sense of this, I started with a base price, giving makers additional points for things such as awards, magazine articles written about them, magazine covers featuring their knives, delivery times, aftermarket prices, etc.

Coming as no surprise, the top makers of the day rose to the top of the list. However, each custom knife category had several hundred makers. My objective for this matrix was to show the position of each maker in a category based on my criteria. Let me stress this was my criteria, as was the bias that came along with it. The matrix showed me which knives were overpriced, priced correctly or under-priced. As you can imagine, this information would be invaluable to a fledgling custom knife dealer. This was some serious homework!

UNDERSTAND THE MARKET

The idea of custom knives as investments has generally been received with looks and comments of derision. I was a knife user and became a collector who embraced a mantra. As I paid for these knives, I invested a substantial amount of money into them. My introduction to the aftermarket was the investment of $10,000. No single person or group of people conspired to create the loss I encountered. The loss occurred because of my lack of understanding of the custom knife market. Perhaps the next few paragraphs can give you a better insight into the market that is custom knives.

Custom knives comprise two large market sectors—fixed blades and folders. These increase or decrease in size as smaller market sectors cycle within the larger market sectors. Prior to the Internet, a market sector could remain relatively unchanged for

The fit, finish and flow of Tim Steingass's "Presentation Bastion Dagger" belie his value pricing, while his ability to create a wide range of knives has enthusiasts continually looking at his work. *(SharpByCoop image)*

a decade or more. Today the cycles are there but the knives in the smaller market sectors move in and out of favor much quicker. Within those cycles are even smaller sectors. Those are the trends (see related section in this book) that can last anywhere from a couple months to a couple years. The matrix gave me insight into the pricing of custom knives, and, to be honest, with the choice between two knives of equal quality and materials from makers of equal skill and reputation, more often than not I bought the one that was less expensive.

The issue of buying what I liked nagged at me, as I knew from my own personal experience that it would cost me money in the long run. This made no sense to me before I created my matrix and even less sense to me after. Given there are thousands of knives available worldwide at any given time, why would you buy a knife for your collection knowing, if you went to sell it, you would lose money? Conversely, the question then has to be asked why a maker would price their knives knowing that they won't sell for that price.

In a business environment, pricing is not arbitrary. An example of a basic pricing formula would include such costs as materials and shop time + labor + business costs (marketing, printing, etc.) + profit = price. Other costs can be added or subtracted. After talking with hundreds of knifemakers, I found that few, if any, used a formula. More times than not, a fellow knifemaker helped them price their knives. From a maker's perspective, that can make sense. The consulting maker has been around for a few

▼ The author says John W. Smith's tactical folders, like this "F-5" locking-liner flipper folder in CPM S35VN blade steel, titanium and OD-green Micarta®, are some of the best bargains in the world. You read that correctly, he said "world." *(PointSeven image)*

▲ R.J. Martin is the standard by which other tactical folder makers are judged. His "Overkill" titanium-frame flipper folders have scary sharp CTS 204P blades and vault-like lockup. *(SharpByCoop image)*

years, makes a similar knife and has a feel for the market. For knifemakers reading this, take heed to the lesson in the next two paragraphs.

At the 1991 Knifemakers' Guild Show, I was standing at a well-known maker's table. A new maker approached him, asked him to look at one of the newer maker's knives and give him his opinion. The well-known maker looked the knife over and asked the new maker what he sold this for. The new maker replied $210. The well-known maker smiled and said, "You should be asking $325 for a knife this nice."

The new maker beamed, thanked the well-known maker and went back to his table. He promptly raised the price of his knife 55 percent based on nothing more than his fellow maker's suggestion. In a few minutes a customer approached the well-known maker's table and engaged him in a conversation about the $375 price tag on one of his knives. The potential customer indicated he felt the price was a little high. The well-known maker was quick to point out that his knives were a bargain at that price. Pointing down the row to the new maker he was just talking to, the well-known maker asked, "See that young man down there? He has only been making knives for two years, has a similar knife to the one in your hand on his table, and his price is $325."

To say I was stunned is putting it mildly. While, as a maker, you may not feel that your friend is your competitor, the fact is that he or she is, and you don't ask your competitors to price your knives. A custom knifemaker should know their position in any given market. If they don't, it is incumbent on the collector to know. This will keep you from overpaying for a knife.

VALUE = WHAT SOMEONE WILL PAY

The value of anything is determined by what someone will pay for it. This concept is exactly what can and often does skew the pricing for one maker or even an entire market. There are buyers for whom the retail price does not matter. They will spend what it takes to get the knife, and often the amount paid borders on the absurd. This is particularly true

One of ABS master smith Terry Vandeventer's knives, like the utility hunter in a ladder-pattern-damascus blade and sheep horn handle, would be a worthwhile addition to anyone's collection. *(Ward image)*

Jason Clark's knives offer the collector an extended variety of options and models. The folding bowie boasts a 3.75-inch CPM S35VN blade, a ladder-pattern-damascus bolster and lightning-strike carbon fiber handle scales.

(Ward image)

investing in custom knives at an entry level. It might be helpful to compare investing in custom knives to a certificate of deposit (CD) offered by banks. As of this writing, my bank was paying a .01 percent annual percentage yield for a $2,500 minimum opening deposit for six months. Should I cash in that CD after one year, I would receive $2,525.

Given the cost of a college education today, or a beach house, doing the basic math on the equation above shows us that investing in CDs is not the way to go, either. Applying the same .01 percent yield to a custom knife bought as an investment, if I bought a $500 knife and sold it for $505, I would get exactly the same return as I would on a six-month CD. My bank doesn't even have a six-month CD with a minimum deposit of $500. And I'm not taking into account knife shipping costs, nor am I deducting the capital gains tax on my $25 profit from the bank. Being an investor can take a little spontaneity out of knife buying/collecting.

Knife enthusiasts have no doubt been watching the upward climb of the tactical folder segment within the custom knife market. This segment seems to have no limits. Collectors are leaving other market sectors to get in on the easy money that can be made flipping tactical folders. The crowds at knife shows are so large, special areas have to be set aside for drawings for the folders, and the drawings are exciting. Potential buyers put their names in a box or hat to get the "chance" to buy a knife from a popular maker. As each name is called, there is a range of emotions from total joy to anguish.

But the custom knife market moves in cycles. In the mid 1980s, a new sector captured the collective imagination of the custom knife market. The knife was called the "inter-frame folder," and popularized by Ron Lake. It was basically a 440C blade, a frame of two stainless steel handle scales and generally a

on the bid-up knives that have become the "show within a show" at knife events around the world. As knifemakers find out who the indiscriminate knife buyers are, and what particular style of knife or which makers' knives they buy, the sellers seek them out. The "flips" (buying and selling for a profit immediately) begin, and the "bubble" (economic bubble) begins to form.

Investing in custom knives does not have to be about getting enough return on investment to pay for a child's college education or a beach house. For those who do invest, they probably understand that seldom, if ever, do they make enough from one knife to pay for college or a beach house. I would suggest

Pohan Leu's "Bluephin" model put him on the tactical folder map. This one is executed in CPM S35VN blade steel, a titanium frame and bolster, and lightning-strike carbon fiber scales. *(Ward image)*

lock-back mechanism. A maker milled a pocket into the outer face of the handle scale or scales and inlaid natural handle material, generally elephant ivory, abalone or pearl.

The knives were clean, unique, filled the hand with some heft, and collectors couldn't get enough of them. It wasn't long before the collectors wanted something a little different, so embellishments were offered—engraving, gold inlay and even gemstone inlays became available, all of which added to the delivery delay and increased the demand. Collectors, particularly those outside of the United States, paid ever-increasing aftermarket prices for inter-frame folders. As it happens in world economies, the inter-frame-folder economy suffered a significant downturn. The knives found their way back to U.S. deal-

ers, who in turn sold them again in the aftermarket, with the buyers unaware that the bubble had burst. This left the new owners with very expensive knives that would never return their initial investment. My recommendation is that you view the previous two paragraphs as a cautionary tale.

Whether you are a collector, investor or just buy an occasional custom knife, do your due diligence about where the market cycles are and which way they are moving. Understanding the maker's position in a particular market sector will subsequently indicate what their knives should be selling for. There is nothing that says the mantra can't be changed to "I buy what I like, but at a value price." Who knows, maybe doing a little homework could get you that beach house!

Filigree, Inlay & Piqué—Hot Knife Art Trio

More knifemakers, engravers and artisans practice piqué, metal inlay and filigree than ever before

By Mike Haskew

Fine art meets function when custom knifemakers and artists make bold statements using precious metals and timeless techniques—and the results are dazzling. Although gold and silver inlay, piqué and filigree have been in vogue since ancient times, today's artisans awaken these processes with skill and imagination, embellishing knives that never stray from their original intent—to cut.

Aspiring artists gravitate toward the classroom and the shop to learn. "There is a renewed and growing interest in the art of engraving," advised engraver Julie Warenski, whose body of work stretches back three decades. "There are more new and talented engravers than ever before. With several resources where one can go to learn engraving now, including the Internet to research and share techniques, it is easier to share information and skills, spurring more creativity in all engravers. The desire to learn and try new techniques helps keep you inspired."

Veteran custom knifemaker Jay Hendrickson learned his silver inlay skills from the legendary Bill Moran, and he believes the opportunities to acquire the technique are virtually unlimited. "When I teach bladesmithing, I stress to students

the importance of a well-designed handle," he explained. "I feel that silver wire inlay enhances the beauty of a handle more than any other decorative application. I have always felt that the handle sells the knife, providing everything else is done well."

Hendrickson advises aspiring knifemakers and engravers who are interested in learning more about silver inlay to check into American Bladesmith Society (ABS) hammer-ins where courses are regularly offered.

"Bill Moran taught me how," said Jay. "I should have a t-shirt with this printed on the front. Bill made all his hand tools, and I had an early opportunity to study them. He was a very close friend of mine and a mentor in all phases of bladesmithing. When I saw Bill doing his marvelous silver inlay work, I knew it was what I wanted to do."

Knifemaker Joe Keeslar transitioned into knives from handcrafted Kentucky rifles that he began to create in 1963 after a stint with the U.S. Marine Corps. Silver inlay is prominent on early American flintlock rifles, and naturally the embellishment found its way onto his knives. For Joe, the constant is excellence in the product. Forging, casting brass trigger guards and butt plates, making locks and triggers, wood carving, sculpting the stock, metallurgical techniques and silver wire inlay were just some of the many skills he learned on his own. The basics of this skill set transferred

Joe Keeslar's 50th-anniversary clip-point hunter features elaborate silver handle inlays, a carved handle spacer and pommel, and file work along the blade spine. *(SharpByCoop.com image)*

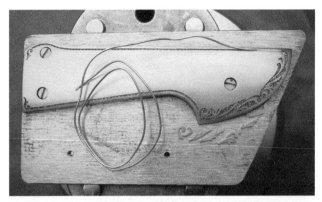

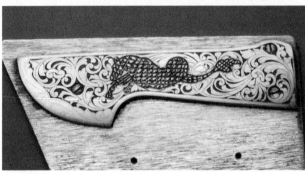

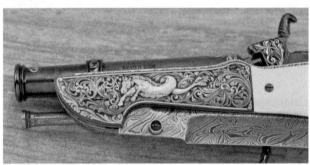

Three images depict how engraver Brian Hochstrat channel-sets gold wire, and the progression of his scrollwork, engraving and gold inlay of a stylized mustang. *(knifeology.com images)*

Joel Chamblin's two-blade "Regal" is aptly named for the maker's checkered piqué work, including 24k-gold pins, on black-lip mother-of-pearl handle scales. *(Chuck Ward image)*

collectors prefer knives that sport a minimum of embellishment. However, his perspective is sensory and analytical, envisioning and leaving an enhanced artistic expression.

"Not everyone likes gold on their knives," Brian noted, "or even engraving for that matter. However, the value it adds, for me as an artist, is that of image separation, color and the overall interest it lends to the engraving. *Bulino* [a method of engraving accomplished with small dots], for example, can be difficult to see in poor light, and by adding color I can create focal points and contrast to create work that visually has more boldness and clarity than that of engraving done all in the steel."

ARTIST TURNED CONSULTANT

Whether he is dealing with a collector or custom knifemaker, Brian utilizes a consultative approach to determine the style and level of engraving or other embellishment that will adorn a particular knife. Discussion is followed by a detailed plan, line drawings, even footnotes, and then an agreement to get started. Still, like a true artist, he says his work is finest when it is done without constraints.

"I do my best work on a loose rein," he laughed, "but I do like to hear ideas and opinions, and above all I want the customer to be happy with what I have done for them. My best work is achieved when I have room to create."

that will grasp and hold the precious metal in place.

Hochstrat got his start as an artisan in saddlery and transitioned into engraving full time in 2008. Saddlery often involves intricate ornamental leather carving, so his move into engraving, already having an understanding of ornamental design, was one of progression.

"I also took a class at the GRS Training Center (located in Emporia, Kansas) in the beginning," said Brian, "and then studied with master engraver Sam Alfano once I became more serious about engraving. After that, I had a solid foundation, and the rest of my skill development came from self study, experimentation and lots of application."

He admits that some custom knifemakers and

Julie Warenski engraved and filigreed a Warren Osborne folder, inlaying 24-karat gold and platinum, and creating a shadow effect. She also carved the white mother-of-pearl handle inlays.

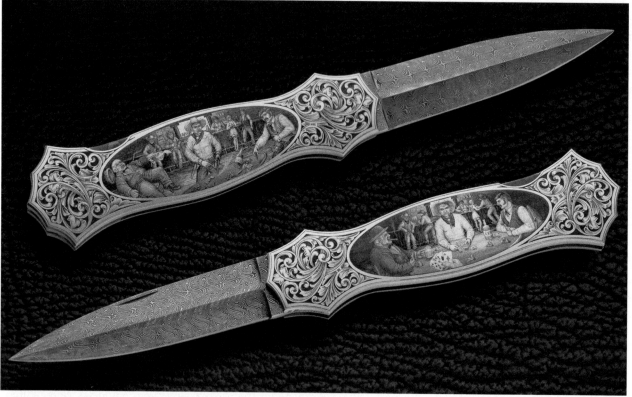

Brian Hochstrat's bulino-style engraving on a Joe Kious folder depicts cowboys playing poker and a subsequent bar fight. Gold scrollwork frames the etching. *(Prairie Digital image)*

The art of piqué is prominent on knives from the old Sheffield, England, production facilities of the 18th and 19th centuries, and examples of these antique knives often serve as inspiration for modern craftsmen. Richard Rogers has been making knives for 18 years, and from time to time, his piqué accents have brought luster to his pieces.

"I have done piqué on traditional folding knives," said Richard, "mainly inspired by old Sheffield fruit knives. It's pretty simple. You just lay out a pattern on the handle material, drill holes, and then glue in lengths of wire. Piqué has been done for a long, long time, mainly as a form of decoration."

While it sounds simple enough, there is definitely an art, an expertise, involved in the piqué process. Measurements must be precise. With any organic handle material, drilling is hazardous. Too much speed may generate excess heat and actually burn the material or cause chipping. Once the silver wire is in place, it must be secured with an adhesive or tapped with a ball peen hammer to a snug fit. The tolerances are tight.

"It is time consuming, and it takes a lot of planning ahead," offered knifemaker Joel Chamblin, whose piqué has often been done in conjunction with checkering on the handle of a Sheffield-style knife. "Still, it isn't rocket science. There isn't a whole lot to learn, but there is some technical challenge to it. When you drill the hole and insert a piece of silver or gold, you then decide how to shape the pins. I have done little gold pins at the top of my checkering, where it comes to a point, and tried to dome the pins a little. I have also done some piqué with the pins finished flat on a flat handle."

TIME INVESTMENT

According to Chamblin, finishing a knife with piqué can require the investment of several hours in the shop. He prefers gold and says that the key to the embellishment is to come up with a design either requested by the customer or that he favors on a planned knife.

"I get most of my ideas for piqué out of books, and I have quite a few of them with pictures of old English knives in them," said Joel. "If I am doing a design, say an oval shape with a bunch of pins, it takes a while to lay out that design and at least a couple of hours of time to work everything out."

Both a first glance and a good long look tell the observer that Warenski's filigree work is intricate, mesmerizing and second to none. Her beautiful main

A Jay Hendrickson Damascus bowie showcases a curly maple handle with silver inlay in a floral design, as well as scrollwork and scalloping. *(Nancy Hendrickson image)*

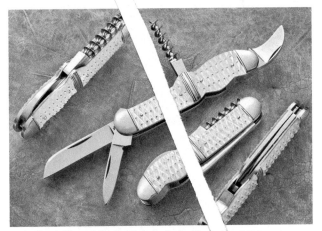

This Joel Chamblin bartender's knife features a checkered mother-of-pearl handle with pink-gold piqué. It sports three blades and a corkscrew.
(SharpByCoop.com image)

gauche, or left-handed dagger, is a tour de force in filigree, and she credits her late husband, knifemaking legend Buster Warenski, with being her inspiration.

"Filigree is the removal of metal to create piercing in the metal," commented Julie. "An example of filigree work is seen on the basket of the main gauche dagger. Filigree can be used on any type of metal where the design can be cut through. The techniques of filigree, inlay and overlay can be incorporated into an engraving and add tremendous adornment to any project."

This beautifully embellished 50th anniversary clip-point hunter by Joe Keeslar includes engraved bolsters and elaborate silver wire handle inlay with gold accents.

(SharpByCoop.com image)

On the main gauche dagger, Julie used a combination of 24-karat gold and platinum inlays with a sterling silver basket that is richly filigreed and sculpted. The blade is Rob Thomas stainless damascus, and the black jade handle is accented with 10-carat diamonds and rubies. Her philosophy is simple.

"Most customers allow me free rein on my engravings," she concluded. "They know they will get my best creativity without confinement and restraint. My goal on every project is always to enhance the beauty of the piece without overtaking the piece."

Since the mid-1980s, Julie has engraved all of Buster's knives and developed quite a following among other custom knifemakers, gaining their trust and handsomely embellishing their work. "I learned how to inlay precious metals and incorporate the inlays into my engravings," she remembered. "In time, I improved and developed my own techniques, as well as making my own tools to do inlay work. It is rare for me to do an engraving project anymore without using any inlay. I have found that at least a touch of gold enhances every project."

SOLE AUTHORSHIP

Although he has collaborated on a few knife projects for non-profit fundraisers and presentation pieces, Keeslar rarely embellishes the work of other knifemakers. He also prefers to maintain sole authorship of his guns and knives, and quickly adds that bad inlay work devalues a knife rather than enhancing it, while well-executed inlay brings out the beauty in the piece and the cost is well worth the investment.

Through it all, he never loses sight of the original purpose of the knife. "Whatever embellishment an artisan or craftsman adds to his or her work, that object must be functional," he asserted. "In the case of a knife, it must cut, hold an edge and do whatever it is supposed to do. Embellishment such as silver wire inlay should not be a substitute for a knife's designed use."

Keeslar draws his inspiration from a variety of sources. Sometimes, it is the client that requests something particular, or he might take a previous design and give it a few tweaks to create something new. Books on engraving and fine woodcarving abound, and as an artisan experiments and learns new techniques, the images of classic work in these books help to stimulate creativity.

"You are constantly looking for new ideas to keep your work fresh and interesting, and also to challenge yourself as a craftsman," Joe offered. "Each knife should surpass in design and reflect better workmanship than the one before. That is the challenge to any artisan whatever field of endeavor they are in."

One of the most gratifying aspects of Keeslar's work is the opportunity to teach others and to lead a new generation of knifemakers and engravers toward excellence. "For those of us who teach, it is a joy to see a student take an idea or technique that you have shown them, improve upon it and take it to a whole new level exceeding the process that you taught them," he smiled. "In the ABS, we take what skills we were taught by the masters who preceded us, hopefully to improve upon them and pass them on to the next generation. It is a very rewarding experience. Pass it on!"

Who Are These Sharp Little Runts?

They're short and sweet, but they've filled a big niche in the world of using knives

By Pat Covert

Runtdom is alive and well! Although there is no timeframe for when a trend becomes a genre, it's safe to say that runts—those short and stubby knives that look like they've been rear-ended by an 18-wheeler—have passed over the threshold. It's been well over six years since custom knifemaker Jim Burke basically defined the pattern with a short, stubby version of one of his full-size tactical folders and gave the genre its "Runt" namesake. Burke's compact yet burly Runt model was duly noted, and the train hasn't stopped since.

Why a runt, you ask? It's a legitimate question. Typically short, light, handy, fancy pocketknives and folders fall into the modern gent's knife category. Some are streamlined versions of larger siblings, and they mirror full-size knives in all regards except for length, weight, high-end materials and embellishments. Because runt knives are beefier than gent's fare, these knives can perform heavier tasks due to blades that can cut deeper, more ample handles that provide a full grip, hardcore materials and little embellishment. Think box cutters with shorter handles, and you get the idea.

For self-defense, short of a heavy blow to one's grip, it is difficult to dislodge a runt from the hand. Nothing protrudes from the grip but the blade, and an attacker wouldn't want to grab or hit that! Runts have the added benefit of being lighter than full-size knives, and some can be worn as neck knives.

Runts may best be described as small knives with

The Spyderco Techno folder exemplifies today's runt knives. The rugged, yet slick Marcin Slysz design has a titanium handle with a sturdy frame-lock mechanism.

The Al Mar SLB (Stout Little Backup), released in 2003, was an early progenitor of the runt-style knife wave that would hit a half a decade later.

an ornery attitude. They have a Napoleon complex, if you will, and owe their very existence to the tactical folder explosion of the past quarter century. As this huge movement gained steam and got more competitive, tactical knives morphed and evolved into other genres, such as fire, police and EMT rescue knives, gent's folders, pry knives and the beloved runt. But there is precedence for small, stubby knives well before the tactical market boom. Small skinners were part of the hunting knife scene long ago. These were, and still are, used for skinning small-to-medium-sized game.

The same goes for folding knives. Back in 2003, Al Mar Knives released a small, stubby folder given the name SLB, an acronym for Stout Little Backup, not a bad definition for the runt genre itself. The SLB, still in the Al Mar stable after a dozen years, is 4.6 inches fully open with a 1.7-inch AUS-8 blade. The knife has all the same traits as the company's larger models—a locking-liner mechanism, Micarta® handle scales and a pocket clip. It is simply a squeezed-down version of larger tactical folders.

A case can also be made for the Boker Plus SubCom, designed by Chad Los Banos and released in late 2005. This 4.5-inch (open) folder became an instant hit and has been one of the company's top sellers ever since. Many incarnations of the small wonder have been produced with variations in blade style and handle color, a rescue version with a webbing cutter in lieu of a blade and a top-of-the-line titanium model. Indeed, there are over a dozen iterations in the SubCom line. In essence, we could go back and find many runts in cutlery history, but they came into their own after Burke's Runt folder.

THE ROAD TO RUNTDOM

For runt knives, or any other knife style for that matter, to become a full-fledged genre requires mass production. This is no knock on custom knifemakers, but the number of handmade pieces compared to production models is minuscule. Runts needed a wide audience, and they got one.

Manufacturers go to great lengths in cost and risk putting a knife model on the market. Design, engineering and tooling are necessary before production ever begins. Then the cost of manufacture, which not only includes material and labor costs, but also administrative, sales and shipping overhead, must be factored in. In short (and runty), a manufacturer is not going to produce a knife unless it promises to be profitable. Runt knives had to cross this barrier before they could ever be considered a knife category.

Two factory knives that helped Runts gain credence and a toehold in the industry were the Benchmade 755 MPR (Mini Pocket Rocket) and Boker Pipsqueak. Both manufacturers went full tilt on these folders. The respective runts were designed in collaboration with noted custom knifemakers and had top-shelf features, like frame-lock mechanisms, quality materials and excellent fabrication.

Introduced in 2010, Benchmade's Shane Sibert-designed 755 MPR became an instant hit. The maker's aggressive styling fit the runt attitude perfectly, and Benchmade did it up right with a titanium Mono-Lock (the company's term for a frame lock), a single green G-10 handle scale and a 2.9-inch

Runts began to pick up steam when manufacturers such as Benchmade and Boker jumped on board. Shown here are the Benchmade MPR (top) and Boker Pipsqueak.

M390 blade. At 6.9 inches open and weighing 5 full ounces, the MPR is a truckload of a knife in a small package.

The Boker Pipsqueak, designed by knifemaker Neil Blackwood, was released in early 2012, and it, too, quickly became a runt fan favorite. The Pipsqueak's lines could best be described as "chunky elegance," and its titanium frame lock, a nicely polished, single, green Micarta handle scale, curvaceous two-tone CPM S30VN blade and flipper one-hand-opening mechanism only added to the appeal. At 6.25 inches overall and weighing 5.1 ounces, the Pipsqueak, like the MPR, was a lot of knife in a compact, hard-working package.

One other past release of note is the Mantis Knives MT-9 folder series, also produced in 2012. Mantis, a young company by knife standards, made a name for itself when it hit the scene around 2008 with a line of *Star Wars*-esque knives designed to break into the lucrative, largely untapped youth market. The MT-9 Pit Boss and MT-9C Tough Tony were, and still are, the most "techie" runts to date. The blades on both models are 2.5 inches in length with elongated one-hand-opening holes that complement the look of the angular handles, which in turn sport more grooves than a Klingon Cruiser.

A WORLD OF RUNTS

Look around the knife industry today and you'll find a world of runts, in fact more today than ever before. As the genre has become entrenched, it has also evolved to include a broader range of locking mechanisms, blade styles and other design tweaks. This is typical as more manufacturers jump on board and their designers are tasked to come up with different styles. The price range has similarly broadened to cover all budgets from expensive to extremely affordable.

If any single knife exemplifies the modern runt breed today it is the Spyderco Techno folder. Designed by Polish knifemaker Marcin Slysz, the Techno combines smooth European lines with the brawn expected of a runt. Spyderco spared no expense on the knife. The Techno features a full titanium frame with a Chris Reeve Integral Lock (frame-lock) mechanism, a top-shelf, 2.55-inch,

Mantis Knives brought hi-tech and youth appeal to the runt equation. The MT-9 Pit Boss (bottom) and MT-9C Tough Tony are still the most futuristic runts to date.

The DPx Gear HEAT/F is a downsized, runt-erized version of the company's wildly popular HEST/F folder, and it's loaded with many of the same features.

4.5mm-thick Carpenter CTS-XHP spear point blade and a wire pocket clip. Fully open, the sturdy folder checks in at just less than 6 inches (5.98 to be exact) and weighs a scant 3.6 ounces.

Another newcomer to the runt fray is the DPx Gear HEAT/F folder. A compact version of the company's popular HEST/F, the runt has many features of its big brother, including a stonewashed, titanium frame lock, a G-10 front handle scale, ample pocket clip and a glass-breaker pommel. The HEAT/F comes with a 2.6-inch, drop-point D2 tool steel blade with dual ambidextrous thumb studs, plus a nifty bottle cap lifter on the blade spine. The HEAT/F, with all its extra functions, is a runt to be taken seriously.

SOG Specialty Knives & Tools' downsized Spec-Elite Mini is a runt-sized version of its big sibling. At 6.5 inches fully open, including a 2.75-inch VG-10 blade, the Spec-Elite Mini folds down to a compact 3.65 inches, almost 1.5 inches shorter than the full-size Spec-Elite! A unique feature of the pint-sized folder is a patented SOG Arc-Lock™, which makes for quick and easy blade deployment. Weighing in at a paltry 2.7 ounces, the lightweight Mini is a folder any enthusiast can carry and conceal in a variety of locations and forget it's there until needed.

The Cold Steel Mini Tuff Lite sports a wicked little 2-inch, wharncliffe-style AUS-8A stainless steel blade mated to a comfortable, nicely sculpted 3-inch Grivory™ handle with a lock-back mechanism. The 1.7-ounce Mini Tuff Lite is available in black or a bright "zombie green" and has a pocket clip, yet it's small and light enough for loose pocket carry.

Small fixed blades make for excellent self-defense knives and can be easily concealed. At top is the Boker Bandit, and below it the CRKT No Bother.

Kershaw Knives has been busy on the runt scene, and the company's Half Ton folder boasts a 2.5-inch 8Cr13MoV stainless spear-point blade teamed up with red glass-reinforced-nylon handle scales, black Santoprene™ inserts and a locking liner. At 6.125 inches open, the Half Ton weighs 3.3 ounces and has a cool pocket clip shaped like a combination hex/open-end wrench.

Equally as cool is the multi-function Kershaw Shuffle model, a locking-liner folder that stretches 5.625 inches fully opened with a stubby 2.375-inch, drop-point blade. The fun begins with a cap lifter on the back of the "K-Textured" glass-filled-nylon handle, as well as a lanyard hole at the handle butt that includes a flathead screwdriver tip. That's one handy design!

REVITALIZED RUNT ROOTS

Paying homage to the early runt pattern and taking it back to its roots are a bevy of modern-day, fixed-blade successors—a wide range of small production knives that do the name proud, ranging from skinners to neck knives.

In the small fixed-blade skinner realm is Benchmade's Hidden Canyon Hunter, a knife that, at 6.32 inches overall, would fit perfectly in a hunting pack. Part of Benchmade's popular HUNT series, this little gem doesn't take up a lot of space yet showcases a 3.6-inch CPM-S30V stainless steel drop-point blade with a deep belly that can tackle some nice-sized game. The Dymondwood™ handle scales have the look of hardwood but are even tougher, and a lanyard hole at the end of the extended tang makes access to the knife easier when needed in a pinch. The Hidden Canyon Hunter is available in a Kydex or pressure-fit-leather belt sheath.

The 6.75-inch Boker Plus Bandit, designed by Hungarian knifemaker Peter Farkas, is an upscale everyday carry fixed blade dressed in carbon fiber handle scales and a handsome stonewashed blade. Jimping (finger grooves) on the spine of the 2.75-inch 440C stainless clip-point blade, as well as a deep finger choil, allow the user to choke up on the knife when using it. When not in use, it tucks away in a leather belt sheath.

The CRKT No Bother fixed blade is an aggressive bit of business designed by knifemaker Ron Johnson of RMJ Tactical. The 2.19-inch 8Cr13MoV blade is a wicked reverse tanto style with a non-reflective, black oxide, stonewashed finish. The No Bother has a thin, tapered, black ABS synthetic handle and matching black leather lanyard. Made for neck or pack carry, it comes with a MOLLE-compatible Kydex® sheath with a quick-release buckle for rapid detachment. The No Bother is no doubt slick.

There is such a wide range of runt folders and fixed blades, choosing just one is the only issue, and that's a good problem to have. The variety and vast number of runts speak directly to the popularity of the knife genre today and for years to come.

World's First Bloomery Steel/Meteorite Razor?

Step-by-step to a one-of-a-kind straight razor

By Tim Zowada

I t is interesting how things work out. It seems a day will start off with a specific plan or schedule. By noon, that plan has often turned into something completely different. Such is the joy of self-employment. A project or production schedule will get started. Then things change. A change in logistics, material supply or even the weather can throw a month or more into a tailspin. Such was the dilemma in making a straight razor for one of my customers, Charles.

Charles floated the idea of me making a straight razor for him in late 2012. He wanted something special. The conversations centered on what could be made and if there could be such a thing as a "dream razor." Charles wanted to own a razor that embodied the ultimate test of a bladesmith's skills. But, he also wanted something the maker could get excited about building.

The decision was made to craft a razor with the entire blade fabricated from scratch. There was to be no purchased, commercial steel. The blade would be crafted from homemade, smelted bloomery steel—crafted by smelting iron to produce "Tamahagane." For visual interest and variation, the Tamahagane would be laminated with iron/nickel meteorite on the top section of the blade. This was a blade to be made in this world and from "out of this world." While bloomery steel and meteorite have been used in concert for centuries, we were not able to find any evidence of them being laminated together in a razor.

The day arrived when Charles had paid his deposit. All the materials were in hand. It was time to start making steel! Then things changed quickly. One Friday afternoon, while I was in a hurry to meet someone, traveling too fast on a dirt road, on a motorcycle ... the results were four broken ribs, a smashed arm and a very messed up production schedule. It is amazing how long it can take to get back into forging shape after such an accident. There was to be no real forging for over nine months. Charles' razor was on hold.

Time went by slowly. Precious time in the shop was spent on other projects while waiting to get back

This is the sand, straight off the beach. When pouring it on the paper, the lighter silica sand went to the outside of the pile. In the close-up, the black stuff is a mixture of magnetite and hematite.

to forging. By late winter 2014, the forging shop was back in business. The time had come to make a very special razor for a very patient customer.

The first step is to smelt the steel. For this razor, two smelts were required, a high-carbon bloom for the cutting edge, and a low-carbon bloom for the back of the blade. The source for the iron ore was Lake Superior beach sand. This sand was sorted and filtered to remove most of the silica sand. The resulting material for the smelt was approximately 60 percent hematite and 40 percent magnetite.

First, the low-carbon bloom was smelted. This is the material that would be laminated with meteorite for the back of the blade. Since the meteorite layers will not harden, it is best if the bloomery steel layers don't harden much either. Low harden-ability would help keep blade distortion to a minimum during heat-treating. A high-carbon bloom was then smelted for the edge material. The finished edge would have a carbon content of about .9 percent and a final hardness of 62 HRC on the Rockwell Hardness Scale.

After the Tamahagane blooms were smelted, the time-consuming work of refining began. During the smelting process, slag and traces of other foreign material are trapped in the bloom. Repeated folding and forge welding helps to work out these inclusions. Usually, each bloom is folded and welded 12-15 times. This results in a bar with several thousand layers. The goal is not to have a lot of layers. All the folding is to remove as much of the slag as possible, and homogenize the carbon content throughout the steel.

GEE WHIZ FACTOR

The next step was to prepare the meteorite for welding to the low-carbon Tamahagane. The sample used is from the Campo del Cielo meteorite found in Argentina. Chunks of it typically contain between six and seven percent nickel. Because of the high nickel content, it will not harden, or allow carbon to migrate through it. As such, it could not be used for

It's hard to believe such a gorgeous straight razor was created from Lake Superior beach sand forged into bloomery steel and combined with meteorite and ivory handle scales.

The Tamahagane/meteorite billet is shown after laminating and taking off the pieces for twisting. The edge was cleaned and etched to show the layers.

The Tamahagane/meteorite billet goes into the forge.

Next, the low-carbon Tamahagane was laminated to the meteorite. A five-layer billet was constructed, three layers of Tamahagane and two layers of meteorite. This billet was forge welded, then folded and welded three additional times to achieve 40 layers. After folding and welding, the Tamahagane/meteorite billet was forged out to four bars, each 1/2-inch square and 8 inches long.

The 40-layer Tamahagane/meteorite bars were then heated and twisted, two clockwise, two counterclockwise. They were then re-forged square, stacked and welded to form a chevron pattern. The composite laminate was forged to .4 inches x .9 inches x 10 inches long. The material for the back of the blade was finally finished.

The high-carbon edge piece of Tamahagane was then prepared. It was forged to .25 inches x .4 inches x 10 inches long. This piece was tack welded to the Tamahagane/meteorite back piece and then forge welded in place. The final bar was forged to .26 inches x .9 inches x 14 inches. This was a lot more steel than is needed for just one razor. But, when a project is challenging and easy to mess up, it is a good idea to make enough material for spare blades, just in case. After all, Charles had been waiting a very long time.

After the smelting, refining, laminating, stacking and re-welding, there was finally enough material to make a couple razors. I admit, with such a large piece of interesting steel, it was tempting to continue forging the piece out and make a short sword. Up until this point, all efforts had been focused on making the blade material. This material could have been used for a variety of different projects. The final bar was normalized and annealed using an electric kiln.

With the laminated blade material in hand, it was time to make the razor blade. The next step was

any part of the cutting edge. It is purely decorative when laminated to the Tamahagane. Some call this the "gee whiz" factor. It goes like this, "Gee whiz! See those pretty silver lines? They fell from the sky!"

Meteorite is also full of inclusions and crud. When forged, meteorite tends to crumble and fall apart. The best way to prepare it for laminating to the Tamahagane is to fold and weld it, to itself, several times. After seven or eight folds, it is "behaving" and ready for laminating to the Tamahagane. At this point, it has been several days of work just to get the materials ready for the initial laminating of the blade.

The meteorite must be folded and welded several times, and after about seven folds, it starts to behave like regular steel. It is heated and pounded during the forging process.

Here are the first blows on the smelted bloom.

to forge a basic bevel, and then grind away everything that didn't look like a razor. While the blade could have been completely forged to shape, the risk of getting the edge out of alignment was pretty high. After all the time, labor, material and supplies that went into making the bar, the decision was made to play it safe, forge a basic bevel, and then grind in the rest of the shape.

Since the blade was to end up as a 6/8's-size razor (that's 3/4 inches wide), the blade was surface ground to .230-inch thick. The tang was profiled, and the cutting edge ground to a thickness of .03 inches.

THE SCARY PART

With any complex project, the heat treatment is always the scary part. It is even scarier when using homemade steel. Samples of the edge material were heat-treated to test temperatures and procedures. Bloomery steel has a very low harden-ability. That means it requires a fast quench to harden fully. Even the famous Parks #50 oil was not a fast enough quench to get the hardness desired. The quench would have to be done in water.

Water quenching can be a bear. Since the cooling of the steel and Martensite transformation is so fast, there can easily be problems with the blade warping or cracking. Careful heating before quenching helps keep things under control. To help make sure the blade was heated evenly, the blade was heated in a molten salt bath to 1,485 degrees Fahrenheit.

The actual water quench is extremely fast and stressful to the steel. The blade temperature drops from 1,485 degrees to less than 900 degrees in less

FEATURES **29**

The finished composite piece displays silver layers of meteorite and dark layers of bloomery steel.

Each Tamahagane/meteorite bar is twisted.

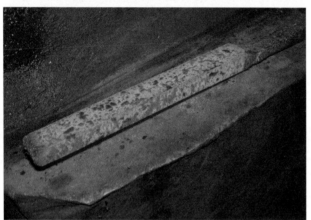

For the cutting edge, it is necessary to weld on a piece of high-carbon Tamahagane.

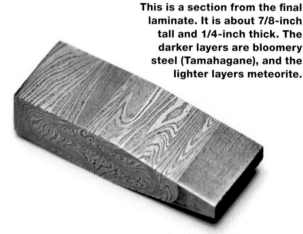

This is a section from the final laminate. It is about 7/8-inch tall and 1/4-inch thick. The darker layers are bloomery steel (Tamahagane), and the lighter layers meteorite.

than a second. After the quench, the blade is brittle and unstable. It was immediately tempered at 380 degrees in a low temperature molten salt bath. The tempering process takes out excess hardness and stress. After three tempering cycles, the edge hardness was 62 HRC, a good hardness for a bloomery steel razor.

Final grinding was next. After heat treatment, the blade was surface ground to a final thickness of .206 inches. Since the spine of a razor also acts as the honing guide, this gives a 16-degree inclusive (both sides of the bevel) angle at the cutting edge. The tang was then tapered and finished.

The final grinding of the main bevel is an exercise in patience. If you try to go to fast, the steel can be

overheated, ruining the edge temper. It is also easy to grind through the edge centerline to the other side of the razor. It is best to go very slowly. Run the belts wet. After this step is completed, the edge is about .001 inches thick with an 800-grit finish.

After all the grinding is completed, it is time to set the actual honing bevel and polish the blade. With most normal damascus, the blade is finished to 600 grit and then etched in ferric chloride. Unfortunately, that would not work with this Tamahagane/meteorite blade. Ferric chloride attacks the minute slag inclusions in the bloomery steel. These slag inclusions are everywhere in bloomery steel, even if they are too small to be seen without magnification. Ferric chloride would turn the blade in to a pitted mess.

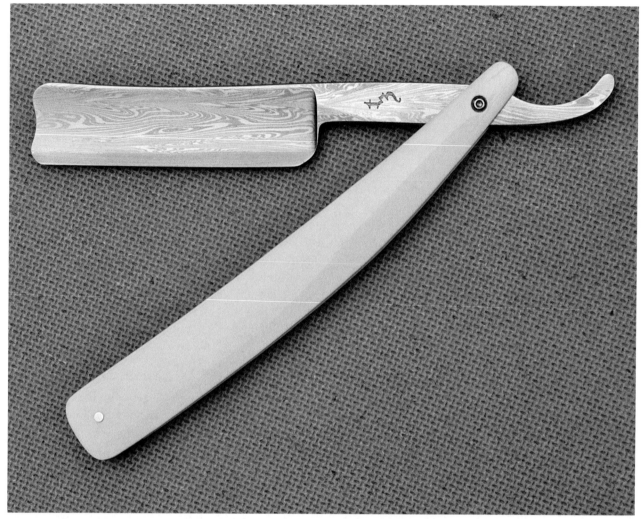

How the blade pattern of the finished razor contrasts against the ivory handle scales is impressive.

For the final polishing, the blade is hand sanded to a 4,000-grit finish. By carefully etching with Nital, the pattern in the Tamahagane/meteorite layers was brought out. Between etchings, the blade is polished with a 3M polishing cloth. The etching and polishing process is repeated until the desired look is achieved.

Charles' Razor was then sharpened using a standard razor honing progression:

- 4,000-grit Norton water stone
- 8,000-grit Norton water stone
- 12,000-grit natural stone
- .5-micron chromium oxide on balsa
- .5-micron chromium oxide on bull-hide hanging strop
- Clean horsehide hanging strop

The neat thing about using bloomery steel for razors is that the blade will stay sharp, almost indefinitely, by simple stropping. Since there are no significant alloys in the steel other than carbon, the steel has very low abrasion resistance, even at a high hardness. That means a simple stropping routine will keep the razor sharp, with rarely having to resort to the bench hones.

Charles' razor was then finished in ivory handle scales, with an adjustable pivot pin. After nearly a year and a half, it was finished. There are a few milestones during the career of a craftsman. Some of those milestones are the ones from projects that stretch abilities, skill and knowledge. This razor was certainly one of those. As of this date, there are only a few bloomery steel/meteorite razors in the world. It is very possible that Charles' was the first. The satisfaction of finishing such a project is beyond words, and that's saying something for a guy who likes to talk!

Wares of the Old World

Bulgarian knives are the product of a people, a place and time, and the villages and wilderness surrounding them

By James Morgan Ayres | All images by ML Ayres

Like many East European cities, Viliko Tarnovo, in Bulgaria, is a blend of the old and new. There is a shiny new shopping center on the edge of town, along with big box stores with all the goods you might find in the United States. The city boasts a university and an English language bookstore. Blocks of apartments built during the Soviet era surround the medieval quarter.

The cobblestone streets of the medieval quarter are lined with timber and plaster buildings with narrow stairs and small rooms, built hundreds of years ago during the Ottoman occupation. On one of these narrow streets, Kirie Dimitrov Dimitrov—that is Kirie, son of Dimitrov, son of Dimitrov—makes knives and swords with his father and his grandfather. In Europe, and particularly in Bulgaria, these are traditional trades, often handed down from father to son. The skill of the craftsmen is tested and certified by a government agency. A certificate from that agency attesting to Kirie's status as master blademaker hangs on the wall of his retail shop.

Here in his small shop, Kirie grinds, polishes and finishes his work, and displays it for the public to see and buy. On occasion, he will, at his forge in his home village near Viliko Tarnovo, forge a few high-carbon-steel blades from rough stock or from an old file or rasp. But most of his work is heat-treating and grinding high-tech Bohler Uddeholm Sleipner steel, and other modern steels at the customer's request.

Kirie's work ranges from folders and hunting knives to recreations of traditional pieces such as the *kindjal*, a knife that has been in use in the Balkans and the Caucasus for longer than anyone can remember. Some experts say the design dates from the Roman Empire, 2,000 years ago, and it is based on the gladius, a Roman short sword. The kindjal has a straight, double-edged blade about 15 inches long, and is still worn in remote areas as a nod to tradition. The gift of a kindjal, usually from father to son,

marks the passage from boyhood to manhood.

Kirie sometimes works with Todor Kushiev, a silversmith whose shop is a few doors from his, and who does silver engraving and chasing on the handles, pommels and sheaths of fancier pieces. The day we first visited, Kirie and Todor had just completed a highly decorated kindjal for a customer in Germany. They displayed it for us and let me handle it. It was light and quick in the hand. The kindjal is not a tool, not meant to hew or carve wood, clear brush or make kindling, but pure weapon, having intention in every part of its design and construction. With its straight, acute clip-point blade, the kindjal appears to be primarily a thrusting weapon. But the edges are sharp and will slice and cleave as well as many curved blades.

The modern countries of Turkey and Bulgaria share a common border, and traces of the 500-year Ottoman occupation are evident in Bulgaria's cuisine, in many of its social customs and in its edged weapons. The yatagan—in Turkish pronounced *yatan*—was and is a favored Turkish blade. In contrast to the straight kindjal blade, the yatagan has a re-curved edge and a slight downward curve to the blade spine toward the point. The antique fighting yatagans I have seen in villages have blades of about the same length as the kindjal, although some of those in museums are of cavalry sword length. The design of the yatagan is clearly optimized for slashing. However, the dropped point is in line with the grip and no doubt would thrust efficiently. Kirie will also make you a classic yatagan if you prefer.

The bulk of Kirie's sales are of hunting knives and either lock-back folders or old Bulgarian folders called "boot knives," not because they're meant to be carried in boots, but rather because the handle butts are made to resemble boots. No one I asked knew why the knives are made this way. To my eye the design resembles the French laguiole folder.

Master silversmith
Todor Kushiev
shows his work on a
kidjal that parades a
silver-chased sheath,
grip and pommel.

GAME DISPATCHERS

The American style of hunting knife with a 4-inch, drop-point blade, used to dress out an autumn buck, has no traction here. Hunting knives in Bulgaria have long blades and are used to actually hunt with, to dispatch game such as wild boar. Also, a long-bladed knife will dress and butcher a wild boar, deer or other game, faster and more effectively than a short blade.

A 4-inch blade is essentially a paring knife in Bulgaria. Hunters there have no limits on some game, such as wild boar, and game can be an important part of their food supply. The ability to quickly process large game is important. Of equal, if not more importance, long blades offer a measure of security for the hunter or woodsman who might be caught away from his rifle or shotgun by a predator.

Protecting oneself from wild predators is not a macho fantasy in these parts, as it might be elsewhere.

Bulgaria is a country about the size of California that has a population less that half that of Los Angeles. There are millions of acres of forest and mountain ranges populated only by wild animals. In addition to deer, ram, hares, ducks and other herbivores, predators including bear, wild boar, fox, wolves and jackals roam everywhere. Fox offer no threat to people. The others sometimes do. Here wolves and other predators do not need to be protected as they do in the United States. There are wolves and bear aplenty, and the largest population of European jackals on the continent. They've been here since the last ice age. These jackals are about the size of a German shepherd and run in packs, sometimes as many as a dozen to a pack.

This traditional Bulgarian hunting knife/pig sticker showcases a convex blade grind and a sturdy oak handle.

When outdoorsmen here venture into forest and mountains, they value a serious blade. The long blade also gets frequent use around the home. Many hunters, woodmen and outdoorsmen live in villages where big knives have many uses, including the slaughter of their own livestock: pigs, goats and sheep.

Big, hefty bowie-style blades are popular with Kirie's local customers, often coupled with a small skinner. These big blades will chop as well as a small hatchet, and so the hunter's load is lightened by the need to carry only one tool/weapon. Even more popular with hunters and outdoorsmen is the traditional Bulgarian hunting and field knife, an all-around utility knife. It's also called a "pig sticker" for its use in slaughtering pigs each autumn. The knife features a slim, single-edged 7- or 8-inch convex-ground blade with a full tang, single guard, a fuller and wood handle scales. Lighter than a bowie, it is an excellent cutting and stabbing blade that has been carried and used by Bulgarian soldiers over many years.

I bought one of these traditional knives made with Sleipner steel for use in the kitchen and around the grounds of our village house, and found it to be a terrific tool. With it, I cleared out last year's wine

grape vines and pruned them down for winter, split kindling for our wood stove, cut up many ducks and roasts, and chopped a small mountain of vegetables. I wasn't set upon by a wild boar or a pack of jackals so can't comment on it as a weapon, but I suspect it would serve.

The blade held its razor edge for about a month of daily use with only a few minutes of stropping on a leather belt every week or so. After some weeks, although it still had a good working edge, I wanted to bring it back to razor sharpness. It was a bit of a job. This is tough steel. I stropped it for 220 strokes on either side of the edge on a piece of 1,200-grit emery paper backed by a piece of foam pad, and then another 100 strokes on a leather belt. I would guess that if I had started with 800-grit or a medium-grit stone, which I did not have, the job would have gone faster.

THE VILLAGE SMITH

In the countryside surrounding Viliko Tarnovo are villages that appear to be lost in time, where adobe walls surround stone houses and sustainability has been a way of life for time out of mind. Everyone has a kitchen garden, a goat or two, chickens and maybe some ducks or geese. Donkeys, rather than pickup trucks, haul produce to market. A smith lives in one of those villages, and makes the ironmongery that holds those carts together, as well as axes, sickles, farm tools, kitchen knives, butcher knives and hunting knives.

Hotnitsa is a village of some 2,000 souls about 15 kilometers from Viliko Tarnovo, and where village culture still prevails. Yourdan Petrov Ivanov is the village smith, a white haired man whose vigor belies his age. He can make you a bearded axe, a coupling for your hay wagon, a hasp for your gate, a traditional forged work knife or hunting knife, or one made to your design. His work is not as smooth as Kirie's—he doesn't use modern high-tech steel—but is more reflective of a true villager's craft, a little rough, totally functional and priced at village prices. Twenty dollars will buy you one his knives.

A short drive over country roads past fields of corn and sunflowers brought us to a narrow lane and Yourdan's home and workshop. An adobe wall surrounds sprawling stone buildings and a vegetable garden. Ducks and chickens wander about pecking at bugs and earthworms. Next to the barn is a rabbit hutch. Yourdan met us with a smile and the powerful handshake of a man who has worked all his life with his hands.

A typical Bulgarian hunting knife dons a large 8-inch Bohler Uddeholm Sleiper steel blade and a stag handle, shown with a companion skinner.

After some refreshment we headed for the workshop. It was a warm day, but not so warm that I was uncomfortable in my light jacket. I was surprised when Yourdan took off his shirt before going to work. It wasn't that hot, even near the forge, and sparks flew all over his arms and chest as he stood at the grinding wheel to work on my knife. Maybe Bulgarians just have tough skin, or smiths do, or Yourdan does. As we watched, Yourdan built up a fire, started his grinding wheel and transformed a rough chunk of steel into a 7-inch knife blade. We left the partially completed knife to allow it to rest while we had lunch.

We dined at a large table next to a fireplace big enough to roast an ox, the door and windows open to the afternoon sun and fresh breezes. Lunch was rabbit, duck, park ribs, a gigantic salad of tomatoes, cucumbers and onions, a cabbage salad, roasted potatoes, home-baked bread fresh from a wood-fired oven and a bottle or two of Ivan's wine, fresh, light and fruity. Lunch was accompanied by much talk and laughter.

After the three-hour lunch, we decided to let my knife "rest" a little longer and to return to see the

The antique knife is a Bulgarian version of the Turkish folding yatagan.

rest of the knifemaking process the following week. Unfortunately, life got in the way of that plan, and we had to unexpectedly return to the United States. We'll be returning to Bulgaria soon. I plan to visit Yourdan again, but this time will come early enough for my knife to be completed before lunch.

Color My Knife World

Blade and handle texturing, heat coloring and other techniques set certain makers' knives apart

By Wally Hayes, ABS master smith

The number of knife texturing techniques and ways of coloring knife parts is ever changing, increasing and evolving. *KNIVES 2016* readers might be interested in a number of techniques that I and other makers use to make our knives stand out and become unique.

This summer, I decided to fashion some chef's knives and sushi knives. I have always wanted to try texturing a blade, a Japanese technique, as far as I can tell, that dates back a long way. I took an old hammer and cut a crosshatch pattern into the hammerhead. I used my side grinder with a 1/8-inch wheel to create the grooves in the hammer face. I heated up a piece of .110-inch-thick 15N20 blade steel and pounded the hot steel on both sides with the crosshatched hammer until I was happy with the texture it created on the 15N20. I had to be careful not to pound near the edge, as it would create nicks upon final sharpening of the blade.

This style of blade making saves a lot of time on sanding and polishing the steel to create a smooth satin, mirror or high-gloss finish, all the while creating something different. The textured blade face serves a purpose, too, when working in the kitchen or at camp, creating air pockets between the blade and food so that meat, fruits and vegetables do not stick to the steel. For fun, I stained the curly maple handles with red food coloring. Then I coated the handle with Krazy Glue to seal it.

Another practice I've been hearing about is applying an acid-etched, stonewashed finish to a knife blade. There are a couple of people, like knifemaker Jason Brous, for example, who employ this method often in their handcraft. One way to achieve the finish is to etch the blade in ferric chloride mixed half-and-half (50/50) with distilled water. The blade is etched (soaked) in the solution for about 30 minutes before it is removed and neutralized in Windex or baking soda in water.

Next the blade is put in a tumbler, like one of sev-

Rick Marchand's D-guard bowie is a complete textured package, including the blade, guard, spacers and even the leather sheath. *(SharpByCoop.com image)*

eral available from Harbor Freight (harborfreight.com). Different makers use a variety of "tumbler media" in the tumblers, such as polishing stones or rock, resin and ceramic abrasives, to tumble against their blades. The blue "rust-cutting resin abrasive" triangles from Harbor Freight work well. Some makers mix in other media, including, but not limited to, small, round rocks. WD-40 is sprayed into the tumbler, and the machine is turned on with the blade inside for about one hour. The blade is then cleaned, re-sharpened and ready to use with its new acid-etched stonewashed finish.

On one of the folders I designed, I engraved a picture into the high-carbon steel handle. Then I went around and embellished or textured the remaining, non-engraved area of the handle frame with a small round burr. Different sized burrs used in a Dremel rotary power tool create varying patterns. The variety of burr choices for a Dremel tool allows the maker to dig deep into the surface of the handle scale or just touch the surface lightly that he or she is working on.

BLUE IT OUT

After engraving the grip and adding texture with the Dremel tool, I blued the handle with cold gun bluing. If a maker were to use a 416 stainless steel handle, rather than the high-carbon steel I used, the stainless steel could be heat blued with a torch instead of cold gun blued. Next, I polished the high spots of the engraving with an eraser (a blue rubber polishing wheel would also work). I then heated the screws with a torch to color them a deep gold/brown. They could also have been heated to a blue color, or heat blued, if that were the desired effect.

Knifemaker Wolfgang Loerchner is a master when it comes to texturing and coloring knives. It would take a whole book to cover everything Wolfe does. In one technique, he uses a Dremel tool with a small round burr to stipple the front and back of his folders. The resulting frosted texture gives an awesome contrast to the high-polished areas of the knives.

Each of his knife handle inlays is cut, filed and polished by hand. You can't get more contrasting colors and textures created in one knife than Wolfe does. He uses 416 or 440C stainless steel, deeply etched nickel damascus, and 18-karat gold, rose gold and black-lip pearl. Wolfe owns a reciprocating profiler but does not use it, as he prefers doing everything by hand. Other makers use mold-making stones, and still others employ tools like the Gess-

Wolfgang Loerchner uses a small bur to texture the handle frame, around the inlays and in the guard area, of his fine folding dagger. *(Murray image)*

Brian Tighe achieves creative handle grooves and texturing using a CNC machine for his Tighe Coon folders, which sport zirconium handles and acid-etched blades, one in "Tighe-ger" stripes. *(PointSeven image)*

Shown is the face of a texturing hammer, with 1/8-inch grooves cut into the hammerhead.

The blade of Jason Brous's streamlined flipper folder is a good example of a stonewashed finish.

pletely covered in dimples. I see some young makers using this technique on the bolsters and/or handle scales of their folders. It is also possible to "hammer forge" a textured surface above the grind lines of a knife blade, a technique usually achieved while the steel is still hot from the forge.

Computer Numerically Controlled (CNC) machines have really changed texturing methods in knifemaking. Many makers use CNC machines to mill out entire knife blades, and this alone allows them to program different blade surface textures right into the machine. Likewise CNC machines are employed to add some great patterns to such handle materials as G-10, Timascus™ and titanium. The patterns that can be programmed into the machine are endless. Knifemaker Brian Tighe has really pushed the envelope and developed CNC machining techniques to create beautiful, original knives.

Texturing and blade surface finishing can end up becoming part of a maker's signature style. An example of this is Rick Marchand of Wildertools. He creates a unique finish on his forged blades, a process involving the use of gun bluing and Javex (commercial bleach by Clorox) to create a completely original textured and etched look. Rick also textures some of his knife handles and sheaths to match in color and style. Many shades of leather stain are used to create a complete package.

DEEP GROOVY GRIPS

Texturing handle materials like G-10 can also be done with a small wheel attachment on a belt grinder. This creates deep grooves for grip, and makes the knife look hard-core tactical. I use a 3/8-inch wheel to texture my G-10 grips, and then give the handles a light bead blast to even out the color. Multi-color G-10 handle scales also look great with added texture.

No discussion on coloring knives would be complete without mentioning Timascus (pattern-welded titanium). This awesome material, developed by Tom Ferry, Chuck Bybee and Bill Cottrell, is beautifully patterned titanium similar to damascus. Upon polishing Timascus and heating it with a torch, knifemakers achieve bright purple, blue and gold hues. You can flame color regular titanium with a torch and also get blues, golds and purples, but custom-made Timascus hardware looks amazing.

A lot of makers use electricity to color-anodize titanium. The process is simple. You make a bath of

wein Power Hand Rotary tool (gesswein.com) with a Z-2X reciprocating profiler. This holds diamond ultra-sonic tools. Very cool!

Another texturing technique that's been in use for quite some time is using a ball peen hammer to peen brass or nickel silver. Brass or nickel silver knife guards, pommels or butt caps are first mirror polished. Then the knifemaker polishes the ball end of a ball peen hammer before tapping the surface of the brass or nickel silver until it is evenly and com-

In this case, Wally Hayes textured around the spooky engravings using a Dremel tool. *(SharpByCoop.com image)*

The "King Tut" folder by Wally Hayes is engraved and titanium painted (the titanium is electronically color anodized using a paint brush). *(SharpByCoop.com image)*

TSP (trisodium phosphate) and distilled water. The anode lead is clipped onto the sheet of titanium in the bath and the cathode is clipped onto the piece to be anodized. The leads are hooked up to a variable DC box for changing the voltage. Twenty-five volts achieves a dark blue color, 12 volts a nice gold, and so on. A knife handle can be engraved or CNC machined, then anodized for color. Afterward, a maker can sand off the highest parts of the engraved areas or CNC-machined textures for a contrasting, light-grey color at the tips of the texturing. How a maker finishes titanium makes a difference in the final appearance. If handle scales are bead blasted, the finish is flat and does not seem to show scratches as much as a high polish.

Anodizing does last longer in the recessed pockets or carved-out sections of a knife handle that are not susceptible to wear. I use a paintbrush to electronically anodize my engravings on titanium. I clip one electronic lead on the handle scale and the other on the bristles of a paintbrush. I dip the paintbrush in water and TSP. I start with the higher voltage colors first and work my way down. So I have to plan the

coloring a bit, but it is a lot of fun. Another method I use is to paint around the edges of a knife handle with the paintbrush, each time turning up the voltage and moving away from the center of the grip. This creates a look of burning paper.

A lot of titanium hardware is now available, including pivot screws for folding knives, stand-offs, pocket clips and 256 screws, so a knifemaker can color coordinate hardware with, say, the liners of folders. Just looking through jewelry supply catalogues from such companies as Gesswein or Rio Grande (riogrande.com) can spark a lot of inspiration for texturing and coloring knives.

I hope I have given readers a couple of ideas and shared enough information to help in navigating and moving forward in the colorful, textured world of knives.

The Three Amigos of the Buck Knives Line

The Compadre Camp Knife, Hatchet and Chopping Froe tackled field chores, no problemo!

By Roderick T. Halvorsen

Every now and then a knife company releases a product line that really grabs my attention. That is the case with the Buck Compadre series. Combining the best of traditional cutting tools with new innovations, this series is utilitarian, well made, and harkens back to field tools of yesteryear. I have little to criticize about Buck's new offering. The Compadres are three good amigos.

Despite the simple model designations of 104, 106 and 108, the tools are aptly named the Camp Knife, Camp Hatchet and Chopping Froe, respectively. Described in company literature as "heavy duty," they are certainly that. This is a series that would make a superb addition to the wreck kit of every 4x4, ATV or light airplane, and no hunter, camper, backpacker or hiker will regret the extra weight on the trail. Somebody at Buck knows a thing or two … or three … about outdoor cutting tools!

The first thing that grabs the eye is the red-as-red-can-be powder coat finish. It will wake a person up from heavy slumber in a sleeping bag, tent, cabin or cot. Tools used heavily in the woods are often dropped or misplaced. It happens. It's impossible for it *not* to happen, and when it does, the Buck Compadre series is more likely to be found by the owner than lost forever.

The Buck Compadres are, from left to right, the Camp Knife, Camp Hatchet and Chopping Froe, shown with their respective black leather sheaths.

Many surveyors and others I know, like me, hit their field tools with a swath of red or blaze-orange spray paint for the same effect. So this idea is hardly new, but it is uncommon for a company to face that fact and just add the red from the start in a production line. The stout coating holds up well indeed. Just what motivated Buck to actually take the plunge into paint I do not know, but the fact it did makes me certain the company is staying in tune with the realities of those in the woods, mountains and bush.

The three Compadres share features. The handles are of laminated "Heritage Walnut Dymondwood." Hard, abrasion-resistant and possessing a smooth yet palpable surface, even when wet, the material looks a lot like it was carved from old German Army gunstocks of the World War II era. Yet due to the use of modern phenolic resins, the material sheds water and holds up well to the elements and to impact when dropped or bumped. TORX-head screws

Cutting the same wood using the Chopping Froe (left) and Camp Hatchet showed the advantages of each. Overall, the hatchet was the better chopper, but the froe was more versatile.

All three Compadres arrived from the factory with shaving-sharp, bright-red blades.

FEATURES **41**

Getting a fire going under soaking-wet conditions was no problem at all with the help of the Camp Hatchet (left) and Chopping Froe (far right).

secure the grips to full tangs, and if Buck were to provide spare handle scales, it would be a cinch to swap out those that got beat up or that a bear gnawed on for lack of food.

The Camp Knife also has a lanyard hole, but I prefer never to have something sharp and pointy lashed to my hand lest it stays too nearby if I trip and fall. Living, working and playing in the mountains on slippery slopes has taught me it is best to chuck the tool if you should unintentionally go down. A couple years ago I was working on a rocky slope on the ranch, slipped and fell face-first into a barbed wire fence, and I am glad my bolo knife didn't add insult to injury. Had it been tied to me, that embarrassing and painful experience might have turned out to be far more serious an accident. Having said all that, the handle hole does make a nice additional spot for a thong to lash it to the sheath if need be.

SHEATH 'EM IF YOU'VE GOT 'EM

The leather sheaths for the Compadre series are stout and well constructed. Welts are a proper thickness, and the rivets are strategically located where the points and edges of the tools contact the leather, except for where the leading edge of the knife touches the sheath, but the knife sheath also includes a plastic insert to guard against cuts when re-holstering the blade. The Camp Knife holster is designed to fit on a 2 1/2-inch belt and has a good snap strap to make sure it doesn't get left behind when pushing through the brush.

While the knife sheath is an easy in/easy out design, the hatchet and froe jobs are not, and that leads to my only real criticism of the series. The hatchet and froe (shake axe) leather sheaths sport "D" rings, but there is no way to secure them to a belt, and the froe scabbard is really more of an edge guard than a scabbard.

Personally I'd prefer a bucket-type scabbard for the Chopping Froe, since such a tool is often used in clearing brush and scrub, or in butchering where it is nice to be able to drop the shake axe into a sheath and pull it out with one hand. Ditto the Camp Hatchet, though in truth the need for a belt sheath for a hatchet is far less than for the other two amigos in the Compadre set.

I commend Buck for the use of 5160 spring steel, heat-treated to 57-59 HRC on the Rockwell Hard-

Dropped in an inconspicuous place, the red powder-coated blade of the Camp Knife stands out clearly and significantly reduces the risk of its loss in the field.

ness Scale, and employed for all three tools. It is certainly true that 5160 requires a bit of caretaking to avoid rust, but the powder coat has held up well for me so far, and even a modicum of effort will take care of the edge. I suppose if I lived and worked in a heavy salt spray environment I might want a little more chromium in the mix, but the general cost and sharpening advantages of Buck's choice outweigh the benefits of most stainless alloys. At least I think so!

Handling the 4 1/2-inch blade Camp Knife, it quickly became apparent that it is a heavy full-tang, slab-gripped, do-anything knife housed in a well-made sheath. With a steel thickness of .156-inch, the stiff blade will adequately meet any chore a knife should face. Overall length of the knife is 9 1/2 inches. The saber-ground edge came hair-shaving sharp right out of the box, and the Camp Knife immediately brought my mind back to the old deck and utility knives of the Big War, like the Cattaraugus 225Q and others of that genre—thick, stout blades with well-backed-up points and hand-filling grips.

It would be hard to find a better design for a guy stuck under a plane wreck in the Alaskan bush or for a backpacker here in my beloved Idaho. The thumb notches on the blade spine gave me a good match striker, though I might add a few more grooves to make it just a bit more effective. No surprise the blade performed camp and kitchen chores without complaint from me, and the red paint stayed put on the blade and didn't rub off on meat, veggies, goat hide or goat carcass when skinning. As for the latter, my good friend and local parish priest from East Africa helped me skin a goat with the Camp Knife and we both found it to be handy for that and other butchering chores.

The edge proved fine enough for jointing and tough enough for cracking a bone here and there. After some time in the woods, in camp and with the goat skinned and cut up, the edge finally needed a touch-up on my hard old Norton stone. It deserved it. This is a Compadre that will make a great companion!

The set was used exclusively for butchering a goat. From skinning to jointing, dicing and making fine cuts, no other tools were necessary.

TOSSING CHIPS

The Model 106 Camp Hatchet reminds me of the traditional one-piece, sheet steel hatchets of the 1950s, but the thickness (.242-inch) and quality make it something completely different. This is a stout hatchet that will stand up to many years of hacking, cutting and pounding. Weight is listed as 23.4 ounces, and in the woods I found it to possess excellent cutting properties. I used it for clearing some trails and cutting and splitting old dry firs for

Though not strictly designed as a skinning knife, the shape and keen edge of the Camp Knife allowed it to perform excellently for the job.

fires. Such cutting media is hard, tough and springy, yet the hatchet did well, biting in deeply and tossing big chips.

I was impressed with the balance and the lack of fatigue developed in my cutting hand. Part of that was the result of the well-designed handle. Identical in shape to that of the froe, the handle allows gripping at the end for maximum power in cutting the bigger stuff, and also permits choking up for fine cutting. It is really two handles in one, again, a feature well thought out by Buck, and the Dymondwood scales held up and provided adequate grip texture, even when covered in blood, fat, rain and icy snow. A hatchet comes in handy for many purposes, some of which involve hammering and pounding, and that is the flaw found in many stamped-steel, one-piece types. Not this one. It is plenty heavy enough for pounding tent pegs and the like.

I have to admit, the tool that got my attention from the beginning was the Model 108 Chopping Froe. It fits smack dab in the middle of the very types of blades I've fashioned in the past and have used extensively for many years. Mostly known as *parangs*, bolos or heavy bush knives, Buck commandeered the word "froe" and turned it upside down, literally. The traditional froe is an old-time splitting tool that requires a striking maul to pound it through the wood to be split, the tool's haft extending upward from the spine. In Buck's froe we have the common arrangement of handle to blade on a tool with uncommon performance.

Firstly, it is a massive tool. At just under 24 ounces, the Chopping Froe has a heavy blade with a sheep's-foot-style tip, the steel being .242-inch thick, and a blade length of 9 1/2 inches. The neat handle design allows a real blade length of 12 inches when gripped at the bottom. This is important because length matters in obtaining blade speed, and blade speed is what cuts brush, saplings and other light material and drives the blade through heavier stuff as well.

Indeed, some Southeast Asian parang and *klewang* type blades have relatively short ground edges with long, dull sections of ricasso, which is the same as the Buck froe when gripped from the base. Adding advantage to effectiveness, the knife can also be grasped at the upper grip section whereby the user gains a great deal of control for fine cutting. It is really a masterful design. In actual testing, I found the froe to be almost as efficient a chopper of heavy material as the hatchet, but not quite. However, the froe far exceeds the hatchet for brush clearing and other light material cutting, making it a more versatile tool.

For pounding, in fact, the hatchet and froe were close in performance, with the hatchet slightly beating out the froe. The froe bettered the hatchet for long, slicing cuts as used during butchering. At the end of the day, what I knew to be true from experience was proven with these tools yet again—a hatchet is a better specialty tool and a parang … oops … froe … is a more versatile tool overall. They are GREAT together.

In the field, the froe turned in an expectedly fine

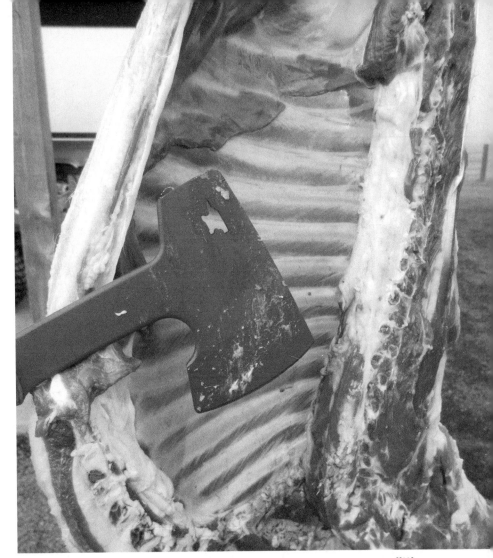

The Camp Hatchet offered fine cleaver-like performance for carcass splitting and similar jobs.

performance. I used it for trail maintenance and in fire making, and also for carcass splitting and cutting up meat back at the ranch. In all chores I found the design to be superb. The swell at the grip butt was sufficient for maintaining comfortable and safe purchase even when wet and/or when I was wearing gloves.

I also appreciated the fine saber-ground edge that came straight from the factory. I cannot emphasize that enough. Nothing is more frustrating than being handed a big knife with a dull-ground, machete-style edge. This one was razor sharp and held up well through all chores, eventually needing sharpening after some abuse near the ground. Again, the paint held up well, and I saw none rub off on the meat we were cutting. The froe is an exceptionally useful tool.

In the end, I found the Buck Compadre blades to be just what Buck called them. The dictionary says "compadre" means "buddy." I couldn't have named these three amigos better myself!

Fix Bayonets!

Did Union edged weapons of the American Civil War change the course of history?

By Edward R. Crews

Col. Joshua Chamberlain had explicit orders on July 2, 1863: "Hold this position at all costs!"

"This position" was the extreme left flank of the Army of the Potomac anchored on a small hill, Little Round Top, at Gettysburg, Pa. "At all costs" meant he was to keep fighting until the men in his command, the 20th Maine, were either dead or disabled. As long as Chamberlain's regiment stood firm, all was well. However, if it faltered, then Confederate troops led by Robert E. Lee could roll up the federal flank, defeat the Union army, threaten Washington and, perhaps, win the war.

Southern commanders knew that the 20th Maine's post was critical to victory. So, on the afternoon of July 2, they sent infantry crashing repeatedly into Chamberlain's command. His men held the line, loading and firing into the gray waves that pounded them. The fighting was so intense that the federal defenders eventually began running out of ammunition.

Short on cartridges but unwilling to retreat or surrender, Chamberlain decided the men would use the only weapons they had left. So, he gave the order: "Fix bayonets!" And, then, he commanded, "Charge!" His regiment swept down the hill. Their bold assault surprised and stunned the Confederates. Lee's veterans halted and then fled. There would be no more attacks on Chamberlain's position. The Army of the Potomac and the American republic were safe.

Chamberlain's famous, heroic attack was not the only time that Union troops would rely on edged weapons in combat during the Civil War. Again and again, federal infantry would use the bayonet in fierce combat at places like Fredericksburg, Va.; Mill Springs, Ky.; Spotsylvania, Va.; Petersburg, Va.; and Chattanooga, Tenn. Likewise, cavalrymen in blue would rely on their sabers on battlefields, including those at Brandy Station, Va.; Gettysburg; Winchester, Va.; and Five Forks, Va.

From the war's start, federal generals believed that bayonets and sabers could win battles. That belief never seriously wavered in four years of brutal, bloody combat. Edged weapons' advocates included some of the North's most prominent military leaders, including George McClellan, James B. McPherson, Gouverneur Warren and Emory Upton.

Confidence in the bayonet was particularly strong. This was reflected in contemporary professional journals like the *Military Gazette*. In it, an author made the case for the weapon: "The public attention is constantly called to the fact that the bayonet is still a weapon of use, and must be relied on in all exigencies of war. It is always ready. No need of ammunition; no fear of failing in its supply of food. It does its work ever so silently, surely and unfailingly."

The 1860 Light Cavalry Saber, with a 34-inch curved blade, was widely issued to Union cavalrymen during the Civil War. The grip was ridged to allow soldiers to hold firmly, and the hand guard protected the soldiers' fingers during sword fights.

RELY ON COLD STEEL

On the eve of battle, generals often told troops to rely on cold steel. For example, Maj. Gen. William Rosecrans sent this message before the Battle of Murfreesboro (Tenn.): "Close steadily in upon the enemy, and when you get within charging distance, rush upon him with the bayonet."

Generals were not the only ones in 1860s America who trusted the bayonet. So did the public. Accordingly, bayonets were mentioned frequently in period articles and editorials, and appeared often in print and magazine illustrations. Given military doctrine and public perceptions, it's no surprise that almost every Union infantryman carried a bayonet, which took two basic forms—socket and sword.

Socket bayonets typically had triangular blades. They were routinely issued with standard U.S. government rifled muskets, including the models 1855 and 1842, as well as the 1861 and 1863 Springfield. One imported weapon, the Austrian Lorenz musket, had a quadrangular bayonet. Socket bayonets essentially were hollow tubes with blades. Each tube sat at the base of the blade and fitted over the musket's barrel where it was locked in place. Socket bayonets were used as stabbing weapons that, theoretically, dispatched an enemy with one swift thrust to a vital organ.

While troops readily accepted socket bayonets, they tended to dislike sword bayonets, also referred to as saber bayonets, which they considered unwieldy. These weapons took their name from their resemblance to swords. Sword bayonets had flat blades that came with sharpened edges and points. They could serve as both stabbing and slashing weapons, attaching to muskets with rings on the hand guards that fit over the guns' muzzles. Slots in the handles engaged lugs on sides of rifle barrels. Sword bayonets were issued with many muskets, most notably the Model 1853 British Enfield, which North and South used.

Although it was a tricky operation, soldiers could

Civil War re-enactors demonstrate a period drill during an event at Jamestown Settlement in Virginia. The men, armed with historically correct weapons, including bayonets and swords, are portraying the 3rd U.S. Infantry Regiment. (Jamestown Settlement image)

load and fire their muskets with either socket or sword bayonets affixed to them. The Union readily supplied thousands of bayonets to its troops thanks to its large industrial sector. Interestingly enough, a huge number of edged weapons came from one producer.

"The Ames Manufacturing Company was one of the most important producers of side arms, swords and light artillery during the Civil War. It began making military swords in 1832 and continued to do so until 1906. By 1865, Ames had manufactured more than 200,000 swords—more than any other company—at their Chicopee, Mass., facility," said Andrew Talkov, vice president for programs at the Virginia Historical Society in Richmond, which holds one of the nation's best Civil War weapons collections.

POLISHED APPEARANCE

Not only did the North have lots of swords and bayonets, these items also had a more polished appearance than those produced in the South.

"Considering that many Confederate-made edged

Edged weapons loomed large in the Victorian imagination and appeared often in contemporary illustrations of combat. In this period print, Union soldiers defend a wounded officer with bayonets and swords.

weapons were variations of U.S. models, they differed in ways that indicated a need for rapid production, use of improvised machinery or shortages in materials. For example, Confederate swords frequently had brass mountings instead of iron, low quality castings, single or no fullers and oilcloth instead of leather grip wrappings," said Talkov, who was a curator for the society's popular exhibition, "An American Turning Point: The Civil War in Virginia," created for the 150th anniversary of the conflict.

Recruits trained extensively with bayonets. Most federal officers had little military experience. So, they relied heavily on two manuals for bayonet instruction: *Infantry Tactics and Bayonet Exercise* by George W. Patten and *Manual of Bayonet Exercise: Prepared For The Use Of The Army Of The United States*, translated by McClellan from a French work.

Both books were well illustrated and focused on teaching the soldier how to attack a foe with thrusts and defend himself with parries. McClellan's manual was more detailed and recommended that the men progress from simple to complex movements. The manual also advocated using stuffed dummies for

practice. Plus, it suggested that men fight each other using blunt bayonets and safety equipment that protected the body, face and eyes.

Interestingly enough, bayonets apparently caused few wounds. In the 1960s, Francis Lord, a distinguished Civil War historian, determined that they caused about 1 percent of all battlefield injuries. This has led many writers to dismiss the bayonet as a weapon.

Recently, a more nuanced view of the bayonet has evolved. The chief cause of this reassessment is work done by Brent Nosworthy, author of *The Bloody Crucible of Courage: Fighting Methods and Combat Experience of the Civil War*. Nosworthy believes that the bayonet's impact was not in casualties produced, but rather in tactical results achieved, a viewpoint shared by an increasing number of historians.

"I think there's an important distinction between a bayonet charge and a soldier using his bayonet to kill an opponent. The bayonet had always been as much a practical weapon as a psychological one, but during the Civil War, attackers were rarely able to advance close enough to use the bayonet, or if they

Thousands of Union troops carried Enfield rifles like this one. Made in England and shipped to the United States, the rifle pictured here is shown with its standard issue bayonet.

did charge, their opponents often fled the field before they arrived," Talkov said. "On the occasions where hand-to-hand combat occurred, it was horrific, brutal and memorable, leaving much blood and ink spilled as a result."

MASS & MOMENTUM

Nosworthy's studies reveal that bayonet charges worked best on open ground where mass and momentum could have a powerful impact. Interestingly enough, Northern and Southern veterans described participating in a bayonet charge as exhilarating. Surrounded by comrades, attackers relieved tension and tried to scare the enemy by screaming. Union troops gave a deep-throated "hurrah," and Confederates preferred the shrill "Rebel yell." As they advanced, the men felt they were an irresistible force, and they often were.

Of course, bayonet attacks could fail. A well-entrenched or determined enemy could thwart an assault, as happened to federal troops at Fredericksburg and Confederates at Gettysburg. When this happened, an attack tended to lose momentum quickly, and the fighting turned into a standoff of musket fire, with attackers often taking huge casualties.

Bayonet fighting in broken terrain was a different experience. Units tended to come apart in these areas. So, men fought alone or in small groups. Often, these fights turned into fierce scraps, characterized by clubbing with rifle butts and stabbing with bayonets. Combat like this happened more often than is widely realized. Notable examples include

The U.S. Army believed firmly that cavalrymen needed sabers as well as pistols and carbines. This period drawing by famous Civil War artist Edwin Forbes shows a cavalry orderly on duty with his mount and his trusty blade at his side.

The Battle of The Wilderness, *The Battle of The Crater* and *Battle for Fort Gregg* at Petersburg, Va.

Besides socket and sword bayonets, several other Union bayonets appeared during the war. The U.S. Navy, for example, developed a knife bayonet to fight with and to clear damaged rigging and lines. One inventor developed a sliding bayonet that worked like a modern gravity knife. Another innovator created

Federal troops make a river crossing in this period print. Note that they are doing so with bayonets fixed.

a saw-toothed bayonet for use by engineering troops and sappers. One of the most curious creations was an experimental shovel bayonet for entrenching.

After the bayonet, the second most common edged weapon in the infantry was the officer's sword. Officer's swords served as badges of rank as well as weapons. On campaign, officers typically carried a Model 1850 sword. For formal occasions, they might own more ornate and delicate dress swords. Another type of these weapons came in the form of presentation swords, which were purely decorative, quite elaborate and expensive. Admirers gave them to officers to recognize major achievements.

Besides bayonets, the most often used edged weapons of the war were cavalry sabers. They typically featured grips and hand guards, and long, curved blades with single sharp edges and pointy ends. These weapons first came into service during the 18th century in Europe. Sabers were a standard item in the U.S. Cavalry, starting with the Revolutionary War.

Union generals believed that the cavalry charge was an irresistible force. This idea was expressed often in professional books, articles and manuals,

including *Regulations and Instructions for the Field Services of the U.S. Cavalry in Time of War* and *Cavalry Tactics, or Regulations for the Instruction, Formations and Movements of the Cavalry of the Army and Volunteers of the United States.* In the latter volume, cavalry commander Philip St. George detailed how to train men with the saber. Practice began on foot. This allowed troops to master parries, slashes and great sweeping movements without harming their mounts. Regiments spent much time on saber drills. Surviving letters indicate that cavalry recruits felt they had truly become soldiers once they mastered this weapon.

SABER SELECTION

The U.S. Army issued three basic types of sabers: the Model 1833, the Model 1840 and the Model 1860. The 1833 saber had a 34-inch blade. The Model 1840 blade was almost a yard long, and, due to its unwieldy nature, was called "Old Wristbreaker."

As the war progressed, the Models 1833 and 1840 fell out of favor. The Model 1860 gained in popularity due to its 30-inch blade, which made it

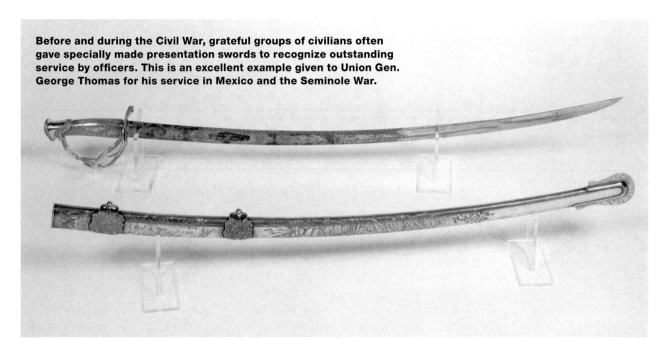

Before and during the Civil War, grateful groups of civilians often gave specially made presentation swords to recognize outstanding service by officers. This is an excellent example given to Union Gen. George Thomas for his service in Mexico and the Seminole War.

comparatively light and easy to handle. Officers and enlisted men carried sabers, although officer models tended to have better fits and finishes. Sabers did see effective service during the war. However, cavalry was deployed in many ways besides the traditional dramatic charge.

"There's nothing as foolish as bringing a knife to a gunfight, and cavalry quickly adapted by transforming themselves into a highly mobile infantry. Typically Civil War cavalry provided reconnaissance, defended the flanks or rear of the army, and executed long-distance raids. The offensive role of cavalry, typified by Napoleon earlier in the century, was effectively ended with the proliferation of rifled weapons on the battlefield," Talkov said.

"There are, of course, examples of cavalrymen pitching into other cavalry troops, like at Gettysburg and Brandy Station, with pistol and saber and a few of mounted cavalry charging into infantry—*First Manassas, The Battle of Third Winchester* and *The Battle of Five Forks*—but the primary weapon of the cavalry became the breach-loading or repeating rifle."

Sabers were utterly useless in forested areas. However, as with the infantry, attacks across open ground could prove effective.

If a cavalry attack hit demoralized infantry or cavalry, then the foe usually fled. However, resolute infantry could slaughter mounted units. Cavalry-on-cavalry fights could turn into melees, characterized by individual combat with men flailing away at one another. Experience soon taught soldiers that a thrust was often more effective than a slash.

Edged weapons figured prominently in military ceremonies during the Civil War. Here, Zouaves (light infantry regiments in the French Army) wear their colorful, exotic uniforms, and, with bayonets fixed, march in a review. Artist Edwin Forbes captured this scene.

While bayonets and sabers did not figure as prominently in the Civil War as they had in previous conflicts, they still played a role—one that they would never have again. Massing troops for an assault ceased to make any sense once machine guns, tanks and airplanes appeared on 20th-century battlefields. Thus, as far as edged weapons were concerned, the Civil War was the last "ancient" conflict where cold steel and determined men could change the course of history.

Inspired by Old Knives in His Collection

This maker takes an occasional coffee break to ponder the designs of the knives he has collected

By Joe Szilaski

I would say that I've been making knives for longer than I like to remember, but I really do love my profession. During my several decades on the "knife circuit," I attended many knife shows and met so many great folks that I now call friends. I have been impressed by the talents of some of my fellow knifemakers, and enjoy swapping stories with them, sharing dinner, drinks and techniques. I have made and sold many knives and tomahawks over the decades, and yes, even purchased a few knives for myself.

My collection is not the biggest. I have seen more impressive collections, some to which, I am proud to say, a few of my knives and tomahawks now belong. Mine is not a high-value collection, as many pieces are simple rusty flea market finds.

But over the years, buying the pieces I could afford led to a decent collection of knives, axes and tools. Most are from the 1840s to late 1900s, a few earlier than that. My knife collection comes from all over the world, but most pieces are from the many knife manufacturers local to me in the northeast United States.

I always enjoy looking at this collection as a whole. My mind often wonders off. I am reminded of a childhood field trip to an arms and armor museum in Budapest. It is one thing to see photos of these ancient weapons and tools in a history book, but quite another to see the actual pieces on display. Some of the thousands of items on display in that Budapest museum are from the stone, copper, bronze, iron and

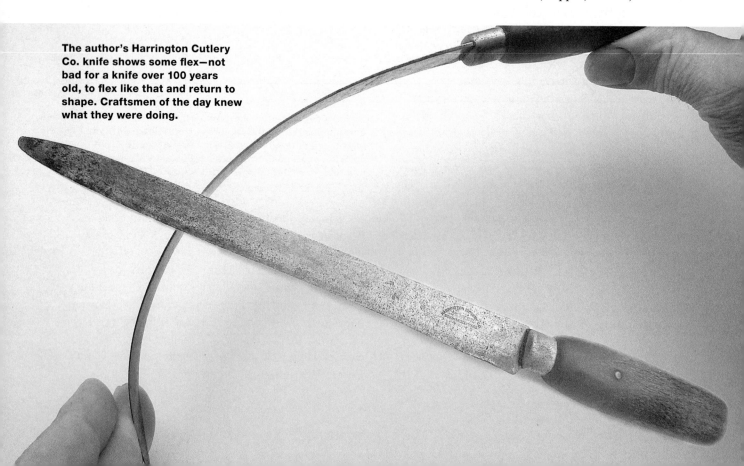

The author's Harrington Cutlery Co. knife shows some flex—not bad for a knife over 100 years old, to flex like that and return to shape. Craftsmen of the day knew what they were doing.

The author says he believes the hand-forged blade is a harvesting knife. Note the serrations, and on the back of the blade, numbers 1 through 10, which may have been a rough measuring device.

steel ages. I remember clearly my amazement over such unbelievable workmanship—knives, swords, war hammers, bows, armor and tools with high-relief carving on bone, wood and ivory, as well as inlays of copper, brass, silver and gold.

Understanding how such works of art were made in days without electricity changes everything. Sometimes, maybe while on a short coffee break, I pick up one of these pieces and take my time to really look at it again.

A particular knife with a "hawk bill"-style blade that often gets my attention is one I found about 35 years ago at an antique store. According to the owner of the store, the knife was made around 1880 and used as a pruning knife. While I thought the size of the knife was much larger than the average pruning knife, the price was reasonable and so I bought it. I bought it because it was certainly a nice, interesting piece.

Most likely a blacksmith, talented farmer or homesteader forged the blade. Whoever forged it knew what he was doing. The blade is forged to shape, all the way down to where it forms a keen cutting edge. Even under a magnifying glass, I could not find one grind or file mark on that blade, but what is most interesting to me is the serrated edge. Full serrations along the cutting edge of the 6 3/8-inch blade were formed using a chisel, which is not as easy as it sounds. To accomplish something like that is tedious work.

Chiseled into the other side of the blade are the numbers 1 to 10, fairly evenly spaced at almost a half-inch apart each. I assume the letters P K that are etched into the blade are the initials of either the owner or the maker, and that the numbers may have

been for taking measurements while using the blade.

It is a well-made knife, and I just had to try it without first sharpening the blade. The knife cut a couple of 1/2-inch-diameter branches with no problem. However, it did much better cutting corn stems, sunflower stalks and some heavy weeds. It is shaped like a pruning knife, and was, according to the seller, used for that purpose. But after testing the blade by cutting a variety of vegetation, I believe the knife was designed to be a multi-purpose harvesting tool. Either way, I love this particular tool; it is simple and well executed, with its own character and beauty. I have never found another one like it, but that does not mean there aren't others out there.

WATCHING GRANDPA WORK

Studying the knife, and the way it was made, I am reminded of my grandpa. He was one of the wisest and most talented men I have ever known. He could figure out how to make and repair things using very basic tooling. Luckily for me, the school I attended was only a block away from where my grandparents lived, and I stopped there almost every day after classes. I am not sure what I enjoyed more—my grandma's cooking or watching Grandpa work on something.

Anyway, one day I remember my grandfather sitting in front of a small post anvil with a boxful of used, bent nails. I watched how he would straighten them out. After a short while he looked up and asked if I would like to help. So that was my first real lesson on how to use and control a hammer. I remember that I missed the nails a lot, but even with bruised fingers and fingernails singing the blues, I was still

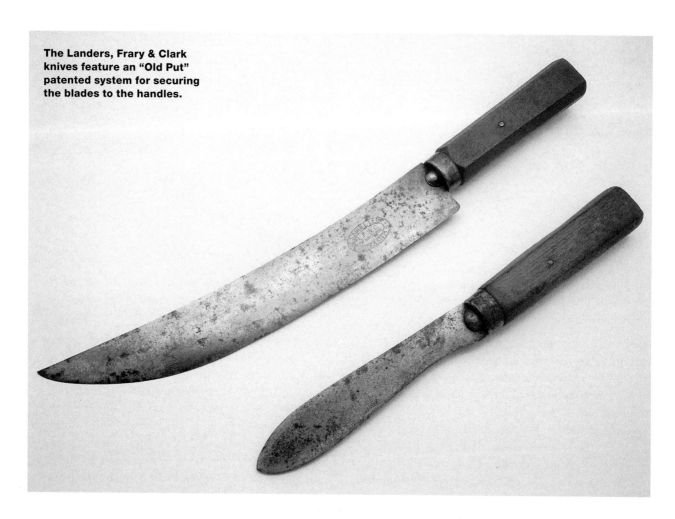

The Landers, Frary & Clark knives feature an "Old Put" patented system for securing the blades to the handles.

one happy kid. Over the years Grandpa taught me how to use a vast number of hand tools.

Looking again at the individual knives that make up my lifetime collection, I am perplexed not only by the impressive workmanship, but also by what the purpose behind each design might have been. Sometimes it is quite challenging to unlock the knife design mystery. If time would allow, I could spend endless hours studying each particular piece because, when I finally think I have found the answer, it feels like I have just met the maker face-to-face.

Sometimes the answer is simply cultural. Every region of the world and any period in time had its style of knives, swords, axes or tomahawks. The design and use of these were based on and dictated by the environment the people lived in, and a move to a new environment is when the style and form of an edged tool or weapon changed dramatically. Hundreds and thousands of years ago, our ancestors started developing the tools and weapons that were best suited to them and their surroundings.

Back when these pieces were made, the craftsmen needed to know how to make their own tools.

This was necessary to be more efficient and more precise in fashioning the particular item. There were no parts or hardware stores. They were their own hardware stores, as well as masters of their craft.

Back when I was in trade school, I was invited to the home of one of my teachers, a 4th-generation blacksmith. Behind his house stood a well-kept old barn. He showed me all of his treasures, the tools and gadgets that his father, grandfather and great grandfather had made. There were endless hand tools, hammers, tongs, chisels, forming blocks, swage blocks and so on. The majority of these tools were handmade. Some were built only for one particular application and used to make very precise parts for machinery. That afternoon proved to be a once-in-a-lifetime experience for me.

After the visit, I was then required to make my own tools and jigs, and so on. A young guy, I did not fully comprehend how important it was back then to be able to make your own tools, but it became a valuable lesson for me.

I consider myself very fortunate to have learned so much from my grandpa and the four master

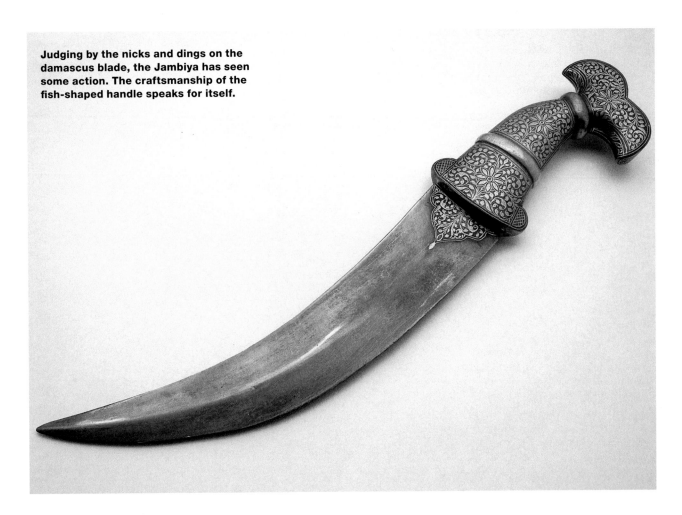

Judging by the nicks and dings on the damascus blade, the Jambiya has seen some action. The craftsmanship of the fish-shaped handle speaks for itself.

smiths I had as teachers in trade school. Each had a different technique to offer. While I learned most everything from them, I still continue to learn by time spent studying these old tools and weapons.

A CLEVER CLAMPING SYSTEM

I have a pair of butcher knives that, in most respects, is not any more special than the next set, but one interesting feature is the way the blades are secured to their handles. Made by Landers, Frary & Clark, the patented "Old Put" never-loosen system was employed, which is actually a clamp system. The clamp is placed over the blade tang and forced into a smaller hole in the wood handle so the wood itself tightly clasps the clamp. The inner edge of the steel ferrule presses against the larger end of the clamp, forcing the clamp tightly up against the blade. On some of the bigger knives, there is also a 1/16-inch pin. This is a clever system.

I've also seen such knives with the right sides of the blades completely flat ground, while the left sides had slight convex grinds to the cutting edges. I am still not 100 percent sure if this was done by

the manufacturer or the owner of each knife as an alteration for his or her own use.

In my collection is a dagger in the style known as a "Qama." It is of Caucasian origin, and later used in most Ottoman and Persian regions. I believe this particular piece is Russian made. The blade is a slim, double-edged dagger or short sword with a nice convex edge. What fascinates me most is what people refer to as blood grooves. The blood grooves on my Qama are off-centered on either side of the blade so that they are not opposite each other, and therefore the blade is not too thin in this area and does not lose strength. This helps with less chance of warping during the blade heat-treating process. Also interesting are the fine craftsmanship and exquisite filigree work on the handle and scabbard.

Another Persian knife in my collection is a *Wahabite*, also known as a long *Jambiya*. A double-edged dagger, it showcases a gracefully curved blade and a convex edge—quite a nasty dagger if you ask me. In experienced hands this dagger could inflict maximum damage and, in my opinion, is more deadly than any straight dagger. Also, it was an

The two smaller leather tools, in a collection that is still quite serviceable after 100 years, were most likely used for harness work.

important part of a man's dress and social standing. Each Arabian region had its particular style of decoration on a dagger hilt and scabbard.

Over 90 percent of the knives I've had the opportunity to study have one thing in common—convexground edges. Don't get me wrong; I am not trying to say there is anything wrong with other types of blade grinds, just that the majority of the pieces I studied had convex grinds. Samples of convex-ground blades can be found from all over the world.

We can learn a lot by studying these old and sometimes ancient pieces made by highly skilled craftsmen of bygone days. They knew more about the design and function of edged weapons and tools than we would have imagined. They were doggone good at their craft. Whether an edged tool or weapon was very ornate or simple, the craftsman's main concern was strength and function. Back then tools were a part of everyday life and existence.

The designs developed thousands of years ago were so perfect that today we don't have much room

to improve upon them. For instance, they have found copper axes dating back to 3300 B.C. of the same shape that we use today. It is true that we have developed better tooling and steel, and therefore we are more efficient and independent, but all that is just a refinement of what our ancestors created.

Of course, even in this modern world, we still have thousands upon thousands of knowledgeable and talented old-fashioned craftsmen. Sadly, that number is decreasing, and a lot of knowledge was lost in an age of mass production. Granted, today we have marvelous tools and materials available to us, but this will never replace the knowledge that our ancestors had.

Like I always say, the question is not how much we know, but how much we don't. Looking at all these old edged tools and weapons, I formed my opinion long ago, that our ancestors were geniuses. I believe that studying and understanding ancient tools and weapons helped make me a better maker.

TRENDS

Year after year, the knifemakers make the book editor's job easy. The Trends in knives practically present themselves, or the knifemakers fashion trendy knives that are relatively easy to spot and categorize once all the images of the finely crafted blades reach the editor's desk. Then the drooling begins, more because of the sheer beauty of the knives than the age of the editor, though it could be a combination of the two.

It's the creativity of the knifemakers that drives Trends in knives. There is always something new on the horizon, even when the craftsmen and ladies are fashioning copies of traditional patterns. They make the patterns their own, adding their own flair and personality, upgrading them with new materials, tweaking the patterns, embellishing them or improving upon the designs. New, high-tech materials help, sure, but often it's a whole new concept that takes root, sprouts, reaches skyward and blossoms. It could be a fantasy scythe, a miniature multi-blade Sheffield-style pocketknife in powder-metal steel, a replaceable-blade folder or a takedown bowie.

How could there be something new in knives when everything's been done before? It's a good thing we don't all ask such questions or knifemakers wouldn't be fashioning pinecone- or cactus-handle flipper folders with bronze bushings and ball-bearing thrust washers. Nor would they build steampunk knives, gent's tacticals, spring assists or compound-ground, laminated blades with meteorite inlays. Year after year, the bar gets raised higher, and the *KNIVES* editor becomes more and more complacent.

Titanium, Tritium & Timascus

Now we all know that knifemakers are innovative, and we've seen incredible creativity in design, blade grinding, handle materials, damascus forging, one-hand-opening folder mechanisms, locks and gadgets. The very title of this section is "Trends," and those don't just happen without innovation. But using a radioactive isotope of hydrogen on a knife? One called *tritium* that contains one proton and two neutrons, an isotope that is rare on earth where trace amounts are formed by the interaction of the atmosphere with cosmic rays? Does it sound like science fiction? No, it's non-fiction, real life, and true that some knifemakers inlay tritium into knife handles because it glows, looks incredibly cool and might actually help a guy stumbling around in the dark find his knife.

That last part might be a stretch, but it's not the first time knifemakers have looked to the stars to find knife handle and blade material. They've been forging meteorite into knife blades and using it in handles for millennia. There's mystique and legend surrounding ancient Egypt, and Tutankhamun, who had meteorite forged into a blade before the use of iron, of gold/meteorite knives among the Mongols or James Black using meteorite in Col. James Bowie's blades.

More commonly, knifemakers shape and often anodize titanium, using it for bolsters, liners and handles, or laminate two or more titanium alloys into patterns resembling damascus and resulting in what is known as *Timascus*. Various alloys color differently by heating or anodizing them, so the color combinations are endless, like the stars in the sky, the cosmos and the galaxies beyond.

◀ **RICK BARRETT: The "Fallout Flipper" is outfitted in a handsome 1095 blade with wispy temper line, a titanium frame lock and a colorful Moku-Ti (mokumé and titanium) handle.** *(Cory Martin Imaging)*

▲ **KIRBY LAMBERT: As colorful as a closet of hippie clothes, the Moku-Ti handle of the multi-ground XHP flipper folder catches the eyes of all passersby. The bolsters are zirconium.** *(SharpByCoop image)*

◀ **GLENN WATERS: The theme of the flipper folder is lightning, bolts of which are engraved in the VG-10 blade, striking out from the titanium handle that has Timascus, titanium and carbon fiber fittings/overlays.**

▼ **BRIAN NADEAU:** Sporty "weaved hex-pattern" titanium handles lead into integral (though colored differently) bolsters and Rob Thomas damascus blades.
(SharpByCoop image)

◄ **RON APPLETON:** The purple and gold hues of the "Voodoo'" one-piece, solid titanium handle play together much better than the Minnesota Vikings. Check out the dimpled A2 blade.
(SharpByCoop image)

◄ **GUSTAVO CECCHINI:** The "Plasma" model is electromagnetic alright, with handle frame materials including titanium, Timascus and the isotopic tritium.
(SharpByCoop image)

▲ **ALLEN ELISHEWITZ:** The "Zirco-Ti" (zirconium and titanium) handle scales will go with most any party pantsuits, and in this case enliven a "Tank" flipper folder with zirconium bolsters and a laminated blade that incorporates Chad Nichols stainless damascus.

Mammoth Markings

▲ **RODNEY WATTS:** Here's a blue tooth, attached to a two-blade fighter in ATS 34 stainless steel, from long before Bluetooth meant wireless technology. *(SharpByCoop image)*

▲ **KURT SWEARINGEN:** The "Saddle Pass" folder moseys along well in mammoth ivory and 416 stainless steel. *(SharpByCoop image)*

▼ **PAUL K. BROWN:** Whether the rings of the cross-cut mammoth ivory are age lines or just well-earned character, the 4-inch hunter with hidden pins is better for them. *(Ward image)*

▼ **KYLE HANSON:** This is proof positive that it's a good idea to dress your damascus utility knife in mammoth ivory. *(SharpByCoop image)*

▲ **BARBIE BELL NOLTE:** It took a dyed mammoth tooth, Al Frisillo engraving and a good knifemaking hand to stack up to the Robert Eggerling mosaic damascus. *(Ward photo)*

▶ **REINHARD TSCHAGER:** Equally stunning are the patterns of the Uwe Heieck damascus blade and mammoth tooth handle, highlighted by engraved gold inlays and pins.

▼ **ANSSI RUUSUVUORI:** Abalone spacers frame the mammoth tooth like ice walls surrounding the frozen tundra.

◀ **JOSH SMITH:** Mammoth ivory handle scales and a sapphire-inlaid thumb stud highlight the mosaic damascus folder with matching bolsters.

(PointSeven image)

▲ **J.W. RANDALL:** Mammoth ivory has the ability to give even more character to a "Texas-wind-pattern"-damascus drop-point hunter than it already has. The ferrule is mosaic damascus next to a fileworked spacer.

▲ **TOM HEARD:** The transition from the stainless damascus blade to the mokumé bolsters and cross-cut mammoth tusk handle scales is seamless on a mid-release auto.

▼ ALAIN and JORIS CHOMILIER: While the Matthias Styrefors mosaic damascus blade and bolsters represent the wooly mammoth and its footprints, the knifemakers say the mammoth bark handle is the same color as the forests of yore, presumably at least!

► LARRY HOSTETTER: The blue mammoth tooth is the cracked ice that cools off the hot fileworked folder. *(PointSeven image)*

▲ WILLIAM C. "BILL" JOHNSON: The ATS 34 fighters attended the ball dressed to the hilts (and sub-hilts) in pinstriped mammoth ivory. *(PointSeven image)*

► PAUL LUSK: The crosscut mammoth ivory is so bold as to almost overpower the Angelo Bee bolster engraving in a hunting dog theme, almost.

(SharpByCoop image)

▲ JOHN GRIFFIN: Antiqued damascus bolsters match beautifully with the mammoth ivory handle scales of the lock-back folder.

▲ **JIM PROVOST:** While the mammoth tooth has a lot of bark left in it, the Damasteel blade does the biting. *(Cory Martin Imaging)*

▲ **ROBERT APPLEBY JR.:** A couple 440C drop-point utility knives illustrate how the color and figure of mammoth ivory can vary from slab to slab, tusk to tusk, beast to wooly beast. *(Ward image)*

▼ **TED BOEZAART:** Milky mammoth ivory hugs the tapered tang of a CPM 154 drop-point fixed blade. *(SharpByCoop image)*

▲ **JOHN COHEA:** Textured bronze and rawhide spacers make for the perfect respite between the lively damascus and mammoth ivory patterns. *(Ward image)*

◄ **MAMORU SHIGENO:** Blue mammoth tooth cuts as deeply as the Special Fighter's ATS 34 blade. *(SharpByCoop image)*

▲ **CHRIS KNAPTON:** Mammoth tooth makes its mark, and so do the Tony Metsala bolsters, amber-inlaid, jeweled thumb stud and upswept CPM 154 blade.

Knee-Bangin' Bowies

You've gotta love the ones that hang from the hip and bang on the knee when you walk. It makes you feel like John Wayne or Alan Ladd in *The Iron Mistress*. Long stretches of steel come to clip points and emit sheens so steely that the glares of cowboys don't measure up to the sight of them. These are knives that make an impression, those with history dating back to The Alamo and before, and are American icons that live up to their namesake, Col. James Bowie.

Bowie makers tend to hearken back to a time when edged tools were forged over a coal fire, handle materials taken from Mother Nature, guards wrestled into place, pommels pounded onto the ends of full tangs and edges honed to shaving sharp. The bowie makers I've known lean toward perfectionism, and polish blades using increasing grits of sandpaper until they find themselves hand rubbing 1,000-grit paper on blade steel that shines like a beacon.

And history is important to such folks, to be learned from, never forgotten and chronicled. These are the folks who keep history alive, through their work, their actions and deeds. It's a difficult lot in life, but one that is ultimately satisfying, like a long blade in a hand-tooled leather sheath, hanging from the hip and banging your knee when you walk.

◄**DOUG CAMPBELL:** Koa wood and a 1095 blade with temper line make the D-guard bowie dance. *(Ward image)*

◄**BEN BREDA:** The bowie in desert ironwood and W2 blade steel is a knee banger and an eye opener. *(PointSeven image)*

▲ **MIKE RUTH:** The damascus was so nice, the maker allowed it to continue past the blade, to the guard, the ferrule and clear to the pommel that caps the ancient walrus ivory handle. *(Caleb Royer Studio image)*

▶ **AKIO SHINOZAKI:** Only stag with nickel silver fittings would do for this Sheffield bowie in a fabulously fileworked ATS 34 blade.
(SharpByCoop image)

◀ **STEVE RANDALL:** The differentially heat-treated, 9-inch W2 blade would cut the slab bacon around the campfire, and more than one dude would want the chance to hold the ironwood grip. *(Ward image)*

▲ **PAUL BRACH:** Exuding tradition is a 14.5-inch I*XL-style bowie in stag and an oval guard. *(PointSeven image)*

▶ **KEN HALL:** This particular bowie hangs down the leg a good 15.5 inches, from the maple butt to the W2 blade tip.
(Ward image)

▲ **LOGAN PEARCE:** This one's called a "Ballroom Bowie," in damascus and box elder burl, and it would be the cat's pajamas to shuffle around the ballroom with it at your side.
(SharpByCoop image)

▼ BILL KIRKES: The walrus-ivory-handle bowie is done up in brass and a length of pointy steel. *(Ward image)*

◄ RICK "BEAR BONE" SMITH: In a dog-bone-style ebony handle, this mirror-polished O1 tool steel bowie is fetching in its own right, complete with German silver escutcheon and a few star-mosaic pins.

◄ LEE BERG: The blade is meteorite that looks like it exploded across the edge, like a star streaking across the sky on a moonlit night. Fossilized walrus anchors the piece, or tails the shooting star. *(Ward image)*

▲ GARY MULKEY: Historically inspired, the George Woodhead reproduction parades a walrus ivory handle, a cast pommel, and nickel silver and sterling silver fittings. *(Ward image)*

▲ JIM BATSON: Crown stag and a forged iron guard were inspired choices for a 17.25-inch 1095 bowie. *(PointSeven image)*

▼ **MARK KNAPP:** The maker manipulated the fossil walrus ivory to look like scales on this trophy of a damascus bowie. *(SharpByCoop image)*

▶ **LIN RHEA:** Big blades like this pattern-welded piece forge their own trails, leaving a wide swath in their wake. Mammoth ivory and stainless fittings trail behind but hold their own.

(Ward image)

◀ **LARAMIE JACKSON:** The brass guard, spacers and pommel add a little golden sparkle to the 440C stainless steel bowie featuring an alternative ivory grip.

◀ **JOHN E. CHASE:** Bocote with nice grains makes for one fine furnishing on the classic O1 bowie.

▲ **PHIL EVANS:** You wouldn't want to cheat at cards if this stag-handle bowie with W2 blade was within reach of your fellow poker players.

(Ward image)

Knee-Bangin' Bowies

▶ **JERRY FISK:** Engraving by the maker adds a little glint to the stainless steel guard, ferrule and pommel of a stag and damascus bowie that, on its own, puts a gleam in the eye. *(Ward photo)*

◀ **DON MCINTOSH:** The brass back strap is an identifying feature of this Joe Musso-style bowie that also sports a 13.25-inch 5160 blade, ironwood handle, and a brass guard and spacers. *(Ward image)*

◀ **RAYMON HUNT:** The fossilized walrus ivory handle of the 5160 bowie wears a wide stripe, accessorizing it with mild steel and gold fittings. *(Ward image)*

▶ **JOHNNY PERRY:** Seven domed nickel silver pins secure the camel bone handle to the 15 7/6-inch George Woodhead-style bowie. *(PointSeven image)*

▲ **STEVE KOSTER:** This D-guard bowie dons a 350-layer damascus blade and a stag grip. *(PointSeven image)*

▶ **MIKE QUESENBERRY:**
The W's-pattern
damascus would dominate
most bowies, but this one
has domed pins and fossil
walrus ivory to balance the
piece, as well as a five-piece
spacer that includes nickel
silver and more damascus.
(SharpByCoop image)

▶ **JEFF CLAIBORNE: A**
13-inch, stag-handle "Texas
Bowie" showcases filework
covering the full-tang L6
blade, as well as the brass
guard and pommel.
(Hoffman image)

▶ **RICK MARCHAND:**
The knifemaker calls
the copper back strap
a "parry strip," and it's
easy to see how one could
ward off blows using the
12.75-inch hand-forged
1095 blade while holding
the hemp-wrapped grip, hand
protected by the D-guard.
(SharpByCoop image)

◀ **CHUCK
RICHARDS:** The
bog oak was
carbon dated to
be 5,460 years
old, and now lives
on as the handle of
a differentially heat
treated W2 bowie.
(BladeGallery.com image)

▲ **J.T. PALIKKO:** The Iron Mistress-
style bowie boasts a mirror-polished
high-carbon-steel blade, a decorated
and darkened brass guard and pommel,
damascus liners and an ebony handle.

▼ J. NEILSON: Three types of meteorite make up the blade—Muonalusta, Odessa and Seymchan—with a core of 1095 high carbon steel next to a Seymchan meteorite guard, and a crown stag and ironwood handle. *(Caleb Royer Studio image)*

▶ GARTH HINDMARCH: There probably wasn't a lot of dyed camel bone available for knife handles in Jim Bowie's day, but there is now, and the modern damascus bowie is the beneficiary.

◀ HENRY TORRES: The 52100 and stag bowie is nearly as straight as an arrow.
(PointSeven image)

▶ STEVE CULVER: Ironwood so beautiful it's framed in nickel silver, and damascus daring enough for more than 8 inches of bowie blade, this one's a looker.
(SharpByCoop image)

◀ JOHN HORRIGAN: The edge isn't really black, just laminated and heat treated to show the smoke, complemented by a hot-blued mild steel guard, gold inlay and a fossil walrus ivory grip.

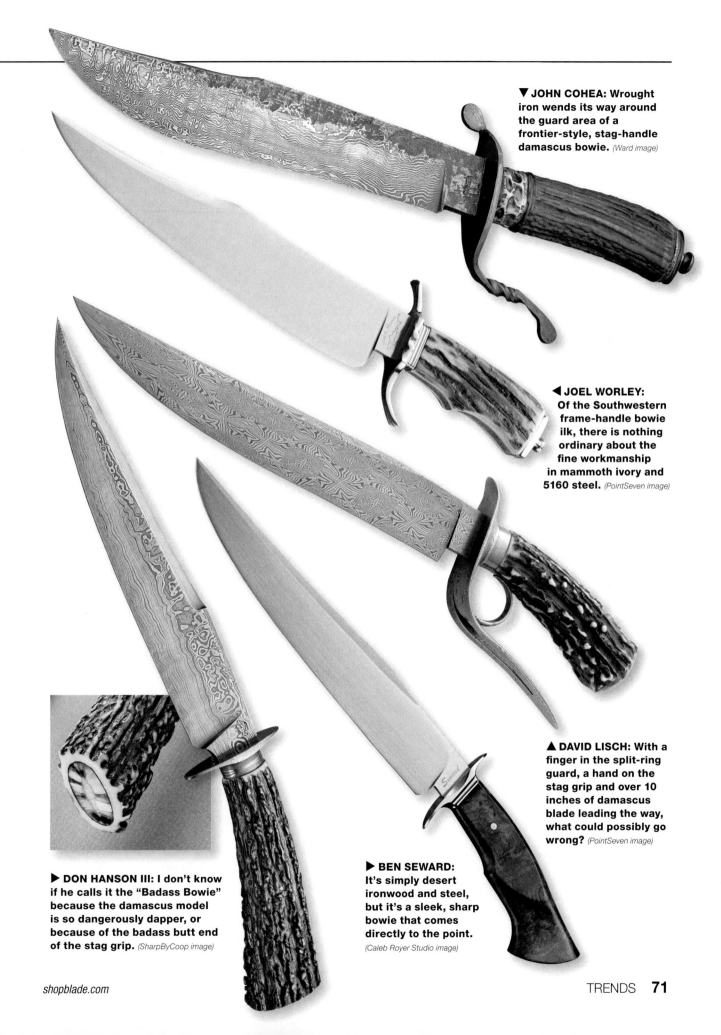

▼ **JOHN COHEA:** Wrought iron wends its way around the guard area of a frontier-style, stag-handle damascus bowie. *(Ward image)*

◄ **JOEL WORLEY:** Of the Southwestern frame-handle bowie ilk, there is nothing ordinary about the fine workmanship in mammoth ivory and 5160 steel. *(PointSeven image)*

▲ **DAVID LISCH:** With a finger in the split-ring guard, a hand on the stag grip and over 10 inches of damascus blade leading the way, what could possibly go wrong? *(PointSeven image)*

► **DON HANSON III:** I don't know if he calls it the "Badass Bowie" because the damascus model is so dangerously dapper, or because of the badass butt end of the stag grip. *(SharpByCoop image)*

► **BEN SEWARD:** It's simply desert ironwood and steel, but it's a sleek, sharp bowie that comes directly to the point. *(Caleb Royer Studio image)*

Bronze Stars

Though the custom knives incorporating bronze into their makeup can never be compared to soldiers awarded Bronze Stars for combat heroism or meritorious service, they are bronze stars in their own right, because they shine. Bronze is such a versatile material, lending industrial and industrious looks to the blades built using the alloy. A bronze patina is a palatable, soothing look, and utilitarian in its strength, solidity and wear resistance.

Besides, it gives knives a golden glow, a hue that might be mimicked through anodizing and heat-treating, but can never be truly duplicated. And bronze is bold, manly and mighty. One can form bronze through lost wax casting, and some of the world's greatest sculptures are bronze. Even busts are bronzed.

Knifemakers tend to be or become experts in materials manipulation. Like sculptors, they form bronze into objects of art and utility, turning what could otherwise be quite mundane into bronze stars that shine like new pennies, only not copper—that would be another book section.

◀ **PETER MASON: Hand sculpted and dimpled bronze fittings highlight the 22-inch short sword in a damascus blade and wild olivewood handle.**

▶ **KEN HALL: Bronze interlocks with ironwood for the guard and handle of a "Keyhole Hunter" equipped with a 5.5-inch W2 blade and smoky temper line.** *(Ward image)*

▲ **ANDERS HOGSTROM: The solid handle of the Damasteel fighter/boot knife was carved in wax, then cast in bronze using the lost wax casting technique.**

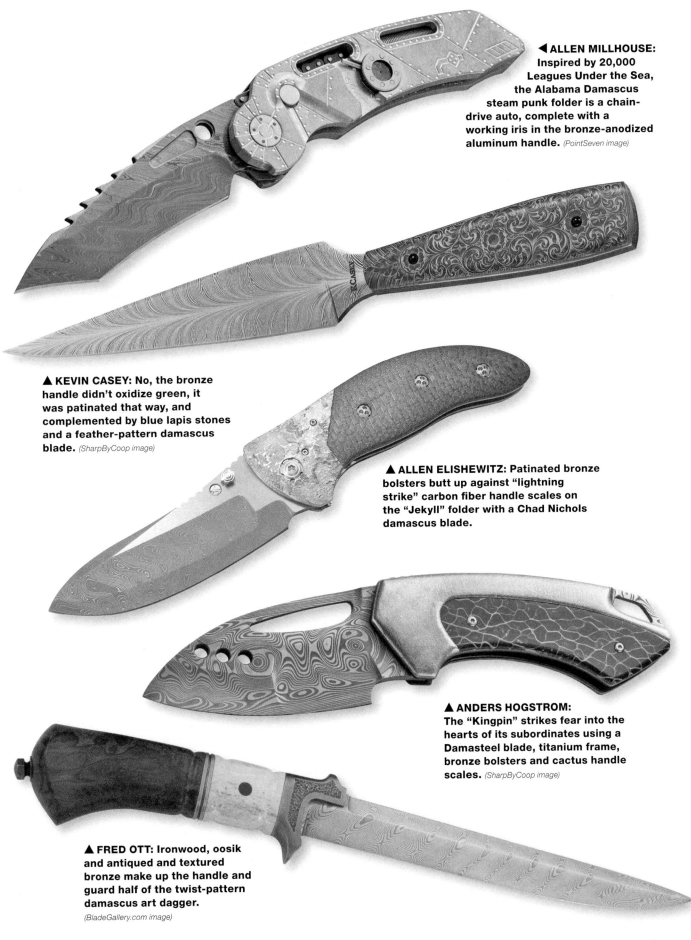

◀ **ALLEN MILLHOUSE:** Inspired by 20,000 Leagues Under the Sea, the Alabama Damascus steam punk folder is a chain-drive auto, complete with a working iris in the bronze-anodized aluminum handle. *(PointSeven image)*

▲ **KEVIN CASEY:** No, the bronze handle didn't oxidize green, it was patinated that way, and complemented by blue lapis stones and a feather-pattern damascus blade. *(SharpByCoop image)*

▲ **ALLEN ELISHEWITZ:** Patinated bronze bolsters butt up against "lightning strike" carbon fiber handle scales on the "Jekyll" folder with a Chad Nichols damascus blade.

▲ **ANDERS HOGSTROM:** The "Kingpin" strikes fear into the hearts of its subordinates using a Damasteel blade, titanium frame, bronze bolsters and cactus handle scales. *(SharpByCoop image)*

▲ **FRED OTT:** Ironwood, oosik and antiqued and textured bronze make up the handle and guard half of the twist-pattern damascus art dagger.

(BladeGallery.com image)

#DopeDaggers

If a guy was going to Tweet about something, "Dope Daggers" would be a good subject, with a hash tag in front, of course, for good measure. Yes, #DopeDaggers is an awesome Twitter message, alongside a .pdf or link to an image of a sweet handmade dagger fresh from the forge. It's not a bad thing to talk about, bring to the forefront or communicate to a mass audience, and much more interesting than the latest thing Kim Kardashian or Miley Cyrus had to say, neither of whom, I'm quite certain, could come close to building an acceptable dagger.

Not many folks have the skills to fashion symmetrically accurate daggers, those with edge-holding blades, comfortable, non-slip grips and protective yet non-clunky or hand-pinching guards. The utilitarian pieces are purpose built for piercing and cutting, ground to even edges and stout but pointy tips, easy to slide into custom sheaths. These are not tools to be taken lightly, but lifesaving measures that serve multiple purposes and satisfy many needs.

Yes, there are worse things to Tweet about than Dope Daggers. One could brag on a hot girlfriend, a great singing voice or the sighting of a movie star on a street corner, you know, such things as those that keep the world spinning on its axis. Or a simple message like "#DopeDaggers" could go out and someone might just contact the Twitter account holder, purchase one of the maker's pieces and carry the tool for a lifetime. #MostAwesomeDude

◄ **PEKKA TUOMINEN:** Fluted fossil walrus ivory spirals toward the mosaic-damascus guard and damascus blade of the stiletto-style dagger.

◄ **DANIEL WATSON:** There's only one custom dagger in the bunch that sports a handle of copper wire strung in a Celtic knot pattern, complete with emerald beads.
(SharpByCoop image)

▲ **MARK KNAPP:** Sheep horn and sunken oak meld together on the grip of a dope damascus dagger.
(SharpByCoop image)

► **RICK MARCHAND:** Deer bone, hemp wrap and a peen-hammered blade do a 1095 dagger proud. *(PointSeven image)*

▲ **LLOYD HALE:** You really do want to shout "hell yeah" to "Gigi's Hale Yeah" dagger in a fluted ebony handle with a silver chain wrap, a 440C blade, sculpted guard and black-lip-pearl pommel inlay. *(SharpByCoop image)*

◄ **ANDERS HOGSTROM:** The walrus ivory handle of the "Punch Dagger" has a natural "tab," or dip, where it meets the bronze fitting, making it perfect for the knife style. This particular piece of walrus was once used as an axe or adze by native Alaskan Inuit Indians.

► **WILLIAM LLOYD:** The carved ivory dragon flashes a toothy grin, hovering over a Bocote wood spacer, talon-like guard and shapely damascus, bladed body. *(PointSeven image)*

◄ **DANIEL ERICKSON:** The "Vested Dagger" does have a vest-like hardwood handle and an integral ladder-pattern damascus blade and frame. The wood is Kamagong, of the ebony genus.

◀ **FRED OTT:** Little did the ancient walrus know that its jaw would make a nice spacer for a fine damascus dagger in an ironwood handle and mammoth ivory pins. The offset dagger blade is sharpened on both sides. *(BladeGallery.com image)*

▶ **DIANNA CASTEEL:** While the dagger blade is orchestrated perfectly in Mike Norris stainless damascus, the picture-frame-style handle is equally ingenious, including a gold-lip-pearl inlay. *(PointSeven image)*

▶ **JAMES BATSON:** The slim waist of the maple handle curves outward to a mokumé guard and damascus dagger blade. *(PointSeven image)*

▶ **DWIGHT PHILLIPS:** From the damascus blade to the silver-wire-wrapped, fluted handle, the quillion dagger is a doozy. *(SharpByCoop image)*

▼ **RAYMON HUNT:** Ebony, silver and O1 tool steel are the key ingredients of a 9.75-inch boot dagger, complete with a coffin-shaped handle. *(Ward image)*

▶ **TIM TABOR:** The Fairbairn-Sykes-style dagger is executed flawlessly in ironwood and 5160 steel.

(Ward image)

▼ **RON NEWTON:** A diamond-pattern damascus blade is pitted against a wire handle that features gun-blued steel and two-toned stainless steel in one funky matrix.

(Caleb Royer Studio image)

▼ **RAY ROGERS:** There's nothing fancy about Micarta® and steel, not, at least, until they're fashioned into a fine fixed-blade dagger.

▼ **MARDI MESHEJIAN:** The fully integral, hand forged, double-edged damascus dagger is of sole authorship and soulful workmanship.

(PointSeven image)

▲ **MICHAEL TYRE:** The mosaic damascus blade is 340 layers, the spacers 150 layers, the frame 240 layers, and the handle all walrus. *(PointSeven image)*

It's Pocket Science

I t's not exactly like a mad scientist crouched over test tubes, with vapors rising into the air as chemicals combine and combust, bubbling over onto the laboratory table where he wipes off the overflow with a white coat sleeve and continues mixing powders into the wee hours of the evening. No, it's not like that, but sometimes the parts of traditional pocketknives are so small, makers use OptiVisors, loupes or other magnifiers just to see and work with them. And most knifemakers don't have dainty hands with long, slender fingers. Fumbling for a folder spring can be a frustrating exercise in futility.

Yet, there is a science to fashioning high-end, quality pocketknives. There's nothing more grating than a folding knife blade that rubs against a liner or handle frame, or an edged implement that flops loosely in and out of the handle like a broken pocket comb. Makers of precise pocketknives deal with tolerances, tensions and all kinds of inner trappings, parts, mechanisms, springs and pivots. Parts must be assembled, fit, finished, tightened and aligned so that each works independently of the others, or if in conjunction, then seamlessly, with no interference among implements.

Does it sound like mad science? It can be maddening, but pocketknife makers aren't mad scientists. They're precision engineers working in the edged implement business. Think of it as pocket science.

◀ **JOEL CHAMBLIN:** Aptly named the "Regal," this one sashays carved black-lip-pearl handle scales, 24k-gold pins, Damasteel bolsters and CPM 154 blades. (Ward image)

◀ **RON NEWTON:** A good pocket scientist uses "popcorn stag," feather-pattern damascus and Celtic knot engraving for a five-blade sowbelly pattern. (Ward image)

▼ **EUGENE SHADLEY:** The "Woodsman" is an auto-assisted opener in stag and stainless, thank you very much.
(SharpByCoop image)

▶ **CALVIN ROBINSON:** A liner-less slip-joint pattern, the big trapper features a 14C28N stainless steel blade and a carbon fiber frame with a stainless escutcheon and shield.

(PointSeven image)

▶ **GARY CROWDER:** Mammoth ivory adds a touch of class to a three-blade stockman in ATS-34 stainless steel. *(Ward image)*

▲ **T.R. OVEREYNDER:** Crediting Tony Bose for the pattern, the maker created his version of a lock-back whittler from CTS-XHP steel, antique Remington bone and 18-karat rose gold. *(PointSeven image)*

▲ **KENDALL SCHORSCH:** A traditional two-blade trapper gets a modern G-10 handle, ATS-34 stainless steel blades and some South Texas "grass burr"-pattern filework.

(PointSeven image)

◀ **RON LAKE:** Known for his patented interframe folders, the maker fashions a couple with special lock-release tabs and stag handle inlays. *(SharpByCoop image)*

▼ **LUKE SWENSON:** Exuding tradition is a stag-handle two-blade trapper in stainless steel and fileworked liners. *(SharpByCoop image)*

◀ **RICHARD TESARIK:** A gent's folder blends hippo and mammoth ivory, as well as titanium and RWL-34 blade steel. Groovy. *(SharpByCoop image)*

▶ **BRUCE BARNETT:** Born into privilege, the two-blade 440C trapper is outfitted in ringed gidgee wood and engraved bolsters. *(PointSeven image)*

▲ **JIM FLEMING:** It's nice to see a "Daddy Barlow" pattern in corncob-jigged red bone, brass, nickel silver, 440C stainless and a half stop so the blade doesn't close on the fingers. *(Cory Martin Imaging)*

Wicked Edges

They're not inherently wicked or evil. In fact, anyone who is a gun or knife enthusiast knows all too well that inanimate objects cannot be or do evil. They need help from devilish, no good, rotten humans with ice in their veins and blackened hearts. So the edges aren't really wicked in terms of meanness. They're wicked in the sense of being sharp, stealth, pointy, curved, claw-like and scary looking. They are made to penetrate, chop, slash, puncture, rip or tear cutting media. And they're utilitarian or fantasy pieces, tactical or military models, artistic renderings or purpose-built, hard-core using knives and tomahawks.

The edges will cut you if you're not careful. The points will prick the skin. They are to be handled with care and respect. That's another thing hunters and shooters will tell you, as well as police and military—to have respect for your weapon. You don't point it where, if misfired, it could injure or kill someone. It is a tool that takes training to operate, practice to perfect and real-life action to master.

These tools are most fun to fashion, I imagine, with edges that swoop up and dip down, points that protrude and serrations that bite. They tear through cutting media like meat-eating animals. They're not evil, not mean, just wicked edges with some nasty bite to them.

▶ **BILL BUXTON:** The spike tomahawk in damascus and wood chops with one end and punctures using the other.
(SharpByCoop image)

▶ **LOGAN PEARCE:** An antique finish gives the blade an even meaner look than the carbon-fiber-handle, claw-like karambit already has.
(SharpByCoop image)

▶ **DANIEL PETERS:** One of the better names for a knife in the book, the "Angry Ginger" holds its own, and its temper, in a CPM 3V blade and a black canvas Micarta handle.

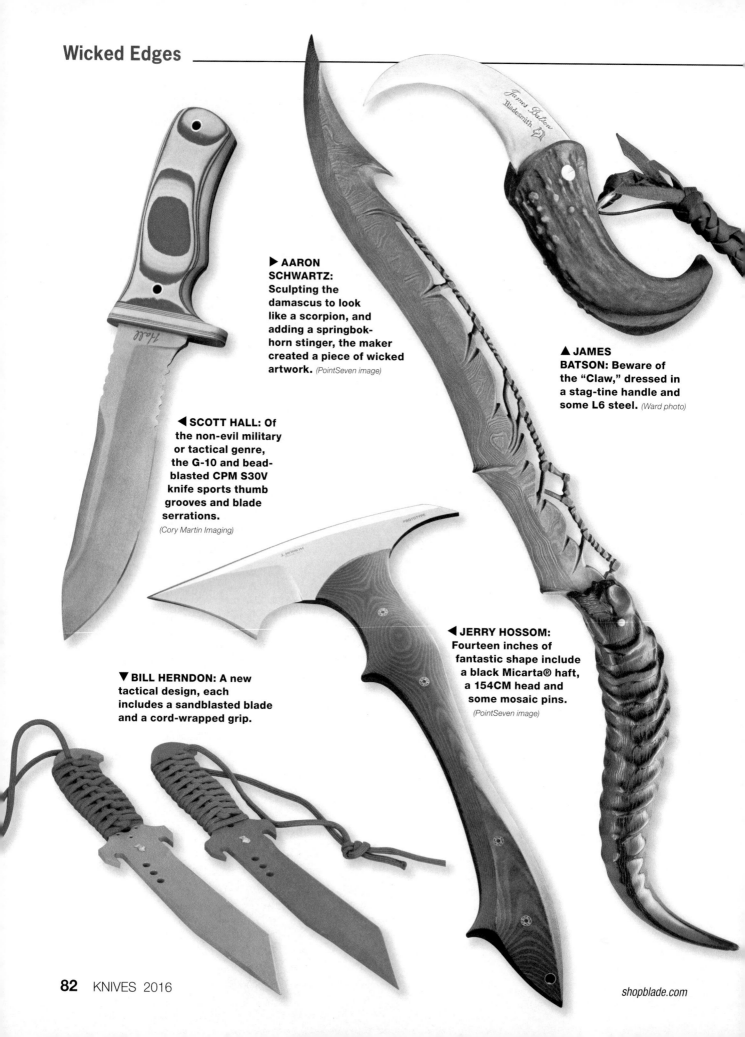

▶ **AARON SCHWARTZ:** Sculpting the damascus to look like a scorpion, and adding a springbok-horn stinger, the maker created a piece of wicked artwork. *(PointSeven image)*

◀ **SCOTT HALL:** Of the non-evil military or tactical genre, the G-10 and bead-blasted CPM S30V knife sports thumb grooves and blade serrations. *(Cory Martin Imaging)*

▲ **JAMES BATSON:** Beware of the "Claw," dressed in a stag-tine handle and some L6 steel. *(Ward photo)*

◀ **JERRY HOSSOM:** Fourteen inches of fantastic shape include a black Micarta® haft, a 154CM head and some mosaic pins. *(PointSeven image)*

▼ **BILL HERNDON:** A new tactical design, each includes a sandblasted blade and a cord-wrapped grip.

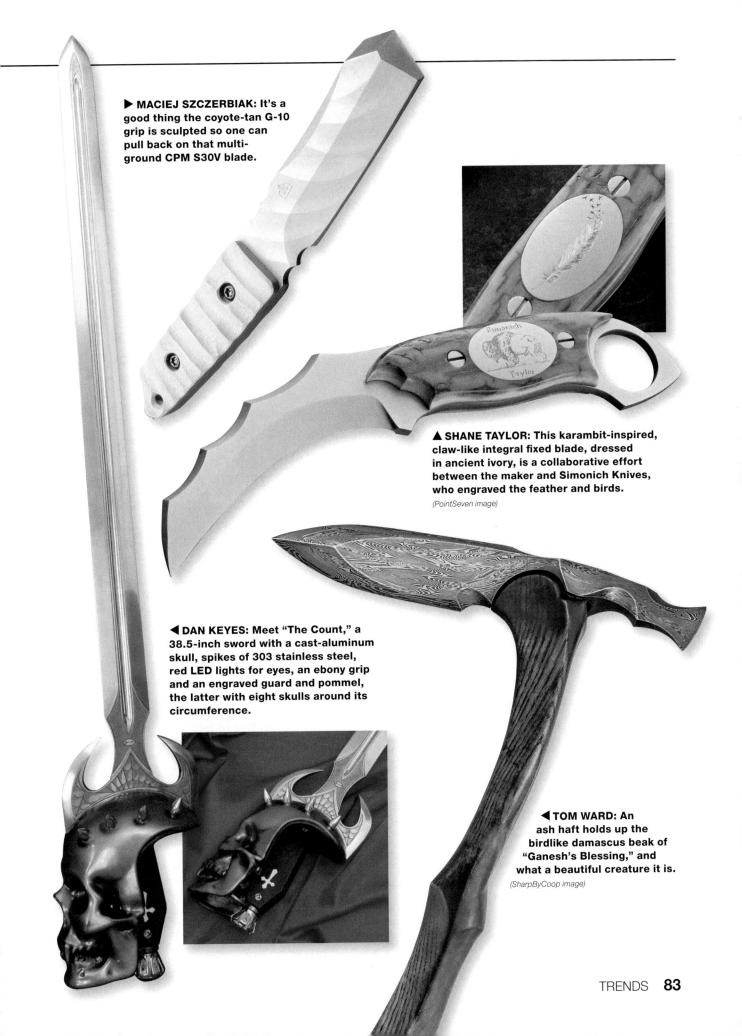

▶ **MACIEJ SZCZERBIAK:** It's a good thing the coyote-tan G-10 grip is sculpted so one can pull back on that multi-ground CPM S30V blade.

▲ **SHANE TAYLOR:** This karambit-inspired, claw-like integral fixed blade, dressed in ancient ivory, is a collaborative effort between the maker and Simonich Knives, who engraved the feather and birds.

(PointSeven image)

◀ **DAN KEYES:** Meet "The Count," a 38.5-inch sword with a cast-aluminum skull, spikes of 303 stainless steel, red LED lights for eyes, an ebony grip and an engraved guard and pommel, the latter with eight skulls around its circumference.

◀ **TOM WARD:** An ash haft holds up the birdlike damascus beak of "Ganesh's Blessing," and what a beautiful creature it is.

(SharpByCoop image)

Edges of the World

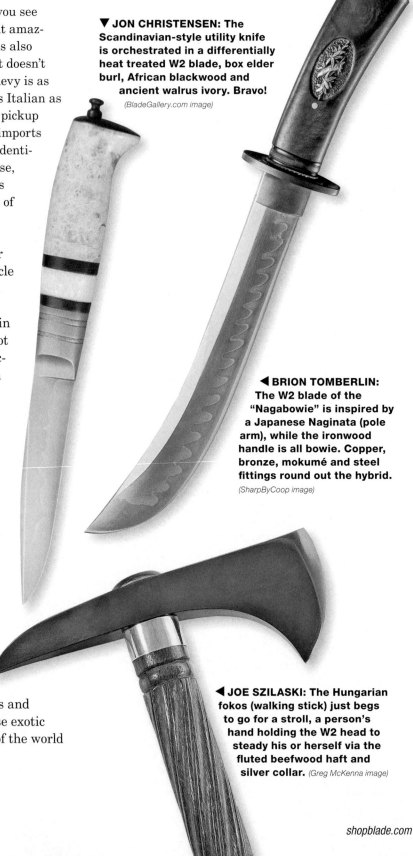

You know it's American when you see it. That's the easy part. Isn't it amazing how something "foreign" is also instantly recognizable? And it doesn't matter which country you live in, a Chevy is as American as a Ford, and a Maserati as Italian as a Ferrari. One doesn't look at a Dodge pickup truck, and say, "Wow, those Japanese imports are sure stylish." The Dodge is easily identified as an American truck. And likewise, even the most novice of car enthusiasts can tell that a Hyundai isn't a product of Detroit, Mich.

So should knives and swords be any different? When you shrink your product down from the size of a vehicle that a person rides inside to a knife he or she carries, one might think that identifying it by country of origin would be more difficult. But that's not the case. Many knife enthusiasts recognize Persian upswept blades when they see them, Scottish basket-hilt swords, Japanese tantos or waki-zashis, French poniards, Napalese kukris and American bowie knives. Those are the easy ones. But can you identify a Hungarian foko or a Spanish belduque? It doesn't take much practice.

Perhaps we're more worldly than we give ourselves credit for. Sure, the average American can't likely name the countries of South Africa, but we know Chinese food when we taste it, a Cuban cigar when we smoke it and a Mexican fiesta when we attend one. Regional recognition isn't limited to geography, but also includes cultures, people, clothing, food, arms and armor. That means knives, and these exotic beauties will take you to the edges of the world and back. Or is the world round?

▼ **JON CHRISTENSEN:** The Scandinavian-style utility knife is orchestrated in a differentially heat treated W2 blade, box elder burl, African blackwood and ancient walrus ivory. Bravo! *(BladeGallery.com image)*

◄ **BRION TOMBERLIN:** The W2 blade of the "Nagabowie" is inspired by a Japanese Naginata (pole arm), while the ironwood handle is all bowie. Copper, bronze, mokumé and steel fittings round out the hybrid. *(SharpByCoop image)*

◄ **JOE SZILASKI:** The Hungarian fokos (walking stick) just begs to go for a stroll, a person's hand holding the W2 head to steady his or herself via the fluted beefwood haft and silver collar. *(Greg McKenna image)*

▼ **VINCE EVANS:** One thing about building a Scottish basket-hilt sword in an 18th-century style is that there's plenty of room for silver and gold wire inlay, and of course for a nearly 32-inch damascus blade. *(SharpByCoop image)*

◄ **J.T. PALIKKO:** I wouldn't have wanted to run into a German Landsknecht, but I love their 15th- and 16th-century swords, this modern rendition in a forged-to-shape high-carbon-steel blade, a fileworked guard and pommel, and an antler grip.

▶ **DENNIS BRADLEY:** Few Persian bowies are executed in hollow-ground, mirror polished stainless steel, with sculpted handles and guards, but perhaps more should be.

(SharpByCoop image)

▲ **DAVID MIRABILE:** A San Mai (laminated) blade is married to a wrapped carbon fiber and Alaskan yellow ash handle, and a copper and titanium guard—an ancient knife design with modern materials. *(SharpByCoop image)*

▶ **WALLY HOSTETTER:** The katana is 28.5 inches long on the cutting edge, and just as long on workmanship, including a cord-wrapped stingray skin hilt, a copper habaki (blade collar) and a textured tsuba (guard). *(PointSeven image)*

◀ **ALLEN ELISHEWITZ:** It doesn't get much better than a Persian bowie in a Chad Nichols damascus blade, dimpled zirconium guard and mastodon-ivory handle, unless of course Lela Milani Khoshbin is holding it.

▲ **SCOTT S. DICKISON:** With a nod to his Scottish heritage, the maker fashions a sgian dubh in a bog oak handle, mosaic pins, a nickel silver guard and a fileworked Alabama Damascus blade. *(Cory Martin Imaging)*

▶ **KEVIN CASHEN:** An exact recreation of a 15th century sword found in a French tomb, this one stretches 42 inches and includes a traditional wire-wrapped handle and an L6 tool steel blade. *(Steve Dean image)*

▶ **WILLIAM LLOYD** and **K.C. LUND:** The impeccably carved ivory hilt, guard and pommel of the damascus Crusader sword elevate the piece to papal status. It comes with an English elm and walnut shield. *(PointSeven image)*

▶ MIKE QUESENBERRY:
The Argentina-silver-wire-wrapped, fluted blackwood hilt of the main gauche (French left-handed dagger) is surrounded by a silver basket and guard, and three-piece damascus spacers at the end of the handle, not to mention a 13 1/8-inch ladder-pattern damascus blade.

(SharpByCoop image)

◀ DON CARLOS ANDRADE: Forged to shape using 52100 blade steel, a pair of French knives includes green maple handles, G-10 inlays and tribal wraps.

▶ MATTHEW GREGORY: This "Kwaiken" awakens the senses, done up in a 5-inch W2 steel blade with distinct hamon (temper line), a tapered tang and a wrapped red stingray skin grip.

◀ JASON BURTON: Of traditional (Japanese) takedown construction is a wakizashi in a 22.5-inch W2 blade, canvas Micarta® hilt, and copper and brass fittings. *(Ward image)*

▼ **RICK BARRETT:** One vicious rendition of a Japanese tanto, with some liberties taken, it features a differentially heat-treated and polished 1095 blade and a cord-wrapped stingray skin handle. *(Cory Martin Imaging)*

◄ **HILL PEARCE:** Though he officially retired in 1990, the maker's fantastic rendition of a Spanish/Mediterranean belduque deserved inclusion herein.

(SharpByCoop image)

▶ **PEKKA TUOMINEN:** Let the Gurkha kukri cutting commence, this version in a spring steel blade, bronze bolster and curly birch handle.

▶ **BADGER BLADES—STEVEN BARKUS and LOUIS BRACHT:** Whether it's the 5160 blade with a long fuller, the guard and pommel that are based on a royal Nordic female burial sword, or the ostrich tibia bone handle (kid you not) carved to resemble a bearded Viking with a herringbone hair braid, this sword sings. *(PointSeven image)*

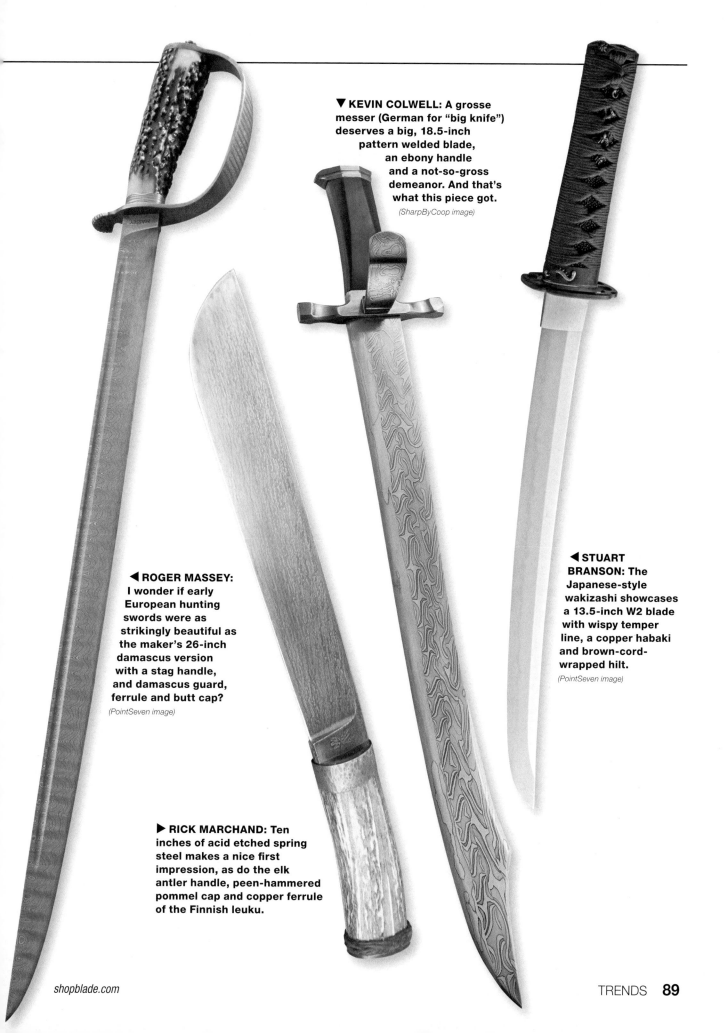

▼ **KEVIN COLWELL:** A grosse messer (German for "big knife") deserves a big, 18.5-inch pattern welded blade, an ebony handle and a not-so-gross demeanor. And that's what this piece got.

(SharpByCoop image)

◄ **ROGER MASSEY:** I wonder if early European hunting swords were as strikingly beautiful as the maker's 26-inch damascus version with a stag handle, and damascus guard, ferrule and butt cap?

(PointSeven image)

◄ **STUART BRANSON:** The Japanese-style wakizashi showcases a 13.5-inch W2 blade with wispy temper line, a copper habaki and brown-cord-wrapped hilt.

(PointSeven image)

► **RICK MARCHAND:** Ten inches of acid etched spring steel makes a nice first impression, as do the elk antler handle, peen-hammered pommel cap and copper ferrule of the Finnish leuku.

Pinecone, Cactus, Coral & Abalone

I see a pinecone, and I think of tree sap that might have seeped between the scales, or its overall conical shape, sharp projections and seeds. I look at a cactus and can almost feel the prickles, or remember the time I ate cooked cactus at an upscale restaurant, savoring the moment, as cactus is quite good when properly prepared. Coral conjures up beautiful images of the blue-green Caribbean, a colorful array of fish and slimy sea creatures. And from those same seas, the brilliant interior of an ear-shaped shell—abalone—evokes visions of nature's hues that can only come from the ocean, translucent, shiny, deep purples, blues, greens, oranges and yellows.

That's not what knifemakers see. Well they might see those things, but they also envision knife handles. Yes, pinecones make knifemakers think of something that could anchor a blade. A tall, old gnarly, prickly cactus suddenly becomes a hilt in the eyes of the artist. Perhaps it's a mirage. And coral and abalone, well, they inspire craftsmen and ladies to fashion grips for their new hunters or folders.

It is not all the knifemakers' doing. If we had to pinpoint the true culprits, then knife materials handlers would take the stand. The suppliers are the ones who blend cactus or pinecone with epoxy to come up with hard, stable handles. Yes, when they see pinecone, cactus, coral and abalone, they don't just see plants, trees and oceanic offerings. They envision hardcore knife handles.

◄ **TRAVIS PAYNE:** The pinecone handle is downright palpable, and the fileworked 440C blade and bolsters engraved by Matt Litz are palatable in their own right. *(PointSeven image)*

◄ **ALAIN and JORIS CHOMILIER:** Leaf-like bronze fittings envelop the coral handle, and grapes sprout from the high-carbon, mosaic-damascus blade forged by Joel Davis.

▲ **ROSS MITSUYUKI:** The whale engraved on the titanium bolster lunges up from the sea, hinting at the origins of the colorful handle material—pink coral—and toward another sea of Devin Thomas damascus.

▼ **DENNIS BRADLEY:** A prickly pear cactus cast in epoxy became the handle of a "Copperhead" hunter in CPM 154 steel and a copper guard and bolts. The sheath is, what else, copperhead-snakeskin leather.

◄ **ALEX DANIELS:** Abalone adds the right aesthetic to a 440C custom fixed blade.

(PointSeven image)

◄ **JIM SORNBERGER:** The California-style art knife called for a silver handle with California abalone inlays, and a finely finished ATS 34 stainless steel blade. It comes in a fully engraved sheath.

◄ **BILL REDD:** Abalone gives the snakeskin-pattern-damascus, drop-point skinner a bit of an aesthetic advantage.

▲ **ANSSI RUUSUVUORI:** Tiger coral shows its stripes along the grip of a zone-tempered 1080 steel blade, complete with nickel silver bolster.

Pack and Field Blades

Venturing out into the wide blue yonder, an exhilarating experience as it may be, isn't to be taken lightly. Respect for the great outdoors and all it has to offer is nothing to be scoffed at. There are hidden dangers. You could slip on a wet rock traversing a stream, get caught in the dark or cold, become lost in the woods, accidentally venture between a mama bear and her cubs, sink in the mud or break through lake ice.

It's nice to have a pack knife, a field blade, axe, tomahawk or neck knife along to help get yourself out of such situations. Such could be used for cutting cloth for a tourniquet, stabbing into ice or the bank of a stream, sparking a flint, cutting wood or tent stakes, skinning game animals, filleting fish or sharpening a pole into a spear. Pack and field blades are those used to make meals, cut clearings and split kindling. They help us to survive and be comfortable in the outdoors. Pack and field blades are using knives and edged tools that go with us when we're on the go.

Knifemakers generally aren't the sit at home and watch TV types, and neither are knife users or active outdoors people. And active lifestyles can be healthy lifestyles … as long as you tote a pack and field blade wherever you go.

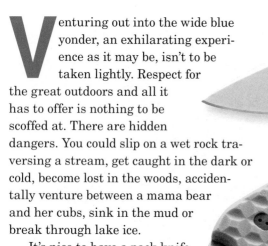

▲ **BRAD LARKIN:** Grooved, green G-10 makes for a good grip on the "Guardian 3" model, as attached to the tang of a 3-inch, drop-point M390 blade. (*PointSeven image*)

▶ **JOE SZILASKI: A prime example of the genre is a "Back Packer's Belt Ax," this one in a W2 tool steel head and hickory haft.**

(*Greg McKenna image*)

◀ **LEVI GRAHAM: Matched walnut handle scales hug the tapered tang of a forged 1095 high-carbon-steel belt knife. The textured metal bolster is wrapped with rawhide.**

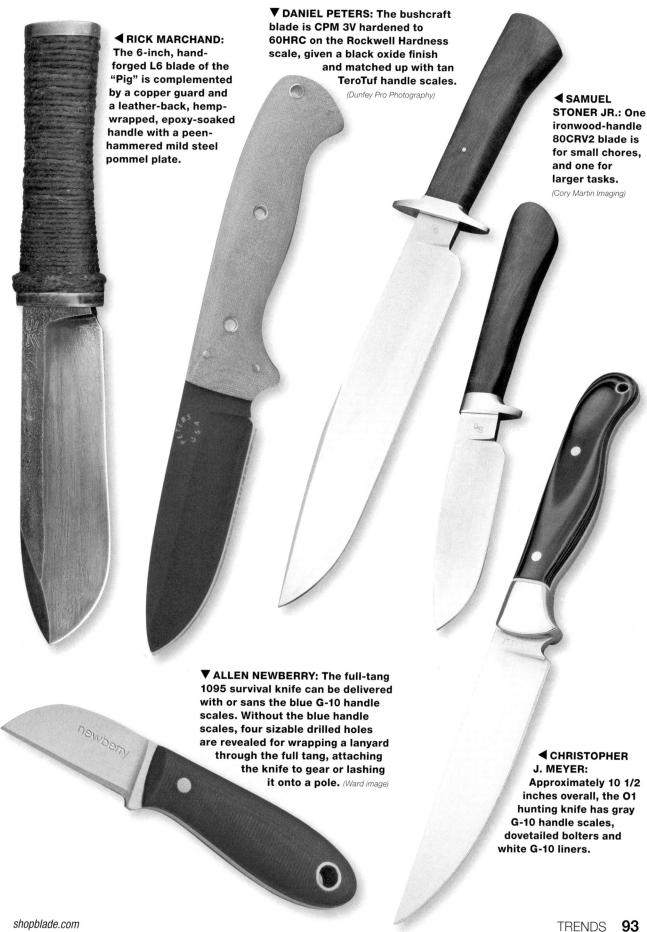

◀ **RICK MARCHAND:** The 6-inch, hand-forged L6 blade of the "Pig" is complemented by a copper guard and a leather-back, hemp-wrapped, epoxy-soaked handle with a peen-hammered mild steel pommel plate.

▼ **DANIEL PETERS:** The bushcraft blade is CPM 3V hardened to 60HRC on the Rockwell Hardness scale, given a black oxide finish and matched up with tan TeroTuf handle scales. *(Dunfey Pro Photography)*

◀ **SAMUEL STONER JR.:** One ironwood-handle 80CRV2 blade is for small chores, and one for larger tasks. *(Cory Martin Imaging)*

▼ **ALLEN NEWBERRY:** The full-tang 1095 survival knife can be delivered with or sans the blue G-10 handle scales. Without the blue handle scales, four sizable drilled holes are revealed for wrapping a lanyard through the full tang, attaching the knife to gear or lashing it onto a pole. *(Ward image)*

◀ **CHRISTOPHER J. MEYER:** Approximately 10 1/2 inches overall, the O1 hunting knife has gray G-10 handle scales, dovetailed bolsters and white G-10 liners.

Pack and Field Blades

▼ **JOHN COHEA:** What says "frontier knife" better than a 1095 tool steel blade, and some copper, rawhide and elk stag? *(SharpByCoop image)*

▲ **JAMES SCROGGS:** A handy pack and field blade boasts a 6-inch, spear-point CPM 154 blade and a Bastogne walnut handle. *(Ward image)*

◄ **KEVIN CROSS:** Spalted ash, African blackwood and brass anchor the 12 3/4-inch CPM S35VN chopper/camp knife. *(SharpByCoop image)*

► **LUDWIG JANSEN VAN VUUREN:** This hollow-ground outdoors knife sports a Sandvik 12C27 blade and an African leadwood (Ceratostigma) handle, along with mosaic and aluminum pins.

◄ **JOHN E. CHASE:** The D2 spay blade of the hunter has as much heft as the black linen Micarta® handle.

▲ **STEVEN J. TEDFORD:** Designed for field dressing game, the Talon, with its ATS 34 blade, cocobolo handle and full, tapered tang, would suffice for many outdoor chores.

◀ **RICK POIRIER:** More than 12 inches of completely fileworked O1 blade, complete with single, integral guard, make for a burly pack knife with a handle to match. *(SharpByCoop image)*

▲ **NATHAN CAROTHERS:** It's hard not to like the clean CPM 3V fixed blade handled in checkered G-10. *(SharpByCoop image)*

▲ **MICHAEL DEIBERT:** The rustically beautiful camp knife incorporates a Brut de Forge-style 5160 blade and an amboyna burl handle. *(PointSeven image)*

▲ **FRED OTT:** For the fancy outdoors person, the Colorado Camp Knife comes in a silver-wire-inlaid curly maple handle, a crown-stag butt, antique wrought iron S-guard and a W2 blade with wavy temper line. *(BladeGallery.com image)*

The Ivory Handlers

Not to be confused with the elephant handlers seen at the circus, zoo or in a parade, those with colorful clothing and wide-brimmed hats, these are ivory handlers, ones who prepare ancient or legal elephant ivory for the grips of knives. Some of the knifemakers wear colorful clothing and wide-brimmed hats, but it is not a prerequisite. Neither is the spraying down of enormous pachyderms or the collection of elephant dung in the job description of the ivory handler. No, they stick to blade making and using the natural resources, i.e. ivory, that elephants have left in their thunderous wakes.

Ivory is a stable, hard, beautiful material in its simplicity and purity, giving off a milky white or golden hue. Ivory knife handles are primed and ready for scrimshaw artists to come along and ply their trade deep within the pores of the material. Or, left of its own accord, as is the case with the knives in this "The Ivory Handlers" section, the knife grips allow damascus blades or fancy guards room to stretch out. Pure, white ivory is an elegant touch on a damascus bowie or a drop-point hunter.

The Ivory Handlers do not straddle the backs of elephants or ride within their twisted trunks, but rather treat, shape and save ivory tusks, giving them a second life and a utilitarian purpose as knife grips. The two are not to be confused.

◄ **LIN RHEA: A curvaceous D-guard wraps around the mammoth ivory handle of a damascus bowie.** (Ward image)

► **WADE COLTER: The little neck dagger is big on materials—a damascus blade, checkered ivory handle and sterling silver fittings.** (PointSeven image)

◄ **ELDON TALLEY: Mammoth ivory handle scales sandwich the tapered tang of a double-hollow-ground CPM 154 fixed blade.** (SharpByCoop image)

▶ **KYLE HANSON:** Mammoth ivory makes the small damascus fighter even more palpable than it already is.

(Ward image)

◀ **STEVE RANDALL:** With damascus blade, end cap and ferrule, as well as a hot-blued guard, the ivory handle is the icing on the cake.

(SharpByCoop image)

◀ **ADAM DESROSIERS:** Named for the "Orc Nouveau" damascus blade pattern, the "Orc Angel" is itself angelic in walrus ivory handle scales.

(Caleb Royer Studio image)

▶ **E.R. "RUSS" ANDREWS II:** You've gotta climb that ladder-pattern-damascus blade before you get to the interior-mammoth-ivory handle, and what a view from on high!

(Caleb Royer Studio image)

▲ **MIKE QUESENBERRY:** The smooth ivory handle and 52100 blade add equal parts of shine to the integral hunter.

(Caleb Royer Studio image)

Buffed Fighters

▶ **CLARENCE DEYONG:** In the "Stiletto Fighter" realm is a wickedly winsome blade fashioned from a mill file and anchored by layered G-10 and carbon fiber. *(Cory Martin Imaging)*

▼ **KEVIN KLEIN:** At 18 inches overall, "The Long Haul" fighter is in it for the duration, including a 15N20-and-1084 blade and integral bolster, a Bocote handle and silver spacer and pins. *(SharpByCoop image)*

▲ **MARCUS LIN:** Just because it's a Bob Loveless design doesn't mean the integral D2 and sambar stag chute knife was easy to execute, but just the opposite. *(SharpByCoop image)*

▲ **KEN HALL:** The keyhole shape where the ironwood meets the guard of the "Keyhole Fighter" might seem the toughest part to fashion, but the W2 blade with temper line is no easy feat, either. *(Ward image)*

▲ **SHAYNE CARTER:** Almost too pretty to fight (almost) is a feather-pattern-damascus model in desert ironwood and a dashing demeanor. Watch those suave ones! *(PointSeven image)*

► **KEVIN CASEY:** It's so easy to state that it's a "Feather Fighter" without truly taking time to appreciate the tight feather pattern of the damascus or the finely finished fossil walrus ivory grip. *(SharpByCoop image)*

◄ **DAVID SHARP:** A knife based on the profile of a Loveless Big Bear, its copper tsuba (guard) and habaki (blade collar) are of Japanese tradition, and how about the blade fullers, bevels and flats? *(SharpByCoop image)*

◄ **DON HANSON III:** The centerline of the "W's"-pattern damascus follows the fighter blade shape, dipping at just the right place, and anchored by an ancient ivory handle. *(SharpByCoop image)*

► **MIKE RUTH JR.:** The ladder-pattern-damascus blade and all fittings are from the same billet of steel, a pretty one at that, as is the ancient walrus ivory used for the handle and spacer. *(Caleb Royer Studio image)*

▲ **MIKE QUESENBERRY:** The only things not integral to the 52100 fighter are the clean pre-ban-ivory handle and domed sterling silver pins. *(Caleb Royer Studio image)*

Buffed Fighters

▼ **DAVID LOUKIDES:** You know you're on a roll when you start fashioning stag-handle sub-hilt fighters in pairs, these with 10- and 11-plus-inch damascus blades. *(SharpByCoop image)*

◄ **PAUL LEBATARD:** This recurved bowie, in stag and peen-hammered stainless steel, has some reach, doesn't it? It's 16.5 inches to be exact.
(PointSeven image)

▲ **RODNEY WATTS:** A tag team attack might call for self-defense using a two-blade fighter, like this one in ATS 34 stainless steel and carbon fiber. *(SharpByCoop image)*

▲ **NEILL SCHUTTE:** Burgundy linen Micarta was a Bob Loveless staple, perfect here for a Big Bear sub-hilt fighter of the Bohler N690 steel kind. *(PointSeven image)*

► **FRED OTT:** His "Blackwatch Fighter" has a fighting chance in a 7-inch, "twist"-damascus blade, a nickel silver guard, pierced ferrule and carved ebony handle.

▼ **BEN SEWARD:** Now the "Solstice Fighter," that's a rare bird one sees only twice a year, when the sun is at its highest, all the better to view the wavy temper line and ironwood grains.

(Caleb Royer Studio image)

► **MAMORU SHIGENO:** The "Special Fighter" has a fetching sculpted pommel and double guard, so I guess the stag-handle beauty is special at that.

(SharpByCoop image)

◄ **TONY BAKER:** If one were in the market for a "Camp Fighter," he could do much worse than the CPM 154 model in large-weave carbon fiber handle scales.

(PointSeven image)

► **J. NEILSON:** A Ka-Bar-style combat knife is prepared in a forged and antiqued 5160 blade with a saw-tooth spine, milled fuller, a black-canvas-Micarta handle and a hex nut pommel with tapered skull crusher.

Buffed Fighters

▶ **BILL BUXTON:** The damascus blade is a full 10 7/8 inches, jutting out from a damascus guard, titanium spacers and a stag handle like a tongue looking to give a lashing. *(Ward image)*

◀ **EDMUND DAVIDSON:** Specializing in full-integral knives, with blades, guards and pommels all one piece of steel, the maker shows us how a 17.5-inch piece looks in desert ironwood. *(PointSeven image)*

▲ **BILL BURKE:** Touches like a mokumé inlay within the artifact ivory handle, a cord wrap and the raised blade clip give this one some swagger.

(PointSeven image)

◀ **SEAN MCWILLIAMS:** A pair of "Kandhari Desert Fighters" would do well in the heat of conflict, considering the integral CPM S35VN blades, tapered tangs and cord-wrapped grips.

▶ **RICHARD CLOW:** You've gotta love the Loveless-style chute knives (parachute knives for Spec Ops pilots). Well, you don't have to, but considering the 4.5-inch CPM 154 blade, it's advisable. *(PointSeven image)*

◀ **STEVE GATLIN:** The Loveless Big Bear style remains popular, and it's easy to see why when looking at this example in stainless steel and ancient ivory. *(PointSeven image)*

▲ **LANDON ROBBINS:** Smoky temper lines blow across the 1084 blade of a beefy blackwood-handle fighter. *(Ward image)*

▲ **CALEB WHITE:** With a foreboding sense of elegance and lethal nature, the "Black Lily" has a sculpted Micarta handle in the shape of the rare, beautiful and ominous flower that is its namesake.

▲ **DANIEL WINKLER:** Synchronize your watch to exactly 0200 hours, grab the Micarta handle, I've got the maple grip, and we roll in 10 minutes. The Bontoc is a collaborative design between Winkler and Rafael Kayanan of Sayoc Kali (Filipino martial arts) fame. *(PointSeven image)*

▶ **PETER PRUYN:** With a San Mai blade of 1085 and anchor-chain wrought iron, this one's ready for the vessel launching dressed up in redwood burl and brass. *(SharpByCoop image)*

▶ **DAVID LISCH:** A split-ring ball guard separates the stag from the damascus, not that they don't go together beautifully. *(Ward image)*

◀ **MACE VITALE:** Don't worry—the blister-curl-maple grip won't give you blisters unless you really abuse the 1075 blade.

(SharpByCoop image)

▶ **BILL LUCKETT:** The "Combat Raptor" preys on other animals using a CPM 154 beak, a Masur birch body and stainless steel appendages.

(PointSeven image)

◀ **DANIEL ERICKSON:** Two knives made for military helicopter pilots, one side of each Micarta handle has a pin for over 100 missions, and the second side showcases pilot wings.

Gorgeous Grains

If a tree falls in the woods, we know one thing—a knifemaker will hear it. It's apparent that knifemakers spend a lot of time in the woods scrounging, scavenging and scaring up some of the prettiest burls this side of the Redwood Forest. Of course, the resourceful makers might also circumvent the felling of a redwood and go straight to their local knife handle supplier, or skip the log scrounging in favor of a materials dealer. I wouldn't put hunting for highly figured burls past them, though. These are guys (and gals!) who make their own handle screws, fashion pivots and even build the tools used to make the knives, by hand, without a production or assembly line. Chopping a little wood pales in comparison.

One thing that doesn't pale is the exterior beauty and gorgeous grains of the exotic, stable and stabilized woods the craftsmen and women attach to sharp blades. Each has its own character and lines, and like the knives themselves, no two handles are ever alike. Some are stained or oiled, sure, but most are simply sanded and polished to bring out the natural beauty, then sealed with a final coat for some lucky knife enthusiast who just purchased a brand new blade. The wood handles look so good with blades tucked into leather sheaths, too, handsome, classy and just downright pretty. They are truly gorgeous grains, and if a few trees were felled in the process, we hope responsible conservation was practiced. If occasionally a tree falls on its own, fear not, a knifemaker will hear it.

▲ **TOM HEARD:** With a Zoe Crist damascus blade and bronze-anodized bolsters, fileworked liners and buckeye burl handle scales, the mid-release automatic has a lot of patterns to palpate.

◄ **KYLE GAHAGAN:** An octagonal, dyed maple handle will make your fingers curl over, your eyes bug out and your knife enthusiasm bubble over. *(Caleb Royer Studio image)*

◄ **MICHAEL ZIEBA:** Some lucky sushi chef will own a pair of CPM S35VN blades in stabilized maple handles, and the thinner the slices shall become. *(SharpByCoop image)*

Gorgeous Grains

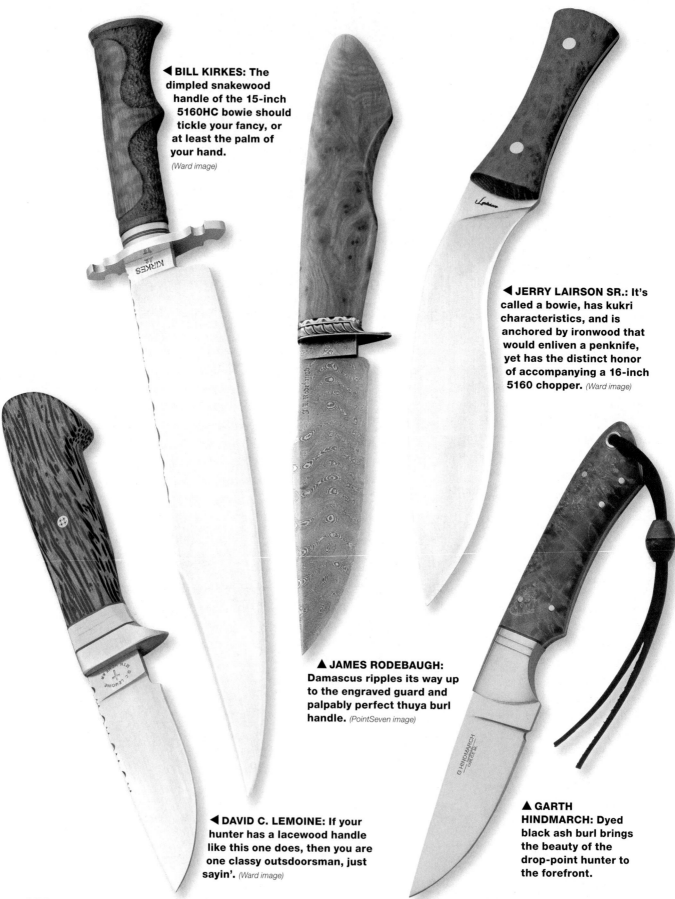

◀ **BILL KIRKES:** The dimpled snakewood handle of the 15-inch 5160HC bowie should tickle your fancy, or at least the palm of your hand. *(Ward image)*

◀ **JERRY LAIRSON SR.:** It's called a bowie, has kukri characteristics, and is anchored by ironwood that would enliven a penknife, yet has the distinct honor of accompanying a 16-inch 5160 chopper. *(Ward image)*

▲ **JAMES RODEBAUGH:** Damascus ripples its way up to the engraved guard and palpably perfect thuya burl handle. *(PointSeven image)*

◀ **DAVID C. LEMOINE:** If your hunter has a lacewood handle like this one does, then you are one classy outsdoorsman, just sayin'. *(Ward image)*

▲ **GARTH HINDMARCH:** Dyed black ash burl brings the beauty of the drop-point hunter to the forefront.

▼ **BRUCE BINGENHEIMER:** Which has more character, the "tiled-W's"-damascus blade or the koa wood handle? *(Caleb Royer Studio image)*

◀ **ROB HUDSON:** Matching up black ash and maple burl for the Damasteel clip-point fixed blade was ingenious, like crossbreeding a plum and an apricot.

◀ **ROSS MITSUYUKI:** Stabilized curly koa is as fetching as the engraved bolsters of a CPM 154 folder.

▲ **JERRY HOSSOM:** The full tang of the PSF-27 steel knife follows the flared butt of the amboyna burl grip all the way to the end, highlighted by a mosaic pin and some fancy workmanship. *(PointSeven image)*

▲ **TANNER WOLFE:** Try this one in a nicely shaped tulipwood handle and CPM S30V blade. *(PointSeven image)*

Gorgeous Grains

◀ **ROBERT BURNS:** A lovely length of timber, the bocote wood grip is complemented by a damascus blade, bronze guard and copper inlay. *(SharpByCoop image)*

▼ **JIM SISKA:** Snakewood is an apt choice for the thin, tapered bird-and-trout knife in a CPM 154 blade. *(SharpByCoop image)*

▶ **DOUN T. ROSE:** A maple burl and 440C stainless steel chef's knife will turn a fry cook into a Sous-Chef in no time. *(David Ricardo image)*

▲ **CHRISTOPHER MEYER:** Orange liners both underlay and highlight the olivewood handle of the 154CM neck knife.

◀ **RAYMOND L. SMITH:** Three mosaic pins secure the stabilized buckeye burl handle to the tang of the damascus push dagger/neck knife.

▶ **KEVIN CROSS:** Amboyna burl and white cedar are the winsome woods of a hunter equipped with a 4.5-inch CPM S35VN blade.
(SharpByCoop image)

◀ **MICKEY YURCO:** Spalted maple is one cool cat in the company of Alabama damascus.
(PointSeven image)

◀ **ERIK FRITZ:** Close the hand around the cocobolo and let the eye follow the 5160 blade down to the tip.
(PointSeven image)

▲ **GENE BASKETT:** The maker made good use of California buckeye burl on his fantastic folder in CPM 154 steel, gold-tone screws and thumb stud, titanium liners and some fancy filework.
(PointSeven image)

▲ **JAMES SCROGGS:** A favorite for large-caliber rifles because of its closed pores and hardness, Bastogne walnut apparently also works beautifully for CPM 154 sub-hilt bowies. *(Ward image)*

TRENDS **109**

▶ **RON ROSENBAUGH:** A bocote wood handle, yellow/orange box elder burl bolsters and mosaic pins make the mirror-polished ATS-34 stainless steel pack knife well worth packing.

▶ **GLEN MIKOLAJCZYK:** Does it get any better than a tiger maple and damascus pipe tomahawk with a walrus ivory mouth piece? Maybe if there was some tobacco and a chief present.
(Cory Martin Imaging)

▼ **EDMUND DAVIDSON:** Folks are green with envy over the stabilized box elder burl handle of an all-integral, hand-rubbed-finished CPM 154 fixed blade.
(PointSeven image)

▼ **MIKE SANDERS:** If a spalted-maple-handle drop-point hunter is your thing, and if not it should be, then the model with mosaic pins, nickel-silver guard and hand-rubbed 440C blade should suffice. *(Allen Alliston image)*

▲ **RON NEWTON:** The maker's new 15-facet handle design is executed here in cocobolo wood married with a 6.75-inch, double-ground, "diamond"-damascus blade.
(Caleb Royer Studio image)

◄ **MICHAEL RADER:** He put some blood, sweat and shine into the koa wood handle, pairing it with a damascus blade and guard, and mammoth-ivory, G-10 and copper spacers.

(Caleb Royer Studio image)

◄ **JOHN DOYLE:** One big bowie boasts a damascus blade and guard, a stabilized curly koa handle and a fileworked bronze spacer.

(BladeGallery.com image)

▼ **DANIEL ERICKSON:** For his 100th knife, the maker forged a "firestorm"-pattern damascus blade, fashioned a ring guard from a 100-year-old wrought iron anchor chain, and pieced together redwood burl and stabilized silver vine for the handle.

▲ **RALPH TURNBULL:** The folding fighter is scintillating, and titillating, in a snakewood grip, superconductor bolsters, a Rob Thomas "herringbone"-damascus blade and a tiger eye thumb stud.

▲ **STEVEN J. TEDFORD:** The dense, tough bocote wood was hand picked by the maker for his "Master Fillet Knife" because of its natural resistance to moisture, adding a 7-inch ATS-34 stainless steel blade.

Show Those Pearly Whites

We reserved this section for the white pearl—mother-of-pearl—not black-lip mother-of-pearl or gold-lip pearl or pink pearl, or any of the others, just white pearl. And she's a purdy girl, that white mother-of-pearl, a bride in a wedding dress, belle of the ball, gloved lady attending the opera, 20-something girl in etiquette class, head turner, princess and ballet dancer all rolled into one. She sparkles when she turns, translucent in her beauty, soft and sheer.

White evokes purity, class and innocence. It softens the looks of knives and denotes elegance. Knives with mother-of-pearl handles are often referred to as gent's knives, art knives or fine knives. Some say they are the "Sunday go to meeting" knives or dress knives. Yet the material is not fragile or weak. On the contrary it's fairly stable, does not shrink or soften in the elements, and can be quite utilitarian.

Such can be said for ladies who dance in heels yet, like Cinderella, labor away with the strength of 10 men. The illusion is in the luminosity, and sometimes it's nice to be treated like a lady. So show those pearly whites, and how hard you work will be our little secret.

◀ **CHICCHI YONEYAMA:** It's nice to see laminated blades on a traditional pocketknife, and just as sweet to see the mother-of-pearl.

(SharpByCoop image)

▶ **FRANK FISCHER:** Small subtleties like hidden hardware securing the mother-of-pearl handle, a jeweled frame, Timascus pocket clip and eggshell-style integral bolsters set the big Elmax flipper folder apart. *(SharpByCoop image)*

▲ **AAD VAN RYSWYK:** Gold piqué work adorns the checked pearl grip of the locking-liner folder that also features engraved gold chimeras on the bolsters and a gold bail trailing off the end of the handle.

▲ **CRAIG BREWER:** The Jerry Rados damascus blade is shaving sharp and the mother-of-pearl smooth as silk.

▲ **EUGENE SHADLEY:** The 14k-gold pins, shield and bail enrich the mother-of-pearl handle and stainless steel bolsters and blades. *(SharpByCoop image)*

◀ **BUTCH BALL:** Damascus and pearl—she's an exquisite girl. Chad Nichols is credited for the damascus.

(PointSeven image)

▲ **MAMORU SHIGENO:** Mother-of-pearl sandwiches the tapered tang of the "Little Horn" model in a Super Gold 2 blade and SUS-303 bolsters.

(SharpByCoop image)

◀ **KYLE HANSON:** Pearl and damascus, the latter in a "W's" pattern, is a positively pointed affair.

(Cory Martin Imaging)

Show Those Pearly Whites

▼ **LARAMIE JACKSON:** The folder parades a pearl handle and thumb stud, and a Rob Thomas damascus blade and bolsters.

▲ **J.W. RANDALL:** The two blades wear their damascus stripes proudly, and the mother-of-pearl handle shimmers in the light.
(Tammy T. Randall image)

▼ **DOUG CAMPBELL:** He differentially heat-treated the blade, coined the bolsters and gave pearl a whirl.
(Caleb Royer Studio image)

▶ **ALAIN and JORIS CHOMILIER:** Look close and you'll see diamonds in the white gold pins, flowers in the Ed Schempp mosaic-damascus blade, and translucency in the mother-of-pearl handle.

◀ **STEVE GATLIN:** There's something about a hollow-ground stainless steel blade and a mother-of-pearl handle that bespeaks culture and class.
(SharpByCoop image)

Some Class Tacts

▲ **JEREMY HORTON and KIRBY LAMBERT:** The Chad Nichols Zircuti (zirconium and titanium) bolster sets off the chisel ground and groovy CTS XHP flipper folder. *(SharpByCoop image)*

▶ **BRANDON MCFARLAND:** The O1 flipper folder flaunts 6AL-4V-titanium handle scales anodized a multi-blue by David Beck of the Qerim 37 company.

▲ **ERNEST EMERSON:** The CQC-6 model was made for a charity auction to benefit the families of the U.S. Navy SEAL Team Six frogmen killed during a rescue mission in Afghanistan. It has a real blade and a sister blade made from World Trade Center steel.

▲ **JASON CLARK:** A stealthy black Persian flipper folder sports a San Mai blade and carbon fiber handle scales. *(Ward image)*

◀ **CHRIS KNAPTON:** Orange-green G-10 handle scales enliven a D2 locking-liner folder with titanium hardware.

In Memory of Operation Extortion 17 August 5, 2011

▲ **KEN ONION:** The maker's sculpted folders are instantly recognizable as a style all his own—some real class tacts from a real class act. *(SharpByCoop image)*

▲ **RICHARD ROGERS:** The "Sharpy" would make a mark considering its slim CPM 154 blade, titanium frame, lightning-strike carbon fiber handle scales and anodized bronze pocket clip, end cap and liners. *(SharpByCoop image)*

▲ **ANDRE THORBURN:** With zirconium bolsters embellished by Marietjie Thorburn, the fancy flipper folder also showcases lightning-strike carbon fiber handle scales, a titanium frame and a Bohler M390 blade. *(SharpByCoop image)*

▶ **DON HANSON III:** Stag and damascus do duty on a classy folder of the locking-liner kind. *(SharpByCoop image)*

◀ **BRIAN TIGHE:** Not only does the maker machine-groove the G-10 frames of his button-lock flipper folders into lightning-bolt-like forms, he also compound-grinds the RWL 34 blades. *(PointSeven image)*

◀ **CHAD NELL:** With one in silver-twill carbon fiber and one in red-and-black Kirinite, there's a dress tactical folder for just about any occasion. *(SharpByCoop image)*

▲ **DAVID SHARP:** That's one sharp dressed blade, in "tuxedo"-pattern stainless damascus, Westinghouse ivory Micarta® and titanium. It's based on the Loveless "Stiff Horn" fixed blade. *(SharpByCoop image)*

▶ **DARRIEL CASTON:** The creatively designed folder is offered in a Cobalt 6 blade and a choice of a brushed stainless steel or mokumé handle. *(SharpByCoop image)*

◀ **JOE SANGSTER:** Three highly patterned materials— musk ox horn, mokumé and damascus—cunningly coalesce within the confines of a fine locking-liner folder. *(PointSeven image)*

▲ **JENS ANSO:** Of 46-piece construction, the "Mojo Extreme" includes Chad Nichols "blackout" damascus handle inlays and a hollow-ground damascus blade with "swedge" along the spine. *(SharpByCoop image)*

▼ **ERIC OCHS:** The "Orca" flipper folder features a harpoon-style Chad Nichols "boomerang" San Mai damascus blade with an XHP core, GTC bearings, Rob Thomas "typhoon" mokumé bolsters and a Westinghouse ivory paper Micarta handle.

▼ **KEITH OUYE:** Even though the "Oda Nobunaga" flipper folder comes with a low-riding pocket clip, you'll want to let it ride high so people can see the Bruce Shaw engraving on the titanium frame.
(SharpByCoop image)

▲ **JEREMY KRAMMES:** Copper is sculpted into a molten-lava-like-form spilling over the carbon fiber handle of an N690 tactical folder.
(SharpByCoop image)

▲ **TIM BRITTON:** As its name implies, the blade and titanium handle slabs of the "Blackout Big T-10" frame-lock folder are machined and blacked out.
(SharpByCoop image)

▲ **PHILIP BOOTH:** An orange stripe breaks up the olive-drab G-10 handle scales, not that any of the 154CM flipper folder is drab at all. This pattern is called "Badenov" (Russian for bad boy). *(Cory Martin Imaging)*

▶ **BILL BEHNKE:** Feather damascus and amber bone step out together to cut the rug. *(Ward image)*

◀ **GUSTAVO CECCHINI:** The "Scarface" CPM 154 assisted opening folder is too pretty for its name, including a grooved and sculpted titanium handle. *(SharpByCoop image)*

▲ **BILL DUFF:** The handle duo is giraffe bone and damascus, while the blade is all 440C stainless steel. *(Ward image)*

▲ **PETER MARTIN:** Style comes in the form of Super Conductor bolsters, a choice of San Mai or feather-damascus steel and C-Tek handle material. *(Cory Martin Imaging)*

▲ **GAIL LUNN:** The wood and steel folder is like pocket jewelry, isn't it, especially with the inlaid thumb stud and damascus bolsters? *(Ward image)*

▶ **MATT DISKIN:** From the looks of the sleek tactical folder, it would indeed be fun to fire open the "Fire" dual-action special edition in a double-ground blade. *(SharpByCoop image)*

▼ **SEAN O'HARE:** The colorful Mokuti handle of the frame-lock flipper folder called for a more subtle but ultimately interesting stonewashed CPM 154 blade.

▼ **CLIFF PARKER:** Walrus ivory gets a tusk up on the competition, here within the confines of a damascus locking liner folder including an 18k-rose-gold thumb stud. *(Cory Martin Imaging)*

▶ **RICK BARRETT:** With an industrial and industrious look, the "Biohazard Fallout Flipper" folder cuts through hazardous waste using a 4.25-inch W1 and 15N20 blade, a titanium handle and MokuTi pocket clip. *(Cory Martin Imaging)*

▼ **A. BRETT SCHALLER:** The "Nighthawk" dress tactical folder, with Mike Norris damascus blade, is black and blued all over. *(SharpByCoop image)*

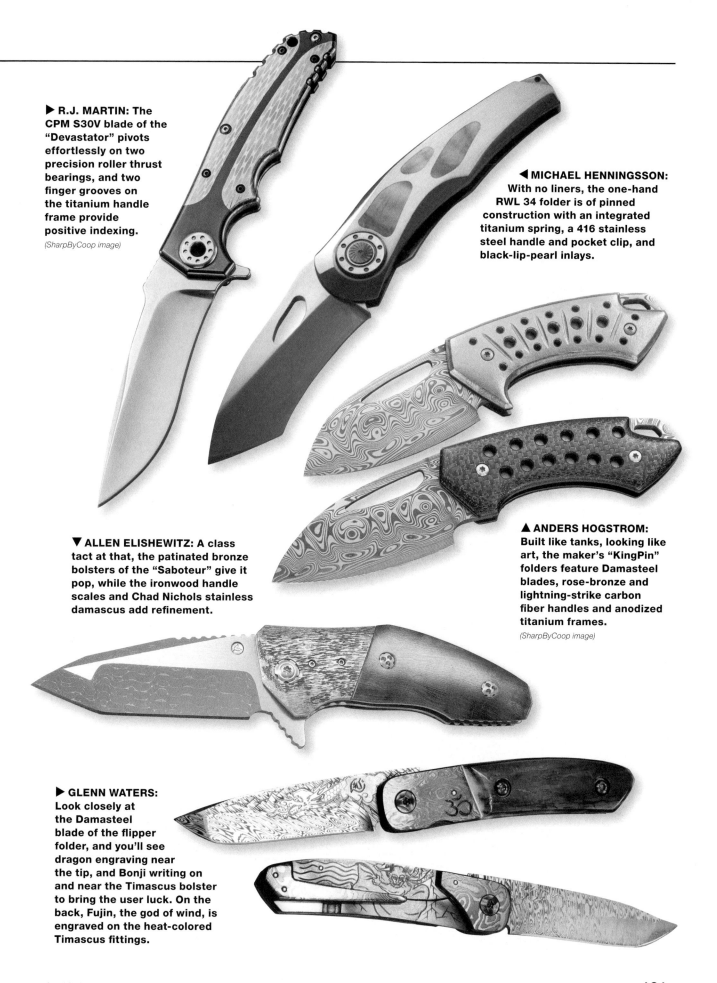

▶ **R.J. MARTIN:** The CPM S30V blade of the "Devastator" pivots effortlessly on two precision roller thrust bearings, and two finger grooves on the titanium handle frame provide positive indexing.
(SharpByCoop image)

◀ **MICHAEL HENNINGSSON:** With no liners, the one-hand RWL 34 folder is of pinned construction with an integrated titanium spring, a 416 stainless steel handle and pocket clip, and black-lip-pearl inlays.

▼ **ALLEN ELISHEWITZ:** A class tact at that, the patinated bronze bolsters of the "Saboteur" give it pop, while the ironwood handle scales and Chad Nichols stainless damascus add refinement.

▲ **ANDERS HOGSTROM:** Built like tanks, looking like art, the maker's "KingPin" folders feature Damasteel blades, rose-bronze and lightning-strike carbon fiber handles and anodized titanium frames.
(SharpByCoop image)

▶ **GLENN WATERS:** Look closely at the Damasteel blade of the flipper folder, and you'll see dragon engraving near the tip, and Bonji writing on and near the Timascus bolster to bring the user luck. On the back, Fujin, the god of wind, is engraved on the heat-colored Timascus fittings.

Temper Lines Flare

▶ **DOUG CAMPBELL:** Traditionally clay hardening the 10-inch W2 bowie blade, the maker achieved a nice hamon (temper line) as pretty as the amber stag grip.
(BladeGallery.com image)

▼ **JON CHRISTENSEN:** Clay hardened W2 wears its temper line with pride, parading it like a big bowie with a carved ironwood handle should.
(Caleb Royer Studio image)

▼ **TIMOTHY STEINGASS:** The fixed-blade "Persistent Hunter" has a persistent temper line along the face of the W2 blade, with full, tapered tang, and a sambar stag handle to boot. *(SharpByCoop image)*

▲ **BRION TOMBERLIN:** A temper line bounces along the 1095 bowie blade toward a stainless steel guard and stag handle.
(Ward image)

▲ **LARAMIE JACKSON:** There's not a straight line on the bowie/fighter, much less on the face of the 1095 blade, this one handled in water buffalo horn with a turquoise spacer.

▼ DON CARLOS ANDRADE: One of two cleavers in the group, this one has a forged W2 blade with a wavy temper line, a maple handle and circular ebony inlay.

▼ SAM LURQUIN: Like the lines of an electrocardiogram printout, the healthy temper line of a W2 blade is just happy to serve the purpose of showing where the hard edge meets the soft spine. *(SharpByCoop image)*

◄ DAVID MIRABILE: The San Mai blade is W2 laminated to stainless steel, while the handle marries ancient walrus ivory with a carbon fiber wrap. *(SharpByCoop image)*

▶ KYLE GAHAGAN: The 1075 bowie blade is differentially heat treated to show a temper line, the bronze spacers fileworked to add a little highlight, and the stainless butt cap carved to match the grooves of the stag grip. *(Caleb Royer Studio image)*

◄ STEVE RANDALL: A W2 blade with wispy temper line pulls duty on a stag-handle fighter.
(SharpByCoop image)

◄ **JOHN WHITE:** Though John sadly passed away in 2014, we couldn't help but show his big camp knife in stag and a full 10 inches of differentially heat-treated W2 steel. *(Ward image)*

▶ **KYLE HANSON:** The temper line looks as toothy as one imagines the W2 blade bevel would be under a microscope, or as the tusked walrus that lent the ivory handle. *(Cory Martin Imaging)*

▼ **JIM CROWELL:** The temper line is as distinct as the clip point of this walrus-ivory-handled bowie in a 10-inch W2 blade and blued steel fittings. *(Ward image)*

▶ **TAD LYNCH:** The differentially tempered W2 blade and the Micarta® handle are jet black and battle ready. *(Ward image)*

◄ **CALEB WHITE:** The visually pleasing profile of the "Gauntlet" hunting/dress knife is enhanced by a clay-quenched W2 blade, a bronze bolster and an African blackwood handle.

◀ **E. SCOTT MCGHEE:** The fang of the "Cottonmouth" is W1 with a distinct hamon, and the body is African blackwood. *(SharpByCoop image)*

◀ **MICHAEL DEIBERT:** The clay-hardened 1095 blade shows it stripes, as does the ironwood grip. *(SharpByCoop image)*

◀ **JOEL AUSTIN:** If one were weary of the same-old same old, they could bust out the ironwood-handle bowie with 1095 blade and cloudy temper line for a refreshing pace. *(Ward image)*

▲ **BEN SEWARD:** The heat treated 1075 blade looks too hot to touch, but is as cool as the carbon fiber handle and heat-colored, fileworked spacer. *(Caleb Royer Studio image)*

▲ **DON HANSON III:** The "5400 Cleaver" is named for the 5,400-layer W2-and-wrought iron blade, as well as the 5,400-year-old bog oak handle. *(SharpByCoop image)*

Chopped Champions

For those who don't watch the Food Network, you likely won't understand what the headline references. But that's OK, it's fairly straightforward—the custom kitchen knives in this section are choppers, and they're champs. Others who have watched "Chopped" on the Food Network have witnessed how chaos in the kitchen often results in savory dishes judged by a panel of renowned chefs. It's not such a stretch to compare the frenzy of making a meal in a short period, given time restraints, to the chaos and frenzy of fashioning kitchen knives and trying to make a living doing so.

Makers of household cutlery, for many of whom it is a part-time job after arriving home from a full day at work, must be smart and efficient. There is no time for checking their Facebook pages and reading the daily news. Most enjoy what they do, and so knifemakers who dabble in kitchen knives consider it a labor of love. They take pride in forging, shaping and finishing fine edges, attaching guards and fitting comfortable handles that will feel nice in the hands of novice and skilled cooks and chefs. In a way, they're the Chopped Champions of the knife world, where a busy day in the dust-choked shop is better than a day at work anytime.

◀ **KEVIN CROSS: The chef should have no problem washing and wiping down the high-carbon Brad Vice damascus blade and stabilized koa handle after use to keep it clean and pristine.** *(SharpByCoop image)*

◀ **PETE PRUYN: The "Urban Cleaver," with pinecone and polymer resin handle, chisel-ground damascus blade and copper bolsters, was named by people at the New York Custom Knife Show who felt it was as well suited for the streets as it was for the kitchen.** *(SharpByCoop image)*

▼ **THOMAS HASLINGER: The stainless steel and mammoth ivory carving set is simple elegance for the kitchen.**

▼ **DAN LEEPER:** A temper line shows where the maker forged and differentially tempered the 52100 blade for a hard edge and soft spine, adding maple burl handle scales onto the 7-inch chef's knife. *(SharpByCoop image)*

▼ **KEVIN CROSS:** Like a creamy gourmet dessert, the "tapioca"-mammoth-ivory handle sweetens the pot, as does the Randy Haas feather-damascus blade. *(PointSeven image)*

◄ **MICHAEL ZIEBA:** Stabilized maple and high-carbon 52100 ball bearing steel just scream "classic chef's knife." *(SharpByCoop image)*

► **MIKE MOONEY:** Called a Nikiri Bocho, the Japanese-style veggie chopper employs a thin edge on its 8-inch CPM S30V blade, an octagonal California buckeye burl handle and an African blackwood bolster.

Chopped Champions

▼ **TONY HUGHES:** A powerfully patterned 8-inch chef's knife is outfitted in an eye-popping "W's" damascus blade and a stabilized spalted maple handle.

► **PETER MARTIN:** The high-end kitchen knife is done up in style, with cherry burl and a San Mai damascus blade. *(Cory Martin Imaging)*

▲ **MARDI MESHEJIAN:** The cleaver shape is so clever, and the carved greenheart wood handle so exotic.

(BladeGallery.com image)

▲ **J. NEILSON:** The 400-layer damascus blade of the kitchen knife might be of a "forced random" pattern, but the overall design flows, and the stabilized burl handle is a natural beauty. *(Caleb Royer Studio image)*

▲ **JOHN HORRIGAN:** Part of a three-knife set, the knife comes with laminated 1095- and-410 blade and a stabilized spalted maple handle.

Wood, Bone, Horn & Stag Hunters

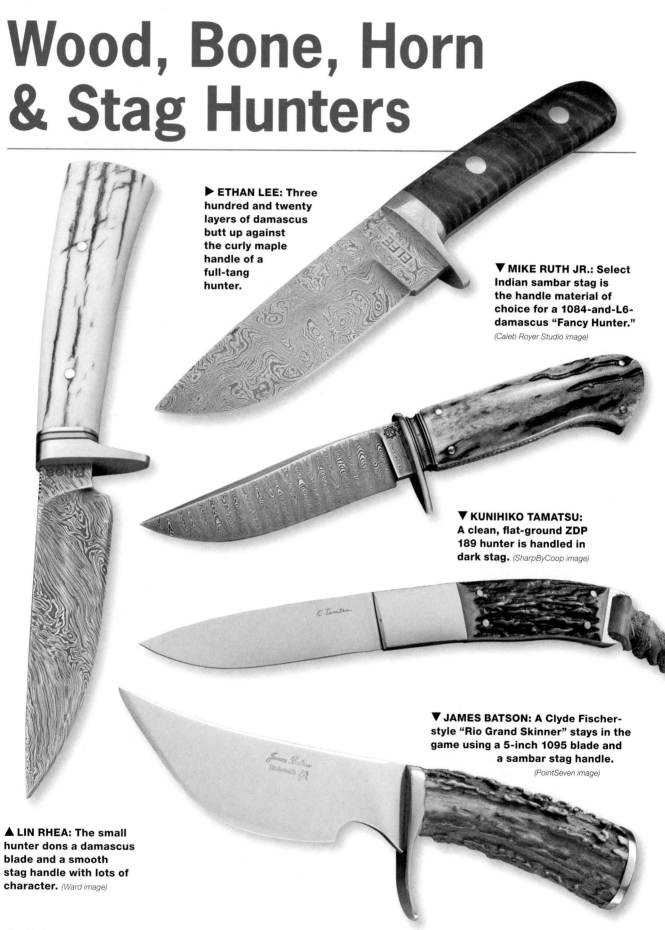

▶ **ETHAN LEE:** Three hundred and twenty layers of damascus butt up against the curly maple handle of a full-tang hunter.

▼ **MIKE RUTH JR.:** Select Indian sambar stag is the handle material of choice for a 1084-and-L6-damascus "Fancy Hunter." *(Caleb Royer Studio image)*

▼ **KUNIHIKO TAMATSU:** A clean, flat-ground ZDP 189 hunter is handled in dark stag. *(SharpByCoop image)*

▼ **JAMES BATSON:** A Clyde Fischer-style "Rio Grand Skinner" stays in the game using a 5-inch 1095 blade and a sambar stag handle. *(PointSeven image)*

▲ **LIN RHEA:** The small hunter dons a damascus blade and a smooth stag handle with lots of character. *(Ward image)*

▶ MAMORU SHIGENO: A fine drop-point hunter is executed in stag and ATS 34 stainless steel.

(SharpByCoop image)

▼ ALAN HUTCHINSON: Walnut is a good way to go when attempting a traditional drop-point hunter, and success is sweet. *(Ward image)*

◀ BEN SEWARD: Ironwood enlivens a 4 1/8-inch hunter as much as the smoky temper line of the 1075 blade. The knife comes with a David Seward carved and stitched leather sheath.

(Ward image)

▼ JERRY FISK: If the 5-inch damascus blade doesn't grab you, the engraved guard and surely the sheep-horn handle should pull you in.

(Ward image)

▲ JIM FLEMING: The finished blade looks nothing like the black diamond file it started out as, and the sambar stag handle has been cut to fit the drop-point hunter. *(Cory Martin Imaging)*

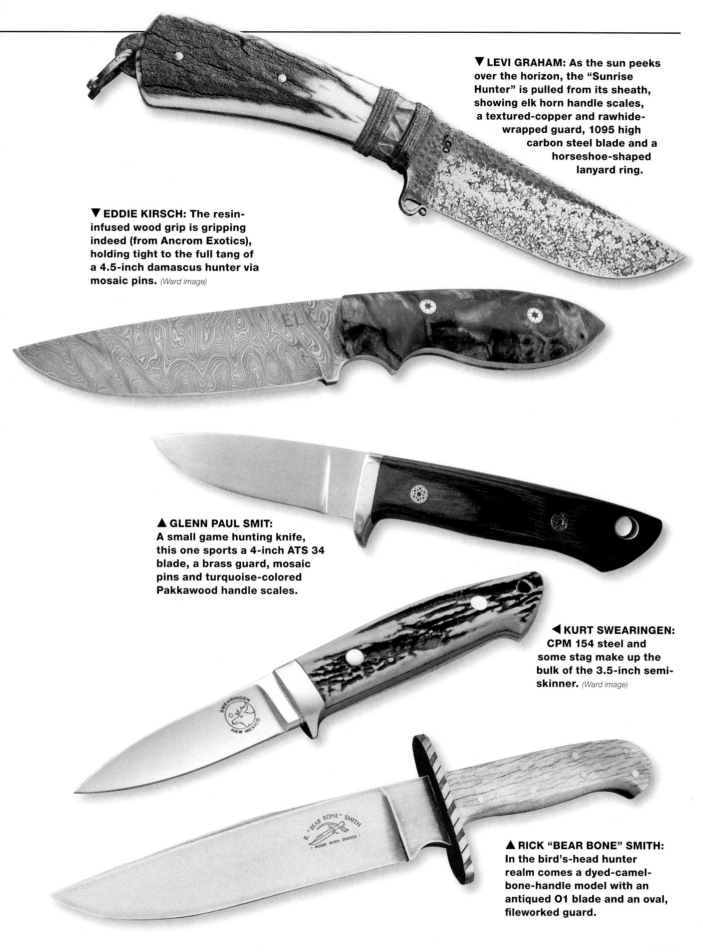

▼ **LEVI GRAHAM:** As the sun peeks over the horizon, the "Sunrise Hunter" is pulled from its sheath, showing elk horn handle scales, a textured-copper and rawhide-wrapped guard, 1095 high carbon steel blade and a horseshoe-shaped lanyard ring.

▼ **EDDIE KIRSCH:** The resin-infused wood grip is gripping indeed (from Ancrom Exotics), holding tight to the full tang of a 4.5-inch damascus hunter via mosaic pins. *(Ward image)*

▲ **GLENN PAUL SMIT:** A small game hunting knife, this one sports a 4-inch ATS 34 blade, a brass guard, mosaic pins and turquoise-colored Pakkawood handle scales.

◄ **KURT SWEARINGEN:** CPM 154 steel and some stag make up the bulk of the 3.5-inch semi-skinner. *(Ward image)*

▲ **RICK "BEAR BONE" SMITH:** In the bird's-head hunter realm comes a dyed-camel-bone-handle model with an antiqued O1 blade and an oval, fileworked guard.

▼ **STEVE CULVER:** A 5160 drop-point hunter handled in walnut exudes tradition, and class.

(Ward image)

▲ **RON ROSENBAUGH:** Buffalo horn and stabilized box elder burl lend some black and orange to an ATS 34 finger-choil hunter.

▶ **STEVE GATLIN:** With the length of stag in hand, the hollow-ground ATS 34 blade would be a pleasure to use on a game animal. *(SharpByCoop image)*

▲ **TOM R. LEWIS:** A turquoise profile of a longhorn steer is creatively inlaid into the stabilized maple burl handle of a wire-damascus knife. Mosaic pins complete the roundup.

▲ **BILL REDD:** Damascus and green jigged bone make for fine bedfellows on a drop-point hunter. It comes with a snakeskin-inlaid leather sheath.

▶ **GARY HOUSE:** A continuously curved drop-point hunter features a 1080-and-15N20 damascus blade, a "blossom and lace"-pattern mosaic damascus buttcap and pommel nut, stag handle, blackwood and copper spacers and a stainless steel guard engraved by Tom Ferry. *(PointSeven image)*

▼ **JOHN E. CHASE:** Just when you think you've seen every wood that can be put on a knife handle, a maker comes up with Jarrah (eucalyptus marginata), and on a bowie/hunter with an O1 blade, no less.

▲ **JASON FRY:** Sambar stag and stacked leather share similar brown tones, and when married to a brass guard and 1080 blade, make for a fine hunter. *(Cory Martin Imaging)*

▲ **RUSTY WAIDE:** More of a tusk than a horn or bone, the ancient walrus ivory makes for a handsome handle on a mosaic-damascus hunter with an anodized-titanium frame. *(SharpByCoop image)*

▲ **DAVID SHARP:** The high, hollow grind of the CPM-D2 blade, the straight grooves of stag, simple single guard and flush pins unite for a fantastic cause. *(Caleb Royer Studio image)*

▶ **EDDIE KIRSCH:** The damascus and amboyna burl patterns bounce right along the full length of the husky 11.5-inch hunter. *(Ward image)*

▼ **PHIL EVANS:** Giraffe bone gives even more personality to an already handsome hunter in a 6-inch W2 blade and a mosaic pin. *(Ward image)*

▼ **BUTCH DEVERAUX:** The maker combines 52100 steel, lacey she-oak, sheep horn and brass like a chemist mixes powders and liquids. *(SharpByCoop image)*

▲ **EDMUND DAVIDSON:** As clean as a whistle, the integral CTS-PD1 hunter is outfitted in a desert ironwood handle and given a hand-rubbed finish. *(PointSeven image)*

▲ **ROBERT MOSLEY:** If all ironwood is as pretty as this, then the ironwood forest would be a far-out place to visit, particularly carrying such a nice damascus hunter on the hip. *(Ward image)*

▼ **ERIC EDQUIST: Dark hues of damascus and ironwood combine for a singular skinner.** *(Ward image)*

▶ **PETE PRUYN: Alaskan birch burl makes an appearance on a 1095 hunter with a damascus guard, and we are all graced by its presence.**

(SharpByCoop image)

◀ **JOHN DOYLE: The dimpled surface of the African blackwood handle is a nice touch, as is the forged and fileworked 1095 blade, and the combination stainless steel/blued-mild-steel guard.**

(SharpByCoop image)

▲ **JOE SZILASKI: Engraved copper bolsters match the tip of the leather sheath, and go together nicely with the antler handle scales of the forged early American-style skinner.**

STATE OF THE ART

"I taught my self to engrave."

"I wanted to add gemstones to my knives, so I made a few bezels, bought and polished the stones, and fit and set them."

"I wanted to scrimshaw the ivory handle, so I attended some scrimshaw classes and just started out small and worked my way up to scrimming entire handles and even some of the ivory-inlaid pommels, spacers, guards and sheaths."

"The handle of the knife was too squared off, with too many rough edges, so I sculpted and sanded it until it felt better in the hand."

"I etched the blade with natural images to match the overall flow and fluidity of the knife."

In my experience, skilled artisans who say such things aren't bragging or looking for kudos, but perhaps take their talents and natural gifts for granted. Or maybe they believe that anyone can accomplish such artistic aptitude with some patience and practice. But those of us with zero artistic ability know those statements to be astounding, unbelievable and awe inspiring. I, for one, can't draw a human face, much less scrimshaw, etch or engrave one, and if I did, the poor person would come off looking like Frankenstein, squared jaw and head, steel rods jutting off his neck.

No one begrudges the knifemakers', embellishers' and craftsmen's and women's abilities. We just want them to know that we admire and appreciate their work, that it moves us and lifts our spirits. The knives in the State Of The Art section are truly beautiful, and for that we're glad the artisans taught themselves to engrave, inlay precious jewels, scrimshaw, sculpt, etch and basically create!

Wire Inlay the William Moran Way

▼ **DWIGHT TOWELL:** Gold wire inlay enhances the desert ironwood handle of the skinner, while engraving highlights it.

TOWELL

OTT

OTT

▲ **FRED OTT:** Twist-damascus hunters are the beneficiaries of heirloom-quality silver-wire-inlaid maple handles.

▼ **BILL LYONS:** Follow the wire around the perimeter of the maple handle, and the blade steel to the point of the hunting knife.

(Ward image)

LYONS

▲ **MATT PARKINSON:** The heart cutout in the head of the tomahawk is a theme revisited by the wire inlay along the wood haft.

(SharpByCoop image)

It's a Hard Rock Knife

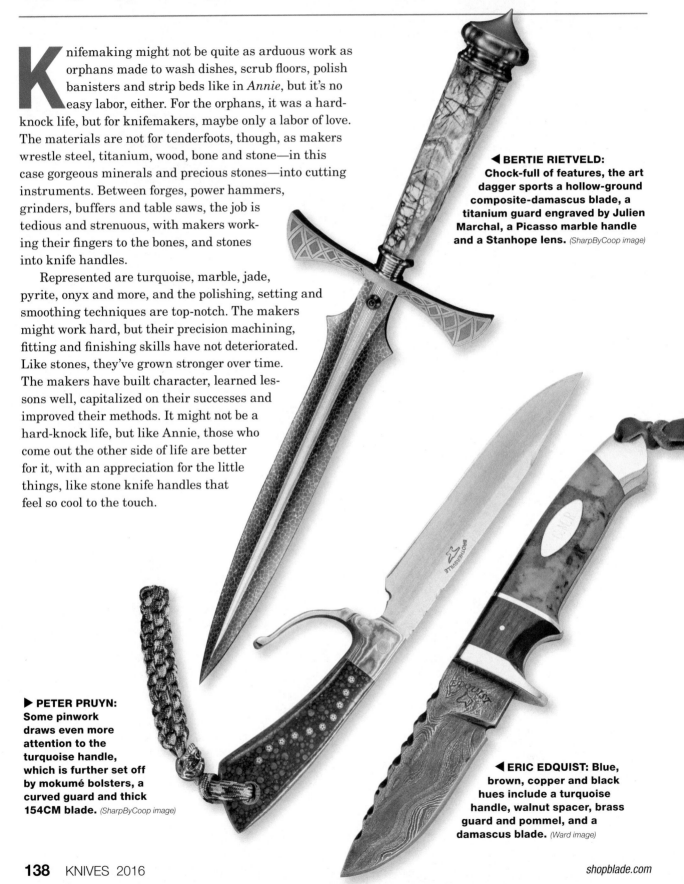

Knifemaking might not be quite as arduous work as orphans made to wash dishes, scrub floors, polish banisters and strip beds like in *Annie*, but it's no easy labor, either. For the orphans, it was a hard-knock life, but for knifemakers, maybe only a labor of love. The materials are not for tenderfoots, though, as makers wrestle steel, titanium, wood, bone and stone—in this case gorgeous minerals and precious stones—into cutting instruments. Between forges, power hammers, grinders, buffers and table saws, the job is tedious and strenuous, with makers working their fingers to the bones, and stones into knife handles.

Represented are turquoise, marble, jade, pyrite, onyx and more, and the polishing, setting and smoothing techniques are top-notch. The makers might work hard, but their precision machining, fitting and finishing skills have not deteriorated. Like stones, they've grown stronger over time. The makers have built character, learned lessons well, capitalized on their successes and improved their methods. It might not be a hard-knock life, but like Annie, those who come out the other side of life are better for it, with an appreciation for the little things, like stone knife handles that feel so cool to the touch.

◀ **BERTIE RIETVELD:** Chock-full of features, the art dagger sports a hollow-ground composite-damascus blade, a titanium guard engraved by Julien Marchal, a Picasso marble handle and a Stanhope lens. *(SharpByCoop image)*

▶ **PETER PRUYN:** Some pinwork draws even more attention to the turquoise handle, which is further set off by mokumé bolsters, a curved guard and thick 154CM blade. *(SharpByCoop image)*

◀ **ERIC EDQUIST:** Blue, brown, copper and black hues include a turquoise handle, walnut spacer, brass guard and pommel, and a damascus blade. *(Ward image)*

▶ **JAY FISHER:** The "Achelous" (Greek mythological patron deity of the "silver-swirling" Achelous River) dagger swirls with engraved stainless steel and an Indian green moss agate gemstone handle.

▲ **CLIFF PARKER:** Judging by the verdite handle, the maker's first time working with stone was a resounding success! He's better know for his damascus, and that's equally evident. *(Cory Martin Imaging)*

▶ **STEPHANIE LEMELIN:** The tiger-eye handle and 18k-gold engraving in a lion motif give an inside look into the artist's skills and sensibilities. *(PointSeven image)*

◀ **WAYNE HENSLEY:** White jade was worked into the ATS-34 stainless steel knife equation nicely. *(PointSeven image)*

▲ **DON LOZIER:** The maker's first art deco piece enlists an onyx/pyrite matrix handle, a Mike Norris ladder-pattern-damascus blade and pointy double guard engraved and gold inlaid by Jeff Parke. *(PointSeven image)*

A Mosaic Damascus Menagerie

▲ **PAUL SEVECEK:** The honey-of-a-blade is "bear" mosaic damascus, complete with paw prints.

▲ **SHANE TAYLOR:** Steampunk gears are forged throughout the niter-blued mosaic damascus blade, and the theme furthered through engraved gold and copper gears in the fine silver window of the textured bronze handle. *(PointSeven image)*

◄ **TOM MCGINNIS:** Dyed mammoth tooth and mosaic damascus are true blue bedfellows to the engraved guard of a utility knife. *(Ward image)*

▲ **MARK KNAPP:** With personality to spare, the bowie blends mosaic damascus, ancient ivory, horn and mokumé. *(SharpByCoop image)*

► **RICK DUNKERLEY:** The blade and bolsters are forged from three composite bars of pictorial mosaic damascus, while walrus ivory handle scales add more personality and symmetry to the folder. *(PointSeven image)*

▶ **DAVID LISCH:** "Fighting dragons" mosaic damascus gives knife enthusiasts lots to look at for 10 3/8 inches of a fine stag-handle fighter. *(Caleb Royer Studio image)*

◀ **RON NEWTON:** The hammer rang while the mosaic damascus integral ring-guard bowie was being forged, complete with interlocking ebony handle and a lot of imagination. *(Ward image)*

▲ **KEVIN CROSS:** Like cells under a microscope, the Doug Ponzio mosaic damascus pattern multiplies across the 7.5-inch blade, stopping only at a dimpled guard and African blackwood grip. *(PointSeven image)*

▼ **CLIFF PARKER:** So if you're a master steel manipulator, you forge a mosaic hippo blade and bolsters to go along with your hippo tooth handle. *(Ward image)*

▲ **MICHAEL TYRE:** The blued "agave cactus" mosaic-damascus blade pattern, with matching bolsters, coordinates well with the blue mammoth ivory handle scales and blue sapphire-inlaid thumb stud.

(PointSeven image)

A Mosaic Damascus Menagerie

▲ **DAMON SOILEAU:** The Robert Eggerling mosaic-damascus blade pays tribute to those incredible armadillo-skin handle scales, and Chad Nichols mosaic damascus bolsters add some more shell armor. *(Cory Martin Imaging)*

▲ **EDDIE KIRSCH:** Webs of blued mosaic damascus patterning spider across the blade, while a maple burl handle with G-10 and nickel silver spacers contrasts effectively. *(Ward image)*

▲ **GENE BASKETT:** The harmonious folder combination is blued Robert Eggerling mosaic damascus, mammoth tooth and anodized titanium engraved by Paul Markow. *(PointSeven image)*

◀ **PETER MASON:** A fine art dagger delivers the goods in the form of carved cocobolo, sculpted and stippled bronze and shapely blued mosaic damascus.

▲ **DON HANSON III:** With mammoth ivory handle scales and a prettily patterned mosaic damascus blade and bolsters, the locking-liner folder is not just another face in the crowd. *(SharpByCoop image)*

A Materials Matrix

▶ **MARK KNAPP:** The mixed-media herringbone handle is a hot commodity, in line with, say, the damascus blade of the drop-point hunter.

(SharpByCoop image)

▼ **RON LAKE:** The ivory inlays of the tab-lock frame-lock folder fall into lines. *(SharpByCoop image)*

◀ **TOM R. LEWIS:** A mosaic handle of sycamore and African blackwood is as impressive as the forged Harley-Davidson motorcycle chain damascus blade.

▶ **ANSSI RUUSUVUORI:** Varnished pieces of photographs covering a solid curly birch core make up a knife handle worth a 1,000 words.

▲ **CHARLES HAWKINS:** Referring to the handle as a black and white matrix, the maker had the wherewithal to pair it up with a damascus blade and custom pins.

Damascus for the Best of Us

▲ **ROB HUDSON:** With a Mike Norris stainless damascus blade, a guard engraved by Jere Davidson and a buffalo-horn and walrus-ivory handle, the fighter seems mild mannered at that.

▲ **JODY MULLER:** The damascus pattern of the flipper folder ingeniously transitions into the worm-grooved titanium handle. *(SharpByCoop image)*

▲ **CHUCK RICHARDS:** The feather damascus patterning flares out toward the edge, spine and S-guard of the walrus-ivory-handle bowie. *(BladeGallery.com image)*

▲ **RON NEWTON:** A "Tsunami Wave" washes over the 9-inch fighter blade, crashing onto the carbon-fiber-inlaid stainless steel guard and sculpted carbon fiber handle. *(Caleb Royer Studio image)*

▲ **RICK "BEAR BONE" SMITH:** The damascus blade of the coffin-handle bowie is personalized with the name of the owner, in case of loss during a Sandbar Fight or melee.

▼ **ADAM DESROSIERS:** A horizontal line running right down the center of the fighter blade is like the quill or stem of the feather in the patterned damascus blade.

(Caleb Royer Studio image)

◄ **TAD LYNCH:** The 10.25-inch blade shows its stripes, proud to be grouped with a bog oak handle and wrought iron guard.

(Caleb Royer Studio image)

▼ **BILL REDD:** "Caviar" damascus is a tasteful rendering, and so is the leaf filework along the spine of the drop-point skinner.

▲ **REINHARD TSCHAGER:** The "Nicker" model comes with a detailed damascus blade by Heinz Denig, a richly engraved gold spacer and a fossil walrus ivory handle.

▲ **LUDWIG J. VAN VUUREN:** Just look at those dimples on the handsome damascus boy dressed in giraffe bone.

▲ MARDI MESHEJIAN: Piercing the damascus blade, and adding an antiqued-copper guard and textured ancient walrus ivory handle—they were all good choices by the craftsman. *(BladeGallery.com image)*

▲ KYLE ROYER: I don't know if his forge or bellows blew in the "West Texas Wind"-pattern damascus blade, but it was a godsend, as is the mother-of-pearl handle, engraving, clamshell guard and rear bolsters, and 24k-gold pins and inlays.

(Caleb Royer Studio image)

◄ GARY MULKEY: The damascus patterning bursts out from the center line of the dagger blade, complementing the fluted blackwood handle and stainless steel guard and pommel. *(Ward image)*

◄ STEVE KOSTER: The tight damascus pattern of the 10.5-inch bowie blade is some hot handiwork akin to that of the finely fileworked liners and closely fit fiddleback-walnut handle.

(PointSeven image)

▲ RAYMOND L. SMITH: It's good that he let the canister-ball-bearing damascus out of the can, and allowed the oosic handle to breathe.

► **JOSH SMITH:** The oh-so-pointy, leaf-shaped damascus blade sprouts out from damascus bolsters, a mammoth-ivory handle and scroll-engraved gold back spacer by Steve Dunn.

(PointSeven image)

► **LANDON ROBBINS:** The hot little ironwood-handle hunter shows off a tightly patterned damascus blade.

(Ward image)

◄ **KEVIN CROSS:** I can't even imagine the giddiness of bringing out this carving set in Mike Norris damascus and Honduran rosewood to cut the ham for Thanksgiving.

(PointSeven image)

◄ **BRIAN TIGHE:** Three-dimensionally-machined titanium handles are like lightning bolts striking the Damasteel tanto blades of the button-lock flipper folders. *(PointSeven image)*

◄ **DAVID LISCH:** The gray grain lines of the walrus ivory handle work well with the 1075-1080-and-15N20-damascus blade. *(PointSeven image)*

◄ **GARY HOUSE:** The pretty damascus blade pattern was deserving of the mokumé guard, stag handle and even the Indianhead nickel inlaid into the pommel. *(PointSeven image)*

▲ **MANUEL QUIROGA:** The long damascus blade nearly dominates the striking blackwood-handle bowie. *(Ward image)*

▲ **MICHAEL TYRE:** Explosion-pattern damascus was contained well within the blade and bolsters of the "Organ Pipe Dress Knife" that also sports a bark-mammoth-ivory handle and 18k-gold screws. *(PointSeven image)*

▲ **TONY HUGHES:** A multi-bar Turkish-twist damascus blade, and damascus guard and buttcap corral the mastodon ivory handle of the foot-long fancy fixed blade. *(PointSeven image)*

▼ **PAVEL SEVECEK:** Leapin' lizards, the mosaic frog damascus has the swamp buzzin' and the flies taking flight. The turquoise and elephant ivory handle will put some spring in the hind legs, too.

◄ **BEN SEWARD:** Where the damascus pattern dips down, the edge sweeps upward, and the blackwood-handle hunter rises through the ranks.
(Caleb Royer Studio image)

► **JASON KNIGHT:** A long blade fuller and sharpened top edge give the damascus blade even more character than it had initially. A curly koa handle helps the patterning along.
(SharpByCoop image)

◄ **MICHAEL RUTH JR.:** When you have a Ws-ladder-pattern damascus blade this beautiful, you let it stretch 20.5 inches, making up the bulk of a "Maritime Law" sword handled in pre-ban elephant ivory.
(Caleb Royer Studio image)

► **STEVE CULVER:** The winning hat trick of knife materials and embellishments is damascus, mammoth ivory and engraving.
(Caleb Royer Studio image)

STATE OF THE ART **149**

Damascus for the Best of Us

▶ **JAMES RODEBAUGH:** The blue-gray hues of mammoth ivory blend beautifully with the nine-bar Turkish-twist-pattern damascus blade. That's a little tiger-eye-inlaid thumb stud. *(PointSeven image)*

◀ **JERRY FISK:** "Dog star" damascus bursts across the 11-inch blade of a Southwest bowie with engraved guard. *(SharpByCoop image)*

▼ **JAMES R. COOK:** Only a "transition"-pattern damascus blade could complete with those carved pearl handle scales, and engraved guard, ferrule and tang. *(Caleb Royer Studio image)*

◀ **CALVIN ROBINSON:** The feather pattern of the damascus and the red stag of the grip embody natural forms that Nathan Dickinson scroll engraving complements yet contrasts tastefully. *(PointSeven image)*

▲ **PAUL K. BROWN:** With ironwood, "honey horn" and nickel silver on one end, and heat-colored Robert Eggerling damascus on the other, there's no camouflaging the handsome-as-all-get-out hunter. *(Ward image)*

▲ **TERRY LEE RENNER:** Heat colored "dragon skin" damascus emits a rainbow of hues on the blade and bolsters of the mammoth-tooth-handle, scimitar-style butterfly knife. *(SharpByCoop image)*

▶ **MIKE QUESENBERRY:** The 1080-and-15N20 "directional"-pattern damascus knows the direction, alright, but is anchored in ebony as to not wander too far away. *(Caleb Royer Studio image)*

▶ **T.C. ROBERTS:** As if the damascus blade wasn't impressive enough, the maker added a choice stag handle and a horned toad poised and ready to leap off the damascus butt cap. *(Ward image)*

◀ **LOGAN PEARCE:** The blue box elder burl handle of the 14 1/8-inch bowie is the perfect counterpart to the "West Texas wind"-pattern damascus blade and fittings. *(Caleb Royer Studio image)*

▼ **MARK NEVLING:** One pattern (Turkish damascus) leads to another (mokumé) and another (mammoth ivory).

▲ **JERRY HOSSOM:** Did the damascus pattern come first, or the blade shape, and could the same question be asked about the buckeye burl or the handle shape that takes its own quasi-natural form? *(PointSeven image)*

Stacked and Secure

▼ **RANDY LEE:** The handle of the CPM 154 stainless steel sub-hilt fighter is 11 layers of alternate ivory, maroon Micarta, ironwood and silver pinecone resin.

(BladeGallery.com image)

◄ **MIKE SANDERS:** Bone and desert ironwood, with stainless steel fittings, are the stacked handle materials of choice for a 440C fixed blade.

(Allen Alliston image)

► **JIM BEHRING:** Just the way William Scagel would have done it, the maker fashions a pair of convex-ground fixed blades in stag and stacked-leather handles. *(SharpByCoop image)*

◄ **NESTOR LORENZO RHO:** With a blade forged from an old railway screw, the skinner also boasts a handle combination of two types of Micarta—bronze and resin—and a "popcorn" red deer stag tine.

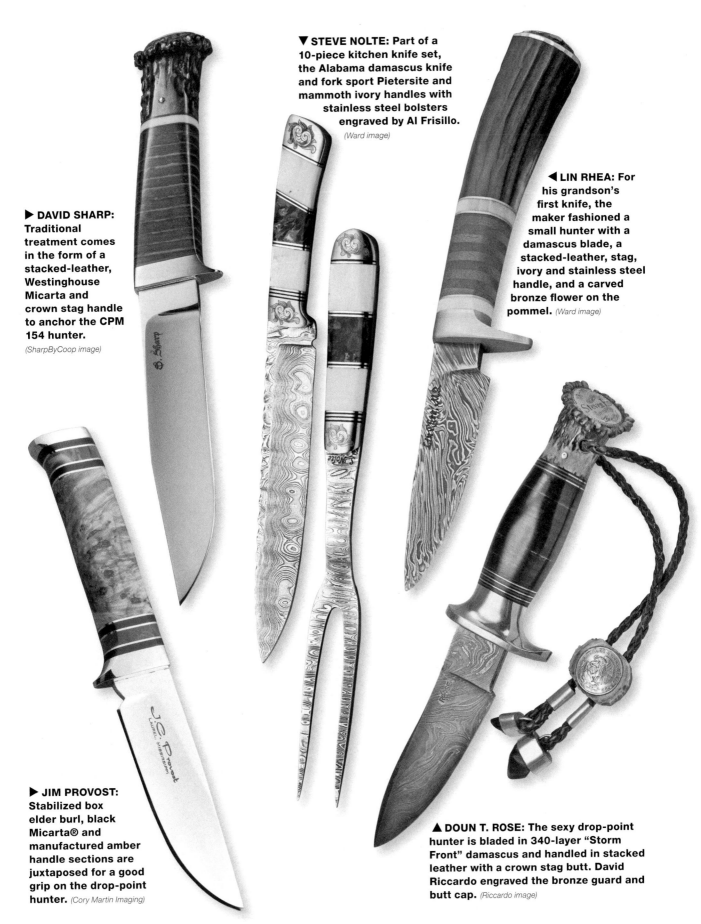

▶ **DAVID SHARP:** Traditional treatment comes in the form of a stacked-leather, Westinghouse Micarta and crown stag handle to anchor the CPM 154 hunter.

(SharpByCoop image)

▼ **STEVE NOLTE:** Part of a 10-piece kitchen knife set, the Alabama damascus knife and fork sport Pietersite and mammoth ivory handles with stainless steel bolsters engraved by Al Frisillo.

(Ward image)

◀ **LIN RHEA:** For his grandson's first knife, the maker fashioned a small hunter with a damascus blade, a stacked-leather, stag, ivory and stainless steel handle, and a carved bronze flower on the pommel. *(Ward image)*

▶ **JIM PROVOST:** Stabilized box elder burl, black Micarta® and manufactured amber handle sections are juxtaposed for a good grip on the drop-point hunter. *(Cory Martin Imaging)*

▲ **DOUN T. ROSE:** The sexy drop-point hunter is bladed in 340-layer "Storm Front" damascus and handled in stacked leather with a crown stag butt. David Riccardo engraved the bronze guard and butt cap. *(Riccardo image)*

Filigree & Filework

Rather than engraving gold and silver jewelry, the ancient Greeks and Etruscans soldered together beads of precious metal, building them up for a granular, artistic motif that suggested the look of lace. Often an underlay of wire added to the effect. Such delicate metalwork was common in French and Italian metalwork from 1660 to the late 19th century, and remains popular in India and Asia. Known as filigree, knifemakers have adapted it quite nicely for the handles of their finest blades. Zaza Revishvili comes to mind as the knifemaker who popularized filigree in the American custom knife industry, perhaps bringing the practice with him from his Russian homeland. There's one beautiful example of a filigreed handle by knifemaker Logan Pierce in this section.

Filework is another form of knife embellishment that strays from engraving in that gravers are set aside for small hand files used to cut away material and create repetitive patterns, often climbing, repeating vine patterns along blade spines, tangs and back spacers, in particular. Though vines are popular, there are a variety of repetitive shapes and figures, even Celtic knots or Texas grass burrs, accomplished through creative filework.

◀ **LOGAN PEARCE:** Silver filigree wraps around and fans out from the black-lip-pearl handle inlays of the 11.5-inch damascus art knife. *(Ward image)*

▲ **KENDALL SCHORSCH:** The smooth bone handle scales of the double-blade trapper called for some contrasting filework, in a "South Texas grass burr" pattern, along the back spacer.
(PointSeven image)

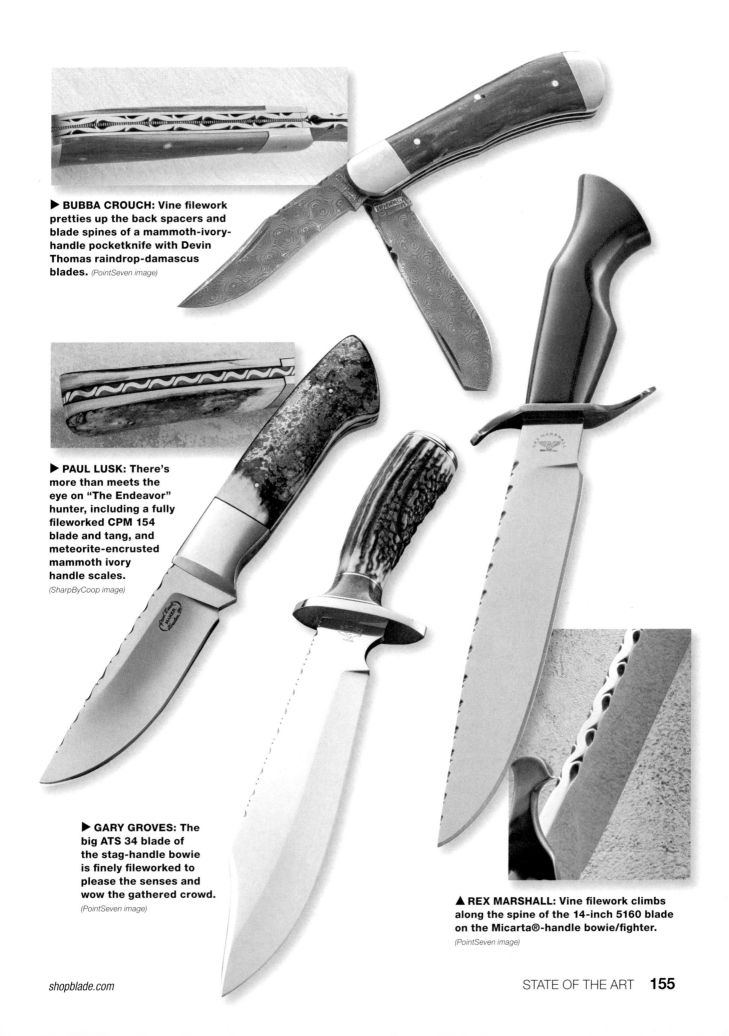

▶ **BUBBA CROUCH:** Vine filework pretties up the back spacers and blade spines of a mammoth-ivory-handle pocketknife with Devin Thomas raindrop-damascus blades. *(PointSeven image)*

▶ **PAUL LUSK:** There's more than meets the eye on "The Endeavor" hunter, including a fully fileworked CPM 154 blade and tang, and meteorite-encrusted mammoth ivory handle scales.

(SharpByCoop image)

▶ **GARY GROVES:** The big ATS 34 blade of the stag-handle bowie is finely fileworked to please the senses and wow the gathered crowd.

(PointSeven image)

▲ **REX MARSHALL:** Vine filework climbs along the spine of the 14-inch 5160 blade on the Micarta®-handle bowie/fighter.

(PointSeven image)

STATE OF THE ART **155**

Sculpted Bods

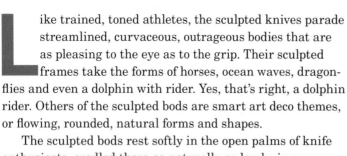

Like trained, toned athletes, the sculpted knives parade streamlined, curvaceous, outrageous bodies that are as pleasing to the eye as to the grip. Their sculpted frames take the forms of horses, ocean waves, dragonflies and even a dolphin with rider. Yes, that's right, a dolphin rider. Others of the sculpted bods are smart art deco themes, or flowing, rounded, natural forms and shapes.

The sculpted bods rest softly in the open palms of knife enthusiasts, cradled there as naturally as lambs in mangers, with nary a sharp edge to poke the skin and only rounded grips for palpability and purchase. The sculpted knives are as utilitarian as they are artistic creations, and such is the allure of art knives in general, as versatile cutting tools that double as painters' pallets, so to speak. The sculpting tools were working overtime on these toned bodies, and their profiles are proof positive of that.

◀ **STEPHANIE LEMELIN: A silver horse with flowing mane is the centerpiece of a damascus and ebony art knife.** *(PointSeven image)*

▼ **KEN STEIGERWALT: Like a unit of luminous flux, the "Lumen" CPM 154 folder emits light via its multi-bevel, stepped Art Deco-style blade and handle, and those translucent black-lip-pearl inlays.**

(SharpByCoop image)

◀ **JOSH SMITH: The elegant form of the handle scales seemingly crashing like waves over a tortoise shell inlay give the knife more movement than the intricate mosaic-damascus blade already provides.**

(PointSeven image)

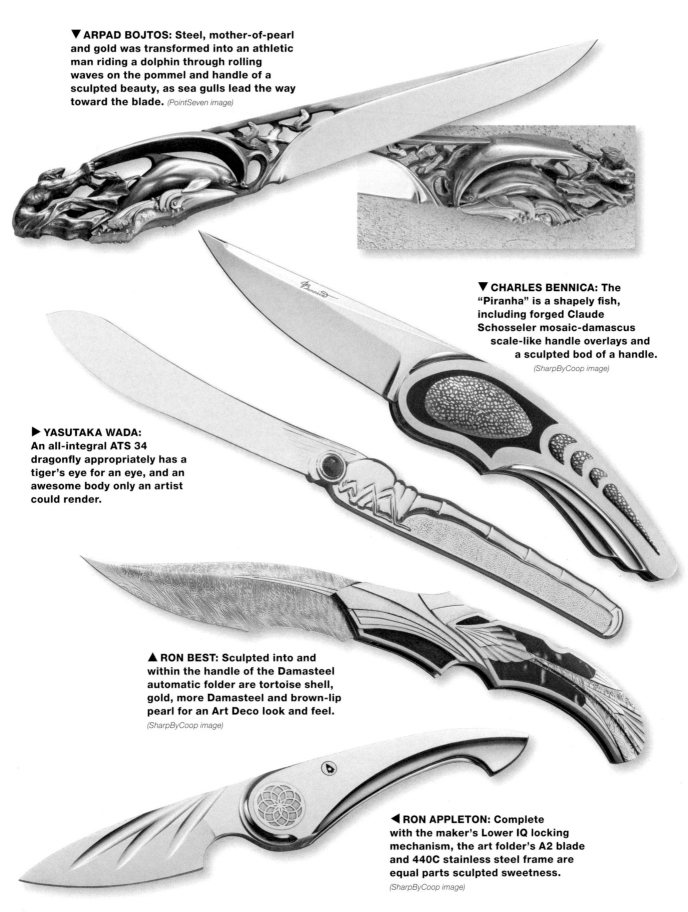

▼ **ARPAD BOJTOS:** Steel, mother-of-pearl and gold was transformed into an athletic man riding a dolphin through rolling waves on the pommel and handle of a sculpted beauty, as sea gulls lead the way toward the blade. *(PointSeven image)*

▼ **CHARLES BENNICA:** The "Piranha" is a shapely fish, including forged Claude Schosseler mosaic-damascus scale-like handle overlays and a sculpted bod of a handle.

(SharpByCoop image)

▶ **YASUTAKA WADA:** An all-integral ATS 34 dragonfly appropriately has a tiger's eye for an eye, and an awesome body only an artist could render.

▲ **RON BEST:** Sculpted into and within the handle of the Damasteel automatic folder are tortoise shell, gold, more Damasteel and brown-lip pearl for an Art Deco look and feel.

(SharpByCoop image)

◀ **RON APPLETON:** Complete with the maker's Lower IQ locking mechanism, the art folder's A2 blade and 440C stainless steel frame are equal parts sculpted sweetness.

(SharpByCoop image)

Slack-Jaw Scrimshaw

MIKE HASBUN: If you're going to scrimshaw the ivory Micarta® handle of a Pete Pruyn Japanese-style damascus tanto, you might as well choose a Samurai skeleton motif. *(SharpByCoop image)*

LORI RISTINEN: African wildlife scenes accomplished in dark ink on mammoth ivory handles make for subtle yet striking images adorning a pair of engraved Kirk Rexroat knives. *(PointSeven image)*

TERRY SCHREINER: Someone tied a fly and inked it into the walrus ivory pores of a Damasteel bird-and-trout knife with mosaic-damascus bolsters. *(Ward image)*

ANNE FELLOWS: The shapely and realistic wolf head scrimshaw in ivory for the handle of a Mike Fellows locking-liner folder follows the shape of the grip and the "ripple twist"-pattern damascus bolsters.

JANE TUKARSKI: The ultra-artistic rendering of an elephant in ivory on Mark Knapp's "Tembo Bowie" was a selling point for the lucky collector who purchased the damascus piece, with proceeds going to help fight the federal ivory ban. *(PointSeven image)*

◄ BOYD ASHWORTH: The little ivory handle folder has a duck-shaped, color-scrimshawed handle and a beak of a blade. *(PointSeven image)*

◄ DR. PETER JENSEN: The nude color scrimshaw in fossil walrus ivory quickens the pulse and enlivens a Reinhard Tschager knife that sports a fileworked gold-ring guard and a Johan Gustafsson damascus blade.

◄ DEBI RUCKER: Freedom comes at a cost, as depicted by an angel over a kneeling soldier scrimshawed on the composite handle of a Thomas Rucker CPM S35VN fixed blade with engraved bolsters. *(PointSeven image)*

► JIM SMITH: A nod to traditional whaler's art, the sea creatures scrimshawed on each side of a walrus ivory handle are further highlighted by a damascus blade and a nickel silver sheath engraved by Roland J. Robidoux.

(PointSeven image)

▲ RON SKAGGS: Though knifemaker W.W. Cronk passed away in 1983, his push dagger scrimshawed in a vampire motif lives on for generations to come.

(SharpByCoop image)

▲ LINDA KARST STONE: One for the pooches, or pooch lovers, the color scrimshaw in ivory gracing the Jerry Moen fixed blade is complemented by Nathan Dickinson engraving. *(PointSeven image)*

The Carvers' Corner

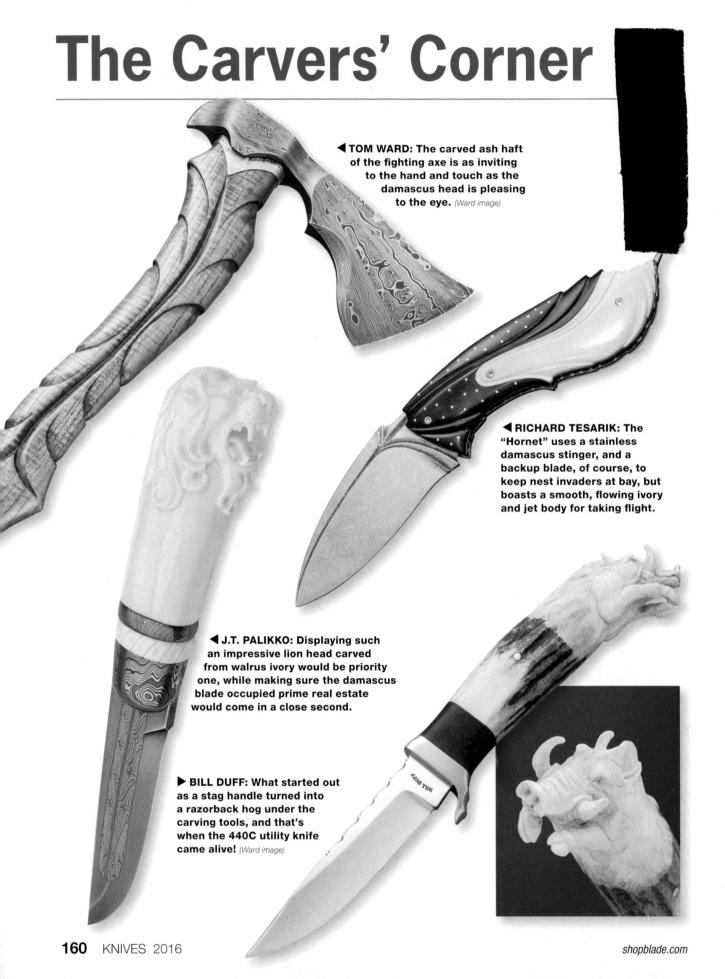

◀ **TOM WARD:** The carved ash haft of the fighting axe is as inviting to the hand and touch as the damascus head is pleasing to the eye. *(Ward image)*

◀ **RICHARD TESARIK:** The "Hornet" uses a stainless damascus stinger, and a backup blade, of course, to keep nest invaders at bay, but boasts a smooth, flowing ivory and jet body for taking flight.

◀ **J.T. PALIKKO:** Displaying such an impressive lion head carved from walrus ivory would be priority one, while making sure the damascus blade occupied prime real estate would come in a close second.

▶ **BILL DUFF:** What started out as a stag handle turned into a razorback hog under the carving tools, and that's when the 440C utility knife came alive! *(Ward image)*

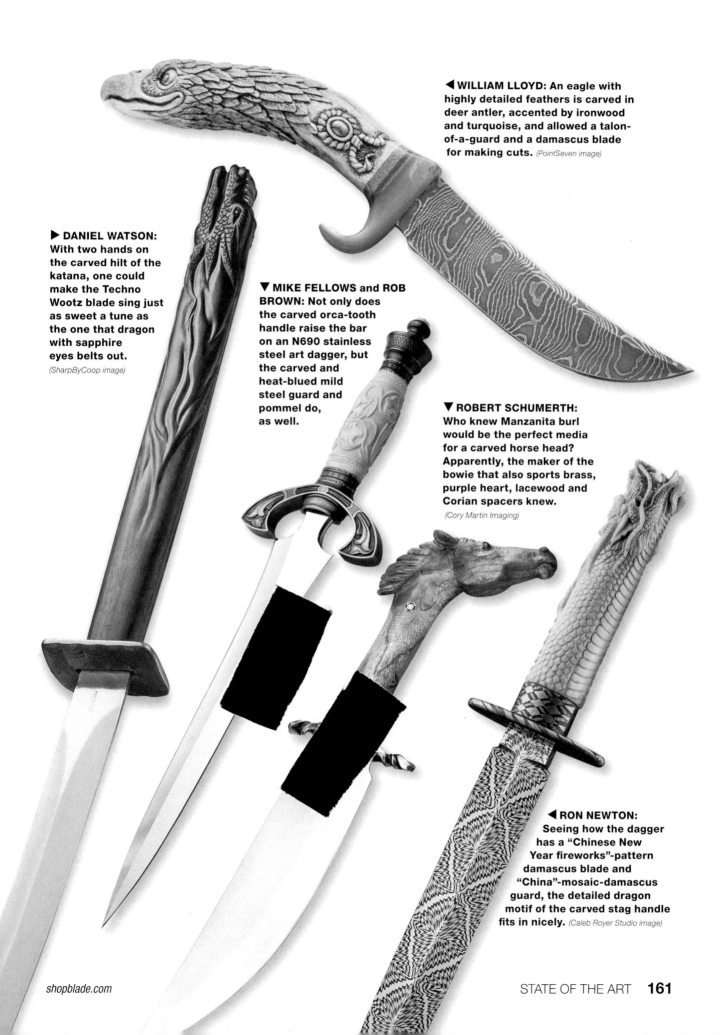

◄ **WILLIAM LLOYD:** An eagle with highly detailed feathers is carved in deer antler, accented by ironwood and turquoise, and allowed a talon-of-a-guard and a damascus blade for making cuts. *(PointSeven image)*

▶ **DANIEL WATSON:** With two hands on the carved hilt of the katana, one could make the Techno Wootz blade sing just as sweet a tune as the one that dragon with sapphire eyes belts out.

(SharpByCoop image)

▼ **MIKE FELLOWS** and **ROB BROWN:** Not only does the carved orca-tooth handle raise the bar on an N690 stainless steel art dagger, but the carved and heat-blued mild steel guard and pommel do, as well.

▼ **ROBERT SCHUMERTH:** Who knew Manzanita burl would be the perfect media for a carved horse head? Apparently, the maker of the bowie that also sports brass, purple heart, lacewood and Corian spacers knew.

(Cory Martin Imaging)

◄ **RON NEWTON:** Seeing how the dagger has a "Chinese New Year fireworks"-pattern damascus blade and "China"-mosaic-damascus guard, the detailed dragon motif of the carved stag handle fits in nicely. *(Caleb Royer Studio image)*

Golden Touches

GLENN WATERS: Butterflies, flowers and a dragon in a windstorm are the engraved, inlaid and overlaid theme of a flipper folder in stainless steel, gold, green gold, pink gold, white gold, titanium and mammoth ivory.

KEN STEIGERWALT: The "Gold Astrum" (ancient Greek for gold star) folder twinkles via its 14k-gold frame, black-lip pearl handle inlays and gold bolsters. *(SharpByCoop image)*

AAD VAN RYSWYK: A golden eagle stares out from the engraved bolsters of a lapis-lazuli-handle lock-back folder.

KOJI HARA: Gold Maki-e (Japanese lacquer sprinkled with gold powder) is overlaid on the black-lip-pearl handle inlays of the spear-point folding dagger, which also features a Ranma (transom) groove in the center of the blade that is pierce engraved with "silk spider" in Kanji characters. *(SharpByCoop image)*

MATTHEW LERCH: Framing the etchings (each side of the handle) of sensuous warrior girls are gold and platinum inlays by Brian Hochstrat, with damascus carried through the blade and handle. *(Prairie Digital image)*

▶ **LEONARDO FRIZZI:** Engraving tipped in 24-karat gold depicts Egyptian king and queen Ramesses and Nefertari (reverse handle side) in full regalia for an RWL-34 locking-liner folder.

◀ **MIKE ZSCHERNY:** Fine touches like the engraved gold bolsters by Damon Soileau, black-lip-pearl handle inlays, a gold bale, damascus blade and fileworked back spacer flourish on the fancy folder. *(Cory Martin Imaging)*

◀ **SALVATORE PUDDU:** Art nouveau scroll engraving and reverse gold inlay by Brian Hochstrat is the perfect golden touch, or gilded touch, to frame the antique tortoise shell inlays of a two-blade folder. *(Prairie Digital image)*

◀ **OWEN WOOD:** A herringbone-pattern damascus folding dagger gets the golden treatment, as well as some beryllium copper, black-lip pearl, titanium and stainless steel.

(SharpByCoop image)

▲ **JOHN HORRIGAN:** Gold wire inlay follows the sweep of the upswept Turkish-twist-pattern damascus blade, with more 24-karat gold along the mild steel guard, all anchored by an ebony handle.

A Life Savings of Engravings

◀ **DAMON SOILEAU:** Details like the three gold dots on the damascus blade of the Stephen Olszewski folder, which play off the gold-inlaid and engraved bolsters, add up to an embellished beauty of a blade.
(Cory Martin Imaging)

◀ **BRUCE SHAW:** Beguiling imagery of flowers and skulls attempts to soften the look of the tough Keith Ouye CPM 154 folding tanto.
(SharpByCoop image)

▼ **VALERIO PELI:** Engraved gold inlays house 15 diamonds, enriching a Reinhard Tschager dagger that also sashays an Ettore Gianferrari damascus blade and a lapis lazuli handle.
(Francesco Pachi image)

◀ **JULIEN MARCHAL:** The Pietersite gemstone handle inlay of a Des Horn folder, complete with Damasteel blade, may have inspired the gold inlay and engraving that elevates the piece.
(Francesco Pachi image)

▼ **MICHAEL HENNINGSSON:** Bulino-style engraving and 24k-gold and copper inlays capture King Kong in all his glory, and within the stainless steel confines of a one-hand-opening folder.

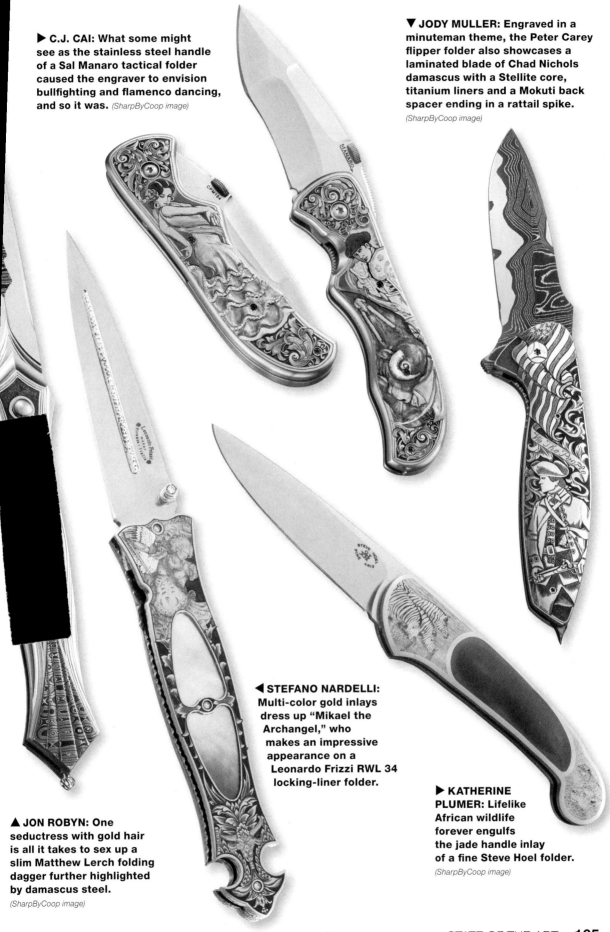

▶ **C.J. CAI:** What some might see as the stainless steel handle of a Sal Manaro tactical folder caused the engraver to envision bullfighting and flamenco dancing, and so it was. *(SharpByCoop image)*

▼ **JODY MULLER:** Engraved in a minuteman theme, the Peter Carey flipper folder also showcases a laminated blade of Chad Nichols damascus with a Stellite core, titanium liners and a Mokuti back spacer ending in a rattail spike. *(SharpByCoop image)*

◀ **STEFANO NARDELLI:** Multi-color gold inlays dress up "Mikael the Archangel," who makes an impressive appearance on a Leonardo Frizzi RWL 34 locking-liner folder.

▲ **JON ROBYN:** One seductress with gold hair is all it takes to sex up a slim Matthew Lerch folding dagger further highlighted by damascus steel. *(SharpByCoop image)*

▶ **KATHERINE PLUMER:** Lifelike African wildlife forever engulfs the jade handle inlay of a fine Steve Hoel folder. *(SharpByCoop image)*

A Life Savings of Engravings

► **BRUCE CHRISTENSEN:** The gray hues of the mammoth tooth handle that anchors the Rodney Watts drop-point hunter are replicated in the scroll-engraved bolsters.

▼ **MIKE TARANGO:** While the Lesswing ATS 34 drop-point h might not demolish buildings, giraffe-bone-handle fixed blad might at least do some damag
(SharpByCoop image)

▲ **VERONIKA TESARIKOVA:** Scroll and leaf engraving furthers the natural flow of a Richard Tesar damascus folder featuring a flower-bud-shaped, carved mammoth ivory grip.

◄ **JIM SMALL** Stout man handle, trappe great and g doub
(Caleb Royer Studio

► **JON ROBYN:** No building, or knife handle for that matter, can corral King Kong, and the color engraving that graces the late, great knifemaker Joe Kious's folding dagger is unrestrained.
(SharpByCoop image)

▲ **DWIGHT TOWELL:** Calling his "Cuddy Mountain Hunter the maker engraved and gold inlaid the bolsters of the mother-of-pearl-handle fixed blade, complete with a cattle brand in the oval inlay.

► **NATHAN DICKINSON:** When knifemaker Marvin Winn saw how the stainless steel handle of his folder turned out after some gold inlay and engraving, he pocketed the knife and silently slinked away. *(PointSeven image)*

◄ **NATHAN DICKINSON:** The rose-pattern Damasteel blade of Calvin Robinson's "Pappy's Jackknife" called for some fancy engraved and gold-inlaid bolsters, as well as elephant ivory handle scales. *(PointSeven image)*

▲ **BEN MIDGLEY JR. & SR.:** It takes a second glance before realizing that the pattern of the engraved stainless steel bolsters is continued in scrimshaw (not an all-steel grip) on the ivory handle scales of the folder. *(Ward image)*

► **VLADIMIR VANCURA:** Engraving brass spells class on a Garth Hindmarch damascus hunter with a mammoth-ivory handle and mosaic pins.

◄ **LLOYD MCCONNELL:** The big fighter boasts a 5-inch 154CM stainless steel blade, a nice blue-mammoth-tooth handle and bolster engraving by the maker. *(PointSeven image)*

▲ **GLENN WATERS:** Through engraved Damasteel and Timascus, as well as engraved gold inlays, the art folder depicts cherry blossoms and butterflies in a most winsome way.

A Life Savings of Engravings

▶ **DAVID RICCARDO:** The feathery theme engraved into the stainless steel bolsters of a Kevin Casey dress folder is repeated in Casey's feather-damascus blade and complemented by mammoth ivory handle scales and sapphire bolster and thumb stud inlays.

(SharpByCoop image)

▼ **NATHAN PETERSON:** Crisscrossing and sandwiching the mammoth ivory handle inlays of a Chester Deubel damascus folder is some fine leaf and scroll engraving.

(Ward image)

▲ **JODY MULLER:** Brown-lip pearl and scroll engraving go hand-in-hand, or bolster-and-blade, with the stainless damascus of a W.D. Pease lock-back folder. *(PointSeven image)*

▲ **BARB SLOBODIAN:** Japanese floral engraving adorns the solid sterling silver handle of Anders Hogstrom's "Okinawa Flower" folder in a random-pattern damascus blade. *(SharpByCoop image)*

▲ **ED LARY:** Both sides of the ATS 34 blade are heat colored and relief-engraved with mammoths, a nod to the rich bark-mammoth-ivory handle scales. *(Cory Martin Imaging)*

◀ **JODY MULLER:** The skulls are apparently from folks who lived by the rules, ascending into an afterlife of gold, diamonds and damascus. *(SharpByCoop image)*

▼ **JOE MASON:** The engraver knew just what to depict on Tom Overeynder's sexy CTS-XHP folding art dagger. *(SharpByCoop image)*

◀ **RICK EATON:** The damascus pearl-handle folding dagger is adorned with curly leaf engraving of the most fertile kind from a fertile mind. *(PointSeven image)*

▲ **DAVID RICCARDO:** An Egyptian woman holding serpents straddles the bolsters of a Chuck Gedraitis double-guard flipper folder, this one in a forged 1095 blade with temper line. *(Cory Martin Imaging)*

▲ **NATHAN DICKINSON:** A slip-joint trapper from the hands of Jerry Moen, "The Roundup" is engraved and gold inlaid on every inch of its 416 stainless steel frame. *(PointSeven image)*

A Life Savings of Engravings

▶ **JIM SMALL:** Follow the Joel Chamblin folder from its CPM 154 blades across the gold-inlaid and engraved bolsters, onto the mammoth ivory handle, with a brief rest at the 14k-gold shield.
(Ward image)

▼ **GIL RUDOLF:** Given a pearl-handle Dennis Friedly boot knife with a tapered tang, the engraver gave it some organic engraving topped with gold flowers.
(SharpByCoop image)

▲ **JIM SORNBE____R:** The blue lapis lazuli handle w___ ___e and diamond inlays is blissfully _____ ___he engraved 14k-gold frame of a ____ ___ ___older. There's a diamond in the thu___ ___ ___ood measure.

▲ **___ _____RDO:** Futuristic alie___ ____led, choosing the ___ ___r a Stan Wilson tactical folder inlaid with glowing material, no less.
(SharpByCoop image)

▲ **NATHAN DICKINSON:** Golden scrolls grace the bolsters of a pearl-handle Terry Schreiner gent's folder in a Damasteel blade. *(Ward image)*

◄ **BRIAN HOCHSTRAT:** This sultry beauty by the late Joe Kious pays tribute to the classic pinup girls of Antonio Vargas and includes gold inlay and unequalled engraving that carefully complements the ingenious pattern of the damascus blade.

(Prairie Digital image)

▲ **MARIAN SAWBY:** The Northwest coastal Indian theme, including copper inlays, engraved into the bolsters of a Scott Sawby jade-handle folder will never be replicated.

(SharpByCoop image)

STATE OF THE ART **171**

And a P

▶ DAVID SEWARD: The maker stuck out his neck with some ostrich skin overlay on the tip and loops of the carved-leather sheath. *(Caleb Royer Studio image)*

▶ **JOHN HORRIGAN:** Winner of the Best Sheath award at the 2014 Arkansas Custom Knife Show, the silver bullet comes with a black stingray skin inlay. *(Ward image)*

FACTORY TRENDS

When looking at what's new, or trending, in factory fixed blades and folders, whether flipper folders, bushcraft blades, survival knives or food prep edges, the word that continues to rise to the top is "tactical." What traditionalists have a difficult time grasping (and believe me, I say "traditionalists" with the utmost respect in this industry, which is built on tradition) is that "tactical" isn't used in the sense of black blades and handles for soldiers, police, self-defense instructors and mall ninjas.

No, the term tactical, used in a more modern knife sense, is closer in meaning to "tactile," or easy to use, useful, easily manipulated, easy to access, easy to pocket, retrieve and handle. And there's nothing wrong with any of those attributes when it comes to one's daily carry knife.

If you look at the categories in this year's "Factory Trends" section, there is, indeed, a focus on tactical folders, gent's tactical folders and tactical fixed blades. And in the middle of all the tactical knives are factory models designed by custom knifemakers, or "Custom Designed Cutters," which is another ongoing, longstanding trend in the industry. After all, production knife company offerings have been driven by the handmade knife industry for some time now, and the benefits are immeasurable. So enjoy all the knives that are easy to manipulate, and that integrate fantastic designs. We all benefit from such features.

Tactical Folders Continue Meteoric Rise

Educated knife enthusiasts gravitate toward hot tactical folders loaded with features and benefits

By Dexter Ewing

The tactical folder segment gets stronger and hotter every year, building on its already successful history and further cementing it as a bona fide knife style and genre. Every year there's another round of exciting, innovative tactical folders released to an eager consumer and professional market, and the knife buying public laps it up with enthusiasm.

The current crop of tactical folders is slick and refined, and loaded with features and benefits that cater to educated knife enthusiasts. Let's take a look at what is currently hot on the tactical folder market. Mind you, there's a lot more selection than what is discussed herein, so keep your mind open and your eyes peeled for what interests you most, and just go for it!

The Boker Plus brand has gained widespread recognition for its varied tactical folders and fixed blades, some designed by today's hottest custom knifemakers. Michael Burch of Burchtree Bladeworks designed the Boker Plus Impetus flipper folder, of which Boker product specialist Terry Trahan says, "From a utilitarian perspective, this is a very nice, strong general purpose folder that meets the legal blade limits in most jurisdictions."

Including a 3.25-inch sheepsfoot-style 440C stainless steel blade, the army-tank-of-a-folder commands attention due to its overbuilt frame, comfortable G-10 handle scales, well-defined main finger groove for indexing one's grip, steel bolsters and an integral hand guard. Due to the attention to detail it takes to finely fit bolsters to handle scales, it has become a rarity to even see bolsters on factory folders. The execution of the Boker Plus Impetus, however, is perfect.

The transition from the G-10 handle scales to the bolsters is smooth, and the handle is contoured to the degree of a fine custom knife. Double titanium liners, one of which doubles as the blade lock, provide a solid backbone to the handle, and a notched-steel handle spacer rounds out the package.

The blade edge sweeps gently upward to form a tip that is ultimately

Designed by Michael Burch, the Boker Plus Impetus is a stout folder featuring a sheepsfoot-style 440C stainless steel blade, steel bolsters, titanium liners and black G-10 handle scales.

The Spyderco Paramilitary 2 was born out of customer demand for a smaller version of the Military that would be easier to carry in the pocket.

useful despite its blunt sheepsfoot appearance. The stonewashed blade rides on an IKBS (Ikoma Korth Bearing System) pivot for smooth opening and closing.

"The IKBS and flipper make for smooth opening," Trahan confirms. Weighing in at 7.5 ounces, the Impetus has the heft of a quality tool that can be used with confidence for tough cutting jobs. While Burch reasserts himself as a maker to watch, the Boker Plus Impetus provides an opportunity to obtain one of his folders at a great price point and without the waiting list inherent to many popular knifemakers.

MILITARY LINEAGE

Spyderco's C81 Paramilitary 2 traces its lineage back to the company's popular C36 Military model, a large, high-performance folder featuring a flat-ground blade and ergonomic handle. The folder is in response to Spyderco customers asking for a smaller, more compact version of the Military model that is easier to carry but retains the same level of high performance as the full-size version.

"The original Paramilitary was designed by [Spyderco founder] Sal Glesser," says Sal's son, Eric. "After years of producing the original model and its gaining a great reputation for performance, I took the already popular design and added some new refinements through gained knowledge and years of customer feedback and manufacturing improvements."

The Military design was elevated to the next level with the addition of Spyderco's own Compression Lock®, which works off of the stainless steel handle liner and is reportedly safer to use than a regular LinerLock®. With the Compression Lock, a user's fingers do not cross the path of the rotating blade. All digits stay out of the way during blade closing! The blade itself rides on a bronze pivot bushing, which not only helps to bolster handle strength and rigidity, but also promotes glassy smooth action.

The 3 7/16-inch CPM S30V blade has the same full, flat grind and distal taper as the full-size Military model, and the Paramilitary 2 retains the same basic handle shape, complete with finger choil for choking up on the blade during controlled cuts. The upgraded model features full-length steel liners nested into a black or "digi-camo" G-10 handle, creating a strong but thin folder that rides easily in the pocket. Other notable improvements are a four-way pocket clip, flush screws, a large lanyard hole and refined ergonomics. All of this adds up to another superb Spyderco cutting tool.

When discussing tactical folders, it's almost impossible to not mention Benchmade Knife Co., which has been on the forefront of the market since the mid-1990s and has yet to show any signs of easing up on the throttle. Case in point, the Benchmade Model 5400 Serum Double Action (DA) Axis Lock™ folder. This is the first Axis Lock model with a double-action opening mechanism—the blade can be opened manually via ambidextrous thumb studs, or fired like a switchblade.

The Zero Tolerance (ZT) 0562 combines the design prowess of Rick Hinderer with the manufacturing excellence that Kai USA, parent of ZT, is well known for.

"The design was inspired by some in-house discussion regarding dual actions in general and how they have proven to be quite popular as of late," says Jason France, Benchmade design engineer. "We wanted to take the versatility and strength of the Axis Lock and give it even more versatility with the option of manual or automatic opening." Thus was born the 5400, and with which, France points out, there is no need to plan or choose opening methods before using the folder, regardless of manual or automatic preference.

"You can activate either opening mode without pushing a secondary button, slide, switch, etc.," he explains. Furthermore, France says a secondary

mechanism that prevents dry fire was engineered into the knife to prevent the user from breaking the torsion spring. "We define 'dry firing' as the tendency for a torsion spring that is held in its loaded state to release suddenly without any resistance," he begins. "This, in turn, results in the spring snapping back to its free position and generally results in catastrophic failure." In other words, the spring will break.

FAILSAFE OPENING

"The mechanism protects against this by not allowing the spring to fire if the blade is in any position *except* fully closed," France notes. There is a failsafe mechanism built into the Serum DA Axis Lock, and if the main auto spring does happen to break, the knife still functions perfectly using the manual thumb studs.

The 5400 Serum comes with a 3.47-inch, modified drop-point 154CM stainless steel blade in a black or satin finish, and a plain or semi-serrated edge. Other features include a machined G-10 handle, a G-10 back spacer, double full-length steel liners and a tip-up, ambidextrous pocket clip. The workmanship is top notch on the easy-to-carry, extremely utilitarian folder.

The majority of the Emerson Knives, Inc., product line is of top-shelf tactical folders made in the U.S.A. In 2013, the company unveiled the Patriot, a formidable folding bowie with a 4-inch, recurved 154CM blade. Ernest Emerson, founder and president of the company, as well as an accomplished custom knifemaker in his own right, had the opportunity to acquire some special wood from a tree that grew on George Washington's historic Mount Vernon estate.

As he was going through knife design possibilities to use in concert with the proprietary wood handle, Emerson details, "I settled on a design influence that would reflect George Washington's era." By that, Emerson says it reflects a time in history when a knife was built for all-around use—camping, hunting, utility, and if necessary, as a weapon.

"The knife had to fulfill any role asked of it," he surmises, "one that a soldier of that era could carry and use. As far as size is concerned, it's a middle-of-the-road design."

With distinct bowie design influences, the blade

gives the knife a masculine attitude, while the recurved edge makes for easy slicing. The ergonomic handle is comfortable in either forward or reverse grips, thanks to the thoughtful handle engineering that includes a generous finger groove in the front and a subtle pinky catch at the rear. In between those two points is a gentle flowing curve that helps the user lock in his or her grip and not let go!

The Patriot comes in a collector-grade version sporting a stonewashed blade with a satin finish and a die-struck medallion of George Washington's profile inlaid into the Mount Vernon wood handle. A copy of a survey map that was drawn up by Washington himself shows exactly where the tree was located on the property.

A PATRIOTIC CHOICE

A user-grade version of the Patriot sports a textured G-10 handle with a manufacturer's suggested retail price of $259.95, as compared to $499.99 for the collector-grade model. Regardless of preference, the Emerson Knives Patriot is an impressive, high-performance knife that makes quite a statement. As with all Emerson folders, the Patriot comes with the Wave feature on the blade spine, allowing the user to rapidly open the folder by catching the wave-shaped extension on a pants pocket hem while simultaneously pulling the knife from the pocket.

Kai USA proudly manufactures Zero Tolerance (ZT) tactical folders in the U.S.A., selling them alongside the company's sibling brands—Kershaw Knives and Shun Cutlery. Some of the newest ZT tactical folders are collaborative efforts between the company and Rick Hinderer of Hinderer Knives, including the Model 0550 frame-lock folder, the 0560 family of tactical folders patterned after Hinderer's wildly popular XM-18 model and now the new 0562 folder featuring Hinderer's "slicer"-ground blade.

Thomas Welk, director of sales and marketing for Kai USA, says, "We refined the design even further for the 0562," particularly smaller jimping (or finger groove texturing) on the blade spine, a shorter lock bar and a narrowed and domed blade stop. "Specifically, the knife is designed to be opened via the flipper," Welk stresses. "The studs on the blade are *not* thumb studs, but rather sturdy blade stops."

The ELMAX steel holds an edge and resists corrosion, while a 3.5-inch drop-point blade configuration lends itself to a variety of tasks both indoors and out, and the slicer grind no doubt enhances the knife's usefulness. "Users love Rick's slicer grind," Welk asserts. "The beveled edge is slightly thicker toward the back of the blade for cutting tougher items, and slimmer toward the middle and tip for super-easy slicing."

Welk says there's plenty of steel left at the tip to reinforce it and prevent the blade from bending or breaking. A titanium frame lock is paired with a front-side, textured G-10 handle scale, and as with all of Hinderer's folders, there is a steel liner on the non-lock side to add rigidity to the handle and strength for the blade stop when the folder is open. A deep-carry, tip-up pocket clip allows discreet carry and easy access.

A fancier 0562CF version of model boasts the same dimensions as the 0562, but with an M390 blade and a carbon fiber handle scale. Hinderer's design expertise paired with Zero Tolerance's manufacturing prowess equates to a must-have tactical folder.

Honestly, each of these tactical folders is a joy to own and use, and when paired with solid market demand for the ever-evolving knife genre, it remains a "get 'em while they're hot" proposition. And, of course, it's the choosing of a tactical folder that's the hardest part.

The bowie-shaped blade of the Emerson Knives, Inc., Patriot is given a recurved edge for easy slicing action, while the ergonomic handle makes the knife easy to use for extended periods.

Gentlemanly Tactical

▶ Among the first gentlemanly tactical folders that Ken Onion (who calls them "genticals") designed for Kershaw over a decade ago is the Leek (green handle). One of several he's designed recently for CRKT is the Ripple II (black handle).

▶ High-end steels and short blades—the Bear Ops Rancor blade is 2.875 inches long—are among the requisites of a bona fide gentlemanly tactical.

◀ The Brous Blades Bionic includes a 3-inch D2 blade, an anodized aluminum handle and a strong locking liner for secure use.

▲ Though advertised as a "gentleman's auto," the Benchmade Impel has many features of a gent's tactical, including a 1.98-inch CPM S30V stainless steel blade, a machined aluminum handle and a textured G10 inlay.

Custom Designed Cutters

▼ A Matthew Lerch design, the CRKT Argus assisted-opening folder sports a 3.6-inch, satin-finished AUS 8 stainless steel blade and a 6061-T6-aluminum handle. Closed length: 4.6 inches.

◄ Jerry Hossom designed the Outdoor Edge "Brush Demon" to include a 13.5-inch black-powder-coated 65Mn high carbon steel blade, a thermoplastic rubber handle and a nylon sheath.

▲ Designed by knifemaker Mike Snody, the KA-BAR "Snody Snake Charmer" boasts a 2 5/16-inch CPM S35V stainless steel blade and a hard plastic sheath.

► United Cutlery's "Brother's Keeper" is a Wes Hibben-designed bowie in a 7-inch 7Cr17MoV stainless steel blade and a Micarta® handle.

◀ Tony Bose has designed several successful knives for Case Cutlery, a couple of the latest being a lock-back whittler (left) and a teardrop folder, both in a stainless steel blades.

▲ Designed by Bob Terzuola, the Spyderco "Double Bevel" features the efficient edge geometry of a flat grind toward the tip of the VG 10 stainless steel blade and the strength of a hollow grind below the opening hole.

▶ An assisted-opening folder designed by Grant and Gavin Hawk, the blade of the Boker Griploc is secured open when a knife user squeezes the anodized-aluminum and polycarbonate grip.

Tactical Fixed Blades

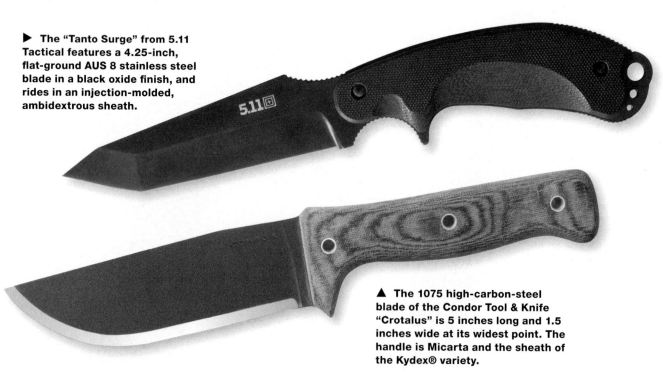

▶ The "Tanto Surge" from 5.11 Tactical features a 4.25-inch, flat-ground AUS 8 stainless steel blade in a black oxide finish, and rides in an injection-molded, ambidextrous sheath.

▲ The 1075 high-carbon-steel blade of the Condor Tool & Knife "Crotalus" is 5 inches long and 1.5 inches wide at its widest point. The handle is Micarta and the sheath of the Kydex® variety.

◄ The "Adept 1010" from Steel Will sports a precision-ground tanto blade of N690Co stainless and a 3D-machine-milled G10 handle. The Kydex sheath accommodates Tek-Lok® and MOLLE carry.

▲ Blackhawk's "Gideon Tanto" has an impressive 5-inch, black-titanium-nitride-coated AUS 8A stainless steel blade and a CNC-machined, textured G-10 handle.

▲ Busse Combat Knife Co.'s "Son of Badger" is an upgrade of the original Badger model released in 1994. "It continues to be a favorite among Busse customers," a company spokesperson noted, "and is powered by INFI steel under the hood."

► TOPS Knives offers its "Firestrike 4.5" in a 7-inch, 1095 high-carbon-steel blade with black traction coating and a black linen Micarta handle. Weight: 20 ounces.

◄ The "Emperor" from Medford Knife & Tool features a 3 5/8-inch blade of D2 tool steel with a combo/flat-ground tip and hollow-ground edge. The butt includes a glass breaker.

▼ Boasting a 4.5-inch 8Cr13MoV stainless steel blade and a choice of synthetic handles, the SOG Specialty Knives & Tools "BladeLight Tactical" features six red LED lights for use in low-visibility conditions.

Knives Marketplace

INTERESTING PRODUCT NEWS FOR BOTH THE CUTLER AND THE KNIFE ENTHUSIAST

The companies and individuals represented on the following pages will be happy to provide additional information — feel free to contact them.

BLADE SHOW 2016

MARK YOUR CALENDARS NOW!

SAVE THE DATE:
JUNE 3 – 5 | ATLANTA | COBB GALLERIA

Stay connected to BLADE Show all year:
BladeShow.com

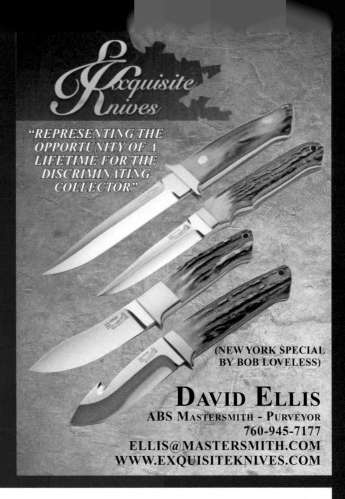

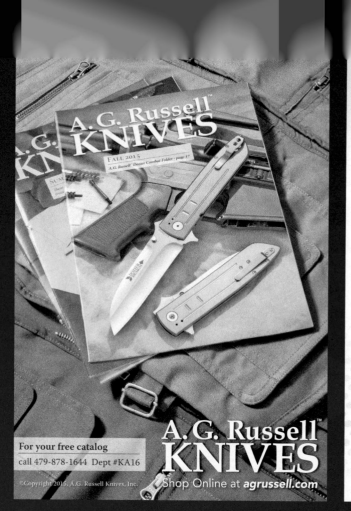
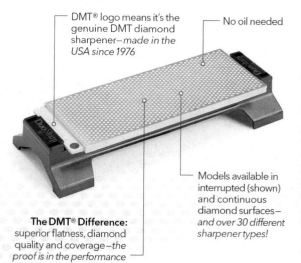

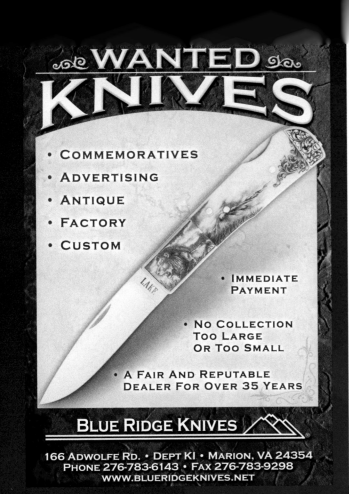
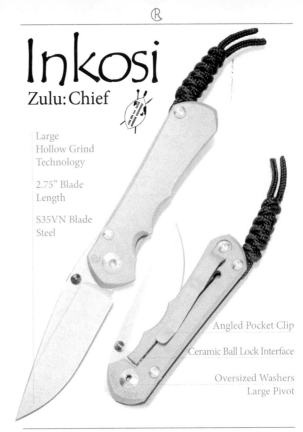

MATT AXELSON

Navy SEAL...
American Warrior...
Husband...
Brother...
Son...

BUSSE COMBAT
KNIFE COMPANY
is proud to be part of this tribute
to Navy SEAL Matt Axelson

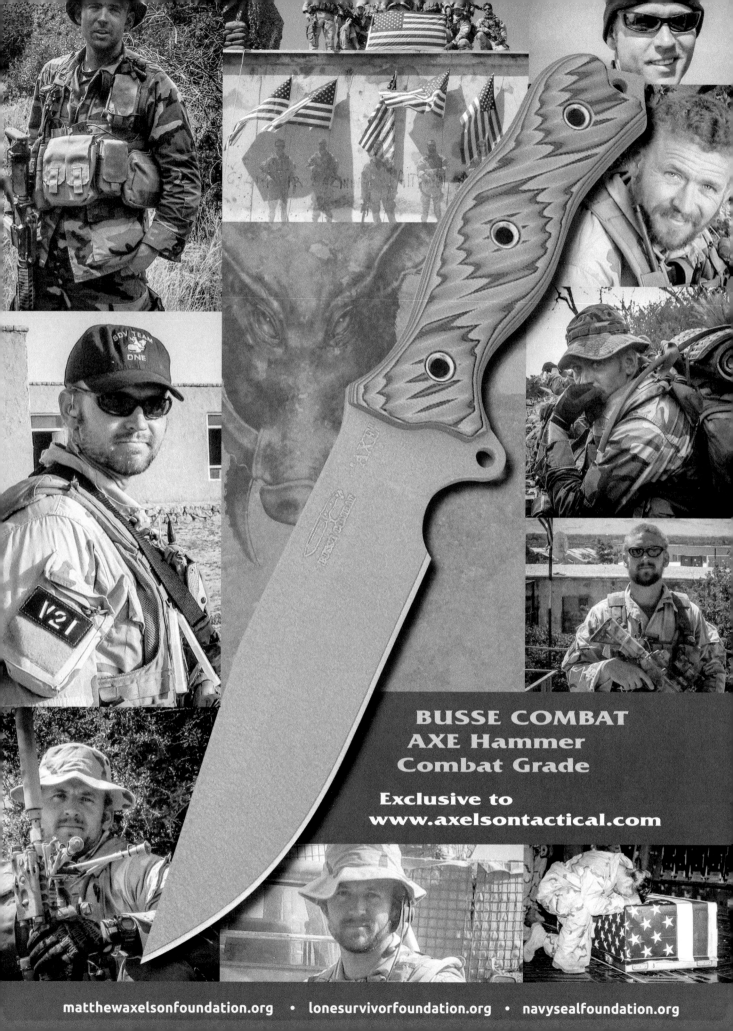

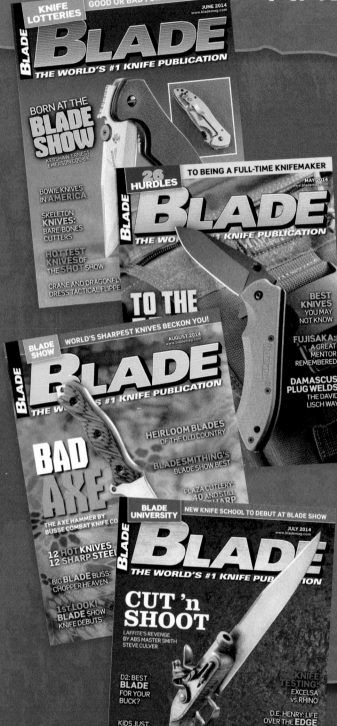

LETHAL FORCE LAW:
Get the Facts

Massad Ayoob's first book on the use of deadly force by the private citizen in defense of self and others, *In the Gravest Extreme*, is considered the authoritative text in its field. *Deadly Force* is the follow-up to this groundbreaking guide, incorporating Ayoob's thirty extra years of experience, during which he's been an expert witness in weapons cases, chair of the Firearms Committee of the American Society of Law Enforcement Trainers, and much more.

This guide will help you understand any legal and ethical issues concerning the use of lethal force by private citizens. You'll also learn about the social and psychological issues surrounding the use of lethal force for self-defense or in defense of others. In addition to exploring these issues, Ayoob also discusses the steps a responsible armed citizen can and should take in order to properly prepare for or help mitigate a lethal force situation.

Retail: $21.99 • ISBN: 9781440240614

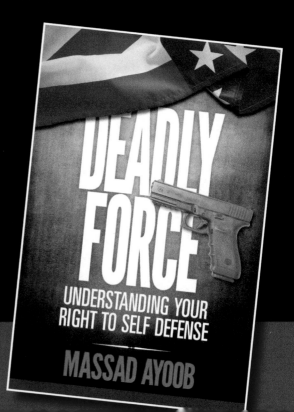

Get our *LOWEST* prices online at
GunDigestStore.com
or call **855.840.5120** (M-F 7am-6pm MT)

MICROTECH

WHEN GREAT MINDS INTERTWINE. THE RESULTS ARE EXTRAORDINARY.

DIRECTORY

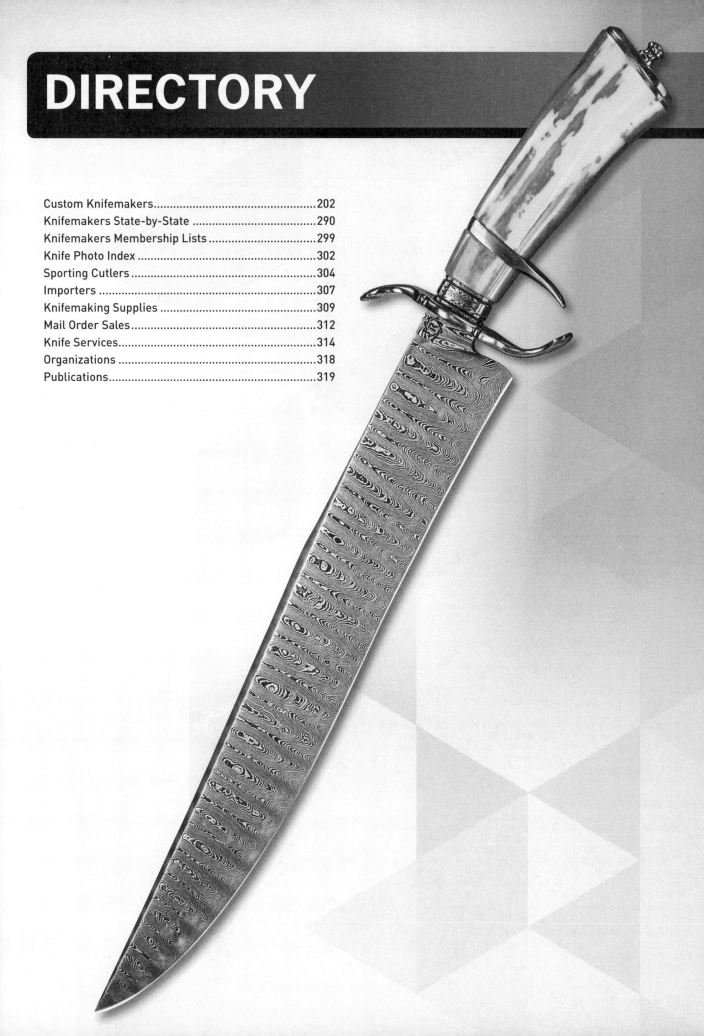

A

ABEGG, ARNIE
5992 Kenwick Cr, Huntington Beach, CA 92648, Phone: 714-848-5697

ABERNATHY, LANCE
Sniper Bladeworks, 15477 N.W. 123rd St., Platte City, MO 64079, Phone: 816-585-1595, lanceabernathy@sbcglobal.net; Web: www.sniperbladeworks.com
Specialties: Tactical frame-lock and locking-liner folding knives.

ACCAWI, FUAD
130 Timbercrest Dr., Oak Ridge, TN 37830, Phone: 865-414-4836, gaccawi@comcast.net; Web: www.acremetalworks.com
Specialties: I create one of a kind pieces from small working knives to performance blades and swords. **Patterns:** Styles include, and not limited to hunters, Bowies, daggers, swords, folders and camp knives. **Technical:** I forge primarily 5160, produces own Damascus and does own heat treating. **Prices:** $150 to $3000. **Remarks:** I am a full-time bladesmith. I enjoy producing Persian and historically influenced work. **Mark:** My mark is an eight sided Middle Eastern star with initials in the center.

ACKERSON, ROBIN E
119 W Smith St, Buchanan, MI 49107, Phone: 616-695-2911

ADAMS, JIM
1648 Camille Way, Cordova, TN 38016, Phone: 901-326-0441, jim@JimAdamsKnives.com Web: www.jimadamsknives.com
Specialties: Fixed blades in classic design. **Patterns:** Hunters, fighters, and Bowies. **Technical:** Grinds Damascus, O1, others as requested. **Prices:** Starting at $150. **Remarks:** Full-time maker. **Mark:** J. Adams, Cordova, TN.

ADAMS, LES
6413 NW 200 St, Hialeah, FL 33015, Phone: 305-625-1699
Specialties: Working straight knives of his design. **Patterns:** Fighters, tactical folders, law enforcing autos. **Technical:** Grinds ATS-34, 440C and D2. **Prices:** $100 to $500. **Remarks:** Part-time maker; first knife sold in 1989. **Mark:** First initial, last name, Custom Knives.

ADDISON, KYLE A
588 Atkins Trail, Hazel, KY 42049-8629, Phone: 270-492-8120, kylest2@yahoo.com
Specialties: Hand forged blades including Bowies, fighters and hunters. **Patterns:** Custom leather sheaths. **Technical:** Forges 5160, 1084, and his own Damascus. **Prices:** $175 to $1500. **Remarks:** Part-time maker, first knife sold in 1996. ABS member. **Mark:** First and middle initial, last name under "Trident" with knife and hammer.

ADKINS, RICHARD L
138 California Ct, Mission Viejo, CA 92692-4079

AIDA, YOSHIHITO
26-7 Narimasu 2-chome, Itabashi-ku, Tokyo, JAPAN 175-0094, Phone: 81-3-3939-0052, Fax: 81-3-3939-0058, Web: http://riverside-land.com/
Specialties: High-tech working straight knives and folders of his design. **Patterns:** Bowies, lockbacks, hunters, fighters, fishing knives, boots. **Technical:** Grinds CV-134, ATS-34; buys Damascus; works in traditional Japanese fashion for some handles and sheaths. **Prices:** $700 to $1200; some higher. **Remarks:** Full-time maker; first knife sold in 1978. **Mark:** Initial logo and Riverside West.

ALBERT, STEFAN
U Lucenecka 434/4, Filakovo 98604, SLOVAKIA, albert@albertknives.com Web: www.albertknives.com
Specialties: Art Knives, Miniatures, Scrimshaw, Bulino. **Prices:** From USD $500 to USD $25000. **Mark:** Albert

ALCORN, DOUGLAS A.
14687 Fordney Rd., Chesaning, MI 48616, Phone: 989-845-6712, fortalcornknives@centurytel.net
Specialties: Gentleman style and presentation knives. **Patterns:** Hunters, miniatures, and military type fixed blade knives and axes. **Technical:** Blades are stock removal and forged using best quality stainless, carbon, and damascus steels. Handle materials are burls, ivory, pearl, leather and other exotics. **Prices:** $300 and up. Motto: Simple, Rugged, Elegant, Handcrafted **Remarks:** Knife maker since 1989 and full time since 1999, Knife Makers Guild (voting member), member of the Bladesmith Society. **Mark:** D.A. Alcorn (Loveless style mark), Maker, Chesaning, MI.

ALDERMAN, ROBERT
2655 Jewel Lake Rd., Sagle, ID 83860, Phone: 208-263-5996
Specialties: Classic and traditional working straight knives in standard patterns or to customer specs and his design; period pieces. **Patterns:** Bowies, fighters, hunters and utility/camp knives. **Technical:** Casts, forges and grinds 1084; forges and grinds L6 and O1. Prefers an old appearance. **Prices:** $100 to $350; some to $700. **Remarks:** Full-time maker; first knife sold in 1975. Doing business as Trackers Forge. Knife-making school. Two-week course for beginners; covers forging, stock removal, hardening, tempering, case making. All materials supplied; $1250. **Mark:** Deer track.

ALEXANDER, EUGENE
Box 540, Ganado, TX 77962-0540, Phone: 512-771-3727

ALEXANDER,, OLEG, AND COSSACK BLADES
15460 Stapleton Way, Wellington, FL 33414, Phone: 443-676-6111, Web: www.cossackblades.com
Technical: All knives are made from hand-forged Damascus (3-4 types of steel are used

to create the Damascus) and have a HRC of 60-62. Handle materials are all natural, including various types of wood, horn, bone and leather. Embellishments include the use of precious metals and stones, including gold, silver, diamonds, rubies, sapphires and other unique materials. All knives include hand-made leather sheaths, and some models include wooden presentation boxes and display stands. **Prices:** $395 to over $10,000, depending on design and materials used. **Remarks:** Full-time maker, first knife sold in 1993. **Mark:** Rectangle enclosing a stylized Cyrillic letter "O" overlapping a stylized Cyrillic "K."

ALLAN, TODD
TODD ALLAN KNIVES, 6525 W. Kings Ave., Glendale, AZ 85306, Phone: 623-210-3766, todd@toddallanknives.com; www.toddallanknives.com
Patterns: Fixed-blade hunters and camp knives. **Technical:** Stock-removal method of blade making using 154CM, high-carbon damascus, stainless damascus, 5160 and 1095 blade steels. Handle materials include various Micartas, stabilized woods and mammoth ivory. **Prices:** $175 to $1,000. **Remarks:** Full-time maker.

ALLEN, MIKE "WHISKERS"
12745 Fontenot Acres Rd, Malakoff, TX 75148, Phone: 903-489-1026, whiskersknives@aol.com; Web: www.whiskersknives.com
Specialties: Working and collector-quality lockbacks, liner locks, automatic folders and assisted openers of his own proprietary mechanisms. **Patterns:** Folders and fixed blades. **Technical:** Makes Damascus, 440C and ATS-34, engraves. **Prices:** $200 and up. **Remarks:** Full-time maker since 1984. **Mark:** Whiskers and month and year.

ALLRED, BRUCE F
1764 N. Alder, Layton, UT 84041, Phone: 801-825-4612, allredbf@msn.com
Specialties: Custom hunting and utility knives. **Patterns:** Custom designs that include a unique grind line, thumb and mosaic pins. **Technical:** ATS-34, 154CM and 440C. **Remarks:** The handle material includes but not limited to Micarta (in various colors), natural woods and reconstituted stone.

ALLRED, ELVAN
31 Spring Terrace Court, St. Charles, MO 63303, Phone: 636-936-8871, allredknives@yahoo.com; Web: www.allredcustomknives.com
Specialties: Innovative sculpted folding knives designed by Elvan's son Scott that are mostly one of a kind. **Patterns:** Mostly folders but some high-end straight knives. **Technical:** ATS-34 SS, 440C SS, stainless Damascus, S30V, 154cm; inlays are mostly natural materials such as pearl, coral, ivory, jade, lapis, and other precious type **Prices:** $500 to $4000, some higher. **Remarks:** Started making knives in the shop of Dr. Fred Carter in the early 1990s. Full-time maker since 2006, first knife sold in 1993. Take some orders but work mainly on one-of-a-kind art knives. **Mark:** Small oval with signature Eallred in the center and handmade above.

ALVERSON, TIM (R.V.)
209 Spring Rd. SE, Arab, AL 35016, Phone: 256-224-9620, alvie35@yahoo.com Web: cwknives.blogspot.com
Specialties: Fancy working knives to customer specs; other types on request. **Patterns:** Bowies, daggers, folders and miniatures. **Technical:** Grinds 440C, ATS-34; buys some Damascus. **Prices:** Start at $100. **Remarks:** Full-time maker; first knife sold in 1981. **Mark:** R.V.A. around rosebud.

AMERI, MAURO
Via Riaello No. 20, Trensasco St Olcese, Genova, ITALY 16010, Phone: 010-8357077, mauro.ameri@gmail.com
Specialties: Working and using knives of his design. **Patterns:** Hunters, Bowies and utility/camp knives. **Technical:** Grinds 440C, ATS-34 and 154CM. Handles in wood or Micarta; offers sheaths. **Prices:** $200 to $1200. **Remarks:** Spare-time maker; first knife sold in 1982. **Mark:** Last name, city.

AMMONS, DAVID C
6225 N. Tucson Mtn. Dr, Tucson, AZ 85743, Phone: 520-471-4433, dcammons@msn.com
Specialties: Will build to suit. **Patterns:** Yours or his. **Prices:** $250 to $2000. **Mark:** AMMONS.

AMOS, CHRIS
PO Box 1519, Riverton, WY 82501, Phone: 520-271-9752, caknives@yahoo.com
Specialties: HEPK (High Endurance Performance Knives). **Patterns:** Hunters, fighters, bowies, kitchen knives and camp knives. **Technical:** Hand-forged, high rate of reduction 52100 and 5160 steel. **Prices:** $150 to $1,500. **Remarks:** Part-time maker since 1997, full time since 2012. Coach/instructor at Ed Fowler's Knifemaking School. HEPK mastersmith rating, 2013. **Mark:** Early **Mark:** CAK stamped; current **Mark:** Amos on right side.

AMOUREUX, A W
PO Box 776, Northport, WA 99157, Phone: 509-732-6292
Specialties: Heavy-duty working straight knives. **Patterns:** Bowies, fighters, camp knives and hunters for world-wide use. **Technical:** Grinds 440C, ATS-34 and 154CM. **Prices:** $80 to $2000. **Remarks:** Full-time maker; first knife sold in 1974. **Mark:** ALSTAR.

ANDERS, DAVID
157 Barnes Dr, Center Ridge, AR 72027, Phone: 501-893-2294
Specialties: Working straight knives of his design. **Patterns:** Bowies, fighters and hunters. **Technical:** Forges 5160, 1080 and Damascus. **Prices:** $225 to $3200. **Remarks:** Part-time maker; first knife sold in 1988. Doing business as Anders Knives. **Mark:** Last name/MS.

ANDERS, JEROME
14560 SW 37th St, Miramar, FL 33027, Phone: 305-613-2990, web:www.andersknives.com
  Specialties: Case handles and pin work. **Patterns:** Layered and mosaic steel. **Prices:** $275 and up. **Remarks:** All his knives are truly one-of-a-kind. **Mark:** J. Anders in half moon.

ANDERSEN, HENRIK LEFOLII
Jagtvej 8, Groenholt, Fredensborg, DENMARK 3480, Phone: 0011-45-48483026
  Specialties: Hunters and matched pairs for the serious hunter. **Technical:** Grinds A2; uses materials native to Scandinavia. **Prices:** Start at $250. **Remarks:** Part-time maker; first knife sold in 1985. **Mark:** Initials with arrow.

ANDERSEN, KARL B.
20200 TimberLodge Rd., Warba, MN 55793, Phone: 218-398-4270, Karl@andersenforge.com Web: www.andersenforge.com
  Specialties: Hunters, bowies, fighters and camp knives forged from high carbon tool steels and Andersen Forge Damascus. **Technical:** All types of materials used. Styles include hidden-tang and full-tang fixed blades, Brut de Forge, integrals and frame-handle construction. **Prices:** Starting at $450 and up. **Remarks:** Full-time maker. ABS journeyman smith. All knives sole authorship. Andersen Forge was instrumental in paving the way for take-down knife construction to be more recognized and broadly accepted in knifemaking today. **Mark:** Andersen in script on obverse. J.S. on either side, depending on knife.

ANDERSON, GARY D
2816 Reservoir Rd, Spring Grove, PA 17362-9802, Phone: 717-229-2665
  Specialties: From working knives to collectors quality blades, some folders. **Patterns:** Traditional and classic designs; customer patterns welcome. **Technical:** Forges Damascus carbon and stainless steels. Offers silver inlay, mokume, filework, checkering. **Prices:** $250 and up. **Remarks:** Part-time maker; first knife sold in 1985. Some engraving, scrimshaw and stone work. **Mark:** GAND, MS.

ANDERSON, MEL
29505 P 50 Rd, Hotchkiss, CO 81419-8203, Phone: 970-872-4882, Fax: 970-872-4882, artnedap@tds.net, melsscratchyhand.com and Web: www.scratchyhand.com
  Specialties: Full-size, miniature and one-of-a-kind straight knives and folders of his design. **Patterns:** Tantos, Bowies, daggers, fighters, hunters and pressure folders. **Technical:** Grinds 440C, 5160, D2, 1095. **Prices:** Start at $175. **Remarks:** Knifemaker and sculptor, full-time maker; first knife sold in 1987. **Mark:** Scratchy Hand.

ANDERSON, TOM
955 Canal Rd. Extd., Manchester, PA 17345, Phone: 717-266-6475, andersontech1@comcast.net Web: artistryintitanium.com
  Specialties: Battle maces and war hammers.

ANDRADE, DON CARLOS
CALIFORNIA CUSTOM KNIVES, 1824 Sunny Hill Ave., Los Osos, CA 93402, Phone: 805-528-8837 or 805-550-2324, andradeartworks@gmail.com; www.californiacustomknives.com
  Specialties Chef knife specialist, also integrally forged personal knives and camp knives. **Technical:** Forges to shape, and a small number of stain-resistant, stock-removal blades. All heat-treating in house. Uses 1095, W2, W1, 1084, 52100, 1065, 1070 and 13C26 blade steels. **Prices:** $250 to $1,650. **Remarks:** Full-time maker; first knife made in 2006 under tutorship of mentor Tai Goo. **Mark:** Initials "DCA" and two circles with a strike running through them (maker's version of infinity/continuity.)

ANDREWS, ERIC
132 Halbert Street, Grand Ledge, MI 48837, Phone: 517-627-7304
  Specialties: Traditional working and using straight knives of his design. **Patterns:** Full-tang knives, skinners and utility knives. **Technical:** Forges carbon steel; heat-treats. All knives come with sheath; most handles are of wood. **Prices:** $80 to $160. **Remarks:** Part-time maker; first knife sold in 1990. Doing business as The Tinkers Bench.

ANDREWS, RUSS
PO Box 7732, Sugar Creek, MO 64054, Phone: 816-252-3344, russandrews@sbcglobal.net; Web:wwwrussandrewsknives.com
  Specialties: Hand forged bowies & hunters. **Mark:** E. R. Andrews II. ERAII.

ANGELL, JON
22516 East C R1474, Hawthorne, FL 32640, Phone: 352-475-5380, syrjon@aol.com

ANKROM, W.E.
14 Marquette Dr, Cody, WY 82414, Phone: 307-587-3017, weankrom@hotmail.com
  Specialties: Best quality folding knives of his design. Bowies, fighters, chute knives, boots and hunters. **Patterns:** Lock backs, liner locks, single high art. **Technical:** ATS-34 commercial Damascus, CPM 154 steel. **Prices:** $500 and up. **Remarks:** Full-time maker; first knife sold in 1975. **Mark:** Name or name, city, state.

ANSO, JENS
GL. Skanderborgvej 116, Sporup, DENMARK 8472, Phone: 45 86968826, info@ansoknives.com; Web: www.ansoknives.com
  Specialties: Working knives of his own design. **Patterns:** Balisongs, swords, folders, drop-points, sheepsfoots, hawkbill, tanto, recurve. **Technical:** Grinds RWL-34 Damasteel S30V, CPM 154CM. Handrubbed or beadblasted finish. **Price:** $400 to $1200, some up to $3500. **Remarks:** Full-time maker since January 2002. First knife sold 1997. Doing business as ANSOKNIVES. **Mark:** ANSO and/or ANSO with logo.

APELT, STACY E
8076 Moose Ave, Norfolk, VA 23518, Phone: 757-583-5872, sapelt@cox.net
  Specialties: Exotic wood and burls, ivories, Bowies, custom made knives to order. **Patterns:** Bowies, hunters, fillet, professional cutlery and Japanese style blades and swords. **Technical:** Hand forging, stock removal, scrimshaw, carbon, stainless and Damascus steels. **Prices:** $65 to $5000. **Remarks:** Professional Goldsmith. **Mark:** Stacy E. Apelt -Norfolk VA.

APLIN, SPENCER
5151 County Rd. 469, Brazoria, TX 77422, Phone: 979-964-4448, spenceraplin@aol.com; Web: www.stacustomknives.com
  Specialties: Custom skinners, fillets, bowies and kitchen knives. **Technical:** Stainless steel powder metals, stainless damascus. Handles include stabilized woods, various ivory and Micarta. Guard and butt-cap materials are brass, copper, nickel silver and Mokume. **Prices:** $250 and up. **Remarks:** First knife sold in 1989. Knives made to order only, nothing is pre-made. All blades are hand drawn, then cut from sheet stock. No two are exactly the same. **Mark:** Signature and date completed.

APPLEBY, ROBERT
746 Municipal Rd, Shickshinny, PA 18655, Phone: 570-864-0879, applebyknives@yahoo.com; Web: www.applebyknives.com
  Specialties: Working using straight knives and folders of his own and popular and historical designs. **Patterns:** Variety of straight knives and folders. **Technical:** Hand forged or grinds O1, 1084, 5160, 440C, ATS-34, commercial Damascus, makes own sheaths. **Prices:** Starting at $75. **Remarks:** Part-time maker, first knife sold in 1995. **Mark:** APPLEBY over SHICKSHINNY, PA.

APPLETON, RON
315 Glenn St, Bluff Dale, TX 76433, Phone: 254-707-2922; cell: 254-396-9328, ronappleton@hotmail.com; Web: www.appletonknives.com
  Specialties: One-of-a-kind folding knives. **Patterns:** Unique folding multi-locks and high-tech patterns. **Technical:** All parts machined, D2, S7, 416, 440C, 6A14V et.al. **Prices:** Start at $23,000. **Remarks:** Full-time maker; first knife sold in 1996. **Mark:** Initials in anvil or initials in arrowhead. Usually only shows at the Art Knife Invitational every 2 years in San Diego, CA.

ARBUCKLE, JAMES M
114 Jonathan Jct, Yorktown, VA 23693, Phone: 757-867-9578, a_r_buckle@hotmail.com
  Specialties: One-of-a-kind of his design; working knives. **Patterns:** Mostly chef's knives and hunters. **Technical:** Forged and stock removal blades using exotic hardwoods, natural materials, Micarta and stabilized woods. Forge 5160 and 1084; stock removal D2, ATS-34, 440C and 154CM. Makes own pattern welded steel. **Prices:** $195 to $700. **Remarks:** Forge, grind, heat-treat, finish and embellish all knives himself. Does own leatherwork. Part-time maker. ABS Journeyman smith 2007; ASM member. **Mark:** J. Arbuckle or J. ARBUCKLE MAKER.

ARCHER, RAY AND TERRI
4207 South 28 St., Omaha, NE 68107, Phone: 402-505-3084, archerrt@cox.net Web: www.archersknives.com
  Specialties: Basic high-finish working knives. **Patterns:** Hunters, skinners camp knives. **Technical:** Flat grinds various steels like 440C, ATS-34 and CPM-S30V. **Prices:** $75 to $500. **Remarks:** Full-time maker. Makes own sheaths; first knife sold 1994. **Mark:** Last name over knives.

ARDWIN, COREY
2117 Cedar Dr., Bryant, AR 72019, Phone: 501-413-1184, ardwinca@gmail.com

ARM-KO KNIVES
PO Box 76280, Marble Ray, KZN, SOUTH AFRICA 4035, Phone: 27 31 5771451, arm-koknives.co.za; Web: www.arm-koknives.co.za
  Specialties: They will make what your fastidious taste desires. Be it cool collector or tenacious tactical with handles of mother-of-pearl, fossil & local ivories. Exotic dye/ stabilized burls, giraffe bone, horns, carbon fiber, g10, and titanium etc. **Technical:** Via stock removal, grinding Damasteel, carbon & mosaic. Damascus, ATS-34, N690, 440A, 440B, 12C27, RWL34 and high carbon EN 8, 5160 all heat treated in house. **Prices:** From $200 and up. **Remarks:** Father a part-time maker for well over 10 years and member of Knifemakers Guild in SA. Son full-time maker over 3 years. **Mark:** Logo of initials A R M and H A R M "Edged Tools."

ARMS, ERIC
11153 7 Mile Road, Tustin, MI 49688, Phone: 231-829-3726, ericarms@netonecom.net
  Specialties: Working hunters, high performance straight knives. **Patterns:** Variety of hunters, scagel style, Ed Fowler design and drop point. **Technical:** Forge 52100, 5160, 1084 hand grind, heat treat, natural handle, stag horn, elk, big horn, flat grind, convex, all leather sheath work. **Prices:** Starting at $150 **Remarks:** Part-time maker **Mark:** Eric Arms

ARNOLD, JOE
47 Patience Cres, London, ON, CANADA N6E 2K7, Phone: 519-686-2623, arnoldknivesandforge@bell.net
  Specialties: Traditional working and using straight knives of his design and to customer specs. **Patterns:** Fighters, hunters and Bowies. **Technical:** Grinds 440C, ATS-34, 5160, and Forges 1084-1085 **Prices:** $75 to $500; some to $2500. **Remarks:** Full-time maker; first knife sold in 1988. **Mark:** Last name, country.

ARROWOOD, DALE
556 Lassetter Rd, Sharpsburg, GA 30277, Phone: 404-253-9672
  Specialties: Fancy and traditional straight knives of his design and to customer specs. **Patterns:** Bowies, fighters and hunters. **Technical:** Grinds ATS-34 and 440C; forges high-carbon steel. Engraves and scrimshaws. **Prices:** $125 to $200; some to $245. **Remarks:**

Part-time maker; first knife sold in 1989. **Mark:** Anvil with an arrow through it; Old English "Arrowood Knives."

ASHBY, DOUGLAS
10123 Deermont Trail, Dallas, TX 75243, Phone: 214-929-7531, doug@ashbycustomknives.com Web: ashbycustomknives.com
Specialties: Traditional and fancy straight knives and folders of his design or to customer specs. **Patterns:** Skinners, hunters, utility/camp knives, locking liner folders. **Technical:** Grinds ATS-34, commercial Damascus, and other steels on request. **Prices:** $125 to $1000. **Remarks:** Part-time maker; first knife sold in 1990. **Mark:** Name, city.

ASHWORTH, BOYD
1510 Bullard Place, Powder Springs, GA 30127, Phone: 404-583-5652, boydashworthknives@comcast.net; Web: www.boydashworthknives.com
Specialties: Gentlemen's and figurative folders. **Patterns:** Fighters, hunters and gents. **Technical:** Forges own Damascus; offers filework; uses exotic handle materials. **Prices:** $500 to $5,000. **Remarks:** Part-time maker; first knife sold in 1993. **Mark:** Last name.

ATHEY, STEVE
3153 Danube Way, Riverside, CA 92503, Phone: 951-850-8612, stevelonnie@yahoo.com
Specialties: Stock removal. **Patterns:** Hunters & Bowies. **Prices:** $100 to $500. **Remarks:** Part-time maker. **Mark:** Last name with number on blade.

ATKINSON, DICK
General Delivery, Wausau, FL 32463, Phone: 850-638-8524
Specialties: Working straight knives and folders of his design; some fancy. **Patterns:** Hunters, fighters, boots; locking folders in interframes. **Technical:** Grinds A2, 440C and 154CM. Likes filework. **Prices:** $85 to $300; some exceptional knives. **Remarks:** Full-time maker; first knife sold in 1977. **Mark:** Name, city, state.

AYARRAGARAY, CRISTIAN L.
Buenos Aires 250, Parana, Entre Rios, ARGENTINA 3100, Phone: 043-231753
Specialties: Traditional working straight knives of his design. **Patterns:** Fishing and hunting knives. **Technical:** Grinds and forges carbon steel. Uses native Argentine woods and deer antler. **Prices:** $150 to $250; some to $400. **Remarks:** Full-time maker; first knife sold in 1980. **Mark:** Last name, signature.

B

BAARTMAN, GEORGE
PO Box 1116, Bela-Bela, LP, SOUTH AFRICA 0480, Phone: 27 14 736 4036, Fax: 086 636 3408, thabathipa@gmail.com
Specialties: Fancy and working LinerLock® folders of own design and to customers specs. Specialize in pattern filework on liners. **Patterns:** LinerLock® folders. **Technical:** Grinds 12C27, ATS-34, and Damascus, prefer working with stainless damasteel. Hollow grinds to hand-rubbed and polished satin finish. Enjoys working with mammoth, warthog tusk and pearls. **Prices:** Folders from $380 to $1000. **Remarks:** Part-time maker. Member of the Knifemakers Guild of South Africa since 1993. **Mark:** BAARTMAN.

BACHE-WIIG, TOM
N-5966, Eivindvik, NORWAY, Phone: 475-778-4290, Fax: 475-778-1099, tom.bache-wiig@enivest.net; Web: tombachewiig.com
Specialties: High-art and working knives of his design. **Patterns:** Hunters, utility knives, hatchets, axes and art knives. **Technical:** Grinds Uddeholm Elmax, powder metallurgy tool stainless steel. Handles made of rear burls of Nordic woods stabilized with vacuum/high-pressure technique. **Prices:** $430 to $900; some to $2300. **Remarks:** Part-time maker; first knife sold 1988. **Mark:** Etched name and eagle head.

BACON, DAVID R.
906 136th St E, Bradenton, FL 34202-9694, Phone: 813-996-4289

BAGLEY, R. KEITH
OLD PINE FORGE, 4415 Hope Acres Dr, White Plains, MD 20695, Phone: 301-932-0990, keithbagley14@verizon.net; Web: www.oldpineforge.com
Specialties: Folders. **Technical:** Use ATS-34, 5160, O1, 1085 and 1095. **Patterns:** Ladder-wave lightning bolt. **Prices:** $275 to $750. **Remarks:** Farrier for 37 years, blacksmith for 37 years, knifemaker for 25 years. **Mark:** KB inside horseshoe and anvil.

BAILEY, I.R.
Lamorna Cottage, Common End, Colkirk, ENGLAND NR 21 7JD, Phone: 01-328-856-183, admin@grommitbaileyknives.com; Web: www.grommitbaileyknives.com
Specialties: Hunters, utilities, Bowies, camp knives, fighters. Mainly influenced by Moran, Loveless and Lile. **Technical:** Primarily stock removal using flat ground 1095, 1075, and 80CrV2. Occasionally forges including own basic Damascus. Uses both native and exotic hardwoods, stag, Leather, Micarta and other synthetic handle materials, with brass or 301 stainless fittings. Does some filework and leather tooling. Does own heat treating. **Remarks:** Part-time maker since 2005. All knives and sheaths are sole authorship. **Mark:** Last name stamped.

BAILEY, JOSEPH D.
3213 Jonesboro Dr, Nashville, TN 37214, Phone: 615-889-3172, jbknfemkr@aol.com
Specialties: Working and using straight knives; collector pieces. **Patterns:** Bowies, hunters, tactical, folders. **Technical:** 440C, ATS-34, Damascus and wire Damascus. Offers scrimshaw. **Prices:** $85 to $1200. **Remarks:** Part-time maker; first knife sold in 1988. **Mark:** Joseph D Bailey Nashville Tennessee.

BAIR, MARK
386 E. 475 N, Firth, ID 83236, Phone: 208-681-7533, markbair@gmail.com
Specialties: Fixed blades. Hunters, bowies, kitchen, utility, custom orders. **Technical:**

High-end damascus, San Mai steel, stainless steel and 52100. Also mammoth ivory and other exotic handles, custom hand filework, and works with high-end custom engravers. **Prices:** $300 to $7,500. **Remarks:** Part-time maker; first knife made in 1988. **Mark:** MB Custom Knives.

BAKER, HERB
14104 NC 87 N, Eden, NC 27288, Phone: 336-627-0338

BAKER, RAY
PO Box 303, Sapulpa, OK 74067, Phone: 918-224-8013
Specialties: High-tech working straight knives. **Patterns:** Hunters, fighters, Bowies, skinners and boots of his design and to customer specs. **Technical:** Grinds 440C, 1095 spring steel or customer request; heat-treats. Custom-made scabbards for any knife. **Prices:** $125 to $500; some to $1000. **Remarks:** Full-time maker; first knife sold in 1981. **Mark:** First initial, last name.

BAKER, TONY
707 Lake Highlands Dr, Allen, TX 75002, Phone: 214-543-1001, tonybakerknives@yahoo.com
Specialties: Hunting knives, integral made **Technical:** 154cm, S30V, and S90VPrices: Starting at $500. **Prices:** $200-$1200 **Remarks:** First knife made in 2001

BAKER, WILD BILL
Box 361, Boiceville, NY 12412, Phone: 914-657-8646
Specialties: Primitive knives, buckskinners. **Patterns:** Skinners, camp knives and Bowies. **Technical:** Works with L6, files and rasps. **Prices:** $100 to $350. **Remarks:** Part-time maker; first knife sold in 1989. **Mark:** Wild Bill Baker, Oak Leaf Forge, or both.

BALL, BUTCH
2161 Reedsville Rd., Floyd, VA 24091, Phone: 540-392-3485, ballknives@yahoo.com
Specialties: Fancy and Tactical Folders and Automatics. **Patterns:** Fixed and folders. **Technical:** Use various Damascus and ATS34, 154cm. **Prices:** $300 -$1500. **Remarks:** Part-time maker. Sold first knife in 1990. **Mark:** Ball or BCK with crossed knives.

BALL, KEN
127 Sundown Manor, Mooresville, IN 46158, Phone: 317-834-4803
Specialties: Classic working/using straight knives of his design and to customer specs. **Patterns:** Hunters and utility/camp knives. **Technical:** Flat-grinds ATS-34. Offers filework. **Prices:** $150 to $400. **Remarks:** Part-time maker; first knife sold in 1994. Doing business as Ball Custom Knives. **Mark:** Last name.

BALLESTRA, SANTINO
via D. Tempesta 11/17, Ventimiglia, ITALY 18039, Phone: 0184-215228, ladasin@libero.it
Specialties: Using and collecting straight knives. **Patterns:** Hunting, fighting, skinners, Bowies, medieval daggers and knives. **Technical:** Forges ATS-34, D2, O2, 1060 and his own Damascus. Uses ivory and silver. **Prices:** $500 to $2000; some higher. **Remarks:** Full-time maker; first knife sold in 1979. **Mark:** First initial, last name.

BALLEW, DALE
PO Box 1277, Bowling Green, VA 22427, Phone: 804-633-5701
Specialties: Miniatures only to customer specs. **Patterns:** Bowies, daggers and fighters. **Technical:** Files 440C stainless; uses ivory, abalone, exotic woods and some precious stones. **Prices:** $100 to $800. **Remarks:** Part-time maker; first knife sold in 1988. **Mark:** Initials and last name.

BANAITIS, ROMAS
84 Winthrop St., Medway, MA 02053, Phone: 774-248-5851, rbanaitis@verizon.net
Specialties: Designing art and fantasy knives. **Patterns:** Folders, daggers and fixed blades. **Technical:** Hand-carved blades, handles and fittings in stainless steel, sterling silver and titanium. **Prices:** Moderate to upscale. **Remarks:** First knife sold in 1996. **Mark:** Romas Banaitis.

BANKS, DAVID L.
99 Blackfoot Ave, Riverton, WY 82501, Phone: 307-856-3154/Cell: 307-851-5599
Specialties: Heavy-duty working straight knives. **Patterns:** Hunters, Bowies and camp knives. **Technical:** Forges Damascus 1084-15N20, L6-W1 pure nickel, 5160, 52100 and his own Damascus; differential heat treat and tempers. Handles made of horn, antlers and exotic wood. Hand-stitched harness leather sheaths. **Prices:** $300 to $2000. **Remarks:** Part-time maker. **Mark:** Banks Blackfoot forged Dave Banks and initials connected.

BAREFOOT, JOE W.
1654 Honey Hill, Wilmington, NC 28442, Phone: 910-641-1143
Specialties: Working straight knives of his design. **Patterns:** Hunters, fighters and boots; tantos and survival knives. **Technical:** Grinds D2, 440C and ATS-34. Mirror finishes. Uses ivory and stag on customer request only. **Prices:** $50 to $160; some to $500. **Remarks:** Part-time maker; first knife sold in 1980. **Mark:** Bare footprint.

BARKER, JOHN
5725 Boulder Bluff Dr., Cumming, GA 30040, Phone: 678-357-8586, barkerknives@bellsouth.net Web: www.barkerknives.com
Specialties: Tactical fixed blades and folders. **Technical:** Stock removal method and CPM and Carpenter powdered technology steels. **Prices:** $150 and up. **Remarks:** First knife made 2006. **Mark:** Snarling dog with "Barker" over the top of its head and "Knives" below.

BARKER, REGGIE
603 S Park Dr, Springhill, LA 71075, Phone: 318-539-2958, wrbarker@cmaaccess.com; Web: www.reggiebarkerknives.com
Specialties: Camp knives and hatchets. **Patterns:** Bowie, skinning, hunting, camping, fighters, kitchen or customer design. **Technical:** Forges carbon steel and own pattern welded steels. **Prices:** $225 to $2000. **Remarks:** Full-time maker. Winner of 1999 and

2000 Spring Hammering Cutting contest. Winner of Best Value of Show 2001; Arkansas Knife Show and Journeyman Smith. Border Guard Forge. **Mark:** Barker JS.

BARKER, ROBERT G.
2311 Branch Rd, Bishop, GA 30621, Phone: 706-769-7827
Specialties: Traditional working/using straight knives of his design. **Patterns:** Bowies, hunters and utility knives. **Technical:** ABS Journeyman Smith. **Technical:** Hand forged carbon and Damascus. Forges to shape high-carbon 5160, cable and chain. Differentially heat-treats. **Prices:** $200 to $500; some to $1000. **Remarks:** Spare-time maker; first knife sold in 1987. **Mark:** BARKER/J.S.

BARKER, STUART
51 Thorpe Dr., Wigston, Leicester, ENGLAND LE18 1LE, Phone: +447887585411, sc_barker@hotmail.com Web: www.barkerknives.co.uk
Specialties: Fixed blade working knives of his design. **Patterns:** Kitchen, hunter, utility/camp knives. **Technical:** Grinds 01, Rw134 & Damasteel, hand rubbed or shot blast finishes. **Prices:** $150 -$1,000. **Remarks:** Part-time maker; first knife sold 2006. **Mark:** Last initial or last name.

BARKES, TERRY
14844 N. Bluff Rd., Edinburgh, IN 46124, Phone: 812-526-6390, knifenpocket@sbcglobal.net; Web:http:// my.hsonline.net/wizard/TerryBarkesKnives.htm
Specialties: Traditional working straight knives of his designs. **Patterns:** Drop point hunters, boot knives, skinning, fighter, utility, all purpose, camp, and grill knives. **Technical:** Grinds 1095 -1084 -52100 -01, Hollow grinds and flat grinds. Hand rubbed finish from 400 to 2000 grit or High polish buff. Hard edge and soft back, heat treat by maker. Likes File work, natural handle material, bone, stag, water buffalo horn, wildbeast bone, ironwood. **Prices:** $200 and up **Remarks:** Full-time maker, first knifge sold in 2005. Doing business as Barkes Knife Shop. **Marks:** Barkes -USA, Barkes Double Arrow -USA

BARLOW, JANA POIRIER
3820 Borland Cir, Anchorage, AK 99517, Phone: 907-243-4581

BARNES, AUBREY G.
11341 Rock Hill Rd, Hagerstown, MD 21740, Phone: 301-223-4587, a.barnes@myactv.net
Specialties: Classic Moran style reproductions and using knives of his own design. **Patterns:** Bowies, hunters, fighters, daggers and utility/camping knives. **Technical:** Forges 5160, 1085, L6 and Damascus, Silver wire inlays. **Prices:** $500 to $5000. **Remarks:** Full-time maker; first knife sold in 1992. Doing business as Falling Waters Forge. **Mark:** First and middle initials, last name, M.S.

BARNES, GARY L.
112 Brandy Ln., Defuniak Springs, FL 32435, Phone: 410-635-6243, Fax: 410-635-6243, glbarnes@glbarnes.com; Web: www.glbarnes.com
Specialties: Ornate button lock Damascus folders. **Patterns:** Barnes original. **Technical:** Forges own Damascus. **Prices:** Average $2500. **Remarks:** ABS Master Smith since 1983. **Mark:** Hand engraved logo of letter B pierced by dagger.

BARNES, GREGORY
266 W Calaveras St, Altadena, CA 91001, Phone: 626-398-0053, snake@annex.com

BARNES, JACK
PO Box 1315, Whitefish, MT 59937-1315, Phone: 406-862-6078

BARNES, MARLEN R.
904 Crestview Dr S, Atlanta, TX 75551-1854, Phone: 903-796-3668, MRBlives@worldnet.att.net
Specialties: Hammer forges random and mosaic Damascus. **Patterns:** Hatchets, straight and folding knives. **Technical:** Hammer forges carbon steel using 5160, 1084 and 52100 with 15N20 and 203E nickel. **Prices:** $150 and up. **Remarks:** Part-time maker; first knife sold 1999. **Mark:** Script M.R.B., other side J.S.

BARNES, ROGER
BC Cutlery Co., 314 Rosemarie Pl., Bay Point, CA 94565, bccutlerycompany@gmail.com
Specialties: Various styles of fixed-blade knives with an emphasis on quality in performance and simple aesthetics. **Patterns:** Karambits, Bob Loveless-inspired drop-point hunters and choppers. **Technical:** Uses 52100, 1095, 5160, AEB-L and CPM-3V blade steels, and Micartas, carbon fiber and G-10 handle scales, all USA-made materials. **Prices:** $75 to $500. **Remarks:** Wait time two weeks to one month.

BARNES, WENDELL
PO Box 272, Clinton, MT 59825, Phone: 406-825-0908
Specialties: Working straight knives. **Patterns:** Hunters, folders, neck knives. **Technical:** Grinds 440C, ATS-34, D2 and Damascus. **Prices:** Start at $75. **Remarks:** Spare-time maker; first knife sold in 1996. **Mark:** First initial, split heart, last name.

BARNES JR., CECIL C.
141 Barnes Dr, Center Ridge, AR 72027, Phone: 501-893-2267

BARNETT, BRUCE
PO Box 447, Mundaring, WA, AUSTRALIA 6073, Phone: 61-4-19243855, bruce@barnettcustomknives.com; Web: www.barnettcustomknives.com
Specialties: Most types of fixed blades, folders, carving sets. **Patterns:** Hunters, Bowies, Camp Knives, Fighters, Lockback and Slipjoint Folders. **Prices:** $200 up **Remarks:** Part time maker. Member Australian Knifemakers Guild and ABS journeyman smith. **Mark:** Barnett + J.S.

BARNETT, VAN
BARNETT INT'L INC, 1135 Terminal Way Ste #209, Reno, NV 89502,

Phone: 304-727-5512; 775-513-6969; 775-686-9084, ImATimeMachine@gmail.com & illusionknives@gmail.com; Web: www.VanBarnett.com
Specialties: Collector grade one-of-a-kind / embellished high art daggers and art folders. **Patterns:** Art daggers and folders. **Technical:** Forges and grinds own Damascus. **Prices:** Upscale. **Remarks:** Designs and makes one-of-a-kind highly embellished art knives using high karat gold, diamonds and other gemstones, pearls, stone and fossil ivories, carved steel guards and blades, all knives are carved and or engraved, does own engraving, carving and other embellishments, sole authorship; full-time maker since 1981. Does one high art collaboration a year with Dellana. Member of ABS. Member Art Knife Invitational Group (AKI) **Mark:** VBARNETT

BARR, JUDSON C.
1905 Pickwick Circle, Irving, TX 75060, Phone: 214-724-0564, judsonbarrknives@yahoo.com
Specialties: Bowies. **Patterns:** Sheffield and Early American. **Technical:** Forged carbon steel and Damascus. Also stock removal. **Remarks:** Journeyman member of ABS. **Mark:** Barr.

BARRETT, RICK L. (TOSHI HISA)
18943 CR 18, Goshen, IN 46528, Phone: 574-533-4297, barrettrick@hotmail.com
Specialties: Japanese-style blades from sushi knives to katana and fantasy pieces. **Patterns:** Swords, axes, spears/lances, hunter and utility knives. **Technical:** Forges and grinds Damascus and carbon steels, occasionally uses stainless. **Prices:** $250 to $4000+. **Remarks:** Full-time bladesmith, jeweler. **Mark:** Japanese mei on Japanese pieces and stylized initials.

BARRON, BRIAN
123 12th Ave, San Mateo, CA 94402, Phone: 650-341-2683
Specialties: Traditional straight knives. **Patterns:** Daggers, hunters and swords. **Technical:** Grinds 440C, ATS-34 and 1095. Sculpts bolsters using an S-curve. **Prices:** $130 to $270; some to $1500. **Remarks:** Part-time maker; first knife sold in 1993. **Mark:** Diamond Drag "Barron."

BARRY, SCOTT
Box 354, Laramie, WY 82073, Phone: 307-721-8038, scottyb@uwyo.edu
Specialties: Currently producing mostly folders, also make fixed blade hunters & fillet knives. **Technical:** Steels used are ATS 34, 154CM, CPM 154, D2, CPM S30V, Damasteel and Devin Thomas stainless damascus. **Prices:** Range from $300 $1000. **Remarks:** Part-time maker. First knife sold in 1972. **Mark:** DSBarry, etched on blade.

BARRY III, JAMES J.
115 Flagler Promenade No., West Palm Beach, FL 33405, Phone: 561-832-4197
Specialties: High-art working straight knives of his design also high art tomahawks. **Patterns:** Hunters, daggers and fishing knives. **Technical:** Grinds 440C only. Prefers exotic materials for handles. Most knives embellished with filework, carving and scrimshaw. Many pieces designed to stand unassisted. **Prices:** $500 to $10,000. **Remarks:** Part-time maker; first knife sold in 1975. Guild member (Knifemakers) since 1991. **Mark:** Branded initials as a J and B together.

BARTH, J.D.
101 4th St, PO Box 186, Alberton, MT 59820, Phone: 406-722-4557, mtdeerhunter@blackfoot.net; Web: www.jdbarthcustomknives.com
Specialties: Working and fancy straight knives of his design. LinerLock® folders, stainless and Damascus, fully file worked, nitre bluing. **Technical:** Grinds ATS-34, 440-C, stainless and carbon Damascus. Uses variety of natural handle materials and Micarta. Likes dovetailed bolsters. Filework on most knives, full and tapered tangs. Makes custom fit sheaths for each knife. **Mark:** Name over maker, city and state.

BARTLETT, MARK
102 Finn Cir., Lawrenceburg, TN 38464, Phone: 931-477-5444, moosetrax@live.com
Specialties: Mostly hunters and small bowies, but moving into larger bowies. **Technical:** Forges for the most part, with some stock removal, primarily using 1095, 1084 and 52100 blade steels. Has started damascus recently. Uses hardwoods and Micarta mostly for handles. **Prices:** $200 to $500, with some recent orders booked at $900-$1,000. **Remarks:** Part-time maker; first knife made in September 2013. **Mark:** Last name with a dagger through the middle "T."

BARTLOW, JOHN
14 Red Fox Dr., Sheridan, WY 82801, Phone: 307-673-4941, 2jbartlow@gmail.com
Specialties: Skinner/caper sets, classic working patterns, and known for bird-and-trout classics. **Technical:** ATS-34, CPM-154, damascus available on all LinerLocks. **Prices:** $400 to $2,500. **Remarks:** Full-time maker, Guild member from 1988. **Mark:** Bartlow Sheridan, Wyo.

BASKETT, BARBARA
427 Sutzer Ck Rd, Eastview, KY 42732, Phone: 270-862-5019, bgbaskett@yahoo.com; Web: www.baskettknives.com
Specialties: Hunters and LinerLocks. **Technical:** 440-C, CPM 154, S30V. **Prices:** $250 and up. **Mark:** B. Baskett.

BASKETT, LEE GENE
427 Sutzer Ck. Rd., Eastview, KY 42732, Phone: 270-862-5019, Cell: 270-766-8724, baskettknives@hotmail.com Web: www.baskettknives.com
Specialties: Fancy working knives and fancy art pieces, often set up in fancy desk stands. **Patterns:** Fighters, Bowies, and Survial Knives; lockback folders and liner locks along with traditional styles. Cutting competition knives. **Technical:** Grinds 01, 440-c, S30V, power CPM154, CPM 4, D2, buys Damascus. Filework provided on most knives. **Prices:** $250 and up. **Remarks:** Part-time maker, first knife sold in 1980. **Mark:** Baskett

BASSETT, DAVID J.
P.O. Box 69-102, Glendene, Auckland, NEW ZEALAND 0645, Phone: 64 9 818 9083, Fax: 64 9 818 9013, david@customknifemaking.co.nz; Web:www.customknifemaking.co.nz
Specialties: Working/using knives. **Patterns:** Hunters, fighters, boot, skinners, tanto. **Technical:** Grinds 440C, 12C27, D2 and some Damascus via stock removal method. **Prices:** $150 to $500. **Remarks:** Part-time maker, first knife sold in 2006. Also carries range of natural and synthetic handle material, pin stock etc. for sale. **Mark:** Name over country in semi-circular design.

BATSON, JAMES
1316 McClung Ave., Huntsville, AL 35801, Phone: 256-971-6860
Specialties: Forged Damascus blades and fittings in collectible period pieces. **Patterns:** Integral art knives, Bowies, folders, American-styled blades and miniatures. **Technical:** Forges carbon steel and his Damascus. **Prices:** $150 to $1800; some to $4500. **Remarks:** Semi retired full-time maker; first knife sold in 1978. **Mark:** Name, bladesmith with horse's head.

BATSON, RICHARD G.
6591 Waterford Rd, Rixeyville, VA 22737, Phone: 540-937-2318, mbatson6591@comcast.net
Specialties: Military, utility and fighting knives in working and presentation grade. **Patterns:** Daggers, combat and utility knives. **Technical:** Grinds O1, 1095 and 440C. Etches and scrimshaws; offers polished, Parkerized finishes. **Prices:** From $400. **Remarks:** Very limited production to active-dute military and vets only. First knife sold in 1958. **Mark:** Bat in circle, hand-signed and serial numbered.

BATTS, KEITH
500 Manning Rd, Hooks, TX 75561, Phone: 903-277-8466, kbatts@cableone.net
Specialties: Working straight knives of his design or to customer specs. **Patterns:** Bowies, hunters, skinners, camp knives and others. **Technical:** Forges 5160 and his Damascus; offers filework. **Prices:** $245 to $895. **Remarks:** Part-time maker; first knife sold in 1988. **Mark:** Last name.

BAUCHOP, ROBERT
PO Box 330, Munster, KN, SOUTH AFRICA 4278, Phone: +27 39 3192449
Specialties: Fantasy knives; working and using knives of his design and to customer specs. **Patterns:** Hunters, swords, utility/camp knives, diver's knives and large swords. **Technical:** Grinds Sandvick 12C27, D2, 440C. Uses South African hardwoods red ivory, wild olive, African blackwood, etc. on handles. **Prices:** $200 to $800; some to $2000. **Remarks:** Full-time maker; first knife sold in 1986. Doing business as Bauchop Custom Knives and Swords. **Mark:** Viking helmet with Bauchop (bow and chopper) crest.

BAXTER, DALE
291 County Rd 547, Trinity, AL 35673, Phone: 256-355-3626, dale@baxterknives.com
Specialties: Bowies, fighters, and hunters. **Patterns:** No Patterns: all unique true customs. **Technical:** Hand forge and hand finish. Steels: 1095 and L6 for carbon blades, 1095/L6 for Damascus. **Remarks:** Full-time bladesmith and sold first knife in 1998. **Mark:** Dale Baxter (script) and J.S. on reverse.

BEAM, JOHN R.
1310 Foothills Rd, Kalispell, MT 59901, Phone: 406-755-2593
Specialties: Classic, high-art and working straight knives of his design. **Patterns:** Bowies and hunters. **Technical:** Grinds 440C, Damascus and scrap. **Prices:** $175 to $600; some to $3000. **Remarks:** Part-time maker; first knife sold in 1950. Doing business as Beam's Knives. **Mark:** Beam's Knives.

BEASLEY, GENEO
PO Box 339, Wadsworth, NV 89442, Phone: 775-575-2584

BEATTY, GORDON H.
121 Petty Rd, Seneca, SC 29672, Phone: 867-723-2966
Specialties: Working straight knives, some fancy. **Patterns:** Traditional patterns, mini-skinners and letter openers. **Technical:** Grinds ATS-34; makes knives one-at-a-time. **Prices:** $185 and up. **Remarks:** Part-time maker; first knife sold in 1982. **Mark:** Name.

BEATY, ROBERT B.
CUTLER, 1995 Big Flat Rd, Missoula, MT 59804, Phone: 406-549-1818
Specialties: Plain and fancy working knives and collector pieces; will accept custom orders. **Patterns:** Hunters, Bowies, utility, kitchen and camp knives; locking folders. **Technical:** Grinds D-2, ATS-34, Dendritie D-2, makes all tool steel Damascus, forges 1095, 5160, 52100. **Prices:** $150 to $600, some to $1100. **Remarks:** Full-time maker; first knife sold 1995. **Mark:** Stainless: First name, middle initial, last name, city and state. Carbon: Last name stamped on Ricasso.

BEAUCHAMP, GAETAN
125 de la Rivire, Stoneham, QC, CANADA G3C 0P6, Phone: 418-848-1914, Fax: 418-848-6859, knives@gbeauchamp.ca; Web: www.gbeauchamp.ca
Specialties: Working knives and folders of his design and to customer specs. **Patterns:** Hunters, fighters, fantasy knives. **Technical:** Grinds ATS-34, 440C, Damascus. Scrimshaws on ivory; specializes in buffalo horn and black backgrounds. Offers a variety of handle materials. **Prices:** Start at $250. **Remarks:** Full-time maker; first knife sold in 1992. **Mark:** Signature etched on blade.

BECKER, FRANZ
Fakenweg 10, 75328 Shomberg, GERMANY, Phone: 0049 (0) 7084 9346805
Specialties: Stainless steel knives in working sizes. **Patterns:** Semi-and full-integral knives; interframe folders. **Technical:** Grinds stainless steels; likes natural handle materials. **Prices:** $200 to $2000. **Mark:** Name, country.

BEERS, RAY
2501 Lakefront Dr, Lake Wales, FL 33898, Phone: 443-841-4143, rbknives@copper.net

BEETS, MARTY
390 N 5th Ave, Williams Lake, BC, CANADA V2G 2G4, Phone: 250-392-7199
Specialties: Working and collectable straight knives of his own design. **Patterns:** Hunter, skinners, Bowies and utility knives. **Technical:** Grinds various steels-does all his own work including heat treating. Uses a variety of handle material specializing in exotic hardwoods, antler and horn. **Price:** $125 to $400. **Remarks:** Wife, Sandy does handmade/hand stitched sheaths. First knife sold in 1988. Business name Beets Handmade Knives.

BEGG, TODD M.
1341 N. McDowell Blvd., Ste. D, Petaluma, CA 94954, Phone: 707-242-1790, info@beggknives.com; Web: http://beggknives.net
Specialties: High-grade tactical folders and fixed blades. **Patterns:** Folders, integrals, fighters. **Technical:** Specializes in flipper folders using "IKBS" (Ikoma Korth Bearing System). **Prices:** $400 -$15,000. **Remarks:** Uses modern designs and materials.

BEHNKE, WILLIAM
8478 Dell Rd, Kingsley, MI 49649, Phone: 231-263-7447, bill@billbehnkeknives.com Web: www.billbehnkeknives.com
Specialties: Hunters, belt knives, folders, hatchets, straight razors, high-end letter openers and tomahawks. **Patterns:** Traditional styling in moderate-sized straight and folding knives. **Technical:** Forges own damascus, prefers W-2. **Prices:** $150 to $2,000. **Remarks:** Part-time maker. **Mark:** Bill Behnke Knives.

BELL, DON
Box 98, Lincoln, MT 59639, Phone: 406-362-3208, dlb@linctel.net
Patterns: Folders, hunters and custom orders. **Technical:** Carbon steel 52100, 5160, 1095, 1084. Making own Damascus. Flat grinds. Natural handle material including fossil. ivory, pearl, & ironwork. **Remarks:** Full-time maker. First knife sold in 1999. **Mark:** Last name.

BELL, DONALD
2 Division St, Bedford, NS, CANADA B4A 1Y8, Phone: 902-835-2623, donbell@accesswave.ca; Web: www.bellknives.com
Specialties: Fancy knives: carved and pierced folders of his own design. **Patterns:** Locking folders, pendant knives, jewelry knives. **Technical:** Grinds Damascus, pierces and carves blades. **Prices:** $500 to $2000, some to $3000. **Remarks:** Spare-time maker; first knife sold in 1993. **Mark:** Bell symbol with first initial inside.

BELL, GABRIEL
88321 North Bank Lane, Coquille, OR 97423, Phone: 541-396-3605, gabriel@dragonflyforge.com; Web: www.dragonflyforge.com & tomboyama.com
Specialties: Full line of combat quality Japanese swords. **Patterns:** Traditional tanto to katana. **Technical:** Handmade steel and welded cable. **Prices:** Swords from bare blades to complete high art $1500 to $28,000. **Remarks:** Studied with father Michael Bell. Instruction in sword crafts. Working in partnership with Michael Bell.**Mark:** Dragonfly in shield or kunitoshi.

BELL, MICHAEL
88321 N Bank Lane, Coquille, OR 97423, Phone: 541-396-3605, michael@dragonflyforge.com; Web: www. Dragonflyforge.com & tomboyama.com
Specialties: Full line of combat quality Japanese swords. **Patterns:** Traditional tanto to katana. **Technical:** Handmade steel and welded cable. **Prices:** Swords from bare blades to complete high art $1500 to $28,000. **Remarks:** Studied with Japanese master Nakajima Muneyoshi. Instruction in sword crafts. Working in partnership with son, Gabriel.**Mark:** Dragonfly in shield or tombo kunimitsu.

BELL, TONY
PO Box 24, Woodland, AL 36280, Phone: 256-449-2655, tbell905@aol.com
Specialties: Hand forged period knives and tomahawks. Art knives and knives made for everyday use.**Technical:**Makes own Damascus. Forges 1095, 5160,1080,L6 steels. Does own heat treating. **Prices:**$75-$1200. **Remarks:**Full time maker. **Mark:**Bell symbol with initial T in the middle.

BENDIK, JOHN
7076 Fitch Rd, Olmsted Falls, OH 44138

BENJAMIN JR., GEORGE
3001 Foxy Ln, Kissimmee, FL 34746, Phone: 407-846-7259
Specialties: Fighters in various styles to include Persian, Moro and military. **Patterns:** Daggers, skinners and one-of-a-kind grinds. **Technical:** Forges O1, D2, A2, 5160 and Damascus. Favors Pakkawood, Micarta, and mirror or Parkerized finishes. Makes unique para-military leather sheaths. **Prices:** $150 to $600; some to $1200. **Remarks:** Doing business as The Leather Box. **Mark:** Southern Pride Knives.

BENNETT, BRETT C
420 Adamstown Rd., Reinholds, PA 17569, Phone: 307-220-3919, brett@bennettknives.com; Web: www.bennettknives.com
Specialties: Hand-rubbed satin finish on all blades. **Patterns:** Mostly fixed-blade patterns. **Technical:** ATS-34, D-2, 1084/15N20 damascus, 1084 forged. **Mark:** "B.C. Bennett" in script or "Bennett" stamped in script.

BENNETT, GLEN C
5821 S Stewart Blvd, Tucson, AZ 85706

BENNETT, PETER
PO Box 143, Engadine, NSW, AUSTRALIA 2233, Phone: 02-520-4975 (home), Fax: 02-528-8219 (work)

Specialties: Fancy and embellished working and using straight knives to customer specs and in standard patterns. **Patterns:** Fighters, hunters, bird/trout and fillet knives. **Technical:** Grinds 440C, ATS-34 and Damascus. Uses rare Australian desert timbers for handles. **Prices:** $90 to $500; some to $1500. **Remarks:** Full-time maker; first knife sold in 1985. **Mark:** First and middle initials, last name; country.

BENNICA, CHARLES
11 Chemin du Salet, Moules et Baucels, FRANCE 34190, Phone: +33 4 67 73 42 40, cbennica@bennica-knives.com; Web: www.bennica-knives.com
Specialties: Fixed blades and folding knives; the latter with slick closing mechanisms with push buttons to unlock blades. Unique handle shapes, signature to the maker. **Technical:** 416 stainless steel frames for folders and ATS-34 blades. Also specializes in Damascus.

BENSINGER, J. W.
583 Jug Brook Rd., Marshfield, VT 05658, Phone: 802-917-1789, jwbensinger@gmail.com Web: www.vermontbladesmith.com
Specialties: Working hunters, bowies for work and defense, and Finnish patterns. Occasional folders. **Technical:** High performance handforged knives in 5160, 52100, 1080, and in-house damascus. **Prices:** Range from $130 for simple bushcraft knives to $500 for larger knives. Damascus prices on request. **Remarks:** First knife made in 1980 or so. Full-time maker. Customer designs welcome. **Mark:** "JWB" and year in cursive.

BENSON, DON
2505 Jackson St #112, Escalon, CA 95320, Phone: 209-838-7921
Specialties: Working straight knives of his design. **Patterns:** Axes, Bowies, tantos and hunters. **Technical:** Grinds 440C. **Prices:** $100 to $150; some to $400. **Remarks:** Spare-time maker; first knife sold in 1980. **Mark:** Name.

BENTLEY, C L
2405 Hilltop Dr, Albany, GA 31707, Phone: 912-432-6656

BER, DAVE
656 Miller Rd, San Juan Island, WA 98250, Phone: 206-378-7230
Specialties: Working straight and folding knives for the sportsman; welcomes customer designs. **Patterns:** Hunters, skinners, Bowies, kitchen and fishing knives. **Technical:** Forges and grinds saw blade steel, wire Damascus, O1, L6, 5160 and 440C. **Prices:** $100 to $300; some to $500. **Remarks:** Full-time maker; first knife sold in 1985. **Mark:** Last name.

BERG, LEE
PO Box 267, Ketchum, OK 74349, leelanny@wavelinx.net
Specialties: One-of-a-kind and investment-quality straight knives of his own design, incorporating traditional, period, Near East and Asian influence. **Patterns:** Daggers, fighters, hunters, bowies, short swords, full size and miniature. **Technical:** Stock removal with file, damascus, meteorite, O1, D2 and ATS-34. **Prices:** $200 and up. **Remarks:** Part-time maker; first knife sold in 1972. **Mark:** Full name.

BERG, LOTHAR
37 Hillcrest Ln, Kitchener ON, CANADA NZK 1S9, Phone: 519-745-3260; 519-745-3260

BERGER, MAX A.
5716 John Richard Ct, Carmichael, CA 95608, Phone: 916-972-9229, bergerknives@aol.com
Specialties: Fantasy and working/using straight knives of his design. **Patterns:** Fighters, hunters and utility/camp knives. **Technical:** Grinds ATS-34 and 440C. Offers fileworks and combinations of mirror polish and satin finish blades. **Prices:** $200 to $600; some to $2500. **Remarks:** Part-time maker; first knife sold in 1992. **Mark:** Last name.

BERGH, ROGER
Dalkarlsa 291, Bygdea, SWEDEN 91598, Phone: 469-343-0061, knivroger@hotmail.com; Web: www.rogerbergh.com
Specialties: Collectible all-purpose straight-blade knives. Damascus steel blades, carving and artistic design knives are heavily influenced by nature and have an organic hand crafted feel.

BERGLIN, BRUCE
17441 Lake Terrace Place, Mount Vernon, WA 98274, Phone: 360-333-1217, bruce@berglins.com
Specialties: Working fixed blades and folders of his own design. **Patterns:** Hunters, boots, bowies, utility, liner locks and slip joints some with vintage finish. **Technical:** Forges carbon steel, grinds carbon steel. Prefers natural handle material. **Prices:** Start at $300. **Remarks:** Part-time maker since 1998. **Mark:** (2 marks) 1. Last name; or 2. First initial, second initial & last name, surrounded with an oval.

BERTOLAMI, JUAN CARLOS
Av San Juan 575, Neuquen, ARGENTINA 8300, fliabertolami@infovia.com.ar
Specialties: Hunting and country labor knives. All of them unique high quality pieces and supplies collectors too. **Technical:** Austrian stainless steel and elephant, hippopotamus and orca ivory, as well as ebony and other fine woods for the handles.

BERTUZZI, ETTORE
Via Partigiani 3, Seriate, Bergamo, ITALY 24068, Phone: 035-294262, Fax: 035-294262
Specialties: Classic straight knives and folders of his design, to customer specs and in standard patterns. **Patterns:** Bowies, hunters and locking folders. **Technical:** Grinds ATS-34, D3, D2 and various Damascus. **Prices:** $300 to $500. **Remarks:** Part-time maker; first knife sold in 1993. **Mark:** Name etched on ricasso.

BESEDICK, FRANK E
1257 Country Club Road, Monongahela, PA 15063-1057, Phone: 724-292-8016, bxtr.bez3@verizon.net
Specialties: Traditional working and using straight knives of his design. **Patterns:** Hunters, utility/camp knives and miniatures; buckskinner blades and tomahawks. **Technical:** Forges and grinds 5160, O1 and Damascus. Offers filework and scrimshaw. **Prices:** $75 to $300; some to $750. **Remarks:** Part-time maker; first knife sold in 1990. **Mark:** Name or initials.

BESHARA, BRENT (BESH)
PO BOX 557, Holyrood, NL, CANADA A0A 2R0, BESH@beshknives.com
Web: www.beshknives.com
Specialties: Fixed blade tools and knives. **Patterns:** BESH Wedge tools and knives. **Technical:** Custom design work, grinds 0-1, D-2, 440C, 154cm. Offers kydex sheathing **Prices:** Start at $250. **Remarks:** Inventor of BESH Wedge geometry, custom maker and designer since 2000. Retired (24yrs) Special Forces, Special Operations Navy bomb disposal diver. Lifelong martial artist. **Mark:** "BESH" stamped.

BEST, RON
1489 Adams Lane, Stokes, NC 27884, Phone: 252-714-1264, ronbestknives@msn.com; Web: www.ronbestknives.com
Specialties: Folders and automatics. **Patterns:** Everything including butterfly knives. **Technical:** Grinds 440C, D-2 and ATS-34. **Prices:** $600 to $8000.

BETANCOURT, ANTONIO L.
5718 Beefwood Ct., St. Louis, MO 63129, Phone: 314-306-1869, bet2001@charter.net
Specialties: One-of-a-kind fixed blades and art knives. **Patterns:** Hunters and Bowies with embellished handles. **Technical:** Uses cast sterling silver and lapidary with fine gemstones, fossil ivory, and scrimshaw. Grinds Damascus and 440C. **Prices:** $100 to $800. **Remarks:** Part-time maker, first knife sold in 1974. **Mark:** Initials in cursive.

BEUKES, TINUS
83 Henry St, Risiville, Vereeniging, GT, SOUTH AFRICA 1939, Phone: 27 16 423 2053
Specialties: Working straight knives. **Patterns:** Hunters, skinners and kitchen knives. **Technical:** Grinds D2, 440C and chain, cable and stainless Damascus. **Prices:** $80 to $180. **Remarks:** Part-time maker; first knife sold in 1993. **Mark:** Full name, city, logo.

BEVERLY II, LARRY H
PO Box 741, Spotsylvania, VA 22553, Phone: 540-846-5426, beverlyknives@aol.com
Specialties: Working straight knives, slip-joints and liner locks. Welcomes customer designs. **Patterns:** Bowies, hunters, guard less fighters and miniatures. **Technical:** Grinds 440C, A2 and O1. **Prices:** $125 to $1000. **Remarks:** Part-time maker; first knife sold in 1986. **Mark:** Initials or last name in script.

BEZUIDENHOUT, BUZZ
PO BOX 28284, Malvern, KZN, SOUTH AFRICA 4055, Phone: 031-4632827, Fax: 031-4632827, buzzbee@mweb.co.za
Specialties: Working and Fancy Folders, my or customer design. **Patterns:** Boots, hunters, kitchen knives and utility/camp knives. **Technical:** Use 12-C-27 + stainless damascus, some carbon damascus. Uses local hardwoods, horn: kudu, impala, buffalo, giraffe bone and ivory for handles.
Prices: $250 to upscale. **Remarks:** Part-time maker; first knife sold in 1985. Member S.A. Knife Makers Guild **Mark:** First name with a bee emblem.

BILLGREN, PER
Stallgatan 9, Soderfors, SWEDEN 81576, Phone: +46 293 30600, Fax: +46 293 30124, mail@damasteel.se Web: www.damasteel.se
Specialties: Damasteel, stainless Damascus steels. **Patterns:** Bluetongue, Heimskringla, Muhammad's ladder, Rose, Twist, Odin's eye, Vinland, Hakkapelliitta. **Technical:** Modern Damascus steel made by patented powder metallurgy method. **Prices:** $80 to $180. **Remarks:** Damasteel is available through distributors around the globe.

BINGENHEIMER, BRUCE
553 Tiffany Dr., Spring Creek, NV 89815, Phone: 775-934-6295, mbing@citlink.net
Specialties: Forging fixed blade hunters, bowies, fighters. **Technical:** Forges own Damascus. Steel choices 5160, 1084. Damascus steels 15N20, 1080. **Prices:** $300 and up. **Remarks:** ABS Journeyman Smith 2010. Member of Montana Knife Makers Association and Oregon Knife Collector's Association. **Mark:** Bingenheimer (arched over) M B.

BIRDWELL, IRA LEE
PO Box 1448, Congress, AZ 85332, Phone: 928-925-3258, heli.ira@gmail.com
Specialties: Special orders. **Mark:** Engraved signature.

BISH, HAL
9347 Sweetbriar Trace, Jonesboro, GA 30236, Phone: 770-477-2422, hal-bish@hp.com

BISHER, WILLIAM (BILL)
1015 Beck Road, Denton, NC 27239, Phone: 336-859-4686, blackturtleforge@wildblue.net; Web: www.blackturtleforge.com
Specialties: Period pieces, also contemporary belt knives, friction folders. **Patterns:** Own design, hunters, camp/utility, Bowies, belt axes, neck knives, carving sets. **Technical:** Forges straight high carbon steels, and own Damascus, grinds ATS34 and 154CM. Uses natural handle materials (wood, bone, stag horn), micarta and stabilized wood. **Prices:** Starting at $75 -$2500. **Remarks:** Past president of North Carolina Custom Knifemakers Guild, member ABS, Full-time maker as of 2007, first knife made 1989, all work in house, blades and sheaths **Mark:** Last name under crown and turtle

BIZZELL, ROBERT

145 Missoula Ave, Butte, MT 59701, Phone: 406-782-4403, patternweld@yahoo.com **Specialties:** Damascus Bowies. **Patterns:** Composite, mosaic and traditional. **Technical:** Fixed blades & LinerLock® folders. **Prices:** Fixed blades start at $275. Folders start at $500. **Remarks:** Currently not taking orders. **Mark:** Hand signed.

BLACK, EARL

3466 South, 700 East, Salt Lake City, UT 84106, Phone: 801-466-8395 **Specialties:** High-art straight knives and folders; period pieces. **Patterns:** Boots, Bowies and daggers; lockers and gents. **Technical:** Grinds 440C and 154CM. Buys some Damascus. Scrimshaws and engraves. **Prices:** $200 to $1800; some to $2500 and higher. **Remarks:** Full-time maker; first knife sold in 1980. **Mark:** Name, city, state.

BLACK, SCOTT

27100 Leetown Rd, Picayune, MS 39466, Phone: 601-799-5939, copperheadforge@telepak.net **Specialties:** Friction folders; fighters. **Patterns:** Bowies, fighters, hunters, smoke hawks, friction folders, daggers. **Technical:** All forged, all work done by him, own hand-stitched leather work; own heat-treating. **Prices:** $100 to $2200. **Remarks:** ABS Journeyman Smith. Cabel / Damascus/ High Carbone. **Mark:** Hot Mark -Copperhead Snake.

BLACK, TOM

921 Grecian NW, Albuquerque, NM 87107, Phone: 505-344-2549, blackknives@comcast.net **Specialties:** Working knives to fancy straight knives of his design. **Patterns:** Drop-point skinners, folders, using knives, Bowies and daggers. **Technical:** Grinds 440C, 154CM, ATS-34, A2, D2, CPM-154 and damascus. Offers engraving and scrimshaw. **Prices:** $250 and up; some over $8500. **Remarks:** Full-time maker; first knife sold in 1970. **Mark:** Name, city.

BLACKWELL, ZANE

PO BOX 234, Eden, TX 76837, Phone: 325-869-8821, blackwellknives@hotmail.com; Web: www.blackwellknives.com **Specialties:** Hunters, slip-joint folders and kitchen knives. **Patterns:** Drop-point and clip-point hunters, and classic slip-joint patterns like single-blade trappers. **Technical:** CPM 154, ATS-34, 440C and D2 blade steels, and natural handle materials. **Prices:** Hunters start at $250, single-blade folders at $350. **Remarks:** Six-month back log. **Mark:** Zane Blackwell Eden Texas.

BLACKWOOD, NEIL

POB 457, Orlando, FL 33860, Phone: 863-812-5588, nblackwood4@gmail.com; Web: www.blackwoodcustomknives.blogspot.com **Specialties:** Fixed blades and tactical folders. **Technical:** Blade steels D2 Talonite, Stellite, CPM S30V and RWL 34. Handle materials: G-10 carbon fiber and Micarta in the synthetics: giraffe bone and exotic woods on the natural side. **Prices:** $1000 to $1500. **Remarks:** Makes everything from the frames to the stop pins, pivot pins: everything but the stainless screws; one factory/custom collaboration (the Hybrid Hunter) with Outdoor Edge is in place and negotiations are under way for one with Benchmade. Collaborations with Boker. **Mark:** Blackwood

BLANCHARD, G R (GARY)

PO BOX 292, Dandridge, TN 37725, Phone: 865-397-9515, blanchardcustomknives@yahoo.com; Web: www.blanchardcustomknives.com **Specialties:** Fancy folders with patented button blade release and high-art straight knives of his design. **Patterns:** Boots, daggers and locking folders. **Technical:** Grinds 440C and ATS-34 and Damascus. Engraves his knives. **Prices:** $1000 to $15,000 or more. **Remarks:** Full-time maker; first knife sold in 1989. **Mark:** First and middle initials, last name or last name only.

BLAUM, ROY

ROY'S KNIFE & ARCHERY SHOP, 319 N Columbia St, Covington, LA 70433, Phone: 985-893-1060 **Specialties:** Working straight knives and folders of his design; lightweight easy-open folders. **Patterns:** Hunters, boots, fishing and woodcarving/whittling knives. **Technical:** Grinds A2, D2, O1, 154CM and ATS-34. Offers leatherwork. **Prices:** $40 to $800; some higher. **Remarks:** Full-time maker; first knife sold in 1976. **Mark:** Engraved signature or etched logo.

BLOODWORTH CUSTOM KNIVES

3502 W. Angelica Dr., Meridian, ID 83646, Phone: 208-888-7778 **Patterns:** Working straight knives, hunters, skinners, bowies, utility knives of his designs or customer specs. Scagel knives. Period knives and traditional frontier knives and sheaths. **Technical:** Grinds D2, ATS34, 154CM, 5160, 01, Damascus, Heat treats, natural and composite handle materials. **Prices:** $185.00 to $1,500. **Remarks:** Roger Smith knife maker. Full-time maker; first knife sold in 1978 **Mark:** Sword over BLOODWORTH.

BLOOMER, ALAN T

PO Box 154, 116 E 6th St, Maquon, IL 61458, Phone: Cell: 309-371-8520, alant.bloomer@winco.net **Specialties:** Folders & straight knives & custom pen maker. **Patterns:** All kinds. **Technical:** Does own heat treating. **Prices:** $400 to $1000. **Remarks:** Part-time maker. No orders. **Mark:** Stamp Bloomer.

BLUM, KENNETH

1729 Burleson, Brenham, TX 77833, Phone: 979-836-9577 **Specialties:** Traditional working straight knives of his design. **Patterns:** Camp knives, hunters and Bowies. **Technical:** Forges 5160; grinds 440C and D2. Uses exotic woods and Micarta for handles. **Prices:** $150 to $300. **Remarks:** Part-time maker; first knife sold in 1978. **Mark:** Last name on ricasso.

BLYSTONE, RONALD L.

231 Bailey Road, Creekside, PA 15732, Phone: 724-397-2671, taxibly@hotmail.com **Specialties:** Traditional forged working knives. **Patterns:** Hunting utility and skinners of his own design. **Technical:** Forges his own pattern welded Damascus using carbon steel. **Prices:** Starting at $150. **Remarks:** Spare-time maker. **Mark:** Initials -upsidedown R against the B, inside a circle, over the word FORGE

BOARDMAN, GUY

39 Mountain Ridge R, New Germany, KZN, SOUTH AFRICA 3619, Phone: 031-726-921 **Specialties:** American and South African-styles. **Patterns:** Bowies, American and South African hunters, plus more. **Technical:** Grinds Bohler steels, some ATS-34. **Prices:** $100 to $600. **Remarks:** Part-time maker; first knife sold in 1986. **Mark:** Name, city, country.

BOCHMAN, BRUCE

183 Howard Place, Grants Pass, OR 97526, Phone: 541-471-1985, 183bab@gmail.com **Specialties:** Hunting, fishing, bird and tactical knives. **Patterns:** Hunters, fishing and bird knives. **Technical:** ATS34, 154CM, mirror or satin finish. Damascus. **Prices:** $250 to $350; some to $750. **Remarks:** Part-time maker; first knife sold in 1977. **Mark:** Custom Knives by B. Bochman

BODEN, HARRY

Via Gellia Mill, Bonsall Matlock, Derbyshire, ENGLAND DE4 2AJ, Phone: 0629-825176 **Specialties:** Traditional working straight knives and folders of his design. **Patterns:** Hunters, locking folders and utility/camp knives. **Technical:** Grinds Sandvik 12C27, D2 and O1. **Prices:** £70 to £150; some to £300. **Remarks:** Full-time maker; first knife sold in 1986. **Mark:** Full name.

BODOLAY, ANTAL

Rua Wilson Soares Fernandes #31, Planalto, Belo Horizonte, MG, BRAZIL MG-31730-700, Phone: 031-494-1885 **Specialties:** Working folders and fixed blades of his design or to customer specs; some art daggers and period pieces. **Patterns:** Daggers, hunters, locking folders, utility knives and Khukris. **Technical:** Grinds D6, high-carbon steels and 420 stainless. Forges files on request. **Prices:** $30 to $350. **Remarks:** Full-time maker; first knife sold in 1965. **Mark:** Last name in script.

BOEHLKE, GUENTER

Parkstrasse 2, 56412 Grobholbach, GERMANY, Phone: (49) 2602-5440, Fax: (49) 2602-5491, Boehlke-Messer@t-online.de; Web: www.boehlke-messer.de **Specialties:** Classic working/using straight knives of his design. **Patterns:** Hunters, utility/camp knives and ancient remakes. **Technical:** Grinds Damascus, CPM-T-440V and 440C. Inlays gemstones and ivory. **Prices:** $220 to $700; some to $2000. **Remarks:** Spare-time maker; first knife sold in 1985. **Mark:** Name, address and bow and arrow.

BOHRMANN, BRUCE

61 Portland St, Yarmouth, ME 04096, Phone: 207-846-3385, bbohr@maine.rr.com; Web: Bohrmannknives.com **Specialties:** Fixed-blade sporting, camp and hunting knives. **Technical:** Stock-removal maker using 13C26 Sandvik stainless steel hardened to 58-60 Rockwell. **Prices:** $499 for each model. Also, special "Heritage" production using historic certified woods (from Washington's, Jefferson's, Madison's and Henry's Plantations) -$1,250. **Remarks:** Full-time maker; first knife made in 1955. Always developing new models and concepts, such as steak knives, fixed blades and miniatures with special pocket sheaths. All knives serial #'d and can be personalized by etching initials into blades. **Mark:** The letter "B" connected to and lying beneath deer antlers.

BOJTOS, ARPAD

Dobsinskeho 10, 98403 Lucenec, SLOVAKIA, Phone: 00421-47 4333512; Cell: 00421-91 5875066, bojtos@stonline.sk; Web: www.arpadbojtos.sk **Specialties:** Art knives, including over 100 folders. **Patterns:** Daggers, fighters and hunters. **Technical:** Grinds ATS-34 and stainless damascus. Carves on steel, handle materials and sheaths. **Prices:** $5000 to $10,000; some over. **Remarks:** Full-time maker; first knife sold in 1990. **Mark:** AB.

BOLDUC, GARY

1419 Tanglewood Dr., Corona, CA 92882, Phone: 951-739-0137, gary@stillwaterwoods.com; Web: www.bolduckknives.com **Specialties:** Fish fillet knives (larger sizes), medium 8" to large 10"-plus. Replica making of primitive Native Alaskan hunting and cutting tools, kitchen cutlery. **Patterns:** Hunters, skinners, fillet, boning, spear points and kitchen cutlery. **Technical:** High-quality stainless steel, mainly CTS-XHP, CPM-154 and CPM-S35VN for improved edge design. **Prices:** $200-$400 and up. **Remarks:** Full-time maker; first knife sold in 2007. **Mark:** First initial, last name with USA under, or grizzly bear with Bolduc Knives underneath.

BOLEWARE, DAVID

PO Box 96, Carson, MS 39427, Phone: 601-943-5372 **Specialties:** Traditional and working/using straight knives of his design, to customer specs and in standard patterns. **Patterns:** Bowies, hunters and utility/camp knives. **Technical:** Grinds ATS-34, 440C and Damascus. **Prices:** $85 to $350; some to $600. **Remarks:** Part-time maker; first knife sold in 1989. **Mark:** First and last name, city, state.

BOLEY, JAMIE

PO Box 477, Parker, SD 57053, Phone: 605-297-0014, jamie@polarbearforge.com **Specialties:** Working knives and historical influenced reproductions. **Patterns:** Hunters, skinners, scramasaxes, and others. **Technical:** Forges 5160, O1, L6, 52100, W1, W2 makes own Damascus. **Prices:** Starts at $125. **Remarks:** Part-time maker. **Mark:** Polar bear paw print with name on the left side and Polar Bear Forge on the right.

BONASSI, FRANCO
Via Nicoletta 4, Pordenone, ITALY 33170, Phone: 0434-550821, frank.bonassi@alice.it
Specialties: Fancy and working one-of-a-kind folder knives of his design. **Patterns:** Folders, linerlocks and back locks. **Technical:** Grinds CPM, ATS-34, 154CM and commercial Damascus. Uses titanium foreguards and pommels. **Prices:** Start at $350. **Remarks:** Spare-time maker; first knife sold in 1988. Has made cutlery for several celebrities; Gen. Schwarzkopf, Fuzzy Zoeller, etc. **Mark:** FRANK.

BOOCO, GORDON
175 Ash St, PO Box 174, Hayden, CO 81639, Phone: 970-276-3195
Specialties: Fancy working straight knives of his design and to customer specs. **Patterns:** Hunters and Bowies. **Technical:** Grinds 440C, D2 and A2. Heat-treats. **Prices:** $150 to $350; some $600 and higher. **Remarks:** Part-time maker; first knife sold in 1984. **Mark:** Last name with push dagger artwork.

BOOS, RALPH
6018-37A Avenue NW, Edmonton, AB, CANADA T6L 1H4, Phone: 780-463-7094
Specialties: Classic, fancy and fantasy miniature knives and swords of his design or to customer specs. **Patterns:** Bowies, daggers and swords. **Technical:** Hand files O1, stainless and Damascus. Engraves and carves. Does heat bluing and acid etching. **Prices:** $125 to $350; some $1000. **Remarks:** Part-time maker; first knife sold in 1982. **Mark:** First initials back to back.

BOOTH, PHILIP W
301 S Jeffery Ave, Ithaca, MI 48847, Phone: 989-875-2844, pbooth@charter.net; Web: www.philipbooth.com
Specialties: Folding knives of his design using various mechanisms. **Patterns:** New "Twerp" ball-bearing flipper knife. "Minnow" folding knives, a series of small folding knives started in 1996 and changing yearly. One of a kind hot-rod car themed folding knives. **Technical:** Grinds ATS-34, CPM-154 and commercial damascus. Offers gun blue finishes and file work. **Prices:** $200 and up. **Remarks:** Part-time maker, first knife sold in 1991. **Mark:** Last name or name with city and map logo.

BORGER, WOLF
Benzstrasse 8, Graben-Neudorf, GERMANY 76676, Phone: 07255-72303, Fax: 07255-72304, wolf@messerschmied.de; Web: www.messerschmied.de
Specialties: High-tech working and using straight knives and folders, many with corkscrews or other tools, of his design. **Patterns:** Hunters, Bowies and folders with various locking systems. **Technical:** Grinds 440C, ATS-34 and CPM. Uses stainless Damascus. **Prices:** $250 to $900; some to $1500. **Remarks:** Full-time maker; first knife sold in 1975. **Mark:** Howling wolf and name; first name on Damascus blades.

BOSE, REESE
8810 N. County Rd. 375 E, Shelburn, IN 47879, Phone: 812-397-5114
Specialties: Traditional working and using knives in standard patterns and multi-blade folders. **Patterns:** Multi-blade slip-joints. **Technical:** ATS-34, D2, 154CM and CPM 440V. **Prices:** $600 to $3,000. **Remarks:** Full-time maker; first knife sold in 1992. Photos by Jack Busfield. **Mark:** R. Bose.

BOSE, TONY
7252 N. County Rd, 300 E., Shelburn, IN 47879-9778, Phone: 812-397-5114
Specialties: Traditional working and using knives in standard patterns; multi-blade folders. **Patterns:** Multi-blade slip-joints. **Technical:** Grinds commercial Damascus, ATS-34 and D2. **Prices:** $400 to $1200. **Remarks:** Full-time maker; first knife sold in 1972. **Mark:** First initial, last name, city, state.

BOSSAERTS, CARL
Rua Albert Einstein 906, Ribeirao Preto, SP, BRAZIL 14051-110, Phone: 016 633 7063
Specialties: Working and using straight knives of his design, to customer specs and in standard patterns. **Patterns:** Hunters, fighters and utility/camp knives. **Technical:** Grinds ATS-34, 440V and 440C; does filework. **Prices:** 60 to $400. **Remarks:** Part-time maker; first knife sold in 1992. **Mark:** Initials joined together.

BOST, ROGER E
30511 Cartier Dr, Palos Verdes, CA 90275-5629, Phone: 310-541-6833, rogerbost@cox.net
Specialties: Hunters, fighters, boot, utility. **Patterns:** Loveless-style. **Technical:** ATS-34, BG-42, 440C, 59-61RC, stock removal and forge. **Prices:** $300 and up. **Remarks:** First knife sold in 1990. Cal. Knifemakers Assn., ABS. **Mark:** Diamond with initials inside and Palos Verdes California around outside.

BOSWORTH, DEAN
329 Mahogany Dr, Key Largo, FL 33037, Phone: 305-451-1564, DLBOZ@bellsouth.net
Specialties: Free hand hollow ground working knives with hand rubbed satin finish, filework and inlays. **Patterns:** Bird and Trout, hunters, skinners, fillet, Bowies, miniatures. **Technical:** Using 440C, ATS-34, D2, Meier Damascus, custom wet formed sheaths. **Prices:** $250 and up. **Remarks:** Part-time maker; first knife made in 1985. Member Florida Knifemakers Assoc. **Mark:** BOZ stamped in block letters.

BOURBEAU, JEAN YVES
15 Rue Remillard, Notre Dame, Ile Perrot, QC, CANADA J7V 8M9, Phone: 514-453-1069
Specialties: Fancy/embellished and fantasy folders of his design. **Patterns:** Bowies, fighters and locking folders. **Technical:** Grinds 440C, ATS-34 and Damascus. Carves precious wood for handles. **Prices:** $150 to $1000. **Remarks:** Part-time maker; first knife sold in 1994. **Mark:** Interlaced initials.

BOWLES, CHRIS
PO Box 985, Reform, AL 35481, Phone: 205-375-6162
Specialties: Working/using straight knives, and period pieces. **Patterns:** Utility, tactical, hunting, neck knives, machetes, and swords. **Grinds:** 0-1, 154 cm, BG-42, 440V. **Prices:** $50 to $400 some higher. **Remarks:** Full-time maker. **Mark:** Bowles stamped or Bowles etched in script.

BOYD, FRANCIS
1811 Prince St, Berkeley, CA 94703, Phone: 510-841-7210
Specialties: Folders and kitchen knives, Japanese swords. **Patterns:** Push-button sturdy locking folders; San Francisco-style chef's knives. **Technical:** Forges and grinds; mostly uses high-carbon steels. **Prices:** Moderate to heavy. **Remarks:** Designer. **Mark:** Name.

BOYE, DAVID
PO Box 1238, Dolan Springs, AZ 86441, Phone: 800-853-1617, Fax: 928-767-4273, boye@cltlink.net; Web: www.boyeknives.com
Specialties: Folders and Boye Basics. Forerunner in the use of dendritic steel and dendritic cobalt for blades. **Patterns:** Lockback folders and fixed blade sheath knives in cobalt. **Technical:** Casts blades in cobalt. **Prices:** From $129 to $360. **Remarks:** Part-time maker; author of Step-by-Step Knifemaking. **Mark:** Name.

BOYES, TOM
2505 Wallace Lake Rd., West Bend, WI 53090, Phone: 262-391-2172
Specialties: Hunters, skinners and fillets. **Technical:** Grinds ATS-34, 440C, O1 tool steel and Damascus. **Prices:** $60 to $1000. **Remarks:** First knife sold in 1998. Doing business as R. Boyes Knives.

BOYSEN, RAYMOND A
125 E St Patrick, Rapid Ciy, SD 57701, Phone: 605-341-7752
Specialties: Hunters and Bowies. **Technical:** High performance blades forged from 52100 and 5160. **Prices:** $200 and up. **Remarks:** American Bladesmith Society Journeyman Smith. Part-time bladesmith. **Mark:** BOYSEN.

BRACH, PAUL
4870 Widgeon Way, Cumming, GA 30028, Phone: 770-595-8952, Web: www.brachknives.com
Specialties: Standard and one-of-a-kind straight knives and locking folders. Nickel silver sheath fittings and gemstone settings used on high-end pieces. **Patterns:** Hunters, bowies, daggers, antique bowies and titanium-frame folders. **Technical:** Grinds CPM-154 and forges high-carbon steel. Usually flat or full convex grinds. **Prices:** $150 to $1,000+. **Remarks:** Part-time maker; first knife sold in 1984. **Mark:** Etched "Paul Brach maker Cumming, GA" or "Brach" stamped.

BRACKETT, JAMIN
PO Box 387, Fallston, NC 28042, Phone: 704-718-3304, jaminbrackett@bellsouth.net; Web: brackettknives.com
Specialties: Hunting, camp, fishing, tactical, and general outdoor use. Handmade of my own design or to customer specs. **Patterns:** Drop point, tanto, fillet, and small EDC the "Tadpole," as well as large camp and tactical knives. **Technical:** Stock removal method, ATS-34 steel cryogenically treated to HRC 59-61. Mirror polish and bead blasted finishes. Handle materials include exotic woods, stag, buffalo horn, colored laminates, Micarta, and G-10. Come hand stitched 8-9 OZ leather sheaths treated in beeswax saddle oil mixture. Tactical models include reinforced tactical nylon sheaths Mollie system compatible. **Prices:** Standard models $150-$325. Personalized engraving available, for gifts and special occasions. **Remarks:** Part-time maker. First knife made in 2009. Member of NC Custom Knifemakers Guild. **Mark:** "Brackett", in bold. Each knife and sheath numbered.

BRADBURN, GARY
BRADBURN CUSTOM CUTLERY, 1714 Park Place, Wichita, KS 67203, Phone: 316-640-5684, gary@bradburnknives.com; Web:www.bradburnknives.com
Specialties: Specialize in clay-tempered Japanese-style knives and swords. **Patterns:** Also Bowies and fighters. **Technical:** Forge and/or grind carbon steel only. **Prices:** $150 to $1200. **Mark:** Initials GB stylized to look like Japanese character.

BRADFORD, GARRICK
582 Guelph St, Kitchener, ON, CANADA N2H-5Y4, Phone: 519-576-9863

BRADLEY, DENNIS
178 Bradley Acres Rd, Blairsville, GA 30512, Phone: 706-745-4364, bzbtaz@brmemc.net Web: www.dennisbradleyknives.com
Specialties: Working straight knives and folders, some high-art. **Patterns:** Hunters, boots and daggers; slip-joints and two-blades. **Technical:** Grinds ATS-34, D2, 440C and commercial Damascus. **Prices:** $100 to $500; some $2000. **Remarks:** Part-time maker; first knife sold in 1973. **Mark:** BRADLEY KNIVES in double heart logo.

BRADLEY, GAYLE
1383 Old Garner Rd., Weatherford, TX 76088-8720, Phone: 817-504-2262, bradleysblades@aol.com; Web: www.bradleysblades.com
Specialties: High-end folders with wedge locks of maker's own design or lock backs, and work/utility knives. Uses high-end materials, including lapidary work and black-lip-pearl handle inlays. **Technical:** Grinds blades from bar stock, performs own heat treating. **Remarks:** Full-time maker; first knife made in 1988.

BRADLEY, JOHN
PO Box 33, Pomona Park, FL 32181, Phone: 386-649-4739, johnbradleyknives@yahoo.com
Specialties: Fixed-blade using and art knives; primitive folders. **Patterns:** Skinners, Bowies, camp knives and primitive knives. **Technical:** Forged and ground 52100, 1095,

01 and Damascus. **Prices:** $250 to $2000. **Remarks:** Full-time maker; first knife sold in 1988. **Mark:** Last name.

BRANDSEY, EDWARD P
4441 Hawkridge Ct, Janesville, WI 53546, Phone: 608-868-9010, ebrandsey@centurytel.net

Patterns: Large bowies, hunters, neck knives and buckskinner-styles. Native American influence on some. An occasional tanto, art piece. Does own scrimshaw. See Egnath's second book. Now making locking liner folders. **Technical:** ATS-34, CPM154, 440-C, 0-1 and some damascus. Paul Bos heat treating past 20 years. **Prices:** $350 to $800; some to $4,000. **Remarks:** Full-time maker; first knife sold in 1973. **Mark:** Initials connected.

BRANDT, MARTIN W
833 Kelly Blvd, Springfield, OR 97477, Phone: 541-747-5422, oubob747@aol.com

BRANTON, ROBERT
PO BOX 807, Awendaw, SC 29429, Phone: 843-928-3624, www.brantonknives.com

Specialties: Working straight knives of his design or to customer specs; throwing knives. **Patterns:** Hunters, fighters and some miniatures. **Technical:** ATS-34, A2 and 1050; forges 5160, O1. Offers hollow-or convex-grinds. **Prices:** $25 to $400. **Remarks:** Part-time maker; first knife sold in 1985. Doing business as Pro-Flyte, Inc. **Mark:** Last name; or first and last name, city, state.

BRASCHLER, CRAIG W.
HC2 Box 498, Zalma, MO 63787, Phone: 573-495-2203

Specialties: Art knives, Bowies, utility hunters, slip joints, miniatures, engraving. **Technical:** Flat grinds. Does own selective heat treating. Does own engraving. **Prices:** Starting at $200. **Remarks:** Full-time maker since 2003. **Mark:** Braschler over Martin Oval stamped.

BRATCHER, BRETT
11816 County Rd 302, Plantersville, TX 77363, Phone: 936-894-3788, Fax: (936) 894-3790, brett_bratcher@msn.com

Specialties: Hunting and skinning knives. **Patterns:** Clip and drop point. Hand forged. **Technical:** Material 5160, D2, 1095 and Damascus. **Price:** $200 to $500. **Mark:** Bratcher.

BRAY JR., W LOWELL
6931 Manor Beach Rd, New Port Richey, FL 34652, Phone: 727-846-0830, brayknives@aol.com Web: www.brayknives.com

Specialties: Traditional working and using straight knives and collector pieces. **Patterns:** One of a kind pieces, hunters, fighters and utility knives. **Technical:** Grinds 440C and ATS-34; forges 52100 and Damascus. **Prices:** $125 to $800. **Remarks:** Spare-time maker; first knife sold in 1992. **Mark:** Lowell Bray Knives in shield or Bray Primative in shield.

BREDA, BEN
56 Blueberry Hill Rd., Hope, ME 04847, Phone: 207-701-7777, bredaknives@gmail.com

Specialties: High-carbon-steel bowies, fighters, hunters chef's knives and LinerLock folders. **Technical:** Forges W2, W1 and 10xx series steels for blades, using natural and stabilized handle materials. **Prices:** Start at $300. **Remarks:** Part-time maker; ABS journeyman smith.

BREED, KIM
733 Jace Dr, Clarksville, TN 37040, Phone: 931-980-4956, sfbreed@yahoo.com

Specialties: High end through working folders and straight knives. **Patterns:** Hunters, fighters, daggers, Bowies. His design or customers. Likes one-of-a-kind designs. **Technical:** Makes own Mosiac and regular Damascus, but will use stainless steels. Offers filework and sculpted material. **Prices:** $150 to $2000. **Remarks:** Full-time maker. First knife sold in 1990. **Mark:** Last name.

BREND, WALTER
415 County Rd. 782, Etowah, TN 37331, Phone: 256-736-3520, Fax: 256-736-3474, walterbrend@outlook.com or walter@brendknives.com; Web: www.brendknives.com

Specialties: Tactical-style knives, fighters, automatics. **Technical:** Grinds D-2 and 440C blade steels, 154CM steel. **Prices:** Micarta and titanium handles.

BRENNAN, JUDSON
PO Box 1165, Delta Junction, AK 99737, Phone: 907-895-5153, Fax: 907-895-5404

Specialties: Period pieces. **Patterns:** All kinds of Bowies, rifle knives, daggers. **Technical:** Forges miscellaneous steels. **Prices:** Upscale, good value. **Remarks:** Muzzle-loading gunsmith; first knife sold in 1978. **Mark:** Name.

BRESHEARS, CLINT
1261 Keats, Manhattan Beach, CA 90266, Phone: 310-372-0739, Fax: 310-372-0739, breshears1@verizon.net; Web: www.clintknives.com

Specialties: Working straight knives and folders. **Patterns:** Hunters, Bowies and survival knives. Folders are mostly hunters. **Technical:** Grinds 440C, 154CM and ATS-34; prefers mirror finishes. **Prices:** $125 to $750; some to $1800. **Remarks:** Part-time maker; first knife sold in 1978. **Mark:** First name.

BREUER, LONNIE
PO Box 877384, Wasilla, AK 99687-7384

Specialties: Fancy working straight knives. **Patterns:** Hunters, camp knives and axes, folders and Bowies. **Technical:** Grinds 440C, AEB-L and D2; likes wire inlay, scrimshaw, decorative filing. **Prices:** $60 to $150; some to $300. **Remarks:** Part-time maker; first knife sold in 1977. **Mark:** Signature.

BREWER, CRAIG
425 White Cedar, Killeen, TX 76542, Phone: 254-634-6934, craig6@embarqmail.com

Specialties: Folders; slip joints, some lock backs and an occasional liner lock. **Patterns:** I like the old traditional patterns. **Technical:** Grinds CPM steels most being CPM-154, 1095

for carbon and some Damascus. **Prices:** $450 and up. **Remarks:** Full-time maker, first knife sold in 2005.**Mark:** BREWER.

BRITTON, TIM
5645 Murray Rd., Winston-Salem, NC 27106, Phone: 336-923-2062, tim@timbritton.com; Web: www.timbritton.com

Specialties: Small and simple working knives, sgian dubhs, slip joint folders and special tactical designs. **Technical:** Forges and grinds stainless steel. **Prices:** $165 to ???. **Remarks:** Veteran knifemaker. **Mark:** Etched signature.

BROADWELL, DAVID
PO Box 3373, Wichita Falls, TX 76301, Phone: 940-782-4442, david@ broadwellstudios.com; Web: www.broadwellstudios.com

Specialties: Sculpted high-art straight and folding knives. **Patterns:** Daggers, sub-hilted fighters, folders, sculpted art knives and some Bowies. **Technical:** Grinds mostly Damascus; carves; prefers natural handle materials, including stone. Some embellishment. **Prices:** $500 to $4000; some higher. **Remarks:** Full-time maker since 1989; first knife sold in 1981. **Mark:** Stylized emblem bisecting "B"/with last name below.

BROCK, KENNETH L
PO Box 375, 207 N Skinner Rd, Allenspark, CO 80510, Phone: 303-747-2547, brockknives@nedernet.net

Specialties: Custom designs, full-tang working knives and button lock folders of his design. **Patterns:** Hunters, miniatures and minis. **Technical:** Flat-grinds D2 and 440C; makes own sheaths; heat-treats. **Prices:** $75 to $800. **Remarks:** Full-time maker; first knife sold in 1978. **Mark:** Last name, city, state and serial number.

BRODZIAK, DAVID
27 Stewart St, PO Box 1130, Albany, WA, AUSTRALIA 6331, Phone: 61 8 9841 3314, Fax: 61898115065, brodziak3@bigpond.com; Web: www.brodziakcustomknives.com

BROMLEY, PETER
BROMLEY KNIVES, 1408 S Bettman, Spokane, WA 99212, Phone: 509-534-4235 or 509-710-8365, Fax: 509-536-2666, bromleyknives@q.com

Specialties: Period Bowies, folder, hunting knives; all sizes and shapes. **Patterns:** Bowies, boot knives, hunters, utility, folder, working knives. **Technical:** High-carbon steel (1084, 1095 and 5160). Stock removal and forge. **Prices:** $85 to $750. **Remarks:** Almost full-time, first knife sold in 1987. A.B.S. Journeyman Smith. **Mark:** Bromley, Spokane, WA.

BROOKER, DENNIS
55858 260th Ave., Chariton, IA 50049, Phone: 641-862-3263, dbrooker@dbrooker.com Web: www.dbrooker.com

Specialties: Fancy straight knives and folders of his design. Obsidian and glass knives. **Patterns:** Hunters, folders and boots. **Technical:** Forges and grinds. Full-time engraver and designer; instruction available. **Prices:** Moderate to upscale. **Remarks:** Part-time maker. Takes no orders; sells only completed work. **Mark:** Name.

BROOKS, BUZZ
2345 Yosemite Dr, Los Angles, CA 90041, Phone: 323-256-2892

BROOKS, MICHAEL
2811 64th St, Lubbock, TX 79413, Phone: 806-438-3862, chiang@clearwire.net

Specialties: Working straight knives of his design or to customer specs. **Patterns:** Martial art, Bowies, hunters, and fighters. **Technical:** Grinds 440C, D2 and ATS-34; offers wide variety of handle materials. **Prices:** $75 & up. **Remarks:** Part-time maker; first knife sold in 1985. **Mark:** Initials.

BROOKS, STEVE R
1610 Dunn Ave, Walkerville, MT 59701, Phone: 406-782-5114, Fax: 406-782-5114, steve@brooksmoulds.com; Web: brooksmoulds.com

Specialties: Working straight knives and folders; period pieces. **Patterns:** Hunters, Bowies and camp knives; folding lockers; axes, tomahawks and buckskinner knives; swords and stilettos. **Technical:** Damascus and mosaic Damascus. Some knives come embellished. **Prices:** $400 to $2000. **Remarks:** Full-time maker; first knife sold in 1982. **Mark:** Lazy initials.

BROOME, THOMAS A
1212 E. Aliak Ave, Kenai, AK 99611-8205, Phone: 907-283-9128, tomlei@ptialaska.net; Web: www.alaskanknives.com

Specialties: Working hunters and folders **Patterns:** Traditional and custom orders. **Technical:** Grinds ATS-34, BG-42, CPM-S30V. **Prices:** $175 to $350. **Remarks:** Full-time maker; first knife sold in 1979. Doing business as Thom's Custom Knives, Alaskan Man O; Steel Knives. **Mark:** Full name, city, state.

BROTHERS, DENNIS L.
2007 Kent Rd., Oneonta, AL 35121, Phone: 205-466-3276, blademan@brothersblades.com Web: www.brothersblades.com

Specialties: Fixed blade hunting/working knives of maker's deigns. Works with customer designed specifications. **Patterns:** Hunters, camp knives, kitchen/utility, bird, and trout. Standard patterns and customer designed. **Technical:** Stock removal. Works with stainless and tool steels. SS cryo-treatment. Hollow and flat grinds. **Prices:** $200 -$400. **Remarks:** Sole authorship knives and customer leather sheaths. Part-time maker. Find on facebook "Brothers Blades by D.L. Brothers" **Mark:** "D.L. Brothers, 4B, Oneonta, AL" on obverse side of blade.

BROTHERS, ROBERT L
989 Philpott Rd, Colville, WA 99114, Phone: 509-684-8922

Specialties: Traditional working and using straight knives and folders of his design and to customer specs. **Patterns:** Bowies, fighters and hunters. **Technical:** Grinds D2;

forges Damascus. Makes own Damascus from saw steel wire rope and chain; part-time goldsmith and stone-setter. **Prices:** $100 to $400; some higher. **Remarks:** Part-time maker; first knife sold in 1986. **Mark:** Initials and year made.

BROUS, JASON
POB 550, Buellton, CA 93427, Phone: 805-717-7192, jbrous@live.com or brousblades@outlook.com; Web: www.brousblades.com
Patterns: Tactical mid-tech folders, production and customized. **Technical:** Stock removal method using D2 steel. **Prices:** $99 -$700. **Remarks:** Started May 2010.

BROUWER, JERRY
Vennewaard 151, 1824 KD, Alkmaar, NETHERLANDS, Phone: 00-31-618-774146, brouwern1@hotmail.nl; Web: www.brouwerknives.com
Specialties: Tactical fixed blades with epoxy-soaked Japanese wrapped handles, tactical and outdoor knives with Micarta or G-10 handles, tactical frame-lock folders. Fine, embellished knives for the demanding VIP. **Patterns:** Fixed-blade tantos, drop points, either V-ground or chisel ground, hunting knives, outdoor knives, folders, desk knives, pocket tools. **Technical:** Stock removal, only premium powder metallurgy steels and fine stainless damascus. **Prices:** $100 to $1,000. **Remarks:** Part-time maker; first knife sold in 2010. **Mark:** Laser etched "Brouwer" with a jack-o-lantern logo.

BROWER, MAX
2016 Story St, Boone, IA 50036, Phone: 515-432-2938, jmbrower@mchsi.com
Specialties: Hunters. Working/using straight knives. **Patterns:** Hunters. **Technical:** Grinds ATS-34. **Prices:** $300 and up. **Remarks:** Spare-time maker; first knife sold in 1981. **Mark:** Last name.

BROWN, DOUGLAS
1500 Lincolnshire Way, Fort Worth, TX 76134, www.debrownphotography.com

BROWN, HAROLD E
3654 NW Hwy 72, Arcadia, FL 34266, Phone: 863-494-7514, brknives@strato.net
Specialties: Fancy and exotic working knives. **Patterns:** Folders, slip-lock, locking several kinds. **Technical:** Grinds D2 and ATS-34. Embellishment available. **Prices:** $175 to $1000. **Remarks:** Part-time maker; first knife sold in 1976. **Mark:** Name and city with logo.

BROWN, JIM
1097 Fernleigh Cove, Little Rock, AR 72210

BROWN, ROB E
PO Box 15107, Emerald Hill, Port Elizabeth, EC, SOUTH AFRICA 6011, Phone: 27-41-3661086, Fax: 27-41-4511731, rbknives@global.co.za
Specialties: Contemporary-designed straight knives and period pieces. **Patterns:** Utility knives, hunters, boots, fighters and daggers. **Technical:** Grinds 440C, D2, ATS-34 and commercial Damascus. Knives mostly mirror finished; African handle materials. **Prices:** $100 to $1500. **Remarks:** Full-time maker; first knife sold in 1985. **Mark:** Name and country.

BROWNE, RICK
980 West 13th St, Upland, CA 91786, Phone: 909-985-1728
Specialties: Sheffield pattern pocket knives. **Patterns:** Hunters, fighters and daggers. No heavy-duty knives. **Technical:** Grinds ATS-34. **Prices:** Start at $450. **Remarks:** Part-time maker; first knife sold in 1975. **Mark:** R.E. Browne, Upland, CA.

BROWNING, STEVEN W
3400 Harrison Rd, Benton, AR 72015, Phone: 501-316-2450

BRUCE, RICHARD L.
13174 Surcease Mine Road, Yankee Hill, CA 95965, Phone: 530-532-0880, richardkarenbruce@yahoo.com
Specialties: Working straight knives. Prefers natural handle material; stag bone and woods. Admires the classic straight knife look. **Patterns:** Hunters, Fighters, Fishing Knives. **Technical:** Uses 01, 1095, L6, W2 steel. Stock removal method, flat grind, heat treats and tempers own knives. Builds own sheaths; simple but sturdy. **Prices:** $150-$400. **Remarks:** Sold first knife in 2006; part-time maker. **Mark:** RL Bruce.

BRUNCKHORST, LYLE
COUNTRY VILLAGE, 23706 7th Ave SE Ste B, Bothell, WA 98021, Phone: 425-402-3484, bronks@bronksknifeworks.com; Web: www.bronksknifeworks.com
Specialties: Forges own Damascus with 1084 and 15N20, forges 5160, 52100. Grinds CPM 154 CM, ATS-34, S30V. Hosts Biannual Northwest School of Knifemaking and Northwest Hammer In. Offers online and in-house sharpening services and knife sharpeners. Maker of the Double U Hoofknife. Traditional working and using knives, the new patent pending Xross-Bar Lock folders, tomahawks and irridescent RR spike knives. **Patterns:** Damascus Bowies, hunters, locking folders and featuring the ultra strong locking tactical folding knives. **Prices:** $185 to $1500; some to $3750. **Remarks:** Full-time maker; first knife made in 1976. **Mark:** Bucking horse or bronk.

BRUNER, FRED JR.
BRUNER BLADES, E10910W Hilldale Dr, Fall Creek, WI 54742, Phone: 715-877-2496, brunerblades@msn.com
Specialties: Pipe tomahawks, swords, makes his own. **Patterns:** Drop point hunters. **Prices:** $65 to $1500. **Remarks:** Voting member of the Knifemakers Guild. **Mark:** Fred Bruner.

BUCHANAN, THAD
THAD BUCHANAN CUSTOM KNIVES, 16401 S.W. Ranchview Rd., Powell Butte, OR 97753, buchananblades@gmail.com; Web: www.buchananblades.com
Specialties: Fixed blades. **Patterns:** Various hunters, trout, bird, utility, boots & fighters, including most Loveless patterns. **Technical:** Stock removal, high polish, variety handle materials. **Prices:** $450 to $2000. **Remarks:** 2005 and 2008 Blade Magazine handmade award for hunter/utility. 2006 Blade West best fixed blade award; 2008 Blade West

best hunter/utility. 2010 and 2011 Best Fixed Blade at Plaza Cutlery Show. **Mark:** Thad Buchanan -maker

BUCHANAN, ZAC
168 Chapel Dr., Eugene, OR 97404, Phone: 541-815-6706, zacbuchananknives@gmail.com; Web: www.zacbuchananknives.com
Specialties: R.W. Loveless-style fixed blades. **Technical:** Stock-removal knifemaker using CPM-154 blade steel, 416 stainless steel fittings and pre-ban elephant ivory, mammoth ivory, buffalo horn, stag and Micarta handles. **Prices:** $500 to $2,000. **Remarks:** Full-time maker; first knife sold in 2009. **Mark:** Zac Buchanan Eugene, Oregon.

BUCHARSKY, EMIL
37 26321 SH627 Spruce Grove, Alberta, CANADA T7Y 1C7, ebuch@telus.net; Web: www.ebuchknives.com
Specialties: Fancy working utility hunters and art folders, usually carved with overlays or inlays of damascus, hidden frames and screws. **Patterns:** Folders, hunters, bowies of maker's own design. **Technical:** Forges own damascus using 1095, 1084, 15N20 and nickel, stock-removal steels from Crucible, CPM alloys and UHB Elmax, natural handle materials of pearl, ancient ivory, bone, stabilized woods and others such as carbon fiber, titanium, stainless steel, mokume gane and gemstones. **Prices:** $400 to $1,000; art knives $1,500 and up. **Remarks:** Full-time maker; first knife made in 1989. **Mark:** Name, city and province in oval on fixed blades. Hand-engraved first name, initial and last name with year, in lower case, on folders.

BUCHNER, BILL
PO Box 73, Idleyld Park, OR 97447, Phone: 541-498-2247, blazinhammer@earthlink.net; Web: www.home.earthlin.net/~blazinghammer
Specialties: Working straight knives, kitchen knives and high-art knives of his design. **Technical:** Uses W1, L6 and his own Damascus. Invented "spectrum metal" for letter openers, folder handles and jewelry. Likes sculpturing and carving in Damascus. **Prices:** $40 to $3000; some higher. **Remarks:** Full-time maker; first knife sold in 1978. **Mark:** Signature.

BUCKNER, JIMMIE H
PO Box 162, Putney, GA 31782, Phone: 229-436-4182
Specialties: Camp knives, Bowies (one-of-a-kind), liner-lock folders, tomahawks, camp axes, neck knives for law enforcement and hide-out knives for body guards and professional people. **Patterns:** Hunters, camp knives, Bowies. **Technical:** Forges 1084, 5160 and Damascus (own), own heat treats. **Prices:** $195 to $795 and up. **Remarks:** Full-time maker; first knife sold in 1980, ABS Master Smith. **Mark:** Name over spade.

BUDELL, MICHAEL
3733 Wieghat Ln., Brenham, TX 77833, Phone: 979-836-3148, mbbudell@att.net
Specialties: Slip Joint Folders. **Technical:** Grinds 01, 440C. File work springs, blades and liners. Natural material scales giraffe, mastadon ivory, elephant ivory, and jigged bone. **Prices:** $175 -$350. **Remarks:** Part-time maker; first knife sold 2006. **Mark:** XA

BUEBENDORF, ROBERT E
108 Lazybrooke Rd, Monroe, CT 06468, Phone: 203-452-1769
Specialties: Traditional and fancy straight knives of his design. **Patterns:** Hand-makes and embellishes belt buckle knives. **Technical:** Forges and grinds 440C, O1, W2, 1095, his own Damascus and 154CM. **Prices:** $200 to $500. **Remarks:** Full-time maker; first knife sold in 1978. **Mark:** First and middle initials, last name and MAKER.

BULLARD, BENONI
4416 Jackson 4, Bradford, AR 72020, Phone: 501-344-2672, benandbren@earthlink.net
Specialties: Bowies and hunters. **Patterns:** Camp knives, bowies, hunters, slip joints, folders, lock blades, miniatures, Hawks Tech. **Technical:** Makes own Damascus. Forges 5160, 1085, 15 N 20. Favorite is 5160. **Prices:** $150 -$1500. **Remarks:** Part-time maker. Sold first knife in 2006. **Mark:** Benoni with a star over the letter i.

BULLARD, RANDALL
7 Mesa Dr., Canyon, TX 79015, Phone: 806-655-0590
Specialties: Working/using straight knives and folders of his design or to customer specs. **Patterns:** Hunters, locking folders and slip-joint folders. **Technical:** Grinds O1, ATS-34 and 440C. Does file work. **Prices:** $125 to $300; some to $500. **Remarks:** Part-time maker; first knife sold in 1993. Doing business as Bullard Custom Knives. **Mark:** First and middle initials, last name, maker, city and state.

BULLARD, TOM
117 MC 8068, Flippin, AR 72634, Phone: 870-656-3428, tbullard8@live.com
Specialties: Traditional folders and hunters. **Patterns:** Bowies, hunters, single and 2-blade trappers, lockback folders. **Technical:** Grinds 440C, A2, D2, ATS-34 and O1. **Prices:** $175 and up. **Remarks:** Offers filework and engraving by Norvell Foster and Terry Thies. Does not make screw-together knives. **Mark:** T Bullard

BUMP, BRUCE D.
1103 Rex Ln, Walla Walla, WA 99362, Phone: 509-386-8879, brucebump1@gmail.com; Web: www.brucebumpknives.com
Specialties: Slip joints, bowies and muzzle-loading pistol-knife combinations. **Patterns:** Maker's own damascus patterns including double mosaics. **Technical:** One-of-a-kind pieces. **Prices:** Please email for prices. **Remarks:** Full-time maker, ABS master smith since 2003. **Mark:** Bruce D. Bump "Custom", Bruce D. Bump "MS".

BURDEN, JAMES
405 Kelly St, Burkburnett, TX 76354

BURGER, FRED
Box 436, Munster, KZN, SOUTH AFRICA 4278, Phone: 27 39 3192316, info@swordcane.com; Web: www.swordcane.com

Specialties: Sword canes, folders, and fixed blades. **Patterns:** 440C and carbon steel blades. **Technical:** Double hollow ground and Poniard-style blades. **Prices:** $300 to $3000. **Remarks:** Full-time maker with son, Barry, since 1987. Member South African Guild. **Mark:** Last name in oval pierced by a dagger.

BURGER, PON
12 Glenwood Ave, Woodlands, Bulawayo, ZIMBABWE 75514
Specialties: Collector's items. **Patterns:** Fighters, locking folders of traditional styles, buckles. **Technical:** Scrimshaws 440C blade. Uses polished buffalo horn with brass fittings. Cased in buffalo hide book. **Prices:** $450 to $1100. **Remarks:** Full-time maker; first knife sold in 1973. Doing business as Burger Products. **Mark:** Spirit of Africa.

BURGER, TIAAN
69 Annie Botha Ave, Riviera,, Pretoria, GT, SOUTH AFRICA, tiaan_burger@hotmail.com
Specialties: Sliplock and multi-blade folder. **Technical:** High carbon or stainless with African handle materials **Remarks:** Occasional fixed blade knives.

BURKE, BILL
20 Adams Ranch Rd., Boise, ID 83716, Phone: 208-336-3792, billburke@bladegallery.com
Specialties: Hand-forged working knives. **Patterns:** Fowler pronghorn, clip point and drop point hunters. **Technical:** Forges 52100 and 5160. Makes own Damascus from 15N20 and 1084. **Prices:** $450 and up. **Remarks:** Dedicated to fixed-blade high-performance knives. ABS Journeyman. Also makes "Ed Fowler" miniatures. **Mark:** Initials connected.

BURKE, DAN
29 Circular Rd., Springdale, NL, CANADA A0J 1T0, Phone: 709-867-2026, dansknives@eastlink.ca
Specialties: Slip joint folders. **Patterns:** Traditional folders. **Technical:** Grinds D2 and BG-42. Prefers natural handle materials; heat-treats. **Prices:** $440 to $1900. **Remarks:** Full-time maker; first knife sold in 1976. **Mark:** First initial and last name.

BURNLEY, LUCAS
1005 La Font Rd. SW, Albuquerque, NM 87105, Phone: 505-814-9964, burnleyknives@comcast.net; www.burnleyknives.com
Specialties: Contemporary tactical fixed blade, and folder designs, some art knives. **Patterns:** Hybrids, neo Japanese, defensive, utility and field knives. **Technical:** Grinds CPM154, A2, D2, BG42, Stainless Damascus as well as titanium and aerospace composites. **Prices:** Most models $225 to $1,500. Some specialty pieces higher. **Remarks:** Full-time maker, first knife sold in 2003. **Mark:** Last name or BRNLY.

BURNS, ROBERT
104 W. 6th St., Carver, MN 55315, Phone: 412-477-4677, wildernessironworks@gmail.com; www.wildernessironworks.org
Specialties Utility knives, fighters, axes, pattern-welded axes and Viking swords. **Technical:** Trained as a blacksmith in Colonial style, forges 1095, 1090, 1084, 15N20, 5160, W1, W2, D2, 440C and wrought iron. **Prices:** $85 to $1,500-plus. **Remarks:** Full-time maker; first knife made in 2005. **Mark:** A compass rose with all of the cardinal directions, and underneath, in cursive, "Wilderness Ironworks."

BURRIS, PATRICK R
1263 Cty. Rd. 750, Athens, TN 37303, Phone: 423-336-5715, burrispr@gmail.com
Specialties: Traditional straight knives and locking-liner folders. **Patterns:** Hunters, bowies, locking-liner folders. **Technical:** Flat grinds high-grade stainless and damascus. **Remarks:** Offers filework, embellishment, exotic materials and damascus **Mark:** Last name in script.

BURROWS, CHUCK
WILD ROSE TRADING CO, 289 La Posta Canyon Rd, Durango, CO 81303, Phone: 970-259-8396, chuck@wrtcleather.com; Web: www.wrtcleather.com
Specialties: Presentation knives, hawks, and sheaths based on the styles of the American frontier incorporating carving, beadwork, rawhide, braintan, and other period correct materials. Also makes other period style knives such as Scottish Dirks and Moorish jambiyahs. **Patterns:** Bowies, Dags, tomahawks, war clubs, and all other 18th and 19th century frontier style edged weapons and tools. **Technical:** Carbon steel only: 5160, 1080/1084, 1095, O1, Damascus-Our Frontier Shear Steel, plus other styles available on request. Forged knives, hawks, etc. are made in collaborations with bladesmiths. Gib Guignard (under the name of Cactus Rose) and Mark Williams (under the name UB Forged). Blades are usually forge finished and all items are given an aged period look. **Prices:** $500 plus. **Remarks:** Full-time maker, first knife sold in 1973. 40+ years experience working leather. **Mark:** A lazy eight or lazy eight with a capital T at the center. On leather either the lazy eight with T or a WRTC makers stamp.

BURROWS, STEPHEN R
1020 Osage St, Humboldt, KS 66748, Phone: 816-921-1573
Specialties: Fantasy straight knives of his design, to customer specs and in standard patterns; period pieces. **Patterns:** Fantasy, bird and trout knives, daggers, fighters and hunters. **Technical:** Forges 5160 and 1095 high-carbon steel, O1 and his Damascus. Offers lost wax casting in bronze or silver of cross guards and pommels. **Prices:** $65 to $600; some to $2000. **Remarks:** Full-time maker; first knife sold in 1983. Doing business as Gypsy Silk. **Mark:** Etched name.

BUSBIE, JEFF
John 316 Knife Works, 170 Towles Rd., Bloomingdale, GA 31302, Phone: 912-656-8238, jbusbie@comcast.net; Web: www.john316knifeworks.com
Specialties: Working full-tang and hidden-tang fixed blades, locking-liner folders and hard-use knives. **Patterns:** Bowies, skinners, fighters, neck knives, work knives, bird knives, swords, art knives and other creations. **Technical:** Stock-removal maker using Alabama Damascus, CPM stainless steels and D2. Handles from hardwoods, G-10, ivory, bone and exotic materials. **Prices:** $100 to $800 and up. **Remarks:** Part-time maker building 150 to 200 knives a year; first knife sold in 2008. **Mark:** john 316 knife works with a cross in the middle.

BUSCH, STEVE
1989 Old Town Loop, Oakland, OR 97462, Phone: 541-459-2833, steve@buschcustomknives.com; Web: wwwbuschcustomknives.blademakers.com
Specialties: D/A automatic right and left handed, folders, fixed blade working mainly in Damascus file work, functional art knives, nitrate bluing, heat bluing most all scale materials. **Prices:** $150 to $2000. **Remarks:** Trained under Vallotton family 3 1/2 years on own since 2002. **Mark:** Signature and date of completion on all knives.

BUSFIELD, JOHN
153 Devonshire Circle, Roanoke Rapids, NC 27870, Phone: 252-537-3949, Fax: 252-537-8704, busfield@charter.net; Web: www.busfieldknives.com
Specialties: Investor-grade folders; high-grade working straight knives. **Patterns:** Original price-style and trailing-point interframe and sculpted-frame folders, drop-point hunters and semi-skinners. **Technical:** Grinds 154CM and ATS-34. Offers interframes, gold frames and inlays; uses jade, agate and lapis. **Prices:** $275 to $2000. **Remarks:** Full-time maker; first knife sold in 1979. **Mark:** Last name and address.

BUSSE, JERRY
11651 Co Rd 12, Wauseon, OH 43567, Phone: 419-923-6471
Specialties: Working straight knives. **Patterns:** Heavy combat knives and camp knives. **Technical:** Grinds D2, A2, INFI. **Prices:** $1100 to $3500. **Remarks:** Full-time maker; first knife sold in 1983. **Mark:** Last name in logo.

BUTLER, BART
822 Seventh St, Ramona, CA 92065, Phone: 760-789-6431

BUTLER, JOHN
777 Tyre Rd, Havana, FL 32333, Phone: 850-539-5742
Specialties: Hunters, Bowies, period. **Technical:** Damascus, 52100, 5160, L6 steels. **Prices:** $80 and up. **Remarks:** Making knives since 1986. Journeyman (ABS). **Mark:** JB.

BUTLER, JOHN R
20162 6th Ave N E, Shoreline, WA 98155, Phone: 206-362-3847, rjjjrb@sprynet.com

BUXTON, BILL
155 Oak Bend Rd, Kaiser, MO 65047, Phone: 573-348-3577, camper@yhti.net; Web: www.billbuxtonknives.com
Specialties: Forged fancy and working straight knives and folders. Mostly one-of-a-kind pieces. **Patterns:** Fighters, daggers, Bowies, hunters, linerlock folders, axes and tomahawks. **Technical:** Forges 52100, 0-1, 1080. Makes own Damascus (mosaic and random patterns) from 1080, 1095, 15n20, and powdered metals 1084 and 4800a. Offers sterling silver inlay, n/s pin patterning and pewter pouring on axe and hawk handles. **Prices:** $300 to $2,500. **Remarks:** Full-time maker, sold first knife in 1998. **Mark:** First initial and last name.

BUZEK, STANLEY
PO Box 731, Waller, TX 77484, Phone: 936-372-1933, stan@sbuzekknives.com; Web: www.sbuzekknives.com
Specialties: Traditional slip-joint pocketknives, LinerLocks and frame-lock folders, and fixed-blade hunters and skinners. **Technical:** Grinds, heat treats and Rockwell tests CPM-154, and some traditional folders in O1 tool steel. Hand-rubbed finishes. Dyed jigged bone, mammoth ivory and fine stabilized woods. **Prices:** $250 and up. **Remarks:** Serious part-time maker; first knife sold in 2006. **Mark:** S. Buzek on riccasso.

BYBEE, BARRY J
795 Lock Rd. E, Cadiz, KY 42211-8615
Specialties: Working straight knives of his design. **Patterns:** Hunters, fighters, boot knives, tantos and Bowies. **Technical:** Grinds ATS-34, 440C. Likes stag and Micarta for handle materials. **Prices:** $125 to $200; some to $1000. **Remarks:** Part-time maker; first knife sold in 1968. **Mark:** Arrowhead logo with name, city and state.

BYRD, WESLEY L
189 Countryside Dr, Evensville, TN 37332, Phone: 423-775-3826, w.l.byrd@worldnet.att.net
Specialties: Hunters, fighters, Bowies, dirks, sgian dubh, utility, and camp knives. **Patterns:** Wire rope, random patterns. Twists, W's, Ladder, Kite Tail. **Technical:** Uses 52100, 1084, 5160, L6, and 15n20. **Prices:** Starting at $180. **Remarks:** Prefer to work with customer for their design preferences. ABS Journeyman Smith. **Mark:** BYRD, WB <X.

C

CABRERA, SERGIO B
24500 Broad Ave, Wilmington, CA 90744

CAFFREY, EDWARD J
2608 Central Ave West, Great Falls, MT 59404, Phone: 406-727-9102, caffreyknives@gmail.com; Web: www.caffreyknives.net
Specialties: One-of-a-kind using and collector quality pieces. Will accept some customer designs. **Patterns:** Bowies, folders, hunters, fighters, camp/utility, tomahawks and hatchets. **Technical:** Forges all types of Damascus, specializing in Mosaic Damascus, 52100, 5160, 1080/1084 and most other commonly forged steels. **Prices:** Starting at $185; typical hunters start at $400; collector pieces can range into the thousands. **Remarks:** Offers one-on-one basic and advanced bladesmithing classes. ABS Mastersmith. Full-time maker. **Mark:** Stamped last name and MS on straight knives.

Etched last name with MS on folders.

CALDWELL, BILL
255 Rebecca, West Monroe, LA 71292, Phone: 318-323-3025
Specialties: Straight knives and folders with machined bolsters and liners. **Patterns:** Fighters, Bowies, survival knives, tomahawks, razors and push knives. **Technical:** Owns and operates a very large, well-equipped blacksmith and bladesmith shop with six large forges and eight power hammers. **Prices:** $400 to $3500; some to $10,000. **Remarks:** Full-time maker and self-styled blacksmith; first knife sold in 1962. **Mark:** Wild Bill and Sons.

CALLAHAN, F TERRY
PO Box 880, Boerne, TX 78006, Phone: 210-260-2378, ftclaw@gvtc.com
Specialties: Custom hand-forged edged knives, collectible and functional. **Patterns:** Bowies, folders, daggers, hunters & camp knives. **Technical:** Forges damascus and 5160. Offers filework, silver inlay and handmade sheaths. **Prices:** $150 to $500. **Remarks:** First knife sold in 1990. ABS/Journeyman Bladesmith. **Mark:** Initial "F" inside a keystone.

CALVERT JR., ROBERT W (BOB)
911 Julia, Rayville, LA 71269, Phone: 318-348-4490, rcalvert1@gmail.com
Specialties: Using and hunting knives; your design or his. Since 1990. **Patterns:** Forges own Damascus; all patterns. **Technical:** 5160, D2, 52100, 1084. Prefers natural handle material. **Prices:** $250 and up. **Remarks:** TOMB Member, ABS. Journeyman Smith. ABS Board of directors **Mark:** Calvert (Block) J S.

CAMBRON, HENRY
169 Severn Way, Dallas, GA 30132-0317, Phone: 770-598-5721, worldclassknives@bellsouth.net; Web: www.worldclassknives.com
Specialties: Everyday carry, working and small neck knives. **Patterns:** Hunters, bowies, camp, utility and combat. **Technical:** Forge, stock removal, filework. Differential quench. Tuff-etched finish. Hand-sewn and Kydex sheaths. **Prices:** $65 to $650. **Remarks:** Full-time maker. **Mark:** First and last name over USA on blades. HC on sheaths.

CAMERER, CRAIG
3766 Rockbridge Rd, Chesterfield, IL 62630, Phone: 618-753-2147, craig@camererknives.com; Web: www.camererknives.com
Specialties: Everyday carry knives, hunters and Bowies. **Patterns:** D-guard, historical recreations and fighters. **Technical:** Most of his knives are forged to shape. **Prices:** $100 and up. **Remarks:** Member of the ABS and PKA. Journeymen Smith ABS.

CAMERON, RON G
PO Box 183, Logandale, NV 89021, Phone: 702-398-3356, rntcameron@mvdsl.com
Specialties: Fancy and embellished working/using straight knives and folders of his design. **Patterns:** Bowies, hunters and utility/camp knives. **Technical:** Grinds ATS-34, AEB-L and Devin Thomas Damascus or own Damascus from 1084 and 15N20. Does filework, fancy pins, mokume fittings. Uses exotic hardwoods, stag and Micarta for handles. Pearl & mammoth ivory. **Prices:** $175 to $850 some to $1000. **Remarks:** Part-time maker; first knife sold in 1994. Doing business as Cameron Handmade Knives. **Mark:** Last name, town, state or last name.

CAMPBELL, DICK
196 Graham Rd, Colville, WA 99114, Phone: 509-684-6080, dicksknives@aol.com
Specialties: Working straight knives, folders and period pieces. **Patterns:** Hunters, fighters, boots and 19th century bowies. **Technical:** Grinds 440C and 154CM. **Prices:** $350 to $4,500. **Remarks:** Full-time maker. First knife sold in 1975. **Mark:** Name.

CAMPBELL, DOUG
46 W Boulder Rd., McLeod, MT 59052, Phone: 406-222-8153, dkcampbl@yahoo.com
Specialties: Sole authorship of most any fixed blade knife. **Patterns:** Capers, hunters, camp knives, bowies and fighters. **Technical:** Forged from 1084, 5160, 52100 and self-forged pattern-welded damascus. **Prices:** $300-$1,300. **Remarks:** Part-time knifesmith. Built first knife in 1987, tried to make every knife since better than the one before. ABS journeyman smith. **Mark:** Grizzly track surrounded by a "C," or "D Campbell" etched on spine.

CAMPOS, IVAN
R.XI de Agosto 107, Tatui, SP, BRAZIL 18270-000, Phone: 00-55-15-2518092, Fax: 00-55-15-2594368, ivan@ivancampos.com; Web: www.ivancompos.net
Specialties: Brazilian handmade and antique knives.

CANDRELLA, JOE
1219 Barness Dr, Warminster, PA 18974, Phone: 215-675-0143
Specialties: Working straight knives, some fancy. **Patterns:** Daggers, boots, Bowies. **Technical:** Grinds 440C and 154CM. **Prices:** $100 to $200; some to $1000. **Remarks:** Part-time maker; first knife sold in 1985. Does business as Franjo. **Mark:** FRANJO with knife as J.

CANTER, RONALD E
96 Bon Air Circle, Jackson, TN 38305, Phone: 731-668-1780, canterr@charter.net
Specialties: Traditional working knives to customer specs. **Patterns:** Beavertail skinners, Bowies, hand axes and folding lockers. **Technical:** Grinds 440C, Micarta & deer antler. **Prices:** $75 and up. **Remarks:** Spare-time maker; first knife sold in 1973. **Mark:** Three last initials intertwined.

CANTRELL, KITTY D
19720 Hwy 78, Ramona, CA 92076, Phone: 760-788-8304

CAPDEPON, RANDY
553 Joli Rd, Carencro, LA 70520, Phone: 318-896-4113, Fax: 318-896-8753
Specialties: Straight knives and folders of his design. **Patterns:** Hunters and locking folders. **Technical:** Grinds ATS-34, 440C and D2. **Prices:** $200 to $600. **Remarks:** Part-time maker; first knife made in 1992. Doing business as Capdepon Knives. **Mark:** Last name.

CAPDEPON, ROBERT
829 Vatican Rd, Carencro, LA 70520, Phone: 337-896-8753, Fax: 318-896-8753
Specialties: Traditional straight knives and folders of his design. **Patterns:** Boots, hunters and locking folders. **Technical:** Grinds ATS-34, 440C and D2. Hand-rubbed finish on blades. Likes natural horn materials for handles, including ivory. Offers engraving. **Prices:** $250 to $750. **Remarks:** Full-time maker; first knife made in 1992. **Mark:** Last name.

CAREY, PETER
P.O. Box 4712, Lago Vista, TX 78645, Phone: 512-358-4839, Web: www.careyblade.com
Specialties: Tactical folders, Every Day Carry to presentation grade. Working straight knives, hunters, and tactical. **Patterns:** High-tech patterns of his own design, Linerlocks, Framelocks, Flippers. **Technical:** Hollow grinds CPM154, CPM S35VN, stainless Damascus, Stellite. Uses titanium, zirconium, carbon fiber, G10, and select natural handle materials. **Prices:** Starting at $450. **Remarks:** Full-time maker, first knife sold in 2002. **Mark:** Last name in diamond.

CARLISLE, JEFF
PO Box 282 12753 Hwy 200, Simms, MT 59477, Phone: 406-264-5693

CARPENTER, RONALD W
Rt. 4 Box 323, Jasper, TX 75951, Phone: 409-384-4087

CARR, JOSEPH E.
W183 N8974 Maryhill Drive, Menomonee Falls, WI 53051, Phone: 920-625-3607, carsmith1@SBCGlobal.net; Web: Hembrook3607@charter.net
Specialties: JC knives. **Patterns:** Hunters, Bowies, fighting knives, every day carries. **Technical:** Grinds ATS-34 and Damascus. **Prices:** $200 to $750. **Remarks:** Full-time maker for 2 years, being taught by Ron Hembrook.

CARR, TIM
3660 Pillon Rd, Muskegon, MI 49445, Phone: 231-766-3582, tim@blackbearforgemi.com Web:www.blackbearforgemi.com
Specialties: Hunters, camp knives. **Patterns:** His or yours. **Technical:** Hand forges 5160, 52100 and Damascus. **Prices:** $125 to $700. **Remarks:** Part-time maker. **Mark:** The letter combined from maker's initials TRC.

CARRILLO, DWAINE
C/O AIRKAT KNIVES, 1021 SW 15th St, Moore, OK 73160, Phone: 405-503-5879, Web: www.airkatknives.com

CARROLL, CHAD
12182 McClelland, Grant, MI 49327, Phone: 231-834-9183, CHAD724@msn.com
Specialties: Hunters, Bowies, folders, swords, tomahawks. **Patterns:** Fixed blades, folders. **Prices:** $100 to $2000. **Remarks:** ABS Journeyman May 2002. **Mark:** A backwards C next to a forward C, maker's initials.

CARTER, FRED
5219 Deer Creek Rd, Wichita Falls, TX 76302, Phone: 904-723-4020, fcarter40@live.com
Specialties: High-art investor-class straight knives; some working hunters and fighters. **Patterns:** Classic daggers, Bowies; interframe, stainless and blued steel folders with gold inlay. **Technical:** Grinds a variety of steels. Uses no glue or solder. Engraves and inlays. **Prices:** Generally upscale. **Remarks:** Full-time maker. **Mark:** Signature in oval logo.

CARTER, MIKE
2522 Frankfort Ave, Louisville, KY 40206, Phone: 502-387-4844, mike@cartercrafts.com Web: www.cartercrafts.com
Remarks: Voting Member Knifemakers Guild.

CARTER, MURRAY M
22097 NW West Union Rd, Hillsboro, OR 97124, Phone: 503-447-1029, murray@cartercutlery.com; Web: www.cartercutlery.com
Specialties: Traditional Japanese cutlery, utilizing San soh ko (three layer) or Kata-ha (two layer) blade construction. Laminated neck knives, traditional Japanese etc. **Patterns:** Works from over 200 standard Japanese and North American designs. **Technical:** Hot forges and cold forges Hitachi white steel #1, Hitachi blue super steel exclusively. **Prices:** $800 to $10,000. **Remarks:** Owns and operates North America's most exclusive traditional Japanese bladesmithing school; web site available at which viewers can subscribe to 10 free knife sharpening and maintenance reports. **Mark:** Name in cursive, often appearing with Japanese characters. **Other:** Very interestng and informative monthly newsletter.

CARTER, SHAYNE
5302 Rosewood Cir., Payson, UT 84651, Phone: 801-913-0181, shaynemcarter@hotmail.com
Specialties: Fixed blades. **Patterns:** Hunters, bowies and fighters. **Technical:** Flat grinds, hand finishes, forges blade steel, including own damascus, some 1084, 52100 and 5160. **Prices:** Part-time maker; first damascus made in 1984.

CASEY, KEVIN
10583 N. 42nd St., Hickory Corners, MI 49060, Phone: 269-719-7412, kevincasey@tds.net; Web: www.kevincaseycustomknives.com
Specialties: Fixed blades and folders. **Patterns:** Liner lock folders and feather Damascus pattern, mammoth ivory. **Technical:** Forges Damascus and carbon steels. **Prices:** Starting at $500 -$2500. **Remarks:** Member ABS, Knifemakers Guild, Custom Knifemakers Collectors Association.

CASHEN, KEVIN R
Matherton Forge, 5615 Tyler St., Hubbardston, MI 48845, Phone: 989-981-6780, kevin@cashenblades.com; Web: www.cashenblades.com
Specialties: User-oriented straight knives and medieval and renaissance period European

swords and daggers. **Patterns:** Hunters and skinners, bowies and camp knives, swords and daggers. **Technical:** Hand forged blades of O1, L6 and maker's own O1-L6-and-O2 damascus, occasionally W2 or 1095, all heat-treated to exacting metallurgical standards. **Prices:** $200 for small hunters to $9,000+ for museum-quality swords, with an average range of $400-$2,000. **Remarks:** Full-time maker, instructor/speaker/consultant; first knife sold in 1985. **Mark:** Gothic "K.C." with master smith stamp. On period pieces, a crowned castle encircled with "Cashen."

CASTEEL, DIANNA
PO Box 63, Monteagle, TN 37356, Phone: 931-212-4341, ddcasteel@charter.net; Web: www.casteelcustomknives.com
Specialties: Small, delicate daggers and miniatures; most knives one-of-a-kind. **Patterns:** Daggers, boot knives, fighters and miniatures. **Technical:** Grinds 440C. Offers stainless Damascus. **Prices:** Start at $350; miniatures start at $250. **Remarks:** Full-time maker. **Mark:** Di in script.

CASTEEL, DOUGLAS
PO Box 63, Monteagle, TN 37356, Phone: 931-212-4341, Fax: 931-723-1856, ddcasteel@charter.net; Web: www.casteelcustomknives.com
Specialties: One-of-a-kind collector-class period pieces. **Patterns:** Daggers, Bowies, swords and folders. **Technical:** Grinds 440C. Offers gold and silver castings. Offers stainless Damascus **Prices:** Upscale. **Remarks:** Full-time maker; first knife sold in 1982. **Mark:** Last name.

CASTELLUCIO, RICH
220 Stairs Rd., Amsterdam, NY 12010, Phone: 518-843-5540, rcastellucio@nycap.rr.com
Patterns: Bowies, push daggers, and fantasy knives. **Technical:** Uses ATS-34, 440C, 154CM. I use stabilized wood, bone for the handles. Guards are made of copper, brass, stainless, nickle, and mokume.

CASTON, DARRIEL
125 Ashcat Way, Folsom, CA 95630, Phone: 916-539-0744, darrielc@gmail.com

CASWELL, JOE
173 S Ventu Park Rd, Newbury, CA 91320, Phone: 805-499-0707, Web:www.caswellknives.com
Specialties: Historic pattern welded knives and swords, hand forged. Also high precision folding and fixed blade "gentleman" and "tactical" knives of his design, period firearms. Inventor of the "In-Line" retractable pocket clip for folding knives. **Patterns:** Hunters, tactical/utility, fighters, bowies, daggers, pattern welded medieval swords, precision folders. **Technical:** Forges own Damascus especially historic forms. Sometimes uses modern stainless steels and Damascus of other makers. Makes some pieces entirely by hand, others using the latest CNC techniques and by hand. Makes sheaths too. **Prices:** $100-$5,500. **Remarks:** Full time makers since 1995. Making mostly historic recreations for exclusive clientele. Recently moving into folding knives and 'modern' designs. **Mark:** CASWELL or CASWELL USA Accompanied by a mounted knight logo.

CATOE, DAVID R
4024 Heutte Dr, Norfolk, VA 23518, Phone: 757-480-3191
Technical: Does own forging, Damascus and heat treatments. Price: $200 to $500; some higher. **Remarks:** Part-time maker; trained by Dan Maragni 1985-1988; first knife sold 1989. **Mark:** Leaf of a camellia.

CECCHINI, GUSTAVO T.
R. XV Novembro 2841, Sao Jose Rio Preto, SPAIN 15015110, Phone: 55 1732224267, tomaki@terra.com.be Web: www.gtcknives.com
Specialties: Tactical and HiTech folders. **Technical:** Stock removal. Stainless steel fixed blades. S30V, S35Vn, S90V, CowryX, Damasteel, Chad Nichols SS damascus, RWL 34, CPM 154 CM, BG 42. **Prices:** $500 -$1500. **Remarks:** Full-time since 2004. **Mark:** Tang Stamp "GTC"

CEPRANO, PETER J.
213 Townsend Brooke Rd., Auburn, ME 04210, Phone: 207-786-5322, bpknives@gmail.com
Specialties: Traditional working/using straight knives; tactical/defense straight knives. Own designs or to a customer's specs. **Patterns:** Hunters, skinners, utility, Bowies, fighters, camp and survival, neck knives. **Technical:** Forges 1095, 5160, W2, 52100 and old files; grinds CPM154cm, ATS-34, 440C, D2, CPMs30v, Damascus from other makes and other tool steels. Hand-sewn and tooled leather and Kydex sheaths. **Prices:** Starting at $125. **Remarks:** Full-time maker, first knife sold in 2001. Doing business as Big Pete Knives. **Mark:** Bold BPK over small BigPeteKnivesUSA.

CHAFFEE, JEFF L
14314 N. Washington St, PO Box 1, Morris, IN 47033, Phone: 812-212-6188
Specialties: Fancy working and utility folders and straight knives. **Patterns:** Fighters, dagger, hunter and locking folders. **Technical:** Grinds commercial Damascus, 440C, ATS-34, D2 and O1. Prefers natural handle materials. **Prices:** $350 to $2000. **Remarks:** Part-time maker; first knife sold in 1988. **Mark:** Last name.

CHAMBERLAIN, JON A
15 S. Lombard, E. Wenatchee, WA 98802, Phone: 509-884-6591
Specialties: Working and kitchen knives to customer specs; exotics on special order. **Patterns:** Over 100 patterns in stock. **Technical:** Prefers ATS-34, D2, L6 and Damascus. **Prices:** Start at $50. **Remarks:** First knife sold in 1986. Doing business as Johnny Custom Knifemakers. **Mark:** Name in oval with city and state enclosing.

CHAMBERLIN, JOHN A
11535 Our Rd., Anchorage, AK 99516, Phone: 907-346-1524, Fax: 907-562-4583

Specialties: Art and working knives. **Patterns:** Daggers and hunters; some folders;. **Technical:** Grinds ATS-34, 440C, A2, D2 and Damascus. Uses Alaskan handle materials such as oosic, jade, whale jawbone, fossil ivory. **Prices:** Start at $200. **Remarks:** Favorite knives to make are double-edged. Does own heat treating and cryogenic deep freeze. Full-time maker; first knife sold in 1984. **Mark:** Name over English shield and dagger.

CHAMBERS, RONNY
1900 W. Mississippi St., Beebe, AR 72012, Phone: 501-288-1476, chambersronny@yahoo.com; Web: www.chamberscustomknives.net

CHAMBLIN, JOEL
960 New Hebron Church Rd, Concord, GA 30206, Phone: 678-588-6769, chamblinknives@yahoo.com Web: chamblinknives.com
Specialties: Fancy and working folders. **Patterns:** Fancy locking folders, traditional, multi-blades and utility. **Technical:** Uses ATS-34, CPM 154, and commercial Damascus. Offers filework. **Prices:** Start at $400. **Remarks:** Full-time maker; first knife sold in 1989. **Mark:** Last name.

CHAMPION, ROBERT
7001 Red Rock Rd., Amarillo, TX 79118, Phone: 806-622-3970, rchampknives@gmail.com; www.rchampknives.com
Specialties: Traditional working straight knives. **Patterns:** Hunters, skinners, camp knives, bowies and daggers. **Technical:** Grinds 440C, ATS-34, D2 and stainless damascus. **Prices:** $100 to $1,800. **Remarks:** Part-time maker; first knife sold in 1979. Stream-lined hunters. **Mark:** Last name with dagger logo, city and state.

CHAPO, WILLIAM G
45 Wildridge Rd, Wilton, CT 06897, Phone: 203-544-9424
Specialties: Classic straight knives and folders of his design and to customer specs; period pieces. **Patterns:** Boots, Bowies and locking folders. **Technical:** Forges stainless Damascus. Offers filework. **Prices:** $750 and up. **Remarks:** Full-time maker; first knife sold in 1989. **Mark:** First and middle initials, last name, city, state.

CHARD, GORDON R
104 S. Holiday Lane, Iola, KS 66749, Phone: 620-365-2311, Fax: 620-365-2311, gchard@cox.net
Specialties: High tech folding knives in one-of-a-kind styles. **Patterns:** Liner locking folders of own design. Also fixed blade Art Knives. **Technical:** Clean work with attention to fit and finish. Blade steel mostly ATS-34 and 154CM, some CPM440V Vaso Wear and Damascus. **Prices:** $150 to $2500. **Remarks:** First knife sold in 1983. **Mark:** Name, city and state surrounded by wheat on each side.

CHASE, ALEX
208 E. Pennsylvania Ave., DeLand, FL 32724, Phone: 386-734-9918, chase8578@bellsouth.net
Specialties: Historical steels, classic and traditional straight knives of his design and to customer specs. **Patterns:** Art, fighters, hunters and Japanese style. **Technical:** Forges O1-L6 Damascus, meteoric Damascus, 52100, 5160; uses fossil walrus and mastodon ivory etc. **Prices:** $150 to $1000; some to $3500. **Remarks:** Full-time maker; Guild member since 1996. Doing business as Confederate Forge. **Mark:** Stylized initials-A.C.

CHASE, JOHN E
217 Walnut, Aledo, TX 76008, Phone: 817-441-8331, jchaseknives@sbcglobal.net
Specialties: Straight working knives in standard patterns or to customer specs. **Patterns:** Hunters, fighters, daggers and Bowies. **Technical:** Grinds D2 and O1; offers mostly satin finishes. **Prices:** Start at $325. **Remarks:** Part-time maker; first knife sold in 1974. **Mark:** Last name in logo.

CHAUVIN, JOHN
200 Anna St, Scott, LA 70583, Phone: 337-237-6138, Fax: 337-230-7980
Specialties: Traditional working and using straight knives of his design, to customer specs and in standard patterns. **Patterns:** Bowies, fighters, and hunters. **Technical:** Grinds ATS-34, 440C and O1 high-carbon. Paul Bos heat treating. Uses ivory, stag, oosic and stabilized Louisiana swamp maple for handle materials. Makes sheaths using alligator and ostrich. **Prices:** $200 and up. Bowies start at $500. **Remarks:** Part-time maker; first knife sold in 1995. **Mark:** Full name, city, state.

CHAVEZ, RAMON
314 N. 5th St., Belen, NM 87002, Phone: 505-453-6008, ramon@chavesknives.com; Web: www.chavesknives.com
Specialties: Frame-lock folding knives and fixed blades. **Patterns:** Hunters, skinners, bushcraft, tactical, neck knives and utility. **Technical:** Grind/stock removal of CPM D2, D2 and CPM 3V. Handles are mostly titanium and Micarta. Thermal molding plastic for sheaths. **Prices:** Start at $225. **Remarks:** Full-time maker; first knife made in 1993, first knife sold in 2010. **Mark:** CHAVES USA with skeleton key.

CHEATHAM, BILL
PO Box 636, Laveen, AZ 85339, Phone: 602-237-2786, blademan76@aol.com
Specialties: Working straight knives and folders. **Patterns:** Hunters, fighters, boots and axes; locking folders. **Technical:** Grinds 440C. **Prices:** $150 to $350; exceptional knives to $600. **Remarks:** Full-time maker; first knife sold in 1976. **Mark:** Name, city, state.

CHERRY, FRANK J
3412 Tiley N.E., Albuquerque, NM 87110, Phone: 505-883-8643

CHEW, LARRY
3025 De leon Dr., Weatherford, TX 76087, Phone: 817-573-8035, chewman@swbell.net; Web: www.voodooinside.com
Specialties: High-tech folding knives. **Patterns:** Double action automatic and manual

folding patterns of his design. **Technical:** CAD designed folders utilizing roller bearing pivot design known as "VooDoo." Double action automatic folders with a variety of obvious and disguised release mechanisms, some with lock-outs. **Prices:** Manual folders start at $475, double action autos start at $750. **Remarks:** Made and sold first knife in 1988, first folder in 1989. Full-time maker since 1997. **Mark:** Name and location etched in blade, Damascus autos marked on spring inside frame. Earliest knives stamped LC.

CHILDERS, DAVID

15575 Marina Dr., Unit 227, Montgomery, TX 77356, childersdavid@att.net; Web: www.davidchildersknives.com

CHINNOCK, DANIEL T.

380 River Ridge Dr., Union, MO 63084, Phone: 314-276-6936, Web: www. DanChinnock.com; email: Sueanddanc@cs.com

Specialties: One of a kind folders in Damascus and Mammoth Ivory. Performs intricate pearl inlays into snake wood and giraffe bone. Makes matching ivory pistol grips for colt 1911's and Colt SAA. **Patterns:** New folder designs each year, thin ground and delicate gentleman's folders, large "hunting" folders in stainless Damascus and CPM154. Several standard models carried by Internet dealers. **Prices:** $500-$1500 **Remarks:** Full-time maker in 2005 and a voting member of the Knifemakers Guild. Performs intricate file work on all areas of knife. **Mark:** Signature on inside of backbar, starting in 2009 blades are stamped with a large "C" and "Dan" buried inside the "C".

CHOATE, MILTON

1665 W. County 17-1/2, Somerton, AZ 85350, Phone: 928-627-7251, mccustom@juno.com

Specialties: Classic working and using straight knives of his design, to customer specs and in standard patterns. **Patterns:** Bowies, hunters and utility/camp knives. **Technical:** Grinds 440C; grinds and forges 1095 and 5160. Does filework on top and guards on request. **Prices:** $200 to $800. **Remarks:** Full-time maker, first knife made in 1990. All knives come with handmade sheaths by Judy Choate. **Mark:** Knives marked "Choate."

CHOMILIER, ALAIN AND JORIS

20 rue des Hauts de Chanturgue, Clermont-Ferrand, FRANCE 63100, Phone: + 33 4 73 25 64 47, jo_chomilier@yahoo.fr

Specialties: One-of-a-kind knives; exclusive designs; art knives in carved patinated bronze, mainly folders, some straight knives and art daggers. **Patterns:** Liner-lock, side-lock, button-lock, lockback folders. **Technical:** Grind carbon and stainless damascus; also carve and patinate bronze. **Prices:** $400 to $3000, some to $4000. **Remarks:** Spare-time makers; first knife sold in 1995; Use fossil stone and ivory, mother-of-pearl, (fossil) coral, meteorite, bronze, gemstones, high karat gold. **Mark:** A. J. Chomilier in italics.

CHRISTENSEN, JON P

516 Blue Grouse, Stevensville, MT 59870, Phone: 406-697-8377, jpcknives@gmail.com; Web: www.jonchristensenknives.com

Specialties: Hunting/utility knives, folders, art knives. **Patterns:** Mosaic damascus**Technical:** Sole authorship, forges 01, 1084, 52100, 5160, Damascus from 1084/15N20. **Prices:** $220 and up. **Remarks:** ABS Mastersmith, first knife sold in 1999. **Mark:** First and middle initial surrounded by last initial.

CHURCHMAN, T W (TIM)

475 Saddle Horn Drive, Bandera, TX 78003, Phone: 210-240-0317, tim.churchman@nustarenergy.com

Specialties: Fancy and traditional straight knives. Bird/trout knives of his design and to customer specs. **Patterns:** Bird/trout knives, Bowies, daggers, fighters, boot knives, some miniatures. **Technical:** Grinds 440C, D2 and 154CM. Offers stainless fittings, fancy filework, exotic and stabilized woods, elk and other antler, and hand sewed lined sheaths. Also flower pins as a style. **Prices:** $350 to $450; some to $2,250. **Remarks:** Part-time maker; first knife made in 1981 after reading "KNIVES '81." Doing business as "Custom Knives Churchman Made." **Mark:** "Churchman" over Texas outline, "Bandera" under.

CIMMS, GREG

Kayne Custom Knife Works, 2297 Rt. 44, Ste. B, Pleasant Valley, NY 12569, Phone: 845-475-7220, cimms1@aol.com

Patterns: Kitchen knives, hunters, bowies, fighters, small swords, bird-and-trout knives, tactical pieces, tomahawks, axes and bushcraft blades. **Technical:** Damascus and straight-carbon-steel cutlery, with some mosaic-damascus and powder-metal pieces. **Prices:** $300 to $4,000. **Remarks:** Full-time maker since 2014; first knife made in 2013. **Mark:** A compass with a "K" in the middle.

CLAIBORNE, JEFF

1470 Roberts Rd, Franklin, IN 46131, Phone: 317-736-7443, jeff@claiborneknives.com; Web: www.claiborneknives.com

Specialties: Multi blade slip joint folders. All one-of-a-kind by hand, no jigs or fixtures, swords, straight knives, period pieces, camp knives, hunters, fighters, ethnic swords all periods. Handle: uses stag, pearl, oosic, bone ivory, mastadon-mammoth, elephant or exotic woods. **Technical:** Forges high-carbon steel, makes Damascus, forges cable grinds, O1, 1095, 5160, 52100, L6. **Prices:** $250 and up. **Remarks:** Full-time maker; first knife sold in 1989. **Mark:** Stylized initials in an oval.

CLAIBORNE, RON

2918 Ellistown Rd, Knox, TN 37924, Phone: 615-524-2054, Bowie@icy.net

Specialties: Multi-blade slip joints, swords, straight knives. **Patterns:** Hunters, daggers, folders. **Technical:** Forges Damascus: mosaic, powder mosaic. Prefers bone and natural handle materials; some exotic woods. **Prices:** $125 to $2500. **Remarks:** Part-time maker; first knife sold in 1979. Doing business as Thunder Mountain Forge Claiborne Knives. **Mark:** Claiborne.

CLARK, D E (LUCKY)

413 Lyman Lane, Johnstown, PA 15909-1409

Specialties: Working straight knives and folders to customer specs. **Patterns:** Customer designs. **Technical:** Grinds D2, 440C, 154CM. **Prices:** $100 to $200; some higher. **Remarks:** Part-time maker; first knife sold in 1975. **Mark:** Name on one side; "Lucky" on other.

CLARK, HOWARD F

115 35th Pl, Runnells, IA 50237, Phone: 515-966-2126, howard@mvforge.com; Web: mvforge.com

Specialties: Currently Japanese-style swords. **Patterns:** Katana. **Technical:** Forges L6 and 1086. **Prices:** $1200 to 5000. **Remarks:** Full-time maker; first knife sold in 1979. Doing business as Morgan Valley Forge. Prior **Mark:** Block letters and serial number on folders; anvil/initials logo on straight knives. Current **Mark:** Two character kanji "Big Ear."

CLARK, JASON

24896 77th Rd., O'Brien, FL 32071, Phone: 386-935-2922, jclark@clarkcustomknives.com; Web: www.clarkcustomknives.com

Specialties: Frame-lock and LinerLock folders. **Patterns:** Drop points, tantos, Persians, clip points, razors and wharncliffes. **Technical:** Sole authorship of knives, constructing 100 percent in house, including designing, cutting, shaping, grinding, heat treating, fitting and finishing. Top quality materials and components, as well as hand-rubbed finishes, media blasting, stonewashing, anodizing and polishing. Licensed to use IKBS (Ikoma Korth Bearing System). **Remarks:** Part-time maker. **Mark:** Cross with initials incorporated.

CLARK, NATE

604 Baird Dr, Yoncalla, OR 97499, nateclarkknives@hotmail.com; Web: www.nateclarkknives.com

Specialties: Automatics (push button and hidden release) ATS-34 mirror polish or satin finish, Damascus, pearl, ivory, abalone, woods, bone, Micarta, G-10, filework and carving and sheath knives. **Prices:** $100 to $2500. **Remarks:** Full-time knifemaker since 1996. **Mark:** Nate Clark on spring, spacer or blade.

CLARK, R W

R.W. CLARK CUSTOM KNIVES, 17602 W. Eugene Terrace, Surprise, AZ 85388-5047, Phone: 909-279-3494, info@rwclarkknives.com

Specialties: Military field knives and Asian hybrids. Hand carved leather sheaths. **Patterns:** Fixed blade hunters, field utility and military. Also presentation and collector grade knives. **Technical:** First maker to use liquid metals LM1 material in knives. Other materials include S30V, O1, stainless and carbon Damascus. **Prices:** $75 to $2000. Average price $300. **Remarks:** Started knifemaking in 1990, full-time in 2000. **Mark:** R.W. Clark, Custom, Corona, CA in standard football shape. Also uses three Japanese characters, spelling Clark, on Asian Hybrids.

CLINCO, MARCUS

821 Appelby Street, Venice, CA 90291, Phone: 818-610-9640, marcus@clincoknives.com; Web: www.clincoknives.com

Specialties: I make mostly fixed blade knives with an emphasis on everyday working and tactical models. Most of my knives are stock removal with the exception of my sole authored damascus blades. I have several integral models including a one piece tactical model named the viper. **Technical:** Most working knife models in ATS 34. Integrals in O-1, D-2 and 440 C. Damascus in 1080 and 15 N 20. Large camp and Bowie models in 5160 and D-2. Handle materials used include micarta, stabilized wood, G-10 and occasionally stag and ivory. **Prices:** $200 -$600.

COATS, KEN

317 5th Ave, Stevens Point, WI 54481, Phone: 715-544-0115

Specialties: Does own jigged bone scales **Patterns:** Traditional slip joints -shadow patterns **Technical:** ATS-34 Blades and springs. Milled frames. Grinds ATS-34, 440C. Stainless blades and backsprings. Does all own heat treating and freeze cycle. Blades are drawn to 60RC. Nickel silver or brass bolsters on folders are soldered, neutralized and pinned. Handles are jigged bone, hardwoods antler, and Micarta. Cuts and jigs own bone, usually shades of brown or green. **Prices:** $300 and up

COCKERHAM, LLOYD

1717 Carolyn Ave, Denham Springs, IA 70726, Phone: 225-665-1565

COFFEE, JIM

2785 Rush Rd., Norton, OH 44203, Phone: 330-631-3355, jcoffee735@aol.com; Web: jcoffeecustomknives.com

Specialties: Stock Removal, hunters, skinners, fighters. **Technical:** Bowie handle material -stabilized wood, micarta, mammoth ivory, stag. Full tang and hidden tang. Steels -0-1, d-2, 5160, damascus **Prices:** $150 to $500 and up. **Remarks:** Part-time maker since 2008.**Mark:** full name in a football etch.

COFFEY, BILL

68 Joshua Ave, Clovis, CA 93611, Phone: 559-299-4259

Specialties: Working and fancy straight knives and folders of his design. **Patterns:** Hunters, fighters, utility, LinerLock® folders and fantasy knives. **Technical:** Grinds 440C, ATS-34, A-Z and commercial Damascus. **Prices:** $250 to $1000; some to $2500. **Remarks:** Full-time maker. First knife sold in 1993. **Mark:** First and last name, city, state.

COFFMAN, DANNY

541 Angel Dr S, Jacksonville, AL 36265-5787, Phone: 256-435-1619

Specialties: Straight knives and folders of his design. Now making liner locks for $650 to $1200 with natural handles and contrasting Damascus blades and bolsters. **Patterns:** Hunters, locking and slip-joint folders. **Technical:** Grinds Damascus, 440C and D2.

Offers filework and engraving. **Prices:** $100 to $400; some to $800. **Remarks:** Spare-time maker; first knife sold in 1992. Doing business as Customs by Coffman. **Mark:** Last name stamped or engraved.

COHEA, JOHN M
114 Rogers Dr., Nettleton, MS 38855, Phone: 662-322-5916, jhncohea@hotmail.com
Web: http://jmcknives.blademakers.com
   Specialties: Frontier style knives, hawks, and leather. **Patterns:** Bowies, hunters, patch/neck knives, tomahawks, and friction folders. **Technical:** Makes both forged and stock removal knives using high carbon steels and damascus. Uses natural handle materials that include antler, bone, ivory, horn, and figured hardwoods. Also makes rawhide covered sheaths that include fringe, tacks, antique trade beads, and other period correct materials. **Prices:** $100 -$1500, some higher. **Remarks:** Part-time maker, first knife sold in 1999. **Mark:** COHEA stamped on riccasso.

COHEN, N J (NORM)
2408 Sugarcone Rd, Baltimore, MD 21209, Phone: 410-484-3841, inquiry@njcknives.com; Web: www.njcknives.com
   Specialties: Working class knives. **Patterns:** Hunters, skinners, bird knives, push daggers, boots, kitchen and practical customer designs. **Technical:** Stock removal 440C, ATS-34, CPM 154 and D2. Handles of Micarta, Corian and stabilized woods. **Prices:** $50 to $250. **Remarks:** Part-time maker; first knife sold in 1982. **Mark:** NJC engraved.

COLE, JAMES M
505 Stonewood Blvd, Bartonville, TX 76226, Phone: 817-430-0302, dogcole@swbell.net

COLEMAN, JOHN A
7325 Bonita Way, Citrus Heights, CA 95610-3003, Phone: 916-335-1568, slimsknifes@yahoo.com
   Specialties: Minis, hunters, bowies of his design or yours. **Patterns:** Plain to fancy file back working knives. **Technical:** Grinds 440C, ATS-34, 145CM, D2, 1095, 5160, 01. Some hand-forged blades. Exotic woods bone, antler and some ivory. **Prices:** $100 to $500. **Remarks:** Does some carving in handles. Part-time maker. First knife sold in 1989. OKCA 2010 Award winner for best mini of show. **Mark:** Cowboy setting on log whittling Slim's Custom Knives above cowboy and name and state under cowboy.

COLLINS, LYNN M
138 Berkley Dr, Elyria, OH 44035, Phone: 440-366-7101
   Specialties: Working straight knives. **Patterns:** Field knives, boots and fighters. **Technical:** Grinds D2, 154CM and 440C. **Prices:** Start at $200. **Remarks:** Spare-time maker; first knife sold in 1980. **Mark:** Initials, asterisks.

COLTER, WADE
PO Box 2340, Colstrip, MT 59323, Phone: 406-748-4573; Shop: 406-748-2010, Fax: Cell: 406-740-1554
   Specialties: Fancy and embellished straight knives, folders and swords of his design; historical and period pieces. **Patterns:** Bowies, swords and folders. **Technical:** Hand forges 52100 ball bearing steel and L6, 1090, cable and chain Damascus from 5N20 and 1084. Carves and makes sheaths. **Prices:** $250 to $3500. **Remarks:** SemiRetired; first knife sold in 1990. Doing business as "Colter's Hell" Forge. **Mark:** Initials on left side ricasso.

COLWELL, KEVIN
Professor's Forge, 15 Stony Hill Rd., Cheshire, CA 06410, Phone: 203-439-2223, colwellk2@southernct.edu
   Specialties: Swords (Dao, jian, seax, messer, baurnwehr, etc.) and knives (puukko, Viking-style, hunters, skinners, bowies, fighters and chef's knives). **Technical:** Forges blades, vivid pattern welding or subtle pattern welding with beautiful hamon and grain structure. **Prices:** $175 to $500, swords $900 and up, depending upon what customer wants in adornment. **Remarks:** Associate professor of psychology.

CONKLIN, GEORGE L
Box 902, Ft. Benton, MT 59442, Phone: 406-622-3268, Fax: 406-622-3410, 7bbgrus@3rivers.net
   Specialties: Designer and manufacturer of the "Brisket Breaker." **Patterns:** Hunters, utility/camp knives and hatchets. **Technical:** Grinds 440C, ATS-34, D2, 1095, 154CM and 5160. Offers some forging and heat-treats for others. Offers some jewelling. **Prices:** $65 to $200; some to $1000. **Remarks:** Full-time maker. Doing business as Rocky Mountain Knives. **Mark:** Last name in script.

CONLEY, BOB
1013 Creasy Rd, Jonesboro, TN 37659, Phone: 423-753-3302
   Specialties: Working straight knives and folders. **Patterns:** Lockers, two-blades, gents, hunters, traditional-styles, straight hunters. **Technical:** Grinds 440C, 154CM and ATS-34. Engraves. **Prices:** $250 to $450; some to $600. **Remarks:** Full-time maker; first knife sold in 1979. **Mark:** Full name, city, state.

CONN JR., C T
206 Highland Ave, Attalla, AL 35954, Phone: 205-538-7688
   Specialties: Working folders, some fancy. **Patterns:** Full range of folding knives. **Technical:** Grinds O2, 440C and 154CM. **Prices:** $125 to $300; some to $600. **Remarks:** Part-time maker; first knife sold in 1982. **Mark:** Name.

CONNOLLY, JAMES
2486 Oro-Quincy Hwy, Oroville, CA 95966, Phone: 530-534-5363, rjconnolly@sbcglobal.net
   Specialties: Classic working and using knives of his design. **Patterns:** Boots, Bowies, daggers and swords. **Technical:** Grinds ATS-34, BG42, A2, O1. **Prices:** $100 to $500;

some to $1500. **Remarks:** Part-time maker; first knife sold in 1980. Doing business as Gold Rush Designs. **Mark:** First initial, last name, Handmade.

CONNOR, JOHN W
PO Box 12981, Odessa, TX 79768-2981, Phone: 915-362-6901

CONNOR, MICHAEL
Box 502, Winters, TX 79567, Phone: 915-754-5602
   Specialties: Straight knives, period pieces, some folders. **Patterns:** Hunters to camp knives to traditional locking folders to Bowies. **Technical:** Forges 5160, O1, 1084 steels and his own Damascus. **Prices:** Moderate to upscale. **Remarks:** Spare-time maker; first knife sold in 1974. ABS Master Smith 1983. **Mark:** Last name, M.S.

CONTI, JEFFREY D
4441 Feigley Rd. W, Port Orchard, WA 98367, Phone: 253-447-4660, Fax: 253-512-8629
   Specialties: Working straight knives. **Patterns:** Fighters and survival knives; hunters, camp knives and fishing knives. **Technical:** Grinds D2, 154CM and O1. Engraves. **Prices:** Start at $80. **Remarks:** Part-time maker; first knife sold in 1980. Does own heat treating. **Mark:** Initials, year, steel type, name and number of knife.

CONWAY, JOHN
13301 100th Place NE, Kirkland, WA 98034, Phone: 425-823-2821, jcknives@Frontier.com
   Specialties: Folders; working and Damascus. Straight knives, camp, utility and fighting knives. **Patterns:** LinerLock® folders of own design. Hidden tang straight knives of own design. **Technical:** Flat grinds forged carbon steels and own Damascus steel, including mosaic. **Prices:** $300 to $850. **Remarks:** Part-time maker since 1999. **Mark:** Oval with stylized initials J C inset.

COOGAN, ROBERT
1560 Craft Center Dr, Smithville, TN 37166, Phone: 615-597-6801, http://iweb.tntech.edu/rcoogan/
   Specialties: One-of-a-kind knives. **Patterns:** Unique items like ulu-style Appalachian herb knives. **Technical:** Forges; his Damascus is made from nickel steel and W1. **Prices:** Start at $100. **Remarks:** Part-time maker; first knife sold in 1979. **Mark:** Initials or last name in script.

COOK, JAMES R
455 Anderson Rd, Nashville, AR 71852, Phone: 870 845 5173, jr@jrcookknives.com; Web: www.jrcookknives.com
   Specialties: Working straight knives and folders of his design or to customer specs. **Patterns:** Bowies, hunters and camp knives. **Technical:** Forges 1084 and high-carbon Damascus. **Prices:** $500 to $10000. **Remarks:** Full-time maker; first knife sold in 1986. **Mark:** First and middle initials, last name.

COOK, LOUISE
475 Robinson Ln, Ozark, IL 62972, Phone: 618-777-2932
   Specialties: Working and using straight knives of her design and to customer specs; period pieces. **Patterns:** Bowies, hunters and utility/camp knives. **Technical:** Forges 5160. Filework; pin work; silver wire inlay. **Prices:** Start at $50/inch. **Remarks:** Part-time maker; first knife sold in 1990. Doing business as Panther Creek Forge. **Mark:** First name and Journeyman stamp on one side; panther head on the other.

COOK, MIKE
475 Robinson Ln, Ozark, IL 62972, Phone: 618-777-2932
   Specialties: Traditional working and using straight knives of his design and to customer specs. **Patterns:** Bowies, hunters and utility/camp knives. **Technical:** Forges 5160. Filework; pin work. **Prices:** Start at $50/inch. **Remarks:** Spare-time maker; first knife sold in 1991. **Mark:** First initial, last name and Journeyman stamp on one side; panther head on the other.

COOK, MIKE A
10927 Shilton Rd, Portland, MI 48875, Phone: 517-242-1352, macook@hughes.net
Web: www.artofishi.com
   Specialties: Fancy/embellished and period pieces of his design. **Patterns:** Daggers, fighters and hunters. **Technical:** Stone bladed knives in agate, obsidian and jasper. Scrimshaws; opal inlays. **Prices:** $60 to $300; some to $800. **Remarks:** Part-time maker; first knife sold in 1988. Doing business as Art of Ishi. **Mark:** Initials and year.

COOMBS JR., LAMONT
546 State Rt 46, Bucksport, ME 04416, Phone: 207-469-3057, Fax: 207-469-3057, theknifemaker@hotmail.com; Web: www.knivesby.com/coombs-knives.html
   Specialties: Classic fancy and embellished straight knives; traditional working and using straight knives. Knives of his design and to customer specs. **Patterns:** Hunters, folders and utility/camp knives. **Technical:** Hollow-and flat-grinds ATS-34, 440C, A2, D2 and O1; grinds Damascus from other makers. **Prices:** $100 to $500; some to $3500. **Remarks:** Full-time maker; first knife sold in 1988. **Mark:** Last name on banner, handmade underneath.

COON, RAYMOND C
21135 S.E. Tillstrom Rd, Damascus, OR 97089, Phone: 503-658-2252, Raymond@damascusknife.com; Web: Damascusknife.com
   Specialties: Working straight knives in standard patterns. **Patterns:** Hunters, Bowies, daggers, boots and axes. **Technical:** Forges high-carbon steel and Damascus or 97089. **Prices:** Start at $235. **Remarks:** Full-time maker; does own leatherwork, makes own Damascus, daggers; first knife sold in 1995. **Mark:** First initial, last name.

COOPER, PAUL
9 Woods St., Woburn, MA 01801, Phone: 781-938-0519, byksm@yahoo.com
   Specialties: Forged, embellished, hand finished fixed-blade knives. **Patterns:** One of a

kind designs, often inspired by traditional and historic pieces. **Technical:** Works in tool steel, damascus and natural materials. **Prices:** $500 -$2000. **Remarks:** Part-time maker, formally apprenticed under J.D. Smith. Sold first piece in 2006. **Mark:** Letter C inside bleeding heart.

COPELAND, THOM
136 Blue Bayou Ests., Nashville, AR 71852, tcope@cswnet.com
Specialties: Hand forged fixed blades; hunters, Bowies and camp knives. **Remarks:** Member of ABS and AKA (Arkansas Knifemakers Association). **Mark:** Copeland.

COPPINS, DANIEL
8651 B Georgetown Rd., Cambridge, OH 43725, Phone: 740-680-2438, Web: www.battlehorseknives.com or www.kickassknives.com
Specialties: Bushcraft knives, tacticals, hunting. **Technical:** Grinds 440C, D2. Antler handles. **Patterns:** Many. **Prices:** $40 to $600. **Remarks:** Sold first knife in 2002; formally Blind Horse Knives. **Mark:** Horse-Kicking Donkey.

CORBY, HAROLD
218 Brandonwood Dr, Johnson City, TN 37604, Phone: 423-926-9781
Specialties: Large fighters and Bowies; self-protection knives; art knives. Along with art knives and combat knives, Corby now has a all new automatic MO.PB1, also side lock MO LL-1 with titanium liners G-10 handles. **Patterns:** Sub-hilt fighters and hunters. **Technical:** Grinds 154CM, ATS-34 and 440C. **Prices:** $200 to $6000. **Remarks:** Full-time maker; first knife sold in 1969. Doing business as Knives by Corby. **Mark:** Last name.

CORDOVA, JOEY
1594 S. Hill Rd., Bernalillo, NM 87004, Phone: 505-410-3809, joeyscordova@gmail.com; www.joelouiknives.com
Patterns: High-carbon full-tang knives and hidden-tang bowies, as well as small neck knives. **Technical:** Differentially heat-treats blades producing hamons (temper lines). **Prices:** $120 and up. **Remarks:** Full-time knifemaker and part-time ring maker.

CORDOVA, JOSEPH G
1450 Lillie Dr, Bosque Farms, NM 87068, Phone: 505-869-3912, kcordova@rt66.com
Specialties: One-of-a-kind designs, some to customer specs. **Patterns:** Fighter called the 'Gladiator', hunters, boots and cutlery. **Technical:** Forges 1095, 5160; grinds ATS-34, 440C and 154CM. **Prices:** Moderate to upscale. **Remarks:** Full-time maker; first knife sold in 1953. Past chairman of American Bladesmith Society. **Mark:** Cordova made.

CORICH, VANCE
12012 W. Dumbarton Dr., Morrison, CO 80465, Phone: 303-999-1553, vancecorichcutlery@gmail.com; https://sites.google.com/site/vancesproject/
Specialties: Fixed blades, usually 2 to 7 inches, recurved blades, locking-liner folders and friction folders. **Technical:** Differential heat treating on high-carbon steels. **Prices:** $150 to $1,000. **Remarks:** Part-time maker working on going full time. **Mark:** Stamped "VCC" or VANCE.

CORKUM, STEVE
34 Basehoar School Rd, Littlestown, PA 17340, Phone: 717-359-9563, sco7129849@aol.com; Web: www.hawkknives.com

CORNETT, BRIAN
1511 N. College St., McKinney, TX 75069, Phone: 972-310-7289, devildogdesign@tx.rr.com; www.d3devildogdesigns.com
Patterns: Tactical, hunting, neck knives and personal-defense tools. **Technical:** Stock removal of 1095, O1 tool steel, 52100, D2, CPM 154 and damascus. **Prices:** $50 to $300. **Remarks:** Full-time maker; first knife made in 2011. **Mark:** D3.

CORNWELL, JEFFREY
Treasure Art Blades, PO Box 244014, Anchorage, AK 99524, Phone: 907-887-1661, cornwellsjej@alaska.net
Specialties: Organic, sculptural shapes of original design from damascus steel and mokume gane. **Technical:** Blade creations from Robert Eggerling damascus and Mike Sakmar mokume. **Remarks:** Free-time maker. **Mark:** Stylized J inside a circle.

COSTA, SCOTT
409 Coventry Rd, Spicewood, TX 78669, Phone: 830-693-3431
Specialties: Working straight knives. **Patterns:** Hunters, skinners, axes, trophy sets, custom boxed steak sets, carving sets and bar sets. **Technical:** Grinds D2, ATS-34, 440 and Damascus. Heat-treats. **Prices:** $225 to $2000. **Remarks:** Full-time maker; first knife sold in 1985. **Mark:** Initials connected.

COTTRILL, JAMES I
1776 Ransburg Ave, Columbus, OH 43223, Phone: 614-274-0020
Specialties: Working straight knives of his design. **Patterns:** Caters to the boating and hunting crowd; cutlery. **Technical:** Grinds O1, D2 and 440C. Likes filework. **Prices:** $95 to $250; some to $500. **Remarks:** Full-time maker; first knife sold in 1977. **Mark:** Name, city, state, in oval logo.

COUSINO, GEORGE
7818 Norfolk, Onsted, MI 49265, Phone: 517-467-4911, cousinoknives@yahoo.com; Web: www.cousinoknives.com
Specialties: Hunters, Bowies using knives. **Patterns:** Hunters, Bowies, buckskinners, folders and daggers. **Technical:** Grinds 440C. **Prices:** $95 to $300. **Remarks:** Part-time maker; first knife sold in 1981. **Mark:** Last name.

COVER, JEFF
11355 Allen Rd, Potosi, MO 63664, Phone: 573-749-0008, jeffcovercustomknives@hotmail.com
Specialties: Folders and straight knives. **Patterns:** **Technical:** Various knife steels and handle materials. **Prices:** $70 to $500. **Mark:** Jeff Cover J.C. Custom Knives.

COVER, RAYMOND A
16235 State Hwy. U, Mineral Point, MO 63660, Phone: 573-749-3783
Specialties: High-tech working straight knives and folders in working patterns. **Patterns:** Slip joints, lockbacks, multi-blade folders. **Technical:** Various knife steels and handle materials. **Prices:** Swords from bare blades to complete high art $200 to $600. **Mark:** "R Cover"

COWLES, DON
1026 Lawndale Dr, Royal Oak, MI 48067, Phone: 248-541-4619, don@cowlesknives.com; Web: www.cowlesknives.com
Specialties: Straight, non-folding pocket knives of his design. **Patterns:** Gentlemen's pocket knives. **Technical:** Grinds CPM154, S30V, Damascus, Talonite. Engraves; pearl inlays in some handles. **Prices:** Start at $300. **Remarks:** Full-time maker; first knife sold in 1994. **Mark:** Full name with oak leaf.

COX, LARRY
701 W. 13th St, Murfreesboro, AR 71958, Phone: 870-258-2429, Fax: Cell: 870-557-8062
Patterns: Hunters, camp knives, Bowies, and skinners. **Technical:** Forges carbon steel 1084, 1080, 15N29, 5160 and Damascus. Forges own pattern welded Damascus as well as doing own heat treat. **Prices:** $150 and up. **Remarks:** Sole ownership; knives and sheaths. Part-time maker; first knife sold in 2007. Member ABS and Arkansas Knifemakers Association. **Mark:** COX.

COX, SAM
1756 Love Springs Rd, Gaffney, SC 29341, Phone: 864-489-1892, Web: www.coxworks.com
Remarks: Started making knives in 1981 for another maker. 1st knife sold under own name in 1983. Full-time maker 1985-2009. Retired in 2010. Now part time. **Mark:** Different logo each year.

COYE, BILL
PO Box 470684, Tulsa, OK 74147, Phone: 918-232-5721, info@coyeknives.com; Web: www.coyeknives.com
Specialties: Tactical and utility knives. **Patterns:** Fighters and utility. **Technical:** Grinds CPM154CM, 154CM, CTS-XHP and Elmax stainless steels. **Prices:** $210 to $320. **Remarks:** Part-time maker. First knife sold in 2009. **Mark:** COYE.

CRADDOCK, MIKE
300 Blythe Dr., Thomasville, NC 27360, Phone: 336-382-8461, ncbladesmith@gmail.com
Specialties: Fighters, bowies. **Patterns:** Hunters and working knives. **Technical:** Forges and grinds high-carbon steel, and does own damascus. **Prices:** $350 to $1,500. **Mark:** CRADDOCK.

CRAIG, ROGER L
2617 SW Seabrook Ave, Topeka, KS 66614, Phone: 785-249-4109
Specialties: Working and camp knives, some fantasy; all his design. **Patterns:** Fighters, hunter. **Technical:** Grinds 1095 and 5160. Most knives have file work. **Prices:** $50 to $250. **Remarks:** Part-time maker; first knife sold in 1991. Doing business as Craig Knives. **Mark:** Last name-Craig.

CRAIN, JACK W
PO Box 212, Granbury, TX 76048, jack@jackcrainknives.com Web: www.jackcrainknives.com
Specialties: Fantasy and period knives; combat and survival knives. **Patterns:** One-of-a-kind art or fantasy daggers, swords and Bowies; survival knives. **Technical:** Forges Damascus; grinds stainless steel. Carves. **Prices:** $350 to $2500; some to $20,000. **Remarks:** Full-time maker; first knife sold in 1969. Designer and maker of the knives seen in the films Dracula 2000, Executive Decision, Demolition Man, Predator I and II, Commando, Die Hard I and II, Road House, Ford Fairlane and Action Jackson, and television shows War of the Worlds, Air Wolf, Kung Fu: The Legend Cont. and Tales of the Crypt. **Mark:** Stylized crane.

CRAMER, BRENT
PO BOX 99, Wheatland, IN 47597, Phone: 812-881-9961, Bdcramer@juno.com Web: BDCramerKnives.com
Specialties: Traditional and custom working and using knives. **Patterns:** Traditional single blade slip-joint folders and standard fixed blades. **Technical:** Stock removal only. Pivot bushing construction on folders. Steel: D-2, 154 CM, ATS-34, CPM-D2, CPM-154CM, O-1, 52100, A-2. All steels heat treated in shop with LN Cryo. Handle Material: Stag, Bone, Wood, Ivory, and Micarta. **Prices:** $150 -$550. **Remarks:** Part-time maker. First fixed blade sold in 2003. First folder sold in 2007. **Mark:** BDC and B.D.Cramer.

CRAWFORD, PAT AND WES
205 N. Center, West Memphis, AR 72301, Phone: 870-732-2452, patcrawford1@earthlink.com; Web: www.crawfordknives.com
Specialties: Stainless steel Damascus. High-tech working self-defense and combat types and folders. **Patterns:** Tactical-more fancy knives now. **Technical:** Grinds S30V. **Prices:** $400 to $2000. **Remarks:** Full-time maker; first knife sold in 1973. **Mark:** Last name.

CRAWLEY, BRUCE R
16 Binbrook Dr, Croydon, VIC, AUSTRALIA 3136
Specialties: Folders. **Patterns:** Hunters, lockback folders and Bowies. **Technical:** Grinds 440C, ATS-34 and commercial Damascus. Offers filework and mirror polish. **Prices:** $160 to $3500. **Remarks:** Part-time maker; first knife sold in 1990. **Mark:** Initials.

CRENSHAW, AL
Rt 1 Box 717, Eufaula, OK 74432, Phone: 918-452-2128
Specialties: Folders of his design and in standard patterns. **Patterns:** Hunters, locking folders, slip-joint folders, multi blade folders. **Technical:** Grinds 440C, D2 and ATS-34. Does filework on back springs and blades; offers scrimshaw on some handles. **Prices:** $150 to $300; some higher. **Remarks:** Full-time maker; first knife sold in 1981. Doing business as A. Crenshaw Knives. **Mark:** First initial, last name, Lake Eufaula, state stamped; first initial last name in rainbow; Lake Eufaula across bottom with Okla. in middle.

CREWS, RANDY
627 Cricket Trail Rd., Patriot, OH 45658, Phone: 740-379-2329, randy.crews@sbcglobal.net
Specialties: Fixed blades, bowies and hunters. **Technical:** 440C, Alabama Damascus, 1095 with file work. Stock removal method. **Prices:** Start at $150. **Remarks:** Collected knives for 30 years. Part-time maker; first knife made in 2002. **Mark:** Crews Patriot OH.

CRIST, ZOE
2274 Deep Gap Rd., Flat Rock, NC 28731, Phone: 828-275-6689, zoe@zoecristknives.com Web: www.zoecristknives.com
Specialties: San mai and stainless steel. Custom damascus and traditional damascus working and art knives. Also makes Mokume. Works to customer specs. **Patterns:** All damascus hunters, bowies, fighters, neck, boot and high-end art knives. **Technical:** Makes all his own damascus steel from 1095, L6, 15n20. Forges all knives, heat treats, filework, differential heat treat. **Prices:** $150 -$2500. **Remarks:** Full-time maker, has been making knives since 1988, went full-time 2009. Also makes own leather sheaths. **Mark:** Small "z" with long tail on left side of blade at ricasso.

CROCKFORD, JACK
1859 Harts Mill Rd, Chamblee, GA 30341, Phone: 770-457-4680
Specialties: Lockback folders. **Patterns:** Hunters, fishing and camp knives, traditional folders. **Technical:** Grinds A2, D2, ATS-34 and 440C. Engraves and scrimshaws. **Prices:** Start at $175. **Remarks:** Part-time maker; first knife sold in 1975. **Mark:** Name.

CROSS, KEVIN
5 Pear Orchard Rd., Portland, CT 06480, Phone: 860-894-2385, kevincross@comcast.net; Web: www.kevincrossknives.com
Specialties: Working/using and presentation grade fixed-blade knives and custom kitchen knives. **Patterns:** Hunters, skinners, fighters. Bowies, camp knives. **Technical:** Stock removal maker. Uses O1, 1095, 154 CPM as well as Damascus from Eggerling, Ealy, Donnelly, Nichols, Thomas and others. Most handles are natural materials such as burled and spalted woods, stag and ancient ivory. **Prices:** $200 -$1,200. **Remarks:** Part-time maker. First knife sold around 1997. **Mark:** Name.

CROSS, ROBERT
RMB 200B, Manilla Rd, Tamworth, NSW, AUSTRALIA 2340, Phone: 067-618385

CROTTS, DAN
PO Box 68, Elm Springs, AR 72728, Phone: 479-248-7116, dancrottsknives@yahoo.com Web: www.facebook.com/dancrottsknives
Specialties: User grade, hunting, tactical and folders. **Technical:** High-end tool steel. **Prices:** $2200. **Remarks:** Specializes in making performance blades. **Mark:** Crotts.

CROUCH, BUBBA
POB 461, Pleasanton, TX 78064, Phone: 210-846-6890, tommycrouch69@gmail.com
Specialties: Slip joints, straight blades. **Patterns:** Case style. Offers filework. **Technical:** ATS-34 and commercial damascus. Using stag, bone and mammoth ivory handle material. **Prices:** $250 to $1,200. **Remarks:** Part-time maker, first knife sold in 2010. **Mark:** Crouch.

CROWDER, GARY L
461401 E. 1125 Rd., Sallisaw, OK 74955, Phone: 918-775-9009, gcrowder99@yahoo.com
Specialties: Folders, multi-blades. **Patterns:** Traditional with a few sheath knives. **Technical:** Flat grinds ATS-34, D2 and others, as well as Damascus via stock-removal. **Prices:** $150 to $600. **Remarks:** Retired, part-time maker. First knife sold in 1994. **Mark:** small acid-etched "Crowder" on blade.

CROWDER, ROBERT
Box 1374, Thompson Falls, MT 59873, Phone: 406-827-4754
Specialties: Traditional working knives to customer specs. **Patterns:** Hunters, Bowies, fighters and fillets. **Technical:** Grinds ATS-34, 154CM, 440C, Vascowear and commercial Damascus. **Prices:** $225 to $500; some to $2500. **Remarks:** Full-time maker; first knife sold in 1985. **Mark:** R Crowder signature & Montana.

CROWELL, JAMES L
676 Newnata Cutoff, Mtn. View, AR 72560, Phone: 870-746-4215, crowellknives@yahoo.com; Web: www.crowellknives.com
Specialties: Bowie knives; fighters and working knives. **Patterns:** Hunters, fighters, Bowies, daggers and folders. Period pieces: War hammers, Japanese and European. **Technical:** Forges 10 series carbon steels as well as O1, L6, W2 and his own damascus. "Flame painted" hamons (temper lines). **Prices:** $525 to $5,500; some to $8,500. **Remarks:** Full-time maker; first knife sold in 1980. Earned ABS Master Bladesmith in 1986. 2011 Marked 25 years as an ABS Mastersmith. **Mark:** A shooting star.

CROWL, PETER
5786 County Road 10, Waterloo, IN 46793, Phone: 260-488-2532, pete@petecrowlknives.com; Web: www.petecrowlknives.com
Specialties: Bowie, hunters. **Technical:** Forges 5160, 1080, W2, 52100. **Prices:** $200 and up. **Remarks:** ABS Journeyman smith. **Mark:** Last name in script.

CROWNER, JEFF
2621 Windsor Pl., Plano, TX 75075, Phone: 541-201-3182, Fax: 541-579-3762
Specialties: Custom knife maker. I make some of the following: wilderness survival blades, martial art weapons, hunting blades. **Technical:** I differentially heat treat every knife. I use various steels like 5160, L-6, Cable Damascus, 52100, 6150, and some stainless types. I use the following for handle materials: TeroTuf by Columbia Industrial products and exotic hardwoods and horn. I make my own custom sheaths as well with either kydex or leather.

CROWTHERS, MARK F
PO Box 4641, Rolling Bay, WA 98061-0641, Phone: 206-842-7501

CUCCHIARA, MATT
387 W. Hagler, Fresno, CA 93711, Phone: 559-917-2328, matt@cucchiaraknives.com Web: www.cucchiaraknives.com
Specialties: I make large and small, plain or hand carved Ti handled Tactical framelock folders. All decoration and carving work done by maker. Also known for my hand carved Ti pocket clips. **Prices:** Start at around $400 and go as high as $1500 or so.

CULHANE, SEAN K.
8 Ranskroon Dr., Horizon, Roodepoort, 1740, SOUTH AFRICA, Phone: +27 82 453-1741, sculhane@wbs.co.za; www.culhaneknives.co.za
Specialties Traditional working straight knives and folders in standard patterns and to customer specifications. **Patterns:** Fighters, hunters, kitchen cutlery, utility and Scottish dirks and sgian dubhs. **Technical:** Hollow grinding Sandvik 12C27 and commercial damascus. Full process, including heat treating and sheaths done by maker. **Prices:** From $180 up, depending on design and materials. **Remarks:** Part-time maker; first knife sold in 1988. **Mark:** First and surname in Gothic script curved over the word "Maker."

CULVER, STEVE
5682 94th St, Meriden, KS 66512, Phone: 785-230-2505, Web: www.culverart.com; Facebook: Steve Culver Knives; YouTube: SteveCulverMS1
Specialties: Edged weapons. Spiral-welded damascus gun barrels, collectible and functional. **Patterns:** Bowies, daggers, hunters, folders and combination weapons. **Technical:** Forges carbon steels and his own damascus. Stock removal of stainless steel for some folders. **Prices:** $500 to $50,000. **Remarks:** Full-time maker; also builds muzzle-loading pistols. **Mark:** Last name, MS.

CUMMING, BOB
CUMMING KNIVES, 35 Manana Dr, Cedar Crest, NM 87008, Phone: 505-286-0509, cumming@comcast.net; Web: www.cummingknives.com
Specialties: One-of-a-kind exhibition grade custom Bowie knives, exhibition grade and working hunters, bird & trout knives, salt and fresh water fillet knives. Low country oyster knives, custom tanto's plains Indian style sheaths & custom leather, all types of exotic handle materials, scrimshaw and engraving. Added folders in 2006. Custom oyster knives. **Prices:** $95 to $3500 and up. **Remarks:** Mentored by the late Jim Nolen, sold first knife in 1978 in Denmark. Retired U.S. Foreign Service Officer. Member NCCKG. **Mark:** Stylized CUMMING.

CURTISS, DAVID
Curtiss Knives, PO Box 902, Granger, IN 46530, Phone: 574-651-2158, david@curtissknives.com; Web: www.curtissknives.com
Specialties: Specialize in custom tactical-style folders and flipper folders, with some of the best sellers being in the Nano and Cruze series. The Nano is now being produced by Boker Knives. Many new knife designs coming soon.

CURTISS, STEVE L
PO Box 448, Eureka, MT 59914, Phone: 406-889-5510, Fax: 406-889-5510, slc@bladerigger.com; Web: http://www.bladerigger.com
Specialties: True custom and semi-custom production (SCP), specialized concealment blades; advanced sheaths and tailored body harnessing systems. **Patterns:** Tactical/personal defense fighters, swords, utility and custom patterns. **Technical:** Grinds A2 and Talonite®; heat-treats. Sheaths: Kydex or Kydex-lined leather laminated or Kydex-lined with Rigger Coat™. Exotic materials available. **Prices:** $50 to $10,000. **Remarks:** Full-time maker. Doing business as Blade Rigger L.L.C. Martial artist and unique defense industry tools and equipment. **Mark:** For true custom: Initials and for SCP: Blade Rigger.

D

DAILEY, G E
577 Lincoln St, Seekonk, MA 02771, Phone: 508-336-5088, gedailey@msn.com; Web: www.gedailey.com
Specialties: One-of-a-kind exotic designed edged weapons. **Patterns:** Folders, daggers and swords. **Technical:** Reforges and grinds Damascus; prefers hollow-grinding. Engraves, carves, offers filework and sets stones and uses exotic gems and gold. **Prices:** Start at $1100. **Remarks:** Full-time maker. First knife sold in 1982. **Mark:** Last name or stylized initialed logo.

DAKE, C M
19759 Chef Menteur Hwy, New Orleans, LA 70129-9602, Phone: 504-254-0357, Fax: 504-254-9501
Specialties: Fancy working folders. **Patterns:** Front-lock lockbacks, button-lock folders. **Technical:** Grinds ATS-34 and Damascus. **Prices:** $500 to $2500; some higher. **Remarks:** Full-time maker; first knife sold in 1988. Doing business as Bayou Custom Cutlery. **Mark:** Last name.

DAKE, MARY H
Rt 5 Box 287A, New Orleans, LA 70129, Phone: 504-254-0357

DALEY, MARK
P.O. Box 427, Waubaushene, Ontario, CANADA L0K 2C0, Phone: 705-543-1080, mark@markdaleyknives.com
Specialties: Art knives with handles made of stainless steel, bronze, gold, silver, pearl and Shibuichi. Many of the maker's knives are also textured and/or carved. Mark Engraved "Mark Daley" or chiseled initials "MD."

DALLYN, KELLY
124 Deerbrook Place S.E., Calgary, AB, CANADA T2J 6J5, Phone: 403-475-3056, info@dallyn-knives.com Web: dallyn-knives.com
Specialties: Kitchen, utility, and hunting knives

DAMASTEEL STAINLESS DAMASCUS
3052 Isim Rd., Norman, OK 73026, Phone: 888-804-0683; 405-321-3614, damascus@newmex.com; Web: www.ssdamacus.com
Patterns: Rose, Odin's eye, 5, 20, 30 twists Hakkapelitta, TNT, and infinity, Big Rose, Mumin

DAMLOVAC, SAVA
10292 Bradbury Dr, Indianapolis, IN 46231, Phone: 317-839-4952
Specialties: Period pieces, fantasy, Viking, Moran type all Damascus daggers. **Patterns:** Bowies, fighters, daggers, Persian-style knives. **Technical:** Uses own Damascus, some stainless, mostly hand forges. **Prices:** $150 to $2500; some higher. **Remarks:** Full-time maker; first knife sold in 1993. Specialty, Bill Moran all Damascus dagger sets, in Moran-style wood case. **Mark:** "Sava" stamped in Damascus or etched in stainless.

D'ANDREA, JOHN
8517 N Linwood Loop, Citrus Springs, FL 34433-5045, Phone: 352-489-2803, shootist1@tampabay.rr.com
Specialties: Fancy working straight knives and folders with filework and distinctive leatherwork. **Patterns:** Hunters, fighters, daggers, folders and an occasional sword. **Technical:** Grinds ATS-34, 154CM, 440C and D2. **Prices:** $220 to $1000. **Remarks:** Part-time maker; first knife sold in 1986. **Mark:** First name, last initial imposed on samurai sword.

D'ANGELO, LAURENCE
14703 NE 17th Ave, Vancouver, WA 98686, Phone: 360-573-0546
Specialties: Straight knives of his design. **Patterns:** Bowies, hunters and locking folders. **Technical:** Grinds D2, ATS-34 and 440C. Hand makes all sheaths. **Prices:** $100 to $200. **Remarks:** Full-time maker; first knife sold in 1987. **Mark:** Football logo—first and middle initials, last name, city, state, Maker.

DANIEL, TRAVIS E
PO Box 1223, Thomaston, GA 30286, Phone: 252-362-1229, tedsknives@mail.com
Specialties: Traditional working straight knives of his design or to customer specs. **Patterns:** Hunters, fighters and utility/camp knives. **Technical:** Grinds ATS-34, 440-C, 154CM, forges his own Damascus. Stock removal. **Prices:** $90 to $1200. **Remarks:** Full-time maker; first knife sold in 1976. **Mark:** TED.

DANIELS, ALEX
1416 County Rd 415, Town Creek, AL 35672, Phone: 256-685-0943, akdknives@gmail.com; Web: http://alexdanielscustomknives.com
Specialties: Working and using straight knives and folders; period pieces, reproduction Bowies. **Patterns:** Mostly reproduction Bowies but offers full line of knives. **Technical:** BG-42, 440C, 1095, 52100 forged blades. **Prices:** $350 to $5500. **Remarks:** Full-time maker; first knife sold in 1963. **Mark:** First and middle initials, last name, city and state.

DANNEMANN, RANDY
RIM RANCH, 27752 P25 Rd, Hotchkiss, CO 81419, randann14@gmail.com
Specialties: Hunting knives. **Patterns:** Utility hunters, trout. **Technical:** 440C and D2.Price: $95 to $450. **Remarks:** First knife sold 1974. **Mark:** R. Dannemann Colorado or stamped Dannemann.

DARBY, DAVID T
30652 S 533 Rd, Cookson, OK 74427, Phone: 918-457-4868, knfmkr@fullnet.net
Specialties: Forged blades only, all styles. **Prices:** $350 and up. **Remarks:** ABS Journeyman Smith. **Mark:** Stylized quillion dagger incorporates last name (Darby).

DARBY, JED
7878 E Co Rd 50 N, Greensburg, IN 47240, Phone: 812-663-2696
Specialties: Traditional working/using straight knives of his design and to customer specs. **Patterns:** Bowies, hunters and utility/camp knives. **Technical:** Grinds 440C, ATS-34 and Damascus. **Prices:** $70 to $550; some to $1000. **Remarks:** Full-time maker; first knife sold in 1992. Doing business as Darby Knives. **Mark:** Last name and year.

DARBY, RICK
71 Nestingrock Ln, Levittown, PA 19054
Specialties: Working straight knives. **Patterns:** Boots, fighters and hunters with mirror finish. **Technical:** Grinds 440C and CPM440V. **Prices:** $125 to $300. **Remarks:** Part-time maker; first knife sold in 1974. **Mark:** First and middle initials, last name.

DARCEY, CHESTER L
1608 Dominik Dr, College Station, TX 77840, Phone: 979-696-1656, DarceyKnives@yahoo.com
Specialties: Lockback, LinerLock® and scale release folders. **Patterns:** Bowies, hunters and utilities. **Technical:** Stock removal on carbon and stainless steels, forge own Damascus. **Prices:** $200 to $1000. **Remarks:** Part-time maker, first knife sold in 1999. **Mark:** Last name in script.

DARK, ROBERT
2218 Huntington Court, Oxford, AL 36203, Phone: 256-831-4645, dark@darkknives.com; Web: www.darkknives.com
Specialties: Fixed blade working knives of maker's designs. Works with customer designed specifications. **Patterns:** Hunters, Bowies, camp knives, kitchen/utility, bird and trout. Standard patterns and customer designed. **Technical:** Forged and stock removal. Works with high carbon, stainless and Damascus steels. Hollow and flat grinds. **Prices:** $175 to $750. **Remarks:** Sole authorship knives and custom leather sheaths. Full-time maker. **Mark:** "R Dark" on left side of blade.

DARPINIAN, DAVE
PO Box 2643, Olathe, KS 66063, Phone: 913-244-7114, darpo1956@yahoo.com Web: www.kansasknives.org
Specialties: Hunters and Persian fighters with natural handle materials. **Patterns:** Full range of straight knives including art daggers. **Technical:** Art grinds damascus and clay-tempered 1095. **Prices:** $300 to $1000. **Remarks:** First knife sold in 1986, part-time maker, member of Kansas Custom Knifemakers Association. **Mark:** Last name on the spline.

DAUGHTERY, TONY
18661 Daughtery Ln., Loxley, AL 36551, Phone: 251-964-5670 or 251-213-0461

DAVIDSON, EDMUND
3345 Virginia Ave, Goshen, VA 24439, Phone: 540-997-5651, davidson.edmund@gmail.com; Web: www.edmunddavidson.com
Specialties: High class art integrals. **Patterns:** Many hunters and art models. **Technical:** CPM 154-CM. **Prices:** $100 to infinity. **Remarks:** Full-time maker; first knife sold in 1986. **Mark:** Name in deer head or custom logos.

DAVIDSON, SCOTT
SOLID ROCK KNIVES, 149 Pless Cir., Alto, GA 30510, Phone: 678-316-1318, Fax: 770-869-0882, solidrockknives@bellsouth.net
Specialties: Tactical knives, some hunters, skinners, bird-and-trout and neck knives. **Technical:** Stock-removal method of blade making, using CPM S30V, 440C and ATS-34 steels, also O1 and 1095HC tool steels. **Prices:** $100 to $1,200, depending on materials used. **Remarks:** Part-time maker; first knife made in 1996. **Mark:** "Ichthys," the Christian fish, with maker's name and address in or around the fish.

DAVIS, BARRY L
4262 US 20, Castleton, NY 12033, Phone: 518-477-5036, daviscustomknives@yahoo.com
Specialties: Collector grade Damascus folders. Traditional designs with focus on turn-of-the-century techniques employed. Sole authorship. Forges own Damascus, does all carving, filework, gold work and piquet. Uses only natural handle material. Enjoys doing multi-blade as well as single blade folders and daggers. **Prices:** Prices range from $2000 to $7000. **Remarks:** First knife sold in 1980.

DAVIS, CHARLIE
ANZA KNIVES, PO Box 457, Lakeside, CA 92040-9998, Phone: 619-561-9445, Fax: 619-390-6283, sales@anzaknives.com; Web: www.anzaknives.com
Specialties: Fancy and embellished working straight knives of his design. **Patterns:** Hunters, camp and utility knives. **Technical:** Grinds high-carbon files. **Prices:** $20 to $185, custom depends. **Remarks:** Full-time maker; first knife sold in 1980. Now offers custom. **Mark:** ANZA U.S.A.

DAVIS, DON
8415 Coyote Run, Loveland, CO 80537-9665, Phone: 970-669-9016, Fax: 970-669-8072
Specialties: Working straight knives in standard patterns or to customer specs. **Patterns:** Hunters, utility knives, skinners and survival knives. **Technical:** Grinds 440C, ATS-34. **Prices:** $75 to $250. **Remarks:** Full-time maker; first knife sold in 1985. **Mark:** Signature, city and state.

DAVIS, JESSE W
3853 Peyton Rd., Coldwater, MS 38618, Phone: 901-849-7250, jessewdavis@yahoo.com
Specialties: Working straight knives and boots in standard patterns and to customer specs. **Patterns:** Boot knives, daggers, fighters, subhilts & Bowies. **Technical:** Grinds A2, D2, 440C and commercial Damascus. **Prices:** $125 to $1000. **Remarks:** Full-time maker; first knife sold in 1977. Former member Knifemakers Guild (in good standing). **Mark:** Name or initials.

DAVIS, JOEL
74538 165th, Albert Lea, MN 56007, Phone: 507-377-0808, joelknives@yahoo.com
Specialties: Complete sole authorship presentation grade highly complex pattern-welded mosaic Damascus blade and bolster stock. **Patterns:** To date Joel has executed over 900 different mosaic Damascus patterns in the past four years. Anything conceived by maker's imagination. **Technical:** Uses various heat colorable "high vibrancy" steels, nickel 200 and some powdered metal for bolster stock only. Uses 1095, 1075 and 15N20. High carbon steels for cutting edge blade stock only. **Prices:** 15 to $50 per square inch and up depending on complexity of pattern. **Remarks:** Full-time mosaic Damascus metal smith focusing strictly on never-before-seen mosaic patterns. Most of maker's work is used for art knives ranging between $1500 and $4500.

DAVIS, JOHN
235 Lampe Rd, Selah, WA 98942, Phone: 509-697-3845, 509-945-4570, jdwelds@charter.net
Specialties: Damascus and mosaic Damascus, working knives, working folders, art knives and art folders. **Technical:** Some ATS-34 and stainless Damascus. Embellishes with fancy stabilized wood, mammoth and walrus ivory. **Prices:** Start at $150. **Remarks:** Part-time maker; first knife sold in 1996. **Mark:** Name city and state on Damascus stamp initials; name inside back RFR.

DAVIS, STEVE
3370 Chatsworth Way, Powder Springs, GA 30127, Phone: 770-427-5740, bsdavis@bellsouth.net

Specialties: Gents and ladies folders. **Patterns:** Straight knives, slip-joint folders, locking-liner folders. **Technical:** Grinds ATS-34 forges own Damascus. Offers filework; prefers hand-rubbed finishes and natural handle materials. Uses pearl, ivory, stag and exotic woods. **Prices:** $250 to $800; some to $1500. **Remarks:** Full-time maker; first knife sold in 1988. Doing business as Custom Knives by Steve Davis. **Mark:** Name engraved on blade.

DAVIS, TERRY
Box 111, Sumpter, OR 97877, Phone: 541-894-2307

Specialties: Traditional and contemporary folders. **Patterns:** Multi-blade folders, whittlers and interframe multiblades; sunfish patterns. **Technical:** Flat-grinds ATS-34. **Prices:** $400 to $1000; some higher. **Remarks:** Full-time maker; first knife sold in 1985. **Mark:** Name in logo.

DAVIS, W C
1955 S 1251 Rd, El Dorado Springs, MO 64744, Phone: 417-876-1259

Specialties: Fancy working straight knives and folders. **Patterns:** Folding lockers and slip-joints; straight hunters, fighters and Bowies. **Technical:** Grinds A2, ATS-34, 154, CPM T490V and CPM 530V. **Prices:** $100 to $300; some to $1000. **Remarks:** Full-time maker; first knife sold in 1972. **Mark:** Name.

DAVIS JR., JIM
5129 Ridge St, Zephyrhills, FL 33541, Phone: 813-779-9213 813-469-4241 Cell, jimdavisknives@aol.com

Specialties: Presentation-grade fixed blade knives w/composite hidden tang handles. Employs a variety of ancient and contemporary ivories. **Patterns:** One-of-a-kind gents, personal, and executive knives and hunters w/unique cam-lock pouch sheaths and display stands. **Technical:** Flat grinds ATS-34 and stainless Damascus w/most work by hand w/assorted files. **Prices:** $300 and up. **Remarks:** Full-time maker, first knives sold in 2000. **Mark:** Signature w/printed name over "HANDCRAFTED."

DAVISON, TODD A.
230 S. Wells St., Kosciusko, MS 39090, Phone: 662-739-7440, crazyknifeblade@yahoo.com; Web: www.tadscustomknives.com

Specialties: Making working/using and collector folders of his design. All knives are truly made one of a kind. Each knife has a serial number inside the liner. **Patterns:** Single and double blade traditional slip-joint pocket knives. **Technical:** Free hand hollow ground blades, hand finished. Using only the very best materials possible. Holding the highest standards to fit & finish and detail. Does his own heat treating. ATS34 and D2 steel. **Prices:** $450 to $900, some higher. **Remarks:** Full time maker, first knife sold in 1981. **Mark:** T.A. DAVISON USA.

DAWKINS, DUDLEY L
221 NW Broadmoor Ave., Topeka, KS 66606-1254, Phone: 785-817-9343, dawkind@reagan.com or dawkind@sbcglobal.net

Specialties: Stylized old or "Dawkins Forged" with anvil in center. New tang stamps. **Patterns:** Straight knives. **Technical:** Mostly carbon steel; some Damascus-all knives forged. **Prices:** Knives: $275 and up; Sheaths: $95 and up. **Remarks:** All knives supplied with wood-lined sheaths. ABS Member, sole authorship. **Mark:** Stylized "DLD or Dawkins Forged with anvil in center.

DAWSON, BARRY
7760 E Hwy 69, Prescott Valley, AZ 86314, Phone: 928-255-9830, dawsonknives@yahoo.com; Web: www.dawsonknives.com

Specialties: Samurai swords, combat knives, collector daggers, tactical, folding and hunting knives. **Patterns:** Offers over 60 different models. **Technical:** Grinds 440C, ATS-34, own heat-treatment. **Prices:** $75 to $1500; some to $5000. **Remarks:** Full-time maker; first knife sold in 1975. **Mark:** Last name, USA in print or last name in script.

DAWSON, LYNN
7760 E Hwy 69 #C-5 157, Prescott Valley, AZ 86314, Phone: 928-713-2812, lynnknives@yahoo.com; Web: www.lynnknives.com

Specialties: Swords, hunters, utility, and art pieces. **Patterns:** Over 25 patterns to choose from. **Technical:** Grinds 440C, ATS-34, own heat treating. **Prices:** $80 to $1000. **Remarks:** Custom work and her own designs. **Mark:** The name "Lynn" in print or script.

DE BRAGA, JOSE C.
1341 9e Rue, Trois Rivieres, QC, CANADA G8Y 2Z2, Phone: 418-948-5864, josedebraga@cgocable.ca

Specialties: Art knives, fantasy pieces and working knives of his design or to customer specs. **Patterns:** Knives with sculptured or carved handles, from miniatures to full-size working knives. **Technical:** Grinds and hand-files 440C and ATS-34. A variety of steels and handle materials available. Offers lost wax casting. **Prices:** Start at $300. **Remarks:** Full-time maker; wax modeler, sculptor and knifemaker; first knife sold in 1984. **Mark:** Initials in stylized script and serial number.

DE MARIA JR., ANGELO
12 Boronda Rd, Carmel Valley, CA 93924, Phone: 831-659-3381, Fax: 831-659-1315, angelodemaria1@mac.com

Specialties: Damascus, fixed and folders, sheaths. **Patterns:** Mosiac and random. **Technical:** Forging 5160, 1084 and 15N20. **Prices:** $200+. **Remarks:** Part-time maker. **Mark:** Angelo de Maria Carmel Valley, CA etch or AdM stamp.

DE MESA, JOHN
1565 W. Main St., STE. 208 #229, Lewisville, TX 75057, Phone: 972-310-3877, TogiArts@me.com; Web: http://togiarts.com/ and http://togiarts.com/CSC/index.html

Specialties: Japanese sword polishing. **Technical:** Traditional sword polishing of Japanese swords made by sword makers in Japan and U.S.**Prices:** Starting at $75 per inch. **Remarks:** Custom Swords Collaborations IN collaboration with Jose De Braga, we can mount Japanese style sword with custom carved handles, sword fittings and scabbards to customer specs.

DE WET, KOBUS
2601 River Road, Yakima, WA 98902, Phone: 509-728-3736, kobus@moderndamascus.com, Web: www.moderndamascus.com

Specialties: Working and art knives. **Patterns:** Every knife is unique. Fixed blades and folders. Hunting, Bowie, Tactical and Utility knives. **Technical:** I enjoy forging my own damascus steel, mainly from 15N20 and 1084. I also use stock removal and stainless steels.**Prices:** Starting at $200**Remarks:** Part time maker, started in 2007**Mark:** Circled "K" / Modern Damascus -Kobus de Wet

DEAN, HARVEY J
3266 CR 232, Rockdale, TX 76567, Phone: 512-446-3111, Fax: 512-446-5060, dean@tex1.net; Web: www.harveydean.com

Specialties: Collectible, functional knives. **Patterns:** Bowies, hunters, folders, daggers, swords, battle axes, camp and combat knives. **Technical:** Forges 1095, O1 and his Damascus. **Prices:** $350 to $10,000. **Remarks:** Full-time maker; first knife sold in 1981. **Mark:** Last name and MS.

DEBAUD, JAKE
2403 Springvale Lane, Dallas, TX 75234, Phone: 214-916-1891, jake.debaud@gmail.com Web: www.debaudknives.com

Specialties: Custom damascus art knives, hunting knives and tactical knives. **Technical:** A2, D2, O1, 1095 and some stainless if requested ATS-34 or 154CM and S30V. **Remarks:** Full-time maker. Have been making knives for three years.

DEBRAGA, JOVAN
141 Notre Dame des Victoir, Quebec, CANADA G2G 1J3, Phone: 418-997-0819/418-877-1915, jovancdebraga@msn.com

Specialties: Art knives, fantasy pieces and working knives of his design or to customer specs. **Patterns:** Knives with sculptured or carved handles, from miniatures to full-sized working knives. **Technical:** Grinds and hand-files 440C, and ATS-34. A variety of steels and handle materials available. **Prices:** Start at $300. **Remarks:** Full time maker. Sculptor and knifemaker. First knife sold in 2003. **Mark:** Initials in stylized script and serial number.

DEIBERT, MICHAEL
LP-114 Las Piedrecitas, Managua, NICARAGUA, Phone: 205-994-2971, mike@deibertknives.com; Web: www.deibertknives.com

Specialties: Large hidden-tang knives such as bowies, choppers and hunters, as well as full-tang fixed blades and integrals. **Technical:** Forges 1095, W1, O1 and 5160 blade steels, clay-hardening and differentially heat treating to achieve a nice hamon (temper line). Also forges pattern-welded steels. **Remarks:** Part-time maker; first knife made in 2000. **Mark:** An anvil with a flaming "D" over it.

DEIBERT, MICHAEL
7570 Happy Hollow Rd., Trussville, AL 35173, mike@deibertknives.com; Web: deibertknives.com

Specialties: Working straight knives in full or hidden tangs, in mono or damascus steel. **Patterns:** Choppers, bowies, hunters and bird-and-trout knives. **Technical:** Makes own damascus, forges all blades and does own heat treating. **Remarks:** ABS journeyman smith, part-time maker. **Mark:** Flaming "D" over an anvil.

DEL RASO, PETER
28 Mayfield Dr, Mt. Waverly, VIC, AUSTRALIA 3149, Phone: 613 98060644, delraso@optusnet.com.au

Specialties: Fixed blades, some folders, art knives. **Patterns:** Daggers, Bowies, tactical, boot, personal and working knives. **Technical:** Grinds ATS-34, commercial Damascus and any other type of steel on request. **Prices:** $100 to $1500. **Remarks:** Part-time maker, first show in 1993. **Mark:** Maker's surname stamped.

DELAROSA, JIM
502 Fairview Cir., Waterford, WI 53185, Phone: 262-422-8604, D-knife@hotmail.com

Specialties: Working straight knives and folders of his design or customer specs. **Patterns:** Hunters, skinners, fillets, utility and locking folders. **Technical:** Grinds ATS-34, 440-C, D2, O1 and commercial Damascus. **Prices:** $100 to $500; some higher. **Remarks:** Part-time maker. **Mark:** First and last name.

DELL, WOLFGANG
Am Alten Berg 9, Owen-Teck, GERMANY D-73277, Phone: 49-7021-81802, wolfgang@dell-knives.de; Web: www.dell-knives.de

Specialties: Fancy high-art straight of his design and to customer specs. **Patterns:** Fighters, hunters, Bowies and utility/camp knives. **Technical:** Grinds ATS-34, RWL-34, Elmax, Damascus (Fritz Schneider). Offers high gloss finish and engraving. **Prices:** $500 to $1000; some to $1600. **Remarks:** Full-time maker; first knife sold in 1992. **Mark:** Hopi hand of peace.

DELLANA
STARLANI INT'L INC, 1135 Terminal Way Ste #209, Reno, NV 89502, Phone: 304-727-5512; 702-569-7827, 1dellana@gmail.com; Web: www.dellana.cc

Specialties: Collector grade fancy/embellished high art folders and art daggers. **Patterns:** Locking folders and art daggers. **Technical:** Forges her own Damascus and W-2. Engraves, does stone setting, filework, carving and gold/platinum fabrication. Prefers exotic, high karat gold, platinum, silver, gemstone and mother-of-pearl handle materials. Price: Upscale. **Remarks:** Sole authorship, full-time maker, first knife sold in 1994. Also does one high art collaboration a year with Van Barnett. Member: Art Knife Invitational and ABS. **Mark:** First name.

DELONG, DICK

PO Box 1024, Centerville, TX 75833-1024, Phone: 903-536-1454

Specialties: Fancy working knives and fantasy pieces. **Patterns:** Hunters and small skinners. **Technical:** Grinds and files O1, D2, 440C and Damascus. Offers cocobolo and Osage orange for handles. **Prices:** Start at $50. **Remarks:** Part-time maker. Member of Art Knife Invitational. Voting member of Knifemakers Guild. Member of ABS. **Mark:** Last name; some unmarked.

DEMENT, LARRY

PO Box 1807, Prince Fredrick, MD 20678, Phone: 410-586-9011

Specialties: Fixed blades. **Technical:** Forged and stock removal. **Prices:** $75 to $200. **Remarks:** Affordable, good feelin', quality knives. Part-time maker.

DENNEHY, JOHN D

2959 Zachary Drive, Loveland, CO 80537, Phone: 970-218-7128, www.thewildirishrose.com

Specialties: Working straight knives, throwers, and leatherworker's knives. **Technical:** 440C, & O1, heat treats own blades, part-time maker, first knife sold in 1989. **Patterns:** Small hunting to presentation Bowies, leatherworks round and head knives. **Prices:** $200 and up. **Remarks:** Custom sheath maker, sheath making seminars at the Blade Show.

DENNING, GENO

CAVEMAN ENGINEERING, 135 Allenvalley Rd, Gaston, SC 29053, Phone: 803-794-6067, cden101656@aol.com; Web: www.cavemanengineering.com

Specialties: Mirror finish. **Patterns:** Hunters, fighters, folders. **Technical:** ATS-34, 440V, S-30-V D2. **Prices:** $100 and up. **Remarks:** Full-time maker since 1996. Sole income since 1999. Instructor at Montgomery Community College (Grinding Blades). A director of SCAK: South Carolina Association of Knifemakers. **Mark:** Troy NC.

DERESPINA, RICHARD

info@derespinaknives.com; Web: www.derespinaknives.com

Specialties: Custom fixed blades and folders, Kris and Karambit. **Technical:** I use the stock removal method. Steels I use are S30V, 154CM, D2, 440C, BG42. Handles made of G10 particularly Micarta, etc. **Prices:** $150 to $550 depending on model. **Remarks:** Full-time maker. **Mark:** My etched logos are two, my last name and Brooklyn NY mark as well as the Star/Yin Yang logo. The star being both representative of various angles of attack common in combat as well as being three triangles, each points to levels of metaphysical understanding. The Yin and Yang have my company initials on each side D & K. Yin and Yang shows the ever present physics of life.

DERINGER, CHRISTOPH

625 Chemin Lower, Cookshire, QC, CANADA J0B 1M0, Phone: 819-345-4260, cdsab@sympatico.ca

Specialties: Traditional working/using straight knives and folders of his design and to customer specs. **Patterns:** Boots, hunters, folders, art knives, kitchen knives and utility/camp knives. **Technical:** Forges 5160, O1 and Damascus. Offers a variety of filework. **Prices:** Start at $250. **Remarks:** Full-time maker; first knife sold in 1989. **Mark:** Last name stamped/engraved.

DERR, HERBERT

413 Woodland Dr, St. Albans, WV 25177, Phone: 304-727-3866

Specialties: Damascus one-of-a-kind knives, carbon steels also. **Patterns:** Birdseye, ladder back, mosaics. **Technical:** All styles functional as well as artistically pleasing. **Prices:** $90 to $175 carbon, Damascus $250 to $800. **Remarks:** All Damascus made by maker. **Mark:** H.K. Derr.

DESAULNIERS, ALAIN

100 Pope Street, Cookshire, QC, CANADA J0B 1M0, pinklaperez@sympatico.ca Web: www.desoknives.com

Specialties: Mostly Loveless style knives. **Patterns:** Double grind fighters, hunters, daggers, etc. **Technical:** Stock removal, ATS-34, CPM. High-polished blades, tapered tangs, high-quality handles. **Remarks:** Full-time. Collaboration with John Young. **Prices:** $425 and up. **Mark:** Name and city in logo.

DESROSIERS, ADAM

PO Box 1954, Petersburg, AK 99833, Phone: 907-518-4570, adam@alaskablades.com Web: www.alaskablades.com

Specialties: High performance, forged, carbon steel and damascus camp choppers, and hunting knives. Hidden tang, full tang, and full integral construction. High performance heat treating. Knife designs inspired by life in Alaskan bush. **Technical:** Hand forges tool steels and damascus. Sole authorship. Full range of handle materials, micarta to Ivory. Preferred steels: W-2, O-1, L-6, 15n20, 1095. **Prices:** $200 -$3000. **Remarks:** ABS member. Has trained with Masters around the world. **Mark:** DrsRosiers over Alaska, underlined with a rose.

DESROSIERS, HALEY

PO Box 1954, Petersburg, AK 99833, Phone: 907-518-1416, haley@alaskablades.com Web: www.alaskablades.com

Specialties: Hunting knives, integrals and a few choppers, high performance.**Technical:** Hand forged blades designed for hard use, exotic wood, antler and ivory handles. **Prices:** $300 -$1500. **Remarks:** Forged first knife in 2001. Part-time bladesmith all year except for commercial fishing season. **Mark:** Capital HD.

DETMER, PHILLIP

14140 Bluff Rd, Breese, IL 62230, Phone: 618-526-4834, jpdetmer@att.net

Specialties: Working knives. **Patterns:** Bowies, daggers and hunters. **Technical:** Grinds ATS-34 and D2. **Prices:** $60 to $400. **Remarks:** Part-time maker; first knife sold in 1977. **Mark:** Last name with dagger.

DEUBEL, CHESTER J.

6211 N. Van Ark Rd., Tucson, AZ 85743, Phone: 520-440-7255, cjdeubel@yahoo.com; Web: www.cjdeubel.com

Specialties: Fancy working straight knives and folders of his or customer design, with intricate file work. **Patterns:** Fighters, Bowies, daggers, hunters, camp knives, and cowboy. **Technical:** Flat guard, hollow grind, antiqued, all types Damascus, 154cpm Stainsteel, high carbon steel, 440c Stainsteel. **Prices:** From $250 to $3500. **Remarks:** Started making part-time in 1980; went to full-time in 2000. Don Patch is my engraver. **Mark:** C.J. Deubel.

DEVERAUX, BUTCH

PO Box 1356, Riverton, WY 82501, Phone: 307-851-0601, bdeveraux@wyoming.com; Web: www.deverauxknives.com

Specialties: High-performance working straight knives. **Patterns:** Hunters, fighters, EDC's, miniatures and camp knives. **Technical:** Forged 52100 blade steel, brass guards, sheephorn handles, as well as stag, cocobolo, she-oak and ironwood. **Prices:** $400 to $3,000. **Remarks:** Part-time maker; first knife sold in 2005. **Mark:** Deveraux on right ricasso.

DEYONG, CLARENCE

8716 Camelot Trace, Sturtevant, WI 53177, Phone: 630-465-6761, cmdeyong@yahoo.com; Web: www.deyongknives.com

Patterns: Mainly creates full-tang hunters, skinners and fighters. **Technical:** Stock removal with some forging, using rasps and files for blade stock with an emphasis on natural handle materials. **Prices:** $150 to $300 with custom sheaths. **Remarks:** Making knives since 1981. **Mark:** DeYong and blade # engraved on the blade.

DIAZ, JOSE

409 W. 12th Ave, Ellensburg, WA 98926, jose@diaztools.com Web: www.diaztools.com

Specialties: Affordable custom user-grade utility and camp knives. Also makes competition cutting knives. **Patterns:** Mas. **Technical:** Blade materials range from high carbon steels and Damascus to high performance tool and stainless steels. Uses both forge and stock removal methods in shaping the steel. Handle materials include Tero Tuf, Black Butyl Burl, Micarta, natural woods and G10. **Prices:** $65-$700. **Remarks:** Part-time knife maker; made first knife in 2008. **Mark:** Reclining tree frog with a smile, and "Diaz Tools."

DICK, DAN

P.O. Box 2303, Hutchinson, KS 67504-2303, Phone: 620-669-6805, Dan@DanDickKnives.com; Web: www.dandickknives.com

Specialties: Traditional working/using fixed bladed knives of maker's design. **Patterns:**Hunters, skinners and utility knives. **Technical:** Stock removal maker using CTS-XHP and D2. Prefers such materials as exotic and fancy burl woods. Makes his own sheaths, all leather with tooling. **Prices:**$135 and up. **Remarks:**Part-time maker since 2006. Marks: Name in outline border of Kansas.

DICKERSON, GAVIN

PO Box 7672, Petit, GT, SOUTH AFRICA 1512, Phone: +27 011-965-0988, Fax: +27 011-965-0988

Specialties: Straight knives of his design or to customer specs. **Patterns:** Hunters, skinners, fighters and Bowies. **Technical:** Hollow-grinds D2, 440C, ATS-34, 12C27 and Damascus upon request. Prefers natural handle materials; offers synthetic handle materials. **Prices:** $190 to $2500. **Remarks:** Part-time maker; first knife sold in 1982. **Mark:** Name in full.

DICKISON, SCOTT S

179 Taylor Rd, Portsmouth, RI 02871, Phone: 401-847-7398, squared22@cox .net; Web: http://sqauredknives.com

Specialties: Straight knives, locking folders and slip joints of his design. **Patterns:** Sgain dubh, bird and trout knives. **Technical:** Forges and grinds commercial Damascus, D2, O1 and sandvik stainless. **Prices:** $400 to $1000; some higher. **Remarks:** Part-time maker; first knife sold in 1989. **Mark:** Stylized initials.

DICRISTOFANO, ANTHONY P

10519 Nevada Ave., Melrose Park, IL 60164, Phone: 847-845-9598, sukemitsu@sbcglobal.net Web: www.namahagesword.com or www.sukemitsu.com

Specialties: Japanese-style swords. **Patterns:** Katana, Wakizashi, Otanto, Kozuka. **Technical:** Tradition and some modern steels. All clay tempered and traditionally hand polished using Japanese wet stones. **Remarks:** Part-time maker. **Prices:** Varied, available on request. **Mark:** Blade tang signed in "SUKEMITSU."

DIETZ, HOWARD

421 Range Rd, New Braunfels, TX 78132, Phone: 830-885-4662

Specialties: Lock-back folders, working straight knives. **Patterns:** Folding hunters, high-grade pocket knives. **Technical:** ATS-34, 440C, CPM 440V, D2 and stainless Damascus. **Prices:** $300 to $1000. **Remarks:** Full-time gun and knifemaker; first knife sold in 1995. **Mark:** Name, city, and state.

DIETZEL, BILL

779 Baycove Ct., Middleburg, FL 32068, Phone: 904-282-1091, wdms97@bellsouth.net

Specialties: Forged straight knives and folders. **Patterns:** His interpretations. **Technical:** Forges his Damascus and other steels. **Prices:** Middle ranges. **Remarks:** Likes natural materials; uses titanium in folder liners. Master Smith (1997). **Mark:** Name.

DIGANGI, JOSEPH M

PO Box 257, Los Ojos, NM 87551, Phone: 505-929-2987, Fax: 505-753-8144, Web: www.digangidesigns.com

Specialties: Kitchen and table cutlery. **Patterns:** French chef's knives, carving sets, steak knife sets, some camp knives and hunters. Holds patents and trademarks for "System ll" kitchen cutlery set. **Technical:** Grinds ATS-34. **Prices:** $150 to $595; some to $1200. **Remarks:** Full-time maker; first knife sold in 1983. **Mark:** DiGangi Designs.

DILL, DAVE
7404 NW 30th St, Bethany, OK 73008, Phone: 405-789-0750
Specialties: Folders of his design. **Patterns:** Various patterns. **Technical:** Hand-grinds 440C, ATS-34. Offers engraving and filework on all folders. **Prices:** Starting at $450. **Remarks:** Full-time maker; first knife sold in 1987. **Mark:** First initial, last name.

DILL, ROBERT
1812 Van Buren, Loveland, CO 80538, Phone: 970-667-5144, Fax: 970-667-5144, dillcustomknives@msn.com
Specialties: Fancy and working knives of his design. **Patterns:** Hunters, Bowies and fighters. **Technical:** Grinds 440C and D2. **Prices:** $100 to $800. **Remarks:** Full-time maker; first knife sold in 1984. **Mark:** Logo stamped into blade.

DINTRUFF, CHUCK
1708 E. Martin Luther King Blvd., Seffner, FL 33584, Phone: 813-381-6916, DINTRUFFKNIVES@aol.com; Web: dintruffknives.com and spinwellfab.com

DION, GREG
3032 S Jackson St, Oxnard, CA 93033, Phone: 519-981-1033
Specialties: Working straight knives, some fancy. Welcomes special orders. **Patterns:** Hunters, fighters, camp knives, Bowies and tantos. **Technical:** Grinds ATS-34, 154CM and 440C. **Prices:** $85 to $300; some to $600. **Remarks:** Part-time maker; first knife sold in 1985. **Mark:** Name.

DIOTTE, JEFF
DIOTTE KNIVES, 159 Laurier Dr, LaSalle, ON, CANADA N9J 1L4, Phone: 519-978-2764

DIPPOLD, AL
90 Damascus Ln, Perryville, MO 63775, Phone: 573-547-1119, adippold@midwest.net
Specialties: Fancy one-of-a-kind locking folders. **Patterns:** Locking folders. **Technical:** Forges and grinds mosaic and pattern welded Damascus. Offers filework on all folders. **Prices:** $500 to $3500; some higher. **Remarks:** Full-time maker; first knife sold in 1980. **Mark:** Last name in logo inside of liner.

DISKIN, MATT
PO Box 653, Freeland, WA 98249, Phone: 360-730-0451, info@volcanknives.com; Web: www.volcanknives.com
Specialties: Damascus autos. **Patterns:** Dirks and daggers. **Technical:** Forges mosaic Damascus using 15N20, 1084, 02, 06, L6; pure nickel. **Prices:** Start at $500. Remarks: Full-time maker. **Mark:** Last name.

DIXON JR., IRA E
PO Box 26, Cave Junction, OR 97523, irasknives@yahoo.com
Specialties: Straight knives of his design. **Patterns:** All patterns include art knives. **Technical:** Grinds CPM materials, Damascus and some tool steels. **Prices:** $275 to $2000. **Remarks:** Full-time maker; first knife sold in 1993. **Mark:** First name, Handmade.

DOBRATZ, ERIC
25371 Hillary Lane, Laguna Hills, CA 92653, Phone: 949-233-5170, knifesmith@gmail.com
Specialties: Differentially quenched blades with Hamon of his design or with customer input. **Patterns:** Hunting, camp, kitchen, fighters, bowies, traditional tanto, and unique fixed blade designs. **Technical:** Hand-forged high carbon and damascus. Prefers natural material for handles; rare/exotic woods and stag, but also uses micarta and homemade synthetic materials. **Prices:** $150 -$1500. **Remarks:** Part-time maker; first knife made in 1995. **Mark:** Stylized Scarab beetle.

DODD, ROBERT F
4340 E Canyon Dr, Camp Verde, AZ 86322, Phone: 928-567-3333, rfdknives@commspeed.net; Web: www.rfdoddknives.com
Specialties: Folders, fixed blade hunter/skinners, Bowies, daggers. **Patterns:** Drop point. **Technical:** ATS-34 and Damascus. **Prices:** $250 and up. **Remarks:** Hand tooled leather sheaths. **Mark:** R. F. Dodd, Camp Verde AZ.

DOIRON, DONALD
6 Chemin Petit Lac des Ced, Messines, QC, CANADA JOX-2JO, Phone: 819-465-2489

DOMINY, CHUCK
PO Box 593, Colleyville, TX 76034, Phone: 817-498-4527
Specialties: Titanium LinerLock® folders. **Patterns:** Hunters, utility/camp knives and LinerLock® folders. **Technical:** Grinds 440C and ATS-34. **Prices:** $250 to $3000. **Remarks:** Full-time maker; first knife sold in 1976. **Mark:** Last name.

DOOLITTLE, MIKE
13 Denise Ct, Novato, CA 94947, Phone: 415-897-3246
Specialties: Working straight knives in standard patterns. **Patterns:** Hunters and fishing knives. **Technical:** Grinds 440C, 154CM and ATS-34. **Prices:** $125 to $200; some to $750. **Remarks:** Part-time maker; first knife sold in 1981. **Mark:** Name, city and state.

DORNELES, LUCIANO OLIVERIRA
Rua 15 De Novembro 2222, Nova Petropolis, RS, BRAZIL 95150-000, Phone: 011-55-54-303-303-90, tchebufalo@hotmail.com
Specialties: Traditional "true" Brazilian-style working knives and to customer specs. **Patterns:** Brazilian hunters, utility and camp knives, Bowies, Dirk. A master at the making of the true "Faca Campeira Gaucha," the true camp knife of the famous Brazilian Gauchos. A Dorneles knife is 100 percent hand-forged with sledge hammers only. Can make spectacular Damascus hunters/daggers. **Technical:** Forges only 52100 and his own

Damascus, can put silver wire inlay on customer design handles on special orders; uses only natural handle materials. **Prices:** $250 to $1000. **Mark:** Symbol with L. Dorneles.

DOTSON, TRACY
1280 Hwy C-4A, Baker, FL 32531, Phone: 850-537-2407
Specialties: Folding fighters and small folders. **Patterns:** LinerLock® and lockback folders. **Technical:** Hollow-grinds ATS-34 and commercial Damascus. **Prices:** Start at $250. **Remarks:** Part-time maker; first knife sold in 1995. **Mark:** Last name.

DOUCETTE, R
CUSTOM KNIVES, 19 Evelyn St., Brantford, ON, CANADA N3R 3G8, Phone: 519-756-9040, randy@randydoucetteknives.com; Web: www.randydoucetteknives.com
Specialties: High-end tactical folders with filework and multiple grinds. **Patterns:** Tactical folders. **Technical:** All knives are handmade. The only outsourcing is heat treatment. **Prices:** $900 to $2,500. **Remarks:** Full-time knifemaker; 2-year waiting list. Maker is proud to produce original knife designs every year!lm **Mark:** R. Doucette

DOURSIN, GERARD
Chemin des Croutoules, Pernes les Fontaines, FRANCE 84210
Specialties: Period pieces. **Patterns:** Liner locks and daggers. **Technical:** Forges mosaic Damascus. **Prices:** $600 to $4000. **Remarks:** First knife sold in 1983. **Mark:** First initial, last name and I stop the lion.

DOUSSOT, LAURENT
1008 Montarville, St. Bruno, QC, CANADA J3V 3T1, Phone: 450-441-3298, doussot@skalja.com; Web: www.skalja.com, www.doussot-knives.com
Specialties: Fancy and embellished folders and fantasy knives. **Patterns:** Fighters and locking folders. **Technical:** Grinds ATS-34 and commercial Damascus. Scale carvings on all knives; most bolsters are carved titanium. **Prices:** $350 to $3000. **Remarks:** Part-time maker; first knife was sold in 1992. **Mark:** Stylized initials inside circle.

DOWNIE, JAMES T
1295 Sandy Ln., Apt. 1208, Sarnia, Ontario, CANADA N7V 4K5, Phone: 519-491-8234
Specialties: Serviceable straight knives and folders; period pieces. **Patterns:** Hunters, Bowies, camp knives, fillet and miniatures. **Technical:** Grinds D2, 440C and ATS-34, Damasteel, stainless steel Damascus. **Prices:** $195 and up. **Remarks:** Full-time maker, first knife sold in 1978. **Mark:** Signature of first and middle initials, last name.

DOWNING, LARRY
12268 State Route 181 N, Bremen, KY 42325, Phone: 270-525-3523, larrydowning@bellsouth.net; Web: www.downingknives.com
Specialties: Working straight knives and folders. **Patterns:** From mini-knives to daggers, folding lockers to interframes. **Technical:** Forges and grinds 154CM, ATS-34 and his own Damascus. **Prices:** $195 to $950; some higher. **Remarks:** Part-time maker; first knife sold in 1979. **Mark:** Name in arrowhead.

DOWNING, TOM
2675 12th St, Cuyahoga Falls, OH 44223, Phone: 330-923-7464
Specialties: Working straight knives; period pieces. **Patterns:** Hunters, fighters and tantos. **Technical:** Grinds 440C, ATs-34 and CPM-T-440V. Prefers natural handle materials. **Prices:** $150 to $900, some to $1500. **Remarks:** Part-time maker; first knife sold in 1979. **Mark:** First and middle initials, last name.

DOWNS, JAMES F
2247 Summit View Rd, Powell, OH 43065, Phone: 614-766-5350, jfdowns1@yahoo.com
Specialties: Working straight knives of his design or to customer specs. **Patterns:** Folders, Bowies, boot, hunters, utility. **Technical:** Grinds 440C and other steels. Prefers mastodon ivory, all pearls, stabilized wood and elephant ivory. **Prices:** $75 to $1200. **Remarks:** Full-time maker; first knife sold in 1980. **Mark:** Last name.

DOX, JAN
Zwanebloemlaan 27, Schoten, BELGIUM B 2900, Phone: 32 3 658 77 43, jan.dox@scarlet.be; Web: doxblades.weebly.com
Specialties: Working/using knives, from kitchen to battlefield. **Patterns:** Own designs, some based on traditional ethnic patterns (Scots, Celtic, Scandinavian and Japanese) or to customer specs. **Technical:** Grinds D2/A2 and stainless, forges carbon steels, convex edges. Handles: Wrapped in modern or traditional patterns, resin impregnated if desired. Natural or synthetic materials, some carved. **Prices:** $50 and up. **Remarks:** Spare-time maker, first knife sold 2001. **Mark:** Name or stylized initials.

DOYLE, JOHN
4779 W. M-61, Gladwin, MI 48624, Phone: 989-802-9470, jdoyleknives@gmail.com
Specialties Hunters, camp knives and bowies. **Technical:** Forges 1075, 1080, 1084, 1095 and 5160. Will practice stock-removal method of blademaking on small knives at times. **Remarks:** Full-time maker; first knife made in 2009. **Mark:** J. Doyle in "Invitation" style print font

DOZIER, BOB
Dozier Knives and Arkansas Made Dozier, PO Box 1941, Springdale, AR 72765, Phone: 888-823-0023/479-756-0023, Fax: 479-756-9139, info@dozierknives.com; Web www.dozierknives.com
Specialties: Folding knives and collector-grade knives (Dozier Knives) and hunting and tactical fixed blades (Arkansas Dozier Made). **Technical:** Uses D2. **Prices:** Start at $205 (Arkansas Made Dozier) or $500 (Dozier Knives). **Remarks:** Full-time maker; first knife sold in 1965. **Mark:** Dozier with an arrow through the D and year over arrow for foldiers, or R.L. Dozier, maker, St. Paul, AR in an oval for the collector-grad knives (Dozier Knives); and Arkansas, Made, Dozier in a circle (Arkansas Dozier Made).

DRAPER, AUDRA
#10 Creek Dr, Riverton, WY 82501, Phone: 307-856-6807 or 307-851-0426 cell, adraper@wyoming.com; Web: www.draperknives.com
Specialties: One-of-a-kind straight and folding knives. Also pendants, earring and bracelets of Damascus. **Patterns:** Design custom knives, using, Bowies, and minis. **Technical:** Forge Damascus; heat-treats all knives. **Prices:** Vary depending on item. **Remarks:** Full-time maker; master bladesmith in the ABS. Member of the PKA; first knife sold in 1995. **Mark:** Audra.

DRAPER, MIKE
#10 Creek Dr, Riverton, WY 82501, Phone: 307-856-6807, adraper@wyoming.com
Specialties: Mainly folding knives in tactical fashion, occasonal fixed blade. **Patterns:** Hunters, Bowies and camp knives, tactical survival. **Technical:** Grinds S30V stainless steel. **Prices:** Starting at $250+. **Remarks:** Full-time maker; first knife sold in 1996. **Mark:** Initials M.J.D. or name, city and state.

DREW, GERALD
213 Hawk Ridge Dr, Mill Spring, NC 28756, Phone: 828-713-4762
Specialties: Blade ATS-34 blades. Straight knives. **Patterns:** Hunters, camp knives, some Bowies and tactical. **Technical:** ATS-34 preferred. **Price:** $65 to $400. **Mark:** GL DREW.

DRISCOLL, MARK
4115 Avoyer Pl, La Mesa, CA 91941, Phone: 619-670-0695, markdriscoll91941@yahoo.com
Specialties: High-art, period pieces and working/using knives of his design or to customer specs; some fancy. **Patterns:** Swords, Bowies, fighters, daggers, hunters and primitive (mountain man-styles). **Technical:** Forges 52100, 5160, 01, L6, 1095, 15n20, W-2 steel and makes his own Damascus and mokume; also does multiple quench heat treating. Uses exotic hardwoods, ivory and horn, offers fancy file work, carving, scrimshaws. **Prices:** $150 to $550; some to $1500. **Remarks:** Part-time maker; first knife sold in 1986. Doing business as Mountain Man Knives. **Mark:** Double "M."

DROST, JASON D
Rt 2 Box 49, French Creek, WV 26218, Phone: 304-472-7901
Specialties: Working/using straight knives of his design. **Patterns:** Hunters and utility/camp knives. **Technical:** Grinds 154CM and D2. **Prices:** $125 to $5000. **Remarks:** Spare-time maker; first knife sold in 1995. **Mark:** First and middle initials, last name, maker, city and state.

DROST, MICHAEL B
Rt 2 Box 49, French Creek, WV 26218, Phone: 304-472-7901
Specialties: Working/using straight knives and folders of all designs. **Patterns:** Hunters, locking folders and utility/camp knives. **Technical:** Grinds ATS-34, D2 and CPM-T-440V. Offers dove-tailed bolsters and spacers, filework and scrimshaw. **Prices:** $125 to $400; some to $740. **Remarks:** Full-time maker; first knife sold in 1990. Doing business as Drost Custom Knives. **Mark:** Name, city and state.

DRUMM, ARMIN
Lichtensteinstrasse 33, Dornstadt, GERMANY 89160, Phone: 49-163-632-2842, armin@drumm-knives.de; Web: www.drumm-knives.de
Specialties: One-of-a-kind forged and Damascus fixed blade knives and folders. **Patterns:** Classic Bowie knives, daggers, fighters, hunters, folders, swords. **Technical:** Forges own Damascus and carbon steels, filework, carved handles. **Prices:** $250 to $800, some higher. **Remarks:** First knife sold in 2001, member of the German Knifemakers Guild. **Mark:** First initial, last name.

DUCKER, BRIAN
Lamorna Cottage, Common End, Colkirk, ENGLAND NR21 7JD, Phone: 01-328-856-183, admin@grommitbaileyknives.com; Web: www.grommitbaileyknives.com
Specialties: Hunters, utility pieces, bowies, camp knives, fighters and folders. **Technical:** Stock removal and forged 1095, 1075 and 80CrV2. Forging own damascus, using exotic and native hardwoods, stag, leather, Micarta and other synthetic materials, with brass and 301 stainless steel fittings. Own leatherwork and heat treating. **Remarks:** Part-time maker since 2009, full time Dec. 2013. All knives and sheaths are sole authorship. **Mark:** GROMMIT UK MAKER & BAILEY GROMMIT MAKERS.

DUFF, BILL
2801 Ash St, Poteau, OK 74953, Phone: 918-647-4458
Specialties: Straight knives and folders, some fancy. **Patterns:** Hunters, folders and miniatures. **Technical:** Grinds 440-C and commercial Damascus. **Prices:** $250 and up. **Remarks:** First knife sold in 1976. **Mark:** Bill Duff.

DUFOUR, ARTHUR J
8120 De Armoun Rd, Anchorage, AK 99516, Phone: 907-345-1701
Specialties: Working straight knives from standard patterns. **Patterns:** Hunters, Bowies, camp and fishing knives—grinded thin and pointed. **Technical:** Grinds 440C, ATS-34, AEB-L. Tempers 57-58R; hollow-grinds. **Prices:** $135; some to $250. **Remarks:** Part-time maker; first knife sold in 1970. **Mark:** Prospector logo.

DUGDALE, DANIEL J.
11 Eleanor Road, Walpole, MA 02081, Phone: 508-404-6509, dlpdugdale@comcast.net
Specialties: Button-lock and straight knives of his design. **Patterns:** Utilities, hunters, skinners, and tactical. **Technical:** Falt grinds D-2 and 440C, aluminum handles with anodized finishes. **Prices:** $150 to $500. **Remarks:** Part-time maker since 1977. **Mark:** Deer track with last name, town and state.

DUNCAN, RON
5090 N. Hwy. 63, Cairo, MO 65239, Phone: 660-263-8949, www.duncanmadeknives.com

Remarks: Duncan Made Knives

DUNKERLEY, RICK
PO Box 601, Lincoln, MT 59639, Phone: 406-210-4101, dunkerleyknives@gmail.com Web: www.dunkerleyknives.com
Specialties: Mosaic Damascus folders and carbon steel utility knives. **Patterns:** One-of-a-kind folders, standard hunters and utility designs. **Technical:** Forges 52100, Damascus and mosaic Damascus. Prefers natural handle materials. **Prices:** $200 and up. **Remarks:** Full-time maker; first knife sold in 1984, ABS Master Smith. Doing business as Dunkerley Custom Knives. Dunkerley handmade knives, sole authorship. **Mark:** Dunkerley, MS.

DUNLAP, JIM
800 E. Badger Lee Rd., Sallisaw, OK 74955, Phone: 918-774-2700, dunlapknives@gmail.com
Specialties: Traditional slip-joint folders. **Patterns:** Single-and multi-blade traditional slip joints. **Technical:** Grinds ATS-34, CPM-154 and damascus. **Prices:** $250 and up. **Remarks:** Part-time maker; first knife sold in 2009. **Mark:** Dunlap.

DUNN, STEVE
376 Biggerstaff Rd, Smiths Grove, KY 42171, Phone: 270-563-9830, dunnknives@windstream.net; Web: www.stevedunnknives.com
Specialties: Working and using straight knives of his design; period pieces. Offers engraving and gold inlay. **Patterns:** Hunters, skinners, Bowies, fighters, camp knives, folders, swords and battle axes. **Technical:** Forges own Damascus, 1075, 15N20, 52100, 1084, L6. **Prices:** Moderate to upscale. **Remarks:** Full-time maker; first knife sold in 1990. **Mark:** Last name and MS.

DURAN, JERRY T
PO Box 9753, Albuquerque, NM 87119, Phone: 505-873-4676, jtdknives@hotmail.com; Web: http://www.google.com/profiles/jtdknivesLLC
Specialties: Tactical folders, Bowies, fighters, liner locks, autopsy and hunters. **Patterns:** Folders, Bowies, hunters and tactical knives. **Technical:** Forges own Damascus and forges carbon steel. **Prices:** Moderate to upscale. **Remarks:** Full-time maker; first knife sold in 1978. **Mark:** Initials in elk rack logo.

DURHAM, KENNETH
BUZZARD ROOST FORGE, 10495 White Pike, Cherokee, AL 35616, Phone: 256-359-4287, www.home.hiwaay.net/~jamesd/
Specialties: Bowies, dirks, hunters. **Patterns:** Traditional patterns. **Technical:** Forges 1095, 5160, 52100 and makes own Damascus. **Prices:** $85 to $1600. **Remarks:** Began making knives about 1995. Received Journeyman stamp 1999. Got Master Smith stamp in 2004. **Mark:** Bull's head with Ken Durham above and Cherokee AL below.

DURIO, FRED
144 Gulino St, Opelousas, LA 70570, Phone: 337-948-4831/cell 337-351-2652, fdurio@yahoo.com
Specialties: Folders. **Patterns:** Liner locks; plain and fancy. **Technical:** Makes own Damascus. **Prices:** Moderate to upscale. **Remarks:** Full-time maker. **Mark:** Last name-Durio.

DUVALL, FRED
10715 Hwy 190, Benton, AR 72015, Phone: 501-778-9360
Specialties: Working straight knives and folders. **Patterns:** Locking folders, slip joints, hunters, fighters and Bowies. **Technical:** Grinds D2 and CPM440V; forges 5160. **Prices:** $100 to $400; some to $800. **Remarks:** Part-time maker; first knife sold in 1973. **Mark:** Last name.

DWYER, DUANE
565 Country Club Dr., Escondido, CA 92029, Phone: 760-471-8275, striderguys@striderknives.com; Web: www.striderknives.com
Specialties: Primarily tactical. **Patterns:** Fixed and folders. **Technical:** Primarily stock removal specializing in highly technical materials. **Prices:** $100 and up, based on the obvious variables. **Remarks:** Full-time maker since 1996.

DYER, DAVID
4531 Hunters Glen, Granbury, TX 76048, Phone: 817-573-1198
Specialties: Working skinners and early period knives. **Patterns:** Customer designs, his own patterns. **Technical:** Coal forged blades; 5160 and 52100 steels. Grinds D2, 1095, L6. **Prices:** $150 for neck knives and small (3" to 3-1/2"). To $600 for large blades and specialty blades. **Mark:** Last name DYER electro etched.

DYESS, EDDIE
1005 Hamilton, Roswell, NM 88201, Phone: 505-623-5599, eddyess@msn.com
Specialties: Working and using straight knives in standard patterns. **Patterns:** Hunters and fighters. **Technical:** Grinds 440C, 154CM and D2 on request. **Prices:** $150 to $300, some higher. **Remarks:** Spare-time maker; first knife sold in 1980. **Mark:** Last name.

E

EAKER, ALLEN L
416 Clinton Ave Dept KI, Paris, IL 61944, Phone: 217-466-5160
Specialties: Traditional straight knives and folders of his design. **Patterns:** Hunters, locking folders and slip-joint folders. **Technical:** Grinds 440C; inlays. **Prices:** $200 to $500. **Remarks:** Spare-time maker; first knife sold in 1994. **Mark:** Initials in tankard logo stamped on tang, serial number and surname on back.

EALY, DELBERT
PO Box 121, Indian River, MI 49749, Phone: 231-238-4705

EATON, FRANK L JR
5365 W. Meyer Rd., Farmington, MO 63640, Phone: 703-314-8708,

eatontactical@me.com; Web: www.frankeatonknives.com
Specialties: Full tang/hidden tang fixed working and art knives of his own design. **Patterns:** Hunters, skinners, fighters, Bowies, tacticals and daggers. **Technical:** Stock removal maker, prefer using natural materials. **Prices:** $175 to $400. **Remarks:** Part-time maker -Active Duty Airborn Ranger-Making 4 years. **Mark:** Name over 75th Ranger Regimental Crest.

EATON, RICK
313 Dailey Rd, Broadview, MT 59015, Phone: 406-667-2405, rick@eatonknives.com; Web: www.eatonknives.com
Specialties: Interframe folders and one-hand-opening side locks. **Patterns:** Bowies, daggers, fighters and folders. **Technical:** Grinds 154CM, ATS-34, 440C and other maker's Damascus. Makes own mosaic Damascus. Offers high-quality hand engraving, Bulino and gold inlay. **Prices:** Upscale. **Remarks:** Full-time maker; first knife sold in 1982. **Mark:** Full name or full name and address.

EBISU, HIDESAKU
3-39-7 Koi Osako, Nishi Ku, Hiroshima, JAPAN 733 0816

ECHOLS, RODGER
2853 Highway 371 W, Nashville, AR 71852-7577, Phone: 870-845-9173 or 870-845-0400, bladmanechols@aol.com; Web: www.echolsknives.com
Specialties: Liner locks, auto-scale release, lock backs. **Patterns:** His or yours. **Technical:** Autos. **Prices:** $500 to $1700. **Remarks:** Likes to use pearl, ivory and Damascus the most. Made first knife in 1984. Part-time maker; tool and die maker by trade. **Mark:** Name.

EDDY, HUGH E
211 E Oak St, Caldwell, ID 83605, Phone: 208-459-0536

EDGE, TOMMY
1244 County Road 157, Cash, AR 72421, Phone: 870-897-6150, tedge@tex.net
Specialties: Fancy/embellished working knives of his design. **Patterns:** Bowies, hunters and utility/camping knives. **Technical:** Grinds 440C, ATS-34 and D2. Makes own cable Damascus; offers filework. **Prices:** $70 to $250; some to $1500. **Remarks:** Part-time maker; first knife sold in 1973. **Mark:** Stamped first initial, last name and stenciled name, city and state in oval shape.

EDMONDS, WARRICK
Adelaide Hills, SOUTH AUSTRALIA, Phone: 61-8-83900339, warrick@riflebirdknives.com Web: www.riflebirdknives.com
Specialties: Fixed blade knives with select and highly figured exotic or unique Australian wood handles. Themed collectors knives to individually designed working knives from Damascus, RWL34, 440C or high carbon steels. **Patterns:** Hunters, utilities and workshop knives, cooks knives with a Deco to Modern flavour. Hand sewn individual leather sheaths. **Technical:** Stock removal using only steel from well known and reliable sources. **Prices:** $250Aust to $1000Aust. **Remarks:** Part-time maker since 2004. **Mark:** Name stamped into sheath.

EDWARDS, MITCH
303 New Salem Rd, Glasgow, KY 42141, Phone: 270-404-0758 / 270-404-0758, medwards@glasgow-ky.com; Web: www.traditionalknives.com
Specialties: Period pieces. **Patterns:** Neck knives, camp, rifleman and Bowie knives. **Technical:** All hand forged, forges own Damascus O1, 1084, 1095, L6, 15N20. **Prices:** $200 to $1000. **Remarks:** Journeyman Smith. **Mark:** Broken heart.

EHRENBERGER, DANIEL ROBERT
1213 S Washington St, Mexico, MO 65265, Phone: 573-633-2010
Specialties: Affordable working/using straight knives of his design and to custom specs. **Patterns:** 10" western Bowie, fighters, hunting and skinning knives. **Technical:** Forges 1085, 1095, his own Damascus and cable Damascus. **Prices:** $80 to $500. **Remarks:** Full-time maker, first knife sold 1994. **Mark:** Ehrenberger JS.

EKLUND, MAIHKEL
Fone Stam V9, Farila, SWEDEN 82041, info@art-knives.com; Web: www.art-knives.com
Specialties: Collector-grade working straight knives. **Patterns:** Hunters, Bowies and fighters. **Technical:** Grinds ATS-34, Uddeholm and Dama steel. Engraves and scrimshaws. **Prices:** $200 to $2000. **Remarks:** Full-time maker; first knife sold in 1983. **Mark:** Initials or name.

ELDRIDGE, ALLAN
7731 Four Winds Dr, Ft. Worth, TX 76133, Phone: 817-370-7778; Cell: 817-296-3528
Specialties: Fancy classic straight knives in standard patterns. **Patterns:** Hunters, Bowies, fighters, folders and miniatures. **Technical:** Grinds O1 and Damascus. Engraves silver-wire inlays, pearl inlays, scrimshaws and offers filework. **Prices:** $50 to $500; some to $1200. **Remarks:** Spare-time maker; first knife sold in 1965. **Mark:** Initials.

ELISHEWITZ, ALLEN
875 Hwy. 321 N, Ste. 600, #212, Lenoir City, TN 37771, Phone: 865-816-3309, allen@elishewitzknives.com; Web: elishewitzknives.com
Specialties: Collectible high-tech working straight knives and folders of his design. **Patterns:** Working, utility and tactical knives. **Technical:** Designs and uses innovative locking mechanisms. All designs drafted and field-tested. **Prices:** $600 to $1000. **Remarks:** Full-time maker; first knife sold in 1989. **Mark:** Gold medallion inlaid in blade.

ELLEFSON, JOEL
PO Box 1016, 310 S 1st St, Manhattan, MT 59741, Phone: 406-284-3111
Specialties: Working straight knives, fancy daggers and one-of-a-kinds. **Patterns:** Hunters, daggers and some folders. **Technical:** Grinds A2, 440C and ATS-34. Makes own mokume in bronze, brass, silver and shibuishi; makes brass/steel blades. **Prices:**

$100 to $500; some to $2000. **Remarks:** Part-time maker; first knife sold in 1978. **Mark:** Stylized last initial.

ELLERBE, W B
3871 Osceola Rd, Geneva, FL 32732, Phone: 407-349-5818
Specialties: Period and primitive knives and sheaths. **Patterns:** Bowies to patch knives, some tomahawks. **Technical:** Grinds Sheffield O1 and files. **Prices:** Start at $35. **Remarks:** Full-time maker; first knife sold in 1971. Doing business as Cypress Bend Custom Knives. **Mark:** Last name or initials.

ELLIOTT, JERRY
4507 Kanawha Ave, Charleston, WV 25304, Phone: 304-925-5045, elliottknives@gmail.com
Specialties: Classic and traditional straight knives and folders of his design and to customer specs. **Patterns:** Hunters, locking folders and Bowies. **Technical:** Grinds ATS-34, 154CM, O1, D2 and T-440-V. All guards silver-soldered; bolsters are pinned on straight knives, spot-welded on folders. **Prices:** $80 to $265; some to $1000. **Remarks:** Full-time maker; first knife sold in 1972. **Mark:** First and middle initials, last name, knife maker, city, state.

ELLIS, WILLIAM DEAN
2767 Edgar Ave, Sanger, CA 93657, Phone: 559-314-4459, urleebird@comcast.net; Web: www.billysblades.com
Specialties: Classic and fancy knives of his design. **Patterns:** Boots, fighters and utility knives. **Technical:** Grinds ATS-34, D2 and Damascus. Offers tapered tangs and six patterns of filework; tooled multi-colored sheaths. **Prices:** $250 to $1500 **Remarks:** Part-time maker; first knife sold in 1991. Doing business as Billy's Blades. Also make shave-ready straight razors for actual use. **Mark:** "B" in a five-point star next to "Billy," city and state within a rounded-corner rectangle.

ELLIS, WILLY B
1025 Hamilton Ave., Tarpon Springs, FL 34689, Phone: 727-942-6420, Web: www.willyb.com
Specialties: One-of-a-kind high art and fantasy knives of his design. Occasional customs full size and miniatures. **Patterns:** Bowies, fighters, hunters and others. **Technical:** Grinds 440C, ATS-34, 1095, carbon Damascus, ivory bone, stone and metal carving. **Prices:** $175 to $15,000. **Remarks:** Full-time maker, first knife made in 1973. Member Knifemakers Guild and FEGA. Jewel setting inlays. **Mark:** Willy B. or WB'S C etched or carved.

ELROD, ROGER R
58 Dale Ave, Enterprise, AL 36330, Phone: 334-347-1863

EMBRETSEN, KAJ
FALUVAGEN 67, Edsbyn, SWEDEN 82830, Phone: 46-271-21057, Fax: 46-271-22961, kay.embretsen@telia.com Web:www.embretsenknives.com
Specialties: Damascus folding knives. **Patterns:** Uses mammoth ivory and some pearl. **Technical:** Uses own Damascus steel. **Remarks:** Full time since 1983. **Prices:** $2500 to $8000. **Mark:** Name inside the folder.

EMERSON, ERNEST R
1234 W. 254th, Harbor City, CA 90710, Phone: 310-539-5633, info@emersonknives.com; Web: www.emersonknives.com
Specialties: High-tech folders and combat fighters. **Patterns:** Fighters, LinerLock® combat folders and SPECWAR combat knives. **Technical:** Grinds 154CM and Damascus. Makes folders with titanium fittings, liners and locks. Chisel grind specialist. **Prices:** $550 to $850; some to $10,000. **Remarks:** Full-time maker; first knife sold in 1983. **Mark:** Last name and Specwar knives.

EMMERLING, JOHN
1368 Pacific Way, Gearheart, OR 97138, Phone: 800-738-5434, ironwerks@linet.com

ENCE, JIM
145 S 200 East, Richfield, UT 84701, Phone: 435-896-6206
Specialties: High-art period pieces (spec in California knives) art knives. **Patterns:** Art, boot knives, fighters, Bowies and occasional folders. **Technical:** Grinds 440C for polish and beauty boys; makes own Damascus. **Prices:** Upscale. **Remarks:** Full-time maker; first knife sold in 1977. Does own engraving, gold work and stone work. Guild member since 1977. Founding member of the AKI. **Mark:** Ence, usually engraved.

ENGLAND, VIRGIL
1340 Birchwood St, Anchorage, AK 99508, Phone: 907-274-9494, WEB: www.virgilengland.com
Specialties: Edged weapons and equipage, one-of-a-kind only. **Patterns:** Axes, swords, lances and body armor. **Technical:** Forges and grinds as pieces dictate. Offers stainless and Damascus. **Prices:** Upscale. **Remarks:** A veteran knifemaker. No commissions. **Mark:** Stylized initials.

ENGLE, WILLIAM
16608 Oak Ridge Rd, Boonville, MO 65233, Phone: 816-882-6277
Specialties: Traditional working and using straight knives of his design. **Patterns:** Hunters, Bowies and fighters. **Technical:** Grinds 440C, ATS-34 and 154 CM. **Prices:** $250 to $500; some higher. **Remarks:** Part-time maker; first knife sold in 1982. All knives come with certificate of authenticity. **Mark:** Last name in block lettering.

ENGLISH, JIM
14586 Olive Vista Dr, Jamul, CA 91935, Phone: 619-669-0833
Specialties: Traditional working straight knives to customer specs. **Patterns:** Hunters, bowies, fighters, tantos, daggers, boot and utility/camp knives. **Technical:** Grinds 440C, ATS-34, commercial Damascus and customer choice. **Prices:** $130 to $350. **Remarks:**

Part-time maker; first knife sold in 1985. In addition to custom line, also does business as Mountain Home Knives. **Mark:** Double "A," Double "J" logo.

ENNIS, RAY
1220S 775E, Ogden, UT 84404, Phone: 800-410-7603, Fax: 501-621-2683, nifmakr@hotmail.com; Web:www.ennis-entrekusa.com

ENOS III, THOMAS M
12302 State Rd 535, Orlando, FL 32836, Phone: 407-239-6205, tmenos3@att.net
Specialties: Heavy-duty working straight knives; unusual designs. **Patterns:** Swords, machetes, daggers, skinners, filleting, period pieces. **Technical:** Grinds 440C. **Prices:** $75 to $1500. **Remarks:** Full-time maker; first knife sold in 1972. No longer accepting custom requests. Will be making his own designs. Send SASE for listing of items for sale. **Mark:** Name in knife logo and year, type of steel and serial number.

EPTING, RICHARD
4021 Cody Dr, College Station, TX 77845, Phone: 979-690-6496, rgeknives@hotmail.com; Web: www.eptingknives.com
Specialties: Folders and working straight knives. **Patterns:** Hunters, Bowies, and locking folders. **Technical:** Forges high-carbon steel and his own Damascus. **Prices:** $200 to $800; some to $1800. **Remarks:** Part-time maker, first knife sold 1996. **Mark:** Name in arch logo.

ERICKSON, DANIEL
Ring Of Fire Forge, 20011 Welch Rd., Snohomish, WA 98296, Phone: 206-355-1793, Web: www.ringoffireforge.com
Specialties: Likes to fuse traditional and functional with creative concepts. **Patterns:** Hunters, fighters, bowies, folders, slip joints, art knives, the Phalanx. **Technical:** Forges own pattern-welded damascus blades (1080/15N20), 5160, CruForgeV, 52100 and W2. Uses figured burls, stabilized woods, fossil ivories and natural and unique materials for handles. Custom stands and sheaths. **Prices:** $250 to $1,500. **Remarks:** Sole authorship, designer and inventor. Started making in 2003; first knife sold in 2004. ABS journeyman smith. **Mark:** "Ring of Fire" with Erickson moving through it.

ERICKSON, L.M.
1379 Black Mountain Cir, Ogden, UT 84404, Phone: 801-737-1930
Specialties: Straight knives; period pieces. **Patterns:** Bowies, fighters, boots and hunters. **Technical:** Grinds 440C, 154CM and commercial Damascus. **Prices:** $200 to $900; some to $5000. **Remarks:** Part-time maker; first knife sold in 1981. **Mark:** Name, city, state.

ERICKSON, WALTER E.
22280 Shelton Tr, Atlanta, MI 49709, Phone: 989-785-5262, wberic@src-milp.com
Specialties: Unusual survival knives and high-tech working knives. **Patterns:** Butterflies, hunters, tantos. **Technical:** Grinds ATS-34 or customer choice. **Prices:** $150 to $500; some to $1500. **Remarks:** Full-time maker; first knife sold in 1981. **Mark:** Using pantograph with assorted fonts (no longer stamping).

ERIKSEN, JAMES THORLIEF
dba VIKING KNIVES, 3830 Dividend Dr, Garland, TX 75042, Phone: 972-494-3667, Fax: 972-235-4932, VikingKnives@aol.com
Specialties: Heavy-duty working and using straight knives and folders utilizing traditional, Viking original and customer specification patterns. Some high-tech and fancy/embellished knives available. **Patterns:** Bowies, hunters, skinners, boot and belt knives, utility/camp knives, fighters, daggers, locking folders, slip-joint folders and kitchen knives. **Technical:** Hollow-grinds 440C, D2, ASP-23, ATS-34, 154CM, Vascowear. **Prices:** $150 to $300; some to $600. **Remarks:** Full-time maker; first knife sold in 1985. Doing business as Viking Knives. For a color catalog showing 50 different models, mail $5 to above address. **Mark:** VIKING or VIKING USA for export.

ERNEST, PHIL (PJ)
PO Box 5240, Whittier, CA 90607-5240, Phone: 562-556-2324, hugger883562@yahoo.com; Web:www.ernestcustomknives.com
Specialties: Fixed blades. **Patterns:** Wide range. Many original as well as hunters, camp, fighters, daggers, bowies and tactical. Specialzin in Wharncliff's of all sizes. **Technical:** Grinds commercial Damascus, Mosaid Damascus. ATS-34. and 440C. Full Tangs with bolsters. Handle material includes all types of exotic hardwood, abalone, peal mammoth tooth, mammoth ivory, Damascus steel and Mosaic Damascus. **Remarks:** Full time maker. First knife sold in 1999. **Prices:** $200 to $1800. Some to $2500. **Mark:** Owl logo with PJ Ernest Whittier CA or PJ Ernest.

ESPOSITO, EMMANUEL
Via Reano 70, Buttigliera Alta TO, ITALY 10090, Phone: 39-011932-16-21, www.emmanuelmaker.it
Specialties: Folding knife with his patent system lock mechanism with mosaic inlay.

ESSEGIAN, RICHARD
7387 E Tulare St, Fresno, CA 93727, Phone: 309-255-5950
Specialties: Fancy working knives of his design; art knives. **Patterns:** Bowies and some small hunters. **Technical:** Grinds A2, D2, 440C and 154CM. Engraves and inlays. **Prices:** Start at $600. **Remarks:** Part-time maker; first knife sold in 1986. **Mark:** Last name, city and state.

ESTABROOK, ROBBIE
1014 Madge Ct., Conway, SC 29526, Phone: 843-489-2331, r1956e@hotmail.com
Specialties: Traditional working straight knives. **Patterns:** Hunters and fishing knives. **Technical:** Hand grinds ATS 34 and D2. **Prices:** $100 and up. **Remarks:** Part-time maker. **Mark:** ESTABROOK.

ETZLER, JOHN
11200 N Island, Grafton, OH 44044, Phone: 440-748-2460, jetzler@bright.net;

Web: members.tripod.com/~etzlerknives/
Specialties: High-art and fantasy straight knives and folders of his design and to customer specs. **Patterns:** Folders, daggers, fighters, utility knives. **Technical:** Forges and grinds nickel Damascus and tool steel; grinds stainless steels. Prefers exotic, natural materials. **Prices:** $250 to $1200; some to $6500. **Remarks:** Full-time maker; first knife sold in 1992. **Mark:** Name or initials.

EVANS, BRUCE A
409 CR 1371, Booneville, MS 38829, Phone: 662-720-0193, beknives@avsia.com; Web: www.bruceevans.homestead.com/open.html
Specialties: Forges blades. **Patterns:** Hunters, Bowies, or will work with customer. **Technical:** 5160, cable Damascus, pattern welded Damascus. **Prices:** $200 and up. **Mark:** Bruce A. Evans Same with JS on reverse of blade.

EVANS, CARLTON
PO Box 46, Gainesville, TX 76241, Phone: 817-886-9231, carlton@carltonevans.com; Web: www.carltonevans.com
Specialties: High end folders and fixed blades. **Technical:** Uses the stock removal methods. The materials used are of the highest quality. **Remarks:** Full-time knifemaker, voting member of Knifemakers Guild, member of the Texas Knifemakers and Collectors Association.

EVANS, PHIL
594 SE 40th, Columbus, KS 66725, Phone: 620-249-0639, phil@glenviewforge.com Web: www.glenviewforge.com
Specialties: Working knives, hunters, skinners, also enjoys making Bowies and fighters, high carbon or Damascus. **Technical:** Forges own blades and makes own Damascus. Uses all kinds of ancient Ivory and bone. Stabilizes own native hardwoods. **Prices:** $150 -$1,500. **Remarks:** Part-time maker. Made first knife in 1995. **Mark:** EVANS.

EVANS, RONALD B
209 Hoffer St, Middleton, PA 17057-2723, Phone: 717-944-5464

EVANS, VINCENT K AND GRACE
HC 1 Box 5275, Keaau, HI 96749-9517, Phone: 808-966-8978, evansvk@gmail.com Web: www.picturetrail.com/vevans
Specialties: Period pieces; swords. **Patterns:** Scottish, Viking, central Asian. **Technical:** Forges 5160 and his own Damascus. **Prices:** $700 to $4000; some to $8000. **Remarks:** Full-time maker; first knife sold in 1983. **Mark:** Last initial with fish logo.

EWING, JOHN H
3276 Dutch Valley Rd, Clinton, TN 37716, Phone: 865-457-5757, johnja@comcast.net
Specialties: Working straight knives, hunters, camp knives. **Patterns:** Hunters. **Technical:** Grinds 440-D2. Forges 5160, 1095 prefers forging. **Prices:** $150 and up. **Remarks:** Part-time maker; first knife sold in 1985. **Mark:** First initial, last name, some embellishing done on knives.

F

FAIRLY, DANIEL
2209 Bear Creek Canyon Rd, Bayfield, CO 81122, danielfairlyknives@gmail.com; Web: www.danielfairlyknives.com
Specialties: "Craftsmanship without compromise. **Patterns:** Ultralight titanium utilities, everyday carry, folders, kitchen knives, Japanese-influenced design. **Technical:** Grinds mostly tool steel and carbidized titanium in .050" to .360" thick material. Uses heavy duty handle materials and flared test tube fasteners or epoxy soaked wrapped handles. Most grinds are chisel; flat convex and hollow grinds used. **Prices:** $85 to $1,850. **Remarks:** Full-time maker since first knife sold in Feb. 2011. **Mark:** Fairly written in all capitals with larger F.

FANT JR., GEORGE
1983 CR 3214, Atlanta, TX 75551-6515, Phone: (903) 846-2938

FARID, MEHR R
8 Sidney Close, Tunbridge Wells, Kent, ENGLAND TN2 5QQ, Phone: 011-44-1892 520345, farid@faridknives.com; Web: www.faridknives.com
Specialties: Hollow handle survival knives. High tech knives. **Patterns:** Flat grind blades & chisel ground LinerLock® folders. **Technical:** Grinds 440C, CPMT-440V, CPM-420V, CPM-15V, CPM5125V, and T-1 high speed steel. **Prices:** $550 to $5000. **Remarks:** Full-time maker; first knife sold in 1991. **Mark:** First name stamped.

FARR, DAN
6531 E. Poleline Ave., Post Falls, ID 83854, Phone: 585-721-1388
Specialties: Hunting, camping, fighting and utility. **Patterns:** Fixed blades. **Technical:** Forged or stock removal. **Prices:** $150 to $750.

FASSIO, MELVIN G
420 Tyler Way, Lolo, MT 59847, Phone: 406-544-1391, fassiocustomknives@gmail.com; Web: www.fassiocustomknives.com
Specialties: Working folders to customer specs. **Patterns:** Locking folders, hunters and traditional-style knives. **Technical:** Grinds 440C. **Prices:** $125 to $350. **Remarks:** Part-time maker; first knife sold in 1975. **Mark:** Name and city, dove logo.

FAUCHEAUX, HOWARD J
PO Box 206, Loreauville, LA 70552, Phone: 318-229-6467
Specialties: Working straight knives and folders; period pieces. Also a hatchet with capping knife in the handle. **Patterns:** Traditional locking folders, hunters, fighters and Bowies. **Technical:** Forges W2, 1095 and his own Damascus; stock removal D2. **Prices:** Start at $200. **Remarks:** Full-time maker; first knife sold in 1969. **Mark:** Last name.

custom knifemakers

FAUST, JOACHIM
Kirchgasse 10, Goldkronach, GERMANY 95497

FELIX, ALEXANDER
PO Box 4036, Torrance, CA 90510, Phone: 310-320-1836, sgiandubh@dslextreme.com
Specialties: Straight working knives, fancy ethnic designs. **Patterns:** Hunters, Bowies, daggers, period pieces. **Technical:** Forges carbon steel and Damascus; forged stainless and titanium jewelry, gold and silver casting. **Prices:** $110 and up. **Remarks:** Jeweler, ABS Journeyman Smith. **Mark:** Last name.

FELLOWS, MIKE
P.O. Box 184, Riversdale 6670, SOUTH AFRICA, Phone: 27 82 960 3868, karatshin@gmail.com
Specialties Miniatures, art knives and folders with occasional hunters and skinners. **Patterns:** Own designs. **Technical:** Uses own damascus. **Prices:** Upon request. **Remarks:** Uses only indigenous materials. Exotic hardwoods, horn and ivory. Does all own embellishments. **Mark:** "SHIN" letter from Hebrew alphabet over Hebrew word "Karat." Other: Member of Knifemakers Guild of South Africa.

FERGUSON, JIM
4652 Hackett St., Lakewood, CA 90713, Phone: 562-342-4890, jim@twistednickel.com; Web: www.twistednickel.com www.howtomakeaknife.net
Specialties: Bowies and push blades. **Patterns:** All styles. **Technical:** Flat and hollow grinds. Sells in U.S. and Canada. **Prices:** $100 to $1,200. **Mark:** Push blade with "Ferguson-USA." Also makes swords, battle axes and utilities.

FERGUSON, JIM
3543 Shadyhill Dr, San Angelo, TX 76904, Phone: 325-655-1061
Specialties: Straight working knives and folders. **Patterns:** Working belt knives, hunters, Bowies and some folders. **Technical:** Grinds ATS-34, D2 and Vascowear. Flat-grinds hunting knives. **Prices:** $200 to $600; some to $1000. **Remarks:** Full-time maker; first knife sold in 1987. **Mark:** First and middle initials, last name.

FERGUSON, LEE
1993 Madison 7580, Hindsville, AR 72738, Phone: 479-443-0084, info@fergusonknives.com; Web: www.fergusonknives.com
Specialties: Straight working knives and folders, some fancy. **Patterns:** Hunters, daggers, swords, locking folders and slip-joints. **Technical:** Grinds D2, 440C and ATS-34; heat-treats. **Prices:** $50 to $600; some to $4000. **Remarks:** Full-time maker; first knife sold in 1977. **Mark:** Full name.

FERRARA, THOMAS
122 Madison Dr, Naples, FL 33942, Phone: 813-597-3363, Fax: 813-597-3363
Specialties: High-art, traditional and working straight knives and folders of all designs. **Patterns:** Boots, Bowies, daggers, fighters and hunters. **Technical:** Grinds 440C, D2 and ATS-34; heat-treats. **Prices:** $100 to $700; some to $1300. **Remarks:** Part-time maker; first knife sold in 1983. **Mark:** Last name.

FERRIER, GREGORY K
3119 Simpson Dr, Rapid City, SD 57702, Phone: 605-342-9280

FERRY, TOM
16005 SE 322nd St, Auburn, WA 98092, Phone: 253-939-4468, tomferryknives@Q.com; Web: tomferryknives.com
Specialties: Presentation grade knives. **Patterns:** Folders and fixed blades. **Technical:** Specialize in Damascus and engraving. **Prices:** $500 and up. **Remarks:** DBA: Soos Creek Ironworks. ABS Master Smith. **Mark:** Combined T and F in a circle and/or last name.

FILIPPOU, IOANNIS-MINAS
23 Vryouron Str, Nea Smyrni 17122, Athens, GREECE 17122, Phone: (1) 935-2093, knifemaker_gr@yahoo.gr

FINCH, RICKY D
1179 Hwy 844, West Liberty, KY 41472, Phone: 606-743-7151, finchknives@mrtc.com; Web: www.finchknives.com
Specialties: Traditional working/using straight knives of his design or to customer spec. **Patterns:** Hunters, skinners and utility/camp knives. LinerLock® of his design. **Technical:** Grinds 440C, ATS-34 and CPM154, hand rubbed stain finish, use Micarta, stabilized wood, natural and exotic. **Prices:** $85 to $225. **Remarks:** Part-time maker, first knife made 1994. Doing business as Finch Knives. **Mark:** Last name inside outline of state of Kentucky.

FINNEY, GARETT
7181 Marcob Way, Loomis, CA 95650, Phone: 650-678-7332, garett@finneyknives.com; Web: www.finneyknives.com
Specialties: Customizes knives utilizing materials that couldn't be used for handle materials until the maker casts them into acrylic. He then combines the cast items with exotic natural materials via inlays in order to create unique, one-of-a-kind works of art. **Technical:** Most knives are mirror polished with fileworked blade spines and engraved bolsters. Price: $80 to $900, depending on knife and materials. Remarks Full-time maker. Mark Maker signs his name via engraving, and also uses a stamp for stock-removal or forged pieces.

FIORINI, BILL
703 W. North St., Grayville, IL 62844, Phone: 618-375-7191, smallflowerlonchura@yahoo.com
Specialties: Fancy working knives. **Patterns:** Hunters, boots, Japanese-style knives and kitchen/utility knives and folders. **Technical:** Forges own Damascus, mosaic and mokune-gane. **Prices:** Full range. **Remarks:** Full-time metal smith researching pattern materials. **Mark:** Orchid crest with name KOKA in Japanese.

FISHER, JAY
1405 Edwards, Clovis, NM 88101, jayfisher@jayfisher.com Web: www.JayFisher.com
Specialties: High-art, working and collector's knives of his design and client's designs. Military working and commemoratives. Gemstone handles, Locking combat sheaths. **Patterns:** Hunters, daggers, folding knives, museum pieces and high-art sculptures. **Technical:** 440C, ATS-34, CPMS30V, D2, O1, CPM154CM, CPMS35VN. Prolific maker of stone-handled knives and swords. **Prices:** $850 to $150,000. **Remarks:** Full-time maker; first knife sold in 1980. High resolution etching, computer and manual engraving. **Mark:** Signature "JaFisher"

FISHER, JOSH
JN Fisher Knives, 8419 CR 3615, Murchison, TX 75778, Phone: 903-203-2130, fisherknives@aol.com; Web: www.jnfisherknives.com
Specialties: Frame-handle fighters. **Technical:** Forge 5160 and 1084 blade steels. **Prices:** $125 to $1,000. **Remarks:** Part-time maker; first knife made in 2007. ABS journeyman smith. **Mark:** Josh Fisher etched. "JS" also etched on the reverse.

FISHER, LANCE
9 Woodlawn Ave., Pompton Lakes, NJ 07442, Phone: 973-248-8447, lance.fisher@sandvik.com
Specialties: Wedding cake knives and servers, forks, etc. Including velvet lined wood display cases. **Patterns:** Drop points, upswept skinners, Bowies, daggers, fantasy, medieval, San Francisco style, chef or kitchen cutlery. **Technical:** Stock removal method only. Steels include but are not limited to CPM 154, D2, CPM S35VN, CPM S90V and Sandvik 13C26. Handle materials include stag, sheep horn, exotic woods, micarta, and G10 as well as reconstituted stone. **Prices:** $350 -$2000. **Remarks:** Part-time maker, will become full-time on retirement. Made and sold first knife in 1981 and has never looked back. **Mark:** Tang stamp.

FISK, JERRY
10095 Hwy 278 W, Nashville, AR 71852, Phone: 870-845-4456, jerry@jerryfisk.com; Web: www.jerryfisk.com or Facebook: Jerry Fisk, MS Custom Knives
Specialties: Edged weapons, collectible and functional. **Patterns:** Bowies, daggers, swords, hunters, camp knives and others. **Technical:** Forges carbon steels and his own pattern welded steels. **Prices:** $1100 to $20,000. **Remarks:** National living treasure. **Mark:** Name, MS.

FISTER, JIM
PO Box 307, Simpsonville, KY 40067
Specialties: One-of-a-kind collectibles and period pieces. **Patterns:** Bowies, camp knives, hunters, buckskinners, and daggers. **Technical:** Forges, 1085, 5160, 52100, his own Damascus, pattern and turkish. **Prices:** $150 to $2500. **Remarks:** Part-time maker; first knife sold in 1982. **Mark:** Name and MS.

FITCH, JOHN S
45 Halbrook Rd, Clinton, AR 72031-8910, Phone: 501-893-2020

FITZ, ANDREW A. SR. AND JR.
63 Bradford Hwy., Milan, TN 38358, Phone: 731-420-0139, fitzknives@yahoo.com
Specialties: Tactical utility flipper folders and fixed blades of the makers' designs. **Patterns:** High-tech utility/defense folders and fixed blades. **Technical:** Grinds CPM 154, CTS B75P, PSF27, Elmax and CTS XHP. Titanium and carbon fiber handles, or G-10 on tactical utility folders. **Prices:** $600 to $1,300 (Andrew Sr.) and $200 to $500 (Andrew Jr.). **Remarks:** Fitz Sr. made and sold first knife in 2002. Fitz Jr. made first knife in 2013 and sold first knife in 2014. **Mark:** Fitz Sr.: Last name Fitz; and Fitz Jr.: Last name with Jr. in the Z.

FITZGERALD, DENNIS M
4219 Alverado Dr, Fort Wayne, IN 46816-2847, Phone: 219-447-1081
Specialties: One-of-a-kind collectibles and period pieces. **Patterns:** Skinners, fighters, camp and utility knives; period pieces. **Technical:** Forges 1085, 1095, L6, 5160, 52100, his own pattern and Turkish Damascus. **Prices:** $100 to $500. **Remarks:** Part-time maker; first knife sold in 1985. Doing business as The Ringing Circle. **Mark:** Name and circle logo.

FLINT, ROBERT
2902 Aspen, Anchorage, AK 99517, Phone: 907-243-6706
Specialties: Working straight knives and folders. **Patterns:** Utility, hunters, fighters and gents. **Technical:** Grinds ATS-34, BG-42, D2 and Damascus. **Prices:** $150 and up. **Remarks:** Part-time maker, first knife sold in 1998. **Mark:** Last name; stylized initials.

FLOURNOY, JOE
5750 Lisbon Rd, El Dorado, AR 71730, Phone: 870-863-7208, flournoy@ipa.net
Specialties: Working straight knives and folders. **Patterns:** Hunters, Bowies, camp knives, folders and daggers. **Technical:** Forges only high-carbon steel, steel cable and his own Damascus. **Prices:** $350 Plus. **Remarks:** First knife sold in 1977. **Mark:** Last name and MS in script.

FLUDDER, KEITH
3 Olive Ln., Tahmoor, New South Wales, AUSTRALIA 2573, Phone: 612 46843236 or 61 412687868, keith@knifemaker.com.au; Web: www.bladesmith.com.au
Specialties: Damascus and carbon steel fixed blades and art knives. **Patterns:** Bowies, fighters, hunters, tantos, wakizashis, katanas and kitchen knives. **Technical:** Forges and makes own damascus, including mosaics and multi-bars from 1075 and 15N20. Also uses 1084, W2, O1, 52100 and 5160. **Prices:** $275 to $3,000. **Remarks:** Full-time maker

since 2000; ABS journeyman smith since 2014; first knife made in 1989. **Mark:** Reverse K on F centered in Southern Cross constellation. Fludder on spine.

FLYNT, ROBERT G

15173 Christy Lane, Gulfport, MS 39503, Phone: 228-832-3378 or cell: 228-265-0410, robertflynt@cableone.net; Web: www.flyntstoneknifeworks.com

Specialties: All types of fixed blades: drop point, clip point, trailing point, bull-nose hunters, tactical, fighters and bowies. LinerLock, slip-joint and lockback folders. **Technical:** Using 154CM, CPM-154, ATS-34, 440C, CPM-3V and 52100 steels. Most blades made by stock removal, hollow and flat grind methods. Forges some cable damascus and uses numerous types of damascus purchased in billets from various makers. All filework and bluing done by the maker. Various wood handles, bone and horn materials, including some with wire inlay and other embellishments. Most knives sold with custom-fit leather sheaths, most include exotic skin inlay when appropriate. **Prices:** $150 and up, depending on embellishments on blade and sheath. **Remarks:** Full-time maker; first knife made in 1966. Knifemakers' Guild member. **Mark:** Last name in cursive letters or a knife striking a flint stone.

FOGARIZZU, BOITEDDU

via Crispi 6, Pattada, ITALY 07016

Specialties: Traditional Italian straight knives and folders. **Patterns:** Collectible folders. **Technical:** forges and grinds 12C27, ATS-34 and his Damascus. **Prices:** $200 to $3000. **Remarks:** Full-time maker; first knife sold in 1958. **Mark:** Full name and registered logo.

FONTENOT, GERALD J

901 Maple Ave, Mamou, LA 70554, Phone: 318-468-3180

FORREST, BRIAN

FORREST KNIVES, PO Box 611, Descanso, CA 91916, Phone: 619-445-6343, forrestforge@gmail.com; Web: www.forrestforge.biz

Specialties: Forged tomahawks, working knives, big Bowies. **Patterns:** Traditional and extra large Bowies. **Technical:** Hollow grinds: 440C, 1095, S160 Damascus. Prices"$125 and up. **Remarks:** Member of California Knifemakers Association. Full-time maker. First knife sold in 1971. **Mark:** Forrest USA/Tomahawks marked FF (Forrest Forge).

FORTHOFER, PETE

5535 Hwy 93S, Whitefish, MT 59937, Phone: 406-862-2674

Specialties: Interframes with checkered wood inlays; working straight knives. **Patterns:** Traditional-style hunting knives. **Technical:** Grinds D2, 440C, 154CM and ATS-34, and prefers mammoth ivory handles and mokume guards. **Prices:** $650 to $850. **Remarks:** Part-time maker; full-time gunsmith. First knife sold in 1979. **Mark:** Name and logo.

FOSTER, AL

118 Woodway Dr, Magnolia, TX 77355, Phone: 936-372-9297

Specialties: Straight knives and folders. **Patterns:** Hunting, fishing, folders and Bowies. **Technical:** Grinds 440-C, ATS-34 and D2. **Prices:** $100 to $1000. **Remarks:** Full-time maker; first knife sold in 1981. **Mark:** Scorpion logo and name.

FOSTER, BURT

23697 Archery Range Rd, Bristol, VA 24202, Phone: 276-669-0121, burt@burtfoster.com; Web:www.burtfoster.com

Specialties: Working straight knives, laminated blades, and some art knives of his design. **Patterns:** Bowies, hunters, daggers. **Technical:** Forges 52100, W-2 and makes own Damascus. Does own heat treating. **Remarks:** ABS MasterSmith. Full-time maker, believes in sole authorship. **Mark:** Signed "BF" initials.

FOSTER, NORVELL C

7945 Youngsford Rd, Marion, TX 78124-1713, Phone: 830-914-2078

Specialties: Engraving; ivory handle carving. **Patterns:** American-large and small scroll-oak leaf and acorns. **Prices:** $25 to $400. **Remarks:** Have been engraving since 1957. **Mark:** N.C. Foster -Marion -Tex and current year.

FOSTER, RONNIE E

95 Riverview Rd., Morrilton, AR 72110, Phone: 501-354-5389

Specialties: Working, using knives, some period pieces, work with customer specs. **Patterns:** Hunters, fighters, Bowies, liner-lock folders, camp knives. **Technical:** Forge-5160, 1084, O1, 15N20-makes own Damascus. **Prices:** $200 (start). **Remarks:** Part-time maker. First knife sold 1994. **Mark:** Ronnie Foster MS.

FOSTER, TIMOTHY L

723 Sweet Gum Acres Rd, El Dorado, AR 71730, Phone: 870-863-6188

FOWLER, CHARLES R

226 National Forest Rd 48, Ft McCoy, FL 32134-9624, Phone: 904-467-3215

FOWLER, ED A.

Willow Bow Ranch, PO Box 1519, Riverton, WY 82501, Phone: 307-856-9815

Specialties: High-performance working and using straight knives. **Patterns:** Hunter, camp, bird, and trout knives and Bowies. New model, the gentleman's Pronghorn. **Technical:** Low temperature forged 52100 from virgin 5-1/2 round bars, multiple quench heat treating, engraves all knives, all handles domestic sheep horn processed and aged at least 5 years. Makes heavy duty hand-stitched waxed harness leather pouch type sheaths. **Prices:** $800 to $7000. **Remarks:** Full-time maker. First knife sold in 1962. **Mark:** Initials connected.

FOWLER, STEPHAN

1142 Reading Dr. NW, Acworth, GA 30102, Phone: 770-726-9706, stephan@fowlerblades.com; Web: www.fowlerblades.com

Specialties: Bowies. **Patterns:** Bowies, hunters, chef's knives (American and Japanese style). **Technical:** Primarily W2 blade steel, also 52100, 1084, 1095 and various damascus

patterns. **Prices:** $200 and up. **Remarks:** Part-time maker since 2004. **Mark:** Fowler.

FRALEY, D B

1355 Fairbanks Ct, Dixon, CA 95620, Phone: 707-678-0393, dbtfnives@sbcglobal.net; Web:www.dbfraleyknives.com

Specialties Usable gentleman's fixed blades and folders. **Patterns:** Four locking-liner and frame-lock folders in four different sizes. **Technical:** Grinds CPM S30V, 154CM and 6K Stellite. **Prices:** $250 and up. **Remarks:** Part-time maker. First knife sold in 1990. **Mark:** First and middle initials, last name over a buffalo.

FRAMSKI, WALTER P

24 Rek Ln, Prospect, CT 06712, Phone: 203-758-5634

FRANCE, DAN

Box 218, Cawood, KY 40815, Phone: 606-573-6104

Specialties: Traditional working and using straight knives of his design. **Patterns:** Hunters, Bowies and utility/camp knives. **Technical:** Forges and grinds O1, 5160 and L6. **Prices:** $35 to $125; some to $350. **Remarks:** Spare-time maker; first knife sold in 1985. **Mark:** First name.

FRANCIS, JOHN D

FRANCIS KNIVES, 18 Miami St., Ft. Loramie, OH 45845, Phone: 937-295-3941, jdfrancis72@gmail.com

Specialties: Utility and hunting-style fixed bladed knives of 440 C and ATS-34 steel; Micarta, exotic woods, and other types of handle materials. **Prices:** $90 to $150 range. **Remarks:** Exceptional quality and value at factory prices. **Mark:** Francis-Ft. Loramie, OH stamped on tang.

FRANK, HEINRICH H

1147 SW Bryson St, Dallas, OR 97338, Phone: 503-831-1489, Fax: 503-831-1489

Specialties: High-art investor-class folders, handmade and engraved. **Patterns:** Folding daggers, hunter-size folders and gents. **Technical:** Grinds 07 and O1. **Prices:** $2,100 to $16,000. **Remarks:** Full-time maker; first knife sold in 1965. Doing business as H.H. Frank Knives. **Mark:** Name, address and date.

FRANKLIN, LARRY

Mya Knives, 418 S. 7th St., Stoughton, WI 53589, Phone: 608-719-2758

Specialties: Fixed-blade hunters, kitchen knives and bird-and-trout knives. **Technical:** Forges 20 percent of blades and uses stock-removal method of blade making on the other 80 percent, with favorite steels being 1095, D2, 440C and 14-4 CrMo steels. **Prices:** $85 to $500. **Remarks:** Started making knives around 2005. **Mark:** Daughter's name with a leaf for her favorite season.

FRANKLIN, MIKE

12040 Garnet Dr., Clermont, FL 34711, Phone: 937-549-2598

Specialties: High-tech tactical folders. **Patterns:** Tactical folders. **Technical:** Grinds CPM-T-440V, 440-C, ATS-34; titanium liners and bolsters; carbon fiber scales. Uses radical grinds and severe serrations. **Prices:** $100 to $1000. **Remarks:** Full-time maker; first knife sold in 1969. All knives made one at a time, 100% by the maker. **Mark:** Stylized boar with HAWG.

FRAPS, JOHN R

3810 Wyandotte Tr, Indianapolis, IN 46240-3422, Phone: 317-849-9419, jfraps@att.net; Web: www.frapsknives.com

Specialties: Working and collector grade LinerLock® and slip joint folders. **Patterns:** One-of-a-kind linerlocks and traditional slip joints. **Technical:** Flat and hollow grinds ATS-34, Damascus, Talonite, CPM S30V, 154Cm, Stellite 6K; hand rubbed or mirror finish. **Prices:** $200 to $1500, some higher. **Remarks:** Voting member of the Knifemaker's Guild; Full-time maker; first knife sold in 1997. **Mark:** Cougar Creek Knives and/or name.

FRAZIER, JIM

6315 Wagener Rd., Wagener, SC 29164, Phone: 803-564-6467, jbfrazierknives@gmail.com; Web: www.jbfrazierknives.com

Specialties: Hunters, semi skinners, oyster roast knives, bird and trout, folders, many patterns of own design with George Herron/Geno Denning influence. **Technical:** Stock removal maker using CPM-154, ATS-34, CPM-S30V and D2. Hollow grind, mainly mirror finish, some satin finish. Prefer to use natural handle material such as stag, horn, mammoth ivory, highly figured woods, some Micarta, others on request. Makes own leather sheaths on 1958 straight needle sticher. **Prices:** $125 to $600. **Remarks:** Part-time maker since 1989. **Mark:** JB Frazier in arch with Knives under it. Stamp on sheath is outline of state of SC, JB Frazier Knives Wagener SC inside outline.

FRED, REED WYLE

3149 X S, Sacramento, CA 95817, Phone: 916-739-0237

Specialties: Working using straight knives of his design. **Patterns:** Hunting and camp knives. **Technical:** Forges any 10 series, old files and carbon steels. Offers initialing upon request; prefers natural handle materials. **Prices:** $30 to $300. **Remarks:** Part-time maker; first knife sold in 1994. Doing business as R.W. Fred Knifemaker. **Mark:** Engraved first and last initials.

FREDEEN, GRAHAM

5121 Finadene Ct., Colorado Springs, CO 80916, Phone: 719-331-5665, fredeenblades@hotmail.com Web: www.fredeenblades.com

Specialties: Working class knives to high-end custom knives. Traditional pattern welding and mosaic Damascus blades. **Patterns:** All types: Bowies, fighters, hunters, skinners, bird and trout, camp knives, utility knives, daggers, etc. Occasionally swords, both European and Asian. **Technical:** Differential heat treatment and Hamon. Damascus steel rings and jewelry. Hand forged blades and Damascus steel. High carbon blade steels:

1050, 1075/1080, 1084, 1095, 5160, 52100, W1, W2, O1, 15n20 **Prices:** $100 -$2,000. **Remarks:** Sole authorship. Part-time maker. First blade produced in 2005. Member of American Bladesmith Society and Professional Knifemaker's Association **Mark:** "Fredeen" etched on the ricasso or on/along the spine of the blade.

FREDERICK, AARON
272 Brooks Ln, West Liberty, KY 41472-8961, Phone: 606-743-2015, aaronf@mrtc.com; Web: www.frederickknives.com
Specialties: Makes most types of knives, but as for now specializes in the Damascus folder. Does all own Damascus and forging of the steel. Also prefers natural handle material such as ivory and pearl. Prefers 14k gold screws in most of the knives he do. Also offer several types of file work on blades, spacers, and liners. Has just recently started doing carving and can do a limited amount of engraving.

FREEMAN, MATT
9286 N. Archie Ave., Fresno, CA 93720, Phone: 559-375-4408, cmftwknives@gmail.com; Web: www.youtube.com/cmftwknives
Specialties: Fixed blades and butterfly knives. **Technical:** Using mostly 1084, 154CM, D2 and file steel, works in any requested materials via stock removal. Also does knife modifications and leather/Kydex work. Three months or less waiting list. **Prices:** $75+. **Mark:** CMFTW.

FREER, RALPH
114 12th St, Seal Beach, CA 90740, Phone: 562-493-4925, Fax: same, ralphfreer@adelphia.net
Specialties: Exotic folders, liner locks, folding daggers, fixed blades. Patters: All original. **Technical:** Lots of Damascus, ivory, pearl, jeweled, thumb studs, carving ATS-34, 420V, 530V. **Prices:** $400 to $2500 and up. **Mark:** Freer in German-style text, also Freer shield.

FREY JR., W FREDERICK
305 Walnut St, Milton, PA 17847, Phone: 570-742-9576, wffrey@ptd.net
Specialties: Working straight knives and folders, some fancy. **Patterns:** Wide range miniatures, boot knives and lock back folders. **Technical:** Grinds A2, O1 and D2; vaseo wear, cru-wear and CPM S90V. **Prices:** $100 to $250; some to $1200. **Remarks:** Spare-time maker; first knife sold in 1983. All knives include quality hand stitched leather sheaths. **Mark:** Last name in script.

FRIEDLY, DENNIS E
12 Cottontail Lane E, Cody, WY 82414, Phone: 307-527-6811, friedlyknives@hotmail.com Web: www.friedlyknives.com
Specialties: Fancy working straight knives and daggers, lock back folders and liner locks. Also embellished bowies. **Patterns:** Hunters, fighters, short swords, minis and miniatures; new line of full-tang hunters/boots. **Technical:** Grinds 440C, commercial Damascus, mosaic Damascus and ATS-34 blades; prefers hidden tangs and full tangs. Both flat and hollow grinds. **Prices:** $350 to $2500. Some to $10,000. **Remarks:** Full-time maker; first knife sold in 1972. **Mark:** D.E. Friedly-Cody, WY. Friedly Knives

FRIESEN, DAVE J
Qualicum Beach, British Columbia, CANADA, Phone: 250-927-4113, info@islandblacksmith.ca; Web: www.islandblacksmith.ca
Specialties: Charcoal-forged classical tanto and fusion-style takedown knives crafted by hand from reclaimed and natural materials using traditional techniques.

FRIGAULT, RICK
1189 Royal Pines Rd, Golden Lake, ON, CANADA K0J 1X0, Phone: 613-401-2869, Web: www.rfrigaultknives.ca
Specialties: Fixed blades. **Patterns:** Hunting, tactical and large Bowies. **Technical:** Grinds ATS-34, 440-C, D-2, CPMS30V, CPMS60V, CPMS90V, BG42 and Damascus. Use G-10, Micarta, ivory, antler, ironwood and other stabilized woods for carbon fiber handle material. Makes leather sheaths by hand. Tactical blades include a Concealex sheath made by "On Scene Tactical." **Remarks:** Sold first knife in 1997. Member of Canadian Knifemakers Guild. **Mark:** RFRIGAULT.

FRITZ, ERIK L
837 River St Box 1203, Forsyth, MT 59327, Phone: 406-351-1101, tacmedic45@yahoo.com
Specialties: Forges carbon steel 1084, 5160, 52100 and Damascus. **Patterns:** Hunters, camp knives, bowies and folders as well as forged tactical. **Technical:** Forges own Mosaic and pattern welded Damascus as well as doing own heat treat. **Prices:** A$200 and up. **Remarks:** Sole authorship knives and sheaths. Part time maker first knife in 2004. ABS member. **Mark:** E. Fritz in arc on left side ricasso.

FRITZ, JESSE
900 S. 13th St, Slaton, TX 79364, Phone: 806-828-5083
Specialties: Working and using straight knives in standard patterns. **Patterns:** Hunters, utility/camp knives and skinners with gut hook, Bowie knives, kitchen carving sets by request. **Technical:** Grinds 440C, O1 and 1095. Uses 1095 steel. Fline-napped steel design, blued blades, filework and machine jewelling. Inlays handles with turquoise, coral and mother-of-pearl. Makes sheaths. **Prices:** $85 to $275; some to $500. **Mark:** Last name only (FRITZ).

FRIZZELL, TED
14056 Low Gap Rd, West Fork, AR 72774, Phone: 501-839-2516, mmhwaxes@aol.com Web: www.mineralmountain.com
Specialties: Swords, axes and self-defense weapons. **Patterns:** Small skeleton knives to large swords. **Technical:** Grinds 5160 almost exclusively—1/4" to 1/2"— bars some O1 and A2 on request. All knives come with Kydex sheaths. **Prices:** $45 to $1200. **Remarks:** Full-time maker; first knife sold in 1984. Doing business as Mineral Mountain Hatchet

Works. Wholesale orders welcome. **Mark:** A circle with line in the middle; MM and HW within the circle.

FRIZZI, LEONARDO
Via Kyoto 31, Firenze, ITALY 50126, Phone: 335-344750, postmaster@frizzi-knives.com; Web: www.frizzi-knives.com
Specialties: Fancy handmade one-of-a kind folders of his own design, some fixed blade and dagger. **Patterns:** Folders liner loch and back locks. **Technical:** Grinds rwl 34, cpm 154, cpm s30v, stainless damascus and the best craft damascus, own heat treating. I usually prefer satin finish the flat of the blade and mirror polish the hollow grind; special 18k gold, filework. **Prices:** $600 to $4,000. **Remarks:** Part-time maker, first knife sold in 2003. **Mark:** Full name, city, country, or initial, last name and city, or initial in square logo.

FRONEFIELD, DANIEL
20270 Warriors Path, Peyton, CO 80831, Phone: 719-749-0226, dfronfld@hiwaay.com
Specialties: Fixed and folding knives featuring meteorites and other exotic materials. **Patterns:** San-mai Damascus, custom Damascus. **Prices:** $500 to $3000.

FROST, DEWAYNE
1016 Van Buren Rd, Barnesville, GA 30204, Phone: 770-358-1426, lbrtyhill@aol.com
Specialties: Working straight knives and period knives. **Patterns:** Hunters, Bowies and utility knives. **Technical:** Forges own Damascus, cable, etc. as well as stock removal. **Prices:** $150 to $500. **Remarks:** Part-time maker ABS Journeyman Smith. **Mark:** Liberty Hill Forge Dewayne Frost w/liberty bell.

FRUHMANN, LUDWIG
Stegerwaldstr 8, Burghausen, GERMANY 84489
Specialties: High-tech and working straight knives of his design. **Patterns:** Hunters, fighters and boots. **Technical:** Grinds ATS-34, CPM-T-440V and Schneider Damascus. Prefers natural handle materials. **Prices:** $200 to $1500. **Remarks:** Spare-time maker; first knife sold in 1990. **Mark:** First initial and last name.

FRY, JASON
1701 North Willis, Abilene, TX 79603, Phone: 325-669-4805, frycustomknives@gmail.com; Web: www.frycustomknives.com
Specialties: Prefers drop points, both with or without bolsters. Prefers native Texas woods and often does contrasting wood bolsters. Also does own leather work. **Patterns:** Primarily EDC and hunting/skinning knives under 8 inches. Also slip-joint folders, primarily single-blade trappers and jacks. **Technical:** 1080 carbon steel, D2 tool steel, and 154CM stainless. Makes knives by stock removal and does own heat treating in a digitally controlled kiln. **Prices:** $150 to $500. **Remarks:** Part-time maker since July 2008, and 2013 probationary member of the Knifemakers' Guild. **Mark:** Jason Fry over Abilene, TX.

FUEGEN, LARRY
617 N Coulter Circle, Prescott, AZ 86303, Phone: 928-776-8777, fuegen@cableone.net; Web: www.larryfuegen.com
Specialties: High-art folders and classic and working straight knives. **Patterns:** Forged scroll folders, lockback folders and classic straight knives. **Technical:** Forges 5160, 1095 and his own Damascus. Works in exotic leather; offers elaborate filework and carving; likes natural handle materials, now offers own engraving. **Prices:** $1,200 to $26,000. **Remarks:** Full-time maker; first knife sold in 1975. Sole authorship on all knives. ABS Mastersmith. **Mark:** Initials connected.

FUJIKAWA, SHUN
Sawa 1157, Kaizuka, Osaka, JAPAN 597 0062, Phone: 81-724-23-4032, Fax: 81-726-23-9229
Specialties: Folders of his design and to customer specs. **Patterns:** Locking folders. **Technical:** Grinds his own steel. **Prices:** $450 to $2500; some to $3000. **Remarks:** Part-time maker.

FUKUTA, TAK
38-Umeagae-cho, Seki-City, Gifu, JAPAN, Phone: 0575-22-0264
Specialties: Bench-made fancy straight knives and folders. **Patterns:** Sheffield-type folders, Bowies and fighters. **Technical:** Grinds commercial Damascus. **Prices:** Start at $300. **Remarks:** Full-time maker. **Mark:** Name in knife logo.

FULLER, BRUCE A
3366 Ranch Rd. 32, Blanco, TX 78606, Phone: 832-262-0529, fullcoforg@aol.com
Specialties: One-of-a-kind working/using straight knives and folders of his designs. **Patterns:** Bowies, hunters, folders, and utility/camp knives. **Technical:** Forges high-carbon steel and his own Damascus. Prefers El Solo Mesquite and natural materials. Offers filework. **Prices:** $200 to $500; some to $1800. **Remarks:** Spare-time maker; first knife sold in 1991. Doing business as Fullco Forge. **Mark:** Fullco, M.S.

FULLER, JACK A
7103 Stretch Ct, New Market, MD 21774, Phone: 301-798-0119
Specialties: Straight working knives of his design and to customer specs. **Patterns:** Fighters, camp knives, hunters, tomahawks and art knives. **Technical:** Forges 5160, O1, W2 and his own Damascus. Does silver wire inlay and own leather work, wood lined sheaths for big camp knives. **Prices:** $400 and up. **Remarks:** Part-time maker. Master Smith in ABS; first knife sold in 1979. **Mark:** Fuller's Forge, MS.

FULTON, MICKEY
406 S Shasta St, Willows, CA 95988, Phone: 530-934-5780
Specialties: Working straight knives and folders of his design. **Patterns:** Hunters, Bowies, lockback folders and steak knife sets. **Technical:** Hand-filed, sanded, buffed ATS-

34, 440C and A2. **Prices:** $65 to $600; some to $1200. **Remarks:** Full-time maker; first knife sold in 1979. **Mark:** Signature.

G

GADBERRY, EMMET
82 Purple Plum Dr, Hattieville, AR 72063, Phone: 501-354-4842

GADDY, GARY LEE
205 Ridgewood Lane, Washington, NC 27889, Phone: 252-946-4359
Specialties: Working/using straight knives of his design; period pieces. **Patterns:** Bowies, hunters, utility/camp knives, oyster knives. **Technical:** Grinds ATS-34, 01; forges 1095. **Prices:** $175+ **Remarks:** Spare-time maker; first knife sold in 1991. No longer accepts orders. **Mark:** Quarter moon stamp.

GAETA, ANGELO
R. Saldanha Marinho 1295, Centro Jau, SP, BRAZIL 17201-310, Phone: 0146-224543, Fax: 0146-224543
Specialties: Straight using knives to customer specs. **Patterns:** Hunters, fighting, daggers, belt push dagger. **Technical:** Grinds D6, ATS-34 and 440C stainless. Titanium nitride golden finish upon request. **Prices:** $60 to $300. **Remarks:** Full-time maker; first knife sold in 1992. **Mark:** First initial, last name.

GAHAGAN, KYLE
200 Preachers Bottom Dr., Moravian Falls, NC 28654, Phone: 919-359-9220, kylegahagan78@yahoo.com; Web: www.gahaganknives.com
Specialties: Bowies and fighters. **Patterns:** Custom designs from maker or customer. **Technical:** Forges 1095, W2, 1075, 1084 and damascus blade steels. **Prices:** $200 and up. **Remarks:** Full-time bladesmith; sold first knife in 2011. **Mark:** Gahagan crest with Gahagan underneath.

GAINES, BUDDY
GAINES KNIVES, 155 Red Hill Rd., Commerce, GA 30530, Web: www.gainesknives.com
Specialties: Collectible and working folders and straight knives. **Patterns:** Folders, hunters, Bowies, tactical knives. **Technical:** Forges own Damascus, grinds ATS-34, D2, commercial Damascus. Prefers mother-of-pearl and stag. **Prices:** Start at $200. **Remarks:** Part-time maker, sold first knife in 1985. **Mark:** Last name.

GAINEY, HAL
904 Bucklevel Rd, Greenwood, SC 29649, Phone: 864-223-0225, Web: www.scak.org
Specialties: Traditional working and using straight knives and folders. **Patterns:** Hunters, slip-joint folders and utility/camp knives. **Technical:** Hollow-grinds ATS-34 and D2; makes sheaths. **Prices:** $95 to $145; some to $500. **Remarks:** Full-time maker; first knife sold in 1975. **Mark:** Eagle head and last name.

GALLAGHER, BARRY
313 W. Bebb St., Lewistown, MT 59457, Phone: 406-538-7056, Web: www.gallagherknives.com
Specialties: One-of-a-kind Damascus folders. **Patterns:** Folders, utility to high art, some straight knives, hunter, Bowies, and art pieces. **Technical:** Forges own mosaic Damascus and carbon steel, some stainless. **Prices:** $400 to $5000+. **Remarks:** Full-time maker; first knife sold in 1993. Doing business as Gallagher Custom Knives. **Mark:** Last name.

GAMBLE, ROGER
18515 N.W. 28th Pl., Newberry, FL 32669, ROGERLGAMBLE@COX.NET
Specialties: Traditional working/using straight knives and folders of his design. **Patterns:** Liner locks and hunters. **Technical:** Grinds ATS-34 and Damascus. **Prices:** $150 to $2000. **Remarks:** Part-time maker; first knife sold in 1982. Doing business as Gamble Knives. **Mark:** First name in a fan of cards over last name.

GANN, TOMMY
2876 State Hwy. 198, Canton, TX 75103, Phone: 903-848-9375
Specialties: Art and working straight knives of my design or customer preferences/design. **Patterns:** Bowie, fighters, hunters, daggers. **Technical:** Forges Damascus 52100 and grinds ATS-34 and D2. **Prices:** $200 to $2500. **Remarks:** Full-time knifemaker, first knife sold in 2002. ABS journey bladesmith. **Mark:** TGANN.

GANSHORN, CAL
123 Rogers Rd., Regina, SK, CANADA S4S 6T7, Phone: 306-584-0524, cganshorn@accesscomm.ca or cganshorn@myaccess.ca
Specialties: Working and fancy fixed blade knives. **Patterns:** Bowies, hunters, daggers, and filleting. **Technical:** Makes own forged Damascus billets, ATS, salt heat treating, and custom forges and burners. **Prices:** $250 to $1500. **Remarks:** Part-time maker. **Mark:** Last name etched in ricasso area.

GARAU, MARCELLO
Via Alagon 42, Oristano, ITALY 09170, Phone: 00393479073454, marcellogarau@libero.it Web: www.knifecreator.com
Specialties: Mostly lock back folders with interframe. **Technical:** Forges own damascus for both blades and frames. **Prices:** 200 -2,700 Euros. **Remarks:** Full-time maker; first knife made in 1995. Attends Milano Knife Show and ECCKSHOW yearly. **Mark:** M.Garau inside handle.

GARCIA, MARIO EIRAS
Rua Edmundo Scannapieco 300, Caxingui, SP, BRAZIL 05516-070, Phone: 011-37218304, Fax: 011-37214528
Specialties: Fantasy knives of his design; one-of-a-kind only. **Patterns:** Fighters, daggers, boots and two-bladed knives. **Technical:** Forges car leaf springs. Uses only natural handle material. **Prices:** $100 to $200. **Remarks:** Part-time maker; first knife sold

in 1976. **Mark:** Two "B"s, one opposite the other.

GARDNER, ROBERT
13462 78th Pl. N, West Palm Beach, FL 33412
Specialties: Straight blades, forged and clay hardened or differentialy heat treated. Kydex and leather sheath maker. **Patterns:** Working/using knives, some to customer specs, and high-end knives, daggers, bowies, ethnic knives, and Steelhead and Lil' Chub woodland survival/bushcraft knife set with an elaborate, versatile sheath system. Affordable hard-use production line of everyday carry belt knives, and less-expensive forged knives, neck knives and "wrench" knives. **Technical:** Grinds, forges and heat treats high-carbon 1084, 1095, 1075, W1, W2, 5160 and 52100 steels, some natural handle materials and Micarta for full-tang knives. **Prices:** $60 and up; sheaths $30 and up. **Remarks:** Full-time maker since 2010; first knife sold in 1986. **Mark:** Initials in angular script, stamped, engraved or etched.

GARNER, GEORGE
7527 Calhoun Dr. NE, Albuquerque, NM 87109, Phone: 505-797-9317, razorbackblades@msn.com and Web: www.razorbackblades.com
Specialties: High art locking liner folders and Daggers of his own design. Working and high art straight knives. **Patterns:** Bowies, daggers, fighters and locking liner folders. **Technical:** Grinds 440C, CPM-154, ATS34 and others. Damascus, Mosaic Damascus and Mokume. Makes own custom leather sheaths. **Prices:** $150 -$2,500. **Remarks:** Part-time maker since 1993. Full-time maker as of 2011. Company name is Razorback Blades. **Mark:** GEORGE GARNER

GARNER, LARRY W
13069 FM 14, Tyler, TX 75706, Phone: 903-597-6045, lwgarner@classicnet.net
Specialties: Fixed blade hunters and Bowies. **Patterns:** His designs or yours. **Technical:** Hand forges 5160. **Prices:** $200 to $500. **Remarks:** Apprentice bladesmith. **Mark:** Last name.

GARVOCK, MARK W
RR 1, Balderson, ON, CANADA K1G 1A0, Phone: 613-833-2545, Fax: 613-833-2208, garvock@travel-net.com
Specialties: Hunters, Bowies, Japanese, daggers and swords. **Patterns:** Cable Damascus, random pattern welded or to suit. **Technical:** Forged blades; hi-carbon. **Prices:** $250 to $900. **Remarks:** CKG member and ABS member. Shipping and taxes extra. **Mark:** Big G with M in middle.

GATLIN, STEVE
103 Marian Ct., Leesburg, GA 31763, Phone: 229-328-5074, stevegatlinknives@hotmail.com; Web: www.stevegatlinknives.com
Specialties: Loveless-style knives, double-ground fighters and traditional hunters. Some tactical models of maker's design. Fixed blades only. **Technical:** Grinds CPM-154, ATS-34 and 154CM. **Prices:** $450 to $1,500 on base models. **Remarks:** Voting member of Knifemakers' Guild since 2009; first knife sold in 2008. **Mark:** Typical football shape with name on top and city below.

GEDRAITIS, CHARLES J
GEDRAITIS HAND CRAFTED KNIVES, 444 Shrewsbury St, Holden, MA 01520, Phone: 508-963-1861, gedraitisknives@yahoo.com; Web: www.gedraitisknives.com
Specialties: One-of-a-kind folders & automatics of his own design. **Patterns:** One-of-a-kind. **Technical:** Forges to shape mostly stock removal. **Prices:** $300 to $2500. **Remarks:** Full-time maker. **Mark:** 3 scallop shells with an initial inside each one: CJG.

GENOVESE, RICK
PO Box 226, 182 Purtill Tr., Tonto Basin, AZ 85553, Phone: 928-274-7739, genoveseknives@hotmail.com; Web: www.rickgenoveseknives.com
Specialties Interframe-style folders. **Patterns:** Sleek folders in gentleman's designs. Also folding dirks and daggers. **Technical:** Main blade material is CPM 154. Also uses damascus by Devin Thomas and Jerry Rados. Inlays gemstones such as lapis lazuli, jade, opal, dinosaur bone, tiger eye, jasper, agate, malachite, petrified wood, as well as various pearls. **Prices:** $1,500-$10,000. **Remarks:** Full-time maker; first knife sold in 1975. **Mark:** Genovese in stylized letters.

GEORGE, HARRY
3137 Old Camp Long Rd, Aiken, SC 29805, Phone: 803-649-1963, hdkk-george@scescape.net
Specialties: Working straight knives of his design or to customer specs. **Patterns:** Hunters, skinners and utility knives. **Technical:** Grinds ATS-34. Prefers natural handle materials, hollow-grinds and mirror finishes. **Prices:** Start at $70. **Remarks:** Part-time maker; first knife sold in 1985. Trained under George Herron. Member SCAK. Member Knifemakers Guild. **Mark:** Name, city, state.

GEORGE, LES
4833 Saratoga Blvd., #401, Corpus Christi, TX 78413, Phone: 361-288-9777, les@georgeknives.com; Web: www.georgeknives.com
Specialties: Tactical frame locks and fixed blades. **Patterns:** Folders, balisongs, and fixed blades. **Technical:** CPM154, S30V, Chad Nichols Damascus. **Prices:** $200 to $800. **Remarks:** Full-time maker, first knife sold in 1992. Doing business as www.georgeknives.com. **Mark:** Last name over logo.

GEORGE, TOM
550 Aldbury Dr, Henderson, NV 89014, tagmaker@aol.com
Specialties: Working straight knives, display knives, custom meat cleavers, and folders of his design. **Patterns:** Hunters, Bowies, daggers, buckskinners, swords and folders. **Technical:** Uses D2, 440C, ATS-34 and 154CM. **Prices:** $500 to $13,500. **Remarks:** Custom orders not accepted "at this time". Full-time maker. First knife1982; first 350 knives were numbered; after that no numbers. Almost all his knives today are Bowies and swords. Creator and maker of the "Past Glories" series of knives. **Mark:** Tom George maker.

GEPNER, DON

2615 E Tecumseh, Norman, OK 73071, Phone: 405-364-2750

Specialties: Traditional working and using straight knives of his design. **Patterns:** Bowies and daggers. **Technical:** Forges his Damascus, 1095 and 5160. **Prices:** $100 to $400; some to $1000. **Remarks:** Spare-time maker; first knife sold in 1991. Has been forging since 1954; first edged weapon made at 9 years old. **Mark:** Last initial.

GERNER, THOMAS

PO Box 301, Walpole, WA, AUSTRALIA 6398, gerner@bordernet.com.au; Web: www.deepriverforge.com

Specialties: Forged working knives; plain steel and pattern welded. **Patterns:** Tries most patterns heard or read about. **Technical:** 5160, L6, O1, 52100 steels; Australian hardwood handles. **Prices:** $220 and up. **Remarks:** Achieved ABS Master Smith rating in 2001. **Mark:** Like a standing arrow and a leaning cross, T.G. in the Runic (Viking) alphabet.

GHIO, PAOLO

4330 Costa Mesa, Pensacola, FL 32504-7849, Phone: 850-393-0135, paologhio@hotmail.com

Specialties: Folders, fillet knives and skinners. **Patterns:** Maker's own design, or will work from a customer's pattern. **Technical:** Stock removal, all work in house, including heat treat. **Prices:** $200 to $500. **Mark:** PKG.

GIAGU, SALVATORE AND DEROMA MARIA ROSARIA

Via V Emanuele 64, Pattada (SS), ITALY 07016, Phone: 079-755918, Fax: 079-755918, coltelligiagupattada@tiscali.it Web: www.culterpattada.it

Specialties: Using and collecting traditional and new folders from Sardegna. **Patterns:** Folding, hunting, utility, skinners and kitchen knives. **Technical:** Forges ATS-34, 440, D2 and Damascus. **Prices:** $200 to $2000; some higher. **Mark:** First initial, last name and name of town and muflon's head.

GIBERT, PEDRO

Los Alamos 410, San Martin de los Andes, Neuquen, ARGENTINA 8370, Phone: 054-2972-410868, rosademayo@infovia.com.ar

Specialties: Hand forges: Stock removal and integral. High quality artistic knives of his design and to customer specifications. **Patterns:** Country (Argentine gaucho-style), knives, folders, Bowies, daggers, hunters. Others upon request. **Technical:** Blade: Bohler k110 Austrian steel (high resistance to waste). Handles: (Natural materials) ivory elephant, killer whale, hippo, walrus tooth, deer antler, goat, ram, buffalo horn, bone, rhea, sheep, cow, exotic woods (South America native woods) hand carved and engraved guards and blades. Stainless steel guards, finely polished: semi-matte or shiny finish. Sheaths: Raw or tanned leather, hand-stitched; rawhide or cotton yarn embroidered. Box: One wood piece, hand carved. Wooden hinges and locks. **Prices:** $600 and up. **Remarks:** Full-time maker. Made first knife in 1987. **Mark:** Only a rose logo. Buyers initials upon request.

GIBO, GEORGE

PO Box 4304, Hilo, HI 96720, Phone: 808-987-7002, geogibo@hilo808.net

Specialties: Straight knives and folders. **Patterns:** Hunters, bird and trout, utility, gentlemen and tactical folders. **Technical:** Grinds ATS-34, BG-42, Talonite, Stainless Steel Damascus. **Prices:** $250 to $1000. **Remarks:** Spare-time maker; first knife sold in 1995. **Mark:** Name, city and state around Hawaiian "Shaka" sign.

GILBERT, CHANTAL

291 Rue Christophe-Colomb est #105, Quebec City, QC, CANADA G1K 3T1, Phone: 418-525-6961, Fax: 418-525-4666, gilbertc@medion.qc.ca; Web:www.chantalgilbert.com

Specialties: Straight art knives that may resemble creatures, often with wings, shells and antennae, always with a beak of some sort, fixed blades in a feminine style. **Technical:** ATS-34 and Damascus. Handle materials usually silver that she forms to shape via special molds and a press; ebony and fossil ivory. **Prices:** Range from $500 to $4000. **Remarks:** Often embellishes her art knives with rubies, meteorite, 18k gold and similar elements.

GILBREATH, RANDALL

55 Crauswell Rd, Dora, AL 35062, Phone: 205-648-3902

Specialties: Damascus folders and fighters. **Patterns:** Folders and fixed blades. **Technical:** Forges Damascus and high-carbon; stock removal stainless steel. **Prices:** $300 to $1500. **Remarks:** Full-time maker; first knife sold in 1979. **Mark:** Name in ribbon.

GILJEVIC, BRANKO

35 Hayley Crescent, Queanbeyan 2620, New South Wales, AUSTRALIA 0262977613

Specialties: Classic working straight knives and folders of his design. **Patterns:** Hunters, Bowies, skinners and locking folders. **Technical:** Grinds 440C. Offers acid etching, scrimshaw and leather carving. **Prices:** $150 to $1500. **Remarks:** Part-time maker; first knife sold in 1987. Doing business as Sambar Custom Knives. **Mark:** Company name in logo.

GINGRICH, JUSTIN

5329 Anna Belle Ln., Wade, NC 28395, Phone: 507-230-0398, justin@gingrichtactical.com Web: www.gingrichtactical.com

Specialties: Anything from bushcraft to tactical, heavy on the tactical. **Patterns:** Fixed blades and folders. **Technical:** Uses all types of steel and handle material, method is stock-removal. **Prices:** $30 -$1000. **Remarks:** Full-time maker. **Mark:** Tang stamp is the old Ranger Knives logo.

GIRTNER, JOE

409 Catalpa Ave, Brea, CA 92821, Phone: 714-529-2388, conceptsinknives@aol.com

Specialties: Art knives and miniatures. **Patterns:** Mainly Damascus (some carved). **Technical:** Many techniques and materials combined. Wood carving knives and tools, hunters, custom orders. **Prices:** $55 to $3000. **Mark:** Name.

GITTINGER, RAYMOND

6940 S Rt 100, Tiffin, OH 44883, Phone: 419-397-2517

GLOVER, RON

5896 Thornhill Ave., Cincinnati, OH 45224, Phone: 513-404-7107, r.glover@zoomtown.com

Specialties: High-tech working straight knives and folders. **Patterns:** Hunters to Bowies; some interchangeable blade models; unique locking mechanisms. **Technical:** Grinds 440C, 154CM; buys Damascus. **Prices:** $70 to $500; some to $800. **Remarks:** Part-time maker; first knife sold in 1981. **Mark:** Name in script.

GLOVER, WARREN D

dba BUBBA KNIVES, PO Box 475, Cleveland, GA 30528, Phone: 706-865-3998, Fax: 706-348-7176, warren@bubbaknives.net; Web: www.bubbaknives.net

Specialties: Traditional and custom working and using straight knives of his design and to customer request. **Patterns:** Hunters, skinners, bird and fish, utility and kitchen knives. **Technical:** Grinds 440, ATS-34 and stainless steel Damascus. **Prices:** $75 to $400 and up. **Remarks:** Full-time maker; sold first knife in 1995. **Mark:** Bubba, year, name, state.

GODDARD, WAYNE

473 Durham Ave, Eugene, OR 97404, Phone: 541-689-8098, wgoddard44@comcast.net

Specialties: Working/using straight knives and folders. **Patterns:** Hunters and folders. **Technical:** Works exclusively with wire Damascus and his own-pattern welded material. **Prices:** $250 to $4000. **Remarks:** Full-time maker; first knife sold in 1963. **Mark:** Blocked initials on forged blades; regular capital initials on stock removal.

GODLESKY, BRUCE F.

1002 School Rd., Apollo, PA 15613, Phone: 724-840-5786, brucegodlesky@yahoo.com; Web: www.birdforge.com

Specialties: Working/using straight knives and tomahawks, mostly forged. **Patterns:** Hunters, birds and trout, fighters and tomahawks. **Technical:** Most forged, some stock removal. Carbon steel only. 5160, O-1, W2, 10xx series. Makes own Damascus and welded cable. **Prices:** Starting at $75. **Mark:** BIRDOG FORGE.

GOERS, BRUCE

3423 Royal Ct S, Lakeland, FL 33813, Phone: 941-646-0984

Specialties: Fancy working and using straight knives of his design and to customer specs. **Patterns:** Hunters, fighters, Bowies and fantasy knives. **Technical:** Grinds ATS-34, some Damascus. **Prices:** $195 to $600; some to $1300. **Remarks:** Part-time maker; first knife sold in 1990. Doing business as Vulture Cutlery. **Mark:** Buzzard with initials.

GOLDBERG, DAVID

321 Morris Rd, Ft Washington, PA 19034, Phone: 215-654-7117, david@goldmountainforge.com; Web: www.goldmountainforge.com

Specialties: Japanese-style designs, will work with special themes in Japanese genre. **Patterns:** Kozuka, Tanto, Wakazashi, Katana, Tachi, Sword canes, Yari and Naginata. **Technical:** Forges his own Damascus and makes his own handmade tamehagane steel from straw ash, iron, carbon and clay. Uses traditional materials, carves fittings handles and cases. Hardens all blades in traditional Japanese clay differential technique. **Remarks:** Full-time maker; first knife sold in 1987. Japanese swordsmanship teacher (jaido) and Japanese self-defense teach (aikido). **Mark:** Name (kinzan) in Japanese Kanji on Tang under handle.

GOLDEN, RANDY

6492 Eastwood Glen Dr, Montgomery, AL 36117, Phone: 334-271-6429, rgolden1@mindspring.com

Specialties: Collectable quality hand rubbed finish, hunter, camp, Bowie straight knives, custom leather sheaths with exotic skin inlays and tooling. **Technical:** Stock removal ATS-34, CPM154, S30V and BG-42. Natural handle materials primarily stag and ivory. **Prices:** $500 to $1500. **Remarks:** Full-time maker, member Knifemakers Guild, first knife sold in 2000. **Mark:** R. R. Golden Montgomery, AL.

GONZALEZ, LEONARDO WILLIAMS

Ituzaingo 473, Maldonado, URUGUAY 20000, Phone: 598 4222 1617, Fax: 598 4222 1617, willyknives@hotmail.com; Web: www.willyknives.com

Specialties: Classic high-art and fantasy straight knives; traditional working and using knives of his design, in standard patterns or to customer specs. **Patterns:** Hunters, Bowies, daggers, fighters, boots, swords and utility/camp knives. **Technical:** Forges and grinds high-carbon and stainless Bohler steels. **Prices:** $100 to $2500. **Remarks:** Full-time maker; first knife sold in 1985. **Mark:** Willy, whale, R.O.U.

GOO, TAI

5920 W Windy Lou Ln, Tucson, AZ 85742, Phone: 520-744-9777, taigoo@msn.com; Web: www.taigoo.com

Specialties: High art, neo-tribal, bush and fantasy. **Technical:** Hand forges, does own heat treating, makes own Damascus. **Prices:** $150 to $500 some to $10,000. **Remarks:** Full-time maker; first knife sold in 1978. **Mark:** Chiseled signature.

GOOD, D.R.

D.R. Good Custom Knives and Weaponry, 6125 W. 100 S., Tipton, IN 46072, Phone: 765-963-6971, drntammigood@bluemarble.net

Specialties: Working knives, own design, Scagel style, "critter" knives, carved handles. **Patterns:** Bowies, large and small, neck knives and miniatures. Offers carved handles, snake heads, eagles, wolves, bear, skulls. **Technical:** Damascus, some stelite, 6K, pearl, ivory, moose. **Prices:** $150 -$1500. **Remarks:** Full-time maker. First knife was Bowie made from a 2-1/2 truck bumper in military. **Mark:** D.R. Good in oval and for minis, DR with a buffalo skull.

GOODE, BEAR
PO Box 6474, Navajo Dam, NM 87419, Phone: 505-632-8184
Specialties: Working/using straight knives of his design and in standard patterns. **Patterns:** Bowies, hunters and utility/camp knives. **Technical:** Grinds 440C, ATS-34, 154-CM; forges and grinds 1095, 5160 and other steels on request; uses Damascus. **Prices:** $60 to $225; some to $500 and up. **Remarks:** Part-time maker; first knife sold in 1993. Doing business as Bear Knives. **Mark:** First and last name with a three-toed paw print.

GOODE, BRIAN
203 Gordon Ave, Shelby, NC 28152, Phone: 704-434-6496, web:www.bgoodeknives.com
Specialties: Flat ground working knives with etched/antique or brushed finish. **Patterns:** Field, camp, hunters, skinners, survival, kitchen, maker's design or yours. Currently full tang only with supplied leather sheath. **Technical:** O-1, D2 and other ground flat stock. Stock removal and differential heat treat preferred. Etched antique/etched satin working finish preferred. Micarta and hardwoods for strength. **Prices:** $150 to $700. **Remarks:** Part-time maker and full-time knife lover. First knife sold in 2004. **Mark:** B. Goode with NC separated by a feather.

GOODPASTURE, TOM
13432 Farrington Road, Ashland, VA 23005, Phone: 804-752-8363, rtg007@aol.com; web: goodpastureknives.com
Specialties: Working/using straight knives of his own design, or customer specs. File knives and primative reproductions. **Patterns:** Hunters, bowies, small double-edge daggers, kitchen, custom miniatures and camp/utility. **Technical:** Stock removal, D-2, O-1, 12C27, 420 HC, 52100. Forged blades of W-2, 1084, and 1095. Flat grinds only. **Prices:** $60 -$300. **Remarks:** Part-time maker, first knife sold at Blade Show 2005. Lifetime guarantee and sharpening. **Mark:** Early mark were initials RTG, current **Mark:** Goodpasture.

GORDON, LARRY B
23555 Newell Cir W, Farmington Hills, MI 48336, Phone: 248-477-5483, lbgordon1@aol.com
Specialties: Folders, small fixed blades. New design rotating scale release automatic. **Patterns:** Rotating handle locker. Ambidextrous fire (R&L) **Prices:** $450 minimum. **Remarks:** High line materials preferred. **Mark:** Gordon.

GORENFLO, JAMES T (JT)
9145 Sullivan Rd, Baton Rouge, LA 70818, Phone: 225-261-5868
Specialties: Traditional working and using straight knives of his design. **Patterns:** Bowies, hunters and utility/camp knives. **Technical:** Forges 5160, 1095, 52100 and his own Damascus. **Prices:** Start at $200. **Remarks:** Part-time maker; first knife sold in 1992. **Mark:** Last name or initials, J.S. on reverse.

GOSHOVSKYY, VASYL
BL.4, C. San Jaime 65, Torreblanca 12596, Castellon de la Plana, SPAIN, Phone: +34-664-838-882, baz_knife@mail.ru; Web: www.goshovskyy-knives.com
Specialties: Presentation and working fixed-blade knives. **Patterns:** R.W. Loveless-pattern knives, primarily hunters and skinners. **Technical:** Stock-removal method. Prefers natural materials for handle scales. Uses primarily RWL-34, CPM-154, N690 or similar blade steel. **Remarks:** Full-time maker.

GOSSMAN, SCOTT
PO Box 41, Whiteford, MD 21160, Phone: 443-617-2444, scogos@peoplepc.com; Web:www.gossmanknives.com
Specialties: Heavy duty knives for big-game hunting and survival. **Patterns:** Modified clip-point/spear-point blades, bowies, hunters and bushcraft. **Technical:** Grinds A2, O1, CPM-154, CPM-3V, S7, flat/convex grinds and convex micro-bevel edges. **Price:** $65 to $500. **Remarks:** Full-time maker doing business as Gossman Knives. **Mark:** Gossman and steel type.

GOTTAGE, DANTE
43227 Brooks Dr, Clinton Twp., MI 48038-5323, Phone: 810-286-7275
Specialties: Working knives of his design or to customer specs. **Patterns:** Large and small skinners, fighters, Bowies and fillet knives. **Technical:** Grinds O1, 440C and 154CM and ATS-34. **Prices:** $150 to $600. **Remarks:** Part-time maker; first knife sold in 1975. **Mark:** Full name in script letters.

GOTTAGE, JUDY
43227 Brooks Dr, Clinton Twp., MI 48038-5323, Phone: 586-286-7275, jgottage@remaxmetropolitan.com
Specialties: Custom folders of her design or to customer specs. **Patterns:** Interframes or integral. **Technical:** Stock removal. **Prices:** $300 to $3000. **Remarks:** Full-time maker; first knife sold in 1980. **Mark:** Full name, maker in script.

GOTTSCHALK, GREGORY J
12 First St. (Ft. Pitt), Carnegie, PA 15106, Phone: 412-279-6692
Specialties: Fancy working straight knives and folders to customer specs. **Patterns:** Hunters to tantos, locking folders to minis. **Technical:** Grinds 440C, 154CM, ATS-34. Now making own Damascus. Most knives have mirror finishes. **Prices:** Start at $150. **Remarks:** Part-time maker; first knife sold in 1977. **Mark:** Full name in crescent.

GOUKER, GARY B
PO Box 955, Sitka, AK 99835, Phone: 907-747-3476
Specialties: Hunting knives for hard use. **Patterns:** Skinners, semi-skinners, and such. **Technical:** Likes natural materials, inlays, stainless steel. **Prices:** Moderate. **Remarks:** New Alaskan maker. **Mark:** Name.

GRAHAM, GORDON
3145 CR 4008, New Boston, TX 75570, Phone: 903-293-2610, Web: www.grahamknives.com
Prices: $325 to $850. **Mark:** Graham.

GRAHAM, LEVI
6608 W. 3rd St. #66, Greeley, CO 80634, Phone: 970-371-0477, lgknives@hotmail.com; www.levigrahamknives.com
Specialties: Forged frontier/period/Western knives. **Patterns:** Hunters, patch knives, skinners, camp, belt and bowies. **Technical:** Forges high-carbon steels and some stock removal in 1095, 1084, 5160, L6, 80CRV2 and 52100. Handle materials include antler, bone, ivory, horn, hardwoods, Micarta and G-10. Rawhide-covered, vegetable-tanned sheaths decorated with deer fringe, quill work for a band or medicine wheel, beads, cones, horse hair, etc. Custom orders welcome. **Prices:** $300 and up. **Remarks:** Member of ABS and PKA. **Mark:** "lg" stamped in lower case letters.

GRANGER, PAUL J
704 13th Ct. SW, Largo, FL 33770-4471, Phone: 727-953-3249, grangerknives@live.com Web: http://palehorsefighters.blogspot.com
Specialties: Working straight knives of his own design and a few folders. **Patterns:** 2.75" to 4" work knives, tactical knives and Bowies from 5"-9." **Technical:** Grinds CPM154-CM, ATS-34 and forges 52100 and 1084. Offers filework. **Prices:** $95 to $500. **Remarks:** Part-time maker since 1997. Sold first knife in 1997. Doing business as Granger Knives and Pale Horse Fighters. Member of ABS and Florida Knifemakers Association. **Mark:** "Granger" or "Palehorse Fighters."

GRAVELINE, PASCAL AND ISABELLE
38 Rue de Kerbrezillic, Moelan-sur-Mer, FRANCE 29350, Phone: 33 2 98 39 73 33, atelier.graveline@wanadoo.fr; Web: www.graveline-couteliers.com
Specialties: French replicas from the 17th, 18th and 19th centuries. **Patterns:** Traditional folders and multi-blade pocket knives; traveling knives, fruit knives and fork sets; puzzle knives and friend's knives; rivet less knives. **Technical:** Grind 12C27, ATS-34, Damascus and carbon steel. **Prices:** $500 to $5000. **Remarks:** Full-time makers; first knife sold in 1992. **Mark:** Last name over head of ram.

GRAVES, DAN
4887 Dixie Garden Loop, Shreveport, LA 71105, Phone: 318-865-8166, Web: wwwtheknifemaker.com
Specialties: Traditional forged blades and Damascus. **Patterns:** Bowies (D guard also), fighters, hunters, large and small daggers. **Remarks:** Full-time maker. **Mark:** Initials with circle around them.

GRAY, BOB
8206 N Lucia Court, Spokane, WA 99208, Phone: 509-468-3924
Specialties: Straight working knives of his own design or to customer specs. **Patterns:** Hunter, fillet and carving knives. **Technical:** Forges 5160, L6 and some 52100; grinds 440C. **Prices:** $100 to $600. **Remarks:** Part-time knifemaker; first knife sold in 1991. Doing business as Hi-Land Knives. **Mark:** HI-L.

GRAY, DANIEL
GRAY KNIVES, POB 718, Brownville, ME 04414, Phone: 207-965-2191, mail@grayknives.com; Web: www.grayknives.com
Specialties: Straight knives, fantasy, folders, automatics and traditional of his own design. **Patterns:** Automatics, fighters, hunters. **Technical:** Grinds O1, 154CM and D2. **Prices:** From $155 to $750. **Remarks:** Full-time maker; first knife sold in 1974. **Mark:** Gray Knives.

GRAY, ROBB
6026 46th Ave. SW, Seattle, WA 98136, Phone: 206-280-7622, robb.gray@graycloud-designs.com; Web: www.graycloud-designs.com
Specialties: Hunting, fishing and leather-workers' knives, along with daggers and utility ranch knives. **Technical:** Stock-removal maker using 440C, CPM-S30V, CPM-154, CPM-12C27, CPM-13C26 and CPM-19C27 stainless steels. Also engraves knives in Sheridan, single point and Western bright cut styles. Owner of "Resinwood," a certified wood fiber product sold to knifemaker supply companies for handle material. **Remarks:** Full-time artist/maker; first knife made in 2009. **Mark:** A rain cloud with name "Graycloud" next to it, surrounded by an oval.

GREBE, GORDON S
107 Weaver Ln., Canon City, CO 81212, Phone: 907-235-8242
Specialties: Working straight knives and folders, some fancy. **Patterns:** Tantos, Bowies, boot fighter sets, locking folders. **Technical:** Grinds stainless steels; likes 1/4" inch stock and glass-bead finishes. **Prices:** $75 to $250; some to $2000. **Remarks:** Full-time maker; first knife sold in 1968. **Mark:** Initials in lightning logo.

GRECO, JOHN
100 Mattie Jones Rd, Greensburg, KY 42743, Phone: 270-932-3335, johngreco@grecoknives.com; Web: www.grecoknives.com
Specialties: Folders. **Patterns:** Tactical, fighters, camp knives, short swords. **Technical:** Stock removal carbon steel. **Prices:** Affordable. **Remarks:** Full-time maker since 1979. First knife sold in 1979. **Mark:** GRECO

GREEN, BILL
6621 Eastview Dr, Sachse, TX 75048, Phone: 972-463-3147
Specialties: High-art and working straight knives and folders of his design and to customer specs. **Patterns:** Bowies, hunters, kitchen knives and locking folders. **Technical:** Grinds ATS-34, D2 and 440V. Hand-tooled custom sheaths. **Prices:** $70 to $350; some to

$750. **Remarks:** Part-time maker; first knife sold in 1990. **Mark:** Last name.

GREEN, WILLIAM (BILL)
46 Warren Rd, View Bank, VIC, AUSTRALIA 3084, Fax: 03-9459-1529
Specialties: Traditional high-tech straight knives and folders. **Patterns:** Japanese-influenced designs, hunters, Bowies, folders and miniatures. **Technical:** Forges O1, D2 and his own Damascus. Offers lost wax castings for bolsters and pommels. Likes natural handle materials, gems, silver and gold. **Prices:** $400 to $750; some to $1200. **Remarks:** Full-time maker. **Mark:** Initials.

GREENAWAY, DON
3325 Dinsmore Tr, Fayetteville, AR 72704, Phone: 501-521-0323
Specialties: Liner locks and bowies. **Prices:** $150 to $1500. **Remarks:** 20 years experience.**Mark:**Greenaway over Fayetteville, Ark.

GREENE, CHRIS
707 Cherry Lane, Shelby, NC 28150, Phone: 704-434-5620

GREENE, DAVID
570 Malcom Rd, Covington, GA 30209, Phone: 770-784-0657
Specialties: Straight working using knives. **Patterns:** Hunters. **Technical:** Forges mosaic and twist Damascus. Prefers stag and desert ironwood for handle material.

GREENE, STEVE
DUNN KNIVES INC, PO Box 307 1449 Nocatee St., Intercession City, FL 33848,
Phone: 800-245-6483, s.greene@earthlink.net; Web: www.dunnknives.com
Specialties: Skinning & fillet knives. **Patterns:** Skinners, drop points, clip points and fillets. **Technical:** CPM-S30V powdered metal steel manufactured by Niagara Specialty Metals. **Prices:** $100 to $350. **Mark:** Dunn by Greene and year. **Remarks:** Full-time knifemaker. First knife sold in 1972. Each knife is handcrafted and includes holster-grade leather sheath.

GREENFIELD, G O
2605 15th St #310, Everett, WA 98201, Phone: 425-244-2902, garyg1946@yahoo.com
Specialties: High-tech and working straight knives and folders of his design. **Patterns:** Boots, daggers, hunters and one-of-a-kinds. **Technical:** Grinds ATS-34, D2, 440C and T-440V. Makes sheaths for each knife. **Prices:** $100 to $800; some to $10,000. **Remarks:** Part-time maker; first knife sold in 1978. **Mark:** Springfield®, serial number.

GREGORY, MATTHEW M.
74 Tarn Tr., Glenwood, NY 14069, Phone: 716-863-1215,
mgregoryknives@yahoo.com; Web: www.mgregoryknives.com
Patterns: Wide variation of styles, as I make what I like to make. Bowies, fighters, Neo-American/Japanese-inspired blades, occasionally kitchen knives. **Technical:** Forging and stock removal, using forging steels such as 1084, 1095, W2 and CruForgeV, as well as high-alloy steels like CPM-3V and CPM-S110V. Hamon (blade temper line) development and polishing. **Prices:** $350 and up. **Remarks:** Part-time maker since 2005. **Mark:** M. Gregory.

GREGORY, MICHAEL
211 Calhoun Rd, Belton, SC 29627, Phone: 864-338-8898, gregom.123@charter.net
Specialties: Interframe folding knives, working hunters and period pieces. Hand rubbed finish, engraving by maker. **Patterns:** Hunters, bowies, daggers and folding knives. **Technical:** Grinds ATS-34 and other makers' damascus. **Prices:** $200 and up. **Remarks:** Full-time maker; first knife sold in 1980. **Mark:** Name, city in logo.

GREINER, RICHARD
1073 E County Rd 32, Green Springs, OH 44836, Phone: 419-483-4613,
rgreiner7295@yahoo.com
Specialties: High-carbon steels, edge hardened. **Patterns:** Most. **Technical:** Hand forged. **Prices:** $125 and up. **Remarks:** Have made knives for 30 years. **Mark:** Maple leaf.

GREISS, JOCKL
Herrenwald 15, Schenkenzell, GERMANY 77773, Phone: +49 7836 95 71 69
or +49 7836 95 55 76, www.jocklgreiss@yahoo.com
Specialties: Classic and working using straight knives of his design. **Patterns:** Bowies, daggers and hunters. **Technical:** Uses only Jerry Rados Damascus. All knives are one-of-a-kind made by hand; no machines are used. **Prices:** $700 to $2000; some to $3000. **Remarks:** Full-time maker; first knife sold in 1984. **Mark:** An "X" with a long vertical line through it.

GREY, PIET
PO Box 363, Naboomspruit, LP, SOUTH AFRICA 0560, Phone: 014-743-3613
Specialties: Fancy working and using straight knives of his design. **Patterns:** Fighters, hunters and utility/camp knives. **Technical:** Grinds ATS-34 and AEB-L; forges and grinds Damascus. Solder less fitting of guards. Engraves and scrimshaws. **Prices:** $125 to $750; some to $1500. **Remarks:** Part-time maker; first knife sold in 1970. **Mark:** Last name.

GRIFFIN, JOHN
26101 Pine Shadows, Hockley, TX 77447, Phone: 281-414-7111, griff6363@yahoo.com
Specialties: Lockbacks, other precision opening and locking folders and fixed blades. **Patterns:** All patterns, including custom-designed pieces. **Technical:** Stainless and damascus blade steels. **Prices:** Start at $800. **Remarks:** Guaranteed for life, very durable and unique designs.

GRIFFIN JR., HOWARD A
14299 SW 31st Ct, Davie, FL 33330, Phone: 954-474-5406, mgriffin18@aol.com
Specialties: Working straight knives and folders. **Patterns:** Hunters, Bowies, locking folders with his own push-button lock design. **Technical:** Grinds 440C. **Prices:** $100 to $200; some to $500. **Remarks:** Part-time maker; first knife sold in 1983. **Mark:** Initials.

GRIMES, MARK
PO BOX 1293, Bedford, TX 76095, Phone: 817-320-7274, ticktock107@gmail.com

Specialties: Qs. **Patterns:** Hunters, fighters, bowies. **Technical:** Custom hand forged 1084 steel blades full and hidden tang, heat treating, sheathes. **Prices:** $150-$400. **Remarks:** Part-time maker, first knife sold in 2009. **Mark:** Last name.

GRIZZARD, JIM
3626 Gunnels Ln., Oxford, AL 36203, Phone: 256-403-1232, grizzardforgiven@aol.com
Specialties: Hand carved art knives inspired by sole authorship. **Patterns:** Fixedblades, folders, and swords. **Technical:** Carving handles, artgrinding, forged and stock removal. **Prices:** Vary. **Remarks:** Uses knives mostly as a ministry to bless others. **Mark:** FOR HIS GLORY CUSTOM KNIVES OR j grizzard in a grizzly bear.

GROSPITCH, ERNIE
18440 Amityville Dr, Orlando, FL 32820, Phone: 407-568-5438, shrpknife@aol.com;
Web: www.erniesknives.com
Specialties: Bowies, hunting, fishing, kitchen, lockback folders, leather craft and knifemaker logo stenciling/blue lightning stencil. **Patterns:** My design or customer's. **Technical:** Stock removal using most available steels. **Prices:** Vary. **Remarks:** Full-time maker, sold first knife in 1990. **Mark:** Etched name over Thunderbird image.

GROSS, W W
109 Dylan Scott Dr, Archdale, NC 27263-3858
Specialties: Working knives. **Patterns:** Hunters, boots, fighters. **Technical:** Grinds. **Prices:** Moderate. **Remarks:** Full-time maker. **Mark:** Name.

GROSSMAN, STEWART
24 Water St #419, Clinton, MA 01510, Phone: 508-365-2291; 800-mysword
Specialties: Miniatures and full-size knives and swords. **Patterns:** One-of-a-kind miniatures—jewelry, replicas—and wire-wrapped figures. Full-size art, fantasy and combat knives, daggers and modular systems. **Technical:** Forges and grinds most metals and Damascus. Uses gems, crystals, electronics and motorized mechanisms. **Prices:** $20 to $300; some to $4500 and higher. **Remarks:** Full-time maker; first knife sold in 1985. **Mark:** G1.

GROVES, GARY
P.O. Box 101, Canvas, WV 26662, ggroves51@gmail.com
Specialties: Fixed blades and hidden-tang knives. **Patterns:** Hunters, skinners and bowies. **Technical:** Stock-removal method using ATS 34 and CPM 154 steels. Handles are mainly natural materials such as bone, horn, stag and wood, with filework on just about all knives. Every knife comes with a made-to-fit sheath. **Prices:** $350 to $1,200. **Remarks:** Full-time knifemaker; first knife sold in 2007. **Mark:** Last name over an anvil and a capital G in the middle of the anvil.

GRUSSENMEYER, PAUL G
310 Kresson Rd, Cherry Hill, NJ 08034, Phone: 856-428-1088,
pgrussentne@comcast.net; Web: www.pgcarvings.com
Specialties: Assembling fancy and fantasy straight knives with his own carved handles. **Patterns:** Bowies, daggers, folders, swords, hunters and miniatures. **Technical:** Uses forged steel and Damascus, stock removal and knapped obsidian blades. **Prices:** $250 to $4000. **Remarks:** Spare-time maker; first knife sold in 1991. **Mark:** First and last initial hooked together on handle.

GUARNERA, ANTHONY R
42034 Quail Creek Dr, Quartzhill, CA 93536, Phone: 661-722-4032
Patterns: Hunters, camp, Bowies, kitchen, fighter knives. **Technical:** Forged and stock removal. **Prices:** $100 and up.

GUINN, TERRY
13026 Hwy 6 South, Eastland, TX 76448, Phone: 254-629-8603,
Web: www.terryguinn.com
Specialties: Working fixed blades and balisongs. **Patterns:** Almost all types of folding and fixed blades, from patterns and "one of a kind". **Technical:** Stock removal all types of blade steel with preference for air hardening steel. Does own heat treating, all knives Rockwell tested in shop. **Prices:** $200 to $2,000. **Remarks:** Part time maker since 1982, sold first knife 1990. **Mark:** Full name with cross in the middle.

GUNTER, BRAD
13 Imnaha Rd., Tijeras, NM 87059, Phone: 505-281-8080

GUNTHER, EDDIE
11 Nedlands Pl Burswood, Auckland, NEW ZEALAND 2013, Phone: 006492722373,
eddit.gunther49@gmail.com
Specialties: Drop point hunters, boot, Bowies. All mirror finished. **Technical:** Grinds D2, 440C, 12c27. **Prices:** $250 to $800. **Remarks:** Part-time maker, first knife sold in 1986. **Mark:** Name, city, country.

H

HAAS, RANDY
HHH Knives, 6518 Chard St., Marlette, MI 48453, Phone: 989-635-7059,
Web: www.hhhcustomknives.com
Specialties: Handmade custom kitchen and culinary knives, hunters, fighters, folders and art knives. **Technical:** Damascus maker and sales. **Remarks:** Full-time maker for 10 years. **Mark:** Three H's with a knife behind the HHH.

HACKNEY, DANA A.
33 Washington St., Monument, CO 80132, Phone: 719-481-3940;
Cell: 719-651-5634, danahackneyknives@gmail.com and dshackney@Q.com;
Web: www.hackneycustomknives.com
Specialties: Hunters, bowies and everyday carry knives, and some kitchen cutlery. **Technical:** ABS journeyman smith who forges 1080 series, 5160, 52100, 01, W2 and his

own damascus. Uses CPM-154 mostly for stainless knives. **Prices:** $150 and up. **Remarks:** Sole ownership knives and sheaths. Full-time maker as of July 2012. Sold first knife in 2005. ABS, MKA and PKA member. **Mark:** Last name, HACKNEY on left-side ricasso.

HAGEN, DOC
POB 58, 702 5th St. SE, 41780 Kansas Point Ln, Pelican Rapids, MN 56572, Phone: 218-863-8503, dochagen@gmail.com; Web: www.dochagencustomknives.com
Specialties: Folders. Autos:bolster release-dual action. Slipjoint folders**Patterns:** Defense-related straight knives; wide variety of folders. **Technical:** Dual action release, bolster release autos. **Prices:** $300 to $800; some to $3000. **Remarks:** Full-time maker; first knife sold in 1975. Makes his own Damascus. **Mark:** DOC HAGEN in shield, knife, banner logo; or DOC.

HAGGERTY, GEORGE S
PO Box 88, Jacksonville, VT 05342, Phone: 802-368-7437, swewater@sover.net
Specialties: Working straight knives and folders. **Patterns:** Hunters, claws, camp and fishing knives, locking folders and backpackers. **Technical:** Forges and grinds W2, 440C and 154CM. **Prices:** $85 to $300. **Remarks:** Part-time maker; first knife sold in 1981. **Mark:** Initials or last name.

HAGUE, GEOFF
Unit 5, Project Workshops, Lains Farm, Quarley, Hampshire, UNITED KINGDOM SP11 8PX, Phone: (+44) 01672-870212, Fax: (+44) 01672 870212, geoff@hagueknives.com; Web: www.hagueknives.com
Specialties: Fixed blade and folding knives. **Patterns:** Back lock, locking liner, slip joint, and friction folders. **Technical:** Grinds D2, RWL-34 and damascus. Mainly natural handle materials. **Prices:** $500 to $2,000. **Remarks:** Full-time maker. **Mark:** Last name.

HAINES, JEFF
Haines Custom Knives, W3678 Bay View Rd., Mayville, WI 53050, Phone: 920-387-0212, knifeguy95@gmail.com; Web: www.hainescustom.com
Patterns: Hunters, skinners, camp knives, customer designs welcome. **Technical:** Forges 1095, 5160, and Damascus, grinds A2. **Prices:** $75 and up. **Remarks:** Part-time maker since 1995. **Mark:** Last name.

HALE, LLOYD
7593 Beech Hill Rd., Pulaski, TN 38478, Phone: 931-424-5846, lloydahale@gmail.com
Specialties: Museum-grade, one-of-a-kind daggers, folders and sub-hilt fighting knives. **Remarks:** Full-time maker for 44+ years. Spent 20+ years creating a one-of-a-kind knife collection for Owsley Brown Frazier of Louisville, KY. I don't accept orders anymore.

HALFRICH, JERRY
340 Briarwood, San Marcos, TX 78666, Phone: 512-353-2582, jerryhalfrich@grandecom.net; Web: www.halfrichknives.com
Specialties: Working knives and specialty utility knives for the professional and serious hunter. Uses proven designs in both straight and folding knives. Pays close attention to fit and finish. Art knives on special request. **Patterns:** Hunters, skinners, and lockback, LinerLock and slip-joint folders. **Technical:** Grinds both flat and hollow D2, Damasteel and CPM 154, makes high precision folders. **Prices:** $450 to $1,500. **Remarks:** Full-time maker since 2000. DBA Halfrich Custom Knives. **Mark:** HALFRICH.

HALL, JEFF
179 Niblick Rd., # 180, Paso Robles, CA 93446, Phone: 562-594-4740, info@nemesis-knives.com; Web: nemesis-knives.com
Specialties: Collectible and working folders and fixed blades of his design. **Technical:** Grinds CPM-S35VN, CPM-154, and various makers' damascus. **Patterns:** Fighters, gentleman's, hunters and utility knives. **Prices:** $100 and up. **Remarks:** Full-time maker. First knife sold 1998. **Mark:** Last name.

HALL, KEN
606 Stevenson Cove Rd., Waynesville, NC 28785, Phone: 828-627-2135, khall@hallenergyconsulting.com; Web: http://www.hallenergyconsulting.com/KHKindex.html
Specialties: Standard and one-of-a-kind fixed-blade knives with leather sheaths. **Patterns:** Hunters, bowies, fighters, chef's knives and tantos. **Technical:** Forges high-carbon steel, flat grinds. **Prices:** $300 to $1,500. **Remarks:** Part-time maker; first knives sold in 2010. **Mark:** Etched "Ken Hall" or "KHall JS."

HALL, SCOTT M.
5 Hickory Hts., Geneseo, IL 61254, Phone: 309-945-2184, smhall@theinter.com; www.hallcustomknives.com
Specialties: Fixed-blade, hollow-ground working knives of his own design and to customer specs. **Patterns:** Designs catering to soldiers and outdoorsmen, including variations of hunters, bowies, fighters and occasionally fillet and kitchen knives. **Technical:** Usually grinds CPM S30V and 154CM, but uses other steels upon request. Handle materials include G-10, Micarta, stag, horn and exotic woods. Most knives are offered with hand-tooled and stitched leather sheaths or Spec Ops sheaths. **Prices:** $150 to $350+. **Remarks:** Part-time maker; first knife sold in 2000. **Mark:** Last name.

HAMLET JR., JOHNNY
300 Billington, Clute, TX 77531, Phone: 979-265-6929, nifeman@swbell.net; Web: www.hamlets-handmade-knives.com
Specialties: Working straight knives and folders. **Patterns:** Hunters, fighters, fillet and kitchen knives, locking folders. Likes upswept knives and trailing-points. **Technical:** Grinds 440C, D2, ATS-34. Makes sheaths. **Prices:** $125 and up. **Remarks:** Full-time maker; sold first knife in 1988. **Mark:** Hamlet's Handmade in script.

HAMMOND, HANK
189 Springlake Dr, Leesburg, GA 31763, Phone: 229-434-1295, godogs57@bellsouth.net
Specialties: Traditional hunting and utility knives of his design. Will also design and produce knives to customer's specifications. **Patterns:** Straight or sheath knives, hunters

skinners as well as Bowies and fighters. **Technical:** Grinds (hollow and flat grinds) CPM 154CM, ATS-34. Also uses Damascus and forges 52100. Offers filework on blades. Handle materials include all exotic woods, red stag, sambar stag, deer, elk, oosic, bone, fossil ivory, Micarta, etc. All knives come with sheath handmade for that individual knife. **Prices:** $100 up to $500. **Remarks:** Part-time maker. Sold first knife in 1981. Doing business as Double H Knives. **Mark:** "HH" inside 8 point deer rack.

HAMMOND, JIM
104 Owens Parkway, Ste. M, Birmingham, AL 35244, Phone: 256-651-1376, jim@jimhammondknives.com; Web: www.jimhammondknives.com
Specialties: High-tech fighters and folders. **Patterns:** Proven-design fighters. **Technical:** Grinds 440C, 440V, S30V and other specialty steels. **Prices:** $385 to $1200; some to $9200. **Remarks:** Full-time maker; first knife sold in 1977. Designer for Columbia River Knife and Tool. **Mark:** Full name, city, state in shield logo.

HAMMOND, RAY
633 Devon Brooke Dr., Woodstock, GA 30188, Phone: 678-300-2883, rayhammond01@yahoo.com; Web: www.biggamehuntingblades.com
Specialties: Fixed blades, primarily hunting knives, utility knives and bowies. **Technical:** Stock removal and forged blades, including 5160, 1095, CPM-154 and damascus blade steels. **Prices:** Start at $300. **Remarks:** Part-time maker; first knife built in 2008. **Mark:** Capital letters RH surrounded by a broken circle, pierced by a knife silhouette, atop the circle is my name, and below the circle the words "custom knives." Will soon alter this to simply my last name.

HANCOCK, TIM
29125 N. 153rd St., Scottsdale, AZ 85262, Phone: 480-998-8849, westernbladesmith@gmail.com
Specialties: High-art and working straight knives and folders of his design and to customer preferences. **Patterns:** Bowies, fighters, daggers, tantos, swords, folders. **Technical:** Forges damascus and 52100; grinds ATS-34. Makes damascus. Silver-wire inlays; offers carved fittings and file work. **Prices:** $500 to $20,000. **Remarks:** Full-time maker; first knife sold in 1988. ABS master smith and AKI member. **Mark:** Last name or heart.

HAND, BILL
PO Box 717, 1103 W. 7th St., Spearman, TX 79081, Phone: 806-659-2967, Fax: 806-659-5139, klinker43@yahoo.com
Specialties: Traditional working and using straight knives and folders of his design or to customer specs. **Patterns:** Hunters, Bowies, folders and fighters. **Technical:** Forges 5160, 52100 and Damascus. **Prices:** Start at $150. **Remarks:** Part-time maker; Journeyman Smith. Current delivery time 12 to 16 months. **Mark:** Stylized initials.

HANKALA, JUKKA
Tuhkurintie 225, 39580 Riitiala, FINLAND, Phone: +358-400-684-625, jukka@hankala.com; www.hankala.com
Specialties: Traditional puukkos and maker's own knife models. **Patterns:** Maker's own puukko models, hunters, folders and ART-knives. **Technical:** Forges Silversteel, Bohler K510, Damasteel stainless damascus and RWL-34 blade steels, as well as his own 15N20-and-1.2842 damascus, mosaic damascus and color damascus. **Prices:** Start at $300. **Remarks:** Full-time maker since 1985. **Mark:** J. Hankala.

HANSEN, LONNIE
PO Box 4956, Spanaway, WA 98387, Phone: 253-847-4632, lonniehansen@msn.com; Web: lchansen.com
Specialties: Working straight knives of his design. **Patterns:** Tomahawks, tantos, hunters, fillet. **Technical:** Forges 1086, 52100, grinds 440V, BG-42. **Prices:** Starting at $300. **Remarks:** Part-time maker since 1989. **Mark:** First initial and last name. Also first and last initial.

HANSEN, ROBERT W
35701 University Ave NE, Cambridge, MN 55008, Phone: 763-689-3242
Specialties: Working straight knives, folders and integrals. **Patterns:** From hunters to minis, camp knives to miniatures; folding lockers and slip-joints in original styles. **Technical:** Grinds O1, 440C and 154CM; likes filework. **Prices:** $100 to $450; some to $600. **Remarks:** Part-time maker; first knife sold in 1983. **Mark:** Fish w/h inside surrounded by Bob Hansen maker.

HANSON III, DON L.
Sunfish Forge, PO Box 13, Success, MO 65570-0013, Phone: 573-674-3045, Web: www.sunfishforge.com; Web: www.donhansonknives.com
Specialties: One-of-a-kind damascus folders, slip joints and forged fixed blades. **Patterns:** Small, fancy pocket knives, large folding fighters and Bowies. **Technical:** Forges own pattern welded Damascus, file work and carving also carbon steel blades with hamons. **Prices:** $800 and up. **Remarks:** Full-time maker, first knife sold in 1984. ABS mastersmith. **Mark:** Sunfish.

HARA, KOJI
292-2 Osugi, Seki-City, Gifu, JAPAN 501-3922, Phone: 0575-24-7569, Fax: 0575-24-7569, info@knifehousehara.com; Web: www.knifehousehara.com
Specialties: High-tech and working straight knives of his design; some folders. **Patterns:** Hunters, locking folders and utility/camp knives. **Technical:** Grinds Cowry X, Cowry Y and ATS-34. Prefers high mirror polish; pearl handle inlay. **Prices:** $400 to $2500. **Remarks:** Full-time maker; first knife sold in 1980. Doing business as Knife House "Hara." **Mark:** First initial, last name in fish.

HARDING, CHAD
12365 Richland Ln, Solsberry, IN 47459, hardingknives@yahoo.com; www.hardingknives.net
Specialties: Hunters and camp knives, occasional fighters or bowies. No folders.

Technical: Hand forge 90% of work. Prefer 10XX steels and tool steels. Makes own damascus and cable and chainsaw chain damascus. 100% sole authorship on knives and sheaths. Mostly natural handle material, prefer wood and stag. **Prices:** $150 to $1,000. **Remarks:** Part-time maker, member of ABS. First knife sold in 2005. **Mark:** Last name.

HARDY, DOUGLAS E
114 Cypress Rd, Franklin, GA 30217, Phone: 706-675-6305

HARDY, SCOTT
639 Myrtle Ave, Placerville, CA 95667, Phone: 530-622-5780, Web: www.innercite.com/~shardy
Specialties: Traditional working and using straight knives of his design. **Patterns:** Most anything with an edge. **Technical:** Forges carbon steels. Japanese stone polish. Offers mirror finish; differentially tempers. **Prices:** $100 to $1000. **Remarks:** Part-time maker; first knife sold in 1982. **Mark:** First initial, last name and Handmade with bird logo.

HARKINS, J A
PO Box 218, Conner, MT 59827, Phone: 406-821-1060, kutter@customknives.net; Web: customknives.net
Specialties: OTFs. **Patterns:** OTFs, Automatics, Folders. **Technical:** Grinds ATS-34. Engraves; offers gem work. **Prices:** $1500 and up. **Remarks:** Celebrating 20th year as full-time maker . **Mark:** First and middle initials, last name.

HARLEY, LARRY W
348 Deerfield Dr, Bristol, TN 37620, Phone: 423-878-5368 (shop); cell: 423-530-1133, Web: www.lonesomepineknives.com
Specialties: One-of-a-kind Persian in one-of-a-kind Damascus. Working knives, period pieces. **Technical:** Forges and grinds ATS-34, 440c, L6, 15, 20, 1084, and 52100. **Patterns:** Full range of straight knives, tomahawks, razors, buck skinners and hog spears. **Prices:** $200 and up. **Mark:** Pine tree.

HARLEY, RICHARD
609 Navaho Trl., Bristol, VA 24201, Phone: 423-878-5368; cell: 423-408-5720
Specialties: Hunting knives, Bowies, friction folders, one-of-a-kind. **Technical:** Forges 1084, S160, 52100, Lg. **Prices:** $150 to $1000. **Mark:** Pine tree with name.

HARM, PAUL W
818 Young Rd, Attica, MI 48412, Phone: 810-724-5582, harm@blclinks.net
Specialties: Early American working knives. **Patterns:** Hunters, skinners, patch knives, fighters, folders. **Technical:** Forges and grinds 1084, O1, 52100 and own Damascus. **Prices:** $75 to $1000. **Remarks:** First knife sold in 1990. **Mark:** Connected initials.

HARNER III, "BUTCH" LLOYD R.
745 Kindig Rd., Littlestown, PA 17340, butch@harnerknives.com; Web: www.harnerknives.com
Specialties: Kitchen knives and straight razors. **Technical:** CPM-3V, CPM-154 and various Carpenter powdered steel alloys. **Remarks:** Full-time maker since 2007. **Mark:** L.R. Harner (2005-Sept. 2012) and Harner III (after Oct. 2012)

HARRINGTON, ROGER
P.O. Box 157, Battle, East Sussex, ENGLAND TN 33 3 DD, Phone: 0854-838-7062, info@bisonbushcraft.co.uk; Web: www.bisonbushcraft.co.uk
Specialties: Working straight knives to his or customer's designs, flat saber Scandinavia-style grinds on full tang knives, also hollow and convex grinds. **Technical:** Grinds O1, D2, Damascus. **Prices:** $200 to $800. **Remarks:** First knife made by hand in 1997 whilst traveling around the world. **Mark:** Bison with bison written under.

HARRIS, CASS
19855 Fraiser Hill Ln, Bluemont, VA 20135, Phone: 540-554-8774, Web: www.tdogforge.com
Prices: $160 to $500.

HARRIS, JAY
991 Johnson St, Redwood City, CA 94061, Phone: 415-366-6077
Specialties: Traditional high-tech straight knives and folders of his design. **Patterns:** Daggers, fighters and locking folders. **Technical:** Uses 440C, ATS-34 and CPM. **Prices:** $250 to $850. **Remarks:** Spare-time maker; first knife sold in 1980.

HARRIS, JOHN
PO Box 2466, Quartzsite, AZ 85346, Phone: 951-653-2755, johnharrisknives@yahoo.com; Web: www.johnharrisknives.com
Specialties: Hunters, daggers, Bowies, bird and trout, period pieces, Damascus and carbon steel knives, forged and stock removal. **Prices:** $200 to $1000.

HARRISON, BRIAN
BFH KNIVES, 2359 E Swede Rd, Cedarville, MI 49719, Phone: 906-430-0720, bfh_knives@yahoo.com
Specialties: High grade fixed blade knives. **Patterns:** Many sizes & variety of patterns from small pocket carries to large combat and camp knives. Mirror and bead blast finishes. All handles of high grade materials from ivory to highly figured stabilized woods to stag, deer & moose horn and Micarta. Hand sewn fancy sheaths for pocket or belt. **Technical:** Flat & hollow grinds usually ATS-34 but some O1, L6 and stellite 6K. **Prices:** $150 to $1200. **Remarks:** Full-time maker, sole authorship. Made first knife in 1980, sold first knife in 1999. Received much knowledge from the following makers: George Young, Eric Erickson, Webster Wood, Ed Kalfayan who are all generous men. **Mark:** Engraved blade outline w/BFH Knives over the top edge, signature across middle & Cedarville, MI underneath.

HARRISON, JIM (SEAMUS)
721 Fairington View Dr, St. Louis, MO 63129, Phone: 314-894-2525, jrh@seamusknives.com; Web: www.seamusknives.com

Specialties: "Crossover" folders, liner-locks and frame-locks. **Patterns:** Uber, Author, Skyyy Folders, Grant Survivor, Fixed blade. **Technical:** Use CPM S30V and 154, Stellite 6k and S.S. Damascus by Norris, Thomas and Damasteel. **Prices:** Folders $375 to $1,000. **Remarks:** Full-time maker since 2008, Maker since 1999. **Mark:** Seamus

HARSEY, WILLIAM H
82710 N. Howe Ln, Creswell, OR 97426, Phone: 541-510-8707, billharsey@gmail.com
Specialties: High-tech kitchen and outdoor knives. **Patterns:** Folding hunters, trout and bird folders; straight hunters, camp knives and axes. **Technical:** Grinds; etches. **Prices:** $125 to $300; some to $1500. Folders start at $350. **Remarks:** Full-time maker; first knife sold in 1979. **Mark:** Full name, state, U.S.A.

HART, BILL
647 Cedar Dr, Pasadena, MD 21122, Phone: 410-255-4981
Specialties: Fur-trade era working straight knives and folders. **Patterns:** Springback folders, skinners, Bowies and patch knives. **Technical:** Forges and stock removes 1095 and 5160 wire Damascus. **Prices:** $100 to $600. **Remarks:** Part-time maker; first knife sold in 1986. **Mark:** Name.

HARTMAN, ARLAN (LANNY)
6102 S Hamlin Cir, Baldwin, MI 49304, Phone: 231-745-4029
Specialties: Working straight knives and folders. **Patterns:** Drop-point hunters, coil spring lockers, slip-joints. **Technical:** Flat-grinds D2, 440C and ATS-34. **Prices:** $300 to $2000. **Remarks:** Part-time maker; first knife sold in 1982. **Mark:** Last name.

HARTMAN, TIM
3812 Pedroncelli Rd NW, Albuquerque, NM 87107, Phone: 505-385-6924, tbonz1@comcast.net
Specialties: Exotic wood scales, sambar stag, filework, hunters. **Patterns:** Fixed blade hunters, skinners, utility and hiking. **Technical:** 154CM, Ats-34 and D2. Mirror finish and contoured scales. **Prices:** Start at $200-$450. **Remarks:** Started making knives in 2004. **Mark:** 3 lines Ti Hartman, Maker, Albuquerque NM

HARVEY, HEATHER
HEAVIN FORGE, PO Box 768, Belfast, MP, SOUTH AFRICA 1100, Phone: 27-13-253-0914, heather@heavinforge.co.za; Web: www.heavinforge.co.za
Specialties: Integral hand forged knives, traditional African weapons, primitive folders and by-gone forged-styles. **Patterns:** All forged knives, war axes, spears, arrows, forks, spoons, and swords. **Technical:** Own carbon Damascus and mokume. Also forges stainless, brass, copper and titanium. Traditional forging and heat-treatment methods used. **Prices:** $300 to $5000, average $1000. **Remarks:** Full-time maker and knifemaking instructor. Master bladesmith with ABS. First Damascus sold in 1995, first knife sold in 1998. Often collaborate with husband, Kevin (ABS MS) using the logo "Heavin." **Mark:** First name and sur name, oval shape with "M S" in middle.

HARVEY, KEVIN
HEAVIN FORGE, PO Box 768, Belfast, LP, SOUTH AFRICA 1100, Phone: 27-13-253-0914, info@heavinforge.co.za Web: www.heavinforge.co.za
Specialties: Large knives of presentation quality and creative art knives. **Patterns:** Fixed blades of Bowie, dagger and fighter-styles, occasionally folders and swords. **Technical:** Stock removal of stainless and forging of carbon steel and own Damascus. Indigenous African handle materials preferred. Own engraving Often collaborate with wife, Heather (ABS MS) under the logo "Heavin." **Prices:** $500 to $5000 average $1500. **Remarks:** Full-time maker and knifemaking instructor. Master bladesmith with ABS. First knife sold in 1984. **Mark:** First name and surname, oval with "M S" in the middle.

HARVEY, MAX
6 Winchester Way, Leeming, Perth, Western Australia 6149, AUSTRALIA, Phone: 61 (8) 93101103 or 61-478-633-356, mcharveyknives@outlook.com; http://mcharveycustomknives.com/wordpress/?page_id=84
Specialties: Fixed-blade knives of all styles. **Patterns:** Camp knives, skinners, bowies, daggers and high-end art knives. **Technical:** Stock-removal using ATS-34, 154CM, 440C and damascus. Do all my own faceting of gem stones in the high-end knives. **Prices:** $250 to $5,000. **Remarks:** Full-time maker; first knife sold in 1981, and founding member of the Australian Knife Makers Guild. **Mark:** First and middle initials, and surname (M C Harvey).

HARVEY, MEL
P.O. Box 176, Nenana, AK 99760, Phone: 907-832-5660, tinker1@nenana.net
Specialties: Fixed blade knives for hunting and fishing. **Patterns:** Hunters, skinners. **Technical:** Stock removal on ATS-34, 440C, O1, 1095; Damascus blades using 1095 and 15N20. **Prices:** Starting at $350. **Remarks:** ABS member, attended Bill Moran School; 50+ knives sold since 2007. **Mark:** Mel Harvey over serial number over Nenana, AK.

HASLINGER, THOMAS
6460 Woodland Dr., British Columbia V1B 3G7, CANADA, Phone: 250-558-9962, Web: www.haslinger-knives.com; www.haslinger-culinary.com
Specialties: One-of-a-kind using, working and art knives HCK signature sweeping grind lines. Maker of New Generation and Evolution Chef series. Differential heat treated stainless steel. **Patterns:** Likes to work with customers on design. **Technical:** Grinds various specialty alloys, including Damascus, High end satin finish. Prefers natural handle materials e.g. ancient ivory stag, pearl, abalone, stone and exotic woods. Does inlay work with stone, some sterling silver, niobium and gold wire work. Custom sheaths using matching woods or hand stitched with unique leather. Offers engraving. **Prices:** $300 and up. **Remarks:** Full-time maker; first knife sold in 1994. Doing business as Haslinger Custom Knives. **Mark:** Two marks used, high end work uses stylized initials, other uses elk antler with Thomas Haslinger, Canada, handcrafted above.

HAWES, CHUCK
HAWES FORGE, PO Box 176, Weldon, IL 61882, Phone: 217-736-2479
Specialties: 95 percent of all work in own Damascus. **Patterns:** Slip-joints liner locks, hunters, Bowie's, swords, anything in between. **Technical:** Forges everything, uses all high-carbon steels, no stainless. **Prices:** $150 to $4000. **Remarks:** Like to do custom orders, his style or yours. Sells Damascus. Full-time maker since 1995. **Mark:** Small football shape. Chuck Hawes maker Weldon, IL.

HAWK, GRANT AND GAVIN
Box 401, Idaho City, ID 83631, Phone: 208-392-4911, blademaker25@msn.com; www.hawkknifedesigns.com
Specialties: Large folders with unique locking systems, D.O.G. lock, toad lock. **Technical:** Grinds ATS-34, titanium folder parts. **Prices:** $450 and up. **Remarks:** Full-time maker. **Mark:** First initials and last names.

HAWKINS, BUDDY
PO Box 5969, Texarkana, TX 75505-5969, Phone: 903-838-7917, buddyhawkins@cableone.net

HAWKINS JR., CHARLES R.
2764 Eunice, San Angelo, TX 76901, Phone: 325-947-7875, chawk12354@aol.com; Web: www.hawkcustomknives.com
Specialties: Custom knives, fixed blades, railroad spike knives and rasp file knives. **Technical:** Stock removal and some forging, using 1095 and 440C steel. **Prices:** $135 and up. **Remarks:** Part-time maker; first knife sold in 2008. **Mark:** Full name, city and state.

HAYES, WALLY
9960, 9th Concession, RR#1, Essex, ON, CANADA N8M-2X5, Phone: 519-776-1284, hayesknives@hayesknives.com; Web: www.hayesknives.com
Specialties: Classic and fancy straight knives and folders. **Patterns:** Daggers, Bowies, fighters, tantos. **Technical:** Forges own Damascus and O1; engraves. **Prices:** $150 to $14,000. **Mark:** Last name, M.S. and serial number.

HAYNES, JERRY
260 Forest Meadow Dr, Gunter, TX 75058, Phone: 903-433-1424, jhaynes@arrow-head.com; Web: http://www.arrow-head.com
Specialties: Working straight knives and folders of his design, also historical blades. **Patterns:** Hunters, skinners, carving knives, fighters, renaissance daggers, locking folders and kitchen knives. **Technical:** Grinds ATS-34, CPM, Stellite 6K, D2 and acquired Damascus. Prefers exotic handle materials. Has B.A. in design. Studied with R. Buckminster Fuller. **Prices:** $200 to $1200. **Remarks:** Part-time maker. First knife sold in 1953. **Mark:** Arrowhead and last name.

HAYS, MARK
HAYS HANDMADE KNIVES, 1008 Kavanagh Dr., Austin, TX 78748, Phone: 512-292-4410, markhays@austin.rr.com
Specialties: Working straight knives and folders. Patterns inspired by Randall and Stone. **Patterns:** Bowies, hunters and slip-joint folders. **Technical:** 440C stock removal. Repairs and restores Stone knives. **Prices:** Start at $200. **Remarks:** Part-time maker, brochure available, with Stone knives 1974-1983, 1990-1991. **Mark:** First initial, last name, state and serial number.

HEADRICK, GARY
122 Wilson Blvd, Juan Les Pins, FRANCE 06160, Phone: 033 610282885, headrick-gary@wanadoo.fr; Web: couteaux-scrimshaw
Specialties: Hi-tech folders with natural furnishings. Back lock & back spring. **Patterns:** Damascus and mokumes. **Technical:** Self made Damascus all steel (no nickel). All chassis titanium. **Prices:** $500 to $2000. **Remarks:** Full-time maker for last 7 years. German Guild-French Federation. 10 years active. **Mark:** HEADRICK on ricosso is new marking.

HEANEY, JOHN D
9 Lefe Court, Haines City, FL 33844, Phone: 863-422-5823, jdh199@msn.com; Web: www.heaneyknives.com
Specialties: Forged 5160, O1 and Damascus. Prefers using natural handle material such as bone, stag and oosic. Plans on using some of the various ivories on future knives. **Prices:** $250 and up. **Remarks:** ABS member. Received journeyman smith stamp in June. **Mark:** Heaney JS.

HEARD, TOM
Turning Point Knives, 2240 Westwood Dr., Waldorf, MD 20601, Phone: 301-843-8626; cell: 301-752-1944, turningpointknives@comcast.net
Specialties: Gent's working/using LinerLocks, automatics and flipper folders of his design. **Patterns:** Fixed blades of varying styles, folders and neck knives. **Technical:** Flat grinds 1095, O1, damascus and 154CM. Offers acid-etched blade embellishments, scrimshaw and hand-tooled custom leather sheaths. Does own heat-treating. **Prices:** $100 to $700. **Remarks:** Full-time maker since retiring; first knife sold in 2012. **Mark:** TH over last name.

HEASMAN, H G
28 St Mary's Rd, Llandudno, N. Wales, UNITED KINGDOM LL302UB, Phone: (UK)0492-876351
Specialties: Miniatures only. **Patterns:** Bowies, daggers and swords. **Technical:** Files from stock high-carbon and stainless steel. **Prices:** $400 to $600. **Remarks:** Part-time maker; first knife sold in 1975. Doing business as Reduced Reality. **Mark:** NA.

HEATH, WILLIAM
PO Box 131, Bondville, IL 61815, Phone: 217-863-2576
Specialties: Classic and working straight knives, folders. **Patterns:** Hunters and Bowies LinerLock® folders. **Technical:** Grinds ATS-34, 440C, 154CM, Damascus, handle materials Micarta, woods to exotic materials snake skins cobra, rattle snake, African flower snake. Does own heat treating. **Prices:** $75 to $300 some $1000. **Remarks:** Full-time maker. First knife sold in 1979. **Mark:** W. D. HEATH.

HEBEISEN, JEFF
310 19th Ave N, Hopkins, MN 55343, Phone: 952-935-4506, jhebeisen@peoplepc.com
Specialties: One of a kind fixed blade of any size up to 16". **Patterns:** Miniature, Hunters, Skinners, Daggers, Bowies, Fighters and Neck knives. **Technical:** Stock removal using CPM-154, D2, 440C. Handle mterial varies depending on intended use, mostly natural materials such as bone, horn, antler, and wood. Filework on many. Heavy duty sheaths made to fit. **Prices:** From $100 to $750. **Remarks:** Full-time maker. First knife sold in 2007. **Mark:** Started new mark in 2012: J. Hebeisen, Hopkins, MN. Older **Mark:** arched name over buffalo skull.

HEDGES, DEE
192 Carradine Rd., Bedfordale, WA, AUSTRALIA 6112, dark_woods_forge@yahoo.com.au; Web: www.darkwoodsforge.com
Patterns: Makes any and all patterns and style of blades from working blades to swords to Japanese inspired. Favors exotic and artistic variations and unique one-off pieces. **Technical:** Forges all blades from a range of steels, favoring 1084, W2, 52100, 5160 and Damascus steels she makes from a 1084/15n20 mix. **Prices:** Start at $200. **Remarks:** Full-time bladesmith and jeweller. Started making blades professionally in 1999, earning my Journeyman Smith rating in 2010. **Mark:** "Dark Woods" atop an ivy leaf, with "Forge" underneath.

HEDLUND, ANDERS
Samstad 400, Brastad, SWEDEN 45491, Phone: 46-523-139 48, anderskniv@passagen.se; Web: http://hem.passagen.se/anderskniv
Specialties: Fancy high-end collectible folders, high-end collectible Nordic hunters with leather carvings on the sheath. Carvings combine traditional designs with own designs. **Patterns:** Own designs. **Technical:** Grinds most steels, but prefers mosaic Damascus and RWL-34. Prefers mother-of-pearl, mammoth, and mosaic steel for folders. Prefers desert ironwood, mammoth, stabilized arctic birch, willow burl, and Damascus steel or RWL-34 for stick tang knives. **Prices:** Starting at $750 for stick tang knives and staring at $1500 for folders. **Remarks:** Part-time maker, first knife sold in 1988. Nordic champion (five countries) several times and Swedish champion 20 times in different classes. **Mark:** Stylized initials or last name.

HEDRICK, DON
131 Beechwood Hills, Newport News, VA 23608, Phone: 757-877-8100, donaldhedrick@cox.net; Web: www.donhedrickknives.com
Specialties: Working straight knives; period pieces and fantasy knives. **Patterns:** Hunters, boots, Bowies and miniatures. **Technical:** Grinds 440C and commercial Damascus. Also makes micro-mini Randall replicas. **Prices:** $150 to $550; some to $1200. **Remarks:** Part-time maker; first knife sold in 1982. **Mark:** First initial, last name in oval logo.

HEETER, TODD S.
9569 Polo Place N., Mobile, AL 36695, Phone: 251-490-5107, toddheeter78@yahoo.com; Web: www.heeterknifeworks.com
Specialties: Complete range of handforged knives, one-of-a-kind custom pieces. **Patterns:** Military-style frame-lock folders, neck knives, railroad spike folders. **Technical:** Handforged blades, including 1095 and D2, stainless steel, Alabama Damascus, doing one-sided chisel grinds and all ranges of flat grinds. Specializes in war-torn look, hand-hammered copper, pattern etching, antique copper and brass handle scales. **Prices:** $150 to $950. **Remarks:** Part-time maker, full-time fabricator and machinist, tool and die maker; first knife sold in 2009. **Mark:** Stamped first initial, middle initial and full last name, logo: HK with a dagger crossing letters.

HEGE, JOHN B.
P.O. Box 316, Danbury, NC 27106, Phone: 336-593-8324, jbhege@embarqmail.com; www.jbhegecustomknives.com
Specialties: Period-style knives and traditional bowies, utility hunters and fancy pieces. **Technical:** Forges larger pieces and often uses stock removal for knives 6 inches and smaller. **Remarks:** ABS journeyman smith since 2013.

HEGWALD, J L
1106 Charles, Humboldt, KS 66748, Phone: 316-473-3523
Specialties: Working straight knives, some fancy. **Patterns:** Makes Bowies, miniatures. **Technical:** Forges or grinds O1, L6, 440C; mixes materials in handles. **Prices:** $35 to $200; some higher. **Remarks:** Part-time maker; first knife sold in 1983. **Mark:** First and middle initials.

HEHN, RICHARD KARL
Lehnmuehler Str 1, Dorrebach, GERMANY 55444, Phone: 06724 3152
Specialties: High-tech, full integral working knives. **Patterns:** Hunters, fighters and daggers. **Technical:** Grinds CPM T-440V, CPM T-420V, forges his own stainless Damascus. **Prices:** $1000 to $10,000. **Remarks:** Full-time maker; first knife sold in 1963. **Mark:** Runic last initial in logo.

HEIMDALE, J E
7749 E 28 CT, Tulsa, OK 74129, Phone: 918-640-0784, heimdale@sbcglobal.net
Specialties: Art knives **Patterns:** Bowies, daggers **Technical:** Makes allcomponents and handles -exotic woods and sheaths. Uses Damascus blades by other Blademakers, notably R.W. Wilson. **Prices:** $300 and up. **Remarks:** Part-time maker. First knife sold in 1999. **Marks:** JEHCO

HEINZ, JOHN
611 Cafferty Rd, Upper Black Eddy, PA 18972, Phone: 610-847-8535,

Web: www.herugrim.com

Specialties: Historical pieces / copies. **Technical:** Makes his own steel. **Prices:** $150 to $800. **Mark:** "H."

HEITLER, HENRY

8106 N Albany, Tampa, FL 33604, Phone: 813-933-1645

Specialties: Traditional working and using straight knives of his design and to customer specs. **Patterns:** Fighters, hunters, utility/camp knives and fillet knives. **Technical:** Flat-grinds ATS-34; offers tapered tangs. **Prices:** $135 to $450; some to $600. **Remarks:** Part-time maker; first knife sold in 1990. **Mark:** First initial, last name, city, state circling double H's.

HELSCHER, JOHN W

2645 Highway 1, Washington, IA 52353, Phone: 319-653-7310

HELTON, ROY

HELTON KNIVES, 2941 Comstock St., San Diego, CA 92111, Phone: 858-277-5024

HEMPERLEY, GLEN

13322 Country Run Rd, Willis, TX 77318, Phone: 936-228-5048, hemperley.com

Specialties: Specializes in hunting knives, does fixed and folding knives.

HENDRICKS, SAMUEL J

2162 Van Buren Rd, Maurertown, VA 22644, Phone: 703-436-3305

Specialties: Integral hunters and skinners of thin design. **Patterns:** Boots, hunters and locking folders. **Technical:** Grinds ATS-34, 440C and D2. Integral liners and bolsters of N-S and 7075 T6 aircraft aluminum. Does leatherwork. **Prices:** $50 to $250; some to $500. **Remarks:** Full-time maker; first knife sold in 1992. **Mark:** First and middle initials, last name, city and state in football-style logo.

HENDRICKSON, E JAY

4204 Ballenger Creek Pike, Frederick, MD 21703, Phone: 301-663-6923, Fax: 301-663-6923, ejayhendrickson@comcast.net

Specialties: Specializes in silver wire inlay. **Patterns:** Bowies, Kukri's, camp, hunters, and fighters. **Technical:** Forges 06, 1084, 5160, 52100, D2, L6 and W2; makes Damascus. Moran-styles on order. **Prices:** $400 to $8,000. **Remarks:** Full-time maker; first knife made in 1972; first knife sold in 1974. **Mark:** Last name, M.S.

HENDRICKSON, SHAWN

2327 Kaetzel Rd, Knoxville, MD 21758, Phone: 301-432-4306

Specialties: Hunting knives. **Patterns:** Clip points, drop points and trailing point hunters. **Technical:** Forges 5160, 1084 and L6. **Prices:** $175 to $400.

HENDRIX, JERRY

HENDRIX CUSTOM KNIVES, 17 Skyland Dr. Ext., Clinton, SC 29325, Phone: 864-833-2659

Specialties: Traditional working straight knives of all designs. **Patterns:** Hunters, utility, boot, bird and fishing. **Technical:** Grinds ATS-34 and 440C. **Prices:** $85 to $275. **Remarks:** Full-time maker. Hand stitched, waxed leather sheaths. **Mark:** Full name in shape of knife.

HENDRIX, WAYNE

9636 Burton's Ferry Hwy, Allendale, SC 29810, Phone: 803-584-3825, Fax: 803-584-3825, whendrixknives@gmail.com Web: www.hendrixknives.com

Specialties: Working/using knives of his design. **Patterns:** Hunters and fillet knives. **Technical:** Grinds ATS-34, D2 and 440C. **Prices:** $100 and up. **Remarks:** Full-time maker; first knife sold in 1985. **Mark:** Last name.

HENNINGSSON, MICHAEL

Klingkarrsvagen 8, 430 83 Vrango (Gothenburg), SWEDEN, Phone: +46 76 626 06 51, michael.henningsson@gmail.com; Web: henningssonknives.com

Specialties: Handmade folding knives, mostly tactical linerlocks and framelocks. **Patterns:** Own design in both engravings and knife models. **Technical:** All kinds of stee; such as Damascus, but prefer clean RWL-43. Tweaking a lot with hand engraving and therefore likes clean steel mostly. Work a lot with inlays of various materials. **Prices:** Starting at $1200 and up, depending on decoration and engravings. **Remarks:** Part-time maker, first knife sold in 2010. **Mark:** Hand engraved name or a Viking sail with initials in runes

HENSLEY, WAYNE

PO Box 904, Conyers, GA 30012, Phone: 770-483-8938

Specialties: Period pieces and fancy working knives. **Patterns:** Boots to bowies, locking folders to miniatures. Large variety of straight knives. **Technical:** Grinds ATS-34, 440C, D2 and commercial damascus. **Prices:** $175 and up. **Remarks:** Full-time maker; first knife sold in 1974. **Mark:** Hensley USA.

HERBST, GAWIE

PO Box 59158, Karenpark, Akasia, GT, SOUTH AFRICA 0118, Phone: +27 72 060 3687, Fax: +27 12 549 1876, gawie@herbst.co.za Web: www.herbst.co.za

Specialties: Hunters, Utility knives, Art knives and Liner lock folders.

HERBST, PETER

Komotauer Strasse 26, Lauf a.d. Pegn., GERMANY 91207, Phone: 09123-13315, Fax: 09123-13379

Specialties: Working/using knives and folders of his design. **Patterns:** Hunters, fighters and daggers; interframe and integral. **Technical:** Grinds CPM-T-440V, UHB-Elmax, ATS-34 and stainless Damascus. **Prices:** $300 to $3000; some to $8000. **Remarks:** Full-time maker; first knife sold in 1981. **Mark:** First initial, last name.

HERBST, THINUS

PO Box 59158, Karenpark, Akasia, GT, SOUTH AFRICA 0118, Phone: +27 82 254 8016, thinus@herbst.co.za; Web: www.herbst.co.za

Specialties: Plain and fancy working straight knives of own design and liner lock folders. **Patterns:** Hunters, utility knives, art knives, and liner lock folders. **Technical:** Prefer exotic materials for handles. Most knives embellished with file work, carving and scrimshaw. **Prices:** $200 to $2000. **Remarks:** Full-time maker, member of the Knifemakers Guild of South Africa.

HERMAN, TIM

517 E. 126 Terrace, Olathe, KS 66061-2731, Phone: 913-839-1924, HermanKnives@comcast.net

Specialties: Investment-grade folders of his design; interframes and bolster frames. **Patterns:** Interframes and new designs in carved stainless. **Technical:** Grinds ATS-34 and damasteel Damascus. Engraves and gold inlays with pearl, jade, lapis and Australian opal. **Prices:** $1500 to $20,000 and up. **Remarks:** Full-time maker; first knife sold in 1978. Inventor of full-color bulino engraving since 1993. **Mark:** Etched signature.

HERNDON, WM R "BILL"

32520 Michigan St, Acton, CA 93510, Phone: 661-269-5860, bherndons1@roadrunner.com

Specialties: Straight knives, plain and fancy. **Technical:** Carbon steel (white and blued), Damascus, stainless steels. **Prices:** Start at $175. **Remarks:** Full-time maker; first knife sold in 1972. American Bladesmith Society journeyman smith. **Mark:** Signature and/or helm logo.

HERRING, MORRIS

Box 85 721 W Line St, Dyer, AR 72935, Phone: 501-997-8861, morrish@ipa.com

HETHCOAT, DON

Box 1764, Clovis, NM 88101, Phone: 575-762-5721, dhethcoat@plateautel.net; Web: www.donhethcoat.com

Specialties: Liner locks, lock backs and multi-blade folder patterns. **Patterns:** Hunters, Bowies. **Technical:** Grinds stainless; forges Damascus. **Prices:** Moderate to upscale. **Remarks:** Full-time maker; first knife sold in 1969. **Mark:** Last name on all.

HEWITT, RONALD "COTTON"

P.O. Box 326, Adel, GA 31620, Phone: 229-896-6366 or 229-237-4378, gobbler12@msn.com, www.hewittknives.com

Specialties: LinerLock folders, including spring-assisted models. **Technical:** Grinds 440C and 1095 blade steels. **Prices:** $350 and up. **Remarks:** Full-time maker; first knife sold in 1975. **Mark:** Last name.

HIBBEN, DARYL

PO Box 172, LaGrange, KY 40031-0172, Phone: 502-222-0983, dhibben1@bellsouth.net

Specialties: Working straight knives, some fancy to customer specs. **Patterns:** Hunters, fighters, Bowies, short sword, art and fantasy. **Technical:** Grinds 440C, ATS-34, 154CM, Damascus; prefers hollow-grinds. **Prices:** $275 and up. **Remarks:** Full-time maker; first knife sold in 1979. **Mark:** Etched full name in script.

HIBBEN, GIL

PO Box 13, LaGrange, KY 40031, Phone: 502-222-1397, Fax: 502-222-2676, gil@hibbenknives.com Web: www.hibbenknives.com

Specialties: Working knives and fantasy pieces to customer specs. **Patterns:** Full range of straight knives, including swords, axes and miniatures; some locking folders. **Technical:** Grinds ATS-34, 440C and D2. **Prices:** $300 to $2000; some to $10,000. **Remarks:** Full-time maker; first knife sold in 1957. Maker and designer of Rambo III knife; made swords for movie Marked for Death and throwing knife for movie Under Seige; made belt buckle knife and knives for movie Perfect Weapon; made knives featured in movie Star Trek the Next Generation, Star Trek Nemesis. 1990 inductee Cutlery Hall of Fame; designer for United Cutlery. Official klingon armourer for Star Trek. Knives also for movies of the Expendables and the Expendables sequel. Over 37 movies and TV productions. President of the Knifemakers Guild. Celebrating 55 years since first knife sold. **Mark:** Hibben Knives. City and state, or signature.

HIBBEN, JOLEEN

PO Box 172, LaGrange, KY 40031, Phone: 502-222-0983, dhibben1@bellsouth.net

Specialties: Miniature straight knives of her design; period pieces. **Patterns:** Hunters, axes and fantasy knives. **Technical:** Grinds Damascus, 1095 tool steel and stainless 440C or ATS-34. Uses wood, ivory, bone, feathers and claws on/for handles. **Prices:** $60 to $600. **Remarks:** Spare-time maker; first knife sold in 1991. Design knives, make & tool leather sheathes. Produced first inlaid handle in 2005, used by Daryl on a dagger. **Mark:** Initials or first name.

HIBBEN, WESTLEY G

14101 Sunview Dr, Anchorage, AK 99515

Specialties: Working straight knives of his design or to customer specs. **Patterns:** Hunters, fighters, daggers, combat knives and some fantasy pieces. **Technical:** Grinds 440C mostly. Filework available. **Prices:** $200 to $400; some to $3000. **Remarks:** Part-time maker; first knife sold in 1988. **Mark:** Signature.

HICKS, GARY

341 CR 275, Tuscola, TX 79562, Phone: 325-554-9762

HIELSCHER, GUY

PO Box 992, 6550 Otoe Rd., Alliance, NE 69301, Phone: 308-762-4318, g-hielsc@bbcwb.net Web: www.ghknives.com

Specialties: Working Damascus fixed blade knives. **Patterns:** Hunters, fighters, capers, skinners, bowie, drop point. **Technical:** Forges own Damascus using 1018 and 0-1 tool steels. **Prices:** $285 and up. **Remarks:** Member of PKA. Part-time maker; sold first knife in 1988. **Mark:** Arrowhead with GH inside.

HIGH, TOM

5474 S 1128 Rd, Alamosa, CO 81101, Phone: 719-589-2108, www.rockymountainscrimshaw.com

Specialties: Hunters, some fancy. **Patterns:** Drop-points in several shapes; some semi-skinners. Knives designed by and for top outfitters and guides. **Technical:** Grinds ATS-34; likes hollow-grinds, mirror finishes; prefers scrimable handles. **Prices:** $300 to $8000. **Remarks:** Full-time maker; first knife sold in 1965. Limited edition wildlife series knives. **Mark:** Initials connected; arrow through last name.

HILL, RICK

20 Nassau, Maryville, IL 62062-5618, Phone: 618-288-4370

Specialties: Working knives and period pieces to customer specs. **Patterns:** Hunters, locking folders, fighters and daggers. **Technical:** Grinds D2, 440C and 154CM; forges his own Damascus. **Prices:** $75 to $500; some to $3000. **Remarks:** Part-time maker; first knife sold in 1983. **Mark:** Full name in hill shape logo.

HILL, STEVE E

217 Twin Lake Tr., Spring Branch, TX 78070, Phone: 830-624-6258 (cell) or 830-885-6108 (home), kingpirateboy2@juno.com or kingpirateboy2@gvtc.com; Web: www.stevehillknives.com

Specialties: Fancy manual and automatic LinerLock® folders, small fixed blades and classic Bowie knives. **Patterns:** Classic to cool folding and fixed blade designs. **Technical:** Grinds Damascus and occasional 440C, D2. Prefers natural materials; offers elaborate filework, carving, and inlays. **Prices:** $400 to $6000, some higher. **Remarks:** Full-time maker; first knife sold in 1978. Google search: Steve Hill custom knives. **Mark:** First initial, last name and handmade. (4400, D2). Damascus folders: mark inside handle.

HILLMAN, CHARLES

225 Waldoboro Rd, Friendship, ME 04547, Phone: 207-832-4634

Specialties: Working knives of his own or custom design. Heavy Scagel influence. **Patterns:** Hunters, fishing, camp and general utility. Occasional folders. **Technical:** Grinds D2 and 440C. File work, blade and handle carving, engraving. Natural handle materials-antler, bone, leather, wood, horn. Sheaths made to order. **Prices:** $60 to $500. **Remarks:** Part-time maker; first knife sold 1986. **Mark:** Last name in oak leaf.

HINDERER, RICK

5373 Columbus Rd., Shreve, OH 44676, Phone: 330-263-0962, Fax: 330-263-0962, rhind64@earthlink.net; Web: www.rickhindererknives.com

Specialties: Working tactical knives, and some one-of-a kind. **Patterns:** Makes his own. **Technical:** Grinds Duratech 20 CV and CPM S30V. **Prices:** $150 to $4000. **Remarks:** Full-time maker doing business as Rick Hinderer Knives, first knife sold in 1988. **Mark:** R. Hinderer.

HINDMARCH, GARTH

PO Box 135, Carlyle, SK, CANADA S0C 0R0, Phone: 306-453-2568

Specialties: Working and fancy straight knives, bowies. **Patterns:** Hunters, skinners, bowies. **Technical:** Grinds 440C, ATS 34, some damascus. **Prices:** $250 to $1,100. **Remarks:** Part-time maker; first knife sold 1994. All knives satin finished. Does filework, offers engraving, stabilized wood, giraffe bone, some Micarta. **Mark:** First initial, last name, city, province.

HINK III, LES

1599 Aptos Lane, Stockton, CA 95206, Phone: 209-547-1292

Specialties: Working straight knives and traditional folders in standard patterns or to customer specs. **Patterns:** Hunting and utility/camp knives; others on request. **Technical:** Grinds carbon and stainless steels. **Prices:** $80 to $200; some higher. **Remarks:** Part-time maker; first knife sold in 1980. **Mark:** Last name, or last name 3.

HINMAN, THEODORE

186 Petty Plain Road, Greenfield, MA 01301, Phone: 413-773-0448, armenemargosian@verizon.net

Specialties: Tomahawks and axes. Offers classes in bladesmithing and toolmaking.

HINSON AND SON, R

2419 Edgewood Rd, Columbus, GA 31906, Phone: 706-327-6801

Specialties: Working straight knives and folders. **Patterns:** Locking folders, liner locks, combat knives and swords. **Technical:** Grinds 440C and commercial Damascus. **Prices:** $200 to $450; some to $1500. **Remarks:** Part-time maker; first knife sold in 1983. Son Bob is co-worker. **Mark:** HINSON, city and state.

HINTZ, GERALD M

5402 Sahara Ct, Helena, MT 59602, Phone: 406-458-5412

Specialties: Fancy, high-art, working/using knives of his design. **Patterns:** Bowies, hunters, daggers, fish fillet and utility/camp knives. **Technical:** Forges ATS-34, 440C and D2. Animal art in horn handles or in the blade. **Prices:** $75 to $400; some to $1000. **Remarks:** Part-time maker; first knife sold in 1980. Doing business as Big Joe's Custom Knives. Will take custom orders. **Mark:** F.S. or W.S. with first and middle initials and last name.

HIRAYAMA, HARUMI

4-5-13 Kitamachi, Warabi City, Saitama, JAPAN 335-0001, Phone: 048-443-2248, Fax: 048-443-2248, swanbird3@gmail.com; Web: www.ne.jp/asahi/harumi/knives

Specialties: High-tech working knives of her design. **Patterns:** Locking folders, interframes, straight gents and slip-joints. **Technical:** Grinds 440C or equivalent; uses natural handle materials and gold. **Prices:** Start at $2500. **Remarks:** Part-time maker; first knife sold in 1985. **Mark:** First initial, last name.

HIROTO, FUJIHARA

2-34-7 Koioosako, Nishi-ku, Hiroshima, JAPAN, Phone: 082-271-8389, fjhr8363@crest.ocn.ne.jp

HOBART, GENE

100 Shedd Rd, Windsor, NY 13865, Phone: 607-655-1345

HOCKENSMITH, DAN

104 North Country Rd 23, Berthoud, CO 80513, Phone: 970-231-6506, blademan@skybeam.com; Web: www.dhockensmithknives.com

Specialties: Traditional working and using straight knives of his design. **Patterns:** Hunters, Bowies, folders and utility/camp knives. **Technical:** Uses his Damascus, 5160, carbon steel, 52100 steel and 1084 steel. Hand forged. **Prices:** $250 to $1500. **Remarks:** Part-time maker; first knife sold in 1987. **Mark:** Last name or stylized "D" with H inside.

HODGE III, JOHN

422 S 15th St, Palatka, FL 32177, Phone: 904-328-3897

Specialties: Fancy straight knives and folders. **Patterns:** Various. **Technical:** Pattern-welded Damascus—"Southern-style." **Prices:** To $1000. **Remarks:** Part-time maker; first knife sold in 1981. **Mark:** JH3 logo.

HOEL, STEVE

PO Box 283, Pine, AZ 85544-0283, Phone: 928-476-6523

Specialties: Investor-class folders, straight knives and period pieces of his design. **Patterns:** Folding interframes lockers and slip-joints; straight Bowies, boots and daggers. **Technical:** Grinds 154CM, ATS-34 and commercial Damascus. **Prices:** $600 to $1200; some to $7500. **Remarks:** Full-time maker. **Mark:** Initial logo with name and address.

HOFER, LOUIS

BOX 125, Rose Prairie, BC, CANADA V0C 2H0, Phone: 250-827-3999, anvil_needles@hotmail.cq; www.anvilandneedles.com

Specialties: Damascus knives, working knives, fixed blade bowies, daggers. **Patterns:** Hunting, skinning, custom. **Technical:** Wild damascus, random damascus. **Prices:** $450 and up. **Remarks:** Part-time maker since 1995. **Mark:** Logo of initials.

HOFFMAN, JAY

Hoffman Haus + Heraldic Device, 911 W Superior St., Munising, MI 49862, Phone: 906-387-3440, hoffmanhaus1@yahoo.com; Web: www.hoffmanhausknives.com

Technical: Scrimshaw, metal carving, own casting of hilts and pommels, etc. Most if not all leather work for sheaths. **Remarks:** Has been making knives for 50 + years. Professionally since 1991. **Mark:** Early knives marked "Hoffman Haus" and year. Now marks "Hoffman Haus Knives" on the blades. Starting in 2010 uses heraldic device. Will build to your specs. Lag time 1-2 months.

HOFFMAN, JESS

W7089 Curt Black Rd., Shawano, WI 54166, Phone: 715-584-2466, mooseyard@gmail.com; Web: www.jhoffmanknives.com

Specialties: Working fixed blades. **Technical:** Stock removal of carbon, stainless and damascus steels. Handles range from paper Micarta to exotic hardwoods. **Prices:** Start at $75. **Remarks:** Part-time knifemaker. **Mark:** Ancestral lower-case "h" and/or J. Hoffman.

HOFFMAN, KEVIN L

28 Hopeland Dr, Savannah, GA 31419, Phone: 912-920-3579, Fax: 912-920-3579, kevh052475@aol.com; Web: www.KLHoffman.com

Specialties: Distinctive folders and fixed blades. **Patterns:** Titanium frame lock folders. **Technical:** Sculpted guards and fittings cast in sterling silver and 14k gold. Grinds ATS-34, CPM S30V damascus. Makes kydex sheaths for his fixed blade working knives. **Prices:** $400 and up. **Remarks:** Full-time maker since 1981. **Mark:** KLH.

HOGAN, THOMAS R

2802 S. Heritage Ave, Boise, ID 83709, Phone: 208-362-7848

HOGSTROM, ANDERS T

Halmstadsvagen 36, Johanneshov, SWEDEN 12153, Phone: 46 702 674 574, andershogstrom@hotmail.com or info@andershogstrom.com; Web: www.andershogstrom.com

Specialties: Short and long daggers, fighters and swords For select pieces makes wooden display stands. **Patterns:** Daggers, fighters, short knives and swords and an occasional sword. **Technical:** Grinds 1050 High Carbon, Damascus and stainless, forges own Damasus on occasion, fossil ivories. Does clay tempering and uses exotic hardwoods. **Prices:** Start at $850. **Marks:** Last name in maker's own signature.

HOKE, THOMAS M

3103 Smith Ln, LaGrange, KY 40031, Phone: 502-222-0350

Specialties: Working/using knives, straight knives. Own designs and customer specs. **Patterns:** Daggers, Bowies, hunters, fighters, short swords. **Technical:** Grind 440C, Damascus and ATS-34. Filework on all knives. Tooling on sheaths (custom fit on all knives). Any handle material, mostly exotic. **Prices:** $100 to $700; some to $1500. **Remarks:** Full-time maker, first knife sold in 1986. **Mark:** Dragon on banner which says T.M. Hoke.

HOLBROOK, H L

PO Box 483, Sandy Hook, KY 41171, Phone: Cell: 606-794-1497, hhknives@mrtc.com

Specialties: Traditional working using straight knives of his design, to customer specs and in standard patterns. Stabilized wood. **Patterns:** Hunters, mild tacticals and neck knives with kydex sheaths. **Technical:** Grinds CPM154CM, 154CM. Blades have hand-rubbed satin finish. Uses exotic woods, stag and Micarta. Hand-sewn sheath with each straight knife. **Prices:** $165 to $485. **Remarks:** Part-time maker; first knife sold in 1983. Doing business as Holbrook Knives. **Mark:** Name, city, state.

HOLDER, D'ALTON
18910 McNeil Rd., Wickenburg, AZ 85390, Phone: 928-684-2025, Fax: 623-878-3964, dholderknives@commspeed.net; Web: dholder.com
Specialties: Deluxe working knives and high-art hunters. **Patterns:** Drop-point hunters, fighters, Bowies. **Technical:** Grinds ATS-34; uses amber and other materials in combination on stick tangs. **Prices:** $400 to $1000; some to $2000. **Remarks:** Full-time maker; first knife sold in 1966. **Mark:** D'HOLDER, city and state.

HOLLOWAY, PAUL
714 Burksdale Rd, Norfolk, VA 23518, Phone: 757-547-6025, houdini969@yahoo.com
Specialties: Working straight knives and folders to customer specs. **Patterns:** Lockers, fighters and boots, push knives, from swords to miniatures. **Technical:** Grinds A2, D2, 154CM, 440C and ATS-34. **Prices:** $210 to $1,200; some to $1,500, higher. **Remarks:** Retired; first knife sold in 1981. USN 28 years, deputy sheriff 16 years. **Mark:** Name and city in logo.

HOOK, BOB
3247 Wyatt Rd, North Pole, AK 99705, Phone: 907-488-8886, grayling@alaska.net; Web: www.alaskaknifeandforge.com
Specialties: Forged carbon steel. Damascus blades. **Patterns:** Pronghorns, bowies, drop point hunters and knives for the kitchen. **Technical:** 5160, 52100, carbon steel and 1084 and 15N20 pattern welded steel blades are hand forged. Heat treated and ground by maker. Handles are natural materials from Alaska. I favor sole authorship of each piece. **Prices:** $300-$1000. **Remarks:** Journeyman smith with ABS. I have attended the Bill Moran School of Bladesmithing. Knife maker since 2000. **Mark:** Hook.

HORN, DES
PO Box 322, Onrusrivier, WC, SOUTH AFRICA 7201, Phone: 27283161795, Fax: +27866280824, deshorn@usa.net
Specialties: Folding knives. **Patterns:** Ball release side lock mechanism and interframe automatics. **Technical:** Prefers working in totally stainless materials. **Prices:** $800 to $7500. **Remarks:** Full-time maker. Enjoys working in gold, titanium, meteorite, pearl and mammoth. **Mark:** Des Horn.

HORN, JESS
2526 Lansdown Rd, Eugene, OR 97404, Phone: 541-463-1510, jandahorn@earthlink.net
Specialties: Investor-class working folders; period pieces; collectibles. **Patterns:** High-tech design and finish in folders; liner locks, traditional slip-joints and featherweight models. **Technical:** Grinds ATS-34, 154CM. **Prices:** Start at $1000. **Remarks:** Full-time maker; first knife sold in 1968. **Mark:** Full name or last name.

HORNE, GRACE
The Old Public Convenience, 469 Fulwood Road, Sheffield, UNITED KINGDOM S10 3QA, gracehorne@hotmail.co.uk Web: www.gracehorn.co.uk
Specialties: Knives of own design, mainly slip-joint folders. **Technical:** Grinds RWL34, Damasteel and own Damascus for blades. Scale materials vary from traditional (coral, wood, precious metals, etc) to unusual (wool, fabric, felt, etc), **Prices:** $500 -$1500**Remarks:** Part-time maker. **Mark:** 'gH' and 'Sheffield'.

HORRIGAN, JOHN
433 C.R. 200 D, Burnet, TX 78611, Phone: 512-756-7545 or 512-636-6562, jhorrigan@yahoo.com Web: www.eliteknives.com
Specialties: High-end custom knives. **Prices:** $200 -$8,500. **Remarks:** Part-time maker. Obtained Mastersmith stamp 2005. First knife made in 1982. **Mark:** Horrigan M.S.

HORTON, SCOT
PO Box 451, Buhl, ID 83316, Phone: 208-543-4222
Specialties: Traditional working stiff knives and folders. **Patterns:** Hunters, skinners, utility, hatchets and show knives. **Technical:** Grinds ATS-34 and D-2 tool steel. **Prices:** $400 to $2500. **Remarks:** First knife sold in 1990. **Mark:** Full name in arch underlined with arrow, city, state.

HOSSOM, JERRY
3585 Schilling Ridge, Duluth, GA 30096, Phone: 770-449-7809, jerry@hossom.com; Web: www.hossom.com
Specialties: Working straight knives of his own design. **Patterns:** Fighters, combat knives, modern Bowies and daggers, modern swords, concealment knives for military and LE uses. **Technical:** Grinds 154CM, S30V, CPM-3V, CPM-154 and stainless Damascus. Uses natural and synthetic handle materials. **Prices:** $350-1500, some higher. **Remarks:** Full-time maker since 1997. First knife sold in 1983. **Mark:** First initial and last name, includes city and state since 2002.

HOSTETLER, LARRY
10626 Pine Needle Dr., Fort Pierce, FL 34945, Phone: 772-465-8352, hossknives@bellsouth.net Web: www.hoss-knives.com
Specialties: EDC working knives and custom collector knives. Utilizing own designs and customer designed creations. Maker uses a wide variety of exotic materials. **Patterns:** Bowies, hunters and folders. **Technical:** Stock removal, grinds ATS-34, carbon and stainless Damascus, embellishes most pieces with file work. **Prices:** $200 -$1500. Some custom orders higher. **Remarks:** Motto: "EDC doesn't have to be ugly." First knife made in 2001, part-time maker, voting member in the Knife Maker's Guild. Doing business as "Hoss Knives." **Mark:** "Hoss" etched into blade with a turn of the century fused bomb in place of the "O" in Hoss.

HOSTETTER, WALLY
P.O. Box 404, San Mateo, FL 32187, Phone: 386-649-0731, shiningmoon_13@yahoo.com; www.shiningmoon13.com
Specialties: Japanese swords and pole arms, and all their mountings from different time periods, other sword styles. **Technical:** Hand forges 1075 on up to 1095 steels, some with vanadium alloys. **Prices:** $1,200 to $6,500. **Remarks:** Full-time maker; first sword was a katana in 1999. **Mark:** Signature on tang in Japanese kanji is Wally San.

HOUSE, CAMERON
2001 Delaney Rd Se, Salem, OR 97306, Phone: 503-585-3286, chouse357@aol.com
Specialties: Working straight knives. **Patterns:** Hunters, Bowies, fighters. **Technical:** Grinds ATS-34, 530V, 154CM. **Remarks:** Part-time maker, first knife sold in 1993. **Prices:** $150 and up. **Mark:** HOUSE.

HOUSE, GARY
2851 Pierce Rd, Ephrata, WA 98823, Phone: 509-754-3272, spindry101@aol.com
Specialties: Bowies, hunters, daggers and some swords. **Patterns:** Unlimited, SW Indian designs, geometric patterns, bowies, hunters and daggers. **Technical:** Mosaic damascus bar stock, forged blades, using 1084, 15N20 and some nickel. Forged company logos and customer designs in mosaic damascus. **Prices:** $500 & up. **Remarks:** Some of the finest and most unique patterns available. ABS master smith. **Marks:** Initials GTH, G hanging T, H.

HOWARD, DURVYN M.
4220 McLain St S, Hokes Bluff, AL 35903, Phone: 256-504-1853
Specialties: Collectible upscale folders; one-of-a-kind, gentlemen's folders. Unique mechanisms and multiple patents. **Patterns:** Conceptual designs; each unique and different. **Technical:** Uses natural and exotic materials and precious metals. **Prices:** $7,500 to $35,000. **Remarks:** Full-time maker; 52 years experience. **Mark:** Howard.

HOWE, TORI
30020 N Stampede Rd, Athol, ID 83801, Phone: 208-449-1509, wapiti@knifescales.com; Web:www.knifescales.com
Specialties Custom knives, knife scales & Damascus blades. **Remarks:** Carry James Luman polymer clay knife scales.

HOWELL, JASON G
1112 Sycamore, Lake Jackson, TX 77566, Phone: 979-297-9454, tinyknives@yahoo.com; Web:www.howellbladesmith.com
Specialties: Fixed blades and LinerLock® folders. Makes own Damascus. **Patterns:** Clip and drop point. **Prices:** $150 to $750. **Remarks:** Likes making Mosaic Damascus out of the ordinary stuff. Member of TX Knifemakers and Collectors Association; apprentice in ABS; working towards Journeyman Stamp. **Mark:** Name, city, state.

HOWELL, KEITH A.
67 Hidden Oaks Dr., Oxford, AL 36203, Phone: 256-283-3269, keith@howellcutlery.com; Web: www.howellcutlery.com
Specialties: Working straight knives and folders of his design or to customer specs. **Patterns:** Hunters, utility pieces, neck knives, everyday carry knives and friction folders. **Technical:** Grinds damascus, 1095 and 154CM. **Prices:** $100 to $250. **Remarks:** Part-time maker; first knife sold in 2007. **Mark:** Last name.

HOWELL, LEN
550 Lee Rd 169, Opelika, AL 36804, Phone: 334-749-1942
Specialties: Traditional and working knives of his design and to customer specs. **Patterns:** Buckskinner, hunters and utility/camp knives. **Technical:** Forges cable Damascus, 1085 and 5160; makes own Damascus. **Mark:** Engraved last name.

HOWELL, TED
1294 Wilson Rd, Wetumpka, AL 36092, Phone: 205-569-2281, Fax: 205-569-1764
Specialties: Working/using straight knives and folders of his design; period pieces. **Patterns:** Bowies, fighters, hunters. **Technical:** Forges 5160, 1085 and cable. Offers light engraving and scrimshaw; filework. **Prices:** $75 to $250; some to $450. **Remarks:** Part-time maker; first knife sold in 1991. Doing business as Howell Co. **Mark:** Last name, Slapout AL.

HOY, KEN
54744 Pinchot Dr, North Fork, CA 93643, Phone: 209-877-7805

HRISOULAS, JIM
SALAMANDER ARMOURY, 284-C Lake Mead Pkwy #157, Henderson, NV 89105, Phone: 702-566-8551, www.atar.com
Specialties: Working straight knives; period pieces. **Patterns:** Swords, daggers and sgian dubhs. **Technical:** Double-edged differential heat treating. **Prices:** $85 to $175; some to $600 and higher. **Remarks:** Full-time maker; first knife sold in 1973. Author of The Complete Bladesmith, The Pattern Welded Blade and The Master Bladesmith. Doing business as Salamander Armory. **Mark:** 8R logo and sword and salamander.

HUCKABEE, DALE
254 Hwy 260, Maylene, AL 35114, Phone: 205-664-2544, huckabeeknives@hotmail.com; Web: http://dalehuckabeeknives.weebly.com
Specialties: Fixed blade hunter and Bowies of his design. **Technical:** Steel used: 5160, 1084, and Damascus. **Prices:** $225 and up, depending on materials used. **Remarks:** Hand forged. Journeyman Smith. Part-time maker. **Mark:** Stamped Huckabee J.S.

HUCKS, JERRY
KNIVES BY HUCKS, 1807 Perch Road, Moncks Corner, SC 29461, Phone: 843-761-6481, Fax: Cell: 843-708-1649, knivesbyhucks@gmail.com
Specialties: Drop points, bowies and oyster knives. **Patterns:** To customer specs or maker's own design. **Technical:** CPM-154, ATS-34, 5160, 15N20, D2 and 1095 mostly for damascus billets. **Prices:** $200 and up. **Remarks:** Full-time maker, retired as a machinist in 1990. Makes sheaths sewn by hand with some carving. Will custom make to order or by sketch. Will also make a miniature bowie on request. **Mark:** Robin Hood hat with Moncks Corner under.

HUDSON, C ROBBIN
116 Hansonville Rd., Rochester, NH 03839, Phone: 603-786-9944, bladesmith8@gmail.com
Specialties: High-art working knives. **Patterns:** Hunters, Bowies, fighters and kitchen knives. **Technical:** Forges W2, nickel steel, pure nickel steel, composite and mosaic Damascus; makes knives one-at-a-time. **Prices:** 500 to $1200; some to $5000. **Remarks:** Full-time maker; first knife sold in 1970. **Mark:** Last name and MS.

HUDSON, ROB
340 Roush Rd, Northumberland, PA 17857, Phone: 570-473-9588, robscustknives@aol.com Web:www.robscustomknives.com
Specialties: Presentation hunters and Bowies. **Technical:** Hollow grinds CPM-154 stainless and stainless Damascus. **Prices:** $400 to $2000. **Remarks:** Full-time maker. Does business as Rob's Custom Knives. **Mark:** Capital R, Capital H in script.

HUDSON, ROBERT
3802 Black Cricket Ct, Humble, TX 77396, Phone: 713-454-7207
Specialties: Working straight knives of his design. **Patterns:** Bowies, hunters, skinners, fighters and utility knives. **Technical:** Grinds D2, 440C, 154CM and commercial Damascus. **Prices:** $85 to $350; some to $1500. **Remarks:** Part-time maker; first knife sold in 1980. **Mark:** Full name, handmade, city and state.

HUGHES, DAN
301 Grandview Bluff Rd, Spencer, TN 38585, Phone: 931-946-3044
Specialties: Working straight knives to customer specs. **Patterns:** Hunters, fighters, fillet knives. **Technical:** Grinds 440C and ATS-34. **Prices:** $55 to $175; some to $300. **Remarks:** Part-time maker; first knife sold in 1984. **Mark:** Initials.

HUGHES, DARYLE
10979 Leonard, Nunica, MI 49448, Phone: 616-837-6623, hughes.builders@verizon.net
Specialties: Working knives. **Patterns:** Buckskinners, hunters, camp knives, kitchen and fishing knives. **Technical:** Forges and grinds 52100 and Damascus. **Prices:** $125 to $1000. **Remarks:** Part-time maker; first knife sold in 1979. **Mark:** Name and city in logo.

HUGHES, ED
280 1/2 Holly Lane, Grand Junction, CO 81503, Phone: 970-243-8547, edhughes26@msn.com
Specialties: Working and art folders. **Patterns:** Buys Damascus. **Technical:** Grinds stainless steels. Engraves. **Prices:** $300 and up. **Remarks:** Full-time maker; first knife sold in 1978. **Mark:** Name or initials.

HUGHES, LAWRENCE
207 W Crestway, Plainview, TX 79072, Phone: 806-293-5406
Specialties: Working and display knives. **Patterns:** Bowies, daggers, hunters, buckskinners. **Technical:** Grinds D2, 440C and 154CM. **Prices:** $125 to $300; some to $2000. **Remarks:** Full-time maker; first knife sold in 1979. **Mark:** Name with buffalo skull in center.

HUGHES, TONY
Tony Hughes Forged Blades, 7536 Trail North Dr., Littleton, CO 80125, Phone: 303-941-1092, tonhug@msn.com
Specialties: Fixed blades, bowies/fighters and hunters of maker's own damascus steel. **Technical:** Forges damascus and mosaic-damascus blades. Fittings are 416 stainless steel, 1095-and-nickel damascus, 1080-and-15N20 damascus or silicon bronze. Prefers ivory, desert ironwood, blackwood, ebony and other burls. **Prices:** $450 and up. **Remarks:** Full-time ABS journeyman smith forging knives for 20 years. **Mark:** Tony Hughes and JS on the other side.

HULETT, STEVE
115 Yellowstone Ave, West Yellowstone, MT 59758-0131, Phone: 406-646-4116, Web: www.seldomseenknives.com
Specialties: Classic, working/using knives, straight knives, folders. Your design, custom specs. **Patterns:** Utility/camp knives, hunters, and LinerLock folders, lock back pocket knives. **Technical:** Grinds 440C stainless steel, O1 Carbon, 1095. Shop is retail and knife shop; people watch their knives being made. We do everything in house: "all but smelt the ore, or tan the hide." **Prices:** Strarting $250 to $7000. **Remarks:** Full-time maker; first knife sold in 1994. **Mark:** Seldom seen knives/West Yellowstone Montana.

HULSEY, HOYT
379 Shiloh, Attalla, AL 35954, Phone: 256-538-6765
Specialties: Traditional working straight knives and folders of his design. **Patterns:** Hunters and utility/camp knives. **Technical:** Grinds 440C, ATS-34, O1 and A2. **Prices:** $75 to $250. **Remarks:** Part-time maker; first knife sold in 1989. **Mark:** Hoyt Hulsey Attalla AL.

HUMENICK, ROY
PO Box 55, Rescue, CA 95672, rhknives@gmail.com; Web: www.humenick.com
Specialties: Traditional multiblades and tactical slipjoints. **Patterns:** Original folder and fixed blade designs, also traditional patterns. **Technical:** Grinds premium steels and Damascus. **Prices:** $350 and up; some to $1500. **Remarks:** First knife sold in 1984. **Mark:** Last name in ARC.

HUMPHREY, LON
4 Western Ave., Newark, OH 43055, Phone: 740-644-1137, lonhumphrey@gmail.com
Specialties: Hunters, tacticals, and bowie knives. **Prices:** I make knives that start in the $150 range and go up to $1000 for a large bowie. **Remarks:** Has been blacksmithing since age 13 and progressed to the forged blade.

HUMPHREYS, JOEL
90 Boots Rd, Lake Placid, FL 33852, Phone: 863-773-0439
Specialties: Traditional working/using straight knives and folders of his design and in standard patterns. **Patterns:** Hunters, folders and utility/camp knives. **Technical:** Grinds ATS-34, D2, 440C. All knives have tapered tangs, mitered bolster/handle joints, handles of horn or bone fitted sheaths. **Prices:** $135 to $225; some to $350. **Remarks:** Part-time maker; first knife sold in 1990. Doing business as Sovereign Knives. **Mark:** First name or "H" pierced by arrow.

HUNT, RAYMON E.
3H's KNIVES, LLC, 600 Milam Ct., Irving, TX 75038, Phone: 214-507-0896, Fax: 972-887-9931, Web: www.3hsknives.com
Specialties: Forged and stock removal for both using and collector-grade knives. **Patterns:** Kitchen cutlery, bowies, daggers, hunters, tactical, utility and straight razors. **Technical:** Steels include 5160, 1075, 1084, 1095, O1, CPM 154, CTS XHP and damascus. Heat treating in-house using oven and torch edge hardening. Uses his own damascus of 1095 and 15N20 and purchases damascus. Engraving and gold inlay by Steve Dunn, filework, peined and polished pins of sterling silver and gold, fire and niter bluing. **Remarks:** American Bladesmith Society, apprentice. **Mark:** 3Hs on left side of blade near the grind line.

HUNTER, HYRUM
285 N 300 W, PO Box 179, Aurora, UT 84620, Phone: 435-529-7244
Specialties: Working straight knives of his design or to customer specs. **Patterns:** Drop and clip, fighters dagger, some folders. **Technical:** Forged from two-piece Damascus. **Prices:** Prices are adjusted according to size, complexity and material used. **Remarks:** Will consider any design you have. Part-time maker; first knife sold in 1990. **Mark:** Initials encircled with first initial and last name and city, then state. Some patterns are numbered.

HUNTER, RICHARD D
7230 NW 200th Ter, Alachua, FL 32615, Phone: 386-462-3150
Specialties: Traditional working/using knives of his design or customer suggestions; filework. **Patterns:** Folders of various types, Bowies, hunters, daggers. **Technical:** Traditional blacksmith; hand forges high-carbon steel (5160, 1084, 52100) and makes own Damascus; grinds 440C and ATS-34. **Prices:** $200 and up. **Remarks:** Part-time maker; first knife sold in 1992. **Mark:** Last name in capital letters.

HURST, JEFF
PO Box 247, Rutledge, TN 37861, Phone: 865-828-5729, jhurst@esper.com
Specialties: Working straight knives and folders of his design. **Patterns:** Tomahawks, hunters, boots, folders and fighters. **Technical:** Forges W2, O1 and his own Damascus. Makes mokume. **Prices:** $250 to $600. **Remarks:** Full-time maker; first knife sold in 1984. Doing business as Buzzard's Knob Forge. **Mark:** Last name; partnered knives are marked with Newman L. Smith, handle artisan, and SH in script.

HUSIAK, MYRON
PO Box 238, Altona, VIC, AUSTRALIA 3018, Phone: 03-315-6752
Specialties: Straight knives and folders of his design or to customer specs. **Patterns:** Hunters, fighters, lock-back folders, skinners and boots. **Technical:** Forges and grinds his own Damascus, 440C and ATS-34. **Prices:** $200 to $900. **Remarks:** Part-time maker; first knife sold in 1974. **Mark:** First initial, last name in logo and serial number.

HUTCHESON, JOHN
SURSUM KNIFE WORKS, 1237 Brown's Ferry Rd., Chattanooga, TN 37419, Phone: 423-667-6193, sursum5071@aol.com; Web: www.sursumknife.com
Specialties: Straight working knives, hunters. **Patterns:** Customer designs, hunting, speciality working knives. **Technical:** Grinds D2, S7, O1 and 5160, ATS-34 on request. **Prices:** $100 to $300, some to $600. **Remarks:** First knife sold 1985, also produces a mid-tech line. Doing business as Sursum Knife Works. **Mark:** Family crest boar's head over 3 arrows.

HUTCHINSON, ALAN
315 Scenic Hill Road, Conway, AR 72034, Phone: 501-470-9653, hutchinsonblades@yahoo.com
Specialties: Hunters, bowies, fighters, combat/survival knives. **Patterns:** Traditional edged weapons and tomahawks, custom patterns. **Technical:** Forges 10 series, 5160, L6, O1, CruForge V, damascus and his own patterns. **Prices:** $250 and up. **Remarks:** Prefers natural handle materials, part-time maker. **Mark:** Last name.

HYTOVICK, JOE "HY"
14872 SW 111th St, Dunnellon, FL 34432, Phone: 800-749-5339, Fax: 352-489-3732, hyclassknives@aol.com
Specialties: Straight, folder and miniature. **Technical:** Blades from Wootz, Damascus and Alloy steel. **Prices:** To $5000. **Mark:** HY.

I

IKOMA, FLAVIO
R Manoel Rainho Teixeira 108, Presidente Prudente, SP, BRAZIL 19031-220, Phone: 0182-22-0115, fikoma@itelesonica.com.br
Specialties: Tactical fixed blade knives, LinerLock® folders and balisongs. **Patterns:** Utility and defense tactical knives built with hi-tech materials. **Technical:** Grinds S30V and Damasteel. **Prices:** $500 to $1000. **Mark:** Ikoma hand made beside Samurai

IMBODEN II, HOWARD L.
620 Deauville Dr, Dayton, OH 45429, Phone: 513-439-1536
Specialties: One-of-a-kind hunting, flint, steel and art knives. **Technical:** Forges and grinds stainless, high-carbon and Damascus. Uses obsidian, cast sterling silver, 14K and

18K gold guards. Carves ivory animals and more. **Prices:** $65 to $25,000. **Remarks:** Full-time maker; first knife sold in 1986. Doing business as Hill Originals. **Mark:** First and last initials, II.

IMEL, BILLY MACE
1616 Bundy Ave, New Castle, IN 47362, Phone: 765-529-1651
Specialties: High-art working knives, period pieces and personal cutlery. **Patterns:** Daggers, fighters, hunters; locking folders and slip-joints with interframes. **Technical:** Grinds D2, 440C and 154CM. **Prices:** $300 to $2000; some to $6000. **Remarks:** Part-time maker; first knife sold in 1973. **Mark:** Name in monogram.

IRIE, MICHAEL L
MIKE IRIE HANDCRAFT, 1606 Auburn Dr., Colorado Springs, CO 80909, Phone: 719-572-5330, mikeirie@aol.com
Specialties: Working fixed blade knives and handcrafted blades for the do-it-yourselfer. **Patterns:** Twenty standard designs along with custom. **Technical:** Blades are ATS-34, BG-43, 440C with some outside Damascus. **Prices:** Fixed blades $95 and up, blade work $45 and up. **Remarks:** Formerly dba Wood, Irie and Co. with Barry Wood. Full-time maker since 1991. **Mark:** Name.

ISAO, OHBUCHI
702-1 Nouso, Yame-City, Fukuoka, JAPAN, Phone: 0943-23-4439, www.5d.biglobe.ne.jp/~ohisao/

ISHIHARA, HANK
86-18 Motomachi, Sakura City, Chiba, JAPAN, Phone: 043-485-3208, Fax: 043-485-3208
Specialties: Fantasy working straight knives and folders of his design. **Patterns:** Boots, Bowies, daggers, fighters, hunters, fishing, locking folders and utility camp knives. **Technical:** Grinds ATS-34, 440C, D2, 440V, CV-134, COS25 and Damascus. Engraves. **Prices:** $250 to $1000; some to $10,000. **Remarks:** Full-time maker; first knife sold in 1987. **Mark:** HANK.

J

JACKS, JIM
344 S. Hollenbeck Ave, Covina, CA 91723-2513, Phone: 626-331-5665
Specialties: Working straight knives in standard patterns. **Patterns:** Bowies, hunters, fighters, fishing and camp knives, miniatures. **Technical:** Grinds Stellite 6K, 440C and ATS-34. **Prices:** Start at $100. **Remarks:** Spare-time maker; first knife sold in 1980. **Mark:** Initials in diamond logo.

JACKSON, CHARLTON R
6811 Leyland Dr, San Antonio, TX 78239, Phone: 210-601-5112

JACKSON, DAVID
214 Oleander Ave, Lemoore, CA 93245, Phone: 559-925-8247, jnbcrea@lemoorenet.com
Specialties: Forged steel. **Patterns:** Hunters, camp knives and bowies. **Prices:** $300 and up. **Mark:** G.D. Jackson -Maker -Lemoore CA.

JACKSON, LARAMIE
POB 442, Claysprings, AZ 85923, Phone: 480-747-3804, ljacksonknives@yahoo.com
Specialties Traditional hunting and working knives and folders, chef's knives. **Patterns:** Bowies, fighters, hunters, daggers and skinners. **Technical:** Grinds 440C, CPM D2, CPM S30V, W2, O1, 52100, 5160, L6, 1095, damascus and whatever customer wants. Offers sheaths. **Prices:** $100-$450+. **Remarks:** Full-time maker; first knife sold in 2010. **Mark:** First initial and last name.

JACQUES, ALEX
28 Junction St., Warwick, RI 02889, Phone: 617-771-4441, customrazors@gmail.com Web: www.customrazors.com
Specialties: One-of-a-kind, heirloom quality straight razors … functional art. **Technical:** Damascus, O1, CPM154, and various other high-carbon and stainless steels. **Prices:** $450 and up. **Remarks:** First knife sold in 2008. **Mark:** Jack-O-Lantern logo with "A. Jacques" underneath.

JAKSIK JR., MICHAEL
427 Marschall Creek Rd, Fredericksburg, TX 78624, Phone: 830-997-1119
Mark: MJ or M. Jaksik.

JANGTANONG, SUCHAT
10901 W. Cave Blvd., Dripping Springs, TX 78620, Phone: 512-264-1501, shakeallpoints@yahoo.com Web: www.mrdamascusknives.com
Specialties: One-of-a-kind handmade art knives, carving pearl and titanium. **Patterns:** Folders (lock back and LinerLock), some fixed blades and butterfly knives. **Technical:** Grinds ATS-34 and damascus steels. **Prices:** $500 to $3,000. **Remarks:** Third-generation, began making knives in 1982; full-time maker who lives in Uthai Thani Province of Thailand. **Mark:** Name (Suchat) on blade.

JANSEN VAN VUUREN, LUDWIG
311 Brighton Rd., Waldronville 9018, Dunedin, NEW ZEALAND, Phone: 64-3-7421012, ludwig@nzhandmadeknives.co.nz; Web: www.nzhandmadeknives.co.nz
Specialties: Fixed-blade knives of his design or custom specifications. **Patterns:** Hunting, fishing, bird-and-trout and chef's knives. **Technical:** Stock-removal maker, Elmax, Sandvik 12C27 and other blade steels on request. Handle material includes Micarta, antler and a wide selection of woods. **Prices:** Starting at $250. **Remarks:** Part-time maker since 2008. **Mark:** L J van Vuuren.

JARVIS, PAUL M
30 Chalk St, Cambridge, MA 02139, Phone: 617-547-4355 or 617-661-3015
Specialties: High-art knives and period pieces of his design. **Patterns:** Japanese and

Mid-Eastern knives. **Technical:** Grinds Myer Damascus, ATS-34, D2 and O1. Specializes in height-relief Japanese-style carving. Works with silver, gold and gems. **Prices:** $200 to $17,000. **Remarks:** Part-time maker; first knife sold in 1978.

JEAN, GERRY
25B Cliffside Dr, Manchester, CT 06040, Phone: 860-649-6449
Specialties: Historic replicas. **Patterns:** Survival and camp knives. **Technical:** Grinds A2, 440C and 154CM. Handle slabs applied in unique tongue-and-groove method. **Prices:** $125 to $250; some to $1000. **Remarks:** Spare-time maker; first knife sold in 1973. **Mark:** Initials and serial number.

JEFFRIES, ROBERT W
Route 2 Box 227, Red House, WV 25168, Phone: 304-586-9780, wvknifeman@hotmail.com; Web: www.jeffriesknieswv.tripod.com
Specialties: Hunters, Bowies, daggers, lockback folders and LinerLock push buttons. **Patterns:** Skinning types, drop points, typical working hunters, folders one-of-a-kind. **Technical:** Grinds all types of steel. Makes his own Damascus. **Prices:** $125 to $600. Private collector pieces to $3000. **Remarks:** Starting engraving. Custom folders of his design. Part-time maker since 1988. **Mark:** Name etched or on plate pinned to blade.

JENKINS, MITCH
194 East 500 South, Manti, Utah 84642, Phone: 435-813-2532, mitch.jenkins@gmail.com Web: MitchJenkinsKnives.com
Specialties: Hunters, working knives. **Patterns:** Johnson and Loveless Style. Drop points, skinners and semi-skinners, Capers and utilities. **Technical:** 154CM and ATS-34. Experimenting with S30V and love working with Damascus on occasion. **Prices:** $150 and up. **Remarks:** Slowly transitioning to full-time maker; first knife made in 2008. **Mark:** Jenkins Manti, Utah and M. Jenkins, Utah.

JENSEN, JOHN LEWIS
JENSEN KNIVES, 146 W. Bellevue Dr. #7, Pasadena, CA 91105, Phone: 626-773-0296, john@jensenknives.com; Web: www.jensenknives.com
Specialties: Designer and fabricator of modern, original one-of-a-kind, hand crafted, custom ornamental edged weaponry. Combines skill, precision, distinction and the finest materials, geared toward the discriminating art collector. **Patterns:** Folding knives and fixed blades, daggers, fighters and swords. **Technical:** High embellishment, BFA 96 Rhode Island School of Design: jewelry and metalsmithing. Grinds carbon and stainless, and carbon/stainless damascus. Works with custom made Damascus to his specs. Uses gold, silver, gemstones, pearl, titanium, fossil mastodon and walrus ivories. Carving, file work, soldering, deep etches Damascus, engraving, layers, bevels, blood grooves. Also forges his own Damascus. **Prices:** Start at $10,000. **Remarks:** Available on a first come basis and via commission based on his designs. **Mark:** Maltese cross/butterfly shield.

JERNIGAN, STEVE
3082 Tunnel Rd., Milton, FL 32571, Phone: 850-994-0802, Fax: 850-994-0802, jerniganknives@att.net
Specialties: Investor-class folders and various theme pieces. **Patterns:** Array of models and sizes in side plate locking interframes and conventional liner construction, including tactical and automatics. **Technical:** Grinds ATS-34, CPM-T-440V and damascus. Inlays mokume (and minerals) in blades and sculpts marble cases. **Prices:** $650 to $1,800; some to $6,000. **Remarks:** Full-time maker, first knife sold in 1982. **Mark:** Last name.

JOBIN, JACQUES
46 St Dominique, Levis, QC, CANADA G6V 2M7, Phone: 418-833-0283, Fax: 418-833-8378
Specialties: Fancy and working straight knives and folders; miniatures. **Patterns:** Minis, fantasy knives, fighters and some hunters. **Technical:** ATS-34, some Damascus and titanium. Likes native snake wood. Heat-treats. **Prices:** Start at $250. **Remarks:** Full-time maker; first knife sold in 1986. **Mark:** Signature on blade.

JOEHNK, BERND
Posadowskystrasse 22, Kiel, GERMANY 24148, Phone: 0431-7297705, Fax: 0431-7297705
Specialties: One-of-a-kind fancy/embellished and traditional straight knives of his design and from customer drawing. **Patterns:** Daggers, fighters, hunters and letter openers. **Technical:** Grinds and file 440C, ATS-34, powder metal orgical, commercial Damascus and various stainless and corrosion-resistant steels. **Prices:** Upscale. **Remarks:** Likes filework. Leather sheaths. Offers engraving. Part-time maker; first knife sold in1990. Doing business as metal design kiel. All knives made by hand. **Mark:** From 2005 full name and city, with certificate.

JOHANNING CUSTOM KNIVES, TOM
1735 Apex Rd, Sarasota, FL 34240 9386, Phone: 941-371-2104, Fax: 941-378-9427, Web: www.survivalknives.com
Specialties: Survival knives. **Prices:** $375 to $775.

JOHANSSON, ANDERS
Konstvartarevagen 9, Grangesberg, SWEDEN 77240, Phone: 46 240 23204, Fax: +46 21 358778, www.scrimart.u.se
Specialties: Scandinavian traditional and modern straight knives. **Patterns:** Hunters, fighters and fantasy knives. **Technical:** Grinds stainless steel and makes own Damascus. Prefers water buffalo and mammoth for handle material. **Prices:** Start at $100. **Remarks:** Spare-time maker; first knife sold in 1994. Works together with scrimshander Viveca Sahlin. **Mark:** Stylized initials.

JOHNS, ROB
1423 S. Second, Enid, OK 73701, Phone: 405-242-2707
Specialties: Classic and fantasy straight knives of his design or to customer specs; fighters for use at Medieval fairs. **Patterns:** Bowies, daggers and swords. **Technical:**

Forges and grinds 440C, D2 and 5160. Handles of nylon, walnut or wire-wrap. **Prices:** $150 to $350; some to $2500. **Remarks:** Full-time maker; first knife sold in 1980. **Mark:** Medieval Customs, initials.

JOHNSON, C E GENE
1240 Coan Street, Chesterton, IN 46304, Phone: 219-787-8324, ddjlady55@aol.com
Specialties: Lock-back folders and springers of his design or to customer specs. **Patterns:** Hunters, Bowies, survival lock-back folders. **Technical:** Grinds D2, 440C, A18, O1, Damascus; likes filework. **Prices:** $100 to $2000. **Remarks:** Full-time maker; first knife sold in 1975. **Mark:** Gene.

JOHNSON, DAVID A
1791 Defeated Creek Rd, Pleasant Shade, TN 37145, Phone: 615-774-3596, artsmith@mwsi.net

JOHNSON, GORDON A.
981 New Hope Rd, Choudrant, LA 71227, Phone: 318-768-2613
Specialties: Using straight knives and folders of my design, or customers. Offering filework and hand stitched sheaths. **Patterns:** Hunters, bowies, folders and miniatures. **Technical:** Forges 5160, 1084, 52100 and my own Damascus. Some stock removal on working knives and miniatures. **Prices:** Mid range. **Remarks:** First knife sold in 1990. ABS apprentice smith. **Mark:** Interlocking initials G.J. or G. A. J.

JOHNSON, JERRY
PO Box 491, Spring City, Utah 84662, Phone: 435-851-3604 or 435-462-3688, Web: sanpetesilver.com
Specialties: Hunter, fighters, camp. **Patterns:** Multiple. **Prices:** $225 -$3000. **Mark:** Jerry E. Johnson Spring City, UT in several fonts.

JOHNSON, JERRY L
29847 260th St, Worthington, MN 56187, Phone: 507-376-9253; Cell: 507-370-3523, doctorj55@yahoo.com
Specialties: Straight knives, hunters, bowies, and fighting knives. **Patterns:** Drop points, trailing points, bowies, and some favorite Loveless patterns. **Technical:** Grinds ATS 34, 440C, S30V, forges own damascus, mirror finish, satin finish, file work and engraving done by self. **Prices:** $250 to $1500. **Remarks:** Part-time maker since 1991, member of knifemakers guild since 2009. **Mark:** Name over a sheep head or elk head with custom knives under the head.

JOHNSON, JOHN R
5535 Bob Smith Ave, Plant City, FL 33565, Phone: 813-986-4478, rottyjohn@msn.com
Specialties: Hand forged and stock removal. **Technical:** High tech. Folders. **Mark:** J.R. Johnson Plant City, FL.

JOHNSON, JOHN R
PO Box 246, New Buffalo, PA 17069, Phone: 717-834-6265, jrj@jrjknives.com; Web: www.jrjknives.com
Specialties: Working hunting and tactical fixed blade sheath knives. **Patterns:** Hunters, tacticals, Bowies, daggers, neck knives and primitives. **Technical:** Flat, convex and hollow grinds. ATS-34, CPM154CM, L6, O1, D2, 5160, 1095 and Damascus. **Prices:** $60 to $700. **Remarks:** Full-time maker, first knife sold in 1996. Doing business as JRJ Knives. Custom sheath made by maker for every knife, **Mark:** Initials connected.

JOHNSON, KEITH R.
9179 Beltrami Line Rd. SW, Bemidji, MN 56601, Phone: 218-368-7482, keith@greatriverforge.com; www.greatriverforge.com
Specialties: Slip-joint and lockback folders. **Patterns:** Mostly traditional patterns but with customer preferences, some of maker's own patterns. **Technical:** Mainly uses CPM 154, sometimes other high-quality stainless steels, Damasteel. Variety of handle materials, including bone, mammoth ivory, Micarta, G-10 and carbon fiber. **Remarks:** Full-time maker; first knife sold in 1986. **Mark:** K.R. JOHNSON (arched) over BEMIDJI.

JOHNSON, MIKE
38200 Main Rd, Orient, NY 11957, Phone: 631-323-3509, mjohnsoncustomknives@hotmail.com
Specialties: Large Bowie knives and cutters, fighters and working knives to customer specs. **Technical:** Forges 5160, O1. **Prices:** $325 to $1200. **Remarks:** Full-time bladesmith. **Mark:** Johnson.

JOHNSON, R B
Box 11, Clearwater, MN 55320, Phone: 320-558-6128, Fax: 320-558-6128, rb@rbjohnsonknives.com; Web: rbjohnsonknives.com
Specialties: Liner locks with titanium, mosaic Damascus. **Patterns:** LinerLock® folders, skeleton hunters, frontier Bowies. **Technical:** Damascus, mosaic Damascus, A-2, O1, 1095. **Prices:** $200 and up. **Remarks:** Full-time maker since 1973. Not accepting orders. **Mark:** R B Johnson (signature).

JOHNSON, RANDY
2575 E Canal Dr, Turlock, CA 95380, Phone: 209-632-5401
Specialties: Folders. **Patterns:** Locking folders. **Technical:** Grinds Damascus. **Prices:** $200 to $400. **Remarks:** Spare-time maker; first knife sold in 1989. Doing business as Puedo Knifeworks. **Mark:** PUEDO.

JOHNSON, RICHARD
W165 N10196 Wagon Trail, Germantown, WI 53022, Phone: 262-251-5772, rlj@execpc.com; Web: http://www.execpc.com/~rlj/index.html
Specialties: Custom knives and knife repair.

JOHNSON, RYAN M
3103 Excelsior Ave., Signal Mountain, TN 37377, Phone: 866-779-6922, contact@rmjtactical.com; Web: www.rmjforge.com www.rmjtactical.com

Specialties: Historical and Tactical Tomahawks. Some period knives and folders. **Technical:** Forges a variety of steels including own Damascus. **Prices:** $500 -$1200 **Remarks:** Full-time maker began forging in 1986. **Mark:** Sledge-hammer with halo.

JOHNSON, STEVEN R
202 E 200 N, PO Box 5, Manti, UT 84642, Phone: 435-835-7941, srj@mail.manti.com; Web: www.srjknives.com
Specialties: Investor-class working knives. **Patterns:** Hunters, fighters, boots. **Technical:** Grinds CPM-154CM and CTS-XHP. **Prices:** $1,500 to $20,000. Engraved knives up to $50,000. **Remarks:** Full-time maker; first knife sold in 1972. Also see SR Johnson forum on www.knifenetwork.com. **Mark:** Registered trademark, including name, city, state, and optional signature mark.

JOHNSON, TOMMY
144 Poole Rd., Troy, NC 27371, Phone: 910-975-1817, tommy@tjohnsonknives.com Web: www.tjohnsonknives.com
Specialties: Straight knives for hunting, fishing, utility, and linerlock and slip joint folders since 1982.

JOHNSON, WM. C. "BILL"
225 Fairfield Pike, Enon, OH 45323, Phone: 937-864-7802, wjohnson64@woh.RR.com
Patterns: From hunters to art knives as well as custom canes, some with blades. **Technical:** Stock removal method utilizing 440C, 154CM, and custom Damascus. **Prices:** $175 to over $2500, depending on design, materials, and embellishments. **Remarks:** Full-time maker. First knife made in 1978. Member of the Knifemakers Guild since 1982. **Mark:** Crescent shaped WM. C. "BILL" JOHNSON, ENON OHIO. Also uses an engraved or electro signature on some art knives and on Damascus blades.

JOHNSTON, DR. ROBT
PO Box 9887 1 Lomb Mem Dr, Rochester, NY 14623

JOKERST, CHARLES
9312 Spaulding, Omaha, NE 68134, Phone: 402-571-2536
Specialties: Working knives in standard patterns. **Patterns:** Hunters, fighters and pocketknives. **Technical:** Grinds 440C, ATS-34. **Prices:** $90 to $170. **Remarks:** Spare-time maker; first knife sold in 1984. **Mark:** Early work marked RCJ; current work marked with last name and city.

JONAS, ZACHARY
204 Village Rd., Wilmot, NH 03287, Phone: 603-877-0128, zack@jonasblade.com; www.jonasblade.com
Specialties: Custom high-carbon damascus, sporting knives, kitchen knives and art knives. Always interested in adding to the repertoire. **Patterns:** Kitchen and bowie knives, hunters, daggers, push daggers, tantos, boot knives, all custom. **Technical:** Forges all damascus blades, works with high-carbon steels to suit the client's individual tastes and needs. **Remarks:** Full-time maker, ABS journeyman smith trained by ABS master smith J.D. Smith, juried member of League of New Hampshire Craftsmen. **Mark:** Sytlized "Z" symbol on one side, "JS" on other, either stamped, engraved or etched.

JONES, BARRY M AND PHILLIP G
221 North Ave, Danville, VA 24540, Phone: 804-793-5282
Specialties: Working and using straight knives and folders of their design and to customer specs; combat and self-defense knives. **Patterns:** Bowies, fighters, daggers, swords, hunters and LinerLock® folders. **Technical:** Grinds 440C, ATS-34 and D2; flat-grinds only. All blades hand polished. **Prices:** $100 to $1000, some higher. **Remarks:** Part-time makers; first knife sold in 1989. **Mark:** Jones Knives, city, state.

JONES, ENOCH
7278 Moss Ln, Warrenton, VA 20187, Phone: 540-341-0292
Specialties: Fancy working straight knives. **Patterns:** Hunters, fighters, boots and Bowies. **Technical:** Forges and grinds O1, W2, 440C and Damascus. **Prices:** $100 to $350; some to $1000. **Remarks:** Part-time maker; first knife sold in 1982. **Mark:** First name.

JONES, JACK P.
17670 Hwy. 2 East, Ripley, MS 38663, Phone: 662-837-3882, jacjones@ripleycable.net
Specialties: Working knives in classic design. **Patterns:** Hunters, fighters, and Bowies. **Technical:** Grinds D2, A2, CPM-154, CTS-XHP and ATS-34. **Prices:** $200 and up. **Remarks:** Full-time maker since retirement in 2005, first knife sold in 1976. **Mark:** J.P. Jones, Ripley, MS.

JONES, ROGER MUDBONE
GREENMAN WORKSHOP, 320 Prussia Rd, Waverly, OH 45690, Phone: 740-739-4562, greenmanworkshop@yahoo.com
Specialties: Working in cutlery to suit working woodsman and fine collector. **Patterns:** Bowies, hunters, folders, hatchets in both period and modern style, scale miniatures a specialty. **Technical:** All cutlery hand forged to shape with traditional methods; multiple quench and draws, limited Damascus production hand carves wildlife and historic themes in stag/antler/ivory, full line of functional and high art leather. All work sole authorship. **Prices:** $50 to $5000 **Remarks:** Full-time maker/first knife sold in 1979. **Mark:** Stamped R. Jones hand made or hand engraved sig. W/Bowie knife mark.

JORGENSEN, CARSON
1805 W Hwy 116, Mt Pleasant, UT 84647, tcjorgensenknife@gmail.com; Web: tcjknives.com
Specialties: Stock removal, Loveless Johnson and young styles. **Prices:** Most $100 to $800.

K

K B S, KNIVES
RSD 181, North Castlemaine, VIC, AUSTRALIA 3450, Phone: 0011 61 3 54 705864
Specialties: Historically inspired bowies, and restoration of fixed and folding knives.
Patterns: Bowies and folders. **Technical:** Flat and hollow grinds, filework. **Prices:** $500
and up. **Remarks:** First knife sold in 1983, foundation member of Australian Knife Guild.
Mark: Initials and address within Southern cross.

KACZOR, TOM
375 Wharncliffe Rd N, Upper London, ON, CANADA N6G 1E4, Phone: 519-645-7640

KAGAWA, KOICHI
1556 Horiyamashita, Hatano-Shi, Kanagawa, JAPAN
Specialties: Fancy high-tech straight knives and folders to customer specs. **Patterns:**
Hunters, locking folders and slip-joints. **Technical:** Uses 440C and ATS-34. **Prices:** $500
to $2000; some to $20,000. **Remarks:** Part-time maker; first knife sold in 1986. **Mark:**
First initial, last name-YOKOHAMA.

KAIN, CHARLES
KAIN DESIGNS, 1736 E. Maynard Dr., Indianapolis, IN 46227, Phone: 317-781-9549,
Fax: 317-781-8521, charles@kaincustomknives.com; Web: www.kaincustomknives.com
Specialties: Unique Damascus art folders. **Patterns:** Any. **Technical:** Specialized &
patented mechanisms. **Remarks:** Unique knife & knife mechanism design. **Mark:** Kain
and Signet stamp for unique pieces.

KANKI, IWAO
691-2 Tenjincho, Ono-City, Hyogo, JAPAN 675-1316, Phone: 07948-3-2555,
Web: www.chiyozurusadahide.jp
Specialties: Plane, knife. **Prices:** Not determined yet. **Remarks:** Masters of traditional
crafts designated by the Minister of International Trade and Industry (Japan). **Mark:**
Chiyozuru Sadahide.

KANSEI, MATSUNO
109-8 Uenomachi, Nishikaiden, Gifu, JAPAN 501-1168, Phone: 81-58-234-8643
Specialties: Folders of original design. **Patterns:** LinerLock® folder. **Technical:** Grinds
VG-10, Damascus. **Prices:** $350 to $2000. **Remarks:** Full-time maker. First knife sold in
1993. **Mark:** Name.

KANTER, MICHAEL
ADAM MICHAEL KNIVES, 14550 West Honey Ln., New Berlin, WI 53151, Phone:
262-860-1136, mike@adammichaelknives.com; Web: www.adammichaelknives.com
Specialties: Fixed blades and folders. **Patterns:** Drop point hunters, Bowies and fighters.
Technical: Jerry Rados Damascus, BG42, CPM, S60V and S30V. **Prices:** $375 and up.
Remarls: Ivory, mammoth ivory, stabilized woods, and pearl handles. **Mark:** Engraved
Adam Michael.

KARP, BOB
PO Box 47304, Phoenix, AZ 85068, Phone: 602 870-1234
602 870-1234, Fax: 602-331-0283
Remarks: Bob Karp "Master of the Blade."

KATO, SHINICHI
Rainbow Amalke 402, Moriyama-ku Nagoya, Aichi, JAPAN 463-0002,
Phone: 81-52-736-6032, skato-402@u0l.gate01.com
Specialties: Flat grind and hand finish. **Patterns:** Bowie, fighter. Hunting and folding
knives. **Technical:** Hand forged,flat grind. **Prices:** $100 to $2000. **Remarks:** Part-time
maker. **Mark:** Name.

KATSUMARO, SHISHIDO
2-6-11 Kamiseno, Aki-ku, Hiroshima, JAPAN, Phone: 090-3634-9054,
Fax: 082-227-4438, shishido@d8.dion.ne.jp

KAUFFMAN, DAVE
158 Jackson Creek Rd., Clancy, MT 59634, Phone: 406-431-8435
Specialties: Field grade and exhibition grade hunting knives and ultra light folders.
Patterns: Fighters, Bowies and drop-point hunters. **Technical:** S30V and SS Damascus.
Prices: $155 to $1200. **Remarks:** Full-time maker; first knife sold in 1989. On the cover
of Knives '94. **Mark:** First and last name, city and state.

KAY, J WALLACE
332 Slab Bridge Rd, Liberty, SC 29657

KAZSUK, DAVID
PO Box 390190, Anza, CA 92539-0190, Phone: 951-238-7460, ddkaz@hotmail.com
Specialties: Hand forged. **Prices:** $150+. **Mark:** Last name.

KEARNEY, JAROD
1505 Parkersburg Turnpike, Swoope, VA 24479, jarodkearney@gmail.com
Web: www.jarodkearney.com
Patterns: Bowies, skinners, hunters, Japanese blades, Sgian Dubhs

KEESLAR, JOSEPH F
391 Radio Rd, Almo, KY 42020, Phone: 270-753-7919, Fax: 270-753-7919,
sjkees@apex.net
Specialties: Classic and contemporary Bowies, combat, hunters, daggers and folders.
Patterns: Decorative filework, engraving and custom leather sheaths available. **Technical:**
Forges 5160, 52100 and his own Damascus steel. **Prices:** $300 to $3000. **Remarks:** Full-
time maker; first knife sold in 1976. ABS Master Smith, and 50 years as a bladesmith (1962-
2012). **Mark:** First and middle initials, last name in hammer, knife and anvil logo, M.S.

KEESLAR, STEVEN C
115 Lane 216 Hamilton Lake, Hamilton, IN 46742, Phone: 260-488-3161,
sskeeslar@hotmail.com
Specialties: Traditional working/using straight knives of his design and to customer
specs. **Patterns:** Bowies, hunters, utility/camp knives. **Technical:** Forges 5160, files
52100 Damascus. **Prices:** $100 to $600; some to $1500. **Remarks:** Part-time maker;
first knife sold in 1976. ABS member. **Mark:** Fox head in flames over Steven C. Keeslar.

KEETON, WILLIAM L
6095 Rehobeth Rd SE, Laconia, IN 47135-9550, Phone: 812-969-2836,
wlkeeton@hughes.net; Web: www.keetoncustomknives.com
Specialties: Plain and fancy working knives. **Patterns:** Hunters and fighters; locking
folders and slip-joints. Names patterns after Kentucky Derby winners. **Technical:** Grinds
any of the popular alloy steels. **Prices:** $195 to $8,000. **Remarks:** Full-time maker; first
knife sold in 1971. **Mark:** Logo of key.

KEHIAYAN, ALFREDO
Cuzco 1455 Ing., Maschwitz, Buenos Aires, ARGENTINA B1623GXU,
Phone: 540-348-4442212, Fax: 54-077-75-4493-5359, alfredo@kehiayan.com.ar;
Web: www.kehiayan.com.ar
Specialties: Functional straight knives. **Patterns:** Utility knives, skinners, hunters and
boots. **Technical:** Forges and grinds SAE 52.100, SAE 6180, SAE 9260, SAE 5160, 440C
and ATS-34, titanium with nitride. All blades mirror-polished; makes leather sheath and
wood cases. **Prices:** From $350 up. **Remarks:** Full-time maker; first knife sold in 1983.
Some knives are satin finish (utility knives). **Mark:** Name.

KEISUKE, GOTOH
105 Cosumo-City Otozu 202, Oita-city, Oita, JAPAN, Phone: 097-523-0750,
k-u-an@ki.rim.or.jp

KELLER, BILL
12211 Las Nubes, San Antonio, TX 78233, Phone: 210-653-6609
Specialties: Primarily folders, some fixed blades. **Patterns:** Autos, liner locks and
hunters. **Technical:** Grinds stainless and Damascus. **Prices:** $400 to $1000, some to
$4000. **Remarks:** Part-time maker, first knife sold 1995. **Mark:** Last name inside outline
of Alamo.

KELLEY, GARY
17485 SW Pheasant Lane, Aloha, OR 97006, Phone: 503-649-7867,
garykelley@theblademaker.com; Web: wwwtheblademaker.com
Specialties: Primitive knives and blades. **Patterns:** Fur trade era rifleman's knives,
tomahawks, and hunting knives. **Technical:** Hand-forges and precision investment casts.
Prices: $35 to $125. **Remarks:** Family business. Doing business as The Blademaker.
Mark: Fir tree logo.

KELLY, DAVE
865 S. Shenandoah St., Los Angeles, CA 90035, Phone: 310-657-7121,
dakcon@sbcglobal.net
Specialties: Collector and user one-of-a-kind (his design) fixed blades, liner lock folders,
and leather sheaths. **Patterns:** Utility and hunting fixed blade knives with hand-sewn
leather sheaths, Gentleman liner lock folders. **Technical:** Grinds carbon steels, hollow,
convex, and flat. Offers clay differentially hardened blades, etched and polished. Uses
Sambar stag, mammoth ivory, and high-grade burl woods. Hand-sewn leather sheaths
for fixed blades and leather pouch sheaths for folders. **Prices:** $250 to $750, some
higher. **Remarks:** Full-time maker, first knife made in 2003. **Mark:** First initial, last name
with large K.

KELLY, STEVEN
11407 Spotted Fawn Ln., Bigfork, MT 59911, Phone: 406-837-1489, www.skknives.com
Technical: Damascus from 1084 or 1080 and 15n20. 52100.

KELSEY, NATE
3867 N. Forestwood Dr., Palmer, AK 99645, Phone: 907-360-4469,
edgealaska@mac.com; Web: www.edgealaska.com
Specialties: Forges high-performance 52100, stock removal on 154CM for Extreme Duty
Worldwide. **Patterns:** Hunters, fighters and bowies. **Prices:** Material dependent, $175 to
$3,000. **Remarks:** Maker since 1990, member ABS. **Mark:** EDGE ALASKA.

KELSO, JIM
577 Collar Hill Rd, Worcester, VT 05682, Phone: 802-229-4254,
Fax: 802-229-0595, kelsomaker@gmail.com; Web:www.jimkelso.com
Specialties: Fancy high-art straight knives and folders that mix Eastern and Western
influences. Only uses own designs. **Patterns:** Daggers, swords and locking folders.
Technical: Works with top bladesmiths. **Prices:** $15,000 to $60,000 . **Remarks:** Full-time
maker; first knife sold in 1980. **Mark:** Stylized initials.

KEMP, LAWRENCE
8503 Water Tower Rd, Ooltewah, TN 37363, Phone: 423-344-2357,
larry@kempknives.com Web: www.kempknives.com
Specialties: Bowies, hunters and working knives. **Patterns:** Bowies, camp knives,
hunters and skinners. **Technical:** Forges carbon steel, and his own Damascus. **Prices:**
$250 to $1500. **Remarks:** Part-time maker, first knife sold in 1991. ABS Journeyman
Smith since 2006. **Mark:** L.A. Kemp.

KENNEDY JR., BILL
PO Box 850431, Yukon, OK 73085, Phone: 405-354-9150, bkfish1@gmail.com;
www.billkennedyjrknives.com
Specialties: Working straight knives and folders. **Patterns:** Hunters, minis, fishing,
and pocket knives. **Technical:** Grinds D2, 440C, ATS-34, BG42. **Prices:** $110 and up.

Remarks: Part-time maker; first knife sold in 1980. **Mark:** Last name and year made.

KERANEN, PAUL
4122 S. E. Shiloh Ct., Tacumseh, KS 66542, Phone: 785-220-2141, pk6269@yahoo.com
Specialties: Specializes in Japanese style knives and swords. Most clay tempered with hamon. **Patterns:** Does bowies, fighters and hunters. **Technical:** Forges and grinds carbons steel only. Make my own Damascus. **Prices:** $75 to $800. **Mark:** Keranen arched over anvil.

KEYES, DAN
6688 King St, Chino, CA 91710, Phone: 909-628-8329

KEYES, GEOFF P.
13027 Odell Rd NE, Duvall, WA 98019, Phone: 425-844-0758, 5ef@polarisfarm.com; Web: www5elementsforge.com
Specialties: Working grade fixed blades, 19th century style gents knives. **Patterns:** Fixed blades, your design or mine. **Technical:** Hnad-forged 5160, 1084, and own Damascus. **Prices:** $200 and up. **Remarks:** Geoff Keyes DBA 5 Elements Forge, ABS Journeyman Smith. **Mark:** Early mark KEYES etched in script. New mark as of 2009: pressed GPKeyes.

KHALSA, JOT SINGH
368 Village St, Millis, MA 02054, Phone: 508-376-8162, Fax: 508-532-0517, jotkhalsa@comcast.net; Web: www.khalsakirpans.com, www.lifeknives.com, and www.thekhalsaraj.com
Specialties: Liner locks, one-of-a-kind daggers, swords, and kirpans (Sikh daggers) all original designs. **Technical:** Forges own Damascus, uses others high quality Damascus including stainless, and grinds stainless steels. Uses natural handle materials frequently unusual minerals. Pieces are frequently engraved and more recently carved. **Prices:** Start at $700.

KHARLAMOV, YURI
Oboronnay 46, Tula, RUSSIA 300007
Specialties: Classic, fancy and traditional knives of his design. **Patterns:** Daggers and hunters. **Technical:** Forges only Damascus with nickel. Uses natural handle materials; engraves on metal, carves on nut-tree; silver and pearl inlays. **Prices:** $600 to $2380; some to $4000. **Remarks:** Full-time maker; first knife sold in 1988. **Mark:** Initials.

KI, SHIVA
5222 Ritterman Ave, Baton Rouge, LA 70805, Phone: 225-356-7274, shivakicustomknives@netzero.net; Web: www.shivakicustomknives.com
Specialties: Working straight knives and folders. **Patterns:** Emphasis on personal defense knives, martial arts weapons. **Technical:** Forges and grinds; makes own Damascus; prefers natural handle materials. **Prices:** $550 to $10,000. **Remarks:** Full-time maker; first knife sold in 1981. **Mark:** Name with logo.

KIEFER, TONY
112 Chateaugay Dr, Pataskala, OH 43062, Phone: 740-927-6910
Specialties: Traditional working and using straight knives in standard patterns. **Patterns:** Bowies, fighters and hunters. **Technical:** Grinds 440C and D2; forges D2. Flat-grinds Bowies; hollow-grinds drop-point and trailing-point hunters. **Prices:** $110 to $300; some to $200. **Remarks:** Spare-time maker; first knife sold in 1988. **Mark:** Last name.

KILBY, KEITH
1902 29th St, Cody, WY 82414, Phone: 307-587-2732
Specialties: Works with all designs. **Patterns:** Mostly Bowies, camp knives and hunters of his design. **Technical:** Forges 52100, 5160, 1095, Damascus and mosaic Damascus. **Prices:** $250 to $3500. **Remarks:** Part-time maker; first knife sold in 1974. Doing business as Foxwood Forge. **Mark:** Name.

KILEY, MIKE AND JANDY
ROCKING K KNIVES, 1325 Florida, Chino Valley, AZ 86323, Phone: 928-910-2647
Specialties: Period knives for cowboy action shooters and mountain men. **Patterns:** Bowies, drop-point hunters, skinners, sheepsfoot blades and spear points. **Technical:** Steels are 1095, 0-1, Damascus and others upon request. Handles include all types of wood, with cocobolo, ironwood, rosewood, maple and bacote being favorites as well as buffalo horn, stag, elk antler, mammoth ivory, giraffe boon, sheep horn and camel bone. **Prices:** $100 to $500 depending on style and materials. Hand-tooled leather sheaths by Jan and Mike. **Mark:** Stylized K on one side; Kiley on the other.

KILPATRICK, CHRISTIAN A
6925 Mitchell Ct, Citrus Hieghts, CA 95610, Phone: 916-729-0733, crimsonkil@gmail.com; www.crimsonknives.com
Specialties: All forged weapons (no firearms) from ancient to modern. All blades produced are first and foremost useable tools, and secondly but no less importantly, artistic expressions. **Patterns:** Hunters, bowies, daggers, swords, axes, spears, boot knives, bird knives, ethnic blades and historical reproductions. Customer designs welcome. **Technical:** Forges and grinds, makes own Damascus. Does file work. **Prices:** $125 to $3200. **Remarks:** 26 year part time maker. First knife sold in 2002.

KIMBERLEY, RICHARD L.
86-B Arroyo Hondo Rd, Santa Fe, NM 87508, Phone: 505-820-2727
Specialties: Fixed-blade and period knives. **Technical:** 01, 52100, 9260 steels. **Remarks:** Member ABS. Marketed under "Kimberleys of Santa Fe." **Mark:** "By D. KIMBERLEY SANTA FE NM."

KIMSEY, KEVIN
198 Cass White Rd. NW, Cartersville, GA 30121, Phone: 770-387-0779 and 770-655-8879
Specialties: Tactical fixed blades and folders. **Patterns:** Fighters, folders, hunters and utility knives. **Technical:** Grinds 440C, ATS-34 and D2 carbon. **Prices:** $100 to $400; some to $600. **Remarks:** Three-time Blade magazine award winner, knifemaker since

1983. **Mark:** Rafter and stylized KK.

KING, BILL
14830 Shaw Rd, Tampa, FL 33625, Phone: 813-961-3455, billkingknives@yahoo.com
Specialties: Folders, lockbacks, liner locks, automatics and stud openers. **Patterns:** Wide varieties; folders. **Technical:** ATS-34 and some Damascus; single and double grinds. Offers filework and jewel embellishment; nickel-silver Damascus and mokume bolsters. **Prices:** $150 to $475; some to $850. **Remarks:** Full-time maker; first knife sold in 1976. All titanium fitting on liner-locks; screw or rivet construction on lock-backs. **Mark:** Last name in crown.

KING, FRED
430 Grassdale Rd, Cartersville, GA 30120, Phone: 770-382-8478, Web: http://www.fking83264@aol.com
Specialties: Fancy and embellished working straight knives and folders. **Patterns:** Hunters, Bowies and fighters. **Technical:** Grinds ATS-34 and D2: forges 5160 and Damascus. Offers filework. **Prices:** $100 to $3500. **Remarks:** Spare-time maker; first knife sold in 1984. **Mark:** Kings Edge.

KING JR., HARVEY G
32170 Hwy K4, Alta Vista, KS 66834, Phone: 785-499-5207, Web: www.harveykingknives.com
Specialties: Traditional working and using straight knives of his design and to customer specs. **Patterns:** Hunters, Bowies and fillet knives. **Technical:** Grinds O1, A2 and D2. Prefers natural handle materials; offers leatherwork. **Prices:** Start at $150. **Remarks:** Full-time maker; first knife sold in 1988. **Mark:** Name, city, state, and serial number.

KINKER, MIKE
8755 E County Rd 50 N, Greensburg, IN 47240, Phone: 812-663-5277, kinkercustomknives@gmail.com
Specialties: Working/using knives, straight knives. Starting to make folders. Your design. **Patterns:** Boots, daggers, hunters, skinners, hatchets. **Technical:** Grind 440C and ATS-34, others if required. Damascus, dovetail bolsters, jeweled blade. **Prices:** $125 to 375; some to $1000. **Remarks:** Part-time maker; first knife sold in 1991. Doing business as Kinker Custom Knives. **Mark:** Kinker

KINNIKIN, TODD
EUREKA FORGE, 7 Capper Dr., Pacific, MO 63069-3603, Phone: 314-938-6248
Specialties: Mosaic Damascus. **Patterns:** Hunters, fighters, folders and automatics. **Technical:** Forges own mosaic Damascus with tool steel Damascus edge. Prefers natural, fossil and artifact handle materials. **Prices:** $1200 to $2400. **Remarks:** Full-time maker; first knife sold in 1994. **Mark:** Initials connected.

KIRK, RAY
PO Box 1445, Tahlequah, OK 74465, Phone: 918-207-8076, ray@rakerknives.com; Web: www.rakerknives.com
Specialties: Folders, skinners fighters, and Bowies. **Patterns:** Neck knives and small hunters and skinners. Full and hidden-tang integrals from 52100 round bar. **Technical:** Forges all knives from 52100 and own damascus. **Prices:** $65 to $3000. **Remarks:** Started forging in 1989; makes own Damascus. **Mark:** Stamped "Raker" on blade.

KIRKES, BILL
235 Oaklawn Cir., Little Rock, AR 72206, Phone: 501-551-0135, bill@kirkesknives.com; Web: www.kirkesknives.com
Specialties: Handforged fixed blades. **Technical:** High-carbon 5160 and 1084 blade steels. Will build to customer's specs, prefers to use natural handle material. **Remarks:** ABS Journeyman smith. **Mark:** Kirkes.

KITSMILLER, JERRY
67277 Las Vegas Dr, Montrose, CO 81401, Phone: 970-249-4290
Specialties: Working straight knives in standard patterns. **Patterns:** Hunters, boots. **Technical:** Grinds ATS-34 and 440C only. **Prices:** $75 to $200; some to $300. **Remarks:** Spare-time maker; first knife sold in 1984. **Mark:** JandS Knives.

KLAASEE, TINUS
PO Box 10221, George, WC, SOUTH AFRICA 6530
Specialties: Hunters, skinners and utility knives. **Patterns:** Uses own designs and client specs. **Technical:** N690 stainless steel 440C Damascus. **Prices:** $700 and up. **Remarks:** Use only indigenous materials. Hardwood, horns and ivory. Makes his own sheaths and boxes. **Mark:** Initials and sur name over warthog.

KLEIN, KEVIN
129 Cedar St., Apt. 2, Boston, MA 02119, Phone: 609-937-8949, kevin.a.klein779@gmail.com
Specialties: Forged damascus blades using 15N20 and 1084. **Remarks:** Full-time maker; first knife made in 2012. Apprentice to J.D. Smith starting in 2012. **Mark:** KAK? or ?, depending on piece.

KNAPP, MARK
Mark Knapp Custom Knives, 1971 Fox Ave, Fairbanks, AK 99701, Phone: 907-452-7477, info@markknappcustomknives.com; Web: www.markknappcustomknives.com
Specialties: Mosaic handles of exotic natural materials from Alaska and around the world. Folders, fixed blades, full and hidden tangs. **Patterns:** Folders, hunters, skinners, and camp knives. **Technical:** Forges own Damascus, uses both forging and stock removal with ATS-34, 154CM, stainless Damascus, carbon steel and carbon Damascus. **Prices:** $800-$3000. **Remarks:** Full time maker, sold first knife in 2000. **Mark:** Mark Knapp Custom Knives Fairbanks, AK.

KNAPTON, CHRIS C.
76 Summerland Dr., Henderson, Aukland, NEW ZEALAND, Phone: 09-835-3598,

knaptch76@gmail.com; Web: www.knappoknives.com

Specialties: Working and fancy straight and folding knives of his own design. **Patterns:** Tactical, utility, hunting fixed and folding knives. **Technical:** Predominate knife steels are Elmax, CPM-154 and D2. All blades made via the stock removal method. **Prices:** $120 -$500. **Remarks:** Part-time maker. **Mark:** Stylized letter K, country name and Haast eagle.

KNICKMEYER, HANK
6300 Crosscreek, Cedar Hill, MO 63016, Phone: 636-285-3210

Specialties: Complex mosaic Damascus constructions. **Patterns:** Fixed blades, swords, folders and automatics. **Technical:** Mosaic Damascus with all tool steel Damascus edges. **Prices:** $500 to $2000; some $3000 and higher. **Remarks:** Part-time maker; first knife sold in 1989. Doing business as Dutch Creek Forge and Foundry. **Mark:** Initials connected.

KNICKMEYER, KURT
6344 Crosscreek, Cedar Hill, MO 63016, Phone: 314-274-0481

KNIGHT, JASON
110 Paradise Pond Ln, Harleyville, SC 29448, Phone: 843-452-1163, jasonknightknives.com

Specialties: Bowies. **Patterns:** Bowies and anything from history or his own design. **Technical:** 1084, 5160, O1, 52102, Damascus/forged blades. **Prices:** $200 and up. **Remarks:** Bladesmith. **Mark:** KNIGHT.

KNIPSCHIELD, TERRY
808 12th Ave NE, Rochester, MN 55906, Phone: 507-288-7829, terry@knipknives.com; Web: www.knipknives.com

Specialties: Folders and fixed blades and leather working knives. **Patterns:** Variations of traditional patterns and his own new designs. **Technical:** Stock removal. Grinds CPM-154CM, ATS-34, stainless Damascus, 01.**Prices:** $60 to $1200 and higher for upscale folders. **Mark:** Etchd logo on blade, KNIP with shield image.

KNOTT, STEVE
KNOTT KNIVES, 203 Wild Rose, Guyton, GA 31312, Phone: 912-536-7651, knottknives@yahoo.com; FaceBook: Knott Knives/Steve Knott

Technical: Uses ATS-34/440C and some commercial Damascus, single and double grinds with mirror or satin finishes. **Patterns:** Hunters, boot knives, bowies, and tantos, slip joint, LinerLock and lock-back folders. Uses a wide variety of handle materials to include ironwood, coca-bola and colored stabilized wood, also horn, bone and ivory upon customer request. **Remarks:** First knife sold in 1991. Part-time maker.

KNOWLES, SHAWN
750 Townsbury Rd, Great Meadows, NJ 07838, Phone: 973-670-3307, skcustomknives@gmail.com Web: shawnknowlescustomknives.com

KNUTH, JOSEPH E
3307 Lookout Dr, Rockford, IL 61109, Phone: 815-874-9597

Specialties: High-art working straight knives of his design or to customer specs. **Patterns:** Daggers, fighters and swords. **Technical:** Grinds 440C, ATS-34 and D2. **Prices:** $150 to $1500; some to $15,000. **Remarks:** Full-time maker; first knife sold in 1989. **Mark:** Initials on bolster face.

KOHLS, JERRY
N4725 Oak Rd, Princeton, WI 54968, Phone: 920-295-3648

Specialties: Working knives and period pieces. **Patterns:** Hunters-boots and Bowies, your designs or his. **Technical:** Grinds, ATS-34 440c 154CM and 1095 and commercial Damascus. **Remarks:** Part-time maker. **Mark:** Last name.

KOJETIN, W
20 Bapaume Rd Delville, Germiston, GT, SOUTH AFRICA 1401, Phone: 27118733305/mobile 27836256208

Specialties: High-art and working straight knives of all designs. **Patterns:** Daggers, hunters and his own Man hunter Bowie. **Technical:** Grinds D2 and ATS-34; forges and grinds 440B/C. Offers "wrap-around" pava and abalone handles, scrolled wood or ivory, stacked filework and setting of faceted semi-precious stones. **Prices:** $185 to $600; some to $11,000. **Remarks:** Spare-time maker; first knife sold in 1962. **Mark:** Billy K.

KOLITZ, ROBERT
W9342 Canary Rd, Beaver Dam, WI 53916, Phone: 920-887-1287

Specialties: Working straight knives to customer specs. **Patterns:** Bowies, hunters, bird and trout knives, boots. **Technical:** Grinds O1, 440C; commercial Damascus. **Prices:** $50 to $100; some to $500. **Remarks:** Spare-time maker; first knife sold in 1979. **Mark:** Last initial.

KOMMER, RUSS
4609 35th Ave N, Fargo, ND 58102, Phone: 701-281-1826, russkommer@yahoo.com Web: www.russkommerknives.com

Specialties: Working straight knives with the outdoorsman in mind. **Patterns:** Hunters, semi-skinners, fighters, folders and utility knives, art knives. **Technical:** Hollow-grinds ATS-34, 440C and 440V. **Prices:** $125 to $850; some to $3000. **Remarks:** Full-time maker; first knife sold in 1995. **Mark:** Bear paw—full name, city and state or full name and state.

KOPP, TODD M
PO Box 3474, Apache Jct., AZ 85217, Phone: 480-983-6143, tmkopp@msn.com

Specialties: Classic and traditional straight knives. Fluted handled daggers. **Patterns:** Bowies, boots, daggers, fighters, hunters, swords and folders. **Technical:** Grinds 5160, 440C, ATS-34. All Damascus steels, or customers choice. Some engraving and filework. **Prices:** $200 to $1200; some to $4000. **Remarks:** Part-time maker; first knife sold in 1989. **Mark:** Last name in Old English, some others name, city and state.

KOSTER, DANIEL
KOSTER KNIVES, 1711 Beverly Ct., Bentonville, AR 72712, Phone: 479-366-7794, dan@kosterknives.com; www.kosterknives.com

Patterns: Bushcraft, survival, outdoor and utility knives. **Technical:** Stock-removal method of blade making, using CPM 3V steel. **Prices:** $150 to $300. **Remarks:** Full-time knifemaker in business since 2005. **Mark:** "K" in a circle, negative shape.

KOSTER, STEVEN C
16261 Gentry Ln, Huntington Beach, CA 92647, Phone: 714-907-7250, kosterknives@verizon.net Web: www.kosterhandforgedknives.com

Specialties: Walking sticks, hand axes, tomahawks, Damascus.**Patterns:** Ladder, twists, round horn. **Technical:** Use 5160, 52100, 1084, 1095 steels. Ladder, twists, **Prices:** $200 to $1000. **Remarks:** Wood and leather sheaths with silver furniture. ABS Journeyman 2003. California knifemakers member. **Mark:** Koster squeezed between lines.

KOVACIK, ROBERT
Zavadska 122, Tomasovce 98401, SLOVAKIA, Phone: Mobil: 00421907644800, kovacikart@gmail.com Web: www.robertkovacik.com

Specialties: Engraved hunting knives, guns engraved; Knifemakers. **Technical:** Fixed blades, folder knives, miniatures. **Prices:** $350 to $10,000 U.S. **Mark:** R.

KOVAR, EUGENE
2626 W 98th St., Evergreen Park, IL 60642, Phone: 708-636-3724/708-790-4115, baldemaster333@aol.com

Specialties: One-of-a-kind miniature knives only. **Patterns:** Fancy to fantasy miniature knives; knife pendants and tie tacks. **Technical:** Files and grinds nails, nickel-silver and sterling silver. **Prices:** $5 to $35; some to $100. **Mark:** GK.

KOYAMA, CAPTAIN BUNSHICHI
3-23 Shirako-cho, Nakamura-ku, Nagoya, Aichi, JAPAN City 453-0817, Phone: 052-461-7070, Fax: 052-461-7070

Specialties: Innovative folding knife. **Patterns:** General purpose one hand. **Technical:** Grinds ATS-34 and Damascus. **Prices:** $400 to $900; some to $1500. **Remarks:** Part-time maker; first knife sold in 1994. **Mark:** Captain B. Koyama and the shoulder straps of CAPTAIN.

KRAFT, STEVE
408 NE 11th St, Abilene, KS 67410, Phone: 785-263-1411

Specialties: Folders, lockbacks, scale release auto, push button auto. **Patterns:** Hunters, boot knives and fighters. **Technical:** Grinds ATS-34, Damascus; uses titanium, pearl, ivory etc. **Prices:** $500 to $2500. **Remarks:** Part-time maker; first knife sold in 1984. **Mark:** Kraft.

KRAMMES, JEREMY
138 W. Penn St., Schuylkill Haven, PA 17972, Phone: 570-617-5753, blade@jkknives.com; Web: www.jkknives.com

Specialties: Working folders and collectible art knives. **Technical:** Stock removal, hollow grinding, carving and engraving. **Prices:** $550+ for working knives, and $1,000+ for art knives. **Remarks:** Part-time maker; first knife sold in 2004. **Mark:** Stylized JK on blade.

KRAPP, DENNY
1826 Windsor Oak Dr, Apopka, FL 32703, Phone: 407-880-7115

Specialties: Fantasy and working straight knives of his design. **Patterns:** Hunters, fighters and utility/camp knives. **Technical:** Grinds ATS-34 and 440C. **Prices:** $85 to $300; some to $800. **Remarks:** Spare-time maker; first knife sold in 1988. **Mark:** Last name.

KRAUSE, JIM
3272 Hwy H, Farmington, MO 63640, Phone: 573-756-7388 or 573-701-7047, james_krause@sbcglobal.net

Specialties: Folders, fixed blades and neck knives. **Patterns:** New pattern for each knife. **Technical:** CPM steels or high-carbon steel on request. **Prices:** $125 and up for neck knives, $250 and up for fixed blades and $450 and up for folders and damascus pieces. **Remarks:** Full-time maker; first knife made in 2000. Makes one knife at a time with the best materials the maker can find. **Mark:** Krause Handmade with Christian fish.

KREGER, THOMAS
1996 Dry Branch Rd., Lugoff, SC 29078, Phone: 803-438-4221, tdkreger@bellsouth.net

Specialties: South Carolina/George Herron style working/using knives. Customer designs considered. **Patterns:** Hunters, skinners, fillet, liner lock folders, kitchen, and camp knives. **Technical:** Hollow and flat grinds of ATS-34, CPM154CM, and 5160. **Prices:** $100 and up. **Remarks:** Full-time maker. President of the South Carolina Association of Knifemakers 2002-2006, and current president since 2013. **Mark:** TDKreger.

KREH, LEFTY
210 Wichersham Way, "Cockeysville", MD 21030

KREIBICH, DONALD L.
1638 Commonwealth Circle, Reno, NV 89503, Phone: 775-746-0533, dmkreno@sbcglobal.net

Specialties: Working straight knives in standard patterns. **Patterns:** Bowies, boots and daggers; camp and fishing knives. **Technical:** Grinds 440C, 154CM and ATS-34; likes integrals. **Prices:** $100 to $200; some to $500. **Remarks:** Part-time maker; first knife sold in 1980. **Mark:** First and middle initials, last name.

KREIN, TOM
P.O. Box 994, 337 E. Main St., Gentry, AR 72734, Phone: 479-233-0508, kreinknives@gmail.com Web: www.kreinknives.net

Specialties LinerLock folders and fixed blades designed to be carried and used. **Technical:** Stock removal using D2, A2, CPM 3V, CPM 154, CPM M4, Stellite 6K and damascus, and makes his own sheaths. **Prices:** $250 to $500 and up. **Remarks:** Full-time maker; first knife made in 1993. **Mark:** Last name and the year the knife was made in the shape of a circle, with a bulldog in the middle.

KRESSLER, D F
Mittelweg 31 i, D-28832 Achim, GERMANY 28832, Phone: +49 (0) 42 02/76-5742, Fax: +49 (0) 42 02/7657 41, info@kresslerknives.com; Web: www.kresslerknives.com
Specialties: High-tech integral and interframe knives. **Patterns:** Hunters, fighters, daggers. **Technical:** Grinds new state-of-the-art steels; prefers natural handle materials. **Prices:** Upscale. **Mark:** Name in logo.

KUBASEK, JOHN A
74 Northhampton St, Easthampton, MA 01027, Phone: 413-527-7917, jaknife01@yahoo.com
Specialties: Left-and right-handed LinerLock® folders of his design or to customer specs. Also new knives made with Ripcord patent. **Patterns:** Fighters, tantos, drop points, survival knives, neck knives and belt buckle knives. **Technical:** Grinds 154CM, S30 and Damascus. **Prices:** $395 to $1500. **Remarks:** Part-time maker; first knife sold in 1985. **Mark:** Name and address etched.

L

LADD, JIM S
1120 Helen, Deer Park, TX 77536, Phone: 713-479-7286
Specialties: Working knives and period pieces. **Patterns:** Hunters, boots and Bowies plus other straight knives. **Technical:** Grinds D2, 440C and 154CM. **Prices:** $125 to $225; some to $550. **Remarks:** Part-time maker; first knife sold in 1965. Doing business as The Tinker. **Mark:** First and middle initials, last name.

LADD, JIMMIE LEE
1120 Helen, Deer Park, TX 77536, Phone: 713-479-7186
Specialties: Working straight knives. **Patterns:** Hunters, skinners and utility knives. **Technical:** Grinds 440C and D2. **Prices:** $75 to $225. **Remarks:** First knife sold in 1979. **Mark:** First and middle initials, last name.

LAINSON, TONY
114 Park Ave, Council Bluffs, IA 51503, Phone: 712-322-5222
Specialties: Working straight knives, liner locking folders. **Technical:** Grinds 154CM, ATS-34, 440C buys Damascus. Handle materials include Micarta, carbon fiber G-10 ivory pearl and bone. **Prices:** $95 to $600. **Remarks:** Part-time maker; first knife sold in 1987. **Mark:** Name and state.

LAIRSON SR., JERRY
H C 68 Box 970, Ringold, OK 74754, Phone: 580-876-3426, bladesmt@brightok.net; Web: www.lairson-custom-knives.net
Specialties: Damascus collector grade knives & high performance field grade hunters & cutting competition knives. **Patterns:** Damascus, random, raindrop, ladder, twist and others. **Technical:** All knives hammer forged. Mar Tempering**Prices:** Field grade knives $300. Collector grade $400 & up. **Mark:** Lairson. **Remarks:** Makes any style knife but prefer fighters and hunters. ABS Mastersmith, AKA member, KGA member. Cutting competition competitor.

LAKE, RON
3360 Bendix Ave, Eugene, OR 97401, Phone: 541-484-2683
Specialties: High-tech working knives; inventor of the modern interframe folder. **Patterns:** Hunters, boots, etc.; locking folders. **Technical:** Grinds 154CM and ATS-34. Patented interframe with special lock release tab. **Prices:** $2200 to $3000; some higher. **Remarks:** Full-time maker; first knife sold in 1966. **Mark:** Last name.

LALA, PAULO RICARDO P AND LALA, ROBERTO P.
R Daniel Martins 636, Presidente Prudente, SP, BRAZIL 19031-260, Phone: 0182-210125, korthknives@terra.com.br; Web: www.ikbsknifetech.com
Specialties: Straight knives and folders of all designs to customer specs. **Patterns:** Bowies, daggers fighters, hunters and utility knives. **Technical:** Grinds and forges D6, 440C, high-carbon steels and Damascus. **Prices:** $60 to $400; some higher. **Remarks:** Full-time makers; first knife sold in 1991. All stainless steel blades are ultra sub-zero quenched. **Mark:** Sword carved on top of anvil under KORTH.

LAMB, CURTIS J
3336 Louisiana Ter, Ottawa, KS 66067-8996, Phone: 785-242-6657

LAMBERT, JARRELL D
2321 FM 2982, Granado, TX 77962, Phone: 512-771-3744
Specialties: Traditional working and using straight knives of his design and to customer specs. **Patterns:** Bowies, hunters, tantos and utility/camp knives. **Technical:** Grinds ATS-34; forges W2 and his own Damascus. Makes own sheaths. **Prices:** $80 to $600; some to $1000. **Remarks:** Part-time maker; first knife sold in 1982. **Mark:** Etched first and middle initials, last name; or stamped last name.

LAMBERT, KIRBY
2131 Edgar St, Regina, SK, CANADA S4N 3K8, kirby@lambertknives.com; Web: www.lambertknives.com
Specialties: Tactical/utility folders. Tactical/utility Japanese style fixed blades. **Prices:** $200 to $1500 U.S. **Remarks:** Full-time maker since 2002. **Mark:** Black widow spider and last name Lambert.

LAMEY, ROBERT M
15800 Lamey Dr, Biloxi, MS 39532, Phone: 228-396-9066, Fax: 228-396-9022, rmlamey@ametro.net; Web: www.lameyknives.com
Specialties: Bowies, fighters, hard use knives. **Patterns:** Bowies, fighters, hunters and camp knives. **Technical:** Forged and stock removal. **Prices:** $125 to $350. **Remarks:** Lifetime reconditioning; will build to customer designs, specializing in hard use, affordable knives. **Mark:** LAMEY.

LANCASTER, C G
No 2 Schoonwinkel St, Parys, Free State, SOUTH AFRICA, Phone: 0568112090
Specialties: High-tech working and using knives of his design and to customer specs. **Patterns:** Hunters, locking folders and utility/camp knives. **Technical:** Grinds Sandvik 12C27, 440C and D2. Offers anodized titanium bolsters. **Prices:** $450 to $750; some to $1500. **Remarks:** Part-time maker; first knife sold in 1990. **Mark:** Etched logo.

LANCE, BILL
12820 E. Scott Rd., Palmer, AK 99645-8863, Phone: 907-694-1487, Web: www.lanceknives.com
Specialties: Ulu sets and working straight knives; limited issue sets. **Patterns:** Several ulu patterns, drop-point skinners. **Technical:** Uses ATS-34 and AEBL; ivory, horn and high-class wood handles. **Prices:** $145 to $500; art sets to $7,500. **Remarks:** First knife sold in 1981. **Mark:** Last name over a lance.

LANCE, LUCAS
3600 N. Charley, Wasilla, AK 99654, Phone: 907-357-0349, lucas@lanceknives.com; Web: www.lanceknives.com
Specialties: Working with materials native to Alaska such as fossilized ivory, bone, musk ox bone, sheep horn, moose antler, all combined with exotic materials from around the world. **Patterns:** Fully functional knives of my own design. **Technical:** Mainly stock removal, flat grinds in ATS-34, 440C, 5160 and various makes of American-made damascus. **Prices:** $165 to $850. **Remarks:** Second-generation knifemaker who grew up and trained in father, Bill Lance's, shop. First knife designed and made in 1994. **Mark:** Last name over a lance.

LANDERS, JOHN
758 Welcome Rd, Newnan, GA 30263, Phone: 404-253-5719
Specialties: High-art working straight knives and folders of his design. **Patterns:** Hunters, fighters and slip-joint folders. **Technical:** Grinds 440C, ATS-34, 154CM and commercial Damascus. **Prices:** $85 to $250; some to $500. **Remarks:** Part-time maker; first knife sold in 1989. **Mark:** Last name.

LANDIS, DAVID E. SR.
4544 County Rd. 29, Galion, OH 44833, Phone: 419-946-3145, del@redbird.net
Specialties: Damascus knives in ladder, twist, double-twist and "W's" patterns. Makes leather sheaths and forges his own damascus. **Prices:** $250 to $500. **Remarks:** Retiree who says knifemaking keeps him learning with new challenges and meeting a lot of great people. **Mark:** DEL.

LANG, DAVID
6153 Cumulus Circle, Kearns, UT 84118, Phone: 801-809-1241, dknifeguy@msn.com
Specialties: Art knives, metal sheaths, push daggers, fighting knives, hunting knives, camp knives, skinning knives, pocketknives, utility knives and three-finger knives. **Patterns:** Prefers to work with own patterns, but will consider other designs. **Technical:** Flat grinds, hollow grinds, hand carving on the blades and handles, and gold and silver casting. **Remarks:** Will work from his designs or to customer specifications. Has been making knives for over 20 years and has learned from some of the best. **Prices:** $250 to $3,000, with most work ranging from $750 to $1,500. **Mark:** Dlang over UTAH.

LANGLEY, GENE H
1022 N. Price Rd, Florence, SC 29506, Phone: 843-669-3150
Specialties: Working knives in standard patterns. **Patterns:** Hunters, boots, fighters, locking folders and slip-joints. **Technical:** Grinds 440C, 154CM and ATS-34. **Prices:** $125 to $450; some to $1000. **Remarks:** Part-time maker; first knife sold in 1979. **Mark:** Name.

LANGLEY, MICK
1015 Centre Crescent, Qualicum Beach, BC, CANADA V9K 2G6, Phone: 250-752-4261
Specialties: Period pieces and working knives. **Patterns:** Bowies, push daggers, fighters, boots. Some folding lockers. **Technical:** Forges 5160, 1084, W2 and his own Damascus. **Prices:** $250 to $2500; some to $4500. **Remarks:** Full-time maker, first knife sold in 1977. **Mark:** Langley with M.S. (for ABS Master Smith)

LANKTON, SCOTT
8065 Jackson Rd. R-11, Ann Arbor, MI 48103, Phone: 313-426-3735
Specialties: Pattern welded swords, krisses and Viking period pieces. **Patterns:** One-of-a-kind. **Technical:** Forges W2, L6 nickel and other steels. **Prices:** $600 to $12,000. **Remarks:** Part-time bladesmith, full-time smith; first knife sold in 1976. **Mark:** Last name logo.

LAPEN, CHARLES
Box 529, W. Brookfield, MA 01585
Specialties: Chef's knives for the culinary artist. **Patterns:** Camp knives, Japanese-style swords and wood working tools, hunters. **Technical:** Forges 1075, car spring and his own Damascus. Favors narrow and Japanese tangs. **Prices:** $200 to $400; some to $2000. **Remarks:** Part-time maker; first knife sold in 1972. **Mark:** Last name.

LAPLANTE, BRETT
4545 CR412, McKinney, TX 75071, Phone: 972-838-9191, blap007@aol.com
Specialties: Working straight knives and folders to customer specs. **Patterns:** Survival knives, Bowies, skinners, hunters. **Technical:** Grinds D2 and 440C. Heat-treats. **Prices:** $200 to $800. **Remarks:** Part-time maker; first knife sold in 1987. **Mark:** Last name in Canadian maple leaf logo.

LARGIN, KEN
KELGIN Knifemakers Co-Op, 2001 S. State Rd. 1, Connersville, IN 47331,

Phone: 765-969-5012, kelginfinecutlery@gmail.com; Web: www.kelgin.com
Specialties: Retired from general knifemaking. Only take limited orders in meteorite damascus or solid meteorite blades. **Patterns:** Any. **Technical:** Stock removal or forged. **Prices:** $500 & up. **Remarks:** Travels the U.S. full time teaching hands-on "History Of Cutting Tools" to Scouts and any interested group. Participants flint knap, forge and keep three tools they make! **Mark:** K.C. Largin (Kelgin mark retired in 2004).

LARK, DAVID
6641 Schneider Rd., Kingsley, MI 49649, Phone: 231-342-1076, dblark58@yahoo.com
Specialties: Traditional straight knives, art knives, folders. **Patterns:** All types. **Technical:** Grinds all types of knife making steel and makes damascus. **Prices:** $600 and up. **Remarks:** Full-time maker, custom riflemaker, and engraver. **Mark:** Lark in script and DBL on engraving.

LAROCHE, JEAN-MARC
16 rue Alexandre Dumas, 78160 Marly le Roi, FRANCE, Phone: +33 1 39 16 16 58, infojmlaroche@orange.fr; Web: www.jmlaroche.com
Specialties: Fantasy pieces to customer specs. **Patterns:** Straight knives and folding knives. **Technical:** Stainless or damascus blade steels. **Prices:** $800 to $4,000, some to $10,000. **Remarks:** Full-time sculptor; full-time knifemaker for 12 years from 1992 to 2004. Awards won include BLADEhandmade "Best In Show" Award in 1997 and "Best Fantasy Knife" at the 1998 BLADE Show West. Artistic design knives are influenced by fantasy movies and comics with handles in bronze, silver or resin, including animal skulls, bones and natural stones. Collaborations with Gil Hibben and Roger Bergh. Recently created a knife capable of mechanical movement: "The Living Knife" with a blade by Bergh. **Mark:** Logo, + name sometimes.

LARSON, RICHARD
549 E Hawkeye Ave, Turlock, CA 95380, Phone: 209-668-1615, lebatardknives@aol.com
Specialties: Sound working knives, lightweight folders, practical tactical knives. **Patterns:** Hunters, trout and bird knives, fish fillet knives, Bowies, tactical sheath knives, one-and two-blade folders. **Technical:** Grinds ATS-34, A2, D2, CPM 3V and commercial. Damascus; forges and grinds 52100, O1 and 1095. Machines folder frames from aircraft aluminum. **Prices:** $40 to $650. **Remarks:** Full-time maker. First knife made in 1974. Offers knife repair, restoration and sharpening. All knives are serial numbered and registered in the name of original purchaser. **Mark:** Stamped last name or etched logo of last name, city, and state.

LARY, ED
951 Rangeline Rd., Mosinee, WI 54455, Phone: 715-630-6202, laryblades@hotmail.com
Specialties: Upscale hunters and art knives with display presentations. **Patterns:** Hunters, period pieces. **Technical:** Grinds all steels, heat treats, fancy filework and engraving. **Prices:** Upscale. **Remarks:** Full-time maker since 1974. **Mark:** Hand engraved "Ed Lary" in script.

LAURENT, KERMIT
1812 Acadia Dr, LaPlace, LA 70068, Phone: 504-652-5629
Specialties: Traditional and working straight knives and folders of his design. **Patterns:** Bowies, hunters, utilities and folders. **Technical:** Forges own Damascus, plus uses most tool steels and stainless. Specializes in altering cable patterns. Uses stabilized handle materials, especially select exotic woods. **Prices:** $100 to $2500; some to $50,000. **Remarks:** Full-time maker; first knife sold in 1982. Doing business as Kermit's Knife Works. Favorite material is meteorite Damascus. **Mark:** First name.

LAURENT, VERONIQUE
Avenue du Capricorne, 53, 1200 Bruxelles, BELGIUM, Phone: 0032 477 48 66 73, whatsonthebench@gmail.com
Specialties: Fixed blades and friction folders. **Patterns:** Bowies, camp knives, "ladies knives" and maker's own designs. **Technical:** Makes own san mai steel with the edges in blue paper steel and the sides in pure nickel and O2, called "Nickwich," meaning nickel in a sandwich. Makes own damascus, numerical milling embellishment, inlays and sheaths. **Prices:** Start at $350. **Remarks:** Part-time knifemaker since 2005 and ABS journeyman smith since 2013.

LAWRENCE, ALTON
201 W Stillwell, De Queen, AR 71832, Phone: 870-642-7643, Fax: 870-642-4023, uncle21@riversidemachine.net; Web: riversidemachine.net
Specialties: Classic straight knives and folders to customer specs. **Patterns:** Bowies, hunters, folders and utility/camp knives. **Technical:** Forges 5160, 1095, 1084, Damascus and railroad spikes. **Prices:** Start at $100. **Remarks:** Part-time maker; first knife sold in 1988. **Mark:** Last name inside fish symbol.

LAY, L J
602 Mimosa Dr, Burkburnett, TX 76354, Phone: 940-569-1329
Specialties: Working straight knives in standard patterns; some period pieces. **Patterns:** Drop-point hunters, Bowies and fighters. **Technical:** Grinds ATS-34 to mirror finish; likes Micarta handles. **Prices:** Moderate. **Remarks:** Full-time maker; first knife sold in 1985. **Mark:** Name or name with ram head and city or stamp L J Lay.

LAY, R J (BOB)
Box 1225, Logan Lake, BC, CANADA V0K 1W0, Phone: 250-523-9923, rjlay@telus.net
Specialties: Traditional-styled, fancy straight knifes of his design. Specializing in hunters. **Patterns:** Bowies, fighters and hunters. **Technical:** Grinds high-performance stainless and tool steels. Uses exotic handle and spacer material. File cut, prefers narrow tang. Sheaths available. **Price:** $200 to $500, some to $5000. **Remarks:** Full-time maker, first knife sold in 1976. Doing business as Lay's Custom Knives. **Mark:** Signature acid etched.

LEAVITT JR., EARL F
Pleasant Cove Rd Box 306, E. Boothbay, ME 04544, Phone: 207-633-3210
Specialties: 1500-1870 working straight knives and fighters; pole arms. **Patterns:** Historically significant knives, classic/modern custom designs. **Technical:** Flat-grinds O1; heat-treats. Filework available. **Prices:** $90 to $350; some to $1000. **Remarks:** Full-time maker; first knife sold in 1981. Doing business as Old Colony Manufactory. **Mark:** Initials in oval.

LEBATARD, PAUL M
14700 Old River Rd, Vancleave, MS 39565, Phone: 228-826-4137, Fax: Cell phone: 228-238-7461, lebatardknives@aol.com
Specialties: Sound working hunting and fillet knives, folding knives, practical tactical knives. **Patterns:** Hunters, trout and bird knives, fish fillet knives, kitchen knives, Bowies, tactical sheath knives,one-and two-blade folders. **Technical:** Grinds ATS-34, D-2, CPM 3-V, CPM-154CM, and commercial Damascus; forges and grinds 1095, O1, and 52100. **Prices:** $75 to $850; some to $1,200. **Remarks:** Full-time maker, first knife made in 1974. Charter member Gulf Coast Custom Knifemakers; Voting member Knifemaker's Guild. **Mark:** Stamped last name, or etched logo of last name, city, and state. **Other:** All knives are serial numbered and registered in the name of the original purchaser.

LEBER, HEINZ
Box 446, Hudson's Hope, BC, CANADA V0C 1V0, Phone: 250-783-5304
Specialties: Working straight knives of his design. **Patterns:** 20 models, from capers to Bowies. **Technical:** Hollow-grinds D2 and M2 steel; mirror-finishes and full tang only. Likes moose, elk, stone sheep for handles. **Prices:** $175 to $1000. **Remarks:** Full-time maker; first knife sold in 1975. **Mark:** Initials connected.

LEBLANC, GARY E
1403 Fairview Ln., Little Falls, MN 56345, Phone: 320-232-0245, butternutcove@hotmail.com
Specialties: Hunting and fishing, some kitchen knives and the Air Assualt tactical knife. Does own leather and Kydex work. **Patterns:** Stock removal. **Technical:** Mostly ATS34 for spec knives--orders, whatever the customer desires. **Prices:** Full range: $85 for parring knife, up $4000 plus fro collector grade hunter and fillet set. **Remarks:** First knife in 1998. **Mark:** Circular with star in center and LEBLANC on upper curve and KNIFEWORKS on lower curve.

LECK, DAL
Box 1054, Hayden, CO 81639, Phone: 970-276-3663
Specialties: Classic, traditional and working knives of his design and in standard patterns; period pieces. **Patterns:** Boots, daggers, fighters, hunters and push daggers. **Technical:** Forges O1 and 5160; makes his own Damascus. **Prices:** $175 to $700; some to $1500. **Remarks:** Part-time maker; first knife sold in 1990. Doing business as The Moonlight Smithy. **Mark:** Stamped: hammer and anvil with initials.

LEE, ETHAN
17200 N. Tucker School Rd., Sturgeon, MO 65284, Phone: 573-682-4364, elee4364@aol.com; Facebook page: ELEE Knives
Specialties: Practical, usable, quality-crafted custom knives. **Technical:** Primarily damascus and hand-forged high-carbon steel, as well as 440C or 154CM stainless. **Prices:** $200-$500. **Remarks:** Part-time knifemaker; first knife made in 2007. **Mark:** ELEE.

LEE, RANDY
PO Box 1873, St. Johns, AZ 85936, Phone: 928-337-2594, randylee.knives@yahoo.com; Web:www.randyleeknives.com
Specialties: Traditional working and using straight knives of his design. **Patterns:** Bowies, fighters, hunters, daggers. **Technical:** Grinds ATS-34, 440C Damascus, and 154CPM. Offers sheaths. **Prices:** $325 to $2500. **Remarks:** Full-time maker; first knife sold in 1979. **Mark:** Full name, city, state.

LEEPER, DAN
10344 Carney Dr. SE, Olympia, WA 98501, Phone: 360-250-2130, leeperd@ymail.com; Web: www.leeperknives.com
Specialties: Hunters, fighters, bowies and chef's knives. **Technical:** Forges 52100, W2, 1084 and 5160 blade steels. Stock removal using CPM 154 stainless and other modern alloy steels. Does own heat treating and leather work. **Prices:** Start at $200. **Remarks:** ABS member. **Mark:** Dan Leeper Olympia WA.

LELAND, STEVE
2300 Sir Francis Drake Blvd, Fairfax, CA 94930-1118, Phone: 415-457-0318, Fax: 415-457-0995, Web: www.stephenleland@comcast.net
Specialties: Traditional and working straight knives and folders of his design. **Patterns:** Hunters, fighters, Bowies, chefs. **Technical:** Grinds O1, ATS-34 and 440C. Does own heat treat. Makes nickel silver sheaths. **Prices:** $150 to $750; some to $1500. **Remarks:** Part-time maker; first knife sold in 1987. Doing business as Leland Handmade Knives. **Mark:** Last name.

LEMAIRE, RYAN M.
14045 Leon Rd., Abbeville, LA 70510, Phone: 337-893-1937, ryanlemaire@yahoo.com
Specialties: All styles. Enjoys early American and frontier styles. Also, office desk sets for hunters and fishermen. **Patterns:** Hunters, camp knives, miniatures and period styles. **Technical:** Stock removal, carbon steel, stainless steel and damascus. Some forging of guards. Leather and wooden sheaths. **Prices:** Vary. **Remarks:** Member of American Bladesmith Society and Louisiana Craft Guild. **Mark:** First name, city and state in oval.

LEMCKE, JIM L
10649 Haddington Ste 180, Houston, TX 77043, Phone: 888-461-8632, Fax: 713-461-8221, jimll@hal-pc.org; Web: www.texasknife.com

Specialties: Large supply of custom ground and factory finished blades; knife kits; leather sheaths; in-house heat treating and cryogenic tempering; exotic handle material (wood, ivory, oosik, horn, stabilized woods); machines and supplies for knifemaking; polishing and finishing supplies; heat treat ovens; etching equipment; bar, sheet and rod material (brass, stainless steel, nickel silver); titanium sheet material. Catalog. $4.

LEMELIN, STEPHANIE

3495 Olivier St., Brossard, CANADA J4Y 2J9, Phone: 514-462-1322, stephlemelin@hotmail.com
Specialties Art knives, mostly ornate. **Patterns:** Knives with sculptured or carved handles. Straight knives and folders. **Technical:** Grinds 440C, CPM 154 and ATS-34, all knives hand filed and flat ground. **Remarks:** Part-time maker, jeweler and knifemaker; first knife sold in 2013. **Mark:** Lemelin.

LEMOINE, DAVID C

239 County Rd. 637, Mountain Home, AR 72653, Phone: 870-656-4730, dlemoine@davidlemoineknives.com; Web: davidlemoineknives.com
Specialties: Superior edge geometry on high performance custom classic and tactical straight blades and liner lock folders. **Patterns:** Hunters, skinners, bird and trout, fillet, camp, tactical, and military knives. Some miniatures. **Technical:** Flat and hollow grinds, CPMS90V, CPMS35V, CPMS30V, D2, A2, O1, 440C, ATS34, 154cm,Damasteel, Chad Nichols, Devin Thomas, and Robert Eggerling Damascus. Hidden and full tapered tangs, ultra-smooth folding mechanisms. File work, will use most all handle materials, does own professional in-house heat treatment and Rockwell testing. Hot blueing. **Prices:** $250 and up. **Remarks:** Part-time maker, giving and selling knives since 1986. Each patron receives a NIV Sportsman's Field Bible. **Mark:** Name, city and state in full oval with cross in the center. Reverse image on other side. The cross never changes.

LENNON, DALE

459 County Rd 1554, Alba, TX 75410, Phone: 903-765-2392, devildaddy1@netzero.net
Specialties: Working / using knives. **Patterns:** Hunters, fighters and Bowies. **Technical:** Grinds high carbon steels, ATS-34, forges some. **Prices:** Starts at $120. **Remarks:** Part-time maker, first knife sold in 2000. **Mark:** Last name.

LEONARD, RANDY JOE

188 Newton Rd, Sarepta, LA 71071, Phone: 318-994-2712

LEONE, NICK

9 Georgetown Dr, Pontoon Beach, IL 62040, Phone: 618-792-0734, nickleone@sbcglobal.net
Specialties: 18th century period straight knives. **Patterns:** Fighters, daggers, bowies. Besides period pieces makes modern designs. **Technical:** Forges 5160, W2, O1, 1098, 52100 and his own Damascus. **Prices:** $100 to $1000; some to $3500. **Remarks:** Full-time maker; first knife sold in 1987. Doing business as Anvil Head Forge. **Mark:** AHF, Leone, NL

LERCH, MATTHEW

N88 W23462 North Lisbon Rd, Sussex, WI 53089, Phone: 262-246-6362, Web: www.lerchcustomknives.com
Specialties: Folders and folders with special mechanisms. **Patterns:** Interframe and integral folders; lock backs, assisted openers, side locks, button locks and liner locks. **Technical:** Grinds ATS-34, 1095, 440 and Damascus. Offers filework and embellished bolsters. **Prices:** $900 and up. **Remarks:** Full-time maker; first knife made in 1986. **Mark:** Last name.

LESSWING, KEVIN

29A East 34th St, Bayonne, NJ 07002, Phone: 551-221-1841, klesswing@excite.com
Specialties: Traditonal working and using straight knives of his design or to customer specs. A few folders. Makes own leather sheaths. **Patterns:** Hunters, daggers, bowies, bird and trout. **Technical:** Forges high carbon and tool steels, makes own Damascus, grinds CPM154CM, Damasteel, and other stainless steels. Does own heat treating. **Remarks:** Voting member of Knifemakers Guild, part-time maker. **Mark:** KL on early knives, LESSWING on Current knives.

LEU, POHAN

PO BOX 15423, Rio Rancho, NM 87174, Phone: 949-300-6412, pohanleu@hotmail.com Web: www.leucustom.com
Specialties: Japanese influenced fixed blades made to your custom specifications. Knives and swords. A2 tool steel, Stock Removal. **Prices:** $180 and up. **Remarks:** Full-time; first knife sold in 2003. **Mark:** LEU or PL.

LEVENGOOD, BILL

15011 Otto Rd, Tampa, FL 33624, Phone: 813-961-5688, bill.levengood@verison.net; Web: www.levengoodknives.com
Specialties: Working straight knives and folders. **Patterns:** Hunters, Bowies, folders and collector pieces. **Technical:** Grinds ATS-34, S-30V, CPM-154 and Damascus. **Prices:** $175 to $1500. **Remarks:** Full time maker; first knife sold in 1983. **Mark:** Last name, city, state.

LEVIN, JACK

201 Brighton 1st Road, Suite 3R, Brooklyn, NY 11235, Phone: 718-415-7911, jacklevin1@yahoo.com
Specialties: Folders with mechanisms.

LEVINE, BOB

101 Westwood Dr, Tullahoma, TN 37388, Phone: 931-454-9943, levineknives@msn.com
Specialties: Working left-and right-handed LinerLock® folders. **Patterns:** Hunters and folders. **Technical:** Grinds ATS-34, 440C, D2, O1 and some Damascus; hollow and some flat grinds. Uses fossil ivory, Micarta and exotic woods. Provides custom leather sheath

with each fixed knife. **Prices:** Starting at $135. **Remarks:** Full-time maker; first knife sold in 1984. Voting member Knifemakers Guild, German Messermaher Guild. **Mark:** Name and logo.

LEWIS, BILL

PO Box 63, Riverside, IA 52327, Phone: 319-461-1609, wildbill37@geticonnect.com
Specialties: Folders of all kinds including those made from one-piece of white tail antler with or without the crown. **Patterns:** Hunters, folding hunters, fillet, Bowies, push daggers, etc. **Prices:** $20 to $200. **Remarks:** Full-time maker; first knife sold in 1978. **Mark:** W.E.L.

LEWIS, MIKE

21 Pleasant Hill Dr, DeBary, FL 32713, Phone: 386-753-0936, dragonsteel@prodigy.net
Specialties: Traditional straight knives. **Patterns:** Swords and daggers. **Technical:** Grinds 440C, ATS-34 and 5160. Frequently uses cast bronze and cast nickel guards and pommels. **Prices:** $100 to $750. **Remarks:** Part-time maker; first knife sold in 1988. **Mark:** Dragon Steel and serial number.

LEWIS, TOM R

1613 Standpipe Rd, Carlsbad, NM 88220, Phone: 575-885-3616, lewisknives@carlsbadnm.com
Specialties: Traditional working straight knives. **Patterns:** Outdoor knives, hunting knives and Bowies. **Technical:** Grinds ATS-34 and CPM-154, forges 5168, W2, 1084 and O1. Makes wire, pattern welded and chainsaw Damascus. **Prices:** $140 to $1500. **Remarks:** Full-time maker; first knife sold in 1980. Doing business as TR Lewis Handmade Knives. **Mark:** Lewis family crest.

LICATA, STEVEN

LICATA CUSTOM KNIVES, 146 Wilson St. 1st Floor, Boonton, NJ 07005, Phone: 973-588-4909, kniveslicata@aol.com; Web: www.licataknives.com
Specialties: Fantasy swords and knives. One-of-a-kind sculptures in steel. **Prices:** $200 to $25,000.

LIEBENBERG, ANDRE

8 Hilma Rd, Bordeaux, Randburg, GT, SOUTH AFRICA 2196, Phone: 011-787-2303
Specialties: High-art straight knives of his design. **Patterns:** Daggers, fighters and swords. **Technical:** Grinds 440C and 12C27. **Prices:** $250 to $500; some $4000 and higher. Giraffe bone handles with semi-precious stones. **Remarks:** Spare-time maker; first knife sold in 1990. **Mark:** Initials.

LIEGEY, KENNETH R

288 Carney Dr, Millwood, WV 25262, Phone: 304-273-9545
Specialties: Traditional working/using straight knives of his design and to customer specs. **Patterns:** Hunters, utility/camp knives, miniatures. **Technical:** Grinds 440C. **Prices:** $125 and up. **Remarks:** Spare-time maker; first knife sold in 1977. **Mark:** First and middle initials, last name.

LIGHTFOOT, GREG

RR #2, Kitscoty, AB, CANADA T0B 2P0, Phone: 780-846-2812; 780-800-1061, Pitbull@lightfootknives.com; Web: www.lightfootknives.com
Specialties: Stainless steel and Damascus. **Patterns:** Boots, fighters and locking folders. **Technical:** Grinds BG-42, 440C, D2, CPM steels, Stellite 6K. Offers engraving. **Prices:** $500 to $2000. **Remarks:** Full-time maker; first knife sold in 1988. Doing business as Lightfoot Knives. **Mark:** Shark with Lightfoot Knives below.

LIN, MARCUS

29233 Via Espada, Murrieta, CA 92563, Phone: 310-720-4368, marcuslin7@gmail.com; Web: www.linknives.com
Specialties: Working knives in the Loveless tradition. **Patterns:** Original patterns direct from the Loveless Shop, designed by R.W. Loveless and, on special request, maker's own patterns. **Technical:** Main blade material is Hitachi's ATS-34; other steels available. Please inquire. **Prices:** $550 to $1,750. **Remarks:** Part-time maker since 2004. Mentored by R.W. Loveless and Jim Merritt. Sole authorship work: knives and sheaths, except for heat treat (which goes to Paul Bos Heat Treat). **Mark:** Main logo is "Marcus Lin, maker, Loveless Design."

LINKLATER, STEVE

8 Cossar Dr, Aurora, ON, CANADA L4G 3N8, Phone: 905-727-8929, knifman@sympatico.ca
Specialties: Traditional working/using straight knives and folders of his design. **Patterns:** Fighters, hunters and locking folders. **Technical:** Grinds ATS-34, 440V and D2. **Prices:** $125 to $350; some to $600. **Remarks:** Part-time maker; first knife sold in 1987. Doing business as Links Knives. **Mark:** LINKS.

LISCH, DAVID K

9239 8th Ave. SW, Seattle, WA 98106, Phone: 206-919-5431, Web: www.davidlisch.com
Specialties: One-of-a-kind collectibles, straight knives and custom kitchen knives of own design and to customer specs. **Patterns:** Hunters, skinners, Bowies, and fighters. **Technical:** Forges all his own Damascus under 360-pound air hammer. Forges and chisels wrought iron, pure iron, and bronze butt caps. **Prices:** Starting at $800. **Remarks:** Full-time blacksmith, part-time bladesmith. **Mark:** D. Lisch J.S.

LISTER JR., WELDON E

116 Juniper Ln, Boerne, TX 78006, Phone: 210-269-0102, wlister@grtc.com; Web: www.weldonlister.com
Specialties: One-of-a-kind fancy and embellished folders. **Patterns:** Locking and slip-joint folders. **Technical:** Commercial Damascus and O1. All knives embellished. Engraves, inlays, carves and scrimshaws. **Prices:** Upscale. **Remarks:** Spare-time maker; first knife sold in 1991. **Mark:** Last name.

LITTLE, GARY M
94716 Conklin Meadows Ln, PO Box 156, Broadbent, OR 97414, Phone: 503-572-2656
Specialties: Fancy working knives. **Patterns:** Hunters, tantos, Bowies, axes and buckskinners; locking folders and interframes. **Technical:** Forges and grinds O1, L6m, 1095, and 15N20; makes his own Damascus; bronze fittings. **Prices:** $120 to $1500. **Remarks:** Full-time maker; first knife sold in 1979. Doing business as Conklin Meadows Forge. **Mark:** Name, city and state.

LITTLE, LARRY
1A Cranberry Ln, Spencer, MA 01562, Phone: 508-885-2301, littcran@aol.com
Specialties: Working straight knives of his design or to customer specs. Likes Scagel-style. **Patterns:** Hunters, fighters, Bowies, folders. **Technical:** Grinds and forges L6, O1, 5160, 1095, 1080. Prefers natural handle material especially antler. Uses nickel silver. Makes own heavy duty leather sheath. **Prices:** Start at $125. **Remarks:** Part-time maker. First knife sold in 1985. Offers knife repairs. **Mark:** Little on one side, LL brand on the other.

LIVESAY, NEWT
3306 S. Dogwood St, Siloam Springs, AR 72761, Phone: 479-549-3356, Fax: 479-549-3357, newt@newtlivesay.com; Web:www.newtlivesay.com
Specialties: Combat utility knives, hunting knives, titanium knives, swords, axes, KYDWX sheaths for knives and pistols, custom orders.

LIVINGSTON, ROBERT C
PO Box 6, Murphy, NC 28906, Phone: 704-837-4155
Specialties: Art letter openers to working straight knives. **Patterns:** Minis to machetes. **Technical:** Forges and grinds most steels. **Prices:** Start at $20. **Remarks:** Full-time maker; first knife sold in 1988. Doing business as Mystik Knifeworks. **Mark:** MYSTIK.

LOCKETT, LOWELL C.
344 Spring Hill Dr., Canton, GA 30115, Phone: 770-846-8114, lcl1932@gmail.com or spur1932@windstream.net
Technical: Forges 5160, 1095 and other blade steels, and uses desert ironwood, ivory and other handle materials. **Prices:** $150 to $1,500. **Remarks:** ABS journeyman smith.

LOCKETT, STERLING
527 E Amherst Dr, Burbank, CA 91504, Phone: 818-846-5799
Specialties: Working straight knives and folders to customer specs. **Patterns:** Hunters and fighters. **Technical:** Grinds. **Prices:** Moderate. **Remarks:** Spare-time maker. **Mark:** Name, city with hearts.

LOERCHNER, WOLFGANG
WOLFE FINE KNIVES, PO Box 255, Bayfield, ON, CANADA N0M 1G0, Phone: 519-565-2196
Specialties: Traditional straight knives, mostly ornate. **Patterns:** Small swords, daggers and stilettos; locking folders and miniatures. **Technical:** Grinds D2, 440C and 154CM; all knives hand-filed and flat-ground. **Prices:** Vary. **Remarks:** Full-time maker; first knife sold in 1983. Doing business as Wolfe Fine Knives. **Mark:** WOLFE.

LOGAN, IRON JOHN
4260 Covert, Leslie, MI 49251, ironjohnlogan@gmail.com; www.ironjohnlogan.com
Patterns: Hunting, camping, outdoor sheath knives, folding knives, axes, tomahawks, historical knives. swords, working chef's knives, and woodwork and leather work knives. **Technical:** Forges low-alloy steels, wrought iron, bloom and hearth materials, or high-alloy steel as the job insists. Makes own damascus and San Mai seel, modern materials and stainlesses. Vegetable-tanned leather sheaths, and American hardwood handles like hickory, walnut and cherry. **Prices:** $200 to $2,000. **Remarks:** Full-time bladesmith; first knife made in 1998. **Mark:** Two horizontal lines crossed by one vertical line and an angle off the bottom to creat a "J."

LONEWOLF, J AGUIRRE
481 Hwy 105, Demorest, GA 30535, Phone: 706-754-4660, Fax: 706-754-8470, lonewolfandsons@windstream.net, Web: www.knivesbylonewolf.com www.eagleswinggallery.com
Specialties: High-art working and using straight knives of his design. **Patterns:** Bowies, hunters, utility/camp knives and fine steel blades. **Technical:** Forges Damascus and high-carbon steel. Most knives have hand-carved moose antler handles. **Prices:** $55 to $500; some to $2000. **Remarks:** Full-time maker; first knife sold in 1980. Doing business as Lonewolf and Sons LLC. **Mark:** Stamp.

LONG, GLENN A
10090 SW 186th Ave, Dunnellon, FL 34432, Phone: 352-489-4272, galong99@att.net
Specialties: Classic working and using straight knives of his design and to customer specs. **Patterns:** Hunters, Bowies, utility. **Technical:** Grinds 440C D2 and 440V. **Prices:** $85 to $300; some to $800. **Remarks:** Part-time maker; first knife sold in 1990. **Mark:** Last name inside diamond.

LONGWORTH, DAVE
1200 Red Oak Ridge, Felicity, OH 45120, Phone: 513-876-2372
Specialties: High-tech working knives. **Patterns:** Locking folders, hunters, fighters and elaborate daggers. **Technical:** Grinds O1, ATS-34, 440C; buys Damascus. **Prices:** $125 to $600; some higher. **Remarks:** Part-time maker; first knife sold in 1980. **Mark:** Last name.

LOOS, HENRY C
210 Ingraham, New Hyde Park, NY 11040, Phone: 516-354-1943, hcloos@optonline.net
Specialties: Miniature fancy knives and period pieces of his design. **Patterns:** Bowies, daggers and swords. **Technical:** Grinds O1 and 440C. Uses sterling, 18K, rubies and emeralds. All knives come with handmade hardwood cases. **Prices:** $90 to $195; some to $250. **Remarks:** Spare-time maker; first knife sold in 1990. **Mark:** Script last initial.

LOUKIDES, DAVID E
76 Crescent Circle, Cheshire, CT 06410, Phone: 203-271-3023, Loussharp1@sbcglobal.net; Web: www.prayerknives.com
Specialties: Hand forged working blades and collectible pieces. **Patterns:** Chef knives, bowies, and hunting knives. . **Technical:** Uses 1084, 1095, 5160, W2, O1 and 1084-and-15N20 damascus. **Prices:** Normally $200 to $1,000. **Remarks:** part-time maker, Journeyman Bladesmith, Full-time Journeyman Toolmaker. **Mark:** Loukides JS.

LOVE, ED
19443 Mill Oak, San Antonio, TX 78258, Phone: 210-497-1021, Fax: 210-497-1021, annaedlove@sbcglobal.net
Specialties: Hunting, working knives and some art pieces. **Technical:** Grinds ATS-34, and 440C. **Prices:** $150 and up. **Remarks:** Part-time maker. First knife sold in 1980. **Mark:** Name in a weeping heart.

LOVESTRAND, SCHUYLER
1136 19th St SW, Vero Beach, FL 32962, Phone: 772-778-0282, Fax: 772-466-1126, lovestranded@aol.com
Specialties: Fancy working straight knives of his design and to customer specs; unusual fossil ivories. **Patterns:** Hunters, fighters, Bowies and fishing knives. **Technical:** Grinds stainless steel. **Prices:** $550 to $2,500. **Remarks:** Part-time maker; first knife sold in 1982. **Mark:** Name in logo.

LOVETT, MICHAEL
PO Box 121, Mound, TX 76558, Phone: 254-865-9956, michaellovett@embarqmail.com
Specialties: The Loveless Connection Knives as per R.W. Loveless-Jim Merritt. **Patterns:** All Loveless Patterns and Original Lovett Patterns. **Technical:** Complicated double grinds and premium fit and finish. **Prices:** $1000 and up. **Remarks:** High degree of fit and finish -Authorized collection by R. W. Loveless **Mark:** Loveless Authorized football or double nude.

LOZIER, DON
5394 SE 168th Ave, Ocklawaha, FL 32179, Phone: 352-625-3576
Specialties: Hand-finished tacticals, collaborative art pieces and sole-authorship fixed blades. **Patterns:** Daggers, fighters, boot knives, and hunters. **Technical:** Grinds ATS-34, 440C and Damascus. Most pieces are highly embellished by notable artisans. Taking limited number of orders per annum. **Prices:** Start at $250; most are $1250 to $3000; some to $12,000. **Remarks:** Full-time maker. **Mark:** Name.

LUCHAK, BOB
15705 Woodforest Blvd, Channelview, TX 77530, Phone: 281-452-1779
Specialties: Presentation knives; start of The Survivor series. **Patterns:** Skinners, Bowies, camp axes, steak knife sets and fillet knives. **Technical:** Grinds 440C. Offers electronic etching; filework. **Prices:** $50 to $1500. **Remarks:** Full-time maker; first knife sold in 1983. Doing business as Teddybear Knives. **Mark:** Full name, city and state with Teddybear logo.

LUCHINI, BOB
1220 Dana Ave, Palo Alto, CA 94301, Phone: 650-321-8095, rwluchin@bechtel.com

LUCIE, JAMES R
9100 Calera Dr., Unit 9, Austin, TX 78735, Phone: 512-436-9202 or 231-557-3084, scagel@netonecom.net
Specialties: William Scagel-style knives. **Patterns:** Authentic scagel-style knives and miniatures. **Technical:** Forges 1084 steel. **Prices:** $1,200 and up. **Remarks:** Full-time maker; first knife sold in 1975. Believes in sole authorship of his work. ABS Journeyman Smith. **Mark:** Scagel-style Kris stamp and maker's name and address.

LUCKETT, BILL
108 Amantes Ln, Weatherford, TX 76088, Phone: 817-320-1568, luckettknives@gmail.com Web: www.billluckettcustomknives.com
Specialties: Uniquely patterned robust straight knives. **Patterns:** Fighters, Bowies, hunters. **Technical:** 154CM stainless.**Prices:** $550 to $1500. **Remarks:** Part-time maker; first knife sold in 1975. Knifemakers Guild Member. **Mark:** Last name over Bowie logo.

LUDWIG, RICHARD O
57-63 65 St, Maspeth, NY 11378, Phone: 718-497-5969
Specialties: Traditional working/using knives. **Patterns:** Boots, hunters and utility/camp knives folders. **Technical:** Grinds 440C, ATS-34 and BG42. File work on guards and handles; silver spacers. Offers scrimshaw. **Prices:** $325 to $400; some to $2000. **Remarks:** Full-time maker. **Mark:** Stamped first initial, last name, state.

LUI, RONALD M
4042 Harding Ave, Honolulu, HI 96816, Phone: 808-734-7746
Specialties: Working straight knives and folders in standard patterns. **Patterns:** Hunters, boots and liner locks. **Technical:** Grinds 440C and ATS-34. **Prices:** $100 to $700. **Remarks:** Spare-time maker; first knife sold in 1988. **Mark:** Initials connected.

LUNDSTROM, JAN-AKE
Mastmostigen 8, Dals-Langed, SWEDEN 66010, Phone: 0531-40270
Specialties: Viking swords, axes and knives in cooperation with handle makers. **Patterns:** All traditional-styles, especially swords and inlaid blades. **Technical:** Forges his own Damascus and laminated steel. **Prices:** $200 to $1000. **Remarks:** Full-time maker; first knife sold in 1985; collaborates with museums. **Mark:** Runic.

LUNDSTROM, TORBJORN (TOBBE)
Norrskenet 4, Are, SWEDEN 83013, 9lundstrm@telia.com Web: http://tobbeiare.se/site/
Specialties: Hunters and collectible knives. **Patterns:** Nordic-style hunters and art knives with unique materials such as mammoth and fossil walrus ivory. **Technical:** Uses forged

blades by other makers, particularly Mattias Styrefors who mostly uses 15N20 and 20C steels and is a mosaic blacksmith. **Remarks:** First knife made in 1986.

LUNN, GAIL
434 CR 1422, Mountain Home, AR 72653, Phone: 870-424-2662, gail@lunnknives.com; Web: www.lunnknives.com
Specialties: Fancy folders and double action autos, some straight blades. **Patterns:** One-of-a-kind, all types. **Technical:** Stock removal, hand made. **Prices:** $300 and up. **Remarks:** Fancy file work, exotic materials, inlays, stone etc. **Mark:** Name in script.

LUNN, LARRY A
434 CR 1422, Mountain Home, AR 72653, Phone: 870-424-2662, larry@lunnknives.com; Web: www.lunnknives.com
Specialties: Fancy folders and double action autos; some straight blades. **Patterns:** All types; his own designs. **Technical:** Stock removal; commercial Damascus. **Prices:** $125 and up. **Remarks:** File work inlays and exotic materials. **Mark:** Name in script.

LUPOLE, JAMIE G
KUMA KNIVES, 285 Main St., Kirkwood, NY 13795, Phone: 607-775-9368, jlupole@stny.rr.com
Specialties: Working and collector grade fixed blades, ethnic-styled blades. **Patterns:** Fighters, Bowies, tacticals, hunters, camp, utility, personal carry knives, some swords. **Technical:** Forges and grinds 10XX series and other high-carbon steels, grinds ATS-34 and 440C, will use just about every handle material available. **Prices:** $80 to $500 and up. **Remarks:** Part-time maker since 1999. Marks: "KUMA" hot stamped, name, city and state-etched, or "Daiguma saku" in kanji.

LURQUIN, SAMUEL
Hameau Du Bois, Hoyaux 10, 7133 Buvrinnes Belgique, Binches, BELGIUM, Phone: 0032-478-349-051, knifespirit@hotmail.com; Web: www.samuel-lurquin.com
Specialties: Forged bowies, fighters, hunters and working knives. **Technical:** Uses, but is not limited to, W1, W2 and L6 blade steels, creates own pattern-welded steel. Commonly uses wood, walrus ivory, mammoth ivory and stag for handles. **Prices:** $500 and up. **Remarks:** Full-time maker beginning in 2014, ABS master smith as of 2015.

LUTZ, GREG
127 Crescent Rd, Greenwood, SC 29646, Phone: 864-229-7340
Specialties: Working and using knives and period pieces of his design and to customer specs. **Patterns:** Fighters, hunters and swords. **Technical:** Forges 1095 and O1; grinds ATS-34. Differentially heat-treats forged blades; uses cryogenic treatment on ATS-34. **Prices:** $50 to $350; some to $1200. **Remarks:** Part-time maker; first knife sold in 1986. Doing business as Scorpion Forge. **Mark:** First initial, last name.

LYLE III, ERNEST L
LYLE KNIVES, PO Box 1755, Chiefland, FL 32644, Phone: 352-490-6693, ernestlyle@msn.com
Specialties: Fancy period pieces; one-of-a-kind and limited editions. **Patterns:** Arabian/Persian influenced fighters, military knives, Bowies and Roman short swords; several styles of hunters. **Technical:** Grinds 440C, D2 and 154 CM. Engraves. **Prices:** $200 -$7500. **Remarks:** Full-time maker; first knife sold in 1972. **Mark:** Lyle Knives over Chiefland, Fla.

LYNCH, TAD
140 Timberline Dr., Beebe, AR 72012, Phone: 501-626-1647, lynchknives@yahoo.com Web: lynchknives.com
Specialties: Forged fixed blades. **Patterns:** Bowies, choppers, fighters, hunters. **Technical:** Hand-forged W-2, 1084, 1095 clay quenched 52100, 5160. **Prices:** Starting at $250. **Remarks:** Part-time maker, also offers custom leather work via wife Amy Lynch. **Mark:** T.D. Lynch over anvil.

LYNN, ARTHUR
29 Camino San Cristobal, Galisteo, NM 87540, Phone: 505-466-3541, lynnknives@aol.com
Specialties: Handforged Damascus knives. **Patterns:** Folders, hunters, Bowies, fighters, kitchen. **Technical:** Forges own Damascus. **Prices:** Moderate.

LYONS, WILLIAM R. (BILL)
36099 U.S. Hwy. 6, Palisade, NE 69040, Phone: 970-219-1600, lyonsknives@reagan.com; Web: www.lyonsknives.com
Specialties: Scrimshaw, ivory inlay, silver wire inlay, hand-carved wood handles, leather handles. **Patterns:** Fighters, bowies, camp knives, integrals, and Moran and Scagel styles. **Technical:** Heat treating to very precise levels, makes damascus and forges O1, O6, W2, 5160, 1084, 1095, 15N20 and L6. **Prices:** $250 to $3,000. **Remarks:** Full-time maker; member of the ABS since 1990. Antique reproductions, all natural handle material, leather sheaths. **Mark:** LYONS.

LYTTLE, BRIAN
Box 5697, High River, AB, CANADA T1V 1M7, Phone: 403-558-3638, brian@lyttleknives.com; Web: www.lyttleknives.com
Specialties: Fancy working straight knives and folders; art knives. **Patterns:** Bowies, daggers, dirks, sgian dubhs, folders, dress knives, tantos, short swords. **Technical:** Forges Damascus steel; engraving; scrimshaw; heat-treating; classes. **Prices:** $450 to $15,000. **Remarks:** Full-time maker; first knife sold in 1983. **Mark:** Last name, country.

M

MACCAUGHTRY, SCOTT F.
Fullerton Forge, 1824 Sorrel St, Camarillo, CA 93010, Phone: 805-750-2137, smack308@hotmail.com
Specialties: Fixed blades and folders. **Technical:** Forges 5160, 52100, W2 and his own damascus using 1084 and 15N20 steels. **Prices:** $275 and up. **Remarks:** ABS journeyman smith. **Mark:** S. MacCaughtry in script, and J.S. on the back side.

MACDONALD, DAVID
2824 Hwy 47, Los Lunas, NM 87031, Phone: 505-866-5866

MACKIE, JOHN
13653 Lanning, Whittier, CA 90605, Phone: 562-945-6104
Specialties: Forged. **Patterns:** Bowie and camp knives. **Technical:** Attended ABS Bladesmith School. **Prices:** $75 to $500. **Mark:** JSM in a triangle.

MACKRILL, STEPHEN
PO Box 1580, Pinegowrie, Johannesburg, GT, SOUTH AFRICA 2123, Phone: 27-11-474-7139, Fax: 27-11-474-7139, info@mackrill.co.za; Web: www.mackrill.net
Specialties: Art fancy, historical, collectors and corporate gifts cutlery. **Patterns:** Fighters, hunters, camp, custom lock back and LinerLock® folders. **Technical:** N690, 12C27, ATS-34, silver and gold inlay on handles; wooden and silver sheaths. **Prices:** $330 and upwards. **Remarks:** First knife sold in 1978. **Mark:** Mackrill fish with country of origin.

MADRULLI, MME JOELLE
Residence Ste Catherine B1, Salon De Provence, FRANCE 13330

MAESTRI, PETER A
S11251 Fairview Rd, Spring Green, WI 53588, Phone: 608-546-4481
Specialties: Working straight knives in standard patterns. **Patterns:** Camp and fishing knives, utility green-river-styled. **Technical:** Grinds 440C, 154CM and 440A. **Prices:** $15 to $45; some to $150. **Remarks:** Full-time maker; first knife sold in 1981. Provides professional cutler service to professional cutters. **Mark:** CARISOLO, MAESTRI BROS., or signature.

MAGEE, JIM
741 S. Ohio St., Salina, KS 67401, Phone: 785-820-6928, jimmagee@cox.net
Specialties: Working and fancy folding knives. **Patterns:** Liner locking folders, favorite is his Persian. **Technical:** Grinds ATS-34, Devin Thomas & Eggerling Damascus, titanium. Liners Prefer mother-of-pearl handles. **Prices:** Start at $225 to $1200. **Remarks:** Part-time maker, first knife sold in 2001. Purveyor since 1982. Past president of the Professional Knifemakers Association **Mark:** Last name.

MAGRUDER, JASON
129 Hillside Ave., Klamath Falls, OR 97601, Phone: 719-210-1579, jason@magruderknives.com; web: MagruderKnives.com
Specialties: Unique and innovative designs combining the latest modern materials with traditional hand craftsmanship. **Patterns:** Fancy neck knives. Tactical gents folders. Working straight knives. **Technical:** Flats grinds CPM3v, CPM154, ATS34, 1080, and his own forged damascus. Hand carves carbon fiber, titanium, wood, ivory, and pearl handles. Filework and carving on blades. **Prices:** $150 and up. **Remarks:** Part-time maker; first knife sold in 2000. **Mark:** Last name.

MAHOMEDY, A R
PO Box 76280, Marble Ray, KZN, SOUTH AFRICA 4035, Phone: +27 31 577 1451, arm-koknives@mweb.co.za; Web: www.arm-koknives.co.za
Specialties: Daggers and elegant folders of own design finished with finest exotic materials currently available. **Technical:** Via stock removal, grinds Damasteel, Damascus and the famous hardenable stainless steels. **Prices:** U.S. $650 and up. **Remarks:** Part-time maker. First knife sold in 1995. Voting member knifemakers guild of SA, FEGA member starting out Engraving. **Mark:** Initials A R M crowned with a "Minaret."

MAHOMEDY, HUMAYD A.R.
PO BOX 76280, Marble Ray, KZN, SOUTH AFRICA 4035, Phone: +27 31 577 1451, arm-koknives@mweb.co.za
Specialties: Tactical folding and fixed blade knives. **Patterns:** Fighters, utilities, tacticals, folders and fixed blades, daggers, modern interpretation of Bowies. **Technical:** Stock-removal knives of Bohler N690, Bohler K110, Bohler K460, Sandvik 12C27, Sandvik RWL 34. Handle materials used are G10, Micarta, Cape Buffalo horn, Water Buffalo horn, Kudu horn, Gemsbok horn, Giraffe bone, Elephant ivory, Mammoth ivory, Arizona desert ironwood, stabilised and dyed burls. **Prices:** $250 -$1000. **Remarks:** First knife sold in 2002. Full-time knifemaker since 2002. First person of color making knives full-time in South Africa. Doing business as HARM EDGED TOOLS. **Mark:** HARM and arrow over EDGED TOOLS.

MAIENKNECHT, STANLEY
38648 S R 800, Sardis, OH 43946

MAINES, JAY
SUNRISE RIVER CUSTOM KNIVES, 5584 266th St., Wyoming, MN 55092, Phone: 651-462-5301, jaymaines@fronternet.net; Web: http://www.sunrisecustomknives.com
Specialties: Heavy duty working, classic and traditional fixed blades. Some high-tech and fancy embellished knives available. **Patterns:** Hunters, skinners, fillet, bowies tantos, boot daggers etc. etc. **Technical:** Hollow ground, stock removal blades of 440C, ATS-34 and CPM S-90V. Prefers natural handle materials, exotic hard woods and stag, rams and buffalo horns. Offers dovetailed bolsters in brass, stainless steel and nickel silver. Custom sheaths from matching wood or hand-stitched from heavy duty water buffalo hide. **Prices:** Moderate to up-scale. **Remarks:** Part-time maker; first knife sold in 1992. Doing business as Sunrise River Custom Knives. Offers fixed blade knives repair and handle conversions. **Mark:** Full name under a Rising Sun logo.

MAISEY, ALAN
PO Box 197, Vincentia, NSW, AUSTRALIA 2540, Phone: 2-4443 7829,

custom knifemakers

tosanaji@excite.com

Specialties: Daggers, especially krisses; period pieces. **Technical:** Offers knives and finished blades in Damascus and nickel Damascus. **Prices:** $75 to $2000; some higher. **Remarks:** Part-time maker; provides complete restoration service for krisses. Trained by a Japanese Kris smith. **Mark:** None, triangle in a box, or three peaks.

MAJORS, CHARLIE

1911 King Richards Ct, Montgomery, TX 77316, Phone: 713-826-3135, charliemajors@sbcglobal.net

Specialties: Fixed-blade hunters and slip-joint and lock-back folders.**Technical:** Practices stock removal method, preferring CPM154 steel and natural handle materials such as ironwood, stag, and mammoth ivory. Also takes customer requests. Does own heat treating and cryogenic quenching. **Remarks:** First knife made in 1980.

MAKOTO, KUNITOMO

3-3-18 Imazu-cho, Fukuyama-city, Hiroshima, JAPAN, Phone: 084-933-5874, kunitomo@po.iijnet.or.jp

MALABY, RAYMOND J

835 Calhoun Ave, Juneau, AK 99801, Phone: 907-586-6981, Fax: 907-523-8031, malaby@gci.net

Specialties: Straight working knives. **Patterns:** Hunters, skiners, Bowies, and camp knives. **Technical:** Hand forged 1084, 5160, O1 and grinds ATS-34 stainless. **Prices:** $195 to $400. **Remarks:** First knife sold in 1994. **Mark:** First initial, last name, city, and state.

MALLOY, JOE

1039 Schwabe St, Freeland, PA 18224, Phone: 570-436-6416, jdmalloy@msn.com

Specialties: Working straight knives and lock back folders—plain and fancy—of his design. **Patterns:** Hunters, utility, folders, tactical designs. **Technical:** 154CM, ATS-34, 440C, D2 and A2, damascus, other exotic steel on request. **Prices:** $100 to $1800. **Remarks:** Part-time maker; first knife sold in 1982. **Mark:** First and middle initials, last name, city and state.

MANARO, SAL

10 Peri Ave., Holbrook, NY 11741, Phone: 631-737-1180, maker@manaroknives.com

Specialties: Tactical folders, bolstered titanium LinerLocks, handmade folders, and fixed blades with hand-checkered components. **Technical:** Compound grinds, hidden fasteners and welded components, with blade steels including CPM-154, damascus, Stellite, D2, S30V and O-1 by the stock-removal method of blade making. **Prices:** $500 and up. **Remarks:** Part-time maker, made first knife in 2001. **Mark:** Last name with arrowhead underline.

MANDT, JOE

3735 Overlook Dr. NE, St. Petersburg, FL 33703, Phone: 813-244-3816, jmforge@mac.com

Specialties: Forged Bowies, camp knives, hunters, skinners, fighters, boot knives, military style field knives. **Technical:** Forges plain carbon steel and high carbon tool steels, including W2, 1084, 5160, O1, 9260, 15N20, cable Damascus, pattern welded Damascus, flat and convex grinds. Prefers natural handle materials, hand-rubbed finishes, and stainless low carbon steel, Damascus and wright iron fittings. Does own heat treat. **Prices:** $150 to $750. **Remarks:** Part-time maker, first knife sold in 206. **Mark:** "MANDT".

MANEKER, KENNETH

RR 2, Galiano Island, BC, CANADA V0N 1P0, Phone: 604-539-2084

Specialties: Working straight knives; period pieces. **Patterns:** Camp knives and hunters; French chef knives. **Technical:** Grinds 440C, 154CM and Vascowear. **Prices:** $50 to $200; some to $300. **Remarks:** Part-time maker; first knife sold in 1981. Doing business as Water Mountain Knives. **Mark:** Japanese Kanji of initials, plus glyph.

MANLEY, DAVID W

3270 Six Mile Hwy, Central, SC 29630, Phone: 864-654-1125, dmanleyknives@bellsouth.net

Specialties: Working straight knives of his design or to custom specs. **Patterns:** Hunters, boot and fighters. **Technical:** Grinds 440C and ATS-34. **Prices:** $80 to $400. **Remarks:** Part-time maker; first knife sold in 1994. **Mark:** First initial, last name, year and serial number.

MANN, MICHAEL L

IDAHO KNIFE WORKS, PO Box 144, Spirit Lake, ID 83869, Phone: 509 994-9394, Web: www.idahoknifeworks.com

Specialties: Working blades-historical reproduction, modern or custom design. **Patterns:** Cowboy Bowies, Mountain Man period blades, old-style folders, designer and maker of "The Cliff Knife", hunter knives, hand ax and fish fillet. **Technical:** High-carbon steel blades-hand forged 5160. Stock removed 15N20 steel. Also Damascus. **Prices:** $130 to $670+. **Remarks:** Made first knife in 1965. Full-time making knives as Idaho Knife Works since 1986. Functional as well as collectible. Each knife truly unique! **Mark:** Four mountain peaks are his initials MM.

MANN, TIM

BLADEWORKS, PO Box 1196, Honokaa, HI 96727, Phone: 808-775-0949, Fax: 808-775-0949, birdman@shaka.com

Specialties: Hand-forged knives and swords. **Patterns:** Bowies, tantos, pesh kabz, daggers. **Technical:** Use 5160, 1050, 1075, 1095 and ATS-34 steels, cable Damascus. **Prices:** $200 to $800. **Remarks:** Just learning to forge Damascus. **Mark:** None yet.

MARAGNI, DAN

RD 1 Box 106, Georgetown, NY 13072, Phone: 315-662-7490

Specialties: Heavy-duty working knives, some investor class. **Patterns:** Hunters, fighters

and camp knives, some Scottish types. **Technical:** Forges W2 and his own Damascus; toughness and edge-holding a high priority. **Prices:** $125 to $500; some to $1000. **Remarks:** Full-time maker; first knife sold in 1975. **Mark:** Celtic initials in circle.

MARCHAND, RICK

Wildertools, 69 Maple Ave., POB 1635, Lunenburg, Nova Scotia, CANADA B0J 2C0, Phone: 226-783-8771, rickmarchand@wildertools.com; Web: www.wildertools.com

Specialties: Specializing in multicultural, period stylized blades and accoutrements. **Technical:** Hand forged from 1070/84/95, L6 and 52100 steel. **Prices:** $175 -$1,500. **Remarks:** Maker since 2007. ABS apprentice smith. **Mark:** Tang stamp: "MARCHAND" along with two Japanese-style characters resembling "W" and "M."

MARINGER, TOM

2692 Powell St., Springdale, AR 72764, maringer@arkansas.net; Web: shirepost.com/cutlery.

Specialties: Working straight and curved blades with stainless steel furniture and wire-wrapped handles. **Patterns:** Subhilts, daggers, boots, swords. **Technical:** Grinds D-2, A-2, ATS-34. May be safely disassembled by the owner via pommel screw or pegged construction. **Prices:** $2000 to $3000, some to $20,000. **Remarks:** Former full-time maker, now part-time. First knife sold in 1975. **Mark:** Full name, year, and serial number etched on tang under handle.

MARKLEY, KEN

7651 Cabin Creek Lane, Sparta, IL 62286, Phone: 618-443-5284

Specialties: Traditional working and using knives of his design and to customer specs. **Patterns:** Fighters, hunters and utility/camp knives. **Technical:** Forges 5160, 1095 and L6; makes his own Damascus; does file work. **Prices:** $150 to $800; some to $2000. **Remarks:** Part-time maker; first knife sold in 1991. Doing business as Cabin Creek Forge. **Mark:** Last name, JS.

MARLOWE, CHARLES

10822 Poppleton Ave, Omaha, NE 68144, Phone: 402-933-5065, cmarlowe1@cox.net; Web: www.marloweknives.com

Specialties: Folding knives and balisong. **Patterns:** Tactical pattern folders. **Technical:** Grind ATS-34, S30V, CPM154, 154CM, Damasteel, others on request. Forges/grinds 1095 on occasion. **Prices:** Start at $450. **Remarks:** First knife sold in 1993. Full-time since 1999. **Mark:** Turtle logo with Marlowe above, year below.

MARLOWE, DONALD

2554 Oakland Rd, Dover, PA 17315, Phone: 717-764-6055

Specialties: Working straight knives in standard patterns. **Patterns:** Bowies, fighters, boots and utility knives. **Technical:** Grinds D2 and 440C. Integral design hunter models. **Prices:** $130 to $850. **Remarks:** Spare-time maker; first knife sold in 1977. **Mark:** Last name.

MARSH, JEREMY

6169 3 Mile NE, Ada, MI 49301, Phone: 616-889-1945, steelbean@hotmail.com; Web: www.marshcustomknives.com

Specialties: Locking liner folders, dressed-up gents knives, tactical knives, and dress tacticals. **Technical:** CPM S30V stainless and Damascus blade steels using the stock-removal method of bladesmithing. **Prices:** $450 to $1500. **Remarks:** Self-taught, part-time knifemaker; first knife sold in 2004. **Mark:** Maker's last name and large, stylized M.

MARSHALL, REX

1115 State Rte. 380, Wilmington, OH 45177, Phone: 937-604-8430, rexmarshall@hotmail.com; www.rexmarshallcustomknives.com

Specialties Hunters, skinners and bowies, plain to fancy. **Technical:** Forges and stock removal, using ATS-34 and 5160 steels. Will custom build to customer's specifications. **Prices:** $125 and up. **Remarks:** First knife made in 2011. **Mark:** Rex Marshall over eagle.

MARTIN, BRUCE E

Rt. 6, Box 164-B, Prescott, AR 71857, Phone: 501-887-2023

Specialties: Fancy working straight knives of his design. **Patterns:** Bowies, camp knives, skinners and fighters. **Technical:** Forges 5160, 1095 and his own Damascus. Uses natural handle materials; filework available. **Prices:** $75 to $350; some to $500. **Remarks:** Full-time maker; first knife sold in 1979. **Mark:** Name in arch.

MARTIN, GENE

PO Box 396, Williams, OR 97544, Phone: 541-846-6755, bladesmith@customknife.com

Specialties: Straight knives and folders. **Patterns:** Fighters, hunters, skinners, boot knives, spring back and lock back folders. **Technical:** Grinds ATS-34, 440C, Damascus and 154CM. Forges; makes own Damascus; scrimshaws. **Prices:** $150 to $2500. **Remarks:** Full-time maker; first knife sold in 1993. Doing business as Provision Forge. **Mark:** Name and/or crossed staff and sword.

MARTIN, HAL W

781 Hwy 95, Morrilton, AR 72110, Phone: 501-354-1682, hal.martin@sbcglobal.net

Specialties: Hunters, Bowies and fighters. **Prices:** $250 and up. **Mark:** MARTIN.

MARTIN, HERB

2500 Starwood Dr, Richmond, VA 23229, Phone: 804-747-1675, hamjlm@hotmail.com

Specialties: Working straight knives. **Patterns:** Skinners, hunters and utility. **Technical:** Hollow grinds ATS-34, and Micarta handles. **Prices:** $125 to $200. **Remarks:** Part-time Maker. First knife sold in 2001. **Mark:** HA MARTIN.

MARTIN, MICHAEL W

Box 572, Jefferson St, Beckville, TX 75631, Phone: 903-678-2161

Specialties: Classic working/using straight knives of his design and in standard patterns. **Patterns:** Hunters. **Technical:** Grinds ATS-34, 440C, O1 and A2. Bead blasted, Parkerized, high polish and satin finishes. Sheaths are handmade. Also hand forges cable Damascus.

Prices: $185 to $280 some higher. **Remarks:** Part-time maker; first knife sold in 1995. Doing business as Michael W. Martin Knives. **Mark:** Name and city, state in arch.

MARTIN, PETER

28220 N. Lake Dr, Waterford, WI 53185, Phone: 262-706-3076, Web: www.petermartinknives.com

Specialties: Fancy, fantasy and working straight knives and folders of his design and in standard patterns. **Patterns:** Bowies, fighters, hunters, locking folders and liner locks. **Technical:** Forges own Mosaic Damascus, powdered steel and his own Damascus. Prefers natural handle material; offers file work and carved handles. **Prices:** Moderate. **Remarks:** Full-time maker; first knife sold in 1988. Doing business as Martin Custom Products. **Mark:** Martin Knives.

MARTIN, RANDALL J

51 Bramblewood St, Bridgewater, MA 02324, Phone: 508-279-0682

Specialties: High tech folding and fixed blade tactical knives employing the latest blade steels and exotic materials. Employs a unique combination of 3d-CNC machining and hand work on both blades and handles. All knives are designed for hard use. Clean, radical grinds and ergonomic handles are hallmarks of RJ's work, as is his reputation for producing "Scary Sharp" knives. **Technical:** Grinds CPM30V, CPM 3V, CPM154CM, A2 and stainless Damascus. Other CPM alloys used on request. Performs all heat treating and cryogenic processing in-house. **Remarks:** Full-time maker since 2001 and materials engineer. Former helicopter designer. First knife sold in 1976.

MARTIN, TONY

PO Box 10, Arcadia, MO 63621, Phone: 573-546-2254, arcadian@charter.net; Web: www.arcadianforge.com

Specialties: Specializes in historical designs, esp. puukko, skean dhu. **Remarks:** Premium quality blades, exotic wood handles, unmatched fit and finish. **Mark:** AF.

MARTIN, JOHN ALEXANDER

821 N Grand Ave, Okmulgee, OK 74447, Phone: 918-758-1099, jam@jamblades.com; Web: www.jamblades.com

Specialties: Inlaid and engraved handles. **Patterns:** Bowies, fighters, hunters and traditional patterns. Swords, fixed blade knives, folders and axes. **Technical:** Forges 5160, 1084, 10XX, O1, L6 and his own Damascus. **Prices:** Start at $300. **Remarks:** Part-time maker. **Mark:** Two initials with last name and MS or 5 pointed star.

MARZITELLI, PETER

19929 35A Ave, Langley, BC, CANADA V3A 2R1, Phone: 604-532-8899, marzitelli@shaw.ca

Specialties: Specializes in unique functional knife shapes and designs using natural and synthetic handle materials. **Patterns:** Mostly folders, some daggers and art knives. **Technical:** Grinds ATS-34, S/S Damascus and others. **Prices:** $220 to $1000 (average $375). **Remarks:** Full-time maker; first knife sold in 1984. **Mark:** Stylized logo reads "Marz."

MASON, BILL

9306 S.E. Venns St., Hobe Sound, FL 33455, Phone: 772-545-3649

Specialties: Combat knives; some folders. **Patterns:** Fighters to match knife types in book Cold Steel. **Technical:** Grinds O1, 440C and ATS-34. **Prices:** $115 to $250; some to $350. **Remarks:** Spare-time maker; first knife sold in 1979. **Mark:** Initials connected.

MASSEY, AL

Box 14 Site 15 RR#2, Mount Uniacke, NS, CANADA B0N 1Z0, Phone: 902-866-4754, armjan@eastlink.ca

Specialties: Working knives and period pieces. **Patterns:** Swords and daggers of Celtic to medieval design, Bowies. **Technical:** Forges 5160, 1084 and 1095. Makes own Damascus. **Prices:** $200 to $500, damascus $300-$1000. **Remarks:** Part-time maker, first blade sold in 1988. **Mark:** Initials and JS on Ricasso.

MASSEY, ROGER

4928 Union Rd, Texarkana, AR 71854, Phone: 870-779-1018, rmassey668@aol.com

Specialties: Traditional and working straight knives and folders of his design and to customer specs. **Patterns:** Bowies, hunters, daggers and utility knives. **Technical:** Forges 1084 and 52100, makes his own Damascus. Offers filework and silver wire inlay in handles. **Prices:** $200 to $1500; some to $2500. **Remarks:** Part-time maker; first knife sold in 1991. **Mark:** Last name, M.S.

MASSEY, RON

61638 El Reposo St., Joshua Tree, CA 92252, Phone: 760-366-9239 after 5 p.m., Fax: 763-366-4620

Specialties: Classic, traditional, fancy/embellished, high art, period pieces, working/using knives, straight knives, folders, and automatics. Your design, customer specs, about 175 standard patterns. **Patterns:** Automatics, hunters and fighters. All folders are side-locking folders. Unless requested as lock books slip joint he specializes or custom designs. **Technical:** ATS-34, 440C, D-2 upon request. Engraving, filework, scrimshaw, most of the exotic handle materials. All aspects are performed by him: inlay work in pearls or stone, handmade Pem' work. **Prices:** $110 to $2500; some to $6000. **Remarks:** Part-time maker; first knife sold in 1976.

MATA, LEONARD

3583 Arruza St, San Diego, CA 92154, Phone: 619-690-6935

MATHEWS, CHARLIE AND HARRY

TWIN BLADES, 121 Mt Pisgah Church Rd., Statesboro, GA 30458, Phone: 912-865-9098, twinblades@bulloch.net; Web: www.twinxblades.com

Specialties: Working straight knives, carved stag handles. **Patterns:** Hunters, fighters, Bowies and period pieces. **Technical:** Grinds D2, CPMS30V, CPM3V, ATS-34 and commercial Damascus; handmade sheaths some with exotic leather, file work. Forges 1095, 1084, and 5160. **Prices:** Starting at $125. **Remarks:** Twin brothers making knives full-time under the label of Twin Blades. Charter members Georgia Custom Knifemakers Guild. Members of The Knifemakers Guild. **Mark:** Twin Blades over crossed knives, reverse side steel type.

MATSUNO, KANSEI

109-8 Uenomachi, Nishikaiden, Gifu-City, JAPAN 501-1168, Phone: 81 58 234 8643

MATSUOKA, SCOT

94-415 Ukalialii Place, Mililani, HI 96789, Phone: 808-625-6658, Fax: 808-625-6658, scottym@hawaii.rr.com; Web: www.matsuokaknives.com

Specialties: Folders, fixed blades with custom hand-stitched sheaths. **Patterns:** Gentleman's knives, hunters, tactical folders. **Technical:** CPM 154CM, 440C, 154, BG42, bolsters, file work, and engraving. **Prices:** Starting price $350. **Remarks:** Part-time maker, first knife sold in 2002. **Mark:** Logo, name and state.

MATSUSAKI, TAKESHI

MATSUSAKI KNIVES, 151 Ono-Cho, Sasebo-shi, Nagasaki, JAPAN, Phone: 0956-47-2938, Fax: 0956-47-2938

Specialties: Working and collector grade front look and slip joint. **Patterns:** Sheffierd type folders. **Technical:** Grinds ATS-34 k-120. **Price:** $250 to $1000, some to $8000. **Remarks:** Part-time maker, first knife sold in 1990. **Mark:** Name and initials.

MAXEN, MICK

2 Huggins Welham Green, Hatfield, Herts, UNITED KINGDOM AL97LR, Phone: 01707 261213, mmaxen@aol.com

Specialties: Damascus and Mosaic. **Patterns:** Medieval-style daggers and Bowies. **Technical:** Forges CS75 and 15N20 / nickel Damascus. **Mark:** Last name with axe above.

MAXFIELD, LYNN

382 Colonial Ave, Layton, UT 84041, Phone: 801-544-4176, lcmaxfield@msn.com

Specialties: Sporting knives, some fancy. **Patterns:** Hunters, fishing, fillet, special purpose; some locking folders. **Technical:** Grinds 440-C, 154-CM, CPM154, D2, CPM S30V, and Damascus. **Prices:** $125 to $400; some to $900. **Remarks:** Part-time maker; first knife sold in 1979. **Mark:** Name, city and state.

MAXWELL, DON

1484 Celeste Ave, Clovis, CA 93611, Phone: 559-299-2197, maxwellknives@aol.com; Web: www.maxwellknives.com

Specialties: Fancy folding knives and fixed blades of his design. **Patterns:** Hunters, fighters, utility/camp knives, LinerLock® folders, flippers and fantasy knives. **Technical:** Grinds 440C, ATS-34, D2, CPM 154, and commercial Damascus. **Prices:** $250 to $1000; some to $2500. **Remarks:** Full-time maker; first knife sold in 1987. **Mark:** Last name only or Maxwell MAX-TAC.

MAY, CHARLES

10024 McDonald Rd., Aberdeen, MS 39730, Phone: 662-369-0404, charlesmayknives@yahoo.com; Web: charlesmayknives.blademakers.com

Specialties: Fixed-blade sheath knives. **Patterns:** Hunters and fillet knives. **Technical:** Scandinavian-ground D2 and S30V blades, black micarta and wood handles, nickel steel pins with maker's own pocket carry or belt-loop pouches. **Prices:** $215 to $495. **Mark:** "Charles May Knives" and a knife in a circle.

MAYNARD, LARRY JOE

PO Box 493, Crab Orchard, WV 25827

Specialties: Fancy and fantasy straight knives. **Patterns:** Big knives; a Bowie with a full false edge; fighting knives. **Technical:** Grinds standard steels. **Prices:** $350 to $500; some to $1000. **Remarks:** Full-time maker; first knife sold in 1986. **Mark:** Middle and last initials.

MAYNARD, WILLIAM N.

2677 John Smith Rd, Fayetteville, NC 28306, Phone: 910-425-1615

Specialties: Traditional and working straight knives of all designs. **Patterns:** Combat, Bowies, fighters, hunters and utility knives. **Technical:** Grinds 440C, ATS-34 and commercial Damascus. Offers fancy filework; handmade sheaths. **Prices:** $100 to $300; some to $750. **Remarks:** Full-time maker; first knife sold in 1988. **Mark:** Last name.

MAYO JR., HOMER

18036 Three Rivers Rd., Biloxi, MS 39532, Phone: 228-326-8298

Specialties: Traditional working straight knives, folders and tactical. **Patterns:** Hunters, fighters, tactical, bird, Bowies, fish fillet knives and lightweight folders. **Technical:** Grinds 440C, ATS-34, D-2, Damascus, forges and grinds 52100 and custom makes sheaths. **Prices:** $100 to $1000. **Remarks:** Part-time maker **Mark:** All knives are serial number and registered in the name of the original purchaser, stamped last name or etched.

MAYO JR., TOM

67 412 Alahaka St, Waialua, HI 96791, Phone: 808-637-6560, mayot001@hawaii.rr.com; Web: www.mayoknives.com

Specialties: Framelocks/tactical knives. **Patterns:** Combat knives, hunters, Bowies and folders. **Technical:** Titanium/stellite/S30V. **Prices:** $500 to $1000. **Remarks:** Full-time maker; first knife sold in 1982. **Mark:** Volcano logo with name and state.

MAYVILLE, OSCAR L

2130 E. County Rd 910S, Marengo, IN 47140, Phone: 812-338-4159

Specialties: Working straight knives; period pieces. **Patterns:** Kitchen cutlery, Bowies, camp knives and hunters. **Technical:** Grinds A2, O1 and 440C. **Prices:** $50 to $350; some to $500. **Remarks:** Full-time maker; first knife sold in 1984. **Mark:** Initials over knife logo.

MCABEE, WILLIAM
27275 Norton Grade, Colfax, CA 95713, Phone: 530-389-8163
Specialties: Working/using knives. **Patterns:** Fighters, Bowies, Hunters. **Technical:** Grinds ATS-34. **Prices:** $75 to $200; some to $350. **Remarks:** Part-time maker; first knife sold in 1990. **Mark:** Stylized WM stamped.

MCCALLEN JR., HOWARD H
110 Anchor Dr, So Seaside Park, NJ 08752

MCCARLEY, JOHN
4165 Harney Rd, Taneytown, MD 21787
Specialties: Working straight knives; period pieces. **Patterns:** Hunters, Bowies, camp knives, miniatures, throwing knives. **Technical:** Forges W2, O1 and his own Damascus. **Prices:** $150 to $300; some to $1000. **Remarks:** Part-time maker; first knife sold in 1977. **Mark:** Initials in script.

MCCARTY, HARRY
1479 Indian Ridge Rd, Blaine, TN 37709, harry@indianridgeforge.com; Web: www.indianridgeforge.com
Specialties: Period pieces. **Patterns:** Trade knives, Bowies, 18th and 19th century folders and hunting swords. **Technical:** Forges and grinds high-carbon steel. **Prices:** $75 to $1300. **Remarks:** Full-time maker; first knife sold in 1977. Doing business as Indian Ridge Forge. **Mark:** Stylized initials inside a shamrock.

MCCLURE, JERRY
3052 Isim Rd, Norman, OK 73026, Phone: 405-321-3614, jerry@jmcclureknives.net; Web: www.jmcclureknives.net
Specialties: Gentleman's folder, linerlock with my jeweled pivot system of eight rubies, forged one-of-a-kind Damascus Bowies, and a line of hunting/camp knives. **Patterns:** Folders, Bowie, and hunting/camp Technical Forges own Damascus, also uses Damasteel and does own heat treating. Prices $500 to $3,000 and up Remarks Full-time maker, made first knife in 1965. Mark J.MCCLURE

MCCLURE, MICHAEL
803 17th Ave, Menlo Park, CA 94025, Phone: 650-323-2596, mikesknives@att.net; Web: www.customknivesbymike.com
Specialties: Working/using straight knives of his design and to customer specs. **Patterns:** Bowies, hunters, skinners, utility/camp, tantos, fillets and boot knives. **Technical:** Forges high-carbon and Damascus; also grinds stainless, all grades. **Prices:** Start at $300. **Remarks:** Part-time maker; first knife sold in 1991. ABS Journeyman Smith. **Mark:** Mike McClure.

MCCONNELL JR., LOYD A
309 County Road 144-B, Marble Falls, TX 78654, Phone: 830-596-3488, ccknives@ccknives.com; Web: www.ccknives.com
Specialties: Working straight knives and folders, some fancy. **Patterns:** Hunters, boots, Bowies, locking folders and slip-joints. **Technical:** Grinds CPM Steels, ATS-34 and BG-42 and commercial Damascus. **Prices:** $450 to $10,000. **Remarks:** Full-time maker; first knife sold in 1975. Doing business as Cactus Custom Knives. Markets product knives under name: Lone Star Knives. **Mark:** Name, city and state in cactus logo.

MCCORNOCK, CRAIG
MCC MTN OUTFITTERS, 4775 Rt. 212/PO 162, Willow, NY 12495, Phone: 845-679-9758, Mccmtn@aol.com; Web: www.mccmtn.com
Specialties: Carry, utility, hunters, defense type knives and functional swords. **Patterns:** Drop points, hawkbills, tantos, waklzashis, katanas **Technical:** Stock removal, forged and Damascus, (yes, he still flints knap). **Prices:** $200 to $2000. **Mark:** McM.

MCCOUN, MARK
14212 Pine Dr, DeWitt, VA 23840, Phone: 804-469-7631, mccounandsons@live.com
Specialties: Working/using straight knives of his design and in standard patterns; custom miniatures. **Patterns:** Locking liners, integrals. **Technical:** Grinds Damascus, ATS-34 and 440C. **Prices:** $150 to $500. **Remarks:** Part-time maker; first knife sold in 1989. **Mark:** Name, city and state.

MCCRACKIN, KEVIN
3720 Hess Rd, House Spings, MO 63051, Phone: 636-677-6066

MCCRACKIN AND SON, V J
3720 Hess Rd, House Springs, MO 63051, Phone: 636-677-6066
Specialties: Working straight knives in standard patterns. **Patterns:** Hunters, Bowies and camp knives. **Technical:** Forges L6, 5160, his own Damascus, cable Damascus. **Prices:** $125 to $700; some to $1500. **Remarks:** Part-time maker; first knife sold in 1983. Son Kevin helps make the knives. **Mark:** Last name, M.S.

MCCULLOUGH, JERRY
274 West Pettibone Rd, Georgiana, AL 36033, Phone: 334-382-7644, ke4er@alaweb.com
Specialties: Standard patterns or custom designs. **Technical:** Forge and grind scrap-tool and Damascus steels. Use natural handle materials and turquoise trim on some. Filework on others. **Prices:** $65 to $250 and up. **Remarks:** Part-time maker. **Mark:** Initials (JM) combined.

MCDONALD, RICH
5010 Carmel Rd., Hillboro, OH 45133, Phone: 937-466-2071, rmclongknives@aol.com; Web: www.longknivesandleather.com
Specialties: Traditional working/using and art knives of his design. **Patterns:** Bowies, hunters, folders, primitives and tomahawks. **Technical:** Forges 5160, 1084, 1095, 52100 and his own Damascus. Fancy filework. **Prices:** $200 to $1500. **Remarks:** Full-time maker; first knife sold in 1994. **Mark:** First and last initials connected.

MCDONALD, ROBERT J
14730 61 Court N, Loxahatchee, FL 33470, Phone: 561-790-1470
Specialties: Traditional working straight knives to customer specs. **Patterns:** Fighters, swords and folders. **Technical:** Grinds 440C, ATS-34 and forges own Damascus. **Prices:** $150 to $1000. **Remarks:** Part-time maker; first knife sold in 1988. **Mark:** Electro-etched name.

MCDONALD, W.J. "JERRY"
7173 Wickshire Cove E, Germantown, TN 38138, Phone: 901-756-9924, wjmcdonaldknives@msn.com; Web: www.mcdonaldknives.com
Specialties: Classic and working/using straight knives of his design and in standard patterns. **Patterns:** Bowies, hunters kitchen and traditional spring back pocket knives. **Technical:** Grinds ATS-34, 154CM, D2, 440V, BG42 and 440C. **Prices:** $125 to $1000. **Remarks:** Full-time maker; first knife sold in 1989. **Mark:** First and middle initials, last name, maker, city and state. Some of his knives are stamped McDonald in script.

MCFALL, KEN
PO Box 458, Lakeside, AZ 85929, Phone: 928-537-2026, Fax: 928-537-8066, knives@citlink.net
Specialties: Fancy working straight knives and some folders. **Patterns:** Daggers, boots, tantos, Bowies; some miniatures. **Technical:** Grinds D2, ATS-34 and 440C. Forges his own Damascus. **Prices:** $200 to $1200. **Remarks:** Part-time maker; first knife sold in 1984. **Mark:** Name, city and state.

MCFARLIN, ERIC E
PO Box 2188, Kodiak, AK 99615, Phone: 907-486-4799
Specialties: Working knives of his design. **Patterns:** Bowies, skinners, camp knives and hunters. **Technical:** Flat and convex grinds 440C, A2 and AEB-L. **Prices:** Start at $200. **Remarks:** Part-time maker; first knife sold in 1989. **Mark:** Name and city in rectangular logo.

MCFARLIN, J W
3331 Pocohantas Dr, Lake Havasu City, AZ 86404, Phone: 928-453-7612, Fax: 928-453-7612, aztheedge@NPGcable.com
Technical: Flat grinds, D2, ATS-34, 440C, Thomas and Peterson Damascus. **Remarks:** From working knives to investment. Customer designs always welcome. 100 percent handmade. Made first knife in 1972. **Prices:** $150 to $3000. **Mark:** Hand written in the blade.

MCGHEE, E. SCOTT
7136 Lisbon Rd., Clarkton, NC 28433, Phone: 910-448-2224, guineahogforge@gmail.com; Web: www.guineahogforge.com
Specialties: Hunting knives, kitchen blades, presentation blades, tactical knives and sword canes. **Technical:** Forge and stock removal, all flat-ground blades, including 1080-and-15N20 damascus, 1084, O1 and W2. **Prices:** $200 to $3,500. **Remarks:** Full-time maker; first knife sold in 2009. Currently an ABS journeyman smith. **Mark:** E. Scott McGhee (large print) above Guinea Hog Forge (small print).

MCGILL, JOHN
PO Box 302, Blairsville, GA 30512, Phone: 404-745-4686
Specialties: Working knives. **Patterns:** Traditional patterns; camp knives. **Technical:** Forges L6 and 9260; makes Damascus. **Prices:** $50 to $250; some to $500. **Remarks:** Full-time maker; first knife sold in 1982. **Mark:** XYLO.

MCGOWAN, FRANK E
12629 Howard Lodge Rd., Sykesville, MD 21784, Phone: 443-745-2611, lizmcgowan31@gmail.com
Specialties: Fancy working knives and folders to customer specs. **Patterns:** Survivor knives, fighters, fishing knives, folders and hunters. **Technical:** Grinds and forges O1, 440C, 5160, ATS-34, 52100, or customer choice. **Prices:** $100 to $1000; some more. **Remarks:** Full-time maker; first knife sold in 1986. **Mark:** Last name.

MCGRATH, PATRICK T
8343 Kenyon Ave, Westchester, CA 90045, Phone: 310-338-8764, hidinginLA@excite.com

MCGRODER, PATRICK J
5725 Chapin Rd, Madison, OH 44057, Phone: 216-298-3405, Fax: 216-298-3405
Specialties: Traditional working/using knives of his design. **Patterns:** Bowies, hunters and utility/camp knives. **Technical:** Grinds ATS-34, D2 and customer requests. Does reverse etching; heat-treats; prefers natural handle materials; custom made sheath with each knife. **Prices:** $125 to $250. **Remarks:** Part-time maker. **Mark:** First and middle initials, last name, maker, city and state.

MCGUANE IV, THOMAS F
410 South 3rd Ave, Bozeman, MT 59715, Phone: 406-586-0248, Web: http://www.thomasmcguane.com
Specialties: Multi metal inlaid knives of handmade steel. **Patterns:** Lock back and LinerLock® folders, fancy straight knives. **Technical:** 1084/1SN20 Damascus and Mosaic steel by maker. **Prices:** $1000 and up. **Mark:** Surname or name and city, state.

MCHENRY, WILLIAM JAMES
Box 67, Wyoming, RI 02898, Phone: 401-539-8353
Specialties: Fancy high-tech folders of his design. **Patterns:** Locking folders with various mechanisms. **Technical:** One-of-a-kind only, no duplicates. Inventor of the Axis Lock. Most pieces disassemble and feature top-shelf materials including gold, silver and gems. **Prices:** Upscale. **Remarks:** Full-time maker; first knife sold in 1988. Former goldsmith. **Mark:** Last name or first and last initials.

MCINTYRE, SHAWN
71 Leura Grove, Hawthornm, E VIC, AUSTRALIA 3123, Phone: 61 3 9813 2049/Cell

61 412 041 062, macpower@netspace.net.au; Web: www.mcintyreknives.com **Specialties:** Damascus & CS fixed blades and art knives. **Patterns:** Bowies, hunters, fighters, kukris, integrals. **Technical:** Forges, makes own Damascus including pattern weld, mosaic, and composite multi-bars form O1 & 15N20 Also uses 1084, W2, and 52100. **Prices:** $275 to $2000. **Remarks:** Full-time maker since 1999. **Mark:** Mcintyre in script.

MCKEE, NEIL
674 Porter Hill Rd., Stevensville, MT 59870, Phone: 406-777-3507, mckeenh@wildblue.net
Specialties: Early American. **Patterns:** Nessmuk, DeWeese, French folders, art pieces. **Technical:** Engraver. **Prices:** $150 to $1000. **Mark:** Oval with initials.

MCKENZIE, DAVID BRIAN
2311 B Ida Rd, Campbell River, BC, CANADA V9W-4V7

MCKIERNAN, STAN
11751 300th St, Lamoni, IA 50140, Phone: 641-784-6873/641-781-0368, slmck@hotmail.com
Specialties: Self-sheathed knives and miniatures. **Patterns:** Daggers, ethnic designs and individual styles. **Technical:** Grinds Damascus and 440C. **Prices:** $200 to $500, some to $1500. **Mark:** "River's Bend" inside two concentric circles.

MCLUIN, TOM
36 Fourth St, Dracut, MA 01826, Phone: 978-957-4899, tmcluin@comcast.net
Specialties: Working straight knives and folders of his design. **Patterns:** Boots, hunters and folders. **Technical:** Grinds ATS-34, 440C, O1 and Damascus; makes his own mokume. **Prices:** $100 to $400; some to $700. **Remarks:** Part-time maker; first knife sold in 1991. **Mark:** Last name.

MCLURKIN, ANDREW
2112 Windy Woods Dr, Raleigh, NC 27607, Phone: 919-834-4693, mclurkincustomknives.com
Specialties: Collector grade folders, working folders, fixed blades, and miniatures. Knives made to order and to his design. **Patterns:** Locking liner and lock back folders, hunter, working and tactical designs. **Technical:** Using patterned Damascus, Mosaic Damascus, ATS-34, BG-42, and CPM steels. Prefers natural handle materials such as pearl, ancient ivory and stabilized wood. Also using synthetic materials such as carbon fiber, titanium, and G10. **Prices:** $250 and up. **Mark:** Last name. Mark is often on inside of folders.

MCNABB, TOMMY
CAROLINA CUSTOM KNIVES, PO Box 327, Bethania, NC 27010,
Phone: 336-924-6053, tommy@tmcnabb.com; Web: carolinaknives.com
Specialties: Classic and working knives of his own design or to customer's specs. **Patterns:** Traditional bowies. Tomahawks, hunters and customer designs. **Technical:** Forges his own Damascus steel, hand forges or grinds ATS-34 and other hi-tech steels. Prefers mirror finish or satin finish on working knives. Uses exotic or natural handle material and stabilized woods. **Price:** $300-$3500. **Remarks:** Full time maker. Made first knife in 1982. Mark "Carolina Custom Knives" on stock removal blades "T. McNabb" on custom orders and Damascus knives.

MCNEES, JONATHAN
15203 Starboard Pl, Northport, AL 35475, Phone: 205-391-8383, jmackusmc@yahoo.com; Web: www.mcneescustomknives.com
Specialties: Tactical, outdoors, utility. **Technical:** Stock removal method utilizing carbon and stainless steels to include 1095, cpm154, A2, cpms35v. **Remarks:** Part-time maker, first knife made in 2007. **Mark:** Jmcnees

MCRAE, J MICHAEL
6100 Lake Rd, Mint Hill, NC 28227, Phone: 704-545-2929, scotia@carolina.rr.com; Web: www.scotiametalwork.com
Specialties: Scottish dirks, sgian dubhs, broadswords. **Patterns:** Traditional blade styles with traditional and slightly non-traditional handle treatments. **Technical:** Forges 5160 and his own Damascus. Prefers stag and exotic hardwoods for handles, many intricately carved. **Prices:** Starting at $125, some to $3500. **Remarks:** Journeyman Smith in ABS, member of ABANA. Full-time maker, first knife sold in 1982. Doing business as Scotia Metalwork. **Mark:** Last name underlined with a claymore.

MCWILLIAMS, SEAN
PO Box 1685, Carbondale, CO 81623, Phone: 970-963-7489, info@seanmcwilliamsforge.com; Web: www.seanmcwilliamsforge.com
Specialties: Tactical, survival and working knives in Kydex-and-nylon sheaths. **Patterns:** Fighters, bowies, hunters and sports knives, period pieces, swords, martial arts blades and some folders. **Technical:** Forges only CPM T440V, CPM S90V and CPM S35VN. **Prices:** $165 to $2,500. **Remarks:** Full-time maker; first knife sold in 1972. **Mark:** Stylized bear paw.

MEERDINK, KURT
248 Yulan Barryville Rd., Barryville, NY 12719-5305, Phone: 845-557-0783
Specialties: Working straight knives. **Patterns:** Hunters, Bowies, tactical and neck knives. **Technical:** Grinds ATS-34, 440C, D2, Damascus. **Prices:** $95 to $1100. **Remarks:** Full-time maker, first knife sold in 1994. **Mark:** Meerdink Maker, Rio NY.

MEERS, ANDREW
1100 S Normal Ave., Allyn Bldg MC 4301, Carbondale, IL 62901, Phone: 774-217-3574, namsuechool@gmail.com
Specialties: Pattern welded blades, in the New England style. **Patterns:** Can do open or closed welding and fancies middle eastern style blades. **Technical:** 1095, 1084, 15n20,

5160, w1, w2 steels **Remarks:** Part-time maker attending graduate school at SIUC; looking to become full-time in the future as well as earn ABS Journeyman status. **Mark:** Korean character for south.

MEIER, DARYL
75 Forge Rd, Carbondale, IL 62903, Phone: 618-549-3234, Web: www.meiersteel.com
Specialties: One-of-a-kind knives and swords. **Patterns:** Collaborates on blades. **Technical:** Forges his own Damascus, W1 and A203E, 440C, 431, nickel 200 and clad steel. **Prices:** $500 and up. **Remarks:** Full-time smith and researcher since 1974; first knife sold in 1974. **Mark:** Name.

MELIN, GORDON C
14207 Coolbank Dr, La Mirada, CA 90638, Phone: 562-946-5753

MELOY, SEAN
7148 Rosemary Lane, Lemon Grove, CA 91945-2105, Phone: 619-465-7173
Specialties: Traditional working straight knives of his design. **Patterns:** Bowies, fighters and utility/camp knives. **Technical:** Grinds 440C, ATS-34 and D2. **Prices:** $125 to $300. **Remarks:** Part-time maker; first knife sold in 1985. **Mark:** Broz Knives.

MENEFEE, RICKY BOB
2440 County Road 1322, Blawchard, OK 73010, rmenefee@pldi.net
Specialties: Working straight knives and pocket knives. **Patterns:** Hunters, fighters, minis & Bowies. **Technical:** Grinds ATS-34, 440C, D2, BG42 and S30V. **Price:** $130 to $1000. **Remarks:** Part-time maker, first knife sold in 2001. Member of KGA of Oklahoma, also Knifemakers Guild. **Mark:** Menefee made or Menefee stamped in blade.

MENSCH, LARRY C
Larry's Knife Shop, 578 Madison Ave, Milton, PA 17847, Phone: 570-742-9554
Specialties: Custom orders. **Patterns:** Bowies, daggers, hunters, tantos, short swords and miniatures. **Technical:** Grinds ATS-34, stainless steel Damascus; blade grinds hollow, flat and slack. Filework; bending guards and fluting handles with finger grooves. **Prices:** $200 and up. **Remarks:** Full-time maker; first knife sold in 1993. Doing business as Larry's Knife Shop. **Mark:** Connected capital "L" and small "m" in script.

MERCER, MIKE
149 N. Waynesville Rd, Lebanon, OH 45036, Phone: 513-932-2837, mmercer08445@roadrunner.com
Specialties: Miniatures and autos. **Patterns:** All folder patterns. **Technical:** Diamonds and gold, one-of-a-kind, Damascus, O1, stainless steel blades. **Prices:** $500 to $5000. **Remarks:** Carved wax -lost wax casting. **Mark:** Stamp -Mercer.

MERCHANT, TED
7 Old Garrett Ct, White Hall, MD 21161, Phone: 410-343-0380
Specialties: Traditional and classic working knives. **Patterns:** Bowies, hunters, camp knives, fighters, daggers and skinners. **Technical:** Forges W2 and 5160; makes own Damascus. Makes handles with wood, stag, horn, silver and gem stone inlay; fancy filework. **Prices:** $125 to $600; some to $1500. **Remarks:** Full-time maker; first knife sold in 1985. **Mark:** Last name.

MERZ III, ROBERT L
1447 Winding Canyon, Katy, TX 77493, Phone: 281-391-2897, bobmerz@consolidated.net; Web: www.merzknives.com
Specialties: Folders. **Prices:** $350 to $1,400. **Remarks:** Full time maker; first knife sold in 1974. **Mark:** MERZ.

MESENBOURG, NICK
2545 Upper 64th Ct. E, Inver Grove Heights, MN 55076, Phone: 651-457-2753 or 651-775-7505, mesenbourg_nicholas@hotmail.com; www.ndmknives.com
Specialties Working straight knives of his design or to customer specs, also sport-themed knives. **Patterns:** Hunters, skinners, bowies, fighters, utility and fillet knives. **Technical:** Grinds 440C stainless steel and commercial damascus. **Prices:** $175-$450, special knives higher. **Remarks:** Part-time maker; first knife sold in 2008. **Mark:** Encircled N D M capital letters.

MESHEJIAN, MARDI
5 Bisbee Court 109 PMB 230, Santa Fe, NM 87508, Phone: 505-310-7441, toothandnail13@yahoo.com
Specialties: One-of-a-kind art knives, folders and kitchen knives. **Patterns:** Swords, daggers, folders and other weapons. **Technical:** Forged steel Damascus and titanium Damascus. **Prices:** $300 to $5000 some to $7000. **Mark:** Stamped stylized "M."

METHENY, H A "WHITEY"
7750 Waterford Dr, Spotsylvania, VA 22551, Phone: 540842-1440, Fax: 540-582-3095, hametheny@aol.com; Web: www methenyknives.com
Specialties: Working and using straight knives of his design and to customer specs. **Patterns:** Hunters and kitchen knives. **Technical:** Grinds 440C and ATS-34. Offers filework; tooled custom sheaths. **Prices:** $350 to $450. **Remarks:** Spare-time maker; first knife sold in 1990. **Mark:** Initials/full name football logo.

METSALA, ANTHONY
30557 103rd St. NW, Princeton, MN 55371, Phone: 763-389-2628, acmetsala@izoom.net; Web: www.metsalacustomknives.com
Specialties: Sole authorship one-off mosaic Damascus liner locking folders, sales of makers finished one-off mosaic Damascus blades. **Patterns:** Except for a couple EDC folding knives, maker does not use patterns. **Technical:** Forges own mosaic Damascus carbon blade and bolster material. All stainless steel blades are heat treated by Paul Bos. **Prices:** $250 to $1500. **Remarks:** Full-time knifemaker and Damascus steel maker, first

custom knifemakers

knife sold in 2005. **Mark:** A.C. Metsala or Metsala.

METZ, GREG T
c/o Yellow Pine Bar HC 83, BOX 8080, Cascade, ID 83611, Phone: 208-382-4336, metzenterprise@yahoo.com
    Specialties: Hunting and utility knives. **Prices:** $350 and up. **Remarks:** Natural handle materials; hand forged blades; 1084 and 1095. **Mark:** METZ (last name).

MEYER, CHRISTOPHER J
737 Shenipsit Lake Rd, Tolland, CT 06084, Phone: 860-875-1826, shenipsitforge.cjm@gmail.com
    Specialties: Handforged tool steels. **Technical:** Forges tool steels, grinds stainless. **Remarks:** Spare-time maker; sold first knife in 2003. **Mark:** Name and/or "Shenipsit Forge."

MICHINAKA, TOSHIAKI
I-679 Koyamacho-nishi, Tottori-shi, Tottori, JAPAN 680-0947, Phone: 0857-28-5911
    Specialties: Art miniature knives. **Patterns:** Bowies, hunters, fishing, camp knives & miniatures. **Technical:** Grinds ATS-34 and 440C. **Prices:** $300 to $900 some higher. **Remarks:** Part-time maker. First knife sold in 1982. **Mark:** First initial, last name.

MICKLEY, TRACY
42112 Kerns Dr, North Mankato, MN 56003, Phone: 507-947-3760, tracy@mickleyknives.com; Web: www.mickleyknives.com
    Specialties: Working and collectable straight knives using mammoth ivory or burl woods, LinerLock® folders. **Patterns:** Custom and classic hunters, utility, fighters and Bowies. **Technical:** Grinding 154-CM, BG-42 forging O1 and 52100. **Prices:** Starting at $325 **Remarks:** Part-time since 1999. **Mark:** Last name.

MIDGLEY, BEN
PO Box 577, Wister, OK 74966, Phone: 918-655-6701, mauricemidgley@windstream.net
    Specialties: Multi-blade folders, slip-joints, some lock-backs and hunters. File work, engraving and scrimshaw. **Patterns:** Reproduce old patterns, trappers, muskrats, stockman, whittlers, lockbacks an hunters. **Technical:** Grinds ATS-34, 440C, 12-C-27, CPM-154, some carbon steel, and commercial Damascus. **Prices:** $385 to $1875. **Remarks:** Full-time maker, first knife sold in 2002. **Mark:** Name, city, and state stamped on blade.

MIKOLAJCZYK, GLEN
4650 W. 7 Mile Rd., Caledonia, WI 53108, Phone: 414-791-0424, Fax: 262-835-9697, glenmikol@aol.com Web: www.customtomahawk.com
    Specialties: Pipe hawks, fancy folders, bowies, long blades, hunting knives, all of his own design. **Technical:** Sole-author, forges own Damascus and powdered steel. Works with ivory, bone, tortoise, horn and antlers, tiger maple, pearl for handle materials. Designs and does intricate file work and custom sheaths. Enjoys exotic handle materials. **Prices:** Moderate. **Remarks:** Founded Weg Von Wennig Forge in 2003, first knife sold in 2004. Also, designs and builds mini-forges. Will build upon request. International sales accepted. **Mark:** Tomahawk and name.

MILES JR., C R "IRON DOCTOR"
1541 Porter Crossroad, Lugoff, SC 29078, Phone: 803-600-9397
    Specialties: Traditional working straight knives of his design or made to custom specs. **Patterns:** Hunters, fighters, utility camp knives and hatches. **Technical:** Grinds O1, D2, ATS-34, 440C, 1095, and 154 CPM. Forges 18th century style cutlery of high carbon steels. Also forges and grinds old files and farrier's rasps to make knives. Custom leather sheaths. **Prices:** $100 and up. **Remarks:** Part-time maker, first knife sold in 1997. **Mark:** Iron doctor plus name and serial number.

MILITANO, TOM
CUSTOM KNIVES, 77 Jason Rd., Jacksonville, AL 36265-6655, Phone: 256-435-7132, jeffkin57@aol.com
    Specialties: Fixed blade, one-of-a-kind knives. **Patterns:** Bowies, fighters, hunters and tactical knives. **Technical:** Grinds 440C, CPM 154CM, A2, and Damascus. Hollow grinds, flat grinds, and decorative filework. **Prices:** $150 plus. **Remarks:** Part-time maker. Sold first knives in the mid to late 1980s. Memberships: Founding member of New England Custom Knife Association. **Mark:** Name engraved in ricasso area -type of steel on reverse side.

MILLARD, FRED G
27627 Kopezyk Ln, Richland Center, WI 53581, Phone: 608-647-5376
    Specialties: Working/using straight knives of his design or to customer specs. **Patterns:** Bowies, hunters, utility/camp knives, kitchen/steak knives. **Technical:** Grinds ATS-34, O1, D2 and 440C. Makes sheaths. **Prices:** $110 to $300. **Remarks:** Full-time maker; first knife sold in 1993. Doing business as Millard Knives. **Mark:** Mallard duck in flight with serial number.

MILLER, CHELSEA GRACE
80 Ainslie St., Brooklyn, NY 11211, Phone: 917-623-7804, chelsea@chelseamillerknives.com; Web: www.chelseamillerknives.com
    Specialties: Selection of rustic cheese knives and kitchen knives. **Technical:** Uses recycled tool steel, such as mechanic's files, wood files and rasps. Forges cheese and smaller kitchen knives, using stock removal to preserve the rasp pattern on large kitchen knives. All the wood for handles is collected from the maker's family farm in Vermont, including spalted maple, apple and walnut. **Prices:** $200 to $500. **Remarks:** Full-time maker; first knife made in 2011. Maker often examines that first knife and admires its simplicity, though it lacks functionality, and uses it as inspiration to remain as imaginative as possible.

MILLER, HANFORD J
1751 Mountain Ranch Rd., Lakespur, CO 80118, Phone: 719-999-2551, hanford.miller@gmail.com
    Specialties: Working knives in Moran styles, Bowie, period pieces, Cinquedea. **Patterns:** Daggers, Bowies, working knives. **Technical:** All work forged: W2, 1095, 5160 and Damascus. ABS methods; offers fine silver repousse, scabboard mountings and wire inlay, oak presentation cases. **Prices:** $400 to $1000; some to $3000 and up. **Remarks:** Full-time maker; first knife sold in 1968. **Mark:** Initials or name within Bowie logo.

MILLER, JAMES P
9024 Goeller Rd, RR 2, Box 28, Fairbank, IA 50629, Phone: 319-635-2294, Web: www.damascusknives.biz
    Specialties: All tool steel Damascus; working knives and period pieces. **Patterns:** Hunters, Bowies, camp knives and daggers. **Technical:** Forges and grinds 1095, 52100, 440C and his own Damascus. **Prices:** $175 to $500; some to $1500. **Remarks:** Full-time maker; first knife sold in 1970. **Mark:** First and middle initials, last name with knife logo.

MILLER, M A
11625 Community Center Dr, Unit #1531, Northglenn, CO 80233, Phone: 303-280-3816
    Specialties: Using knives for hunting. 3-1/2"-4" Loveless drop-point. Made to customer specs. **Patterns:** Skinners and camp knives. **Technical:** Grinds 440C, D2, O1 and ATS-34 Damascus miniatures. **Prices:** $225 to $350; miniatures $75 to $150. **Remarks:** Part-time maker; first knife sold in 1988. **Mark:** Last name stamped in block letters or first and middle initials, last name, maker, city and state with triangles on either side etched.

MILLER, MICHAEL
3030 E Calle Cedral, Kingman, AZ 86401, Phone: 928-757-1359, mike@mmilleroriginals.com
    Specialties: Hunters, Bowies, and skinners with exotic burl wood, stag, ivory and gemstone handles. **Patterns:** High carbon steel knives. **Technical:** High carbon and nickel alloy Damascus and high carbon and meteorite Damascus. Also mosaic Damascus. **Prices:** $235 to $4500. **Remarks:** Full-time maker since 2002, first knife sold 2000; doing business as M Miller Originals. **Mark:** First initial and last name with 'handmade' underneath.

MILLER, MICHAEL E
910146 S. 3500 Rd., Chandler, OK 74834, Phone: 918-377-2411, mimiller1@cotc.net
    Specialties: Traditional working/using knives of his design. **Patterns:** Bowies, hunters and kitchen knives. **Technical:** Grinds ATS-34, CPM 440V; forges Damascus and cable Damascus and 52100. Prefers scrimshaw, fancy pins, basket weave and embellished sheaths. **Prices:** $130 to $500. **Remarks:** Part-time maker; first knife sold in 1984. Doing business as Miller Custom Knives. Member of Knife Group Of Oklahoma. **Mark:** First and middle initials, last name, maker.

MILLER, NATE
Sportsman's Edge, 1075 Old Steese Hwy N, Fairbanks, AK 99712, Phone: 907-460-4718, sportsmansedge@gci.net Web: www.alaskasportsmansedge.com
    Specialties: Fixed blade knives for hunting, fishing, kitchen and collector pieces. **Patterns:** Hunters, skinners, utility, tactical, fishing, camp knives-your pattern or mine. **Technical:** Stock removal maker, ATS-34, 154CM, 440C, D2, 1095, other steels on request. Handle material includes micarta, horn, antler, fossilized ivory and bone, wide selection of woods. **Prices:** $225-$800. **Remarks:** Full time maker since 2002. **Mark:** Nate Miller, Fairbanks, AK.

MILLER, RICK
516 Kanaul Rd, Rockwood, PA 15557, Phone: 814-926-2059
    Specialties: Working/using straight knives of his design and in standard patterns. **Patterns:** Bowies, daggers, hunters and friction folders. **Technical:** Grinds L6. Forges 5160, L6 and Damascus. Patterns for Damascus are random, twist, rose or ladder. **Prices:** $75 to $250; some to $400. **Remarks:** Part-time maker; first knife sold in 1982. **Mark:** Script stamp "R.D.M."

MILLER, RONALD T
12922 127th Ave N, Largo, FL 34644, Phone: 813-595-0378 (after 5 p.m.)
    Specialties: Working straight knives in standard patterns. **Patterns:** Combat knives, camp knives, kitchen cutlery, fillet knives, locking folders and butterflies. **Technical:** Grinds D2, 440C and ATS-34; offers brass inlays and scrimshaw. **Prices:** $45 to $325; some to $750. **Remarks:** Part-time maker; first knife sold in 1984. **Mark:** Name, city and state in palm tree logo.

MILLER, STEVE
1376 Pine St., Clearwater, FL 33756, Phone: 727-461-4180, millknives@aol.com; Web: www.millerknives.com
    Patterns: Bowies, hunters, skinners, folders. **Technical:** 440-C, ATS-34, Sandvic Stainless, CPM-S30-V, Damascus. Exotic hardwoods, bone, horn, antler, ivory, synthetics. All leather work and sheaths made by me and handstitched. **Remarks:** Have been making custom knives for sale since 1990. Part-time maker, hope to go full time in about five and a half years (after retirement from full-time job). **Mark:** Last name inside a pentagram.

MILLER, TERRY
P.O. Box 262, Healy, AK 99743, Phone: 907-683-1239, terry@denalidomehome.com
    Specialties: Alaskan ulus with wood or horn. **Remarks:** New to knifemaking (6 years).

MILLS, LOUIS G
9450 Waters Rd, Ann Arbor, MI 48103, Phone: 734-668-1839
    Specialties: High-art Japanese-style period pieces. **Patterns:** Traditional tantos, daggers and swords. **Technical:** Makes steel from iron; makes his own Damascus by traditional

Japanese techniques. **Prices:** $900 to $2000; some to $8000. **Remarks:** Spare-time maker. **Mark:** Yasutomo in Japanese Kanji.

MILLS, MICHAEL
151 Blackwell Rd, Colonial Beach, VA 22443-5054, Phone: 804-224-0265
Specialties: Working knives, hunters, skinners, utility and Bowies. **Technical:** Forge 5160 differential heat-treats. **Prices:** $300 and up. **Remarks:** Part-time maker, ABS Journeyman. **Mark:** Last name in script.

MINCHEW, RYAN
3310 Cimmaron Ave., Midland, TX 79707-5802, Phone: 806-752-0223, ryan@minchewknives.com Web: www.minchewknives.com
Specialties: Hunters and folders. **Patterns:** Standard hunters and bird-and-trout knives. **Prices:** $150 to $500. **Mark:** Minchew.

MINNICK, JIM & JOYCE
144 North 7th St, Middletown, IN 47356, Phone: 765-354-4108, jmjknives@aol.com; Web: www.minnickknives.com
Specialties: Lever-lock folding art knives, liner-locks. **Patterns:** Stilettos, Persian and one-of-a-kind folders. **Technical:** Grinds and carves Damascus, stainless, and high-carbon. **Prices:** $950 to $7000. **Remarks:** Part-time maker; first knife sold in 1976. Husband and wife team. **Mark:** Minnick and JMJ.

MIRABILE, DAVID
PO BOX 20417, Juneau, AK 99802, Phone: 907-321-1103, dmirabile02@gmail.com; Web: www.mirableknives.com
Specialties: Elegant edged weapons and hard use Alaskan knives. **Patterns:** Fighters, personal carry knives, special studies of the Tlinget dagger. **Technical:** Uses W-2, 1080, 15n20, 1095, 5160, and his own Damascus, and stainless/high carbon San Mai.

MITCHELL, JAMES A
PO Box 4646, Columbus, GA 31904, Phone: 404-322-8582
Specialties: Fancy working knives. **Patterns:** Hunters, fighters, Bowies and locking folders. **Technical:** Grinds D2, 440C and commercial Damascus. **Prices:** $100 to $400; some to $900. **Remarks:** Part-time maker; first knife sold in 1976. Sells knives in sets. **Mark:** Signature and city.

MITCHELL, MAX DEAN AND BEN
3803 VFW Rd, Leesville, LA 71440, Phone: 318-239-6416
Specialties: Hatchet and knife sets with folder and belt and holster all match. **Patterns:** Hunters, 200 L6 steel. **Technical:** L6 steel; soft back, hand edge. **Prices:** $300 to $500. **Remarks:** Part-time makers; first knife sold in 1965. Custom orders only; no stock. **Mark:** First names.

MITCHELL, WM DEAN
2626 Eastbrook Dr., Mesquite, TX 75150, Phone: 972-270-1648, wmdeanmitchell@gmail.com
Specialties: Functional and collectable cutlery. **Patterns:**Personal and collector's designs. **Technical:**Forges own Damascus and carbon steels. **Prices:** Determined by the buyer. **Remarks:**Gentleman knifemaker. ABS Master Smith 1994.**Mark:** Full name with anvil and MS or WDM and MS.

MITSUYUKI, ROSS
PO Box 29577, Honolulu, HI 96820, Phone: 808-778-5907, Fax: 808-671-3335, r.p.mitsuyuki@gmail.com; Web:www.picturetrail.com/homepage/mrbing
Specialties: Working straight knives and folders/engraving titanium & 416 S.S. **Patterns:** Hunting, fighters, utility knives and boot knives. **Technical:** 440C, BG42, ATS-34, S30V, CPM154, and Damascus. **Prices:** $150 and up. **Remarks:** Spare-time maker, first knife sold in 1998. **Mark:** (Honu) Hawaiian sea turtle.

MIVILLE-DESCHENES, ALAIN
1952 Charles A Parent, Quebec, CANADA G2B 4B2, Phone: 418-845-0950, Fax: 418-845-0950, amd@miville-deschenes.com; Web: www.miville-deschenes.com
Specialties: Working knives of his design or to customer specs and art knives. **Patterns:** Bowies, skinner, hunter, utility, camp knives, fighters, art knives. **Technical:** Grinds ATS-34, CPMS30V, 0-1, D2, and sometime forge carbon steel. **Prices:** $250 to $700; some higher. **Remarks:** Part-time maker; first knife sold in 2001. **Mark:** Logo (small hand) and initials (AMD).

MOELLER, HARALD
#17-493 Pioneer Crescent, Parksville, BC, CANADA V9P 1V2, Phone: 250-248-0391, moeknif@shaw.ca; Web: www.collectiblecustomknives.com
Specialties: Collector grade San Sfransisco Dagger; small fighters, Fantasy Axes, Bowies, Survival Knives. Special design award winning liner lock folders; Viper throwing knives. **Technical:** Steels -440-C, ATS34, damascus, etc. Materials: mammoth, Abalone, MOP, Black Water Buffalo, 14K Gold, rubies, diamonds, etc. **Prices:** Throwing knives -$80 to $350; Fighters -$400 to $600; Axe -$3200; Folders -$600 to $3400; Dagger -Up to $9,000. **Remarks:** Now part time maker, first knife sold in 1979. member Southern California Blades; Member Oregon Knife Collectors Assoc.**Mark:** Moeller

MOEN, JERRY
4478 Spring Valley Rd., Dallas, TX 75244, Phone: 972-839-1609, jmoen@moencustomknives.com Web: moencustomknives.com
Specialties: Hunting, pocket knives, fighters tactical, and exotic. **Prices:** $500 to $5,000.

MOIZIS, STAN
8213 109B St., Delta, British Columbia (BC), CANADA V4C 4G9, Phone: 604-597-8929, moizis@telus.net
Specialties: Automatic and spring-assist folding knives and soon to come out-the-fronts.

Patterns: Well-made carry knives with some upper-end materials available for steel and handles. All patterns are freehand, and thus each knife is unique. Marks: "SM" on blade with date and place of manufacture on inside of spacer. On knives with professionally out-of-house machined parts, mark is "BRNO BORN."

MOJZIS, JULIUS
B S Timravy 6, 98511 Halic, SLOVAKIA, julius.mojzis@gmail.com; Web: www.juliusmojzis.com
Specialties: Art Knives. **Prices:** USD $2000. **Mark:** MOJZIS.

MONCUS, MICHAEL STEVEN
1803 US 19 N, Smithville, GA 31787, Phone: 912-846-2408

MONTANO, GUS A
P.O. Box 501264, San Diego, CA 92150, Phone: 619-273-5357
Specialties: Traditional working/using straight knives of his design. **Patterns:** Boots, Bowies and fighters. **Technical:** Grinds 1095 and 5160; grinds and forges cable. Double or triple hardened and triple drawn; hand-rubbed finish. Prefers natural handle materials. **Prices:** $200 to $400; some to $600. **Remarks:** Spare-time maker; first knife sold in 1997. **Mark:** First initial and last name.

MONTEIRO, VICTOR
31 Rue D'Opprebais, Maleves Ste Marie, BELGIUM 1360, Phone: 010 88 0441, victor.monteiro@skynet.be
Specialties: Working and fancy straight knives, folders and integrals of his design. **Patterns:** Fighters, hunters and kitchen knives. **Technical:** Grinds ATS-34, 440C, D2, Damasteel and other commercial Damascus, embellishment, filework and domed pins. **Prices:** $300 to $1000, some higher. **Remarks:** Part-time maker; first knife sold in 1989. **Mark:** Logo with initials connected.

MONTELL, TY
PO BOX 1312, Thatcher, AZ 85552, Phone: 575-538-1610, Fax: Cell: 575-313-4373, montellfamily@aol.com
Specialties: Automatics, slip-joint folders, hunting and miniatures.**Technical:** Stock removal. Steel of choice is CPM-154, Devin Thomas Damascus. **Prices:** $250 and up. **Remarks:** First knife made in 1980. **Mark:** Tang stamp -Montell.

MOONEY, MIKE
19432 E. Cloud Rd., Queen Creek, AZ 85142, Phone: 480-244-7768, mike@moonblades.com; Web: www.moonblades.com
Specialties: Hand-crafted high-performing straight knives of his or customer's design. **Patterns:** Bowies, fighters, hunting, camp and kitchen users or collectible. **Technical:** Flat-grind, hand-rubbed finish. S30V, CMP-154, Damascus, any steel. **Prices:** $300 to $3000. **Remarks:** Doing business as moonblades.com. Commissions are welcome. **Mark:** M. Mooney followed by crescent moon.

MOORE, DAVY
Moyriesk, Quin, Co Clare, IRELAND, Phone: 353 (0)65 6825975, davy@mooreireland.com; Web: http://www.mooreireland.com
Specialties: Traditional and Celtic outdoor hunting and utility knives. **Patterns:** Traditional hunters and skinners, Celtic pattern hunting knives, Bushcrafting, fishing, utility/camp knives. **Technical:** Stock removal knives 01, D2, RWL 34, ATS 34, CPM 154, Damasteel (various).**Prices:** 250-1700 Euros.**Remarks:** Full-time maker, first knife sold in 2004. **Mark:** Three stars over rampant lion / MOORE over Ireland.

MOORE, JAMES B
1707 N Gillis, Ft. Stockton, TX 79735, Phone: 915-336-2113
Specialties: Classic working straight knives and folders of his design. **Patterns:** Hunters, Bowies, daggers, fighters, boots, utility/camp knives, locking folders and slip-joint folders. **Technical:** Grinds 440C, ATS-34, D2, L6, CPM and commercial Damascus. **Prices:** $85 to $700; exceptional knives to $1500. **Remarks:** Full-time maker; first knife sold in 1972. **Mark:** Name, city and state.

MOORE, JON P
304 South N Rd, Aurora, NE 68818, Phone: 402-849-2616, Web: www.sharpdecisionknives.com
Specialties: Working and fancy straight knives using antler, exotic bone, wood and Micarta. Will use customers' antlers on request. **Patterns:** Hunters, skinners, camp and bowies. **Technical:** Hand-forged high carbon steel. Makes his own damascus. **Prices:** Start at $125. **Remarks:** Full-time maker, sold first knife in 2003. Does on-location knife forging demonstrations. **Mark:** Sword through anvil with name.

MOORE, MARVE
HC 89 Box 393, Willow, AK 99688, Phone: 907-232-0478, marvemoore@aol.com
Specialties: Fixed blades forged and stock removal. **Patterns:** Hunter, skinners, fighter, short swords. **Technical:** 100 percent of his work is done by hand. **Prices:** $100 to $500. **Remarks:** Also makes his own sheaths. **Mark:** -MM-.

MOORE, MICHAEL ROBERT
70 Beauliew St, Lowell, MA 01850, Phone: 978-479-0589, Fax: 978-441-1819

MOORE, TED
340 E Willow St, Elizabethtown, PA 17022, Phone: 717-367-3939, tedmoore@tedmooreknives.com; Web: www.tedmooreknives.com
Specialties: Damascus folders, cigar cutters, high art. **Patterns:** Slip joints, linerlock, cigar cutters. **Technical:** Grinds Damascus and stainless steels. **Prices:** $250 and up. **Remarks:** Part-time maker; first knife sold 1993. **Mark:** Moore U.S.A.

MORALES, RAMON
LP-114, Managua, NICARAGUA, Phone: 011-505-824-8950,

nicaraguabladesmith@gmail.com

Specialties: Forges knives and enjoys making brut de forge pieces. **Patterns:** Choppers, bowies and hunters. **Technical:** Does all his own blade heat treating in house and makes his own damascus. **Remarks:** Only ABS journeyman smith in Central America. **Mark:** Initials "RM" inside the outline of Nicaragua.

MORETT, DONALD
116 Woodcrest Dr, Lancaster, PA 17602-1300, Phone: 717-746-4888

MORGAN, JEFF
9200 Arnaz Way, Santee, CA 92071, Phone: 619-448-8430

Specialties: Early American style knives. **Patterns:** Hunters, bowies, etc. **Technical:** Carbon steel and carbon steel damascus. **Prices:** $60 to $400

MORGAN, TOM
14689 Ellett Rd, Beloit, OH 44609, Phone: 330-537-2023

Specialties: Working straight knives and period pieces. **Patterns:** Hunters, boots and presentation tomahawks. **Technical:** Grinds O1, 440C and 154CM. **Prices:** Knives, $65 to $200; tomahawks, $100 to $325. **Remarks:** Full-time maker; first knife sold in 1977. **Mark:** Last name and type of steel used.

MORO, CORRADO
Via Omegna, 22 -Rivoli 10098, Torino, ITALY, Phone: +39 3472451255, info@moroknives.com; Web: www.moroknives.com

Specialties: High-end folders of his own design and to customer specs, unique locking and pivoting systems. **Patterns:** Inspired by nature and technology. **Technical:** Uses ATS 34, 916 and 904L blade steels, and titanium, carbon-lip inlays, precious metals and diamonds. **Prices:** $3,500 to $11,000 and above. **Remarks:** Full-time maker; first knife sold in 2011. **Mark:** MORO on blade.

MORRIS, C H
1590 Old Salem Rd, Frisco City, AL 36445, Phone: 334-575-7425

Specialties: LinerLock® folders. **Patterns:** Interframe liner locks. **Technical:** Grinds 440C and ATS-34. **Prices:** Start at $350. **Remarks:** Full-time maker; first knife sold in 1973. Doing business as Custom Knives. **Mark:** First and middle initials, last name.

MORRIS, ERIC
306 Ewart Ave, Beckley, WV 25801, Phone: 304-255-3951

MORRIS, MICHAEL S.
609 S. Main St., Yale, MI 48097, Phone: 810-887-7817, michaelmorrisknives@gmail.com

Specialties: Hunting and Tactical fixed blade knives of his design made from files. **Technical:** All knives hollow ground on 16" wheel. Hand stitches his own sheaths also. **Prices:** From $60 to $350 with most in the $90 to $125 range. **Remarks:** Machinist since 1980, made his first knife in 1984, sold his first knife in 2004. Now full-time maker. **Mark:** Last name with date of manufacture.

MOSES, STEVEN
1610 W Hemlock Way, Santa Ana, CA 92704

MOSIER, DAVID
1725 Millburn Ave., Independence, MO 64056, Phone: 816-796-3479, dmknives@aol.com Web: www.dmknives.com

Specialties: Tactical folders and fixed blades. **Patterns:** Fighters and concealment blades. **Technical:** Uses S35VN, CPM 154, S30V, 154CM, ATS-34, 440C, A2, D2, Stainless damascus, and Damasteel. Fixed blades come with Kydex sheaths made by maker. **Prices:** $150 to $1000. **Remarks:** Full-time maker, business name is DM Knives. **Mark:** David Mosier Knives encircling sun.

MOULTON, DUSTY
135 Hillview Lane, Loudon, TN 37774, Phone: 865-408-9779, Web: www.moultonknives.com

Specialties: Fancy and working straight knives. **Patterns:** Hunters, fighters, fantasy and miniatures. **Technical:** Grinds ATS-34 and Damascus. **Prices:** $300 to $2000. **Remarks:** Full-time maker; first knife sold in 1991. Now doing engraving on own knives as well as other makers. **Mark:** Last name.

MOYER, RUSS
1266 RD 425 So, Havre, MT 59501, Phone: 406-395-4423

Specialties: Working knives to customer specs. **Patterns:** Hunters, Bowies and survival knives. **Technical:** Forges W2 & 5160. **Prices:** $150 to $350. **Remarks:** Part-time maker; first knife sold in 1980. **Mark:** Initials in logo.

MULKEY, GARY
533 Breckenridge Rd, Branson, MO 65616, Phone: 417-335-0123, gary@mulkeyknives.com; Web: www.mulkeyknives.com

Specialties: Sole authorship damascus and high-carbon steel hunters, bowies and fighters. **Patterns:** Fixed blades (hunters, bowies, and fighters). **Prices:** $450 and up. **Remarks:** Full-time maker since 1997. **Mark:** MUL above skeleton key.

MULLER, JODY
3359 S. 225th Rd., Goodson, MO 65663, Phone: 417-752-3260, mullerforge2@hotmail.com; Web: www.mullerforge.com

Specialties: Hand engraving, carving and inlays, fancy folders and oriental styles. **Patterns:** One-of-a-kind fixed blades and folders in all styles. **Technical:** Forges own Damascus and high carbon steel. **Prices:** $300 and up. **Remarks:** Full-time knifemaker, does hand engraving, carving and inlay. All work done by maker. **Mark:** Muller

MUNJAS, BOB
600 Beebe Rd., Waterford, OH 45786, Phone: 740-336-5538,

Web: hairofthebear.com

Specialties: Damascus and carbon steel sheath knives. **Patterns:** Hunters and neck knives. **Technical:** My own Damascus, 5160, 1095, 1984, L6, and W2. Forge and stock removal. Does own heat treating and makes own sheaths. **Prices:** $100 to $500. **Remarks:** Part-time maker. **Mark:** Moon Munjas.

MURA, DENIS
Via Pesciule 15 56021, Cascina (Pi), ITALY, Phone: +39 3388365277, zeb1d@libero.it; Web: www.denismura.com

Specialties: Straight knives. **Patterns:** Hunters, bowies, camp knives and everyday carry (EDC) knives. **Technical:** Grinds A2, D2, W2; 440C, RWL 34; CPM 154, Sleipner, Niolox, 1095, 1084, 1070, C145SC, Becut, damascus and san mai steels. **Prices:** Start at $250. **Remarks:** Part-time maker; first knife made in 2006. **Mark:** MD.

MURSKI, RAY
12129 Captiva Ct, Reston, VA 22091-1204, Phone: 703-264-1102, rmurski@gmail.com

Specialties: Fancy working/using folders of his design. **Patterns:** Hunters, slip-joint folders and utility/camp knives. **Technical:** Grinds CPM-3V **Prices:** $125 to $500. **Remarks:** Spare-time maker; first knife sold in 1996. **Mark:** Engraved name with serial number under name.

MUTZ, JEFF
8210 Rancheria Dr. Unit 7, Rancho Cucamonga, CA 91730, Phone: 909-559-7129, jmutzknives@hotmail.com; Web: www.jmutzknives.com

Specialties: Traditional working/using fixed blade and slip-jointed knives of own design and customer specs. **Patterns:** Hunters, skinners, and folders. **Technical:** Forges and grinds all steels Offers scrimshaw. **Prices:** $225 to $800. **Remarks:** Full-time maker, first knife sold in 1998. **Mark:** First initial, last name over "maker."

MYERS, PAUL
644 Maurice St, Wood River, IL 62095, Phone: 618-258-1707

Specialties: Fancy working straight knives and folders. **Patterns:** Full range of folders, straight hunters and Bowies; tie tacks; knife and fork sets. **Technical:** Grinds D2, 440C, ATS-34 and 154CM. **Prices:** $100 to $350; some to $3000. **Remarks:** Full-time maker; first knife sold in 1974. **Mark:** Initials with setting sun on front; name and number on back.

MYERS, STEVE
1429 Carolina Ave., Springfield, IL 62702, Phone: 217-416-0800, myersknives@ymail.com

Specialties: Working straight knives and integrals. **Patterns:** Camp knives, hunters, skinners, Bowies, and boot knives. **Technical:** Forges own Damascus and high carbon steels. **Prices:** $250 to $1,000. **Remarks:** Full-time maker, first knife sold in 1985. **Mark:** Last name in logo.

N

NADEAU, BRIAN
SHARPBYDESIGN LLC, 8 Sand Hill Rd., Stanhope, NJ 07874, Phone: 862-258-0792, nadeau@sharpbydesign.com; Web: www.sharpbydesign.com

Specialties: High-quality tactical fixed blades and folders, collector and working blades. All blades and sheaths of maker's own design. Designs, writes programs and machines all components on CNC equipment, nothing water jet, everything hand finished. **Technical:** Works with new CPM steels, but loves to get an order for a W2 blade with a nice hamon or temper line. **Prices:** $100 and up. **Remarks:** Part-time maker. **Mark:** Name in script, or initials "BN" skewed on top of one another.

NARASADA, MAMORU
9115-8 Nakaminowa, Minowa-machi, Kamiina-gun, NAGANO, JAPAN 399-4601, Phone: 81-265-79-3960, Fax: 81-265-79-3960

Specialties: Utility working straight knife. **Patterns:** Hunting, fishing, and camping knife. **Technical:** Grind and forges / ATS34, VG10, 440C, CRM07. **Prices:** $150 to $500, some higher. **Remarks:** First knife sold in 2003. **Mark:** M.NARASADA with initial logo.

NATEN, GREG
1804 Shamrock Way, Bakersfield, CA 93304-3921

Specialties: Fancy and working/using folders of his design. **Patterns:** Fighters, hunters and locking folders. **Technical:** Grinds 440C, ATS-34 and CPM440V. Heat-treats; prefers desert ironwood, stag and mother-of-pearl. Designs and sews leather sheaths for straight knives. **Prices:** $175 to $600; some to $950. **Remarks:** Spare-time maker; first knife sold in 1992. **Mark:** Last name above battle-ax, handmade.

NAUDE, LOUIS
P.O. Box 1103, Okahandja, Namibia, AFRICA 7560, Phone: +264 (0)81-38-36-285, info@louisnaude.co.za Web: www.louisnaude.co.za

Specialties: Folders, Hunters, Custom. **Patterns:** See Website. **Technical:** Stock removal, African materials. **Prices:** See website. **Remarks:** Still the tool! **Mark:** Louis Naude Knives with family crest.

NEALY, BUD
125 Raccoon Way, Stroudsburg, PA 18360, Phone: 570-402-1018, Fax: 570-402-1018, bnealy@ptd.net; Web: www.budnealyknifemaker.com

Specialties: Original design concealment knives with designer multi-concealment sheath system. **Patterns:** Fixed Blades and Folders **Technical:** Grinds CPM 154, XHP, and Damascus. **Prices:** $200 to $2500. **Remarks:** Full-time maker; first knife sold in 1980. **Mark:** Name, city, state or signature.

NEASE, WILLIAM
2336 Front Rd., LaSalle, ON, CANADA Canada N9J 2C4, wnease@hotmail.com

Web: www.unsubtleblades.com
Specialties: Hatchets, choppers, and Japanese-influenced designs. **Technical:** Stock removal. Works A-2, D-2, S-7, O-1, powder stainless alloys, composite laminate blades with steel edges. **Prices:** $125 to $2200. **Remarks:** Part-time maker since 1994. **Mark:** Initials W.M.N. engraved in cursive on exposed tangs or on the spine of blades.

NEDVED, DAN
206 Park Dr, Kalispell, MT 59901, bushido2222@yahoo.com
Specialties: Slip joint folders, liner locks, straight knives. **Patterns:** Mostly traditional or modern blend with traditional lines. **Technical:** Grinds ATS-34, 440C, 1095 and uses other makers Damascus. **Prices:** $95 and up. Mostly in the $150 to $200 range. **Remarks:** Part-time maker, averages 2 a month. **Mark:** Dan Nedved or Nedved with serial # on opposite side.

NEELY, GREG
5419 Pine St, Bellaire, TX 77401, Phone: 713-991-2677, gtneely64@comcast.net
Specialties: Traditional patterns and his own patterns for work and/or collecting. **Patterns:** Hunters, Bowies and utility/camp knives. **Technical:** Forges own Damascus, 1084, 5160 and some tool steels. Differentially tempers. **Prices:** $225 to $5000. **Remarks:** Part-time maker; first knife sold in 1987. **Mark:** Last name or interlocked initials, MS.

NEILSON, J
187 Cistern Ln., Towanda, PA 18848, Phone: 570-721-0470, mountainhollow@epix.net; Web: www.mountainhollow.net
Specialties: Working and collectable fixed blade knives. **Patterns:** Hunter/fighters, Bowies, neck knives and daggers. **Technical:** Multiple high-carbon steels as well as maker's own damascus. **Prices:** $100 to $4,500. **Remarks:** ABS Master Smith, full-time maker, first knife sold in 2000, doing business as Neilson's Mountain Hollow. Each knife comes with a sheath. **Mark:** J. Neilson MS.

NELL, CHAD
2424 E. 2070 S, St. George, UT 84790, Phone: 435-229-6442, chad@nellknives.com; Web: www.nellknives.com
Specialties: Frame-lock folders and fixed blades. **Patterns:** Templar, ESG, Hybrid and Loveless patterns. **Technical:** Grinds CPM-154, ATS-34. **Prices:** Starting at $300. **Remarks:** Full-time maker since Sep 2011, First knife made in May 2010. **Mark:** C. Nell Utah, USA or C. Nell Kona, Hawaii.

NELSON, KEN
2712 17th St., Racine, WI 53405, Phone: 262-456-7519 or 262-664-5293, ken@ironwolfonline.com Web: www.ironwolfonline.com
Specialties: Working straight knives, period pieces. **Patterns:** Utility, hunters, dirks, daggers, throwers, hawks, axes, swords, pole arms and blade blanks as well. **Technical:** Forges 5160, 52100, W2, 10xx, L6, carbon steels and own Damascus. Does his own heat treating. **Prices:** $50 to $350, some to $3000. **Remarks:** Part-time maker. First knife sold in 1995. Doing business as Iron Wolf Forge. **Mark:** Stylized wolf paw print.

NETO JR.,, NELSON AND DE CARVALHO, HENRIQUE M.
R. Joao Margarido No 20-V, Bragança Paulista, SP, BRAZIL 12900-000, Phone: 011-7843-6889, Fax: 011-7843-6889
Specialties: Straight knives and folders. **Patterns:** Bowies, katanas, jambyias and others. **Technical:** Forges high-carbon steels. **Prices:** $70 to $3000. **Remarks:** Full-time makers; first knife sold in 1990. **Mark:** HandN.

NEVLING, MARK
BURR OAK KNIVES, 3567 N. M52, Owosso, MI 48867, Phone: 989-472-3167, burroakknives@aol.com; Web: www.burroakknives.com
Specialties: Tactical folders using stainless over high-carbon San Mai. **Patterns:** Hunters, fighters, bowies, folders and small executive knives. **Technical:** Convex grinds, forges, uses only high-carbon and damascus. **Prices:** $200 to $4,000. **Remarks:** Full-time maker, first knife sold 1988. Apprentice damascus smith to George Werth and Doug Ponzio.

NEWBERRY, ALLEN
PO BOX 301, Lowell, AR 72745, Phone: 479-530-6439, newberry@newberryknives.com Web: www.newberryknives.com
Specialties: Fixed blade knives both forged and stock removal. **Patterns:** Traditional patterns as well as newer designs inspired by historical and international blades. **Technical:** Uses 1095, W2, 5160, 154-CM, other steels by request. **Prices:** $150 to $450+. **Remarks:** Many of the knives feature hamons. **Mark:** Newberry with a capital N for forged pieces and newberry with a lower case n for stock removal pieces.

NEWCOMB, CORBIN
628 Woodland Ave, Moberly, MO 65270, Phone: 660-263-4639
Specialties: Working straight knives and folders; period pieces. **Patterns:** Hunters, axes, Bowies, folders, buckskinned blades and boots. **Technical:** Hollow-grinds D2, 440C and 154CM; prefers natural handle materials. Makes own Damascus; offers cable Damascus. **Prices:** $100 to $500. **Remarks:** Full-time maker; first knife sold in 1982. Doing business as Corbin Knives. **Mark:** First name and serial number.

NEWHALL, TOM
3602 E 42nd Stravenue, Tucson, AZ 85713, Phone: 520-721-0562, gggaz@aol.com

NEWTON, LARRY
1758 Pronghorn Ct, Jacksonville, FL 32225, Phone: 904-537-2066, lnewton1@comcast.net; Web: larrynewtonknives.com
Specialties: Traditional and slender high-grade gentlemen's automatic folders, locking liner type tactical, and working straight knives. **Patterns:** Front release locking folders, interframes, hunters, and skinners. **Technical:** Grinds Damascus, ATS-34, 440C and D2. **Prices:** Folders start at $350, straights start at $150. **Remarks:** Retired teacher. Full-time

maker. First knife sold in 1989. Won Best Folder for 2008 -Blade Magazine. **Mark:** Last name.

NEWTON, RON
223 Ridge Ln, London, AR 72847, Phone: 479-293-3001, rnewton@centurylink.net
Specialties: All types of folders and fixed blades. Blackpowder gun knife combos. **Patterns:** Traditional slip joint, multi-blade patterns, antique bowie repros. **Technical:** Forges traditional and mosaid damascus. Performs engraving and gold inlay. **Prices:** $500 and up. **Remarks:** Creates hidden mechanisms in assisted opening folders. **Mark:** NEWTON M.S. in a western invitation font."

NICHOLS, CALVIN
710 Colleton Rd., Raleigh, NC 27610, Phone: 919-523-4841, calvin.nichols@nicholsknives.com; Web: http://nicholsknives.com
Specialties: Flame-colored high carbon damascus. **Patterns:** Fixed blades or folders, bowies and daggers. **Technical:** Stock removal. **Prices:** Start at $200. **Remarks:** Full-time maker, 22 years experience, own heat treating, 2012 Best Custom and High Art winner, National and North Carolina Knifemakers Guild member. **Mark:** First, last name--city, state.

NICHOLS, CHAD
1125 Cr 185, Blue Springs, MS 38828, Phone: 662-538-5966, chadn28@hotmail.com Web: chadnicholsdamascus.com
Specialties: Gents folders and everyday tactical/utility style knives and fixed hunters. **Technical:** Makes own stainless damascus, mosaic damascus, and high carbon damascus. **Prices:** $450 -$1000. **Mark:** Name and Blue Springs.

NICHOLSON, R. KENT
16502 Garfield Ave., Monkton, MD 21111, Phone: 410-323-6925
Specialties: Large using knives. **Patterns:** Bowies and camp knives in the Moran-style. **Technical:** Forges W2, 9260, 5160; makes Damascus. **Prices:** $150 to $995. **Remarks:** Part-time maker; first knife sold in 1984. **Mark:** Name.

NIELSON, JEFF V
1060 S Jones Rd, Monroe, UT 84754, Phone: 435-527-4242, jvn1u205@hotmail.com
Specialties: Classic knives of his design and to customer specs. **Patterns:** Fighters, hunters; miniatures. **Technical:** Grinds 440C stainless and Damascus. **Prices:** $100 to $1200. **Remarks:** Part-time maker; first knife sold in 1991. **Mark:** Name, location.

NIEMUTH, TROY
3143 North Ave, Sheboygan, WI 53083, Phone: 414-452-2927
Specialties: Period pieces and working/using straight knives of his design and to customer specs. **Patterns:** Hunters and utility/camp knives. **Technical:** Grinds 440C, 1095 and A2. **Prices:** $85 to $350; some to $500. **Remarks:** Full-time maker; first knife sold in 1995. **Mark:** Etched last name.

NILSSON, JONNY WALKER
Akkavare 16, 93391 Arvidsjaur, SWEDEN, Phone: +46 702144207, 0960.13048@telia.com; Web: www.jwnknives.com
Specialties: High-end collectible Nordic hunters, engraved reindeer antler. World class freehand engravings. Matching engraved sheaths in leather, bone and Arctic wood with inlays. Combines traditional techniques and design with his own innovations. Master Bladesmith who specializes in forging mosaic Damascus. Sells unique mosaic Damascus bar stock to folder makers. **Patterns:** Own designs and traditional Sami designs. **Technical:** Mosaic Damascus of UHB 20 C 15N20 with pure nickel, hardness HRC 58-60. **Prices:** $1500 to $6000. **Remarks:** Full-time maker since 1988. Nordic Champion (5 countries) numerous times, 50 first prizes in Scandinavian shows. Yearly award in his name in Nordic Championship. Knives inspired by 10,000 year old indigenous Sami culture. **Mark:** JN on sheath, handle, custom wood box. JWN on blade.

NIRO, FRANK
1948 Gloaming Dr, Kamloops, B.C., CANADA V1S1P8, Phone: 250-372-8332, niro@telus.net
Specialties: Liner locking folding knives in his designs in what might be called standard patterns. **Technical:** Enjoys grinding mosaic Damascus with pure nickel of the make up for blades that are often double ground; as well as meteorite for bolsters which are then etched and heat colored. Uses 416 stainless for spacers with inlays of natural materials, gem stones with also file work. Liners are made from titanium are most often fully file worked and anodized. Only uses natural materials particularly mammoth ivory for scales. **Prices:** $500 to $1500 **Remarks:** Full time maker. Has been selling knives for over thirty years. **Mark:** Last name on the inside of the spacer.

NISHIUCHI, MELVIN S
6121 Forest Park Dr, Las Vegas, NV 89156, Phone: 702-501-3724, msnknives@yahoo.com
Specialties: Collectable quality using/working knives. **Patterns:** Locking liner folders, fighters, hunters and fancy personal knives. **Technical:** Grinds ATS-34 and Devin Thomas Damascus; prefers semi-precious stone and exotic natural handle materials. **Prices:** $375 to $2000. **Remarks:** Part-time maker; first knife sold in 1985. **Mark:** Circle with a line above it.

NOLEN, STEVE
3325 Teton, Longmont, CO 80504-6251, Phone: 720-334-1801, bladesmith@nolenknives.com or stevenolen1@msn.com; Web: www.nolenknives.com
Specialties: Working knives; display pieces. **Patterns:** Wide variety of straight knives, butterflies and buckles. **Technical:** Grind D2, 440C and 154CM. Offer filework; make exotic handles. **Prices:** $150 to $800; some higher. **Remarks:** Full-time maker; Steve is third generation maker. **Mark:** NK in oval logo.

NOLTE, BARBIE
10801 Gram B Cir., Lowell, AR 72745, Phone: 479-283-2095, barbie.b@gmail.com
Specialties: Collector-grade high art knives. **Technical:** Hollow grinds high-carbon, mosaic-damascus blades. Limited supply. **Prices:** Start at $600. All prices include handmade exotic leather sheaths. **Mark:** B Bell and B Nolte.

NOLTE, STEVE
10801 Gram B Cir., Lowell, AR 72745, Phone: 479-629-1676, snolte@alertalarmsys.com; Web: www.snolteknives.com
Specialties: Fancy hunters and skinners, a few fighters, some collector-grade, high-art knives. One-of-a-kind mosaic handle creations including exotic stone work. **Technical:** Mostly high-carbon damascus, some stainless damascus with very few straight stainless blades. Hollow grinds. **Prices:** Start at $400. All prices include handmade sheaths, mostly exotic leathers. **Mark:** S.Nolte.

NORDELL, INGEMAR
SkarpŒvagen 5, FŠrila, SWEDEN 82041, Phone: 0651-23347, ingi@ingemarnordell.se; Web: www.ingemarnordell.se
Specialties: Classic working and using straight knives. **Patterns:** Hunters, Bowies and fighters. **Technical:** Forges and grinds ATS-34, D2 and Sandvik. **Prices:** $300 to $3,000. **Remarks:** Part-time maker; first knife sold in 1985. **Mark:** Initials or name.

NOREN, DOUGLAS E
14676 Boom Rd, Springlake, MI 49456, Phone: 616-842-4247, gnoren@icsdata.com
Specialties: Hand forged blades, custom built and made to order. Hand file work, carving and casting. Stag and stacked handles. Replicas of Scagel and Joseph Rogers. Hand tooled custom made sheaths. **Technical:** Master smith, 5160, 52100 and 1084 steel. **Prices:** Start at $250. **Remarks:** Sole authorship, works in all mediums, ABS Mastersmith, all knives come with a custom hand-tooled sheath. Also makes anvils. Enjoys the challenge and meeting people.

NORFLEET, ROSS W
4110 N Courthouse Rd, Providence Forge, VA 23140-3420, Phone: 804-966-2596, rossknife@aol.com
Specialties: Classic, traditional and working/using knives of his design or in standard patterns. **Patterns:** Hunters and folders. **Technical:** Hollow-grinds 440C and ATS-34. **Prices:** $150 to $550. **Remarks:** Part-time maker; first knife sold in 1992. **Mark:** Last name.

NORTON, DON
95N Wilkison Ave, Port Townsend, WA 98368-2534, Phone: 306-385-1978
Specialties: Fancy and plain straight knives. **Patterns:** Hunters, small Bowies, tantos, boot knives, fillets. **Technical:** Prefers 440C, Micarta, exotic woods and other natural handle materials. Hollow-grinds all knives except fillet knives. **Prices:** $185 to $2800; average is $200. **Remarks:** Full-time maker; first knife sold in 1980. **Mark:** Full name, Hsi Shuai, city, state.

NOWACKI, STEPHEN R.
167 King Georges Ave, Regents Park, Southampton, Hampshire, ENGLAND SO154LD, Phone: 023 81 785 630 or 079 29 737 872, stephen.nowacki@hotmail.co.uk Web: www.whitetigerknives.com
Specialties: Hand-forged, bowies, daggers, tactical blades, hunters and mountain-man style folders. **Technical:** Hitachi white paper steel and stainless carbon San Mai. Heat treats and uses natural handle materials. **Prices:** $200 -$1500. **Remarks:** Full-time maker. First knife sold in 2000. Doing business as White Tiger Knives. **Mark:** Stylized W T.

NOWLAND, RICK
3677 E Bonnie Rd, Waltonville, IL 62894, Phone: 618-279-3170, ricknowland@frontiernet.net
Specialties: Slip joint folders in traditional patterns. **Patterns:** Trapper, whittler, sowbelly, toothpick and copperhead. **Technical:** Uses ATS-34, bolsters and liners have integral construction. **Prices:** $225 to $1000. **Remarks:** Part-time maker. **Mark:** Last name.

NUCKELS, STEPHEN J
1105 Potomac Ave, Hagerstown, MD 21742, Phone: 301-739-1287, sgnucks@myactv.net
Specialties: Traditional using/working/everyday carry knives and small neck knives. **Patterns:** Hunters, bowies, Drop and trailing point knives, frontier styles. **Technical:** Hammer forges carbon steels, stock removal. Modest silver wire inlay and file work. Sheath work. **Remarks:** Spare-time maker forging under Potomac Forge, first knife made in 2008. Member W.F. Moran Jr. Foundation, American Bladesmith Society. **Mark:** Initials.

NUNN, GREGORY
HC64 Box 2107, Castle Valley, UT 84532, Phone: 435-259-8607
Specialties: High-art working and using knives of his design; new edition knife with handle made from anatomized dinosaur bone, first ever made. **Patterns:** Flaked stone knives. **Technical:** Uses gem-quality agates, jaspers and obsidians for blades. **Prices:** $250 to $2300. **Remarks:** Full-time maker; first knife sold in 1989. **Mark:** Name, knife and edition numbers, year made.

O

OATES, LEE
PO BOX 1391, La Porte, TX 77572, Phone: 281-471-6060, bearoates@att.net
Web: www.bearclawknives.com
Specialties: Friction folders, period correct replicas, traditional, working and primitive knives of my design or to customer specs. **Patterns:** Bowies, teflon-coated fighters, daggers, hunters, fillet and kitchen cutlery. **Technical:** Heat treating service for other makers. Teaches blacksmithing/bladesmithing classes. Forges carbon, 440C, D2, and

makes own Damascus, stock removal on SS and kitchen cutlery, Teflon coatings available on custom hunters/fighters, makes own sheaths. **Prices:** $150 to $2500. **Remarks:** Full-time maker and heat treater since 1996. First knife sold in 1988. **Mark:** Harmony (yin/yang) symbol with two bear tracks inside all forged blades; etched "Commanche Cutlery" on SS kitchen cutlery.

O'BRIEN, MIKE J.
3807 War Bow, San Antonio, TX 78238, Phone: 210-256-0673, obrien8700@att.net
Specialties: Quality straight knives of his design. **Patterns:** Mostly daggers (safe queens), some hunters. **Technical:** Grinds 440c, ATS-34, and CPM-154. Emphasis on clean workmanship and solid design. Likes hand-rubbed blades and fittings, exotic woods. **Prices:** $300 to $700 and up. **Remarks:** Part-time maker, made first knife in 1988. **Mark:** O'BRIEN in semi-circle.

OCHS, CHARLES F
124 Emerald Lane, Largo, FL 33771, Phone: 727-536-3827, Fax: 727-536-3827, charlesox@oxforge.com; Web: www.oxforge.com
Specialties: Working knives; period pieces. **Patterns:** Hunters, fighters, Bowies, buck skinners and folders. **Technical:** Forges 52100, 5160 and his own Damascus. **Prices:** $150 to $1800; some to $2500. **Remarks:** Full-time maker; first knife sold in 1978. **Mark:** OX Forge.

OCHS, ERIC
PO BOX 1311, Sherwood, OR 97140, Phone: 503-925-9790, Fax: 503-925-9790, eric@ochs.com Web: www.ochssherworx.com
Specialties: Tactical folders and flippers, as well as fixed blades for tactical, hunting and camping. **Patterns:** Tactical liner- and frame-lock folders with texture in various synthetic and natural materials. **Technical:** Focus on powder metals, including CPM-S30V, Elmax, CPM-154, CPM-3V and CPM-S35VN, as well as damascus steels. Flat, hollow, compound and Loveless-style grinds. **Prices:** $300 -$2,500. **Remarks:** Full-time maker; made first knife in 2008 and started selling knives in mid-2009. **Mark:** The words "Ochs Sherworx" separated by an eight point compass insignia was used through 2013. Beginning in January 2014, "Ochs Worx" separated by navigation star compass insignia.

ODOM JR., VICTOR L.
PO Box 572, North, SC 29112, Phone: 803-247-2749, cell 803-608-0829, vlodom3@tds.net Web: www.knifemakercentral.com
Specialties: Forged knives and tomahawks; stock removal knives. **Patterns:** Hunters, Bowies, George Herron patterns, and folders. **Technical:** Use 1095, 5160, 52100 high carbon and alloy steels, ATS-34, and 154 CM. **Prices:** Straight knives $60 and up. Folders $250 and up. **Remarks:** Student of Mr. George Henron. SCAK.ORG. Secretary of the Couth Carolina Association of Knifemakers. **Mark:** Steel stamp "ODOM" and etched "Odom Forge North, SC" plus a serial number.

OELOFSE, TINUS
P.O. Box 33879, Glenstantia, Pretoria, SOUTH AFRICA 0100, Phone: +27-82-3225090, tinusoelofseknives@gmail.com
Specialties Top-class folders, mainly LinerLocks, and practical fixed blades. **Technical:** Using damascus, mostly Damasteel, and blade billets. Mammoth ivory, mammoth tooth, mother-of-pearl, gold and black-lip-pearl handles for folders. Giraffe bone, warthog ivory, horn and African hardwoods for hunters. Deep relief engraving, mostly leaf and scroll, and daughter Mariscke's scrimshaw. Likes to work on themed knives and special projects. Hand-stitched sheaths by Kitty. **Prices:** $350 to $1,500. **Mark:** Tinus Oelofse in an oval logo with a dagger outline used for the "T."

OGDEN, BILL
OGDEN KNIVES, PO Box 52, Avis, PA 17721, Phone: 570-974-9114
Specialties: One-of-a-kind, liner-lock folders, hunters, skinners, minis. **Technical:** Grinds ATS-34, 440-C, D2, 52100, Damascus, natural and unnatural handle materials, hand-stitched custom sheaths. **Prices:** $50 and up. **Remarks:** Part-time maker since 1992. Marks: Last name or "OK" stamp (Ogden Knives).

OGLETREE JR., BEN R
2815 Israel Rd, Livingston, TX 77351, Phone: 409-327-8315
Specialties: Working/using straight knives of his design. **Patterns:** Hunters, kitchen and utility/camp knives. **Technical:** Grinds ATS-34, W1 and 1075; heat-treats. **Prices:** $200 to $400. **Remarks:** Part-time maker; first knife sold in 1955. **Mark:** Last name, city and state in oval with a tree on either side.

O'HARE, SEAN
1831 Rte. 776, Grand Manan, NB, CANADA E5G 2H9, Phone: 506-662-8524, sean@oharecustomknives.com; Web: www.oharecustomknives.com
Specialties: Fixed blade hunters and folders. **Patterns:** Fixed and folding knives, daily carry to collectible art. **Technical:** Stock removal, flat ground. **Prices:** $250 USD to $2,000 USD. **Remarks:** Strives to balance aesthetics, functionality and durability. **Mark:** S O'Hare.

OLIVE, MICHAEL E
6388 Angora Mt Rd, Leslie, AR 72645, Phone: 870-363-4668
Specialties: Fixed blades. **Patterns:** Bowies, camp knives, fighters and hunters. **Technical:** Forged blades of 1084, W2, 5160, Damascus of 1084, and1572. **Prices:** $250 and up. **Remarks:** Received J.S. stamp in 2005. **Mark:** Olive.

OLIVER, TODD D
719 Artesian Rd. #63, Cheyenne, WY 82007, Phone: 812-821-5928, tdblues7@aol.com
Specialties: Damascus hunters and daggers. High-carbon as well. **Patterns:** Ladder, twist random. **Technical:** Sole author of all his blades. **Prices:** $350 and up. **Remarks:** Learned bladesmithing from Jim Batson at the ABS school and Damascus from Billy

Merritt in Indiana. **Mark:** T.D. Oliver Spencer IN. Two crossed swords and a battle ax.

OLSON, DARROLD E

PO Box 1182, McMinnville, OR 97128, Phone: 541-285-1412

Specialties: Straight knives and folders of his design and to customer specs. **Patterns:** Hunters, liner locks and slip joints. **Technical:** Grinds ATS-34, 154CM and 440C. Uses anodized titanium; sheaths wet-molded. **Prices:** $125 to $550 and up. **Remarks:** Part-time maker; first knife sold in 1989. **Mark:** Name, type of steel and year.

OLSON, JOE

2008 4th Ave., #8, Great Falls, MT 59405, Phone: 406-735-4404, olsonhandmade@hotmail.com; Web: www.olsonhandmade.com

Specialties: Theme based art knives specializing in mosaic Damascus autos, folders, and straight knives, all sole authorship. **Patterns:** Mas. **Technical:** Foix. **Prices:** $300 to $5000 with most in the $3500 range. **Remarks:** Full-time maker for 15 years. **Mark:** Folders marked OLSON relief carved into back bar. Carbon steel straight knives stamped OLSON, forged hunters also stamped JS on reverse side.

OLSON, ROD

Box 373, Nanton, AB, CANADA T0L 1R0, Phone: 403-646-5838, rod.olson@hotmail.com

Patterns: Button lock folders. **Technical:** Grinds RWL 34 blade steel, titanium frames. **Prices:** Mid range. **Remarks:** Part-time maker; first knife sold in 1979. **Mark:** Last name.

OLSZEWSKI, STEPHEN

1820 Harkney Hill Rd, Coventry, RI 02816, Phone: 401-397-4774, blade5377@yahoo.com; Web: www.olszewskiknives.com

Specialties: Lock back, liner locks, automatics (art knives). **Patterns:** One-of-a-kind art knives specializing in figurals. **Technical:** Damascus steel, titanium file worked liners, fossil ivory and pearl. Double actions. **Prices:** $400 to $20,000. **Remarks:** Will custom build to your specifications. Quality work with guarantee. **Mark:** SCO inside fish symbol. Also "Olszewski."

O'MACHEARLEY, MICHAEL

129 Lawnview Dr., Wilmington, OH 45177, Phone: 937-728-2818, omachearleycustomknives@yahoo.com

Specialties: Forged and Stock removal; hunters, skinners, bowies, plain to fancy. **Technical:** ATS-34 and 5160, forges own Damascus. **Prices:** $180-$1000 and up. **Remarks:** Full-time maker, first knife made in 1999. **Mark:** Last name and shamrock.

O'MALLEY, DANIEL

4338 Evanston Ave N, Seattle, WA 98103, Phone: 206-261-1735

Specialties: Custom chef's knives. **Remarks:** Making knives since 1997.

ONION, KENNETH J

47-501 Hui Kelu St, Kaneohe, HI 96744, Phone: 808-239-1300, shopjunky@aol.com; Web: www.kenonionknives.com

Specialties: Folders featuring speed safe as well as other invention gadgets. **Patterns:** Hybrid, art, fighter, utility. **Technical:** S30V, CPM 154V, Cowry Y, SQ-2 and Damascus. **Prices:** $500 to $20,000. **Remarks:** Full-time maker; designer and inventor. First knife sold in 1991. **Mark:** Name and state.

O'QUINN, W. LEE

2654 Watson St., Elgin, SC 29045, Phone: 803-438-8322, wleeoquinn@bellsouth.net; Web: www.creativeknifeworks.com

Specialties: Hunters, utility, working, tactical and neck knives. **Technical:** Grinds ATS-34, CPM-154, 5160, D2, 1095 and damascus steels. **Prices:** Start at $100. **Remarks:** Member of South Carolina Association of Knifemakers. **Mark:** O'Quinn.

ORFORD, BEN

Nethergreen Farm, Ridgeway Cross, Malvern, Worcestershire, ENGLAND WR13 5JS, Phone: 44 01886 880410, web: www.benorford.com

Specialties: Working knives for woodcraft and the outdoorsman, made to his own designs. **Patterns:** Mostly flat Scandinavian grinds, full and partial tang. Also makes specialist woodcraft tools and hook knives. Custom leather sheaths by Lois, his wife. **Technical:** Grinds and forges 01, EN9, EN43, EN45 plus recycled steels. Heat treats. **Prices:** $25 -$650. **Remarks:** Full-time maker; first knife made in 1997. **Mark:** Celtic knot with name underneath.

ORTON, RICH

739 W. Palm Dr., Covina, CA 91722, Phone: 626-332-3441, rorton2@ca.rr.com

Specialties: Straight knives only. **Patterns:** Fighters, hunters, skinners. **Technical:** Grinds ATS-34. Heat treats by Paul Bos. **Prices:** $100 to $1000. **Remarks:** Full-time maker; first knife sold in 1992. Doing business as Orton Knife Works. **Mark:** Last name, city state (maker)

OSBORNE, DONALD H

5840 N McCall, Clovis, CA 93611, Phone: 559-299-9483, Fax: 559-298-1751, oforge@sbcglobal.net

Specialties: Traditional working using straight knives and folder of his design. **Patterns:** Working straight knives, Bowies, hunters, camp knives and folders. **Technical:** Forges carbon steels and makes Damascus. Grinds ATS-34, 154CM, and 440C. **Prices:** $150 and up. **Remarks:** Part-time maker. **Mark:** Last name logo and J.S.

OSBORNE, WARREN

#2-412 Alysa Ln, Waxahachie, TX 75167, Phone: 972-935-0899, Fax: 972-937-9004, ossie6@mac.com Web: www.osborneknives.com

Specialties: Investment grade collectible, interframes, one-of-a-kinds; unique locking mechanisms and cutting competition knives. **Patterns:** Folders; bolstered and interframes; conventional lockers, front lockers and back lockers; some slip-joints; some high-art pieces. **Technical:** Grinds CPM M4, BG42, CPM S30V, Damascus -some forged and stock removed cutting competition knives. **Prices:** $1200 to $3500; some to $5000. Interframes $1250 to $3000. **Remarks:** Full-time maker; first knife sold in 1980. **Mark:** Last name in boomerang logo.

OTT, FRED

1257 Rancho Durango Rd, Durango, CO 81303, Phone: 970-375-9669, fredsknives@wildblue.net

Patterns: Bowies, hunters tantos and daggers. **Technical:** Forges 1086M, W2 and Damascus. **Prices:** $250 to $2,000. **Remarks:** Full-time maker. **Mark:** Last name.

OTT, TED

154 Elgin Woods Ln., Elgin, TX 78621, Phone: 512-413-2243, tedottknives@aol.com

Specialties: Fixed blades, chef knives, butcher knives, bowies, fillet and hunting knives. **Technical:** Use mainly CPM powder steel, also ATS-34 and D-2. B>**Prices:** $250 -$1000, depending on embellishments, including scrimshaw and engraving. **Remarks:** Part-time maker; sold first knife in 1993. Won world cutting competition title in 2010 and 2012, along with the Bladesports championship. **Mark:** Ott Knives Elgin Texas.

OUYE, KEITH

PO Box 25307, Honolulu, HI 96825, Phone: 808-395-7000, keith@keithouyeknives.com; Web: www.keithouyeknives.com

Specialties: Folders with 1/8 blades and titanium handles. **Patterns:** Tactical design with liner lock and flipper. **Technical:** Blades are stainless steel ATS 34, CPM154 and S30V. Titanium liners (.071) and scales 3/16 pivots and stop pin, titanium pocket clip. Heat treat by Paul Bos.**Prices:** $495 to $995, with engraved knives starting at $1,200. **Remarks:** Engraving done by C.J. Cal, Bruce Shaw, Lisa Tomlin and Tom Ferry. Retired, so basically a full time knifemaker. Sold first fixed blade in 2004 and first folder in 2005. **Mark:** Ouye/Hawaii with steel type on back side Other: Selected by Blade Magazine (March 2006 issue) as one of five makers to watch in 2006.

OVEREYNDER, T R

1800 S. Davis Dr, Arlington, TX 76013, Phone: 817-277-4812, Fax: 817-277-4812, trovereynder@gmail.com or tom@overeynderknives.com; Web: www.overeynderknives.com

Specialties: Highly finished collector-grade knives. Multi-blades. **Patterns:** Fighters, Bowies, daggers, locking folders, 70 percent collector-grade multi blade slip joints, 25 percent interframe, 5 percent fixed blade **Technical:** Grinds CPM-D2, CPM-S60V, CPM-S30V, CPM-154, CPM-M4, BG-42, CTS-XHP, PSF27, RWL-34 and vendor supplied damascus. Has been making titanium-frame folders since 1977. **Prices:** $800 to $2,500, some to $9,000. **Remarks:** Full-time maker; first knife sold in 1977. Doing business as TRO Knives. **Mark:** T.R. OVEREYNDER KNIVES, city and state.

OWEN, DAVID J.A.

30 New Forest Rd., Forest Town, Johannesburg, SOUTH AFRICA, Phone: +27-11-486-1086; cell: +27-82-990-7178, djaowen25@gmail.com

Specialties: Steak knife sets, carving sets, bird-and-trout knives, top-end hunting knives, LinerLock folders. **Patterns:** Variety of knives and techniques. **Technical:** Stock-removal method, freehand hollow and flat grinds, exotic handle materials such as African hardwoods, giraffe bone, hippo tooth and warthog tusk. **Prices:** $150 and up. **Remarks:** Full-time maker since 1993. **Mark:** Two knives back-to-back with words "Owen" and "original" acid etched above and below the knives.

OWENS, DONALD

2274 Lucille Ln, Melbourne, FL 32935, Phone: 321-254-9765

OWENS, JOHN

14500 CR 270, Nathrop, CO 81236, Phone: 719-207-0067

Specialties: Hunters. **Prices:** $225 to $425 some to $700. **Remarks:** Spare-time maker. **Mark:** Last name.

OWNBY, JOHN C

708 Morningside Tr., Murphy, TX 75094-4365, Phone: 972-442-7352, john@johnownby.com; Web: www.johnownby.com

Specialties: Hunters, utility/camp knives. **Patterns:** Hunters, locking folders and utility/camp knives. **Technical:** 440C, D2 and ATS-34. All blades are flat ground. Prefers natural materials for handles—exotic woods, horn and antler. **Prices:** $150 to $350; some to $500. **Remarks:** Part-time maker; first knife sold in 1993. Doing business as John C. Ownby Handmade Knives. **Mark:** Name, city, state.

OYSTER, LOWELL R

543 Grant Rd, Corinth, ME 04427, Phone: 207-884-8663

Specialties: Traditional and original designed multi-blade slip-joint folders. **Patterns:** Hunters, minis, camp and fishing knives. **Technical:** Grinds 01; heat-treats. **Prices:** $55 to $450; some to $750. **Remarks:** Full-time maker; first knife sold in 1981. **Mark:** A scallop shell.

P

PACKARD, RONNIE

301 White St., Bonham, TX 75418, Phone: 903-227-3131, packardknives@gmail.com; Web: www.packardknives.com

Specialties: Bowies, folders (lockback, slip joint, frame lock, Hobo knives) and hunters of all sizes. **Technical:** Grinds 440C, ATS-34, D2 and stainless damascus. Makes own sheaths, does heat treating and sub-zero quenching in shop. **Prices:** $160 to $2,000. **Remarks:** Part-time maker; first knife sold in 1975. **Mark:** Last name over year.

PADILLA, GARY
PO Box 5706, Bellingham, WA 98227, Phone: 360-756-7573, gkpadilla@yahoo.com
Specialties: Unique knives of all designs and uses. **Patterns:** Hunters, kitchen knives, utility/camp knives and obsidian ceremonial knives. **Technical:** Grinds 440C, ATS-34 and damascus, with limited flintknapped obsidian. **Prices:** Discounted from $50 to $200 generally. **Remarks:** Retired part-time maker; first knife sold in 1977. **Mark:** Stylized name.

PAGE, LARRY
1200 Mackey Scott Rd, Aiken, SC 29801-7620, Phone: 803-648-0001
Specialties: Working knives of his design. **Patterns:** Hunters, boots and fighters. **Technical:** Grinds ATS-34. **Prices:** Start at $85. **Remarks:** Part-time maker; first knife sold in 1983. **Mark:** Name, city and state in oval.

PAGE, REGINALD
6587 Groveland Hill Rd, Groveland, NY 14462, Phone: 716-243-1643
Specialties: High-art straight knives and one-of-a-kind folders of his design. **Patterns:** Hunters, locking folders and slip-joint folders. **Technical:** Forges O1, 5160 and his own Damascus. Prefers natural handle materials but will work with Micarta. **Remarks:** Spare-time maker; first knife sold in 1985. **Mark:** First initial, last name.

PAINTER, TONY
87 Fireweed Dr, Whitehorse, YT, CANADA Y1A 5T8, Phone: 867-633-3323, yukonjimmies@gmail.com; Web: www.tonypainterdesigns.com
Specialties: One-of-a-kind using knives, some fancy, fixed and folders. **Patterns:** No fixed patterns. **Technical:** Grinds ATS-34, D2, O1, S30V, Damascus satin finish. Prefers to use exotic woods and other natural materials. Micarta and G10 on working knives. **Prices:** Starting at $200. **Remarks:** Full-time knifemaker and carver. First knife sold in 1996. **Mark:** Two stamps used: initials TP in a circle and painter.

PALIKKO, J-T
B30 B1, Suomenlinna, 00190 Helsinki, FINLAND, Phone: +358-400-699687, jt@kp-art.fi; Web: www.art-helsinki.com
Specialties: One-of-a-kind knives and swords. **Patterns:** Own puukko models, hunters, integral & semi-integral knives, swords & other historical weapons and friction folders. **Technical:** Forges 52100 & other carbon steels, Damasteel stainless damascus & RWL-34, makes own damascus steel, makes carvings on walrus ivory and antler. **Prices:** Starting at $250. **Remarks:** Full-time maker; first knife sold in 1989. **Mark:** JT

PALM, RIK
10901 Scripps Ranch Blvd, San Diego, CA 92131, Phone: 858-530-0407, rikpalm@knifesmith.com; Web: www.knifesmith.com
Specialties: Sole authorship of one-of-a-kind unique art pieces, working/using knives and sheaths. **Patterns:** Carved nature themed knives, camp, hunters, friction folders, tomahawks, and small special pocket knives. **Technical:** Makes own Damascus, forges 5160H, 1084, 1095, W2, O1. Does his own heat treating including clay hardening. **Prices:** $80 and up. **Remarks:** American Bladesmith Society Journeyman Smith. First blade sold in 2000. **Mark:** Stamped, hand signed, etched last name signature.

PALMER, TAYLOR
TAYLOR-MADE SCENIC KNIVES INC., 1607 E. 450 S, Blanding, UT 84511, Phone: 435-678-2523, taylormadewoodeu@citlink.net
Specialties: Bronze carvings inside of blade area. **Prices:** $250 and up. **Mark:** Taylor Palmer Utah.

PANAK, PAUL S
6103 Leon Rd., Andover, OH 44003, Phone: 330-442-2724, burn@burnknives.com; Web: www.burnknives.com
Specialties: Italian-styled knives. DA OTF's, Italian style stilettos. **Patterns:** Vintage-styled Italians, fighting folders and high art gothic-styles all with various mechanisms. **Technical:** Grinds ATS-34, 154 CM, 440C and Damascus. **Prices:** $800 to $3000. **Remarks:** Full-time maker, first knife sold in 1998. **Mark:** "Burn."

PANCHENKO, SERGE
5927 El Sol Way, Citrus Heights, CA 95621, Phone: 916-588-8821, serge@sergeknives.com Web: www.sergeknives.com
Specialties: Unique art knives using natural materials, copper and carbon steel for a rustic look. **Patterns:** Art knives, tactical folders, Japanese-and relic-style knives. **Technical:** Forges carbon steel, grinds carbon and stainless steels. **Prices:** $100 to $800. **Remarks:** Part-time maker, first knife sold in 2008. **Mark:** SERGE

PARDUE, JOE
PO Box 569, Hillister, TX 77624, Phone: 409-429-7074, Fax: 409-429-5657, joepardue@hughes.net; Web: http://www.melpardueknives.com/Joepardueknives/index.htm

PARDUE, MELVIN M
4461 Jerkins Rd., Repton, AL 36475, Phone: 251-248-2686, mpardue@frontiernet.net; Web: www.pardueknives.com
Specialties: Folders, collectable, combat, utility and tactical. **Patterns:** Lockback, liner lock, push button; all blade and handle patterns. **Technical:** Grinds 154CM, 440C, 12C27. Forges mokume and Damascus. Uses titanium. **Prices:** $400 to $1600. **Remarks:** Full-time maker, Guild member, ABS member, AFC member. First knife made in 1957; first knife sold professionally in 1974. **Mark:** Mel Pardue.

PARKER, CLIFF
6350 Tulip Dr, Zephyrhills, FL 33544, Phone: 813-973-1682, cooldamascus@aol.com Web: cliffparkerknives.com
Specialties: Damascus gent knives. **Patterns:** Locking liners, some straight knives. **Technical:** Mostly use 1095, 1084, 15N20, 203E and powdered steel. **Prices:** $700 to $2100. **Remarks:** Making own Damascus and specializing in mosaics; first knife sold in 1996. Full-time beginning in 2000. **Mark:** CP.

PARKER, J E
11 Domenica Cir, Clarion, PA 16214, Phone: 814-226-4837, jimparkerknives@hotmail.com Web:www.jimparkerknives.com
Specialties: Fancy/embellished, traditional and working straight knives of his design and to customer specs. Engraving and scrimshaw by the best in the business. **Patterns:** Bowies, hunters and LinerLock® folders. **Technical:** Grinds 440C, 440V, ATS-34 and nickel Damascus. Prefers mastodon, oosik, amber and malachite handle material. **Prices:** $75 to $5200. **Remarks:** Full-time maker; first knife sold in 1991. Doing business as Custom Knife. **Mark:** J E Parker and Clarion PA stamped or etched in blade.

PARKER, ROBERT NELSON
1527 E Fourth St, Royal Oak, MI 48067, Phone: 248-545-8211, rnparkerknives@gmail.com or rnparkerknives@wowway.com; Web: www.classicknifedesign.com
Specialties: Traditional working and using straight knives of his design. **Patterns:** Chutes, subhilts, hunters, and fighters. **Technical:** Grinds CPM-154, CPM-D2, BG-42 and ATS-34, no forging, hollow and flat grinds, full and hidden tangs. Hand-stitched leather sheaths. **Prices:** $400 to $2,000, some to $3,000. **Remarks:** Full-time maker; first knife sold in 1986. I do forge sometimes. **Mark:** Full name.

PARKS, BLANE C
15908 Crest Dr, Woodbridge, VA 22191, Phone: 703-221-4680
Specialties: Knives of his design. **Patterns:** Boots, Bowies, daggers, fighters, hunters, kitchen knives, locking and slip-joint folders, utility/camp knives, letter openers and friction folders. **Technical:** Grinds ATS-34, 440C, D2 and other carbon steels. Offers filework, silver wire inlay and wooden sheaths. **Prices:** Start at $250 to $650; some to $1000. **Remarks:** Part-time maker; first knife sold in 1993. Doing business as B.C. Parks Knives. **Mark:** First and middle initials, last name.

PARKS, JOHN
3539 Galilee Church Rd, Jefferson, GA 30549, Phone: 706-367-4916
Specialties: Traditional working and using straight knives of his design. **Patterns:** Hunters, integral bolsters, and personal knives. **Technical:** Forges 1095 and 5168. **Prices:** $275 to $600; some to $800. **Remarks:** Part-time maker; first knife sold in 1989. **Mark:** Initials.

PARLER, THOMAS O
11 Franklin St, Charleston, SC 29401, Phone: 803-723-9433

PARRISH, ROBERT
271 Allman Hill Rd, Weaverville, NC 28787, Phone: 828-645-2864
Specialties: Heavy-duty working knives of his design or to customer specs. **Patterns:** Survival and duty knives; hunters and fighters. **Technical:** Grinds 440C, D2, O1 and commercial Damascus. **Prices:** $200 to $300; some to $6000. **Remarks:** Part-time maker; first knife sold in 1970. **Mark:** Initials connected, sometimes with city and state.

PARRISH III, GORDON A
940 Lakloey Dr, North Pole, AK 99705, Phone: 907-488-0357, ga-parrish@gci.net
Specialties: Classic and high-art straight knives of his design and to customer specs; working and using knives. **Patterns:** Bowies and hunters. **Technical:** Grinds tool steel and ATS-34. Uses mostly Alaskan handle materials. **Prices:** Starting at $300. **Remarks:** Spare-time maker; first knife sold in 1980. **Mark:** Last name, FBKS. ALASKA

PARSONS, LARRY
539 S. Pleasant View Dr., Mustang, OK 73064, Phone: 405-376-9408, l.j.parsons@sbcglobal.net; parsonssaddleshop.com
Specialties: Variety of sheaths from plain leather, geometric stamped, also inlays of various types. **Prices:** Starting at $35 and up

PARSONS, PETE
5905 High Country Dr., Helena, MT 59602, Phone: 406-202-0181, Parsons14@MT.net; Web: www.ParsonsMontanaKnives.com
Specialties: Forged utility blades in straight steel or Damascus (will grind stainless on customer request). Folding knives of my own design. **Patterns:** Hunters, fighters, Bowies, hikers, camp knives, everyday carry folders, tactical folders, gentleman's folders. Some customer designed pieces. **Technical:** Forges carbon steel, grinds carbon steel and some stainless. Forges own Damascus. **Mark:** Left side of blade PARSONS stamp or Parsons Helena, MT etch.

PARTRIDGE, JERRY D.
P.O. Box 977, DeFuniak Springs, FL 32435, Phone: 850-520-4873, jerry@partridgeknives.com; Web: www.partridgeknives.com
Specialties: Fancy and working straight knives and straight razors of his designs. **Patterns:** Hunters, skinners, chef's knives, straight razors, neck knives, and miniatures. **Technical:** Grinds 440C, ATS-34, carbon Damascus, and stainless Damascus. **Prices:** $250 and up, depending on materials used. **Remarks:** Part-time maker, first knife sold in 2007. **Mark:** Partridge Knives logo on the blade; Partridge or Partridge Knives engraved in script.

PASSMORE, JIMMY D
316 SE Elm, Hoxie, AR 72433, Phone: 870-886-1922

PATRICK, BOB
12642 24A Ave, S. Surrey, BC, CANADA V4A 8H9, Phone: 604-538-6214, Fax: 604-888-2683, bob@knivesonnet.com; Web: www.knivesonnet.com
Specialties: Maker's designs only, No orders. **Patterns:** Bowies, hunters, daggers, throwing knives. **Technical:** D2, 5160, Damascus. **Prices:** Good value. **Remarks:** Full-time maker; first knife sold in 1987. Doing business as Crescent Knife Works. **Mark:** Logo with name and province or Crescent Knife Works.

PATRICK, CHUCK
4650 Pine Log Rd., Brasstown, NC 28902, Phone: 828-837-7627,
chuckandpeggypatrick@gmail.com Web: www.chuckandpeggypatrick.com
    Specialties: Period pieces. **Patterns:** Hunters, daggers, tomahawks, pre-Civil War folders. **Technical:** Forges hardware, his own cable and Damascus, available in fancy pattern and mosaic. **Prices:** $150 to $1000; some higher. **Remarks:** Full-time maker. **Mark:** Hand-engraved name or flying owl.

PATRICK, PEGGY
4650 Pine Log Rd., Brasstown, NC 28902, Phone: 828-837-7627,
chuckandpeggypatrick@gmail.com Web: www.chuckandpeggypatrick.com
    Specialties: Authentic period and Indian sheaths, braintan, rawhide, beads and quill work. **Technical:** Does own braintan, rawhide; uses only natural dyes for quills, old color beads.

PATRICK, WILLARD C
PO Box 5716, Helena, MT 59604, Phone: 406-458-6552, wilamar@mt.net
    Specialties: Working straight knives and one-of-a-kind art knives of his design or to customer specs. **Patterns:** Hunters, Bowies, fish, patch and kitchen knives. **Technical:** Grinds ATS-34, 1095, O1, A2 and Damascus. **Prices:** $100 to $2000. **Remarks:** Full-time maker; first knife sold in 1989. Doing business as Wil-A-Mar Cutlery. **Mark:** Shield with last name and a dagger.

PATTAY, RUDY
8739 N. Zurich Way, Citrus Springs, FL 34434, Phone: 516-318-4538,
dolphin51@att.net; Web: www.pattayknives.com
    Specialties: Fancy and working straight knives of his design. **Patterns:** Bowies, hunters, utility/camp knives, drop point, skinners. **Technical:** Hollow-grinds ATS-34, 440C, O1. Offers commercial Damascus, stainless steel soldered guards; fabricates guard and butt cap on lathe and milling machine. Heat-treats. Prefers synthetic handle materials. Offers hand-sewn sheaths. **Prices:** $100 to $350; some to $500. **Remarks:** Full-time maker; first knife sold in 1990. **Mark:** First initial, last name in sorcerer logo.

PATTERSON, PAT
Box 246, Barksdale, TX 78828, Phone: 830-234-3586, pat@pattersonknives.com
    Specialties: Traditional fixed blades and LinerLock folders. **Patterns:** Hunters and folders. **Technical:** Grinds 440C, ATS-34, D2, O1 and Damascus. **Prices:** $250 to $1000. **Remarks:** Full-time maker. First knife sold in 1991. **Mark:** Name and city.

PATTON, DICK AND ROB
6803 View Ln., Nampa, ID 83687, Phone: 208-468-4123,
grpatton@pattonknives.com; Web: www.pattonknives.com
    Specialties: Custom Damascus, hand forged, fighting knives, Bowie and tactical. **Patterns:** Mini Bowie, Merlin Fighter, Mandrita Fighting Bowie. **Prices:** $100 to $2000.

PATTON, PHILLIP
PO BOX 113, Yoder, IN 46798, phillip@pattonblades.com Web: www.pattonblades.com
    Specialties: Tactical fixed blades, including fighting, camp, and general utility blades. Also makes Bowies and daggers. Known for leaf and recurve blade shapes. **Technical:** Forges carbon, stainless, and high alloy tool steels. Makes own damascus using 1084/15n20 or O1/L6. Makes own carbon/stainless laminated blades. For handle materials, prefers high end woods and sythetics. Uses 416 ss and bronze for fittings. **Prices:** $175 -$1000 for knives; $750 and up for swords. **Remarks:** Full-time maker since 2005. Two-year backlog. ABS member. **Mark:** "Phillip Patton" with Phillip above Patton.

PAULO, FERNANDES R
Raposo Tavares No 213, Lencois Paulista, SP, BRAZIL 18680, Phone: 014-263-4281
    Specialties: An apprentice of Jose Alberto Paschoarelli, his designs are heavily based on the later designs. **Technical:** Grinds tool steels and stainless steels. Part-time knifemaker. **Prices:** Start from $100. **Mark:** P.R.F.

PAWLOWSKI, JOHN R
19380 High Bluff Ln., Barhamsville, VA 23011, Phone: 757-870-4284,
Fax: 757-223-5935, bigjohnknives@yahoo.com; Web: www.bigjohnk.com
    Specialties: Traditional working and using straight knives and folders. **Patterns:** Hunters, Bowies, fighters and camp knives. **Technical:** Stock removal, grinds 440C, ATS-34, 154CM and buys Damascus. **Prices:** $250 and up. **Remarks:** Part-time maker, first knife sold in 1983, Knifemaker Guild Member. **Mark:** Name with attacking eagle.

PAYNE, TRAVIS
T-BONE'S CUSTOM CREATIONS, 1588 CR 2655, Telephone, TX 75488,
Phone: 903-640-6484, tbone7599@yahoo.com, Web: tbonescustomcreations.com
    Specialties: Full-time maker of fixed blades, specializing in a unique style of castration knives, but also hunting and everyday carry (EDC's). **Technical:** Prefers 440C, PSF27, CPM 154 and Damasteel blade steels. **Prices:** $200 to $1,000. **Remarks:** Full-time maker since 1993.

PEAGLER, RUSS
PO Box 1314, Moncks Corner, SC 29461, Phone: 803-761-1008
    Specialties: Traditional working straight knives of his design and to customer specs. **Patterns:** Hunters, fighters, boots. **Technical:** Hollow-grinds 440C, ATS-34 and O1; uses Damascus steel. Prefers bone handles. **Prices:** $85 to $300; some to $500. **Remarks:** Spare-time maker; first knife sold in 1983. **Mark:** Initials.

PEARCE, LOGAN
1013 Dogtown Rd., De Queen, AR 71832, Phone: 580-212-0995,
night_everclear@hotmail.com; Web: www.pearceknives.com
    Specialties: Edged weapons, art knives, stright working knives. **Patterns:** Bowie, hunters, tomahawks, fantasy, utility, daggers, and slip-joint. **Technical:** Fprges 1080, L6,

5160, 440C, steel cable, and his own Damascus. **Prices:** $35 to $500. **Remarks:** Full-time maker, first knife sold in 1992. Doing business as Pearce Knives **Mark:** Name

PEASE, W D
657 Cassidy Pike, Ewing, KY 41039, Phone: 606-845-0387,
Web: www.wdpeaseknives.com
    Specialties: Display-quality working folders. **Patterns:** Fighters, tantos and boots; locking folders and interframes. **Technical:** Grinds ATS-34 and commercial Damascus; has own side-release lock system. **Prices:** $500 to $1000; some to $3000. **Remarks:** Full-time maker; first knife sold in 1970. **Mark:** First and middle initials, last name and state. W. D. Pease Kentucky.

PEDERSEN, OLE
23404 W. Lake Kayak Dr., Monroe, WA 98272, Phone: 425-931-5750, ole@pedersenknives.com; www.pedersenknives.com
    Specialties Fixed blades of own design. **Patterns:** Hunters, working and utility knives. **Technical:** Stock removal, hollow grinds CPM 154 and stainless steel, 416 stainless fittings, makes own custom sheaths. Handles are mostly stabilized burl wood, some G-10. Heat treats and tempers own knives. **Prices:** $275 to $500. **Remarks:** Full-time maker; sold first knife in 2012. **Mark:** Ole Pedersen -Maker.

PEELE, BRYAN
219 Ferry St, PO Box 1363, Thompson Falls, MT 59873, Phone: 406-827-4633,
banana_peele@yahoo.com
    Specialties: Fancy working and using knives of his design. **Patterns:** Hunters, Bowies and fighters. **Technical:** Grinds 440C, ATS-34, D2, O1 and commercial Damascus. **Prices:** $110 to $300; some to $900. **Remarks:** Part-time maker; first knife sold in 1985. **Mark:** The Elk Rack, full name, city, state.

PELLEGRIN, MIKE
MP3 Knives, 107 White St., Troy, IL 62294-1126, Phone: 618-667-6777,
Web: MP3knives.com
    Specialties: Lockback folders with stone inlays, and one-of-a-kind art knives with stainless steel or damascus handles. **Technical:** Stock-removal method of blade making using 440C, Damasteel or high-carbon damascus blades. **Prices:** $800 and up. **Remarks:** Making knives since 2000. **Mark:** MP (combined) 3.

PENDLETON, LLOYD
24581 Shake Ridge Rd, Volcano, CA 95689, Phone: 209-296-3353,
Fax: 209-296-3353
    Specialties: Contemporary working knives in standard patterns. **Patterns:** Hunters, fighters and boots. **Technical:** Grinds and ATS-34; mirror finishes. **Prices:** $400 to $900 **Remarks:** Full-time maker; first knife sold in 1973. **Mark:** First initial, last name logo, city and state.

PENDRAY, ALFRED H
13950 NE 20th St, Williston, FL 32696, Phone: 352-528-6124
    Specialties: Working straight knives and folders; period pieces. **Patterns:** Fighters and hunters, axes, camp knives and tomahawks. **Technical:** Forges Wootz steel; makes his own Damascus; makes traditional knives from old files and rasps. **Prices:** $125 to $1000; some to $3500. **Remarks:** Part-time maker; first knife sold in 1954. **Mark:** Last initial in horseshoe logo.

PENNINGTON, C A
163 Kainga Rd, Kainga Christchurch, NEW ZEALAND 8009, Phone: 03-3237292,
capennington@xtra.co.nz
    Specialties: Classic working and collectors knives. Folders a specialty. **Patterns:** Classical styling for hunters and collectors. **Technical:** Forges his own all tool steel Damascus. Grinds D2 when requested. **Prices:** $240 to $2000. **Remarks:** Full-time maker; first knife sold in 1988. Color brochure $3. **Mark:** Name, country.

PEPIOT, STEPHAN
73 Cornwall Blvd, Winnipeg, MB, CANADA R3J-1E9, Phone: 204-888-1499
    Specialties: Working straight knives in standard patterns. **Patterns:** Hunters and camp knives. **Technical:** Grinds 440C and industrial hack-saw blades. **Prices:** $75 to $125. **Remarks:** Spare-time maker; first knife sold in 1982. Not currently taking orders. **Mark:** PEP.

PERRY, CHRIS
1654 W. Birch, Fresno, CA 93711, Phone: 559-246-7446, chris.perry4@comcast.net
    Specialties: Traditional working/using straight knives of his design. **Patterns:** Boots, hunters and utility/camp knives. **Technical:** Grinds ATS-34, Damascus, 416ss fittings, silver and gold fittings, hand-rubbed finishes. **Prices:** Starting at $250. **Remarks:** Part-time maker, first knife sold in 1995. **Mark:** Name above city and state.

PERRY, JIM
Hope Star PO Box 648, Hope, AR 71801, jenn@comfabinc.com

PERRY, JOHN
9 South Harrell Rd, Mayflower, AR 72106, Phone: 501-470-3043,
jpknives@cyberback.com
    Specialties: Investment grade and working folders; Antique Bowies and slip joints. **Patterns:** Front and rear lock folders, liner locks, hunters and Bowies. **Technical:** Grinds CPM440V, D2 and making own Damascus. Offers filework. **Prices:** $375 to $1200; some to $3500. **Remarks:** Part-time maker; first knife sold in 1991. Doing business as Perry Custom Knives. **Mark:** Initials or last name in high relief set in a diamond shape.

PERRY, JOHNNY
PO Box 35, Inman, SC 29349, Phone: 864-431-6390, perr3838@bellsouth.net
    Mark: High Ridge Forge.

PERSSON, CONNY
PL 588, Loos, SWEDEN 82050, Phone: +46 657 10305, Fax: +46 657 413 435, connyknives@swipnet.se; Web: www.connyknives.com
Specialties: Mosaic Damascus. **Patterns:** Mosaic Damascus. **Technical:** Straight knives and folders. **Prices:** $1000 and up. **Mark:** C. Persson.

PETEAN, FRANCISCO AND MAURICIO
R. Dr. Carlos de Carvalho Rosa 52, Birigui, SP, BRAZIL 16200-000, Phone: 0186-424786
Specialties: Classic knives to customer specs. **Patterns:** Bowies, boots, fighters, hunters and utility knives. **Technical:** Grinds D6, 440C and high-carbon steels. Prefers natural handle material. **Prices:** $70 to $500. **Remarks:** Full-time maker; first knife sold in 1985. **Mark:** Last name, hand made.

PETERS, DANIEL
5589 Poydasheff Ct., Columbus, GA 31907, Phone: 360-451-9386, dan@danpeterscustomknives.com; www.danpeterscustomknives.com
Specialties Hunters, skinners, tactical and combat knives. **Patterns:** Drop points, daggers, folders, hunters, skinners, Kukri style and fillet knives, often to customer's specs. **Technical:** CPM S35VN, CPM 3V, CPM 154 and a few other high-end specialty steels. **Prices:** $75 for bottle openers, and $150 and up on all others. **Remarks:** Part-time maker, full-time military. Member of Georgia Custom Knifemakers Guild and The Knifemakers' Guild (probationary). **Mark:** PETERS USA etched.

PETERSEN, DAN L
10610 SW 81st, Auburn, KS 66402, Phone: 785-220-8043, dan@petersenknives.com; Web: www.petersenknives.com
Specialties: Period pieces and forged integral hilts on hunters and fighters. **Patterns:** Texas-style Bowies, boots and hunters in high-carbon and Damascus steel. **Technical:** Precision heat treatments. Bainite blades with mantensite cores. **Prices:** $800 to $10,000. **Remarks:** First knife sold in 1978. ABS Master Smith. **Mark:** Stylized initials.

PETERSON, CHRIS
Box 143, 2175 W Rockyford, Salina, UT 84654, Phone: 435-529-7194
Specialties: Working straight knives of his design. **Patterns:** Large fighters, boots, hunters and some display pieces. **Technical:** Forges O1 and meteor. Makes and sells his own Damascus. Engraves, scrimshaws and inlays. **Prices:** $150 to $600; some to $1500. **Remarks:** Full-time maker; first knife sold in 1986. **Mark:** A drop in a circle with a line through it.

PETERSON, ELDON G
368 Antelope Trl, Whitefish, MT 59937, Phone: 406-862-2204, draino@digisys.net; Web: http://www.kmg.org/egpeterson
Specialties: Fancy and working folders, any size. **Patterns:** Lockback interframes, integral bolster folders, liner locks, and two-blades. **Technical:** Grinds 440C and ATS-34. Offers gold inlay work, gem stone inlays and engraving. **Prices:** $285 to $5000. **Remarks:** Full-time maker; first knife sold in 1974. **Mark:** Name, city and state.

PETERSON, LLOYD (PETE) C
64 Halbrook Rd, Clinton, AR 72031, Phone: 501-893-0000, wmblade@cyberback.com
Specialties: Miniatures and mosaic folders. **Prices:** $250 and up. **Remarks:** Lead time is 6-8 months. **Mark:** Pete.

PFANENSTIEL, DAN
1824 Lafayette Ave, Modesto, CA 95355, Phone: 209-575-5937, dpfan@sbcglobal.net
Specialties: Japanese tanto, swords. One-of-a-kind knives. **Technical:** Forges simple carbon steels, some Damascus. **Prices:** $200 to $1000. **Mark:** Circle with wave inside.

PHILIPPE, D A
3024 Stepping Stone Path, The Villages, FL 32163, Phone: 352-633-9676, dave.philippe@yahoo.com
Specialties: Traditional working straight knives. **Patterns:** Hunters, trout and bird, camp knives etc. **Technical:** Grinds ATS-34, 440C, A-2, Damascus, flat and hollow ground. Exotic woods and antler handles. Brass, nickel silver and stainless components. **Prices:** $125 to $800. **Remarks:** Full-time maker, first knife sold in 1984. **Mark:** First initial, last name.

PHILLIPS, ALISTAIR
Amaroo, ACT, AUSTRALIA 2914, alistair.phillips@knives.mutantdiscovery.com; Web: http://knives.mutantdiscovery.com
Specialties: Slipjoint folders, forged or stock removal fixed blades. **Patterns:** Single blade slipjoints, smaller neck knives, and hunters. **Technical:** Flat grnds O1, ATS-34, and forged 1055. **Prices:** $80 to $400. **Remarks:** Part-time maker, first knife made in 2005. **Mark:** Stamped signature.

PHILLIPS, DENNIS
16411 West Bennet Rd, Independence, LA 70443, Phone: 985-878-8275
Specialties: Specializes in fixed blade military combat tacticals.

PHILLIPS, DONAVON
905 Line Prairie Rd., Morton, MS 39117, Phone: 662-907-0322, bigdknives@gmail.com
Specialties: Flat ground, tapered tang working/using knives. **Patterns:** Hunters, Capers, Fillet, EDC, Field/Camp/Survival, Competition Cutters. Will work with customers on custom designs or changes to own designs. **Technical:** Stock removal maker using CPM-M4, CPM-154, and other air-hardening steels. Will use 5160 or 52100 on larger knives. G-10 or rubber standard, will use natural material if requested including armadillo. Kydex sheath is standard, outsourced leather available.†Heat treat is done by maker. **Prices:** $100 -$1000 **Remarks:** Part-time/hobbyist maker. First knife made in 2004; first sold 2007. **Mark:** Mark is etched, first and last name forming apex of triangle, city and

state at the base, D in center.

PICKENS, SELBERT
2295 Roxalana Rd, Dunbar, WV 25064, Phone: 304-744-4048
Specialties: Using knives. **Patterns:** Standard sporting knives. **Technical:** Stainless steels; stock removal method. **Prices:** Moderate. **Remarks:** Part-time maker. **Mark:** Name.

PICKETT, TERRELL
66 Pickett Ln, Lumberton, MS 39455, Phone: 601-794-6125, pickettfence66@bellsouth.net
Specialties: Fix blades, camp knives, Bowies, hunters, & skinners. Forge and stock removal and some firework. **Technical:** 5160, 1095, 52100, 440C and ATS-34. **Prices:** Range from $150 to $550. **Mark:** Logo on stock removal T.W. Pickett and on forged knives Terrell Pickett's Forge.

PIENAAR, CONRAD
19A Milner Rd, Bloemfontein, Free State, SOUTH AFRICA 9300, Phone: 027 514364180, Fax: 027 514364180
Specialties: Fancy working and using straight knives and folders of his design, to customer specs and in standard patterns. **Patterns:** Hunters, locking folders, cleavers, kitchen and utility/camp knives. **Technical:** Grinds 12C27, D2 and ATS-34. Uses some Damascus. Embellishments; scrimshaws; inlays gold. Knives come with wooden box and custom-made leather sheath. **Prices:** $300 to $1000. **Remarks:** Part-time maker; first knife sold in 1981. Doing business as C.P. Knifemaker. Makes slip joint folders and liner locking folders. **Mark:** Initials and serial number.

PIERCE, HAROLD L
106 Lyndon Lane, Louisville, KY 40222, Phone: 502-429-5136
Specialties: Working straight knives, some fancy. **Patterns:** Big fighters and Bowies. **Technical:** Grinds D2, 440C, 154CM; likes sub-hilts. **Prices:** $150 to $450; some to $1200. **Remarks:** Full-time maker; first knife sold in 1982. **Mark:** Last name with knife through the last initial.

PIERCE, RANDALL
903 Wyndam, Arlington, TX 76017, Phone: 817-468-0138

PIERGALLINI, DANIEL E
4011 N. Forbes Rd, Plant City, FL 33565, Phone: 813-754-3908 or 813-967-1471, coolnifedad@wildblue.net; Web: www.piergalliniknives.com
Specialties: Traditional and fancy straight knives and folders of his design or to customer's specs. **Patterns:** Hunters, fighters, skinners, working and camp knives. **Technical:** Grinds 440C, O1, D2, ATS-34, some Damascus; forges his own mokume. Uses natural handle material. **Prices:** $450 to $800; some to $1800. **Remarks:** Full-time maker; sold first knife in 1994. **Mark:** Last name, city, state or last name in script.

PIESNER, DEAN
1786 Sawmill Rd, Conestogo, ON, CANADA N0B 1N0, Phone: 519-664-3648, dean47@rogers.com
Specialties: Classic and period pieces of his design and to customer specs. **Patterns:** Bowies, skinners, fighters and swords. **Technical:** Forges 5160, 52100, steel Damascus and nickel-steel Damascus. Makes own mokume gane with copper, brass and nickel silver. Silver wire inlays in wood. **Prices:** Start at $150. **Remarks:** Full-time maker; first knife sold in 1990. **Mark:** First initial, last name, JS.

PITMAN, DAVID
PO Drawer 2566, Williston, ND 58802, Phone: 701-572-3325

PITT, DAVID F
Anderson, CA 96007, Phone: 530-357-2393, handcannons@tds.net; Web: www.bearpawcustoms.blademakers.com
Specialties: Fixed blade, hunters and hatchets. Flat ground mirror finish. **Patterns:** Hatchets with gut hook, small gut hooks, guards, bolsters or guard less. **Technical:** Grinds A2, 440C, 154CM, ATS-34, D2. **Prices:** $150 to $1,000. **Remarks:** All work done in-house including heat treat, and all knives come with hand-stitched, wet-fromed sheaths. **Mark:** Bear paw with David F. Pitt Maker.

PLOPPERT, TOM
1407 2nd Ave. SW, Cullman, AL 35055, Phone: 256-962-4251, tomploppert3@bellsouth.net
Specialties: Highly finished single-to multiple-blade slip-joint folders in standard and traditional patterns, some lockbacks. **Technical:** Hollow grinds CPM-154, 440V, damascus and other steels upon customer request. Uses elephant ivory, mammoth ivory, bone and pearl. **Mark:** Last name stamped on main blade.

PLUNKETT, RICHARD
29 Kirk Rd, West Cornwall, CT 06796, Phone: 860-672-3419; Toll free: 888-KNIVES-8
Specialties: Traditional, fancy folders and straight knives of his design. **Patterns:** Slip-joint folders and small straight knives. **Technical:** Grinds O1 and stainless steel. Offers many different file patterns. **Prices:** $150 to $450. **Remarks:** Full-time maker; first knife sold in 1994. **Mark:** Signature and date under handle scales.

PODMAJERSKY, DIETRICH
9219 15th Ave NE, Seattle, WA 98115, Phone: 206-552-0763, podforge@gmail.com; Web: podforge.com
Specialties: Straight and folding knives that use fine engraving and materials to create technically intricate, artistic visions. **Technical:** Stainless and carbon steel blades, with titanium and precious metal fittings, including Japanese ornamental alloys. **Prices:** $500 and up.

POIRIER, RICK
1149 Sheridan Rd., McKees Mills, New Brunswick E4V 2W7, CANADA,
Phone: 506-525-2818, ripknives@gmail.com; Web: www.ripcustomknives.com
Specialties: Working straight knives of his design or to customer specs, hunters, fighters, bowies, utility, camp, tantos and short swords. **Technical:** Forges own damascus and cable damascus using 1084, 15N20, O1 and mild steel. Forges/grinds mostly O1 and W2. Varied handle materials inlcude G-10, Micarta, wood, bone, horn and Japanese cord wrap. **Prices:** $200 and up. **Remarks:** Full-time maker, apprenticed under ABS master smith Wally Hayes; first knife made in 1998. Marks: R P (pre. 2007), RIP (2007 on), also etches gravestone RIP.

POLK, CLIFTON
4625 Webber Creek Rd, Van Buren, AR 72956, Phone: 479-474-3828,
cliffpolkknives1@aol.com; Web: www.polkknives.com
Specialties: Fancy working folders. **Patterns:** One blades spring backs in five sizes, LinerLock®, automatics, double blades spring back folder with standard drop & clip blade or bird knife with drop and vent hook or cowboy's knives with drop and hoof pick and straight knives. **Technical:** Uses D2 & ATS-34. Makes all own Damascus using 1084, 1095, O1, 15N20, 5160. Using all kinds of exotic woods. Stag, pearls, ivory, mastodon ivory and other bone and horns. **Prices:** $200 to $3000. **Remarks:** Retired fire fighter, made knives since 1974. **Mark:** Polk.

POLK, RUSTY
5900 Wildwood Dr, Van Buren, AR 72956, Phone: 870-688-3009, polkknives@yahoo.com; Web: www.facebook.com/polkknives
Specialties: Skinners, hunters, Bowies, fighters and forging working knives fancy Damascus, daggers, boot knives, survival knives, and folders. **Patterns:** Drop point, and forge to shape. **Technical:** ATS-34, 440C, Damascus, D2, 51/60, 1084, 15N20, does all his forging. **Prices:** $200 to $2000. **Mark:** R. Polk

POLLOCK, WALLACE J
806 Russet Valley Dr., Cedar Park, TX 78613, Phone: 512-918-0528,
jarlsdad@gmail.com; Web: www.pollackknives.com
Specialties: Using knives, skinner, hunter, fighting, camp knives. **Patterns:** Use his own patterns or yours. Traditional hunters, daggers, fighters, camp knives. **Technical:** Grinds ATS-34, D-2, BG-42, makes own Damascus, D-2, O-1, ATS-34, prefer D-2, handles exotic wood, horn, bone, ivory. **Remarks:** Full-time maker, sold first knife 1973. **Prices:** $250 to $2500. **Mark:** Last name, maker, city/state.

POLZIEN, DON
1912 Inler Suite-L, Lubbock, TX 79407, Phone: 806-791-0766, blindinglightknives.net
Specialties: Traditional Japanese-style blades; restores antique Japanese swords, scabbards and fittings. **Patterns:** Hunters, fighters, one-of-a-kind art knives. **Technical:** 1045-1050 carbon steels, 440C, D2, ATS-34, standard and cable Damascus. **Prices:** $150 to $2500. **Remarks:** Full-time maker. First knife sold in 1990. **Mark:** Oriental characters inside square border.

PONZIO, DOUG
10219 W State Rd 81, Beloit, WI 53511, Phone: 608-313-3223,
prfgdoug@hughes.net; Web: www.ponziodamascus.com
Specialties: Mosaic Damascus, stainless Damascus. **Mark:** P.F.

POOLE, MARVIN O
PO Box 552, Commerce, GA 30529, Phone: 803-225-5970
Specialties: Traditional working/using straight knives and folders of his design and in standard patterns. **Patterns:** Bowies, fighters, hunters, locking folders, bird and trout knives. **Technical:** Grinds 440C, D2, ATS-34. **Prices:** $50 to $150; some to $750. **Remarks:** Part-time maker; first knife sold in 1980. **Mark:** First initial, last name, year, serial number.

POTIER, TIMOTHY F
PO Box 711, Oberlin, LA 70655, Phone: 337-639-2229, tpotier@hotmail.com
Specialties: Classic working and using straight knives to customer specs; some collectible. **Patterns:** Hunters, Bowies, utility/camp knives and belt axes. **Technical:** Forges carbon steel and his own Damascus; offers filework. **Prices:** $300 to $1800; some to $4000. **Remarks:** Part-time maker; first knife sold in 1981. **Mark:** Last name, MS.

POTTER, BILLY
6323 Hyland Dr., Dublin, OH 43017, Phone: 614-589-8324,
potterknives@yahoo.com; Web: www.potterknives.com
Specialties: Working straight knives; his design or to customers patterns. **Patterns:** Bowie, fighters, utilities, skinners, hunters, folding lock blade, miniatures and tomahawks. **Technical:** Grinds and forges, carbon steel, L6, O-1, 1095, 5160, 1084 and 52000. Grinds 440C stainless. Forges own Damascus. Handles: prefers exotic hardwood, curly and birdseye maples. Bone, ivory, antler, pearl and horn. Some scrimshaw. **Prices:** Start at $100 up to $800. **Remarks:** Part-time maker; first knife sold 1996. **Mark:** First and last name (maker).

POWELL, ROBERT CLARK
PO Box 321, 93 Gose Rd., Smarr, GA 31086, Phone: 478-994-5418
Specialties: Composite bar Damascus blades. **Patterns:** Art knives, hunters, combat, tomahawks. **Patterns:** Hand forges all blades. **Prices:** $300 and up. **Remarks:** ABS Journeyman Smith. **Mark:** Powell.

POWERS, WALTER R.
PO BOX 82, Lolita, TX 77971, Phone: 361-874-4230, carlyn@laward.net
Web: waltscustomknives.blademakers.com
Specialties: Skinners and hunters. **Technical:** Uses mainly CPMD2, CPM154 and

CPMS35VN, but will occasionally use 3V. Stock removal. **Prices:** $140 -$200. **Remarks:** Part-time maker; first knife made in 2002. **Mark:** WP

PRATER, MIKE
PRATER AND COMPANY, 81 Sanford Ln., Flintstone, GA 30725,
Phone: 706-820-7300, cmprater@aol.com; Web: www.pratercustoms.com
Specialties: Customizing factory knives. **Patterns:** Buck knives, case knives, hen and rooster knives. **Technical:** Manufacture of mica pearl. **Prices:** Varied. **Remarks:** First knife sold in 1980. **Mark:** Mica pearl.

PRESSBURGER, RAMON
59 Driftway Rd, Howell, NJ 07731, Phone: 732-363-0816
Specialties: BG-42. Only knifemaker in U.S.A. that has complete line of affordable hunting knives made from BG-42. **Patterns:** All types hunting styles. **Technical:** Uses all steels; main steels are D-2 and BG-42. **Prices:** $75 to $500. **Remarks:** Full-time maker; has been making hunting knives for 30 years. Makes knives to your patterning. **Mark:** NA.

PRESTI, MATT
5280 Middleburg Rd, Union Bridge, MD 21791, Phone: 410-775-1520;
Cell: 240-357-3592
Specialties: Hunters and chef's knives, fighters, bowies, and period pieces. **Technical:** Forges 5160, 52100, 1095, 1080, W2, and O1 steels as well as his own Damascus. Does own heat treating and makes sheaths. Prefers natural handle materials, particularly antler and curly maple. **Prices:** $150 and up. **Remarks:** Part-time knifemaker who made his first knife in 2001. **Mark:** MCP.

PRICE, DARRELL MORRIS
92 Union, Plymouth, Devon, ENGLAND PL1 3EZ, Phone: 0752 223546
Specialties: Traditional Japanese knives, Bowies and high-art knives. **Technical:** Nickel Damascus and mokume. **Prices:** $1000 to $4000. **Remarks:** Part-time maker; first knife sold in 1990. **Mark:** Initials and Japanese name—Kuni Shigae.

PRICE, TIMMY
PO Box 906, Blairsville, GA 30514, Phone: 706-745-5111

PRIDGEN JR., LARRY
PO Box 5616, Fitzgerald, GA 31750, Phone: 229-457-6522,
pridgencustomknives@gmail.com Web: www.pridgencustomknives.com
Specialties: Custom folders. **Patterns:** Bowie, fighter, skinner, trout, liner lock, and custom orders. **Technical:** I do stock removal and use carbon and stainless Damascus and stainless steel. **Prices:** $300 and up. **Remarks:** Each knife comes with a hand-crafted custom sheath and life-time guarantee. **Mark:** Distinctive logo that looks like a brand with LP and a circle around it.

PRIMOS, TERRY
932 Francis Dr, Shreveport, LA 71118, Phone: 318-686-6625, tprimos@sport.rr.com or terry@primosknives.com; Web: www.primosknives.com
Specialties: Traditional forged straight knives. **Patterns:** Hunters, Bowies, camp knives, and fighters. **Technical:** Forges primarily 1084 and 5160; also forges Damascus. **Prices:** $250 to $600. **Remarks:** Full-time maker; first knife sold in 1993. **Mark:** Last name.

PRINSLOO, THEUNS
PO Box 2263, Bethlehem, Free State, SOUTH AFRICA 9700, Phone: 27824663885, theunsmes@yahoo.com; Web: www.theunsprinsloo.co.za
Specialties: Handmade folders and fixed blades. **Technical:** Own Damascus and mokume. I try to avoid CNC work, laser cutting and machining as much as possible. **Prices:** $650 and up. **Mark:** Handwritten name with bushman rock art and mountain scene.

PRITCHARD, RON
613 Crawford Ave, Dixon, IL 61021, Phone: 815-284-6005
Specialties: Plain and fancy working knives. **Patterns:** Variety of straight knives, locking folders, interframes and miniatures. **Technical:** Grinds 440C, 154CM and commercial Damascus. **Prices:** $100 to $200; some to $1500. **Remarks:** Part-time maker; first knife sold in 1979. **Mark:** Name and city.

PROVENZANO, JOSEPH D
39043 Dutch Lane, Ponchatoula, LA 70454, Phone: 225-615-4846, gespro61@gmail.com
Specialties: Working straight knives and folders in standard patterns. **Patterns:** Hunters, Bowies, folders, camp and fishing knives. **Technical:** Grinds ATS-34, 440C, 154CM, CPM-S60V, CPM-S90V, CPM-3V and damascus. Hollow-grinds hunters. **Prices:** $125 to $300; some to $1,000. **Remarks:** Part-time maker; first knife sold in 1980. **Mark:** Joe-Pro.

PROVOST, J.C.
1634 Lakeview Dr., Laurel, MS 39440, Phone: 601-498-1143,
jcprovost2@gmail.com; Web: www.jcprovost.com
Specialties: Classic working straight knives and folders. **Patterns:** Hunters, skinners, bowies, daggers, fighters, fillet knives, chef's and steak knives, folders and customs. **Technical:** Grinds 440C, CPM-154 and commercial damascus. **Prices:** $175 and up. **Remarks:** Part-time maker; first knife made in 1979. Taught by R.W. Wilson. **Mark:** Name, city and state.

PRUYN, PETER
Brothersville Custom Knives, 110 Reel La., Grants Pass, OR 97527, Phone: 631-793-9052, Fax: 541-479-1889, brothersvilleknife@gmail.com Web: brothersvilleknife.com
Specialties: Chef knives and fighters in damascus and san mai, as well as stainless steels. **Patterns:** Fixed-blade knives of all styles, some folding models. **Technical:** Damascus, high-carbon and stainless steels; does own heat treating. **Prices:** $200 to $2,000, with

a discount to active and retired military personnel. **Remarks:** Full-time maker, first knife sold in 2009. **Mark:** Anvil with "Brothersville" crested above.

PUDDU, SALVATORE
Via Lago Bunnari #12, 09045 Quartu Sant 'Elena, (Cagliari) Sardinia, ITALY, Phone: 0039-070-892208, salvatore.puddu@tin.it
Specialties: Custom knives. **Remarks:** Full-time maker.

PULIS, VLADIMIR
CSA 230-95, 96701 Kremnica, SLOVAKIA, Phone: 00421 903 340076, vpulis@gmail.com; Web: www.vpulis.host.sk
Specialties: Fancy and high-art straight knives of his design. **Patterns:** Daggers and hunters. **Technical:** Forges Damascus steel. All work done by hand. **Prices:** $250 to $3000; some to $10,000. **Remarks:** Full-time maker; first knife sold in 1990. **Mark:** Initials in sixtagon.

PURSLEY, AARON
8885 Coal Mine Rd, Big Sandy, MT 59520, Phone: 406-378-3200
Specialties: Fancy working knives. **Patterns:** Locking folders, straight hunters and daggers, personal wedding knives and letter openers. **Technical:** Grinds O1 and 440C; engraves. **Prices:** $900 to $2500. **Remarks:** Full-time maker; first knife sold in 1975. **Mark:** Initials connected with year.

PURVIS, BOB AND ELLEN
2416 N Loretta Dr, Tucson, AZ 85716, Phone: 520-795-8290, repknives2@cox.net
Specialties: Hunter, skinners, Bowies, using knives, gentlemen folders and collectible knives. **Technical:** Grinds ATS-34, 440C, Damascus, Dama steel, heat-treats and cryogenically quenches. We do gold-plating, salt bluing, scrimshawing, filework and fashion handmade leather sheaths. Materials used for handles include exotic woods, mammoth ivory, mother-of-pearl, G-10 and Micarta. **Prices:** $165 to $800. **Remarks:** Knifemaker since retirement in 1984. Selling them since 1993. **Mark:** Script or print R.E. Purvis ~ Tucson, AZ or last name only.

PUTNAM, DONALD S
590 Wolcott Hill Rd, Wethersfield, CT 06109, Phone: 860-563-9718, Fax: 860-563-9718, dpknives@cox.net
Specialties: Working knives for the hunter and fisherman. **Patterns:** His design or to customer specs. **Technical:** Uses stock removal method, O1, W2, D2, ATS-34, 154CM, 440C and CPM REX 20; stainless steel Damascus on request. **Prices:** $250 and up. **Remarks:** Full-time maker; first knife sold in 1985. **Mark:** Last name with a knife outline.

Q

QUAKENBUSH, THOMAS C
2426 Butler Rd, Ft Wayne, IN 46808, Phone: 219-483-0749

QUARTON, BARR
PO Box 4335, McCall, ID 83638, Phone: 208-634-3641
Specialties: Plain and fancy working knives; period pieces. **Patterns:** Hunters, tantos and swords. **Technical:** Forges and grinds 154CM, ATS-34 and his own Damascus. **Prices:** $180 to $450; some to $4500. **Remarks:** Part-time maker; first knife sold in 1978. Doing business as Barr Custom Knives. **Mark:** First name with bear logo.

QUATTLEBAUM, CRAIG
912 Scooty Dr., Beebe, AR 72012-3454, mustang376@gci.net
Specialties: Traditional straight knives and one-of-a-kind knives of his design; period pieces. **Patterns:** Bowies and fighters. **Technical:** Forges 5168, 1095 and own Damascus. **Prices:** $300 to $2000. **Remarks:** Part-time maker; first knife sold in 1988. **Mark:** Stylized initials.

QUESENBERRY, MIKE
110 Evergreen Cricle, Blairsden, CA 96103, Phone: 775-233-1527, quesenberryknives@gmail.com; Web: www.quesenberryknives.com
Specialties: Hunters, daggers, bowies and integrals. **Technical:** Forges 52100 and W2. Makes own damascus. Will use stainless on customer requests. Does own heat-treating and own leather work. **Prices:** Starting at $400. **Remarks:** Part-time maker. ABS member since 2006. ABS master bladesmith. **Mark:** Last name.

R

RABUCK, JASON
W3080 Hay Lake Road, Springbrook, WI 54875, Phone: 715-766-8220, sales@rabuckhandmadeknives.com; web: www.rabuckhandmadeknives.com
Patterns: Hunters, skinners, camp knives, fighters, survival/tactical, neck knives, kitchen knives. Include whitetail antler, maple, walnut, as well as stabilized woods and micarta. **Technical:** Flat grinds 1095, 5160, and 0-1 carbon steels. Blades are finished with a hand-rubbed satin blade finish. Hand stitched leather sheaths specifically fit to each knife. Boot clips, swivel sheaths, and leg ties include some of the available sheath options. **Prices:** $140 -$560. **Remarks:** Also knife restoration (handle replacement, etc.) Custom and replacement sheath work available for any knife. **Mark:** "RABUCK" over a horseshoe

RACHLIN, LESLIE S
412 Rustic Ave., Elmira, NY 14905, Phone: 607-733-6889, lrachlin@stry.rr.com
Specialties: Classic and working kitchen knives, carving sets and outdoors knives. **Technical:** Grinds 440C or cryogenically heat-treated A2. **Prices:** $65 to $1,400. **Remarks:** Spare-time maker; first knife sold in 1989. Doing business as Tinkermade Knives. **Mark:** LSR

RADER, MICHAEL
23706 7th Ave. SE, Ste. D, Bothell, WA 98021, michael@raderblade.com; Web: www.raderblade.com
Specialties: Swords, kitchen knives, integrals. **Patterns:** Non traditional designs. Inspired by various cultures. **Technical:** Damascus is made with 1084 and 15N-20, forged blades in 52100, W2 and 1084. **Prices:** $350 -$5,000 **Remarks:** ABS Journeyman Smith **Mark:** ABS Mastersmith Mark "Rader" on one side, "M.S." on other

RADOS, JERRY F
134 Willie Nell Rd., Columbia, KY 42728, Phone: 606-303-3334, jerry@radosknives.com Web: www.radosknives.com
Specialties: Deluxe period pieces. **Patterns:** Hunters, fighters, locking folders, daggers and camp knives. **Technical:** Forges and grinds his own Damascus which he sells commercially; makes pattern-welded Turkish Damascus. **Prices:** Start at $900. **Remarks:** Full-time maker; first knife sold in 1981. **Mark:** Last name.

RAFN, DAN C.
Smedebakken 24, Hadsten, DENMARK 8370, contact@dcrknives.com Web: www.dcrknives.com
Specialties: One of a kind collector art knives of own design. **Patterns:** Mostly fantasy style fighters and daggers. But also swords, hunters, and folders. **Technical:** Grinds RWL-34, sleipner steel, damasteel, and hand forges Damascus. **Prices:** Start at $500. **Remarks:** Part-time maker since 2003. **Mark:** Rafn. or DCR. or logo.

RAGSDALE, JAMES D
160 Clear Creek Valley Tr., Ellijay, GA 30536, Phone: 706-636-3180, jimmarrags@etcmail.com
Specialties: Fancy and embellished working knives of his design or to customer specs. **Patterns:** Hunters, folders and fighters. **Technical:** Grinds 440C, ATS-34 and A2. Uses some Damascus **Prices:** $150 and up. **Remarks:** Full-time maker; first knife sold in 1984. **Mark:** Fish symbol with name above, town below.

RAINVILLE, RICHARD
126 Cockle Hill Rd, Salem, CT 06420, Phone: 860-859-2776, w1jo@comcast.net
Specialties: Traditional working straight knives. **Patterns:** Outdoor knives, including fishing knives. **Technical:** L6, 400C, ATS-34. **Prices:** $100 to $800. **Remarks:** Full-time maker; first knife sold in 1982. **Mark:** Name, city, state in oval logo.

RALEY, R. WAYNE
825 Poplar Acres Rd, Collierville, TN 38017, Phone: 901-853-2026

RALPH, DARREL
BRIAR KNIVES, 12034 S. Profit Row, Forney, TX 75126, Phone: 469-728-7242, dralph@earthlink.net; Web: www.darrelralph.com
Specialties: Tactical and tactical dress folders and fixed blades. **Patterns:** Daggers, fighters and swords. **Technical:** High tech. Forges his own damascus, nickel and high-carbon. Uses mokume and damascus, mosaics and special patterns. Engraves and heat treats. Prefers pearl, ivory and abalone handle material; uses stones and jewels. **Prices:** $600 to $30,000. **Remarks:** Full-time maker; first knife sold in 1987. Doing business as Briar Knives. **Mark:** DDR.

RAMONDETTI, SERGIO
VIA MARCONI N 24, CHIUSA DI PESIO (CN), ITALY 12013, Phone: 0171 734490, Fax: 0171 734490, info@ramon-knives.com Web: www.ramon-knives.com
Specialties: Folders and straight knives of his design. **Patterns:** Utility, hunters and skinners. **Technical:** Grinds RWL-34 and Damascus. **Prices:** $500 to $2000. **Remarks:** Part-time maker; first knife sold in 1999. **Mark:** Logo (S.Ramon) with last name.

RAMOS, STEVEN
2466 Countryside Ln., West Jordan, UT 84084, Phone: 801-913-1696, srknives88@gmail.com; Web: www.handmadecustomknives.com
Specialties: Mirror finishes, complex filework, tapered tangs, genuine polished gemstone handles, all original and unique blade designs. **Patterns:** Fixed, full-tang hunters/utility, fighters, modified bowies, daggers, cooking and chef's knives, personalized wedding cake knives and art pieces. **Technical:** Stock removal, predominantly using CPM 154 stainless steel, but also 440C, D2, 154CM and others. Mostly polished gemstone handles, but also Micarta, G-10 and various woods. Sheaths and custom display stands with commemorative engravings also available. **Prices:** $400 to $3,000. **Remarks:** Full-time maker. **Mark:** Signature "Steven Ramos" laser etched on blade.

RAMSEY, RICHARD A
8525 Trout Farm Rd, Neosho, MO 64850, Phone: 417-592-1494, rams@hughes.net or ramseyknives@gmail.com; Web: www.ramseyknives.com
Specialties: Drop point hunters. **Patterns:** Various Damascus. **Prices:** $125 to $1500. **Mark:** RR double R also last name-RAMSEY.

RANDALL, PATRICK
Patrick Knives, 160 Mesa Ave., Newbury Park, CA 91320, Phone: 805-390-5501, pat@patrickknives.com; Web: www.patrickknives.com
Specialties: Chef's and kitchen knives, bowies, hunters and utility folding knives. **Technical:** Preferred materials include 440C, 154CM, CPM-3V, 1084, 1095 and ATS-34. Handle materials include stabilized wood, Micarta, stag and jigged bone. **Prices:** $125 to $225. **Remarks:** Part-time maker since 2005.

RANDALL, STEVE
3438 Oak Ridge Cir., Lincolnton, NC 28092, Phone: 704-472-4957, steve@ksrblades.com; Web: www.ksrblades.com
Specialties: Mostly working straight knives and one-of-a-kind pieces, some fancy fixed

blades. **Patterns:** Bowies, hunters, choppers, camp and utility knives. **Technical:** Forged high-carbon-steel blades; 5160, 52100, W2, CruForgeV, high-carbon simple steels like 1075, 1084 and 1095, and damascus patterns. **Prices:** $275 and up. **Remarks:** Part-time maker, first knife sold in 2009. Earned journeyman smith rating in 2012. Doing business as Knives By Steve Randall or KSR Blades. **Mark:** KS Randall on left side, JS on right side.

RANDALL JR., JAMES W
11606 Keith Hall Rd, Keithville, LA 71047, Phone: 318-925-6480, Fax: 318-925-1709, jw@jwrandall.com; Web: www.jwrandall.com
Specialties: Collectible and functional knives. **Patterns:** Bowies, hunters, daggers, swords, folders and combat knives. **Technical:** Forges 5160, 1084, O1 and his Damascus. **Prices:** $400 to $8000. **Remarks:** Part-time. First knife sold in 1998. **Mark:** JW Randall, MS.

RANDALL MADE KNIVES
4857 South Orange Blossom Trail, Orlando, FL 32839, Phone: 407-855-8075, Fax: 407-855-9054, Web: http://www.randallknives.com
Specialties: Working straight knives. **Patterns:** Hunters, fighters and Bowies. **Technical:** Forges and grinds O1 and 440B. **Prices:** $170 to $550; some to $450. **Remarks:** Full-time maker; first knife sold in 1937. **Mark:** Randall made, city and state in scimitar logo.

RANDOW, RALPH
7 E. Chateau Estates Dr., Greenbrier, AR 72058, Phone: 318-729-3368, randow3368@gmail.com

RANKL, CHRISTIAN
Possenhofenerstr 33, Munchen, GERMANY 81476, Phone: 0049 01 71 3 66 26 79, Fax: 0049 8975967265, Web: http://www.german-knife.com/german-knifemakers-guild.html
Specialties: Tail-lock knives. **Patterns:** Fighters, hunters and locking folders. **Technical:** Grinds ATS-34, D2, CPM1440V, RWL 34 also stainless Damascus. **Prices:** $450 to $950; some to $2000. **Remarks:** Part-time maker; first knife sold in 1989. **Mark:** Electrochemical etching on blade.

RAPP, STEVEN J
8033 US Hwy 25-70, Marshall, NC 28753, Phone: 828-649-1092
Specialties: Gold quartz; mosaic handles. **Patterns:** Daggers, Bowies, fighters and San Francisco knives. **Technical:** Hollow-and flat-grinds 440C and Damascus. **Prices:** Start at $500. **Remarks:** Full-time maker; first knife sold in 1981. **Mark:** Name and state.

RAPPAZZO, RICHARD
142 Dunsbach Ferry Rd, Cohoes, NY 12047, Phone: 518-783-6843
Specialties: Damascus locking folders and straight knives. **Patterns:** Folders, dirks, fighters and tantos in original and traditional designs. **Technical:** Hand-forges all blades; specializes in Damascus; uses only natural handle materials. **Prices:** $400 to $1500. **Remarks:** Part-time maker; first knife sold in 1985. **Mark:** Name, date, serial number.

RARDON, A D
1589 SE Price Dr, Polo, MO 64671, Phone: 660-354-2330
Specialties: Folders, miniatures. **Patterns:** Hunters, buck skinners, Bowies, miniatures and daggers. **Technical:** Grinds O1, D2, 440C and ATS-34. **Prices:** $150 to $2000; some higher. **Remarks:** Full-time maker; first knife sold in 1954. **Mark:** Fox logo.

RARDON, ARCHIE F
1589 SE Price Dr, Polo, MO 64671, Phone: 660-354-2330
Specialties: Working knives. **Patterns:** Hunters, Bowies and miniatures. **Technical:** Grinds O1, D2, 440C, ATS-34, cable and Damascus. **Prices:** $50 to $500. **Remarks:** Part-time maker. **Mark:** Boar hog.

RASSENTI, PETER
218 Tasse, St-Eustache, Quebec J7P 4C2, CANADA, Phone: 450-598-6250, guireandgimble@hotmail.com
Specialties: Tactical mono-frame folding knives.

RAY, ALAN W
1287 FM 1280 E, Lovelady, TX 75851, awray@rayzblades.com; Web: www.rayzblades.com
Specialties: Working straight knives of his design. **Patterns:** Hunters. **Technical:** Forges O1, L6 and 5160 for straight knives. **Prices:** $200 to $1000. **Remarks:** Full-time maker; first knife sold in 1979. **Mark:** Stylized initials.

REBELLO, INDIAN GEORGE
358 Elm St, New Bedford, MA 02740-3837, Phone: 508-999-7090, indgeo@juno.com; Web: www.indiangeorgesknives.com
Specialties: One-of-a-kind fighters and Bowies. **Patterns:** To customer's specs, hunters and utilities. **Technical:** Forges his own Damascus, 5160, 52100, 1084, 1095, cable and O1. Grinds S30V, ATS-34, 154CM, 440C, D2 and A2. **Prices:** Starting at $250. **Remarks:** Full-time maker, first knife sold in 1991. Doing business as Indian George's Knives. Founding father and President of the Southern New England Knife-Makers Guild. Member of the N.C.C.A. **Mark:** Indian George's Knives.

RED, VERNON
2020 Benton Cove, Conway, AR 72034, Phone: 501-450-7284, knivesvr@conwaycorp.net
Specialties: Lock-blade folders, as well as fixed-blade knives of maker's own design or customer's. **Patterns:** Hunters, fighters, Bowies, folders. **Technical:** Hollow grind, flat grind, stock removal and forged blades. Uses 440C, D-2, A-2, ATS-34, 1084, 1095, and Damascus.**Prices:** $225 and up. **Remarks:** Made first knife in 1982, first folder in 1992. Member of (AKA) Arkansas Knives Association. **Mark:** Last name.

REDD, BILL
2647 West 133rd Circle, Broomfield, Colorado 80020, Phone: 303-469-9803, unlimited_design@msn.com
Prices: Contact maker. **Remarks:** Full-time custom maker, member of PKA and RMBC (Rocky Mountain Blade Collectors). **Mark:** Redd Knives, Bill Redd.

REDDIEX, BILL
27 Galway Ave, Palmerston North, NEW ZEALAND, Phone: 06-357-0383, Fax: 06-358-2910
Specialties: Collector-grade working straight knives. **Patterns:** Traditional-style Bowies and drop-point hunters. **Technical:** Grinds 440C, D2 and O1; offers variety of grinds and finishes. **Prices:** $130 to $750. **Remarks:** Full-time maker; first knife sold in 1980. **Mark:** Last name around kiwi bird logo.

REED, JOHN M
3937 Sunset Cove Dr., Port Orange, FL 32129, Phone: 386-310-4569, jreed129@cfl.rr.com
Specialties: Hunter, utility, some survival knives. **Patterns:** Trailing Point, and drop point sheath knives. **Technical:** ATS-34, Rockwell 60 exotic wood or natural material handles. **Prices:** $145 to $500. Depending on handle material. **Remarks:** Likes the stock removal method. "Old Fashioned trainling point blades." Handmade and sewn leather sheaths. **Mark:** "Reed" acid etched on left side of blade.

REEVE, CHRIS
2949 Victory View Way, Boise, ID 83709-2946, Phone: 208-375-0367, Fax: 208-375-0368, crkinfo@chrisreeve.com; Web: www.chrisreeve.com
Specialties: Originator and designer of the One Piece range of fixed blade utility knives and of the Sebenza Integral Lock folding knives made by Chris Reeve Knives. Currently not making or taking custom orders. **Patterns:** Art folders and fixed blades; one-of-a-kind. **Technical:** Grinds specialty stainless steels, damascus and other materials to his own design. **Prices:** $1,000 and up. **Remarks:** Full-time in knife business; first knife sold in 1982. **Mark:** Signature and date.

REEVES, J.R.
5181 South State Line, Texarkana, AR 71854, Phone: 870-773-5777, jos123@netscape.com
Specialties: Working straight knives of my design or customer design if a good flow. **Patterns:** Hunters, fighters, bowies, camp, bird, and trout knives. **Technical:** Forges and grinds 5160, 1084, 15n20, L6, 52100 and some damascus. Also some stock removal 440C, O1, D2, and 154 CM steels. I offer flat or hollow grinds. Natural handle material to include Sambar stag, desert Ironwood, sheep horn, other stabilized exotic woods and ivory. Custom filework offered. **Prices:** $200 -$1500. **Remarks:** Full-time maker, first knife sold in 1985. **Mark:** JR Reeves.

REGEL, JEAN-LOUIS
les ichards, Saint Leger de Fougeret, FRANCE 58120, Phone: 0033-66-621-6185, jregel2@hotmail.com
Specialties: Bowies, camp knives, swords and folders. **Technical:** Forges own Wootz steel by hand, and damascus and high-carbon blade steels. **Remarks:** American Bladesmith Society journeyman smith. **Mark:** Jean-louis on right side of blade.

REGGIO JR., SIDNEY J
PO Box 851, Sun, LA 70463, Phone: 504-886-5886
Specialties: Miniature classic and fancy straight knives of his design or in standard patterns. **Patterns:** Fighters, hunters and utility/camp knives. **Technical:** Grinds 440C, ATS-34 and commercial Damascus. Engraves; scrimshaws; offers filework. Hollow grinds most blades. Prefers natural handle material. Offers handmade sheaths. **Prices:** $85 to $250; some to $500. **Remarks:** Part-time maker; first knife sold in 1988. Doing business as Sterling Workshop. **Mark:** Initials.

REID, JIM
6425 Cranbrook St. NE, Albuquerque, NM 87111, jhrabq7@Q.com
Specialties: Fixed-blade knives.**Patterns:** Hunting, neck, and cowboy bowies. **Technical:** A2, D2, and damascus, stock removal. **Prices:** $125 to $300. **Mark:** Jim Reid over New Mexico zia sign.

RENNER, TERRY
TR Blades, Inc., 707 13th Ave. Cir. W, Palmetto, FL 34221, Phone: 941-729-3226; 941-545-6320, terrylmusic@gmail.com Web: www.trblades.com
Specialties: High art folders and straight-blades, specialty locking mechanisms. Designer of the Neckolas knife by CRKT. Deep-relief carving.**Technical:** Prefer CPM154, S30V, 1095 carbon, damascus by Rob Thomas, Delbert Ealey, Bertie Reitveld, Todd Fischer, Joel Davis. Does own heat treating. **Remarks:** Full-time maker as of 2005. Formerly in bicylce manufacturing business, with patents for tooling and fixtures. President of the Florida Knifemaker's Association since 2009. **Mark:** TR* stylized

REPKE, MIKE
4191 N. Euclid Ave., Bay City, MI 48706, Phone: 517-684-3111
Specialties: Traditional working and using straight knives of his design or to customer specs; classic knives; display knives. **Patterns:** Hunters, Bowies, skinners, fighters boots, axes and swords. **Technical:** Grind 440C. Offer variety of handle materials. **Prices:** $99 to $1500. **Remarks:** Full-time makers. Doing business as Black Forest Blades. **Mark:** Knife logo.

REVERDY, NICOLE AND PIERRE
5 Rue de L'egalite', Romans, FRANCE 26100, Phone: 334 75 05 10 15, Web: http://www.reverdy.com

Specialties: Art knives; legend pieces. Pierre and Nicole, his wife, are creating knives of art with combination of enamel on pure silver (Nicole) and poetic Damascus (Pierre) such as the "La dague a la licorne." **Patterns:** Daggers, folding knives Damascus and enamel, Bowies, hunters and other large patterns. **Technical:** Forges his Damascus and "poetic Damascus"; where animals such as unicorns, stags, dragons or star crystals appear, works with his own EDM machine to create any kind of pattern inside the steel with his own touch. **Prices:** $2000 and up. **Remarks:** Full-time maker since 1989; first knife sold in 1986. Nicole (wife) collaborates with enamels. **Mark:** Reverdy.

REVISHVILI, ZAZA
2102 Linden Ave, Madison, WI 53704, Phone: 608-243-7927
Specialties: Fancy/embellished and high-art straight knives and folders of his design. **Patterns:** Daggers, swords and locking folders. **Technical:** Uses Damascus; silver filigree, silver inlay in wood; enameling. **Prices:** $1000 to $9000; some to $15,000. **Remarks:** Full-time maker; first knife sold in 1987. **Mark:** Initials, city.

REXFORD, TODD
518 Park Dr., Woodland Park, CO 80863, Phone: 719-650-6799, todd@rexfordknives.com; Web: www.rexfordknives.com
Specialties: Dress tactical and tactical folders and fixed blades. **Technical:** I work in stainless steels, stainless damascus, titanium, Stellite and other high performance alloys. All machining and part engineering is done in house.

REXROAT, KIRK
12 Crow Ln., Banner, WY 82832, Phone: 307-689-5430, rexroatknives@gmail.com; Web: www.rexroatknives.com
Specialties: Using and collectible straight knives and folders of his design or to customer specs. **Patterns:** Bowies, hunters, folders. **Technical:** Forges damascus patterns, mosaic and 52100. Does own engraving. **Prices:** $400 and up. **Remarks:** Part-time maker, master smith in the ABS; first knife sold in 1984. Doing business as Rexroat Knives. Designs and builds prototypes for Al Mar Knives. **Mark:** Last name.

REYNOLDS, DAVE
1404 Indian Creek, Harrisville, WV 26362, Phone: 304-643-2889, wvreynolds@zoomintevnet.net
Specialties: Working straight knives of his design. **Patterns:** Bowies, kitchen and utility knives. **Technical:** Grinds and forges L6, 1095 and 440C. Heat-treats. **Prices:** $50 to $85; some to $175. **Remarks:** Full-time maker; first knife sold in 1980. Doing business as Terra-Gladius Knives. **Mark:** Mark on special orders only; serial number on all knives.

REYNOLDS, JOHN C
#2 Andover HC77, Gillette, WY 82716, Phone: 307-682-6076
Specialties: Working knives, some fancy. **Patterns:** Hunters, Bowies, tomahawks and buck skinners; some folders. **Technical:** Grinds D2, ATS-34, 440C and forges own Damascus and knives. Scrimshaws. **Prices:** $200 to $3000. **Remarks:** Spare-time maker; first knife sold in 1969. **Mark:** On ground blades JC Reynolds Gillette, WY, on forged blades, initials make the mark-JCR.

RHEA, LIN
413 Grant 291020, Prattsville, AR 72129, Phone: 870-942-6419, lwrhea@rheaknives.com; Web: www.rheaknives.com
Specialties: Traditional and early American styled Bowies in high carbon steel or Damascus. **Patterns:** Bowies, hunters and fighters. **Technical:** Filework wire inlay. Sole authorship of construction, Damascus and embellishment. **Prices:** $280 to $1500. **Remarks:** Serious part-time maker and rated as a Master Smith in the ABS.

RHO, NESTOR LORENZO
Prinera Junta 589, Junin, Buenos Aires, ARGENTINA CP 6000, Phone: +54-236-154670686, info@cuchillosrho.com.ar; Web: www.cuchillosrho.com.ar
Specialties: Classic and fancy straight knives of his design. **Patterns:** Bowies, fighters and hunters. **Technical:** Grinds 420C, 440C, 1084, 5160, 52100, L6 and W1. Offers semi-precious stones on handles, acid etching on blades and blade engraving. **Prices:** $120 to $600, collector's pieces up to $3,000. **Remarks:** Full-time maker; first knife sold in 1975. **Mark:** Name.

RIBONI, CLAUDIO
Via L Da Vinci, Truccazzano (MI), ITALY, Phone: 02 95309010, Web: www.riboni-knives.com

RICARDO ROMANO, BERNARDES
Ruai Coronel Rennò 1261, Itajuba MG, BRAZIL 37500, Phone: 0055-2135-622-5896
Specialties: Hunters, fighters, Bowies. **Technical:** Grinds blades of stainless and tools steels. **Patterns:** Hunters. **Prices:** $100 to $700. **Mark:** Romano.

RICHARD, RAYMOND
31047 SE Jackson Rd., Gresham, OR 97080, Phone: 503-663-1219, rayskee13@hotmail.com; Web: www.hawknknives.com
Specialties: Hand-forged knives, tomahawks, axes, and spearheads, all one-of-a-kind. **Prices:** $200 and up, some to $3000. **Remarks:** Full-time maker since 1994. **Mark:** Name on spine of blades.

RICHARDS, CHUCK
7243 Maple Tree Lane SE, Salem, OR 97317, Phone: 503-569-5549, woodchuckforge@gmail.com; Web: www.acrichardscustomknives.com
Specialties: Fixed blade Damascus. One-of-a-kind. **Patterns:** Hunters, fighters. **Prices:** $300 to $1,500+ **Remarks:** Likes to work with customers on a truly custom knife. **Mark:** A.C. Richards J.S. or ACR J.S.

RICHARDS, RALPH (BUD)
6413 Beech St, Bauxite, AR 72011, Phone: 501-602-5367, DoubleR042@aol.com; Web: www.ralphrichardscustomknives.com
Specialties: Forges 55160, 1084, and 15N20 for Damascus. S30V, 440C, and others. Wood, mammoth, giraffe and mother of pearl handles.

RICHARDSON, PERCY
1508 Atkinson Dr., Lufkin, TX 75901, Phone: 936-288-1690 or 936-634-1690, richardsonknives@yahoo.com; Web: americasfightingshipsknives.com or richardsonhandmadeknives.com
Specialties: Knives forged from steel off old ships. **Patterns:** Slip joints, lockbacks, hunters, bowies, mostly knives forged from steel from old Navy ships. **Prices:** $300 to $2,000. **Remarks:** Five-year project of ships knives, 2014 until 2019. **Mark:** Richardson over five-point star and Lone Star USA.

RICHARDSON III, PERCY (RICH)
1508 Atkinson Dr., Lufkin, TX 75901, Phone: 318-455-5309 or 936-634-1690, prichardson100@yahoo.com; Web: www.facebook.com/PRichKnives
Specialties: Straight knives of others' damascus, laser etching, some stabilized woods. **Patterns:** Hunters, skinners, small bowies and fighters. **Technical:** Stock removal, hollow grinds using CPM 154, ATS 34, 440C and damascus blade steels. **Prices:** $150 to $600. **Remarks:** Full-time maker, first knife made in 1995. **Mark:** Rich with year after on backbone of blade.

RICHARDSON JR., PERCY
1400 SM Tucker Rd., Pollok, TX 75969, Phone: 936-288-1690, Percy@Richardsonhandmadeknives.com; Web: www.Richardsonhandmadeknives.com
Specialties: Working straight knives and folders. **Patterns:** Hunters, skinners, bowies, fighters and folders. **Technical:** Mostly grinds CPM-154. **Prices:** $175 -$750 some bowies to $1200. **Remarks:** Full-time maker, first knife sold in 1990. Doing business as Richardsons Handmade Knives. **Mark:** Texas star with last name across it.

RICHERSON, RON
P.O. Box 51, Greenburg, KY 42743, Phone: 270-405-0491, Fax: 270-932-5601, RRicherson1@windstream.net
Specialties: Collectible and functional fixed blades, locking liners, and autos of his design. **Technical:** Grinds ATS-34, S30V, S60V, CPM-154, D2, 440, high carbon steel, and his and others' Damascus. Prefers natural materials for handles and does both stock removal and forged work, some with embellishments. **Prices:** $250 to $850, some higher. **Remarks:** Full-time maker. Member American Bladesmith Society. Made first knife in September 2006, sold first knife in December 2006. **Mark:** Name in oval with city and state. Also name in center of oval Green River Custom Knives.

RICKE, DAVE
1209 Adams St, West Bend, WI 53090, Phone: 262-334-5739
Specialties: Working knives; period pieces. **Patterns:** Hunters, boots, Bowies; locking folders and slip joints. **Technical:** Grinds ATS-34, A2, 440C and 154CM. **Prices:** $145 and up. **Remarks:** Full-time maker; first knife sold in 1976. **Mark:** Last name.

RICKS, KURT J.
Darkhammer Forge, 29 N. Center, Trenton, UT 84338, Phone: 435-563-3471, kopsh@hotmail.com; http://darkhammerworks.tripod.com
Specialties: Fixed blade working knives of all designs and to customer specs. **Patterns:** Fighters, daggers, hunters, swords, axes, and spears. **Technical:** Uses a coal fired forge. Forges high carbon, tool and spring steels. Does own heat treat on forge. Prefers natural handle materials. Leather sheaths available. **Prices:** Start at $50 plus shipping. **Remarks:** A knife should be functional first and pretty second. Part-time maker; first knife sold in 1994. **Mark:** Initials.

RIDER, DAVID M
PO Box 5946, Eugene, OR 97405-0911, Phone: 541-343-8747

RIDGE, TIM
SWAMP FOX KNIVES, 1282 W. Creston Rd., Crossville, TN 38571, Phone: 931-484-0216, swampfoxknives@frontiernet.net; www.swampfoxknives.com
Specialties Handforged historical American knives circa 1700 to 1865, colonial through Civil War eras. **Technical:** Forges 1095, 5160, 1084 and 1075 high-carbon steels. **Prices:** $135 to $2,000, depending on style and size of knife. **Remarks:** Full-time maker for 17 years. **Mark:** Patented running fox with TR in the body.

RIDLEY, ROB
RR1, Sundre, AB, CANADA T0M 1X0, Phone: 405-556-1113, rob@rangeroriginal.com; www.rangeroriginal.com, www.knifemaker.ca
Specialties: The knives I make are mainly fixed blades, though I'm exploring the complex world of folders. **Technical:** I favour high-end stainless alloys and exotic handle materials because a knife should provide both cutting ability and bragging rights. **Remarks:** I made my first knife in 1998 and still use that blade today. I've gone from full time, to part time, to hobby maker, but I still treasure time in the shop or spent with other enthusiasts. Operates Canadian Knifemakers Supply

RIEPE, RICHARD A
17604 E 296 St, Harrisonville, MO 64701

RIETVELD, BERTIE
PO Box 53, Magaliesburg, GT, SOUTH AFRICA 1791, Phone: 2783 232 8766, bertie@rietveldknives.com; Web: www.rietveldknives.com
Specialties: Art daggers, Bolster lock folders, Persian designs, embraces elegant designs. **Patterns:** Mostly one-of-a-kind. **Technical:** Sole authorship, work only in own

Damascus, gold inlay, blued stainless fittings. **Prices:** $500 -$8,000 **Remarks:** First knife made in 1979. Annual shows attended: ECCKS, Blade Show, Milan Show, South African Guild Show. Marks: Logo is elephant in half circle with name, enclosed in Stanhope lens

RIGNEY JR., WILLIE
191 Colson Dr, Bronston, KY 42518, Phone: 606-679-4227
   Specialties: High-tech period pieces and fancy working knives. **Patterns:** Fighters, boots, daggers and push knives. **Technical:** Grinds 440C and 154CM; buys Damascus. Most knives are embellished. **Prices:** $150 to $1500; some to $10,000. **Remarks:** Full-time maker; first knife sold in 1978. **Mark:** First initial, last name.

RINKES, SIEGFRIED
Am Sportpl 2, Markterlbach, GERMANY 91459

RITCHIE, ADAM
Koi Knifeworks, 10925 Sheridan Ave. S, Bloomington, MN 55431,
Phone: 651-503-2818, adamkara2@earthlink.net
   Specialties: Japanese-influenced fixed blades. **Patterns:** Small utility knives to larger hunter/tactical pieces, Kwaikens, tantos and Kiridashis. **Technical:** Flat and convex grinds O1 tool steel and 1095, differentially heat treated to 58-60 Rockwell hardness. **Prices:** $150-$1,000. **Remarks:** Part-time maker, full-time firefighter/EMT/FEO. **Mark:** Koi Knifeworks in circle around Kanji or Koi.

RIZZI, RUSSELL J
37 March Rd, Ashfield, MA 01330, Phone: 413-625-2842
   Specialties: Fancy working and using straight knives and folders of his design or to customer specs. **Patterns:** Hunters, locking folders and fighters. **Technical:** Grinds 440C, D2 and commercial Damascus. **Prices:** $150 to $750; some to 2500. **Remarks:** Part-time maker; first knife sold in 1990. **Mark:** Last name, Ashfield, MA.

ROBBINS, BILL
2160 E. Fry Blvd., Ste. C5, Sierra Vista, AZ 85635-2794, billrknifemaker@aol.com
   Specialties: Plain and fancy working straight knives. Makes to his designs and most anything you can draw. **Patterns:** Hunting knives, utility knives, and Bowies. **Technical:** Grinds ATS-34, 440C, tool steel, high carbon, buys Damascus. **Prices:** $70 to $450. **Remarks:** Part-time maker, first knife sold in 2001. **Mark:** Last name or desert scene with name.

ROBBINS, HOWARD P
1310 E. 310th Rd., Flemington, MO 65650, Phone: 417-282-5055, ARobb1407@aol.com
   Specialties: High-tech working knives with clean designs. **Patterns:** Folders, hunters and camp knives. **Technical:** Grinds 440C. Heat-treats; likes mirror finishes. Offers leatherwork. **Prices:** $100 to $500; some to $1000. **Remarks:** Full-time maker; first knife sold in 1982. **Mark:** Name, city and state.

ROBBINS, LANDON
2370 State Hwy. U, Crane, MO 65633, Phone: 417-207-4290, lwrobbins71@gmail.com
   Specialties: Fixed blades using high-carbon damascus. **Patterns:** Hunters, bowies and fighters. **Technical:** Hand-forged, flat-ground 1084, 1074, 5160, 52100 and maker's own damascus. **Prices:** $300 and up. **Remarks:** Part-time maker, ABS journeyman smith. **Mark:** Robbins with an arrow under name.

ROBERTS, CHUCK
PO Box 7174, Golden, CO 80403, Phone: 303-642-2388, chuck@crobertsart.com; Web: www.crobertsart.com
   Specialties: Price daggers, large Bowies, hand-rubbed satin finish. **Patterns:** Bowies and California knives. **Technical:** Grinds 440C, 5160 and ATS-34. Handles made of stag, ivory or mother-of-pearl. **Prices:** $1250. **Remarks:** Full-time maker. Company name is C. Roberts -Art that emulates the past. **Mark:** Last initial or last name.

ROBERTS, JACK
10811 Sagebluff Dr, Houston, TX 77089, Phone: 281-481-1784, jroberts59@houston.rr.com
   Specialties: Hunting knives and folders, offers scrimshaw by wife Barbara. **Patterns:** Drop point hunters and LinerLock® folders. **Technical:** Grinds 440-C, offers file work, texturing, natural handle materials and Micarta. **Prices:** $200 to $800 some higher. **Remarks:** Part-time maker, sold first knife in 1965. **Mark:** Name, city, state.

ROBERTS, MICHAEL
601 Oakwood Dr, Clinton, MS 39056, Phone: 601-540-6222, Fax: 601-213-4891
   Specialties: Working and using knives in standard patterns and to customer specs. **Patterns:** Hunters, Bowies, tomahawks and fighters. **Technical:** Forges 5160, O1, 1095 and his own Damascus. Uses only natural handle materials. **Prices:** $145 to $500; some to $1100. **Remarks:** Part-time maker; first knife sold in 1988. **Mark:** Last name or first and last name in Celtic script.

ROBERTS, T. C. (TERRY)
142131 Lake Forest Heights Rd., Siloam Springs, AR 72761, Phone: 479-373-6502, carolcroberts@cox.net
   Specialties: Working straight knives and folders of the maker's original design. **Patterns:** Bowies, daggers, fighters, locking folders, slip joints to include multiblades and whittlers. **Technical:** Grinds all types of carbon and stainless steels and commercially available Damascus. Works in stone and casts in bronze and silver. Some inlays and engraving. **Prices:** $250 -$3500. **Remarks:** Full-time maker; sold first knife in 1983. **Mark:** Stamp is oval with initials inside.

ROBERTSON, LEO D
3728 Pleasant Lake Dr, Indianapolis, IN 46227, Phone: 317-882-9899, ldr52@juno.com
   Specialties: Hunting and folders. **Patterns:** Hunting, fillet, Bowie, utility, folders and

tantos. **Technical:** Uses ATS-34, 154CM, 440C, 1095, D2 and Damascus steels. **Prices:** Fixed knives $75 to $350, folders $350 to $600. **Remarks:** Handles made with stag, wildwoods, laminates, mother-of-pearl. Made first knife in 1990. Member of American Bladesmith Society. **Mark:** Logo with full name in oval around logo.

ROBINSON, CALVIN
5501 Twin Creek Circle, Pace, FL 32571, Phone: 850 572 1504, calvin@calvinrobinsonknives.com; Web: www.CalvinRobinsonKnives.com
   Specialties: Working knives of my own design. **Patterns:** Hunters, fishing, folding and kitchen and purse knives. **Technical:** Now using 14C28N stainless blade steel, as well as 12C27, 13C26 and D2. **Prices:** $180 to $2500. **Remarks:** Full-time maker. Knifemakers' Guild Board of Directors. **Mark:** Robinson.

ROBINSON, CHUCK
SEA ROBIN FORGE, 1423 Third Ave., Picayune, MS 39466, Phone: 601-798-0060, robi5515@bellsouth.net
   Specialties: Deluxe period pieces and working / using knives of his design and to customer specs. **Patterns:** Bowies, fighters, hunters, utility knives and original designs. **Technical:** Forges own damascus, 52100, O1, W2, L6 and 1070 thru 1095. **Prices:** Start at $225. **Remarks:** First knife 1958. **Mark:** Fish logo, anchor and initials C.R.

ROBINSON III, REX R
10531 Poe St, Leesburg, FL 34788, Phone: 352-787-4587
   Specialties: One-of-a-kind high-art automatics of his design. **Patterns:** Automatics, liner locks and lock back folders. **Technical:** Uses tool steel and stainless Damascus and mokume; flat grinds. Hand carves folders. **Prices:** $1800 to $7500. **Remarks:** First knife sold in 1988. **Mark:** First name inside oval.

ROCHFORD, MICHAEL R
PO Box 577, Dresser, WI 54009, Phone: 715-755-3520, mrrochford@centurytel.net
   Specialties: Working straight knives and folders. Classic Bowies and Moran traditional. **Patterns:** Bowies, fighters, hunters: slip-joint, locking and liner locking folders. **Technical:** Grinds ATS-34, 440C, 154CM and D-2; forges W2, 5160, and his own Damascus. Offers metal and metal and leather sheaths. Filework and wire inlay. **Prices:** $150 to $1000; some to $2000. **Remarks:** Part-time maker; first knife sold in 1984. **Mark:** Name.

RODDY, ROY "TIM"
7640 Hub-Bedford Rd., Hubbard, OH 44425, Phone: 330-770-5921, pfr2rtr@hotmail.com
   Specialties: Any type of knife a customer wants, large knives, small knives and anything in between. **Patterns:** Hunters, fighters, martial arts knives, hide-outs, neck knives, throwing darts and locking-liner folders. Leather or Kydex sheaths with exotic-skin inlays. **Technical:** 440C, D2, ATS-34 or damascus blade steels. **Remarks:** Started making knives 25 years ago. **Mark:** Railroad sign (circle with an X inside and an R on either side of the X).

RODEBAUGH, JAMES L
P.O. Box 404, Carpenter, WY 82054, Phone: 307-649-2394, jlrodebaugh@gmail.com

RODEWALD, GARY
447 Grouse Ct, Hamilton, MT 59840, Phone: 406-363-2192
   Specialties: Bowies of his design as inspired from historical pieces. **Patterns:** Hunters, Bowies and camp/combat. Forges 5160 1084 and his own Damascus of 1084, 15N20, field grade hunters AT-34-440C, 440V, and BG42. **Prices:** $200 to $1500. **Remarks:** Sole author on knives, sheaths done by saddle maker. **Mark:** Rodewald.

RODKEY, DAN
18336 Ozark Dr, Hudson, FL 34667, Phone: 727-863-8264
   Specialties: Traditional straight knives of his design and in standard patterns. **Patterns:** Boots, fighters and hunters. **Technical:** Grinds 440C, D2 and ATS-34. **Prices:** Start at $200. **Remarks:** Full-time maker; first knife sold in 1985. Doing business as Rodkey Knives. **Mark:** Etched logo on blade.

ROEDER, DAVID
426 E. 9th Pl., Kennewick, WA 99336, d.roeder1980@yahoo.com
   Specialties: Fixed blade field and exposition grade knives. **Patterns:** Favorite styles are Bowie and hunter. **Technical:** Forges primarily 5160 and 52100. Makes own Damascus. **Prices:** Start at $150. **Remarks:** Made first knife in September, 1996. **Mark:** Maker's mark is a D and R with the R resting at a 45-degree angle to the lower right of the D.

ROGERS, RAY
PO Box 126, Wauconda, WA 98859, Phone: 509-486-8069, knives @rayrogers.com; Web: www.rayrogers.com
   Specialties: LinerLock® folders. Asian and European professional chef's knives. **Patterns:** Rayzor folders, chef's knives and cleavers of his own and traditional designs, drop point hunters and fillet knives. **Technical:** Stock removal S30V, 440, 1095, O1 Damascus and other steels. Does all own heat treating, clay tempering, some forging G-10, Micarta, carbon fiber on folders, stabilized burl woods on fixed blades. **Prices:** $300 to $700. **Remarks:** Knives are made one-at-a-time to the customer's order. Happy to consider customizing knife designs to suit your preferences and sometimes create entirely new knives when necessary. As a full-time knifemaker is willing to spend as much time as it takes (usually through email) discussing the options and refining details of a knife's design to insure that you get the knife you really want.

ROGERS, RICHARD
PO Box 769, Magdalena, NM 87825, Phone: 575-838-7237, r.s.rogers@gmail.com; Web: www.richardrogersknives.com
   Specialties: Folders. **Patterns:** Modern slip joints, LinerLocks and frame-locks. **Prices:** $300 and up. **Mark:** Last name.

ROGHMANS, MARK
607 Virginia Ave, LaGrange, GA 30240, Phone: 706-885-1273
Specialties: Classic and traditional knives of his design. **Patterns:** Bowies, daggers and fighters. **Technical:** Grinds ATS-34, D2 and 440C. **Prices:** $250 to $500. **Remarks:** Part-time maker; first knife sold in 1984. Doing business as LaGrange Knife. **Mark:** Last name and/or LaGrange Knife.

ROHN, FRED
7675 W Happy Hill Rd, Coeur d'Alene, ID 83814, Phone: 208-667-0774
Specialties: Hunters, boot knives, custom patterns. **Patterns:** Drop points, double edge, etc. **Technical:** Grinds 440 or 154CM. **Prices:** $85 and up. **Remarks:** Part-time maker. **Mark:** Logo on blade; serial numbered.

ROLLERT, STEVE
PO Box 65, Keenesburg, CO 80643-0065, Phone: 303-732-4858, steve@doveknives.com; Web: www.doveknives.com
Specialties: Highly finished working knives. **Patterns:** Variety of straight knives; locking folders and slip-joints. **Technical:** Forges and grinds W2, 1095, ATS-34 and his pattern-welded, cable Damascus and nickel Damascus. **Prices:** $300 to $1000; some to $3000. **Remarks:** Full-time maker; first knife sold in 1980. Doing business as Dove Knives. **Mark:** Last name in script.

ROMEIS, GORDON
1521 Coconut Dr., Fort Myers, FL 33901, Phone: 239-940-5060, gordonromeis@gmail.com Web: Romeisknives.com
Specialties: Smaller using knives. **Patterns:** I have a number of standard designs that include both full tapered tangs and narrow tang knives. Custom designs are welcome. Many different types. No folders. **Technical:** Standard steel is 440C. Also uses Alabama Damascus steel. **Prices:** Start at $165. **Remarks:** I am a part-time maker however I do try to keep waiting times to a minimum. **Mark:** Either my name, city, and state or simply ROMEIS depending on the knife.

RONZIO, N. JACK
PO Box 248, Fruita, CO 81521, Phone: 970-858-0921

ROOSEVELT, RUSSELL
398 County Rd. 450 E, Albion, IL 62806-4753, Phone: 618-445-3226 or 618-302-7272, rroosevelt02@gmail.com
Specialties: Using straight knives of his design and to customers' specs. **Patterns:** Hunters, utility and camp knives. **Technical:** Forges 1084 and high-carbon damascus. **Prices:** $250 to $1,200. **Remarks:** Part-time maker, first knife sold in 1999. **Mark:** Full name left side, ABS JS stamp right side.

ROOT, GARY
644 East 14th St, Erie, PA 16503, Phone: 814-459-0196
Specialties: Damascus Bowies with hand carved eagles, hawks and snakes for handles. Few folders made. **Patterns:** Daggers, fighters, hunter/field knives. **Technical:** Using handforged Damascus from Ray Bybar Jr (M.S.) and Robert Eggerling. Grinds D2, 440C, 1095 and 5160. Some 5160 is hand forged. **Prices:** $80 to $300 some to $1000. **Remarks:** Full time maker, first knife sold in 1976. **Mark:** Name over Erie, PA.

ROSE, BOB
PO BOX 126, Wagontown, PA 19376, Phone: 484-883-3925, bobmedit8@comcast.net Web: www.bobroseknives.com
Patterns: Bowies, fighters, drop point hunters, daggers, bird and trout, camp, and other fixed blade styles. **Technical:** Mostly using 1095 and damascus steel, desert ironwood and other top-of-the-line exotic woods as well as mammoth tooth. **Prices:** $49 -$300. **Remarks:** Been making and selling knives since 2004. "Knife Making is a meditation technique for me."

ROSE, DEREK W
14 Willow Wood Rd, Gallipolis, OH 45631, Phone: 740-446-4627

ROSE II, DOUN T.
Ltc US Special Operations Command (ret.), 1795/96 W Sharon Rd SW, Fife Lake, MI 49633, Phone: 231-645-1369, rosecutlery@gmail.com; Web: www.rosecutlery.com
Specialties: Straight working, collector and presentation knives to a high level of fit and finish. Design in collaboration with customer. **Patterns:** Field knives, Scagel, bowies, tactical, period pieces, axes and tomahawks, fishing and hunting spears and fine kitchen cutlery. **Technical:** Forged and blade ground, high carbon and stainless steel appropriate to end use. Steel from leading industry sources. Some period pieces from recovered stock. Makes own damascus (to include multi-bar and mosaic) and mokume gane. **Remarks:** Full-time maker, ABS since 2000, William Scagel Memorial Scholarship 2002, Bill Moran School of Blade Smithing 2003, apprentice under Master Blacksmith Dan Nickels at Black Rock Forge current. Working at Crooked Pine Forge. **Mark:** Last name ROSE in block letters with five petal "wild rose" in place of O. Doing business as Rose Cutlery.

ROSENBAUGH, RON
2806 Stonegate Dr, Crystal Lake, IL 60012, Phone: 815-477-9233 or 815-345-1633, ron@rosenbaughknives.com; Web: www.rosenbaughknives.com
Specialties: Fancy and plain working knives using own designs, collaborations, and traditional patterns. **Patterns:** Bird, trout, boots, hunters, fighters, some Bowies. **Technical:** Grinds high alloy stainless, tool steels, and Damascus; forges 1084,5160, 52100, carbon and spring steels. **Prices:** $150 to $1000. **Remarks:** Part-time maker, first knife sold in 2004. **Mark:** Last name, logo, city.

ROSENFELD, BOB
1260 hightower Trl., Apt. 305, Atlanta, GA 30350, Phone: 770-867-2647, www.1bladesmith@msn.com

Specialties: Fancy and embellished working/using straight knives of his design and in standard patterns. **Patterns:** Daggers, hunters and utility/camp knives. **Technical:** Forges 52100, A203E, 1095 and L6 Damascus. Offers engraving. **Prices:** $125 to $650; some to $1000. **Remarks:** Full-time maker; first knife sold in 1984. Also makes folders; ABS Journeyman. **Mark:** Last name or full name, Knifemaker.

ROSS, D L
27 Kinsman St, Dunedin, NEW ZEALAND, Phone: 64 3 464 0239, Fax: 64 3 464 0239
Specialties: Working straight knives of his design. **Patterns:** Hunters, various others. **Technical:** Grinds 440C. **Prices:** $100 to $450; some to $700 NZ (not U.S. $). **Remarks:** Part-time maker; first knife sold in 1988. **Mark:** Dave Ross, Maker, city and country.

ROSS, STEPHEN
534 Remington Dr, Evanston, WY 82930, Phone: 307-799-7653
Specialties: One-of-a-kind collector-grade classic and contemporary straight knives and folders of his design and to customer specs; some fantasy pieces. **Patterns:** Combat and survival knives, hunters, boots and folders. **Technical:** Grinds stainless and tool steels. Engraves, scrimshaws. Makes leather sheaths. **Prices:** $160 to $3000. **Remarks:** Part-time maker; first knife sold in 1971. **Mark:** Last name in modified Roman; sometimes in script.

ROSS, TIM
3239 Oliver Rd, Thunder Bay, ON, CANADA P7G 1S9, Phone: 807-935-2667, Fax: 807-935-3179, rosscustomknives@gmail.com
Specialties: Fixed blades, natural handle material. **Patterns:** Hunting, fishing, Bowies, fighters. **Technical:** 440C, D2, 52100, Cable, 5160, 1084, L6, W2. **Prices:** $150 to $750 some higher. **Remarks:** Forges and stock removal. **Mark:** Ross Custom Knives.

ROSSDEUTSCHER, ROBERT N
133 S Vail Ave, Arlington Heights, IL 60005, Phone: 847-577-0404, Web: www.rnrknives.com
Specialties: Frontier-style and historically inspired knives. **Patterns:** Trade knives, Bowies, camp knives and hunting knives, tomahawks and lances. **Technical:** Most knives are hand forged, a few are stock removal. **Prices:** $135 to $1500. **Remarks:** Journeyman Smith of the American Bladesmith Society. **Mark:** Back-to-back "R's", one upside down and backwards, one right side up and forward in an oval. Sometimes with name, town and state; depending on knife style.

ROTELLA, RICHARD A
643 75th St., Niagara Falls, NY 14304, richarpo@roadrunner.com
Specialties: Highly finished working knives of his own design, as well as some Loveless-style designs. **Patterns:** Hunters, fishing, small game, utility, fighters and boot knives. **Technical:** Grinds ATS-34, 154CM, CPM 154 and 440C. **Prices:** $150 to $600. **Remarks:** Part-time maker; first knife sold in 1977. Sells completed knives only and does not take orders; makes about 70 knives a year. **Mark:** Name and city.

ROUGEAU, DERICK
1465 Cloud Peak Dr., Sparks, NV 89436, Phone: 775-232-6167, derick@rougeauknives.com; Web: www.rougeauknives.com
Specialties: A wide range of original designs from practical to tactical and traditional. **Patterns:** Bowies, hunters, fighters, bushcraft blades, tantos, machetes, chef's knives, tomahawks, hatchets, swords, neck and tool knives. Also makes assorted accessories and other cool items. **Technical:** Using stock-removal process. Flat and hollow grinds using a wide range of steels from damascus to 1080, 1095, 5160, 6150, 01, D2, ATS 34, CPM 154 and other CPM stainless steels. Does own heat treating, leather work and Kydex, and uses synthetic materials, stabilized woods and antler. **Prices:** $250 to $650 or more. **Remarks:** Part-time maker, full-time artist/designer. **Mark:** "DR" logo in front of "ROUGEAU."

ROULIN, CHARLES
113 B Rt. de Soral, Geneva, SWITZERLAND 1233, Phone: 022-757-4479, Fax: 079-218-9754, charles.roulin@bluewin.ch; Web: www.coutelier-roulin.com
Specialties: Fancy high-art straight knives and folders of his design. **Patterns:** Bowies, locking folders, slip-joint folders and miniatures. **Technical:** Grinds 440C, ATS-34 and D2. Engraves; carves nature scenes and detailed animals in steel, ivory, on handles and blades. **Prices:** $500 to $3000; some to Euro: 14,600. **Remarks:** Full-time maker; first knife sold in 1988. **Mark:** Symbol of fish with name or name engraved.

ROUSH, SCOTT
Big Rock Forge, 31920 Maki Rd, Washburn, WI 54891, Phone: 715-373-2334, scott@bigrockforge.com; Web: bigrockforge.com
Specialties: Forged blades representing a diversity of styles from trasditional hunters, fighters, camp knives, and EDC's to artistic pieces of cultural and historical inspiration with an emphasis in unique materials. **Technical:** Forges Aldo 1084, W2, low MN 1075, stainless/high carbon san mai, wrought iron/high carbon san mai, damascus. **Prices:** $85 to $1000 **Remarks:** Full-time maker; first knife sold in 2010.**Mark:** Stamped initials (SAR) set in a diamond.

ROWE, FRED
BETHEL RIDGE FORGE, 3199 Roberts Rd, Amesville, OH 45711, Phone: 866-325-2164, fred.rowe@bethelridgeforge.com; Web: www.bethelridgeforge.com
Specialties: Damascus and carbon steel sheath knives. **Patterns:** Bowies, hunters, fillet small kokris. **Technical:** His own Damascus, 52100, O1, L6, 1095 carbon steels, mosaics. **Prices:** $200 to $2000. **Remarks:** All blades are clay hardened. **Mark:** Bethel Ridge Forge.

ROYER, KYLE
9021 State Hwy. M, Clever, MO 65631, Phone: 417-247-5572, royerknifeworks@live.com; Web: www.kyleroyerknives.com

Specialties: Folders and fixed-blade knives. **Technical:** Mosaic damascus and engraving. **Prices:** $350 to $7,500. **Remarks:** ABS master smith. **Mark:** K~ROYER~MS.

ROZAS, CLARK D
1436 W "G" St, Wilmington, CA 90744, Phone: 310-518-0488
Specialties: Hand forged blades. **Patterns:** Pig stickers, toad stabbers, whackers, choppers. **Technical:** Damascus, 52100, 1095, 1084, 5160. **Prices:** $200 to $600. **Remarks:** A.B.S. member; part-time maker since 1995. **Mark:** Name over dagger.

RUA, GARY
400 Snell St., Apt. 2, Fall River, MA 02721, Phone: 508-677-2664
Specialties: Working straight knives of his design. 1800 to 1900 century standard patterns. **Patterns:** Bowies, hunters, fighters, and patch knives. **Technical:** Forges and grinds. Damascus, 5160, 1095, old files. Uses only natural handle material. **Prices:** $350 -$2000. **Remarks:** Part-time maker. (Harvest Moon Forge) **Mark:** Last name.

RUANA KNIFE WORKS
Box 520, Bonner, MT 59823, Phone: 406-258-5368, Fax: 406-258-2895, info@ruanaknives.com; Web: www.ruanaknives.com
Specialties: Working knives and period pieces. **Patterns:** Variety of straight knives. **Technical:** Forges 5160 chrome alloy for Bowies and 1095. **Prices:** $200 and up. **Remarks:** Full-time maker; first knife sold in 1938. Brand new non catalog knives available on ebay under seller name ruanaknives. For free catalog email regular mailing address to info@ruanaknives.com **Mark:** Name.

RUCKER, THOMAS
30222 Mesa Valley Dr., Spring, TX 77386, Phone: 832-216-8122, admin@knivesbythomas.com Web: www.knivesbythomas.com
Specialties: Personal design and custom design. Hunting, tactical, folding knives, and cutlery. **Technical:** Design and grind ATS34, D2, O1, Damascus, and VG10. **Prices:** $150 -$5,000. **Remarks:** Full-time maker and custom scrimshaw and engraving done by wife, Debi Rucker. First knife done in 1969; first design sold in 1975 **Mark:** Etched logo and signature.

RUPERT, BOB
301 Harshaville Rd, Clinton, PA 15026, Phone: 724-573-4569, rbrupert@aol.com
Specialties: Wrought period pieces with natural elements. **Patterns:** Elegant straight blades, friction folders. **Technical:** Forges colonial 7; 1095; 5160; diffuse mokume-gane and Damascus. **Prices:** $150 to $1500; some higher. **Remarks:** Part-time maker; first knife sold in 1980. Evening hours studio since 1980. Likes simplicity that disassembles. **Mark:** R etched in Old English.

RUPLE, WILLIAM H
201 Brian Dr., Pleasanton, TX 78064, Phone: 830-569-0007, bknives@devtex.net
Specialties: Multi-blade folders, slip joints, some lock backs. **Patterns:** Like to reproduce old patterns. Offers filework and engraving. **Technical:** Grinds CPM-154 and other carbon and stainless steel and commercial Damascus. **Prices:** $950 to $2500. **Remarks:** Full-time maker; first knife sold in 1988. **Mark:** Ruple.

RUSNAK, JOSEF
Breclavska 6, 323 00 Plzen, CZECH REPUBLIC, Phone: 00420721329442, rusnak.josef@centrum.cz; Web: http://knife.guaneru.cz
Specialties: Highly artistically designed knives. **Patterns:** Straight knives and folders. Collaboration with Buddy Weston. **Technical:** Engraving in high-quality steel and organic materials (mammoth tusk, giraffe bone, mother-of-pearl, bone), miniature sculpting, casting (Au, Ag, bronze). **Prices:** $1,000 and up. **Remarks:** Part-time maker; first knife sold in 1994. **Mark:** Signature.

RUSS, RON
5351 NE 160th Ave, Williston, FL 32696, Phone: 352-528-2603, RussRs@aol.com
Specialties: Damascus and mokume. **Patterns:** Ladder, rain drop and butterfly. **Technical:** Most knives, including Damascus, are forged from 52100-E. **Prices:** $65 to $2500. **Mark:** Russ.

RUSSELL, MICK
4 Rossini Rd, Pari Park, Port Elizabeth, EC, SOUTH AFRICA 6070
Specialties: Art knives. **Patterns:** Working and collectible bird, trout and hunting knives, defense knives and folders. **Technical:** Grinds D2, 440C, ATS-34 and Damascus. Offers mirror or satin finishes. **Prices:** Start at $100. **Remarks:** Full-time maker; first knife sold in 1986. **Mark:** Stylized rhino incorporating initials.

RUSSELL, TOM
6500 New Liberty Rd, Jacksonville, AL 36265, Phone: 205-492-7866
Specialties: Straight working knives of his design or to customer specs. **Patterns:** Hunters, folders, fighters, skinners, Bowies and utility knives. **Technical:** Grinds D2, 440C and ATS-34; offers filework. **Prices:** $75 to $225. **Remarks:** Part-time maker; first knife sold in 1987. Full-time tool and die maker. **Mark:** Last name with tulip stamp.

RUTH, MICHAEL G
3101 New Boston Rd, Texarkana, TX 75501, Phone: 903-832-7166/cell:903-277-3663, Fax: 903-832-4710, mike@ruthknives.com; Web: www.ruthknives.com
Specialties: Hunters, bowies & fighters. Damascus & carbon steel. **Prices:** $375 & up. **Mark:** Last name.

RUTH, JR., MICHAEL
5716 Wilshire Dr., Texarkana, TX 75503, Phone: 903-293-2663, michael@ruthlesscustomknives.com; Web: www.ruthlesscustomknives.com
Specialties: Custom hand-forged blades, utilizing high carbon and Damascus steels. **Patterns:** Bowies, hunters and fighters ranging from field to presentation-grade pieces. **Technical:** Steels include 5160, 1084, 15n20, W-2, 1095, and O-1. Handle materials

include a variety of premium hardwoods, stag, assorted ivories and micarta. **Mark:** 8-pointed star with capital "R" in center.

RUUSUVUORI, ANSSI
Verkkotie 38, Piikkio, FINLAND 21500, Phone: 358-50-520 8057, anssi.ruusuvuori@akukon.fi; Web: www.arknives.suntuubi.com
Specialties: Traditional and modern puukko knives and hunters. Sole author except for Damascus steel.**Technical:** Forges mostly 1080 steel and grinds RWL-34. **Prices:** $200 to $500; some to $1200. **Remarks:** Part-time maker.**Mark:** A inside a circle (stamped)

RYBAR JR., RAYMOND B
2328 S. Sunset Dr., Camp Verde, AZ 86322, Phone: 928-567-6372
Specialties: Straight knives or folders with customers name, logo, etc. in mosaic pattern. **Patterns:** Common patterns plus mosaics of all types. **Technical:** Forges own Damascus. Primary forging of self smelted steel -smelting classes. **Prices:** $200 to $1200; Bible blades to $10,000. **Remarks:** Master Smith (A.B.S.) Primary focus toward Biblicaly themed blades **Mark:** Rybar or stone church forge or Rev. 1:3 or R.B.R. between diamonds.

RYDBOM, JEFF
PO Box 548, Annandale, MN 55302, Phone: 320-274-9639, jry1890@hotmail.com
Specialties: Ring knives. **Patterns:** Hunters, fighters, Bowie and camp knives. **Technical:** Straight grinds O1, A2, 1566 and 5150 steels. **Prices:** $150 to $1000. **Remarks:** No pinning of guards or pommels. All silver brazed. **Mark:** Capital "C" with J R inside.

RYUICHI, KUKI
504-7 Tokorozawa-Shinmachi, Tokorozawa-city, Saitama, JAPAN, Phone: 042-943-3451

RZEWNICKI, GERALD
8833 S Massbach Rd, Elizabeth, IL 61028-9714, Phone: 815-598-3239

S

SAINDON, R BILL
233 Rand Pond Rd, Goshen, NH 03752, Phone: 603-863-1874, dayskier71@aol.com
Specialties: Collector-quality folders of his design or to customer specs. **Patterns:** Latch release, LinerLock® and lockback folders. **Technical:** Offers limited amount of own Damascus; also uses Damas makers steel. Prefers natural handle material, gold and gems. **Prices:** $500 to $4000. **Remarks:** Full-time maker; first knife sold in 1981. Doing business as Daynia Forge. **Mark:** Sun logo or engraved surname.

SAKAKIBARA, MASAKI
20-8 Sakuragaoka 2-Chome, Setagaya-ku, Tokyo, JAPAN 156-0054, Phone: 81-3-3420-0375

SAKMAR, MIKE
4337 E. Grand River Ave. #113, Howell, MI 48843, Phone: 517-546-6388, Fax: 517-546-6399, sakmarent@yahoo.com; Web: www.sakmarenterprises.com
Specialties: Mokume in various patterns and alloy combinations. **Patterns:** Bowies, fighters, hunters and integrals. **Technical:** Grinds ATS-34, Damascus and high-carbon tool steels. Uses mostly natural handle materials—elephant ivory, walrus ivory, stag, wildwood, oosic, etc. Makes mokume for resale. **Prices:** $250 to $2500; some to $4000. **Remarks:** Part-time maker; first knife sold in 1990. Supplier of mokume. **Mark:** Last name.

SALLEY, JOHN D
3965 Frederick-Ginghamsburg Rd., Tipp City, OH 45371, Phone: 937-698-4588, Fax: 937-698-4131
Specialties: Fancy working knives and art pieces. **Patterns:** Hunters, fighters, daggers and some swords. **Technical:** Grinds ATS-34, 12C27 and W2; buys Damascus. **Prices:** $85 to $1000; some to $6000. **Remarks:** Part-time maker; first knife sold in 1979. **Mark:** First initial, last name.

SALTER, GREGG
Salter Fine Cutlery, POB 384571, Waikoloa, HI 96738-4571, Phone: 808-883-0128, saltent@aol.com; Web: www.salterfinecutlery.com
Specialties: Custom, made-to-order cutlery, chopping boards and boxes, including kitchen knife sets, steak knife sets, carving sets, chef's knives and collectible knives and swords. Work in collaboration with several individual bladesmiths who create blades to our specifications. **Technical:** Variety of steels available, including VG-10, Aogami Super, SG2, OU-31, YSS White Paper Shirogami, YSS Aogami Blue Paper and Tamahagane (swords). Damascus patterns and, in the case of swords, hand-etched scenes available. **Prices:** Range widely, from approximately $250 to over $1 million in the case of one spectacular collectible. Average price for chef's knives in the $500-$750 range. **Remarks:** Full-time business making a range of products based around knives. **Mark:** Hawaiian koa tree with crossed chef's knives and the outline of a crown between them.

SAMPSON, LYNN
381 Deakins Rd, Jonesborough, TN 37659, Phone: 423-348-8373
Specialties: Highly finished working knives, mostly folders. **Patterns:** Locking folders, slip-joints, interframes and two-blades. **Technical:** Grinds D2, 440C and ATS-34; offers extensive filework. **Prices:** Start at $300. **Remarks:** Full-time maker; first knife sold in 1982. **Mark:** Name and city in logo.

SANDBERG, RONALD B
24784 Shadowwood Ln, Brownstown, MI 48134-9560, Phone: 734-671-6866, msc2009@comcast.net
Specialties: Good looking and functional hunting knives, filework, mixing of handle materials. **Patterns:** Hunters, skinners and Bowies. **Prices:** $120 and up. **Remarks:** Full lifetime workmanship guarantee. **Mark:** R.B. SANDBERG

custom knifemakers

SANDERS, BILL
335 Bauer Ave, PO Box 957, Mancos, CO 81328, Phone: 970-533-7223, Fax: 970-533-7390, billsand@frontier.net; Web: www.billsandershandmadeknives.com
Specialties: Survival knives, working straight knives, some fancy and some fantasy, of his design. **Patterns:** Hunters, boots, utility knives, using belt knives. **Technical:** Grinds 440C, ATS-34 and commercial Damascus. Provides wide variety of handle materials. **Prices:** $170 to $800. **Remarks:** Full-time maker. Formerly of Timberline Knives. **Mark:** Name, city and state.

SANDERS, MICHAEL M
PO Box 1106, Ponchatoula, LA 70454, Phone: 985-507-2530, sanders-michael16@yahoo.com
Specialties: Working straight knives and folders, some deluxe. **Patterns:** Hunters, fighters, bowies, daggers, large folders, gentlemen's folders, slip-joint folders and deluxe damascus miniatures. **Technical:** Grinds O1, D2, 440C, CPM 154 and damascus. **Prices:** $75 to $650, and upscale. **Remarks:** Full-time maker; first knife sold in 1967. Fast delivery, takes special custom orders, can do multiple knives for organizations with their logo. **Mark:** Name and state.

SANDOW, BRENT EDWARD
50 O'Halloran Road, Howick, Auckland, NEW ZEALAND 2014, Phone: 64 9 537 4166, knifebug@vodafone.co.nz; Web: www.brentsandowknives.com
Specialties: Tactical fixed blades, hunting, camp, Bowie. **Technical:** All blades made by stock removal method. **Prices:** From US $200 upward. **Mark:** Name etched or engraved.

SANDS, SCOTT
2 Lindis Ln, New Brighton, Christchurch 9, NEW ZEALAND
Specialties: Classic working and fantasy swords. **Patterns:** Fantasy, medieval, celtic, viking, katana, some daggers. **Technical:** Forges own Damascus; 1080 and L6; 5160 and L6; O1 and L6. All hand-polished, does own heat-treating, forges non-Damascus on request. **Prices:** $1500 to $15,000+. **Remarks:** Full-time maker; first blade sold in 1996. **Mark:** Stylized Moon.

SANFORD, DICK
151 London Ln., Chehalis, WA 98532, Phone: 360-748-2128, richardsanfo364@centurytel.net
Remarks: Ten years experience hand forging knives

SANGSTER, JOE
POB 312, Vienna, GA 31092, Phone: 229-322-3407, ssangster@sowega.net; Web: www.sangsterknives.com
Specialties Gent's LinerLock folders with filework. **Patterns:** Traditional LinerLock folders, hunters, skinners and kitchen knives. **Technical:** Grinds ATS-34, CPM 134, 440C and commercial damascus. Handle materials of mammoth ivory, mammoth tooth, pearl, oosic, coral and exotic burl woods. **Prices:** $250 to $500, some up to $1,200. **Remarks:** Full-time maker; first knife sold in 2003. **Mark:** name or name, city and state.

SANTA, LADISLAV "LASKY"
Stara Voda 264/10, 97637 Hrochot, SLOVAKIA, Phone: +421-907-825-2-77, lasky@lasky.sk; Web: www.lasky.sk
Specialties: Damascus hunters, daggers and swords. **Patterns:** Various damascus patterns. **Prices:** $300 to $6,000 U.S. **Mark:** L or Lasky.

SANTIAGO, ABUD
Av Gaona 3676 PB, Buenos Aires, ARGENTINA 1416, Phone: 5411 4612 8396, info@phi-sabud.com; Web: www.phi-sabud.com/blades.html

SANTINI, TOM
101 Clayside Dr, Pikeville, NC 27863, Phone: 586-354-0245, tomsantiniknives@hotmail.com; Web: www.tomsantiniknives.com
Specialties: working/using straight knives, tactical, and some slipjoints **Technical:** Grinds ATS-34, S-90-V, D2, and damascus. I handstitch my leather sheaths. **Prices:** $150 -$500. **Remarks:** Full-time maker, first knife sold in 2004. **Mark:** Full name.

SARGANIS, PAUL
2215 Upper Applegate Rd, Jacksonville, OR 97530, Phone: 541-899-2831, paulsarganis@hotmail.com; Web: www.sarganis.50megs.com
Specialties: Hunters, folders, Bowies. **Technical:** Forges 5160, 1084. Grinds ATS-34 and 440C. **Prices:** $120 to $500. **Remarks:** Spare-time maker, first knife sold in 1987. **Mark:** Last name.

SASS, GARY N
2048 Buckeye Dr, Sharpsville, PA 16150, Phone: 724-866-6165, gnsass@yahoo.com
Specialties: Working straight knives of his design or to customer specifications. **Patterns:** Hunters, fighters, utility knives, push daggers. **Technical:** Grinds 440C, ATS-34 and Damascus. Uses exotic wood, buffalo horn, warthog tusk and semi-precious stones. **Prices:** $50 to $250, some higher. **Remarks:** Part-time maker. First knife sold in 2003. **Mark:** Initials G.S. formed into a diamond shape or last name.

SAVIANO, JAMES
124 Wallis St., Douglas, MA 01516, Phone: 508-476-7644, jimsaviano@gmail.com
Specialties: Straight knives. **Patterns:** Hunters, bowies, fighters, daggers, short swords. **Technical:** Hand-forged high-carbon and my own damascus steel. **Prices:** Starting at $300. **Remarks:** ABS mastersmith, maker since 2000, sole authorship. **Mark:** Last name or stylized JPS initials.

SAWBY, SCOTT
480 Snowberry Ln, Sandpoint, ID 83864, Phone: 208-263-4253, scotmar3@gmail.com; Web: www.sawbycustomknives.com
Specialties: Folders, working and fancy. **Patterns:** Locking folders, patent locking systems and interframes. **Technical:** Grinds D2, 440C, CPM154, ATS-34, S30V, and Damascus. **Prices:** $700 to $3000. **Remarks:** Full-time maker; first knife sold in 1974. Engraving by wife Marian. **Mark:** Last name, city and state.

SCARROW, WIL
c/o LandW Mail Service, PO Box 1036, Gold Hill, OR 97525, Phone: 541-855-1236, willsknife@earthlink.net
Specialties: Carving knives, also working straight knives in standard patterns or to customer specs. **Patterns:** Carving, fishing, hunting, skinning, utility, swords and Bowies. **Technical:** Forges and grinds: A2, L6, W1, D2, 5160, 1095, 440C, AEB-L, ATS-34 and others on request. Offers some filework. **Prices:** $105 to $850; some higher. Prices include sheath (carver's $40 and up). **Remarks:** Spare-time maker; first knife sold in 1983. Two to eight month construction time on custom orders. Doing business as Scarrow's Custom Stuff and Gold Hill Knife works (in Oregon). Carving knives available at Raven Dog Enterprises. Contact at Ravedog@aol.com. **Mark:** SC with arrow and year made.

SCHALLER, ANTHONY BRETT
5609 Flint Ct. NW, Albuquerque, NM 87120, Phone: 505-899-0155, brett@schallerknives.com; Web: www.schallerknives.com
Specialties: Straight knives and locking-liner folders of his design and in standard patterns. **Patterns:** Boots, fighters, utility knives and folders. **Technical:** Grinds CPM154, S30V, and stainless Damascus. Offers filework, hand-rubbed finishes and full and narrow tangs. Prefers exotic woods or Micarta for handle materials, G-10 and carbon fiber to handle materials. **Prices:** $100 to $350; some to $500. **Remarks:** Part-time maker; first knife sold in 1990. **Mark:** A.B. Schaller -Albuquerque NM -handmade.

SCHEID, MAGGIE
124 Van Stallen St, Rochester, NY 14621-3557
Specialties: Simple working straight knives. **Patterns:** Kitchen and utility knives; some miniatures. **Technical:** Forges 5160 high-carbon steel. **Prices:** $100 to $200. **Remarks:** Part-time maker; first knife sold in 1986. **Mark:** Full name.

SCHEMPP, ED
PO Box 1181, Ephrata, WA 98823, Phone: 509-754-2963, Fax: 509-754-3212, edschempp@yahoo.com
Specialties: Mosaic Damascus and unique folder designs. **Patterns:** Primarily folders. **Technical:** Grinds CPM440V; forges many patterns of mosaic using powdered steel. **Prices:** $100 to $400; some to $2000. **Remarks:** Part-time maker; first knife sold in 1991. Doing business as Ed Schempp Knives. **Mark:** Ed Schempp Knives over five heads of wheat, city and state.

SCHEMPP, MARTIN
PO Box 1181, 5430 Baird Springs Rd NW, Ephrata, WA 98823, Phone: 509-754-2963, Fax: 509-754-3212
Specialties: Fantasy and traditional straight knives of his design, to customer specs and in standard patterns. **Patterns:** Paleolithic-styles. **Patterns:** Fighters and Paleolithic designs. **Technical:** Uses opal, Mexican rainbow and obsidian. Offers scrimshaw. **Prices:** $15 to $100; some to $250. **Remarks:** Spare-time maker; first knife sold in 1995. **Mark:** Initials and date.

SCHEURER, ALFREDO E FAES
Av Rincon de los Arcos 104, Col Bosque Res del Sur, Distrito Federal, MEXICO 16010, Phone: 5676 47 63
Specialties: Fancy and fantasy knives of his design. **Patterns:** Daggers. **Technical:** Grinds stainless steel; casts and grinds silver. Sets stones in silver. **Prices:** $2000 to $3000. **Remarks:** Spare-time maker; first knife sold in 1989. **Mark:** Symbol.

SCHIPPNICK, JIM
PO Box 326, Sanborn, NY 14132, Phone: 716-731-3715, ragnar@ragweedforge.com; Web: www.ragweedforge.com
Specialties: Nordic, early American, rustic. **Mark:** Runic R. **Remarks:** Also imports Nordic knives from Norway, Sweden and Finland.

SCHLUETER, DAVID
2136 Cedar Gate Rd., Madison Heights, VA 24572, Phone: 434-384-8642, drschlueter@hotmail.com
Specialties: Japanese-style swords. **Patterns:** Larger blades. O-tanto to Tachi, with focus on less common shapes. **Technical:** Forges and grinds carbon steels, heat-treats and polishes own blades, makes all fittings, does own mounting and finishing. **Prices:** Start at $3000. **Remarks:** Sells fully mounted pieces only, doing business as Odd Frog Forge. **Mark:** Full name and date.

SCHMITZ, RAYMOND E
PO Box 1787, Valley Center, CA 92082, Phone: 760-749-4318

SCHNEIDER, CRAIG M
5380 N Amity Rd, Claremont, IL 62421, Phone: 217-377-5715, raephtownslam@att.blackberry.net
Specialties: Straight knives and folders of his own design. **Patterns:** Bowies, hunters, tactical, bird & trout. **Technical:** Forged high-carbon steel and Damascus. Flat grind and differential heat treatment use a wide selection of handle, guard and bolster material, also offers leather sheaths. **Prices:** $150 to $3,500. **Remarks:** Part-time maker; first knife sold in 1985. **Mark:** Stylized initials with Schneider Claremont IL.

SCHNEIDER, HERMAN J.
14084 Apple Valley Rd, Apple Valley, CA 92307, Phone: 760-946-9096

Specialties: Presentation pieces, Fighters, Hunters. **Prices:** Starting at $900. **Mark:** H.J. Schneider-Maker or maker's last name.

SCHOEMAN, CORRIE

Box 28596, Danhof, Free State, SOUTH AFRICA 9310, Phone: 027 51 4363528 Cell: 027 82-3750789, corries@intekom.co.za

Specialties: High-tech folders of his design or to customer's specs. **Patterns:** Linerlock folders and automatics. **Technical:** ATS-34, Damascus or stainless Damascus with titanium frames; prefers exotic materials for handles. **Prices:** $650 to $2000. **Remarks:** Full-time maker; first knife sold in 1984. All folders come with filed liners and back and jeweled inserts. **Mark:** Logo in knife shape engraved on inside of back bar.

SCHOENFELD, MATTHEW A

RR #1, Galiano Island, BC, CANADA V0N 1P0, Phone: 250-539-2806

Specialties: Working knives of his design. **Patterns:** Kitchen cutlery, camp knives, hunters. **Technical:** Grinds 440C. **Prices:** $85 to $500. **Remarks:** Part-time maker; first knife sold in 1978. **Mark:** Signature, Galiano Is. B.C., and date.

SCHOENINGH, MIKE

49850 Miller Rd, North Powder, OR 97867, Phone: 541-856-3239

SCHOLL, TIM

1389 Langdon Rd, Angier, NC 27501, Phone: 910-897-2051, tschollknives@live.com

Specialties: Fancy and working/using straight knives and folders of his design and to customer specs. **Patterns:** Bowies, hunters, tomahawks, daggers & fantasy knives. **Technical:** Forges high carbon and tool steel makes Damascus, grinds ATS-34 and D2 on request. **Prices:** $150 to $6000. **Remarks:** Part-time maker; first knife sold in 1990. Doing business as Tim Scholl Custom Knives. Member North Carolina Custom Knifemakers Guild. American Bladesmith Society journeyman smith. **Mark:** S pierced by arrow.

SCHORSCH, KENDALL

693 Deer Trail Dr., Jourdanton, TX 78026, Phone: 830-770-0205, schorschknives@gmail.com; Web: www.schorschknives.com

Specialties Slip-joint folders and straight blades. **Patterns:** Single-and double-blade trappers and straight hunting knives, all with or without filework. **Technical:** Grinds CPM 154, ATS-34, D2 and damascus. **Prices:** $350 to $750 and up. **Remarks:** Full-time maker; first knife sold in 2010. **Mark:** Stamped SCHORSCH on the tang or Schorsch Knives etched in a circle with an Arrow "S" in the center.

SCHRADER, ROBERT

55532 Gross De, Bend, OR 97707, Phone: 541-598-7301

Specialties: Hunting, utility, Bowie. **Patterns:** Fixed blade. **Prices:** $150 to $600.

SCHRAP, ROBERT G

CUSTOM LEATHER KNIFE SHEATH CO., 7024 W Wells St, Wauwatosa, WI 53213-3717, Phone: 414-771-6472 or 414-379-6819, Fax: 414-479-9765, knifesheaths@aol.com; Web: www.customsheaths.com

Specialties: Leatherwork. **Prices:** $35 to $100. **Mark:** Schrap in oval.

SCHREINER, TERRY

4310 W. Beech St., Duncan, OK 73533, Phone: 580-255-4880, Rhino969@hotmail.com

Specialties Hunters, bird-and-trout knives, handforged, one-of-a-kind bowies. **Patterns:** Hunters and bird-and-trout knives. **Technical:** Stainless damascus, Damasteel, hand-forged carbon damascus and RWL stainless steels, with handle materials mostly natural, including stag, mastodon ivory, horn and wood. **Prices:** $350 to $1,500. **Remarks:** Part-time maker. **Mark:** TerryJack Knives; TSchreiner with interlocking T&S.

SCHROEN, KARL

4042 Bones Rd, Sebastopol, CA 95472, Phone: 707-823-4057, Fax: 707-823-2914, Web: http://users.ap.net/~schroen

Specialties: Using knives made to fit. **Patterns:** Sgian dubhs, carving sets, wood-carving knives, fishing knives, kitchen knives and new cleaver design. **Technical:** Forges A2, ATS-34, D2 and L6 cruwear S30V S90V. **Prices:** $150 to $6000. **Remarks:** Full-time maker; first knife sold in 1968. Author of The Hand Forged Knife. **Mark:** Last name.

SCHUCHMANN, RICK

1251 Wilson Dunham Hill Rd., New Richmond, OH 45157, Phone: 513-553-4316

Specialties: Replicas of antique and out-of-production Scagels and Randalls, primarily miniatures. **Patterns:** All sheath knives, mostly miniatures, hunting and fighting knives, some daggers and hatchets. **Technical:** Stock removal, 440C and O1 steel. Most knives are flat ground, some convex. **Prices:** $175 to $600 and custom to $4000. **Remarks:** Part-time maker, sold first knife in 1997. Knives on display in the Randall Museum. Sheaths are made exclusively at Sullivan's Holster Shop, Tampa, FL **Mark:** SCAR.

SCHUTTE, NEILL

01 Moffet St., Fichardt Park, Bloemfontein, SOUTH AFRICA 9301, Phone: +27(0) 82 787 3429, neill@schutteknives.co.za; www.schutteknives.co.za

Specialties: Bob Loveless-style knives, George Herron fighters, custom designs and designs/requests from clients. **Technical:** Mainly stock removal of Bohler N690, RWL-34 and ATS-34, if available, blade steels. Uses the materials clients request. **Prices:** $450 to $1,250. **Remarks:** Full-time maker; first knife made at 10 years old, seriously started knifemaking in 2008. **Mark:** Kneeling archer/bowman (maker's surname, Schutte, directly translates to archer or bowman.)

SCHWARTZ, AARON

Woodbridge, VA, Phone: 908-256-3869, big_hammer_forge@yahoo.com

Specialties Fantasy custom designs and one-off custom pieces to order. **Technical:** Stock-removal method of blade making. **Remarks:** Made first knife around eight years ago.

SCHWARZER, LORA SUE

POB 6, Crescent City, FL 32112, Phone: 904-307-0872, auntielora57@yahoo.com

Specialties: Scagel style knives. **Patterns:** Hunters and miniatures **Technical:** Forges 1084 and Damascus. **Prices:** Start at $400. **Remarks:** Part-time maker; first knife sold in 1997. Journeyman Bladesmith, American Bladesmith Society. Now working with Steve Schwarzer on some projects.**Mark:** Full name -JS on reverse side.

SCHWARZER, STEPHEN

POB 6, Crescent City, FL 32112, Phone: 904-307-0872, schwarzeranvil@gmail.com; Web: www.steveschwarzer.com

Specialties: Mosaic Damascus and picture mosaic in folding knives. All Japanese blades are finished working with Wally Hostetter considered the top Japanese lacquer specialist in the U.S.A. Also produces a line of carbon steel knives at $300. **Patterns:** Folders, axes and buckskinner knives. **Technical:** Specializes in picture mosaic Damascus and powder metal mosaic work. Sole authorship; all work including carving done in-house. Most knives have file work and carving. Hand carved steel and precious metal guards. **Prices:** $1500 to $5000, some higher; carbon steel and primitive knives much less. **Remarks:** Full-time maker; first knife sold in 1976, considered by many to be one of the top mosaic Damascus specialists in the world. Mosaic Master level work. I am now working with Lora Schwarzer on some projects. **Mark:** Schwarzer + anvil.

SCIMIO, BILL

4554 Creek Side Ln., Spruce Creek, PA 16683, Phone: 814-632-3751, sprucecreekforge@gmail.com Web: www.sprucecreekforge.com

Specialties: Hand-forged primitive-style knives with curly maple, antler, bone and osage handles.

SCORDIA, PAOLO

Via Terralba 144, Torrimpietra, Roma, ITALY 00050, Phone: 06-61697231, paolo.scordia@uni.net; Web: www.scordia-knives.com

Specialties: Working, fantasy knives, Italian traditional folders and fixed blades of own design. **Patterns:** Any. **Technical:** Forge mosaic Damascus, forge blades, welds own mokume and grinds ATS-34, etc. use hardwoods and Micarta for handles, brass and nickel-silver for fittings. Makes sheaths. **Prices:** $200 to $2000, some to $4000. **Remarks:** Part-time maker; first knife sold in 1988. **Mark:** Sun and moon logo and ititials.

SCROGGS, JAMES A

108 Murray Hill Dr, Warrensburg, MO 64093, Phone: 660-747-2568, jscroggsknives@embarqmail.com

Specialties: Straight knives, prefers light weight. **Patterns:** Hunters, hideouts, and fighters. **Technical:** Grinds CPM-154 stainless plus experiments in steel. Prefers handles of walnut in English, bastonge, American black. Also uses myrtle, maple, Osage orange. **Prices:** $200 to $1000. **Remarks:** 1st knife sold in 1985. Full-time maker. Won "Best Hunter Award" at Branson Hammer-In & Knife Show for 2012 and 2014. **Mark:** SCROGGS in block or script.

SCULLEY, PETER E

340 Sunset Dr, Rising Fawn, GA 30738, Phone: 706-398-0169

SEATON, DAVID D

1028 South Bishop Ave, #237, Rolla, MO 65401, Phone: 573-465-3193, aokcustomknives@gmail.com

Specialties: Gentleman's and Lady's folders. **Patterns:** Liner lock folders of own design and to customer specs, lock backs, slip joints, some stright knives, tactical folders, skinners, fighters, and utility knives. **Technical:** Grinds ATS 34, O1, 1095, 154CM, CPM154, commercial Damascus. Blades are mostly flat ground, some hollow ground. Does own heat treating, tempering, and Nitre Bluing. Prefers natural handle materials such as ivory, mother of pearl, bone, and exotic woods, some use of G10 and micarta on hard use knives. Use gem stones, gold, silver on upscale knives, offers some carving, filework, and engrving. **Prices:** $150 to $600 avg; some to $1500 and up depending on materials and embellishments. **Remarks:** First knife sold in 2002, part-time maker, doing business at AOK Custom Knives. **Mark:** full or last name engraved on blade.

SEIB, STEVE

7914 Old State Road, Evansville, IN 47710, Phone: 812-867-2231, sseib@insightbb.com

Specialties: Working straight knives. Pattern: Skinners, hunters, bowies and camp knives. **Technical:** Forges high-carbon and makes own damascus. **Remarks:** Part-time maker. ABS member. **Mark:** Last name.

SELF, ERNIE

950 O'Neill Ranch Rd, Dripping Springs, TX 78620-9760, Phone: 512-940-7134, ernieself@yahoo.com

Specialties: Traditional and working straight knives and folders of his design and in standard patterns. **Patterns:** Hunters, locking folders and slip-joints. **Technical:** Grinds 440C, D2, 440V, ATS-34 and Damascus. Offers fancy filework. **Prices:** $250 to $1000; some to $2500. **Remarks:** Full-time maker; first knife sold in 1982. Also customizes Buck 110's and 112's folding hunters. **Mark:** In oval shape -Ernie Self Maker Dripping Springs TX.

SELLEVOLD, HARALD

PO Box 4134, S Kleivesmau:2, Bergen, NORWAY N5835, Phone: 47 55-310682, haraldsellevold@c2i.net; Web:knivmakeren.com

Specialties: Norwegian-styles; collaborates with other Norse craftsmen. **Patterns:** Distinctive ferrules and other mild modifications of traditional patterns; Bowies and friction folders. **Technical:** Buys Damascus blades; blacksmiths his own blades. Semi-gemstones used in handles; gemstone inlay. **Prices:** $350 to $2000. **Remarks:** Full-time maker; first knife sold in 1980. **Mark:** Name and country in logo.

SELZAM, FRANK

Martin Reinhard Str 23, Bad Koenigshofen, GERMANY 97631, Phone: 09761-5980, frankselzam.de

Specialties: Hunters, working knives to customers specs, hand tooled and stitched leather sheaths large stock of wood and German stag horn. **Patterns:** Mostly own design. **Technical:** Forged blades, own Damascus, also stock removal stainless. **Prices:** $250 to $1500. Re**Mark:** First knife sold in 1978. **Mark:** Last name stamped.

SENTZ, MARK C

4084 Baptist Rd, Taneytown, MD 21787, Phone: 410-756-2018

Specialties: Fancy straight working knives of his design. **Patterns:** Hunters, fighters, folders and utility/camp knives. **Technical:** Forges 1085, 1095, 5160, 5155 and his Damascus. Most knives come with wood-lined leather sheath or wooden presentation sheath. **Prices:** Start at $275. **Remarks:** Full-time maker; first knife sold in 1989. Doing business as M. Charles Sentz Gunsmithing, Inc. **Mark:** Last name.

SERAFEN, STEVEN E

24 Genesee St, New Berlin, NY 13411, Phone: 607-847-6903

Specialties: Traditional working/using straight knives of his design and to customer specs. **Patterns:** Bowies, fighters, hunters. **Technical:** Grinds ATS-34, 440C, high-carbon steel. **Prices:** $175 to $600; some to $1200. **Remarks:** Part-time maker; first knife sold in 1990. **Mark:** First and middle initial, last name in script.

SEVECEK, PAVEL

Lhota u Konice 7, BRODEK U KONICE, 79845 CZECH REPUBLIC, Phone: 00420 603 545 333, seva.noze@seznam.cz; Web: www.sevaknives.cz

Specialties Production of handforged mosaic damascus knives, all including the plastic engravings and sheaths of his own exclusive work. **Prices:** $800 and up. **Remarks:** First knife sold in 2001. **Mark:** Logo SP in blade.

SEVEY CUSTOM KNIFE

94595 Chandler Rd, Gold Beach, OR 97444, Phone: 541-247-2649, sevey@charter.net; Web: www.seveyknives.com

Specialties: Fixed blade hunters. **Patterns:** Drop point, trailing paint, clip paint, full tang, hidden tang. **Technical:** D-2, and ATS-34 blades, stock removal. Heat treatment by Paul Bos. **Prices:** $225 and up depending on overall length and grip material. **Mark:** Sevey Custom Knife.

SEWARD, BEN

471 Dogwood Ln., Austin, AR 72007, Phone: 501-416-1543, sewardsteel@gmail.com; Web: www.bensewardknives.com

Specialties: Forged blades, mostly bowies and fighters. **Technical:** Forges high-carbon steels such as 1075 and W2. **Remarks:** First knife made in 2005; ABS journeyman smith and member Arkansas Knifemakers Association.

SFREDDO, RODRIGO MENEZES

Rua 7 De Setembro 66 Centro, Nova Petropolis, RS, BRAZIL 95150-000, Phone: 011-55-54-303-303-90, r.sfreddoknives@gmail.com; www.sbccutelaria.org.br

Specialties: Integrals, bowies, hunters, dirks & swords. **Patterns:** Forges his own Damascus and 52100 steel. **Technical:** Specialized in integral knives and Damascus. **Prices:** From $350 and up. Most around $750 to $1000. **Remarks:** Considered by many to be the Brazil's best bladesmith. ABS SBC Member. **Mark:** S. Sfreddo on the left side of the blade.

SHADLEY, EUGENE W

209 NW 17th Street, Grand Rapids, MN 55744, Phone: 218-999-7197 or 218-244-8628, Fax: call first, ShadleyKnives@hotmail.com

Specialties: Gold frames are available on some models. **Patterns:** Whittlers, stockman, sowbelly, congress, trapper, etc. **Technical:** Grinds ATS-34, 416 frames. **Prices:** Starts at $600, some models up to $15,000. **Remarks:** Full-time maker; first knife sold in 1985. Doing business as Shadley Knives. **Mark:** Last name.

SHADMOT, BOAZ

MOSHAV PARAN D N, Arava, ISRAEL 86835, srb@arava.co.il

SHARP, DAVID

17485 Adobe St., Hesperia, CA 92345, Phone: 520-370-1899, sharpwerks@gmail.com or david@sharpwerks.com; Web: www.sharpwerks.com

Specialties: Fixed blades. **Patterns:** Original and real Loveless pattern utilities, hunters and fighters. **Technical:** Stock removal, tool steel and stainless steel, hollow grind, machine finish, full polish, various handle materials. **Prices:** $300 to $1,500. **Remarks:** Part-time maker, first knife sold in 2011. **Mark:** "Sharpwerks" on original designs; "D. Sharp" on Loveless designs.

SHARRIGAN, MUDD

111 Bradford Rd, Wiscasset, ME 04578-4457, Phone: 207-882-9820, Fax: 207-882-9835

Specialties: Custom designs; repair straight knives, custom leather sheaths. **Patterns:** Daggers, fighters, hunters, crooked knives and seamen working knives; traditional Scandinavian-styles. **Technical:** Forges 1095, 5160, and W2. **Prices:** $50 to $325; some to $1200. **Remarks:** Full-time maker; first knife sold in 1982. **Mark:** Swallow tail carving. Mudd engraved.

SHEEHY, THOMAS J

4131 NE 24th Ave, Portland, OR 97211-6411, Phone: 503-493-2843

Specialties: Hunting knives and ulus. **Patterns:** Own or customer designs. **Technical:** 1095/O1 and ATS-34 steel. **Prices:** $35 to $200. **Remarks:** Do own heat treating; forged or ground blades. **Mark:** Name.

SHEELY, "BUTCH" FOREST

15784 Custar Rd., Grand Rapids, OH 43522, Phone: 419-308-3471, sheelyblades@gmail.com

Specialties: Traditional bowies and pipe tomahawks. **Patterns:** Bowies, hunters, integrals, dirks, axes and hawks. **Technical:** Forges 5160, 52100, 1084, 1095, and Damascus.**Prices:** $150 to $1500;**Remarks:** Full-time bladesmith part-time blacksmith; first knife sold in 1982. ABS Journeysmith, sole author of all knives and hawks including hand sewn leather sheaths, doing business as Beaver Creek Forge. **Mark:** First and last name above Bladesmith.

SHEETS, STEVEN WILLIAM

6 Stonehouse Rd, Mendham, NJ 07945, Phone: 201-543-5882

SHIFFER, STEVE

PO Box 471, Leakesville, MS 39451, Phone: 601-394-4425, aiifish2@yahoo.com; Web: wwwchoctawplantationforge.com

Specialties: Bowies, fighters, hard use knives. **Patterns:** Fighters, hunters, combat/utility knives. Walker pattern LinerLock® folders. Allen pattern scale and bolster release autos. **Technical:** Most work forged, stainless stock removal. Makes own Damascus. O1 and 5160 most used also 1084, 440c, 154cm, s30v. **Prices:** $125 to $1000. **Remarks:** First knife sold in 2000, all heat treatment done by maker. Doing business as Choctaw Plantation Forge. **Mark:** Hot mark sunrise over creek.

SHINOSKY, ANDY

3117 Meanderwood Dr, Canfield, OH 44406, Phone: 330-702-0299, andrew@shinosky.com; Web: www.shinosky.com

Specialties: Collectable folders and interframes. **Patterns:** Drop point, spear point, trailing point, daggers. **Technical:** Grinds ATS-34 and Damascus. Prefers natural handle materials. Most knives are engraved by Andy himself. **Prices:** Start at $800. **Remarks:** Part-time maker/engraver. First knife sold in 1992. **Mark:** Name.

SHIPLEY, STEVEN A

800 Campbell Rd Ste 137, Richardson, TX 75081, Phone: 972-644-7981, Fax: 972-644-7985, steve@shipleysphotography.com

Specialties: Hunters, skinners and traditional straight knives. **Technical:** Hand grinds ATS-34, 440C and Damascus steels. Each knife is custom sheathed by his son, Dan. **Prices:** $175 to $2000. **Remarks:** Part-time maker; like smooth lines and unusual handle materials. **Mark:** S A Shipley.

SHOEMAKER, CARROLL

380 Yellowtown Rd, Northup, OH 45658, Phone: 740-446-6695

Specialties: Working/using straight knives of his design. **Patterns:** Hunters, utility/camp and early American backwoodsmen knives. **Technical:** Grinds ATS-34; forges old files, O1 and 1095. Uses some Damascus; offers scrimshaw and engraving. **Prices:** $100 to $175; some to $350. **Remarks:** Spare-time maker; first knife sold in 1977. **Mark:** Name and city or connected initials.

SHOEMAKER, SCOTT

316 S Main St, Miamisburg, OH 45342, Phone: 513-859-1935

Specialties: Twisted, wire-wrapped handles on swords, fighters and fantasy blades; new line of seven models with quick-draw, multi-carry Kydex sheaths. **Patterns:** Bowies, boots and one-of-a-kinds in his design or to customer specs. **Technical:** Grinds A6 and ATS-34; buys Damascus. Hand satin finish is standard. **Prices:** $100 to $1500; swords to $8000. **Remarks:** Part-time maker; first knife sold in 1984. **Mark:** Angel wings with last initial, or last name.

SHOGER, MARK O

875 Taylor Rd., Kalama, WA 98625, Phone: 503-816-8615, mosdds@msn.com

Specialties: Working and using straight knives and folders of his design; fancy and embellished knives. **Patterns:** Hunters, Bowies, daggers and folders. **Technical:** Forges O1, W2, 1084, 5160, 52100 and 1084/15n20 pattern weld. **Remarks:** Spare-time maker. **Mark:** Last name "Shoger" or stamped last initial over anvil.

SHROPSHIRE, SHAWN

PO Box 453, Piedmont, OK 73078, Phone: 405-833-5239, shawn@sdsknifeworks.com; Web: www.sdsknifeworks.com

Specialties: Working straight knives and frontier style period pieces. **Patterns:** Bowies, hunters, skinners, fighters, patch/neck knives.**Technical:** Grinds D2, 154CM and some Damascus, forges 1084, 5160.**Prices:** Starting at $125. **Remarks:** Part-time maker; first knife sold in 1997. Doing business at SDS Knifeworks. **Mark:** Etched "SDS Knifeworks -Oklahoma" in an oval or "SDS" tang stamp.

SHULL, JAMES

5146 N US 231 W, Rensselaer, IN 47978, Phone: 219-866-0436, nbjs@netnitco.net Web: www.shullhandforgedknives.com

Specialties: Working knives of hunting, fillet, Bowie patterns. **Technical:** Forges or uses 1095, 5160, 52100 & O1. **Prices:** $100 to $300. **Remarks:** DBA Shull Handforged Knives. **Mark:** Last name in arc.

SIBERT, SHANE

PO BOX 241, Gladstone, OR 97027, Phone: 503-650-2082, shane.sibert@comcast.net Web: www.sibertknives.com

Specialties: Innovative light weight hiking and backpacking knives for outdoorsman and adventurers, progressive fixed blade combat and fighting knives. One-of-a-kind knives of various configurations. Titanium frame lock folders. **Patterns:** Modern configurations of utility/camp knives, bowies, modified spear points, daggers, tantos, recurves, clip points and spine serrations. **Technical:** Stock removal. Specializes in CPM S30V, CPM S35VN, CPM D2, CPM 3V, stainless damascus. Micarta, G-10, stabilized wood and titanium.

Prices: $200 -$1000, some pieces $1500 and up. **Remarks:** Full-time maker, first knife sold in 1994. **Mark:** Stamped "SIBERT" and occasionally uses electro-etch with oval around last name.

SIBRIAN, AARON
4308 Dean Dr, Ventura, CA 93003, Phone: 805-642-6950
Specialties: Tough working knives of his design and in standard patterns. **Patterns:** Makes a "Viper utility"—a kukri derivative and a variety of straight using knives. **Technical:** Grinds 440C and ATS-34. Offers traditional Japanese blades; soft backs, hard edges, temper lines. **Prices:** $60 to $100; some to $250. **Remarks:** Spare-time maker; first knife sold in 1989. **Mark:** Initials in diagonal line.

SIMMONS, H R
1100 Bay City Rd, Aurora, NC 27806, Phone: 252-916-2241
Specialties: Working/using straight knives of his design. **Patterns:** Fighters, hunters and utility/camp knives. **Technical:** Forges and grinds L6; grinds ATS-34. **Prices:** $150 and up. **Remarks:** Part-time maker; first knife sold in 1987. Doing business as HRS Custom Knives, Royal Forge and Trading Company. **Mark:** HRS.

SIMONELLA, GIANLUIGI
Via Battiferri 33, Maniago, ITALY 33085, Phone: 01139-427-730350
Specialties: Traditional and classic folding and working/using knives of his design and to customer specs. **Patterns:** Bowies, fighters, hunters, utility/camp knives. **Technical:** Forges ATS-34, D2, 440C. **Prices:** $250 to $400; some to $1000. **Remarks:** Full-time maker; first knife sold in 1988. **Mark:** Wilson.

SINCLAIR, J E
520 Francis Rd, Pittsburgh, PA 15239, Phone: 412-793-5778
Specialties: Fancy hunters and fighters, liner locking folders. **Patterns:** Fighters, hunters and folders. **Technical:** Flat-grinds and hollow grind, prefers hand rubbed satin finish. Uses natural handle materials. **Prices:** $185 to $800. **Remarks:** Part-time maker; first knife sold in 1995. **Mark:** First and middle initials, last name and maker.

SINYARD, CLESTON S
27522 Burkhardt Dr, Elberta, AL 36530, Phone: 334-987-1361,
nimoforge1@gulftel.com; Web: www.knifemakersguild.com
Specialties: Working straight knives and folders of his design. **Patterns:** Hunters, buckskinners, Bowies, daggers, fighters and all-Damascus folders. **Technical:** Makes Damascus from 440C, stainless steel, D2 and regular high-carbon steel; forges "forefinger pad" into hunters and skinners. **Prices:** In Damascus $450 to $1500; some $2500. **Remarks:** Full-time maker; first knife sold in 1980. Doing business as Nimo Forge. **Mark:** Last name, U.S.A. in anvil.

SIROIS, DARRIN
Tactical Combat Tools, 6182 Lake Trail Dr., Fayetteville, NC 28304,
Phone: 910-730-0536, knives@tctknives.com; www.tctknives.com
Specialties: Tactical fighters, hunters and camp knives. **Technical:** Stock removal method of blade making, using D2 and 154CM steels. Entire process, including heat treat, done in-house. **Prices:** $80 to $750. **Remarks:** Part-time maker; first knife sold in 2008. **Mark:** Letters TCT surrounded by a triangle, or "Delta Tactical Combat Tools."

SISKA, JIM
48 South Maple St, Westfield, MA 01085, Phone: 413-642-3059,
siskaknives@comcast.net
Specialties: Traditional working straight knives, no folders. **Patterns:** Hunters, fighters, Bowies and one-of-a-kinds; folders. **Technical:** Grinds D2, A2, 154CM and ATS-34, buys damascus and forges some blades. Likes exotic woods. **Prices:** $300 and up. **Remarks:** Part-time. **Mark:** Siska in Old English, or for forged blades, a hammer over maker's name.

SJOSTRAND, KEVIN
1541 S Cain St, Visalia, CA 93292, Phone: 559-625-5254
Specialties: Traditional and working/using straight knives and folders of his design or to customer specs. **Patterns:** Fixed blade hunters, Bowies, utility/camp knives. **Technical:** Grinds ATS-34, 440C and 1095. Prefers high polished blades and full tang. Natural and stabilized hardwoods, Micarta and stag handle material. **Prices:** $250 to $400. **Remarks:** Part-time maker; first knife sold in 1992. **Mark:** SJOSTRAND

SKIFF, STEVEN
SKIFF MADE BLADES, PO Box 537, Broadalbin, NY 12025, Phone: 518-883-4875,
skiffmadeblades@hotmail.com; Web: www.skiffmadeblades.com
Specialties: Custom using/collector grade straight blades and LinerLock® folders of maker's design or customer specifications. **Patterns:** Hunters, utility/camp knives, tactical/fancy art folders. **Prices:** Straight blades $225 and up. Folders $450 and up. **Technical:** Stock removal hollow ground ATS-34, 154 CM, S30V, and tool steel. Damascus-Devon Thomas, Robert Eggerling, Mike Norris and Delbert Ealy. Nickel silver and stainless in-house heat treating. Handle materials: man made and natural woods (stabilized). Horn shells sheaths for straight blades, sews own leather and uses sheaths by "Tree-Stump Leather." **Remarks:** First knife sold 1997. Started making folders in 2000. **Mark:** SKIFF on blade of straight blades and in inside of backspacer on folders.

SLEE, FRED
9 John St, Morganville, NJ 07751, Phone: 732-591-9047
Specialties: Working straight knives, some fancy, to customer specs. **Patterns:** Hunters, fighters, fancy daggers and folders. **Technical:** Grinds D2, 440C and ATS-34. **Prices:** $285 to $1100. **Remarks:** Part-time maker; first knife sold in 1980. **Mark:** Letter "S" in Old English.

SLOAN, DAVID
PO BOX 83, Diller, NE 68342, Phone: 402-793-5755, sigp22045@hotmail.com

Specialties: Hunters, choppers and fighters. **Technical:** Forged blades of W2, 1084 and Damascus. **Prices:** Start at $225. **Remarks:** Part-time maker, made first knife in 2002, received JS stamp 2010. **Mark:** Sloan JS.

SLOAN, SHANE
4226 FM 61, Newcastle, TX 76372, Phone: 940-846-3290
Specialties: Collector-grade straight knives and folders. **Patterns:** Uses stainless Damascus, ATS-34 and 12C27. Bowies, lockers, slip-joints, fancy folders, fighters and period pieces. **Technical:** Grinds D2 and ATS-34. Uses hand-rubbed satin finish. Prefers rare natural handle materials. **Prices:** $250 to $6500. **Remarks:** Full-time maker; first knife sold in 1985. **Mark:** Name and city.

SLOBODIAN, SCOTT
PO Box 1498, San Andreas, CA 95249, Phone: 209-286-1980, Fax: 209-286-1982,
info@slobodianswords.com; Web: www.slobodianswords.com
Specialties: Japanese-style knives and swords, period pieces, fantasy pieces and miniatures. **Patterns:** Small kweikens, tantos, wakazashis, katanas, traditional samurai swords. **Technical:** Flat-grinds 1050, commercial Damascus. **Prices:** Prices start at $1500. **Remarks:** Full-time maker; first knife sold in 1987. **Mark:** Blade signed in Japanese characters and various scripts.

SMALE, CHARLES J
509 Grove Ave, Waukegan, IL 60085, Phone: 847-244-8013

SMALL, ED
Rt 1 Box 178-A, Keyser, WV 26726, Phone: 304-298-4254, coldanvil@gmail.com
Specialties: Working knives of his design; period pieces. **Patterns:** Hunters, daggers, buckskinners and camp knives; likes one-of-a-kinds, very primitive bowies. **Technical:** Forges and grinds W2, L6 and his own Damascus. **Prices:** $150 to $1500. **Remarks:** Full-time maker; first knife sold in 1978. **Mark:** Script initials connected.

SMART, STEVE
907 Park Row Cir, McKinney, TX 75070-3847, Phone: 214-837-4216, Fax: 214-837-4111
Specialties: Working/using straight knives and folders of his design, to customer specs and in standard patterns. **Patterns:** Bowies, hunters, kitchen knives, locking folders, utility/camp, fishing and bird knives. **Technical:** Grinds ATS-34, D2, 440C and O1. Prefers mirror polish or satin finish; hollow-grinds all blades. All knives come with sheath. Offers some filework. **Prices:** $95 to $225; some to $500. **Remarks:** Spare-time maker; first knife sold in 1983. **Mark:** Name, Custom, city and state in oval.

SMIT, GLENN
627 Cindy Ct, Aberdeen, MD 21001, Phone: 410-272-2959,
wolfsknives@comcast.net; Web: www.facebook.com/Wolf'sKnives
Specialties: Working and using straight and folding knives of his design or to customer specs. Customizes and repairs all types of cutlery. Exclusive maker of Dave Murphy Style knives. **Patterns:** Hunters, Bowies, daggers, fighters, utility/camp, folders, kitchen knives and miniatures, Murphy combat, C.H.A.I.K., Little 88 and Tiny 90-styles. **Technical:** Grinds 440C, ATS-34, O1, A2 also grinds 6AL4V titanium allox for blades. Reforges commercial Damascus and makes cast aluminum handles. **Prices:** Miniatures start at $50; full-size knives start at $100. **Remarks:** Spare-time maker; first knife sold in 1986. Doing business as Wolf's Knives. **Mark:** G.P. SMIT, with year on reverse side, Wolf's Knives-Murphy's way with date.

SMITH, J D
69 Highland, Roxbury, MA 02119, Phone: 617-989-0723, jdsmith02119@yahoo.com
Specialties: Fighters, Bowies, Persian, locking folders and swords. **Patterns:** Bowies, fighters and locking folders. **Technical:** Forges and grinds D2, his Damascus, O1, 52100 etc. and wootz-pattern hammer steel. **Prices:** $500 to $2000; some to $5000. **Remarks:** Full-time maker; first knife sold in 1987. Doing business as Hammersmith. **Mark:** Last initial alone or in cartouche.

SMITH, J.B.
21 Copeland Rd., Perkinston, MS 39573, Phone: 228-380-1851
Specialties: Traditional working knives for the hunter and fisherman. **Patterns:** Hunters, Bowies, and fishing knives; copies of 1800 period knives. **Technical:** Grinds ATS-34, 440C. **Prices:** $100 to $800. **Remarks:** Full-time maker, first knife sold in 1972. **Mark:** J.B. Smith MAKER PERKINSTON, MS.

SMITH, JERRY W.
Jerry W. Smith Knives, 1950 CR 5120, Willow Springs, MO 65793, Phone: 417-252-7463, jwdeb93@gmail.com; Web: www.jerrywsmith.com
Specialties: Loveless-style knives, folders/slip joints. **Patterns:** Sway backs and drop-point hunters. **Technical:** Steels used D2, A2, O1, 154CM and CPM 154. Stock removal, heat treat in house, all leather work in house. **Prices:** Start at $200. **Remarks:** Full-time knifemaker. First knife made in 2004. **Mark:** Jerry W Smith USA.

SMITH, JOHN M
3450 E Beguelin Rd, Centralia, IL 62801, Phone: 618-249-6444, jknife@frontiernet.net
Specialties: Folders. **Patterns:** Folders. **Prices:** $250 to $2500. **Remarks:** First knife sold in 1980. Not taking orders at this time on fixed blade knives. Part-time maker. **Mark:** Etched signature or logo.

SMITH, JOHN W
1322 Cow Branch Rd, West Liberty, KY 41472, Phone: 606-743-3599,
jwsknive@mrtc.com; Web: www.jwsmithknives.com
Specialties: Fancy and working locking folders of his design or to customer specs. **Patterns:** Interframes, traditional and daggers. **Technical:** Grinds 530V and his own Damascus. Offers gold inlay, engraving with gold inlay, hand-fitted mosaic pearl inlay and filework. Prefers hand-rubbed finish. Pearl and ivory available. **Prices:** Utility pieces

$375 to $650. Art knives $1200 to $10,000. **Remarks:** Full-time maker. **Mark:** Initials engraved inside diamond.

SMITH, JOSH
Box 753, Frenchtown, MT 59834, Phone: 406-626-5775, joshsmithknives@gmail.com; Web: www.joshsmithknives.com
Specialties: Mosaic, Damascus, LinerLock folders, automatics, Bowies, fighters, etc. **Patterns:** All kinds. **Technical:** Advanced Mosaic and Damascus. **Prices:** $450 and up. **Remarks:** A.B.S. Master Smith. **Mark:** Josh Smith with last two digits of the current year.

SMITH, LACY
PO BOX 188, Jacksonville, AL 36265, Phone: 256-310-4619, sales@smith-knives.com; Web: www.smith-knives.com
Specialties: All styles of fixed-blade knives. **Technical:** Stock removal method of blade making. **Prices:** $100 and up. **Mark:** Circle with three dots and three S's on inside.

SMITH, LENARD C
PO Box D68, Valley Cottage, NY 10989, Phone: 914-268-7359

SMITH, MICHAEL J
1418 Saddle Gold Ct, Brandon, FL 33511, Phone: 813-431-3790, smithknife@hotmail.com; Web: www.smithknife.com
Specialties: Fancy high art folders of his design. **Patterns:** Locking locks and automatics. **Technical:** Uses ATS-34, non-stainless and stainless Damascus; hand carves folders, prefers ivory and pearl. Hand-rubbed satin finish. Liners are 6AL4V titanium. **Prices:** $500 to $3000. **Remarks:** Full-time maker; first knife sold in 1989. **Mark:** Name, city, state.

SMITH, NEWMAN L.
865 Glades Rd Shop #3, Gatlinburg, TN 37738, Phone: 423-436-3322, thesmithshop@aol.com; Web: www.thesmithsshop.com
Specialties: Collector-grade and working knives. **Patterns:** Hunters, slip-joint and lock-back folders, some miniatures. **Technical:** Grinds O1 and ATS-34; makes fancy sheaths. **Prices:** $165 to $750; some to $1000. **Remarks:** Full-time maker; first knife sold in 1984. Partners part-time to handle Damascus blades by Jeff Hurst; marks these with SH connected. **Mark:** First and middle initials, last name.

SMITH, RALPH L
525 Groce Meadow Rd, Taylors, SC 29687, Phone: 864-444-0819, ralph_smith1@charter.net; Web: www.smithhandcraftedknives.com
Specialties: Working knives: straight and folding knives. Hunters, skinners, fighters, bird, boot, Bowie and kitchen knives. **Technical:** Concave Grind D2, ATS 34, 440C, steel hand finish or polished. **Prices:** $125 to $350 for standard models. **Remarks:** First knife sold in 1976. KMG member since 1981. SCAK founding member and past president. **Mark:** SMITH handcrafted knives in SC state outline.

SMITH, RAYMOND L
217 Red Chalk Rd, Erin, NY 14838, Phone: 607-795-5257, Bladesmith@wildblue.net; Web: www.theanvilsedge.com
Specialties: Working/using straight knives and folders to customer specs and in standard patterns; period pieces. **Patterns:** Bowies, hunters, slip joints. **Technical:** Forges 5160, 52100, 1018, 15N20, 1084, ATS 34. Damascus and wire cable Damascus. Filework. **Prices:** $125 to $1500; estimates for custom orders. **Remarks:** Full-time maker; first knife sold in 1991. ABS Master Smith. Doing business as The Anvils Edge. **Mark:** Ellipse with RL Smith, Erin NY MS in center.

SMITH, RICK
BEAR BONE KNIVES, 1843 W Evans Creek Rd., Rogue River, OR 97537, Phone: 541-582-4144, BearBoneSmith@msn.com; Web: www.bearbone.com
Specialties: Classic, historical style Bowie knives, hunting knives and various contemporary knife styles. **Technical:** Blades are either forged or made by stock removal method depending on steel used. Also forge weld wire Damascus. Does own heat treating and tempering using digital even heat kiln. Stainless blades are sent out for cryogenic "freeze treat." Preferred steels are O1, tool, 5160, 1095, 1084, ATS-34, 154CM, 440C and various high carbon Damascus. **Prices:** $350 to $1500. Custom leather sheaths available for knives. **Remarks:** Full-time maker since 1997. Serial numbers no longer put on knives. Official business name is "Bear Bone Knives." **Mark:** Early maker's mark was "Bear Bone" over capital letters "RS" with downward arrow between letters and "Hand Made" underneath letters. Mark on small knives is 3/8 circle containing "RS" with downward arrow between letters. Current mark since 2003 is "R Bear Bone Smith" arching over image of coffin Bowie knife with two shooting stars and "Rogue River, Oregon" underneath.

SMITH, SHAWN
2644 Gibson Ave, Clouis, CA 93611, Phone: 559-323-6234, kslc@sbcglobal.net
Specialties: Working and fancy straight knives. **Patterns:** Hunting, trout, fighters, skinners. **Technical:** Hollow grinds ATS-34, 154CM, A-2. **Prices:** $150.00 and up. **Remarks:** Part time maker. **Mark:** Shawn Smith handmade.

SMITH, STUART
Smith Hand Forged Knives, 32 Elbon Rd., Blairgowrie, Gauteng, SOUTH AFRICA 2123, Phone: +27 84 248 1324, samuraistu@forgedknives.co.za; www.forgedknives.co.za
Specialties: Hand-forged bowie knives and puukos in high-carbon steel and maker's own damascus. **Patterns:** Bowies, puukos, daggers, hunters, fighters, skinners and swords. **Technical:** Forges 5160, 1070, 52100 and SilverSteel, and maker's own damascus from 5160 and Bohler K600 nickel tool steel. Fitted guards and threaded pommels. Own heat treating. Wood and bronze carving. Own sheaths and custom sheaths. **Prices:** $150 to $1,500. **Remarks:** Full-time maker since 2004; first knife sold in 2000. **Mark:** Stamped

outline of an anvil with SMITH underneath on right side of knife. For 2014, anvil and surname with 10Yrs.

SMOCK, TIMOTHY E
1105 N Sherwood Dr, Marion, IN 46952, Phone: 765-664-0123

SNODY, MIKE
910 W. Young Ave., Aransas Pass, TX 78336, Phone: 361-443-0161, snodyknives@yahoo.com; Web: www.snodygallery.com
Specialties: High performance straight knives in traditional and Japanese-styles. **Patterns:** Skinners, hunters, tactical, Kwaiken and tantos. **Technical:** Grinds BG42, ATS-34, 440C and A2. Offers full or tapered tangs, upgraded handle materials such as fossil ivory, coral and exotic woods. Traditional diamond wrap over stingray on Japanese-style knives. Sheaths available in leather or Kydex. **Prices:** $100 to $1000. **Remarks:** Part-time maker; first knife sold in 1999. **Mark:** Name over knife maker.

SNOW, BILL
4824 18th Ave, Columbus, GA 31904, Phone: 706-576-4390, tipikw@knology.net
Specialties: Traditional working/using straight knives and folders of his design and to customer specs. Offers engraving and scrimshaw. **Patterns:** Bowies, fighters, hunters and folders. **Technical:** Grinds ATS-34, 440V, 440C, 420V, CPM350, BG42, A2, D2, 5160, 52100 and O1; forges if needed. Cryogenically quenches all steels; inlaid handles; some integrals; leather or Kydex sheaths. **Prices:** $125 to $700; some to $3500. **Remarks:** Now also have 530V, 10V and 3V steels in use. Full-time maker; first knife sold in 1958. Doing business as Tipi Knife works. **Mark:** Old English scroll "S" inside a tipi.

SOAPER, MAX H.
2375 Zion Rd, Henderson, KY 42420, Phone: 270-827-8143
Specialties: Primitive Longhunter knives, scalpers, camp knives, cowboy Bowies, neck knives, working knives, period pieces from the 18th century. **Technical:** Forges 5160, 1084, 1095; all blades differentially heat treated. **Prices:** $80 to $800. **Remarks:** Part-time maker since 1989. **Mark:** Initials in script.

SOILEAU, DAMON
POB 7292, Kingsport, TN 37664, Phone: 423-297-4665, oiseaumetalarts@gmail.com; Web: www.oiseaumetalarts.etsy.com
Specialties: Natural and exotic materials, slip-joint folders, fixed blades, hidden tang and full tang, hand engraving. **Patterns:** Slip-joint folders, hunters, skinners and art knives. **Technical:** Stock removal of damascus, forges W2, O1 and 1084. **Prices:** $150 to $2,000. **Remarks:** Full-time maker and hand engraver. **Mark:** Hand engraved last name on spine of blade, or inside back spring of folders.

SONNTAG, DOUGLAS W
902 N 39th St, Nixa, MO 65714, Phone: 417-693-1640, dougsonntag@gmail.com
Specialties: Working knives; art knives. **Patterns:** Hunters, boots, straight working knives; Bowies, some folders, camp/axe sets. **Technical:** Grinds D2, ATS-34, forges own Damascus; does own heat treating. **Prices:** $225 and up. **Remarks:** Full-time maker; first knife sold in 1986. **Mark:** Etched name in arch.

SONNTAG, JACOB D
14148 Trisha Dr., St. Robert, MO 65584, Phone: 573-336-4082, Jake0372@live.com
Specialties: Working knives, some art knives. **Patterns:** Hunters, bowies, and tomahawks. **Technical:** Grinds D2, ATS34 and Damascus. Forges some Damascus and tomahawks; does own heat treating. **Prices:** $200 and up. **Remarks:** Part-time maker; first knife sold in 2010. **Mark:** Etched name or stamped

SONNTAG, KRISTOPHER D
902 N 39th St, Nixa, MO 65714, Phone: 417-838-8327, kriss@buildit.us
Specialties: Working fixed blades, hunters, skinners, using knives. **Patterns:** Hunters, bowies, skinners. **Technical:** Grinds D2, ATS 34, Damascus. Makes some Damascus; does own heat treating. **Prices:** $200 and up.**Remarks:** Part-time maker; first knife sold in 2010. **Mark:** Etched name or stamped

SONTHEIMER, G DOUGLAS
14821 Dufief Mill Rd., Gaithersburg, MD 20878, Phone: 301-948-5227
Specialties: Fixed blade knives. **Patterns:** Whitetail deer, backpackers, camp, claws, fillet, fighters. **Technical:** Hollow Grinds. **Price:** $500 and up. **Remarks:** Spare-time maker; first knife sold in 1976. **Mark:** LORD.

SORNBERGER, JIM
25126 Overland Dr, Volcano, CA 95689, Phone: 209-295-7819, sierrajs@volcano.net
Specialties: Master engraver making classic San Francisco-style knives. Collectible straight knives. **Patterns:** Fighters, daggers, bowies, miniatures, hunters, custom canes and LinerLock folders. **Technical:** Grinds 440C, 154CM and ATS-34; engraves, carves and embellishes. **Prices:** $500 to $35,000 in gold with gold quartz inlays. **Remarks:** Full-time maker; first knife sold in 1970. Master engraver. **Mark:** First initial, last name, city and state.

SOWELL, BILL
100 Loraine Forest Ct, Macon, GA 31210, Phone: 478-994-9863, billsowell@reynoldscable.net
Specialties: Antique reproduction Bowies, forging Bowies, hunters, fighters, and most others. Also folders. **Technical:** Makes own Damascus, using 1084/15N20, also making own designs in powder metals, forges 5160-1095-1084, and other carbon steels, grinds ATS-34. **Prices:** Starting at $150 and up. **Remarks:** Part-time maker. Sold first knife in 1998. Does own leather work. ABS Master Smith. **Mark:** Iron Horse Forge -Sowell -MS.

SPAKE, JEREMY
6128 N. Concord Ave., Portland, OR 97217-4735, jeremy@spakeknife.com;

Web: www.spakeknife.com
Specialties: Handmade hidden-tang fixed blades. **Patterns:** Utility, hunting and Nordic-influenced knives, as well as others as the occasion arises. **Technical:** Forges three-layer laminated blades with high-carbon steel cores, also forges W2, O1, L6, 1084 and 1075. Stock removal blades on occasion. For handles, prefers a variety of stabilized woods and other premium natural materials. **Prices:** $350 to $500 and up. **Remarks:** Part-time maker; first knife sold in 2012. American Bladesmith Society member. **Mark:** Last name etched or stamped in Gotham typeface.

SPARKS, BERNARD
PO Box 73, Dingle, ID 83233, Phone: 208-847-1883, dogknifeii@juno.com; Web: www.sparksknives.com
Specialties: Maker engraved, working and art knives. Straight knives and folders of his own design. **Patterns:** Locking inner-frame folders, hunters, fighters, one-of-a-kind art knives. **Technical:** Grinds 530V steel, 440-C, 154CM, ATS-34, D-2 and forges by special order; triple temper, cryogenic soak. Mirror or hand finish. New Liquid metal steel. **Prices:** $300 to $2000. **Remarks:** Full-time maker, first knife sold in 1967. **Mark:** Last name over state with a knife logo on each end of name. Prior 1980, stamp of last name.

SPICKLER, GREGORY NOBLE
5614 Mose Cir, Sharpsburg, MD 21782, Phone: 301-432-2746

SPINALE, RICHARD
4021 Canterbury Ct, Lorain, OH 44053, Phone: 440-282-1565
Specialties: High-art working knives of his design. **Patterns:** Hunters, fighters, daggers and locking folders. **Technical:** Grinds 440C, ATS-34 and 07; engraves. Offers gold bolsters and other deluxe treatments. **Prices:** $300 to $1000; some to $3000. **Remarks:** Spare-time maker; first knife sold in 1976. **Mark:** Name, address, year and model number.

SPIVEY, JEFFERSON
9244 W Wilshire, Yukon, OK 73099, Phone: 405-371-9304, jspivey5@cox.net
Specialties: The Saber tooth: a combination hatchet, saw and knife. **Patterns:** Built for the wilderness, all are one-of-a-kind. **Technical:** Grinds chromemoly steel. The saw tooth spine curves with a double row of biangular teeth. **Prices:** Start at $275. **Remarks:** First knife sold in 1977. As of September 2006 Spivey knives has resumed production of the Sabertooth knife (one word trademark).**Mark:** Name and serial number.

SPRAGG, WAYNE E
252 Oregon Ave, Lovell, WY 82431, Phone: 307-548-7212
Specialties: Working straight knives, some fancy. **Patterns:** Folders. **Technical:** Forges carbon steel and makes Damascus. **Prices:** $200 and up. **Remarks:** All stainless heat-treated by Paul Bos. Carbon steel in shop heat treat. **Mark:** Last name front side w/s initials on reverse side.

SPROKHOLT, ROB
Burgerweg 5, Gatherwood, NETHERLANDS 1754 KB Burgerbrug, Phone: 0031 6 51230225, Fax: 0031 84 2238446, info@gatherwood.nl; Web: www.gatherwood.nl
Specialties: One-of-a-kind knives. Top materials collector grade, made to use. **Patterns:** Outdoor knives (hunting, sailing, hiking), Bowies, man's surviving companions MSC, big tantos, folding knives. **Technical:** Handles mostly stabilized or oiled wood, ivory, Micarta, carbon fibre, G10. Stiff knives are full tang. Characteristic one row of massive silver pins or tubes. Folding knives have a LinerLock® with titanium or Damascus powdersteel liner thumb can have any stone you like. Stock removal grinder: flat or convex. Steel 440-C, RWL-34, ATS-34, PM damascener steel. **Prices:** Start at 320 euro. **Remarks:** Writer of the first Dutch knifemaking book, supply shop for knife enthusiastic. First knife sold in 2000. **Mark:** Gatherwood in an eclipse etched blade or stamped in an intarsia of silver in the spine.

SQUIRE, JACK
350 W. 7th St., McMinnville, OR 97182-5509, Phone: 503-472-7290

ST. AMOUR, MURRAY
2066 Lapasse Rd., Beachburg, Ontario, CANADA K0J 1C0, Phone: 613-587-4194, knives@nrtco.net; Web: www.st-amourknives.com
Specialties: Hunters, fish knives, outdoor knives, bowies and some collectors' pieces. **Technical:** Steels include CPM S30V, CPM S90V, CPM 154, 154CM and ATS 34. **Remarks:** Full-time maker; first knife sold in 1992. **Mark:** St. Amour over Canada or small print st. amour.

ST. CLAIR, THOMAS K
12608 Fingerboard Rd, Monrovia, MD 21770, Phone: 301-482-0264

STAFFORD, RICHARD
104 Marcia Ct, Warner Robins, GA 31088, Phone: 912-923-6372, Cell: 478-508-5821, rnrstafford@cox.net
Specialties: High-tech straight knives and some folders. **Patterns:** Hunters in several patterns, fighters, boots, camp knives, combat knives and period pieces. **Technical:** Grinds ATS-34 and 440C. Machine satin finish offered. **Prices:** Starting at $150. **Remarks:** Part-time maker; first knife sold in 1983. **Mark:** R. W. STAFFORD GEORGIA.

STAINTHORP, GUY
4 Fisher St, Brindley Ford, Stroke-on-Trent, ENGLAND ST8 7QJ, Phone: 07946 469 888, guystainthorp@hotmail.com Web: http://stainthorpknives.co.uk/index.html
Specialties: Tactical and outdoors knives to his own design. **Patterns:** Hunting, survival and occasionally folding knives. **Technical:** Grinds RWL-34, O1, S30V, Damasteel. Micarta, G10 and stabilised wood/bone for handles. **Prices:** $200 -$1000. **Remarks:** Full-time knifemaker. **Mark:** Squared stylised GS over "Stainthorp".

STALCUP, EDDIE
PO Box 2200, Gallup, NM 87305, Phone: 505-863-3107, sharon.stalcup@gmail.com
Specialties: Working and fancy hunters, bird and trout. Special custom orders. **Patterns:** Drop point hunters, locking liner and multi blade folders. **Technical:** ATS-34, 154 CM, 440C, CPM 154 and S30V. **Prices:** $150 to $1500. **Remarks:** Scrimshaw, exotic handle material, wet formed sheaths. Membership Arizona Knife Collectors Association. Southern California blades collectors & professional knife makers assoc. **Mark:** E.F. Stalcup, Gallup, NM.

STANCER, CHUCK
62 Hidden Ranch Rd NW, Calgary, AB, CANADA T3A 5S5, Phone: 403-295-7370, stancerc@telusplanet.net
Specialties: Traditional and working straight knives. **Patterns:** Bowies, hunters and utility knives. **Technical:** Forges and grinds most steels. **Prices:** $175 and up. **Remarks:** Part-time maker. **Mark:** Last name.

STANFORD, PERRY
405N Walnut #9, Broken Arrow, OK 74012, Phone: 918-251-7983 or 866-305-5690, stanfordoutdoors@valornet; Web: www.stanfordoutdoors.homestead.com
Specialties: Drop point, hunting and skinning knives, handmade sheaths. **Patterns:** Stright, hunting and skinners. **Technical:** Grinds 440C, ATS-34 and Damascus. **Prices:** $65 to $275. **Remarks:** Part-time maker, first knife sold in 2007. Knifemaker supplier, manufacturer of paper sharpening systems. Doing business as Stanford Outdoors. **Mark:** Company name and nickname.

STANLEY, JOHN
604 Elm St, Crossett, AR 71635, Phone: 970-304-3005
Specialties: Hand forged fixed blades with engraving and carving. **Patterns:** Scottish dirks, skeans and fantasy blades. **Technical:** Forge high-carbon steel, own Damascus. Prices $70 to $500. **Remarks:** All work is sole authorship. Offers engraving and carving services on other knives and handles. **Mark:** Varies.

STAPEL, CHUCK
Box 1617, Glendale, CA 91209, Phone: 213-705-6433, www.stapelknives.com
Specialties: Working knives of his design. **Patterns:** Variety of straight knives, tantos, hunters, folders and utility knives. **Technical:** Grinds D2, 440C and AEB-L. **Prices:** $185 to $12,000. **Remarks:** Full-time maker; first knife sold in 1974. **Mark:** Last name or last name, U.S.A.

STAPLETON, WILLIAM E
BUFFALO 'B' FORGE, 5425 Country Ln, Merritt Island, FL 32953
Specialties: Classic and traditional knives of his design and customer spec. **Patterns:** Hunters and using knives. **Technical:** Forges, O1 and L6 Damascus, cable Damascus and 5160; stock removal on request. **Prices:** $150 to $1000. **Remarks:** Part-time maker, first knife sold 1990. Doing business as Buffalo "B" Forge. **Mark:** Anvil with S initial in center of anvil.

STATES, JOSHUA C
43905 N 16th St, New River, AZ 85087, Phone: 623-826-3809, Web: www.dosgatosforge.com
Specialties: Design and fabrication of forged working and art knives from O1 and my own damascus. Stock removal from 440C and CM154 upon request. Folders from 440C, CM154 and Damascus. Flat and Hollow grinds. Knives made to customer specs and/or design.**Patterns:** Bowies, hunters, daggers, chef knives, and exotic shapes. **Technical:** Damascus is 1095, 1084, O1 and 15N20. Carved or file-worked fittings from various metals including my own mokume gane and Damascus.**Prices:** $150 to $1500. **Remarks:** Part-time maker with waiting list. First knife sold in 2006. **Mark:** Initials JCS inside small oval, or Dos Gatos Forge. Unmarked knives come with certificate of authorship.

STECK, VAN R
260 W Dogwood Ave, Orange City, FL 32763, Phone: 407-416-1723, van@thudknives.com
Specialties: Specializing in double-edged grinds. Free-hand grinds: folders, spears, bowies, swords and miniatures. **Patterns:** Tomahawks with a crane for the spike, tactical merged with nature.**Technical:** Hamon lines, folder lock of own design, the arm-lock! **Prices:** $50 -$1500. **Remarks:** Builds knives designed by Laci Szabo or builds to customer design. Studied with Reese Weiland on folders and automatics. **Mark:** GEISHA holding a sword with initials and THUD KNIVES in a circle.

STEGALL, KEITH
701 Outlet View Dr, Wasilla, AK 99654, Phone: 907-376-0703, kas5200@yahoo.com
Specialties: Traditional working straight knives. **Patterns:** Most patterns. **Technical:** Grinds 440C and 154CM. **Prices:** $100 to $300. **Remarks:** Spare-time maker; first knife sold in 1987. **Mark:** Name and state with anchor.

STEGNER, WILBUR G
9242 173rd Ave SW, Rochester, WA 98579, Phone: 360-273-0937, wilbur@wgsk.net; Web: www.wgsk.net
Specialties: Working/using straight knives and folders of his design. **Patterns:** Hunters and locking folders. **Technical:** Makes his own Damascus steel. **Prices:** $100 to $1000; some to $5000. **Remarks:** Full-time maker; first knife sold in 1979. Google search key words-"STEGNER KNIVES." Best folder awards NWKC 2009, 2010 and 2011. **Mark:** First and middle initials, last name in bar over shield logo.

STEIER, DAVID
7722 Zenith Way, Louisville, KY 40219, Phone: 502-969-8409, umag300@aol.com; Web: www.steierknives.com
Specialties: Folding LinerLocks, Bowies, slip joints, lockbacks, and straight hunters.

custom knifemakers

Technical: Stock removal blades of 440C, ATS-34, and Damascus from outside sources like Robert Eggerling and Mike Norris. **Prices:** $150 for straight hunters to $1400 for fully decked-out folders. **Remarks:** First knife sold in 1979. **Mark:** Last name STEIER.

STEIGER, MONTE L
Box 186, Genesee, ID 83832, Phone: 208-285-1769, montesharon@genesee-id.com
Specialties: Traditional working/using straight knives of all designs. **Patterns:** Hunters, utility/camp knives, fillet and chefs. Carving sets and steak knives. **Technical:** Grinds 1095, O1, 440C, ATS-34. Handles of stacked leather, natural wood, Micarta or pakkawood. Each knife comes with right-or left-handed sheath. **Prices:** $110 to $600. **Remarks:** Spare-time maker; first knife sold in 1988. Retired librarian **Mark:** First initial, last name, city and state.

STEIGERWALT, KEN
507 Savagehill Rd, Orangeville, PA 17859, Phone: 570-683-5156, Web: www.steigerwaltknives.com
Specialties: Carving on bolsters and handle material. **Patterns:** Folders, button locks and rear locks. **Technical:** Grinds ATS-34, 440C and commercial Damascus. Experiments with unique filework. **Prices:** $500 to $5000. **Remarks:** Full-time maker; first knife sold in 1981. **Mark:** Kasteigerwalt

STEINAU, JURGEN
Julius-Hart Strasse 44, Berlin, GERMANY 01162, Phone: 372-6452512, Fax: 372-645-2512
Specialties: Fantasy and high-art straight knives of his design. **Patterns:** Boots, daggers and switch-blade folders. **Technical:** Grinds 440B, 2379 and X90 Cr.Mo.V. 78. **Prices:** $1500 to $2500; some to $3500. **Remarks:** Full-time maker; first knife sold in 1984. **Mark:** Symbol, plus year, month day and serial number.

STEINBERG, AL
5244 Duenas, Laguna Woods, CA 92653, Phone: 949-951-2889, lagknife@fea.net
Specialties: Fancy working straight knives to customer specs. **Patterns:** Hunters, Bowies, fishing, camp knives, push knives and high end kitchen knives. **Technical:** Grinds O1, 440C and 154CM. **Prices:** $60 to $2500. **Remarks:** Full-time maker; first knife sold in 1972. **Mark:** Signature, city and state.

STEINBRECHER, MARK W
1122 92nd Place, Pleasant Prairie, WI 53158-4939
Specialties: Working and fancy folders. **Patterns:** Daggers, pocket knives, fighters and gents of his own design or to customer specs. **Technical:** Hollow grinds ATS-34, O1 other makers Damascus. Uses natural handle materials: stag, ivories, mother-of-pearl. File work and some inlays. **Prices:** $500 to $1200, some to $2500. **Remarks:** Part-time maker, first folder sold in 1989. **Mark:** Name etched or handwritten on ATS-34; stamped on Damascus.

STEINGASS, T.K.
334 Silver Lake Rd., Bucksport, ME 04416, Phone: 304-268-1161, tksteingass@frontier.com; Web: http://steingassknives.com
Specialties: Loveless style hunters and fighters and sole authorship knives: Man Knife, Silent Hunter, and Silent Fighter. Harpoon Grind Camp Knife and Harpoon Grind Man Hunter. **Technical:** Stock removal, use CPM 154, S3V and occasionally 1095 or O1 for camp choppers.**Prices:** $200 to $500. **Remarks:** Part-time maker; first knife made in 2010. **Mark:** STEINGASS.

STEKETEE, CRAIG A
871 NE US Hwy 60, Billings, MO 65610, Phone: 417-744-2770, stekknives04@yahoo.com
Specialties: Classic and working straight knives and swords of his design. **Patterns:** Bowies, hunters, and Japanese-style swords. **Technical:** Forges his own Damascus; bronze, silver and Damascus fittings, offers filework. Prefers exotic and natural handle materials. **Prices:** $200 to $4000. **Remarks:** Full-time maker. **Mark:** STEK.

STEPHAN, DANIEL
2201 S Miller Rd, Valrico, FL 33594, Phone: 727-580-8617, knifemaker@verizon.net
Specialties: Art knives, one-of-a-kind.

STERLING, MURRAY
693 Round Peak Church Rd, Mount Airy, NC 27030, Phone: 336-352-5110, Fax: 336-352-5105, sterck@surry.net; Web: www.sterlingcustomknives.com
Specialties: Single and dual blade folders. Interframes and integral dovetail frames. **Technical:** Grinds ATS-34 or Damascus by Mike Norris and/or Devin Thomas. **Prices:** $300 and up. **Remarks:** Full-time maker; first knife sold in 1991. **Mark:** Last name stamped.

STERLING, THOMAS J
ART KNIVES BY, 120 N Pheasant Run, Coupeville, WA 98239, Phone: 360-678-9269, Fax: 360-678-9269, netsuke@comcast.net; Web: www.bladegallery.com Or www.sterlingsculptures.com
Specialties: Since 2003 Tom Sterling and Dr. J.P. Higgins have created a unique collaboration of one-of-a-kind, ultra-quality art knives with percussion or pressured flaked stone blades and creatively sculpted handles. Their knives are often highly influenced by the traditions of Japanese netsuke and unique fusions of cultures, reflecting stylistically integrated choices of exotic hardwoods, fossil ivories and semi-precious materials, contrasting inlays and polychromed and pyrographed details. **Prices:** $300 to $900. **Remarks:** Limited output ensures highest quality artwork and exceptional levels of craftsmanship. **Mark:** Signatures Sterling and Higgins.

STETTER, J. C.
115 E College Blvd PMB 180, Roswell, NM 88201, Phone: 505-627-0978

Specialties: Fixed and folding. **Patterns:** Traditional and yours. **Technical:** Forged and ground of varied materials including his own pattern welded steel. **Prices:** Start at $250. **Remarks:** Full-time maker, first knife sold 1989. **Mark:** Currently "J.C. Stetter."

STEYN, PETER
PO Box 76, Welkom, Freestate, SOUTH AFRICA 9460, Phone: 27573522015, Fax: 27573523566, Web:www.petersteynknives.com email:info@petersteynknives.com
Specialties: Fixed blade knives of own design, all with hand-stitched leather sheaths. Folding knives of own design supplied with soft pouches. **Patterns:**Fixed blades: hunters and skinners. Folding knives: friction folders, slip joints and lockbacks. **Technical:**Grinds 12C27 and Damasteel. Blades are bead-blasted in plain or patterned finish. Ceramic wash also available in satin or antiqued finish. Grind syle is convex, concave on the obverse, and convex on the reverse. Works with a wide variety of handle materials, prefers exotic woods and synthetics. **Prices:** $150 to $650. **Remarks:**Full-time maker, first knife sold 2005, member of South African Guild. **Mark:** Letter 'S' in shape of pyramid with full name above and 'Handcrafted' below.

STICE, DOUGLAS W
PO Box 12815, Wichita, KS 67277, Phone: 316-295-6855, doug@sticecraft.com; Web: www.sticecraft.com
Specialties: Working fixed blade knives of own design. **Patterns:** Tacticals, hunters, skinners,utility, and camp knives. **Technical:** Grinds CPM154CM, 154CM, CPM3V, Damascus; uses 18" contact grinds where wheel for hollow grinds, also flat. **Prices:** $100 to $750. **Remarks:** Full-time maker; first professional knife made in 2009. All knives have serial numbers and include certificate of authenticity. **Mark:** Stylized "Stice" stamp.

STIDHAM, DANIEL
3106 Mill Cr. Rd., Gallipolis, Ohio 45631, Phone: 740-446-1673, danstidham@yahoo.com
Specialties: Fixed blades, folders, Bowies and hunters. **Technical:**440C, Alabama Damascus, 1095 with filework. **Prices:** Start at $150. **Remarks:** Has made fixed blades since 1961, folders since 1986. Also sells various knife brands.**Mark:** Stidham Knives Gallipolis, Ohio 45631.

STIMPS, JASON M
374 S Shaffer St, Orange, CA 92866, Phone: 714-744-5866

STIPES, DWIGHT
2651 SW Buena Vista Dr, Palm City, FL 34990, Phone: 772-597-0550, dwightstipes@adelphia.net
Specialties: Traditional and working straight knives in standard patterns. **Patterns:** Boots, Bowies, daggers, hunters and fighters. **Technical:** Grinds 440C, D2 and D3 tool steel. Handles of natural materials, animal, bone or horn. **Prices:** $75 to $150. **Remarks:** Full-time maker; first knife sold in 1972. **Mark:** Stipes.

STOKES, ED
22614 Cardinal Dr, Hockley, TX 77447, Phone: 713-351-1319
Specialties: Working straight knives and folders of all designs. **Patterns:** Boots, Bowies, daggers, fighters, hunters and miniatures. **Technical:** Grinds ATS-34, 440C and D2. Offers decorative butt caps, tapered spacers on handles and finger grooves, nickel-silver inlays, handmade sheaths. **Prices:** $185 to $290; some to $350. **Remarks:** Full-time maker; first knife sold in 1973. **Mark:** First and last name, Custom Knives with Apache logo.

STONE, JERRY
PO Box 1027, Lytle, TX 78052, Phone: 830-709-3042
Specialties: Traditional working and using folders of his design and to customer specs; fancy knives. **Patterns:** Fighters, hunters, locking folders and slip joints. Also make automatics. **Technical:** Grinds 440C and ATS-34. Offers filework. **Prices:** $175 to $1000. **Remarks:** Full-time maker; first knife sold in 1973. **Mark:** Name over Texas star/town and state underneath.

STORCH, ED
RR 4, Mannville, AB, CANADA T0B 2W0, Phone: 780-763-2214, storchknives@gmail.com; Web: www.storchknives.com
Specialties: Working knives, fancy fighting knives, kitchen cutlery and art knives. Knifemaking classes. **Patterns:** Working patterns, Bowies and folders. **Technical:** Forges his own Damascus. Grinds ATS-34. Builds friction folders. Salt heat treating. **Prices:** $100 to $3,000 (U.S.). **Remarks:** Full-time maker; first knife sold in 1984. Classes taught in stock-removal, and damascus and sword making. **Mark:** Last name.

STORMER, BOB
34354 Hwy E, Dixon, MO 65459, Phone: 636-734-2693, bs34354@gmail.com
Specialties: Straight knives, using collector grade. **Patterns:** Bowies, skinners, hunters, camp knives. **Technical:** Forges 5160, 1095. **Prices:** $200 to $500. **Remarks:** Part-time maker, ABS Journeyman Smith 2001. **Mark:** Setting sun/fall trees/initials.

STOUT, CHARLES
RT3 178 Stout Rd, Gillham, AR 71841, Phone: 870-386-5521

STOUT, JOHNNY
1205 Forest Trail, New Braunfels, TX 78132, Phone: 830-606-4067, johnny@stoutknives.com; Web: www.stoutknives.com
Specialties: Folders, some fixed blades. Working knives, some fancy. **Patterns:** Hunters, tactical, Bowies, automatics, liner locks and slip-joints. **Technical:** Grinds stainless and carbon steels; forges own Damascus. **Prices:** $450 to $895; some to $3500. **Remarks:** Full-time maker; first knife sold in 1983. Hosts semi-annual Guadalupe Forge Hammer-in and Knifemakers Rendezvous. **Mark:** Name and city in logo.

STRAIGHT, KENNETH J
11311 103 Lane N, Largo, FL 33773, Phone: 813-397-9817

STRANDE, POUL
Soster Svenstrup Byvej 16, Viby Sj., Dastrup, DENMARK 4130, Phone: 46 19 43 05, Fax: 46 19 53 19, Web: www.poulstrande.com

Specialties: Classic fantasy working knives; Damasceret blade, Nikkel Damasceret blade, Lamineret: Lamineret blade with Nikkel. **Patterns:** Bowies, daggers, fighters, hunters and swords. **Technical:** Uses carbon steel and 15C20 steel. **Prices:** NA. **Remarks:** Full-time maker; first knife sold in 1985. **Mark:** First and last initials.

STRAUB, SALEM F.
324 Cobey Creek Rd., Tonasket, WA 98855, Phone: 509-486-2627, vorpalforge@hotmail.com Web: www.prometheanknives.com

Specialties: Elegant working knives, fixed blade hunters, utility, skinning knives; liner locks. Makes own horsehide sheaths. **Patterns:** A wide range of syles, everything from the gentleman's pocket to the working kitchen, integrals, Bowies, folders, check out my website to see some of my work for ideas. **Technical:** Forges several carbon steels, 52100, W1, etc. Grinds stainless and makes/uses own damascus, cable, san mai, stadard patterns. Likes clay quenching, hamons, hand rubbed finishes. Flat, hollow, or convex grinds. Prefers synthetic handle materials. Hidden and full tapered tangs. **Prices:** $150 -$600, some higher. **Remarks:** Full-time maker. Doing what it takes to make your knife ordering and buying experience positive and enjoyable; striving to exceed expectations. All knives backed by lifetime guarantee. **Mark:** "Straub" stamp or "Promethean Knives" etched. Some older pieces stamped "Vorpal" though no longer using this mark. **Other:** Feel free to call or e-mail anytime. I love to talk knives.

STRICKLAND, DALE
1440 E Thompson View, Monroe, UT 84754, Phone: 435-896-8362

Specialties: Traditional and working straight knives and folders of his design and to customer specs. **Patterns:** Hunters, folders, miniatures and utility knives. **Technical:** Grinds Damascus and 440C. **Prices:** $120 to $350; some to $500. **Remarks:** Part-time maker; first knife sold in 1991. **Mark:** Oval stamp of name, Maker.

STRIDER, MICK
STRIDER KNIVES, 565 Country Club Dr., Escondido, CA 92029, Phone: 760-471-8275, Fax: 503-218-7069, striderguys@striderknives.com; Web: www.striderknives.com

STRONG, SCOTT
1599 Beaver Valley Rd, Beavercreek, OH 45434, Phone: 937-426-9290

Specialties: Working knives, some deluxe. **Patterns:** Hunters, fighters, survival and military-style knives, art knives. **Technical:** Forges and grinds O1, A2, D2, 440C and ATS-34. Uses no solder; most knives disassemble. **Prices:** $75 to $450; some to $1500. **Remarks:** Spare-time maker; first knife sold in 1983. **Mark:** Strong Knives.

STROYAN, ERIC
Box 218, Dalton, PA 18414, Phone: 717-563-2603

Specialties: Classic and working/using straight knives and folders of his design. **Patterns:** Hunters, locking folders, slip-joints. **Technical:** Forges Damascus; grinds ATS-34, D2. **Prices:** $200 to $600; some to $2000. **Remarks:** Part-time maker; first knife sold in 1968. **Mark:** Signature or initials stamp.

STUART, MASON
24 Beech Street, Mansfield, MA 02048, Phone: 508-339-8236, smasonknives@verizon.net Web: smasonknives.com

Specialties: Straight knives of his design, standard patterns. **Patterns:** Bowies, hunters, fighters and neck knives. **Technical:** Forges and grinds. Damascus, 5160, 1095, 1084, old files. Uses only natural handle material. **Prices:** $350 -2,000. **Remarks:** Part-time maker. **Mark:** First initial and last name.

STUART, STEVE
Box 168, Gores Landing, ON, CANADA K0K 2E0, Phone: 905-440-6910, stevestuart@xplornet.com

Specialties: Straight knives. **Patterns:** Tantos, fighters, skinners, file and rasp knives. **Technical:** Uses 440C, CPM154, CPMS30V, Micarta and natural handle materials. **Prices:** $60 to $400. **Remarks:** Part-time maker. **Mark:** SS.

STUCKY, DANIEL
37924 Shenandoah Loop, Springfield, OR 97478, Phone: 541-747-6496, stuckyj1@msn.com, www.stuckyknives.com

Specialties: Tactical, fancy and everyday carry folders, fixed-blade hunting knives, trout, bird and fillet knives. **Technical:** Stock removal maker. Steels include but are not limited to damascus, CPM 154, CPM S30V, CPM S35VN, 154CM and ATS-34. **Prices:** Start at $300 and can go to thousands, depending on materials used. **Remarks:** Full-time maker; first knife sold in 1999. **Mark:** Name over city and state.

STYREFORS, MATTIAS
Unbyn 23, Boden, SWEDEN 96193, infor@styrefors.com

Specialties: Damascus and mosaic Damascus. Fixed blade Nordic hunters, folders and swords. **Technical:** Forges, shapes and grinds Damascus and mosaic Damascus from mostly UHB 15N20 and 20C with contrasts in nickel and 15N20. Hardness HR 58. **Prices:** $800 to $3000. **Remarks:** Full-time maker since 1999. International reputation for high end Damascus blades. Uses stabilized Arctic birch and willow burl, horn, fossils, exotic materials, and scrimshaw by Viveca Sahlin for knife handles. Hand tools and hand stitches leather sheaths in cow raw hide. Works in well equipped former military forgery in northern Sweden. **Mark:** MS.

SUEDMEIER, HARLAN
762 N 60th Rd, Nebraska City, NE 68410, Phone: 402-873-4372

Patterns: Straight knives. **Technical:** Forging hi carbon Damascus. **Prices:** Starting at $175. **Mark:** First initials & last name.

SUGIHARA, KEIDOH
4-16-1 Kamori-Cho, Kishiwada City, Osaka, JAPAN F596-0042, Fax: 0724-44-2677

Specialties: High-tech working straight knives and folders of his design. **Patterns:** Bowies, hunters, fighters, fishing, boots, some pocket knives and liner-lock folders. **Technical:** Grinds ATS-34, COS-25, buys Damascus and high-carbon steels. **Prices:** $60 to $4000. **Remarks:** Full-time maker, first knife sold in 1980. **Mark:** Initial logo with fish design.

SUGIYAMA, EDDY K
2361 Nagayu, Naoirimachi Naoirigun, Oita, JAPAN, Phone: 0974-75-2050

Specialties: One-of-a-kind, exotic-style knives. **Patterns:** Working, utility and miniatures. **Technical:** CT rind, ATS-34 and D2. **Prices:** $400 to $1200. **Remarks:** Full-time maker. **Mark:** Name or cedar mark.

SUMMERS, ARTHUR L
1310 Hess Rd, Concord, NC 28025, Phone: 704-787-9275 Cell: 704-305-0735, arthursummers88@hotmail.com

Specialties: Drop points, clip points, straight blades. **Patterns:** Hunters, Bowies and personal knives. **Technical:** Grinds ATS-34, CPM-D2, CPM-154 and damascus. **Prices:** $250 to $1000. **Remarks:** Full-time maker; first knife sold in 1988. **Mark:** Serial number is the date.

SUMMERS, DAN
2675 NY Rt. 11, Whitney Pt., NY 13862, Phone: 607-692-2391, dansumm11@gmail.com

Specialties: Period knives and tomahawks. **Technical:** All hand forging. **Prices:** Most $100 to $400.

SUMMERS, DENNIS K
827 E. Cecil St, Springfield, OH 45503, Phone: 513-324-0624

Specialties: Working/using knives. **Patterns:** Fighters and personal knives. **Technical:** Grinds 440C, A2 and D2. Makes drop and clip point. **Prices:** $75 to $200. **Remarks:** Part-time maker; first knife sold in 1995. **Mark:** First and middle initials, last name, serial number.

SUNDERLAND, RICHARD
Av Infraganti 23, Col Lazaro Cardenas, Puerto Escondido, OA, MEXICO 71980, Phone: 011 52 94 582 1451, sunamerica@prodigy.net.mx7

Specialties: Personal and hunting knives with carved handles in oosic and ivory. **Patterns:** Hunters, Bowies, daggers, camp and personal knives. **Technical:** Grinds 440C, ATS-34 and O1. Handle materials of rosewoods, fossil mammoth ivory and oosic. **Prices:** $150 to $1000. **Remarks:** Part-time maker; first knife sold in 1983. Doing business as Sun Knife Co. **Mark:** SUN.

SUTTON, S RUSSELL
4900 Cypress Shores Dr, New Bern, NC 28562, Phone: 252-637-3963, srsutton@suddenlink.net; Web: www.suttoncustomknives.com

Specialties: Straight knives and folders to customer specs and in standard patterns. **Patterns:** Boots, hunters, interframes, slip joints and locking liners. **Technical:** Grinds ATS-34, 440C and stainless Damascus. **Prices:** $220 to $2000. **Remarks:** Full-time maker; first knife sold in 1992. Provides relief engraving on bolsters and guards. **Mark:** Etched last name.

SWEARINGEN, KURT
22 Calvary Rd., Cedar Crest, NM 87008, Phone: 575-613-0500, kurt@swearingenknife.com; Web: www.swearingenknife.com

Specialties: Traditional hunting and camp knives, as well as slip-joint and lockback folders of classic design with an emphasis on utility. Hand-carved and tooled sheaths accompany each knife. **Patterns:** Loveless-style hunters, Scagel folders, as well as original designs. **Technical:** Grinds CPM 154 for all standard hunting models and D2 for all folders. Smiths W2 for forged hunters, and 5160 or 1084 for camp knives. **Prices:** Standard models in CPM 154 start at $320, including a custom sheath. **Remarks:** Serious part-time maker and ABS journeyman smith, I personally test each knife in my shop and in the field during hunting season (hunters) and in my work as a forester (camp knives).

SWEAZA, DENNIS
4052 Hwy 321 E, Austin, AR 72007, Phone: 501-941-1886, knives4den@aol.com

SWEENEY, COLTIN D
1216 S 3 St W, Missoula, MT 59801, Phone: 406-721-6782

SWENSON, LUKE
SWENSON KNIVES, 1667 Brushy Creek Dr., Lakehills, TX 78063, Phone: 210-722-3227, luke@swensonknives.com; Web: www.swensonknives.com

Specialties: Fixed blades for outdoor/survival or bushcraft use, some tactical and military patterns, and slip-joint folders. **Technical:** Stock-removal method of blade making. Flat grinds A2 tool steel for fixed blades, and hollow grinds CPM 154 for slip-joint folders. Credits Bill Ruple for mentoring him in the making slip joints. **Prices:** $275 to $600. **Remarks:** Part-time maker/full-time firefighter; first knife made in 2003. **Mark:** Name and city where maker lives.

SWYHART, ART
509 Main St, PO Box 267, Klickitat, WA 98628, Phone: 509-369-3451, swyhart@gorge.net; Web: http://www.knifeoutlet.com/swyhart.htm

Specialties: Traditional working and using knives of his design. **Patterns:** Bowies, hunters and utility/camp knives. **Technical:** Forges 52100, 5160 and Damascus 1084 mixed with either 15N20 or O186. Blades differentially heat-treated with visible temper line. **Prices:** $75 to $250; some to $350. **Remarks:** Part-time maker; first knife sold in 1983. **Mark:** First name, last initial in script.

SYLVESTER, DAVID
465 Sweede Rd., Compton, QC, CANADA, Phone: 819-837-0304, david@swedevilleforge.com Web: swedeville.forge.com
Patterns: I hand forge all my knives and I like to make hunters and integrals and some Bowies and fighters. I work with W2, 1084, 1095, and my damascus. **Prices:** $200 -$1500. **Remarks:** Part-time maker. ABS Journeyman Smith. **Mark:** D.Sylvester

SYMONDS, ALBERTO E
Rambla M Gandhi 485, Apt 901, Montevideo, URUGUAY 11300, Phone: 011 598 27103201, Fax: 011 598 2 7103201, albertosymonds@hotmail.com
Specialties: All kinds including puukos, nice sheaths, leather and wood. **Prices:** $300 to $2200. **Mark:** AESH and current year.

SYSLO, CHUCK
3418 South 116 Ave, Omaha, NE 68144, Phone: 402-333-0647, ciscoknives@cox.net
Specialties: Hunters, working knives, daggers and misc. **Patterns:** Hunters, daggers and survival knives; locking folders. **Technical:** Flat-grinds D2, 440C and 154CM; hand polishes only. **Prices:** $250 to $1,000; some to $3,000. **Remarks:** Part-time maker; first knife sold in 1978. Uses many natural materials. Making some knives, mainly retired from knifemaking. **Mark:** CISCO in logo.

SZCZERBIAK, MACIEJ
Crusader Forge Knives, PO Box 2181, St. George, UT 84771, Phone: 435-574-2193, crusaderforge@yahoo.com; Web: www.crusaderforge.com
Patterns: Drop-point, spear-point and tanto fixed blades and tactical folders. **Technical:** Stock removal using CPM-S30V and D2 steels. Knives designed with the technical operator in mind, and maintain an amazing balance in the user's hand. **Prices:** $300 to $2,500. **Remarks:** First knife made in 1999.

SZILASKI, JOSEPH
School of Knifemaking, 52 Woods Dr., Pine Plains, NY 12567, Phone: 518-398-0309, joe@szilaski.com; Web: www.szilaski.com
Specialties: Straight knives, folders and tomahawks of his design, to customer specs and in standard patterns. Many pieces are one-of-a-kind. Offers knifemaking classes for all levels in 4,000-square-foot shop. Courses are in forging, grinding, damascus, tomahawk engraving and carving. **Patterns:** Bowies, daggers, fighters, hunters, art knives and early American styles. **Technical:** Forges A2, D2, O1 and damascus. **Prices:** $450 to $4,000; some to $10,000. **Remarks:** Full-time maker; first knife sold in 1990. ABS master smith. **Mark:** Snake logo.

T

TABER, DAVID E.
51 E. 4th St., Ste. 300, Winona, MN 55987, Phone: 507-450-1918, dtaber@qwestoffice.net
Specialties: Traditional slip joints, primarily using and working knives. **Technical:** Blades are hollow ground on a 20" wheel, ATS-34 and some damascus steel. **Remarks:** Full-time orthodontist, part-time maker; first knife made in January 2011. **Mark:** dr.t.

TABOR, TIM
18925 Crooked Lane, Lutz, FL 33548, Phone: 813-948-6141, taborknives.com
Specialties: Fancy folders, Damascus Bowies and hunters. **Patterns:** My own design folders & customer requests. **Technical:** ATS-34, hand forged Damascus, 1084, 15N20 mosaic Damascus, 1095, 5160 high carbon blades, flat grind, file work & jewel embellishments. **Prices:** $175 to $1500. **Remarks:** Part-time maker, sold first knife in 2003. **Mark:** Last name

TAKACH, ANDREW
1390 Fallen Timber Rd., Elizabeth, PA 15037, Phone: 724-691-2271, a-takach@takachforge.com; Web: www.takachforge.com
Specialties: One-of-a-kind fixed blade working knives (own design or customer's). Mostly all fileworked. **Patterns:** Hunters, skinners, caping, fighters, and designs of own style. **Technical:** Forges mostly 5160, 1090, O1, an down pattern welded Damascus, nickle Damascus, and cable and various chain Damascus. Also do some San Mai. **Prices:** $100 to $350, some over $550. **Remarks:** Doing business as Takach Forge. First knife sold in 2004. **Mark:** Takach (stamped).

TAKAHASHI, MASAO
39-3 Sekine-machi, Maebashi-shi, Gunma, JAPAN 371 0047, Phone: 81 27 234 2223, Fax: 81 27 234 2223
Specialties: Working straight knives. **Patterns:** Daggers, fighters, hunters, fishing knives, boots. **Technical:** Grinds ATS-34 and Damascus. **Prices:** $350 to $1000 and up. **Remarks:** Part-time maker; first knife sold in 1982. **Mark:** M. Takahashi.

TALLY, GRANT
26961 James Ave, Flat Rock, MI 48134, Phone: 313-414-1618
Specialties: Straight knives and folders of his design. **Patterns:** Bowies, daggers, fighters. **Technical:** Grinds ATS-34, 440C and D2. Offers filework. **Prices:** $250 to $1000. **Remarks:** Part-time maker; first knife sold in 1985. Doing business as Tally Knives. **Mark:** Tally (last name).

TAMATSU, KUNIHIKO
5344 Sukumo, Sukumo City, Kochi-ken, JAPAN 788-0000, Phone: 0880-63-3455, ktamatsu@mb.gallery.ne.jp; Web: www.knife.tamatu.net
Specialties: Loveless-style fighters, sub-hilt fighters and hunting knives. **Technical:** Mirror-finished ATS-34, BG-42 and CPM-S30V blades. **Prices:** $400 to $2,500. **Remarks:** Part-time maker, making knives for eight years. **Mark:** Electrical etching of "K. Tamatsu."

TAMBOLI, MICHAEL
12447 N 49 Ave, Glendale, AZ 85304, Phone: 602-978-4308, mnbtamboli@gmail.com
Specialties: Miniatures, some full size. **Patterns:** Miniature hunting knives to fantasy art knives. **Technical:** Grinds ATS-34 & Damascus. **Prices:** $75 to $500; some to $2000. **Remarks:** Full time maker; first knife sold in 1978. **Mark:** Initials, last name, last name city and state, MT Custom Knives or Mike Tamboli in Japanese script.

TASMAN, KERLEY
9 Avignon Retreat, Pt Kennedy, WA, AUSTRALIA 6172, Phone: 61 8 9593 0554, Fax: 61 8 9593 0554, taskerley@optusnet.com.au
Specialties: Knife/harness/sheath systems for elite military personnel and body guards. **Patterns:** Utility/tactical knives, hunters small game and presentation grade knives. **Technical:** ATS-34 and 440C, Damascus, flat and hollow grids. **Prices:** $200 to $1800 U.S. **Remarks:** Will take presentation grade commissions. Multi award winning maker and custom jeweler. **Mark:** Maker's initials.

TAYLOR, BILLY
10 Temple Rd, Petal, MS 39465, Phone: 601-544-0041
Specialties: Straight knives of his design. **Patterns:** Bowies, skinners, hunters and utility knives. **Technical:** Flat-grinds 440C, ATS-34 and 154CM. **Prices:** $60 to $300. **Remarks:** Part-time maker; first knife sold in 1991. **Mark:** Full name, city and state.

TAYLOR, C. GRAY
560 Poteat Ln, Fall Branch, TN 37656, Phone: 423-348-8304 or 423-765-6434, grayknives@aol.com; Web: www.cgraytaylor.com
Specialties: Traditonal multi-blade lobster folders, also art display Bowies and daggers. **Patterns:** Orange Blossom, sleeveboard and gunstocks. **Technical:** Grinds. **Prices:** Upscale. **Remarks:** Full-time maker; first knife sold in 1975. **Mark:** Name, city and state.

TAYLOR, SHANE
42 Broken Bow Ln, Miles City, MT 59301, Phone: 406-234-7175, shane@taylorknives.com; Web: www.taylorknives.com
Specialties: One-of-a-kind fancy Damascus straight knives and folders. **Patterns:** Bowies, folders and fighters. **Technical:** Forges own mosaic and pattern welded Damascus. **Prices:** $450 and up. **Remarks:** ABS Master Smith, full-time maker; first knife sold in 1982. **Mark:** First name.

TEDFORD, STEVEN J.
14238 Telephone Rd., Colborne, ON, CANADA K0K 1S0, Phone: 613-689-7569, firebornswords@yahoo.com; Web: www.steventedfordknives.com
Specialties: Handmade custom fixed blades, specialty outdoors knives. **Patterns:** Swept Survival Bowie, large, medium and small-size field-dressing/hunting knives, drop-point skinners, and world-class fillet knives. **Technical:** Exclusively using ATS-34 stainless steel, Japanese-inspired, free-hand ground, zero-point edge blade design. **Prices:** All knives are sold wholesale directly from the shop starting at $150 to $500+. **Remarks:** Tedford Knives; Function is beauty. Every knife is unconditionally guaranteed for life.

TENDICK, BEN
798 Nadine Ave, Eugene, OR 97404, Phone: 541-912-1280, bentendick@gmail.com; Web: www.brtbladeworks.com
Specialties: Hunter/utility, tactical, bushcraft, and kitchen. **Technical:** Preferred steel -L6, 5160, and 15N20. Stock Removal. **Prices:** $130 to $700. **Remarks:** Part-time; has been making knives since early 90's but started seriously making knives in 2010. In business at BRT Bladeworks, no website yet but can be found on Facebook. **Mark:** Initials (BRT) with B backwards and T between the B and R, and also use last name.

TERRILL, STEPHEN
16357 Goat Ranch Rd, Springville, CA 93265, Phone: 559-539-3116, slterrill@yahoo.com
Specialties: Deluxe working straight knives and folders. **Patterns:** Fighters, tantos, boots, locking folders and axes; traditional oriental patterns. **Technical:** Forges 1095, 5160, Damascus, stock removal ATS-34. **Prices:** $300+. **Remarks:** Full-time maker; first knife sold in 1972. **Mark:** Name, city, state in logo.

TERZUOLA, ROBERT
10121 Eagle Rock NE, Albuquerque, NM 87122, Phone: 505-856-7077, terzuola@earthlink.net
Specialties: Working folders of his design; period pieces. **Patterns:** High-tech utility, defense and gentleman's folders. **Technical:** Grinds CPM154 and damascus. Offers titanium, carbon fiber and G10 composite for side-lock folders and tactical folders. **Prices:** $1,200 to $3,000. **Remarks:** Full-time maker; first knife sold in 1980. **Mark:** Mayan dragon head, name.

TESARIK, RICHARD
Pisecnik 87, 614 00 Brno, Czech Republic, Phone: 00420-602-834-726, rtesarik@gmail.com; Web: www.tesarikknives.com
Specialties: Handmade art knives. **Patterns:** Daggers, hunters and LinerLock or backlock folders. **Technical:** Grinds RWL-34, N690 and stainless or high-carbon damascus. Carves on blade, handle and other parts. I prefer fossil material and exotic wood, don't use synthetic material. **Prices:** $600 to $2,000. **Remarks:** Part-time maker, full-time hobby; first knife sold in 2009. **Mark:** TR.

THAYER, DANNY O
8908S 100W, Romney, IN 47981, Phone: 765-538-3105, dot61h@juno.com
Specialties: Hunters, fighters, Bowies. **Prices:** $250 and up.

THEIS, TERRY
21452 FM 2093, Harper, TX 78631, Phone: 830-864-4438
Specialties: All European and American engraving styles. **Prices:** $200 to $2000. **Remarks:** Engraver only.

THEVENOT, JEAN-PAUL
16 Rue De La Prefecture, Dijon, FRANCE 21000
Specialties: Traditional European knives and daggers. **Patterns:** Hunters, utility-camp knives, daggers, historical or modern style. **Technical:** Forges own Damascus, 5160, 1084. **Remarks:** Part-time maker. ABS Master Smith. **Mark:** Interlocked initials in square.

THIE, BRIAN
13250 150th St, Burlington, IA 52601, Phone: 319-850-2188, thieknives@gmail.com; Web: www.mepotelco.net/web/tknives
Specialties: Working using knives from basic to fancy. **Patterns:** Hunters, fighters, camp and folders. **Technical:** Forges blades and own Damascus. **Prices:** $250 and up. **Remarks:** ABS Journeyman Smith, part-time maker. Sole author of blades including forging, heat treat, engraving and sheath making. **Mark:** Last name hand engraved into the blade, JS stamped into blade.

THILL, JIM
10242 Bear Run, Missoula, MT 59803, Phone: 406-251-5475, bearrunmt@hotmail.com
Specialties: Traditional and working/using knives of his design. **Patterns:** Fighters, hunters and utility/camp knives. **Technical:** Grinds D2 and ATS-34; forges 10-95-85, 52100, 5160, 10 series, reg. Damascus-mosaic. Offers hand cut sheaths with rawhide lace. **Prices:** $145 to $350; some to $1250. **Remarks:** Full-time maker; first knife sold in 1962. **Mark:** Running bear in triangle.

THOMAS, BOB
Sunset Forge, 3502 Bay Rd., Ferndale, WA 98248, Phone: 360-201-0160, Fax: 360-366-5723, sunsetforge@rockisland.com

THOMAS, DAVID E
8502 Hwy 91, Lillian, AL 36549, Phone: 251-961-7574, redbluff@gulftel.com
Specialties: Bowies and hunters. **Technical:** Hand forged blades in 5160, 1095 and own Damascus. **Prices:** $400 and up. **Mark:** Stylized DT, maker's last name, serial number.

THOMAS, DEVIN
PO Box 568, Panaca, NV 89042, Phone: 775-728-4363, hoss@devinthomas.com; Web: www.devinthomas.com
Specialties: Traditional straight knives and folders in standard patterns. **Patterns:** Bowies, fighters, hunters. **Technical:** Forges stainless Damascus, nickel and 1095. Uses, makes and sells mokume with brass, copper and nickel-silver. **Prices:** $300 to $1200. **Remarks:** Full-time maker; first knife sold in 1979. **Mark:** First and last name, city and state with anvil, or first name only.

THOMAS, KIM
PO Box 531, Seville, OH 44273, Phone: 330-769-9906
Specialties: Fancy and traditional straight knives of his design and to customer specs; period pieces. **Patterns:** Boots, daggers, fighters, swords. **Technical:** Forges own Damascus from 5160, 1010 and nickel. **Prices:** $135 to $1500; some to $3000. **Remarks:** Part-time maker; first knife sold in 1986. Doing business as Thomas Iron Works. **Mark:** KT.

THOMAS, ROCKY
1716 Waterside Blvd, Moncks Corner, SC 29461, Phone: 843-761-7761
Specialties: Traditional working knives in standard patterns. **Patterns:** Hunters and utility/camp knives. **Technical:** ATS-34 and commercial Damascus. **Prices:** $130 to $350. **Remarks:** Spare-time maker; first knife sold in 1986. **Mark:** First name in script and/or block.

THOMPSON, KENNETH
4887 Glenwhite Dr, Duluth, GA 30136, Phone: 770-446-6730
Specialties: Traditional working and using knives of his design. **Patterns:** Hunters, Bowies and utility/camp knives. **Technical:** Forges 5168, O1, 1095 and 52100. **Prices:** $75 to $1500; some to $2500. **Remarks:** Part-time maker; first knife sold in 1990. **Mark:** P/W; or name, P/W, city and state.

THOMPSON, LEON
45723 SW Saddleback Dr, Gaston, OR 97119, Phone: 503-357-2573
Specialties: Working knives. **Patterns:** Locking folders, slip-joints and liner locks. **Technical:** Grinds ATS-34, D2 and 440C. **Prices:** $450 to $1000. **Remarks:** Full-time maker; first knife sold in 1976. **Mark:** First and middle initials, last name, city and state.

THOMPSON, LLOYD
PO Box 1664, Pagosa Springs, CO 81147, Phone: 970-264-5837
Specialties: Working and collectible straight knives and folders of his design. **Patterns:** Straight blades, lock back folders and slip joint folders. **Technical:** Hollow-grinds ATS-34, D2 and O1. Uses sambar stag and exotic woods. **Prices:** $150 to upscale. **Remarks:** Full-time maker; first knife sold in 1985. Doing business as Trapper Creek Knife Co. **Remarks:** Offers three-day knife-making classes. **Mark:** Name.

THOMPSON, TOMMY
4015 NE Hassalo, Portland, OR 97232-2607, Phone: 503-235-5762
Specialties: Fancy and working knives; mostly liner-lock folders. **Patterns:** Fighters, hunters and liner locks. **Technical:** Grinds D2, ATS-34, CPM440V and T15. Handles are either hardwood inlaid with wood banding and stone or shell, or made of agate, jasper, petrified woods, etc. **Prices:** $75 to $500; some to $1000. **Remarks:** Part-time maker; first knife sold in 1987. Doing business as Stone Birds. Knife making temporarily stopped due to family obligations. **Mark:** First and last name, city and state.

THOMSEN, LOYD W
25241 Renegade Pass, Custer, SD 57730, Phone: 605-673-2787, loydt@yahoo.com; Web: horseheadcreekknives.com
Specialties: High-art and traditional working/using straight knives and presentation pieces of his design and to customer specs; period pieces. Hand carved animals in crown of stag on handles and carved display stands. **Patterns:** Bowies, hunters, daggers and utility/camp knives. **Technical:** Forges and grinds 1095HC, 1084, L6, 15N20, 440C stainless steel, nickel 200; special restoration process on period pieces. Makes sheaths. Uses natural materials for handles. **Prices:** $350 to $1000. **Remarks:** Full-time maker; first knife sold in 1995. Doing business as Horsehead Creek Knives. **Mark:** Initials and last name over a horse's head.

THORBURN, ANDRE E.
P.O. Box 1748, Bela Bela, Warmbaths, LP, SOUTH AFRICA 0480, Phone: 27-82-650-1441, Fax: 27-86-750-2765, andrethorburn@gmail.com; Web: www.thorburnknives.co.za
Specialties: Working and fancy folders of own design to customer specs. **Technical:** Uses RWL-34, Damasteel, CPM steels, Bohler N690, and carbon and stainless damascus. **Prices:** Starting at $350. **Remarks:** Full-time maker since 1996; first knife sold in 1990. Member of South African, Italian, and German guilds. **Mark:** Initials and name in a double circle.

THOUROT, MICHAEL W
T-814 Co Rd 11, Napoleon, OH 43545, Phone: 419-533-6832, Fax: 419-533-3516, mike2row@henry-net.com; Web: wwwsafariknives.com
Specialties: Working straight knives to customer specs. Designed two-handled skinning ax and limited edition engraved knife and art print set. **Patterns:** Fishing and fillet knives, Bowies, tantos and hunters. **Technical:** Grinds O1, D2, 440C and Damascus. **Prices:** $200 to $5000. **Remarks:** Part-time maker; first knife sold in 1968. **Mark:** Initials.

THUESEN, ED
21211 Knolle Rd, Damon, TX 77430, Phone: 979-553-1211, Fax: 979-553-1211
Specialties: Working straight knives. **Patterns:** Hunters, fighters and survival knives. **Technical:** Grinds D2, 440C, ATS-34 and Vascowear. **Prices:** $150 to $275; some to $600. **Remarks:** Part-time maker; first knife sold in 1979. Runs knifemaker supply business. **Mark:** Last name in script.

TIENSVOLD, ALAN L
PO Box 355, 3277 U.S. Hwy. 20, Rushville, NE 69360, Phone: 308-360-0613, tiensvoldknives@gpcom.net
Specialties: Working knives, tomahawks and period pieces, high end Damascus knives. **Patterns:** Random, ladder, twist and many more. **Technical:** Hand forged blades, forges own Damascus. **Prices:** Working knives start at $300. **Remarks:** Received Journeyman rating with the ABS in 2002. Does own engraving and fine work. **Mark:** Tiensvold hand made U.S.A. on left side, JS on right.

TIENSVOLD, JASON
PO Box 795, Rushville, NE 69360, Phone: 308-360-2217, jasontiensvoldknives@yahoo.com
Specialties: Working and using straight knives of his design; period pieces. Gentlemen folders, art folders. Single action automatics. **Patterns:** Hunters, skinners, Bowies, fighters, daggers, liner locks. **Technical:** Forges own Damascus using 15N20 and 1084, 1095, nickel, custom file work. **Prices:** $200 to $4000. **Remarks:** Full-time maker, first knife sold in 1994; doing business under Tiensvold Custom Knives. **Mark:** J. Tiensvold on left side, MS on right.

TIGHE, BRIAN
12-111 Fourth Ave, Suite 376 Ridley Square, St. Catharines, ON, CANADA L2S 3P5, Phone: 905-892-2734, Web: www.tigheknives.com
Specialties: Folding knives, bearing pivots. High tech tactical folders. **Patterns:** Boots, daggers and locking. **Technical:** BG-42, RWL-34, Damasteel, 154CM, S30V, CPM 440V and CPM 420V. Prefers natural handle material inlay; hand finishes. **Prices:** $450 to $4000. **Remarks:** Full-time maker; first knife sold in 1989. **Mark:** Etched signature.

TILL, CALVIN E AND RUTH
1010 Maple St., Lot 4, Chadron, NE 69337-6967, Phone: 308-432-6945
Specialties: Straight knives, hunters, Bowies; no folders **Patterns:** Training point, drop point hunters, Bowies. **Technical:** ATS-34 sub zero quench RC59, 61. **Prices:** $700 to $1200. **Remarks:** Sells only the absolute best knives they can make. Manufactures every part in their knives. **Mark:** RC Till. The R is for Ruth.

TILTON, JOHN
24041 Hwy 383, Iowa, LA 70647, Phone: 337-582-6785, john@jetknives.com
Specialties: Bowies, camp knives, skinners and folders. **Technical:** All forged blades. Makes own Damascus. **Prices:** $150 and up. **Remarks:** ABS Journeyman Smith. **Mark:** Initials J.E.T.

TINDERA, GEORGE
BURNING RIVER FORGE, 751 Hadcock Rd, Brunswick, OH 44212-2648, Phone: 330-220-6212
Specialties: Straight knives; his designs. **Patterns:** Personal knives; classic Bowies and fighters. **Technical:** Hand-forged high-carbon; his own cable and pattern welded Damascus. **Prices:** $125 to $600. **Remarks:** Spare-time maker; sold first knife in 1995. Natural handle materials.

TINGLE, DENNIS P
19390 E Clinton Rd, Jackson, CA 95642, Phone: 209-223-4586, dtknives@earthlink.net
Specialties: Swords, fixed blades: small to medium, tomahawks. **Technical:** All blades forged. **Remarks:** ABS, JS. **Mark:** D. Tingle over JS.

TIPPETTS, COLTEN
4068 W Miners Farm Dr, Hidden Springs, ID 83714, Phone: 208-229-7772, coltentippetts@gmail.com

Specialties: Fancy and working straight knives and fancy locking folders of his own design or to customer specifications. **Patterns:** Hunters and skinners, fighters and utility. **Technical:** Grinds BG-42, high-carbon 1095 and Damascus. **Prices:** $200 to $1000. **Remarks:** Part-time maker; first knife sold in 1996. **Mark:** Fused initials.

TODD, RICHARD C

375th LN 46001, Chambersburg, IL 62323, Phone: 217-327-4380, ktodd45@yahoo.com
Specialties: Multi blade folders and silver sheaths. **Patterns:** Jewel setting and hand engraving. **Mark:** RT with letter R crossing the T or R Todd.

TOICH, NEVIO

Via Pisacane 9, Rettorgole di Caldogna, Vincenza, ITALY 36030,
Phone: 0444-985065, Fax: 0444-301254
Specialties: Working/using straight knives of his design or to customer specs. **Patterns:** Bowies, hunters, skinners and utility/camp knives. **Technical:** Grinds 440C, D2 and ATS-34. Hollow-grinds all blades and uses mirror polish. Offers hand-sewn sheaths. Uses wood and horn. **Prices:** $120 to $300; some to $450. **Remarks:** Spare-time maker; first knife sold in 1989. Doing business as Custom Toich. **Mark:** Initials and model number punched.

TOKAR, DANIEL

Box 1776, Shepherdstown, WV 25443
Specialties: Working knives; period pieces. **Patterns:** Hunters, camp knives, buckskinners, axes, swords and battle gear. **Technical:** Forges L6, 1095 and his Damascus; makes mokume, Japanese alloys and bronze daggers; restores old edged weapons. **Prices:** $25 to $800; some to $3000. **Remarks:** Part-time maker; first knife sold in 1979. Doing business as The Willow Forge. **Mark:** Arrow over rune and date.

TOMBERLIN, BRION R

ANVIL TOP CUSTOM KNIVES, 825 W Timberdell, Norman, OK 73072,
Phone: 405-202-6832, anviltopp@aol.com
Specialties: Handforged blades, working pieces, standard classic patterns, some swords and customer designs. **Patterns:** Bowies, hunters, fighters, Persian and eastern-styles. Likes Japanese blades. **Technical:** Forges 1050, 1075, 1084, 1095, 5160, some forged stainless, also does some stock removal in stainless. Also makes own damascus. **Prices:** $350 to $4,000 or higher for swords and custom pieces. **Remarks:** Part-time maker, ABS master smith. Prefers natural handle materials, hand-rubbed finishes. Likes temper lines. **Mark:** BRION with MS.

TOMEY, KATHLEEN

146 Buford Pl, Macon, GA 31204, Phone: 478-746-8454, ktomey@
tomeycustomknives.com; Web: www.tomeycustomknives.com
Specialties: Working hunters, skinners, daily users in fixed blades, plain and embellished. Tactical neck and belt carry. Japanese influenced. Bowies. **Technical:** Grinds O1, ATS-34, flat or hollow grind, filework, satin and mirror polish finishes. High quality leather sheaths with tooling. Kydex with tactical. **Prices:** $150 to $500. **Remarks:** Almost full-time maker. **Mark:** Last name in diamond.

TONER, ROGER

531 Lightfoot Pl, Pickering, ON, CANADA L1V 5Z8, Phone: 905-420-5555
Specialties: Exotic sword canes. **Patterns:** Bowies, daggers and fighters. **Technical:** Grinds 440C, D2 and Damascus. Scrimshaws and engraves. Silver cast pommels and guards in animal shapes; twisted silver wire inlays. Uses semi-precious stones. **Prices:** $200 to $2000; some to $3000. **Remarks:** Part-time maker; first knife sold in 1982. **Mark:** Last name.

TORRES, HENRY

2329 Moody Ave., Clovis, CA 93619, Phone: 559-297-9154, Web: www.htknives.com
Specialties: Forged high-performance hunters and working knives, Bowies, and fighters. **Technical:** 52100 and 5160 and makes own Damascus. **Prices:** $350 to $3000. **Remarks:** Started forging in 2004. Has mastership with American Bladesmith Association.

TOSHIFUMI, KURAMOTO

3435 Higashioda, Asakura-gun, Fukuoka, JAPAN, Phone: 0946-42-4470

TOWELL, DWIGHT L

2375 Towell Rd, Midvale, ID 83645, Phone: 208-355-2419
Specialties: Solid, elegant working knives; art knives, high quality hand engraving and gold inlay. **Patterns:** Hunters, Bowies, daggers and folders. **Technical:** Grinds 154CM, ATS-34, 440C and other maker's Damascus. **Prices:** Upscale. **Remarks:** Full-time maker. First knife sold in 1970. Member of AKI. **Mark:** Towell, sometimes hand engraved.

TOWNSEND, ALLEN MARK

6 Pine Trail, Texarkana, AR 71854, Phone: 870-772-8945

TOWNSLEY, RUSSELL

PO BOX 91, Floral, AR 72534-0091, Phone: 870-307-8069,
circleTRMtownsley@yahoo.com
Specialties: Using knives of his own design. **Patterns:** Hunters, skinners, folders. **Technical:** Hollow grinds D2 and O1. Handle material -antler, tusk, bone, exotic woods. **Prices:** Prices start at $125. **Remarks:** Arkansas knifemakers association. Sold first knife in 2009. Doing business as Circle-T knives. **Mark:** Encircled T.

TRACE RINALDI CUSTOM BLADES

1470 Underpass Rd, Plummer, ID 83851, Trace@thrblades.com;
Web: www.thrblades.com
Technical: Grinds S30V, 3V, A2 and talonite fixed blades. **Prices:** $300-$1000. **Remarks:** Tactical and utility for the most part. **Mark:** Diamond with THR inside.

TRIBBLE, SKYLAR

Cold Handle Custom Knives, 1413 Alabama St., Leakesville, MS 39451,
Phone: 601-394-3490, skylartribble@yahoo.com
Specialties: Fixed blades only. **Patterns:** From small neck knives to large bowie knives. **Technical:** Mainly uses repurposed steels from old files and high-carbon steels, and recently started using 154CM and CPM 154 stainless steels that he enjoys working with. Does both stock removal and forging, saying it's up to the customer. **Prices:** $50+ (up to around $600). **Remarks:** Part-time maker and full-time student; first knife made in 2009 at 13 years old. **Mark:** C with H and K on the tail of the C (for Cold Handle Custom Knives).

TRINDLE, BARRY

1660 Ironwood Trail, Earlham, IA 50072-8611, Phone: 515-462-1237
Specialties: Engraved folders. **Patterns:** Mostly small folders, classical-styles and pocket knives. **Technical:** 440 only. Engraves. Handles of wood or mineral material. **Prices:** Start at $1000. **Mark:** Name on tang.

TRISLER, KENNETH W

6256 Federal 80, Rayville, LA 71269, Phone: 318-728-5541

TRITZ, JEAN-JOSE

Pinneberger Chaussee 48, Hamburg, GERMANY 22523, Phone: +49(40) 49 78 21,
jeanjosetritz@aol.com
Specialties: Scandinavian knives, Japanese kitchen knives, friction folders, swords. **Patterns:** Puukkos, Tollekniven, Hocho, friction folders, swords. **Technical:** Forges tool steels, carbon steels, 52100 Damascus, mokume, San Maj. **Prices:** $200 to $2000; some higher. **Remarks:** Full-time maker; first knife sold in 1989. Does own leatherwork, prefers natural materials. Sole authorship. Speaks French, German, English, Norwegian. **Mark:** Initials in monogram.

TROUT, GEORGE H.

727 Champlin Rd, Wilmington, OH 45177, Phone: 937-382-2331, gandjtrout@msn.com
Specialties: Working knives, some fancy. **Patterns:** Hunters, drop points, Bowies and fighters. **Technical:** Stock removal: ATS-34, 440C Forged: 5160, W2, 1095, O1 Full integrals: 440C, A2, O1. **Prices:** $150 and up. **Remarks:** Makes own sheaths and mosaic pins. Fileworks most knives. First knife 1985. **Mark:** Etched name and state on stock removal. Forged: stamped name and forged.

TRUJILLO, ALBERT M B

2035 Wasmer Cir, Bosque Farms, NM 87068, Phone: 505-869-0428,
trujilloscutups@comcast.net
Specialties: Working/using straight knives of his design or to customer specs. **Patterns:** Hunters, skinners, fighters, working/using knives. File work offered. **Technical:** Grinds ATS-34, D2, 440C, S30V. Tapers tangs, all blades cryogenically treated. **Prices:** $75 to $500. **Remarks:** Part-time maker; first knife sold in 1997. **Mark:** First and last name under logo.

TRUNCALI, PETE

2914 Anatole Court, Garland, TX 75043, Phone: 214-763-7127,
truncaliknives@yahoo.com Web:www.truncaliknives.com
Specialties: Lockback folders, locking liner folders, automatics and fixed blades. Does business as Truncali Custom Knives.

TSCHAGER, REINHARD

S. Maddalena di Sotto 1a, Bolzano, ITALY 39100, Phone: 0471-975005,
Fax: 0471-975005, reinhardtschager@virgilio.it
Specialties: Classic, high-art, collector-grade straight knives of his design. **Patterns:** Jewel knife, daggers, and hunters. **Technical:** Grinds ATS-34, D2 and Damascus. Oval pins. Gold inlay. Offers engraving. **Prices:** $900 to $2000; some to $3000. **Remarks:** Spare-time maker; first knife sold in 1979. **Mark:** Gold inlay stamped with initials.

TUCH, WILLIAM

Troy Studios, 1220 S.W. Morrison St., Lobby A, Portland, OR 97205, Phone: 503-504-1261, tuchknives@gmail.com; Web: www.tuchknives.com
Specialties: Folding knives and daggers, mostly ornate. **Patterns:** One-of-a-kind locking knives, lockbacks, side locks, switchblades, miniatures and more. **Technical:** Flat and hollow grinds, ornate sculpture. All knives are hand filed and hand polished. Materials vary. **Prices:** $1,800 to $10,000 and up. **Remarks:** Full-time maker since 2004. **Mark:** TUCH.

TUOMINEN, PEKKA

Pohjois-Keiteleentie 20, Tossavanlahti, FINLAND 72930, Phone: 358405167853,
puukkopekka@luukku.com; Web: www.puukkopekka.com
Specialties: Puukko knives. **Patterns:** Puukkos, hunters, leukus, and folders. **Technical:** Forges silversteel, 1085, 52100, and makes own Damascus 15N20 and 1095. Grinds RWL-34 and ATS-34. **Prices:** Starting at $300. **Remarks:** Full-time maker. **Mark:** PEKKA; earlier whole name.

TURCOTTE, LARRY

1707 Evergreen, Pampa, TX 79065, Phone: 806-665-9369, 806-669-0435
Specialties: Fancy and working/using knives of his design and to customer specs. **Patterns:** Hunters, kitchen knives, utility/camp knives. **Technical:** Grinds 440C, D2, ATS-34. Engraves, scrimshaws, silver inlays. **Prices:** $150 to $350; some to $1000. **Remarks:** Part-time maker; first knife sold in 1977. Doing business as Knives by Turcotte. **Mark:** Last name.

TURECEK, JIM

12 Elliott Rd, Ansonia, CT 06401, Phone: 203-734-8406, jturecek@sbcglobal.net
Specialties: Exotic folders, art knives and some miniatures. **Patterns:** Trout and bird knives with split bamboo handles and one-of-a-kind folders. **Technical:** Grinds and

forges stainless and carbon damascus. All knives are handmade using no computer-controlled machinery. **Prices:** $2,000 to $10,000. **Remarks:** Full-time maker; first knife sold in 1983. **Mark:** Last initial in script, or last name.

TURNBULL, RALPH A
14464 Linden Dr, Spring Hill, FL 34609, Phone: 352-688-7089, tbull2000@bellsouth.net; Web: www.turnbullknives.com
Specialties: Fancy folders. **Patterns:** Primarily gents pocket knives. **Technical:** Wire EDM work on bolsters. **Prices:** $300 and up. **Remarks:** Full-time maker; first knife sold in 1973. **Mark:** Signature or initials.

TURNER, KEVIN
17 Hunt Ave, Montrose, NY 10548, Phone: 914-739-0535
Specialties: Working straight knives of his design and to customer specs; period pieces. **Patterns:** Daggers, fighters and utility knives. **Technical:** Forges 5160 and 52100. **Prices:** $90 to $500. **Remarks:** Part-time maker; first knife sold in 1991. **Mark:** Acid-etched signed last name and year.

TURNER, MIKE
3065 Cedar Flat Rd., Williams, OR 97544, Phone: 541-846-0204, mike@turnerknives.com Web: www.turnerknives.com
Specialties: Forged and stock removed full tang, hidden and thru tang knives. **Patterns:** Hunters, fighters, Bowies, boot knives, skinners and kitchen knives. **Technical:** I make my own damascus. **Prices:** $200 -$1,000. **Remarks:** Part-time maker, sold my first knife in 2008, doing business as Mike Turner Custom Knives. **Mark:** Name, City, & State.

TYRE, MICHAEL A
1219 Easy St, Wickenburg, AZ 85390, Phone: 928-684-9601/602-377-8432, mtyre86@gmail.com; Web: www.miketyrecustomknives.com
Specialties: Quality folding knives, upscale gents folders, one-of-a-kind collectable models. **Patterns:** Working fixed blades for hunting, kitchen and fancy bowies. Forging my own damascus patterns. **Technical:** Grinds, prefers hand-rubbed satin finishes and uses natural handle materials. **Prices:** $250 to $1,300. **Remarks:** ABS journeyman smith.

TYSER, ROSS
1015 Hardee Court, Spartanburg, SC 29303, Phone: 864-585-7616
Specialties: Traditional working and using straight knives and folders of his design and in standard patterns. **Patterns:** Bowies, hunters and slip-joint folders. **Technical:** Grinds 440C and commercial Damascus. Mosaic pins; stone inlay. Does filework and scrimshaw. Offers engraving and cut-work and some inlay on sheaths. **Prices:** $45 to $125; some to $400. **Remarks:** Part-time maker; first knife sold in 1995. Doing business as RT Custom Knives. **Mark:** Stylized initials.

U

UCHIDA, CHIMATA
977-2 Oaza Naga Shisui Ki, Kumamoto, JAPAN 861-1204

UPTON, TOM
Little Rabbit Forge, 1414 Feast Pl., Rogers, AR 72758, Phone: 479-636-6755, Web: www.upton-knives.com
Specialties: Working fixed blades. **Patterns:** Hunters, utility, fighters, bowies and small hatchets. **Technical:** Forges 5160, 1084 and W2 blade steels, or stock removal using D2, 440C and 154CM. Performs own heat treat. **Prices:** $150 and up. **Remarks:** Part-time maker; first knife sold in 1977. Member of ABS, Arkansas Knifemakers Association and Knife Group Association. **Mark:** Name (Small Rabbit logo), city and state, etched or stamped.

V

VAGNINO, MICHAEL
PO Box 67, Visalia, CA 93279, Phone: 559-636-0501; cell: 559-827-7802, mike@mvknives.com; Web: www.mvknives.com
Specialties: Folders and straight knives, working and fancy. **Patterns:** Folders--locking liners, slip joints, lock backs, double and single action autos. Straight knives--hunters, Bowies, camp and kitchen. **Technical:** Forges 52100, W2, 15N20 and 1084. Grinds stainless. Makes own damascus and does engraving. **Prices:** $300 to $4,000 and above. **Remarks:** Full-time maker, ABS Mastersmith. **Mark:** Logo, last name.

VAIL, DAVE
554 Sloop Point Rd, Hampstead, NC 28443, Phone: 910-270-4456
Specialties: Working/using straight knives of his own design or to the customer's specs. **Patterns:** Hunters/skinners, camp/utility, fillet, Bowies. **Technical:** Grinds ATS-34, 440c, 154 CM and 1095 carbon steel. **Prices:** $90 to $450. **Remarks:** Part-time maker. Member of NC Custom Knifemakers Guild. **Mark:** Etched oval with "Dave Vail Hampstead NC" inside.

VALLOTTON, BUTCH AND AREY
621 Fawn Ridge Dr, Oakland, OR 97462, Phone: 541-459-2216, Fax: 541-459-7473
Specialties: Quick opening knives w/complicated mechanisms. **Patterns:** Tactical, fancy, working, and some art knives. **Technical:** Grinds all steels, uses others' Damascus. Uses Spectrum Metal. **Prices:** From $350 to $4500. **Remarks:** Full-time maker since 1984; first knife sold in 1981. Co/designer, Applegate Fairbarn folding w/Bill Harsey. **Mark:** Name w/ viper head in the "V."

VALLOTTON, RAINY D
1295 Wolf Valley Dr, Umpqua, OR 97486, Phone: 541-459-0465
Specialties: Folders, one-handed openers and art pieces. **Patterns:** All patterns. **Technical:** Stock removal all steels; uses titanium liners and bolsters; uses all finishes. **Prices:** $350 to $3500. **Remarks:** Full-time maker. **Mark:** Name.

VALLOTTON, SHAWN
621 Fawn Ridge Dr, Oakland, OR 97462, Phone: 503-459-2216
Specialties: Left-hand knives. **Patterns:** All styles. **Technical:** Grinds 440C, ATS-34 and Damascus. Uses titanium. Prefers bead-blasted or anodized finishes. **Prices:** $250 to $1400. **Remarks:** Full-time maker. **Mark:** Name and specialty.

VALLOTTON, THOMAS
621 Fawn Ridge Dr, Oakland, OR 97462, Phone: 541-459-2216
Specialties: Custom autos. **Patterns:** Tactical, fancy. **Technical:** File work, uses Damascus, uses Spectrum Metal. **Prices:** From $350 to $700. **Remarks:** Full-time maker. Maker of ProtŽgé 3 canoe. **Mark:** T and a V mingled.

VAN CLEVE, STEVE
Box 372, Sutton, AK 99674, Phone: 907-745-3038, Fax: 907-745-8770, sucents@mtaonline.net; Web: www.alaskaknives.net

VAN DE MANAKKER, THIJS
Koolweg 34, Holland, NETHERLANDS, Phone: 0493539369, www.ehijsvandemanakker.com
Specialties: Classic high-art knives. **Patterns:** Swords, utility/camp knives and period pieces. **Technical:** Forges soft iron, carbon steel and Bloomery Iron. Makes own Damascus, Bloomery Iron and patterns. **Prices:** $20 to $2000; some higher. **Remarks:** Full-time maker; first knife sold in 1969. **Mark:** Stylized "V."

VAN DEN BERG, NEELS
166 Van Heerdan St., Capital Park, Pretoria, Gauteng, SOUTH AFRICA, Phone: +27(0)12-326-5649 or +27(0)83-451-3105, neels@blackdragonforge.com; Web: http://www.blackdragonforge.com or http://www.facebook.com/neels.vandenberg
Specialties: Handforged damascus and high-carbon steel axes, hunters, swords and art knives. **Patterns:** All my own designs and customer collaborations, from axes, hunters, choppers, bowies, swords and folders to one-off tactical prototypes. **Technical:** Flat and hollow grinding. Handforges high-carbon steels and maker's own damascus. Also works in high-carbon stainless steels. **Prices:** $50 to $1,000. **Remarks:** Part-time maker; first knife sold in Oct. 2009. **Mark:** Stylized capital letter "N" resembling a three-tier mountain, normally hot stamped in forged blades.

VAN DEN ELSEN, GERT
Purcelldreef 83, Tilburg, NETHERLANDS 5012 AJ, Phone: 013-4563200, gvdelsen@home.nl
Specialties: Fancy, working/using, miniatures and integral straight knives of the maker's design or to customer specs. **Patterns:** Bowies, fighters, hunters and Japanese-style blades. **Technical:** Grinds ATS-34 and 440C; forges Damascus. Offers filework, differentially tempered blades and some mokume-gane fittings. **Prices:** $350 to $1000; some to $4000. **Remarks:** Part-time maker; first knife sold in 1982. Doing business as G-E Knives. **Mark:** Initials GE in lozenge shape.

VAN DER WESTHUIZEN, PETER
PO Box 1698, Mossel Bay, SC, SOUTH AFRICA 6500, Phone: 27 446952388, pietvdw@telkomsa.net
Specialties: Working knives, folders, daggers and art knives. **Patterns:** Hunters, skinners, bird, trout and sidelock folders. **Technical:** Sandvik, 12627. Damascus indigenous wood and ivory. **Prices:** From $450 to $5500. **Remarks:** First knife sold in 1987. Full-time since 1996. **Mark:** Initial & surname. Handmade RSA.

VAN DIJK, RICHARD
76 Stepney Ave Rd 2, Harwood Dunedin, NEW ZEALAND, Phone: 0064-3-4780401, Web: www.hoihoknives.com
Specialties: Damascus, Fantasy knives, sgiandubhs, dirks, swords, and hunting knives. **Patterns:** Mostly one-offs, anything from bird and trout to swords, no folders. **Technical:** Forges mainly own Damascus, some 5160, O1, 1095, L6. Prefers natural handle materials, over 40 years experience as goldsmith, handle fittings are often made from sterling silver and sometimes gold, manufactured to cap the handle, use gemstones if required. Makes own sheaths. **Prices:** $300 and up. **Remarks:** Full-time maker, first knife sold in 1980. Doing business as HOIHO KNIVES. **Mark:** Stylized initials RvD in triangle.

VAN EIZENGA, JERRY W
14281 Cleveland, Nunica, MI 49448, Phone: 616-638-2275
Specialties: Hand forged blades, Scagel patterns and other styles. **Patterns:** Camp, hunting, bird, trout, folders, axes, miniatures. **Technical:** 5160, 52100, 1084. **Prices:** Start at $250. **Remarks:** Part-time maker, sole author of knife and sheath. First knife made 1970s. ABS member who believes in the beauty of simplicity. **Mark:** J.S. stamp.

VAN ELDIK, FRANS
Ho Flaan 3, Loenen, NETHERLANDS 3632 BT, Phone: 0031 294 233 095, Fax: 0031 294 233 095
Specialties: Fancy collector-grade straight knives and folders of his design. **Patterns:** Hunters, fighters, boots and folders. **Technical:** Forges and grinds D2, 154CM, ATS-34 and stainless Damascus. **Prices:** Start at $450. **Remarks:** Spare-time maker; first knife sold in 1979. Knifemaker 30 years, 25 year member of Knifemakers Guild. **Mark:** Lion with name and Amsterdam.

VAN HEERDEN, ANDRE
P.O. Box 905-417, Garsfontein, Pretoria, GT, SOUTH AFRICA 0042, Phone: 27 82 566 6030, andrevh@iafrica.com; Web: www.andrevanheerden.com
Specialties: Fancy and working folders of his design to customer specs. **Technical:** Grinds RWL34, 19C27, D2, carbon and stainless Damascus. **Prices:** Starting at $350. **Remarks:** Part-time maker, first knife sold in 2003. **Mark:** Initials and name in a double circle.

VAN REENEN, IAN
6003 Harvard St, Amarillo, TX 79109, Phone: 806-236-8333, ianvanreenen@suddenlink.net Web: www.ianvanreenencustomknives.com
Specialties: Pocketknives and hunting knives. **Patterns:** Tactical pocketknives. **Technical:** 14C28N, 12C27 and ATS-34 blade steels. **Prices:** $600 to $1,500. **Remarks:** Specializing in tactical pocketknives. **Mark:** IVR with TEXAS underneath.

VAN RYSWYK, AAD
AVR KNIVES, Werf Van Pronk 8, Vlaardingen, NETHERLANDS 3134 HE, Phone: +31 10 4742952, info@avrknives.com; Web: www.avrknives.com
Specialties: High-art interframe folders of his design. **Patterns:** Hunters and locking folders. **Technical:** Uses semi-precious stones, mammoth ivory, iron wood, etc. **Prices:** $550 to $3800. **Remarks:** Full-time maker; first knife sold in 1993.

VANCE, DAVID
2646 Bays Bend Rd., West Liberty, KY 41472, Phone: 606-743-1465 and 606-362-8339, dtvance@mrtc.com; Web: www.facebook.com/ddcutlery
Specialties: Custom hunting or collectible knives, folders and fixed blades, also unique bullet casing handle pins and filework. **Patterns:** Maker's design or made to customers' specifications. **Technical:** Uses stock removal method on 1095 steel. **Remarks:** Part-time maker; first knife made in 2006. **Mark:** Cursive D&D.

VANDERFORD, CARL G
2290 Knob Creek Rd, Columbia, TN 38401, Phone: 931-381-1488
Specialties: Traditional working straight knives and folders of his design. **Patterns:** Hunters, Bowies and locking folders. **Technical:** Forges and grinds 440C, O1 and wire Damascus. **Prices:** $60 to $125. **Remarks:** Part-time maker; first knife sold in 1987. **Mark:** Last name.

VANDERKOLFF, STEPHEN
5 Jonathan Crescent, Mildmay, ON, CANADA N0g 2JO, Phone: 519-367-3401, steve@vanderkolffknives.com; Web: www.vanderkolffknives.com
Specialties: Fixed blades from gent's pocketknives and drop hunters to full sized Bowies and art knives. **Technical:** Primary blade steel 440C, Damasteel or custom made Damascus. All heat treat done by maker and all blades hardness tested. Handle material: stag, stabilized woods or MOP. **Prices:** $150 to $1200. **Remarks:** Started making knives in 1998 and sold first knife in 2000. Winner of the best of show art knife 2005 Wolverine Knife Show.

VANDEVENTER, TERRY L
3274 Davis Rd, Terry, MS 39170-8719, Phone: 601-371-7414, tvandeventer@comcast.net
Specialties: Bowies, hunters, camp knives, friction folders. **Technical:** 1084, 1095, 15N20 and L6 steels. Damascus and mokume. Natural handle materials. **Prices:** $600 to $3000. **Remarks:** Sole author; makes everything here. First ABS MS from the state of Mississippi. **Mark:** T.L. Vandeventer (silhouette of snake underneath). MS on ricasso.

VANHOY, ED AND TANYA
24255 N Fork River Rd, Abingdon, VA 24210, Phone: 276-944-4885, vanhoyknives@centurylink.net
Specialties: Traditional and working/using straight knives and folders and innovative locking mechanisms. **Patterns:** Fighters, straight knives, folders, hunters, art knives and Bowies. **Technical:** Grinds ATS-34 and carbon/stainless steel Damascus; forges carbon and stainless Damascus. Offers filework and engraving with hammer and chisel. **Prices:** $250 to $3000. **Remarks:** Full-time maker; first knife sold in 1977. Wife also engraves. Doing business as Van Hoy Custom Knives. **Mark:** Acid etched last name.

VARDAMAN, ROBERT
2406 Mimosa Lane, Hattiesburg, MS 39402, Phone: 601-268-3889, rvx222@gmail.com
Specialties: Working straight knives, mainly integrals, of his design or to customer specs. **Patterns:** Mainly integrals, bowies and hunters. **Technical:** Forges 52100, W2 and 1084. Filework. **Prices:** $250 to $1,000. **Remarks:** Part-time maker. First knife sold in 2004. **Mark:** Last name, last name with Mississippi state logo.

VASQUEZ, JOHNNY DAVID
1552 7th St, Wyandotte, MI 48192, Phone: 734-281-2455

VEIT, MICHAEL
3289 E Fifth Rd, LaSalle, IL 61301, Phone: 815-223-3538, whitebear@starband.net
Specialties: Damascus folders. **Technical:** Engraver, sole author. **Prices:** $2500 to $6500. **Remarks:** Part-time maker; first knife sold in 1985. **Mark:** Name in script.

VELARDE, RICARDO
7240 N Greenfield Dr, Park City, UT 84098, Phone: 435-901-1773, velardeknives@mac.com Web: www.velardeknives.com
Specialties: Investment grade integrals and interframs. **Patterns:** Boots, fighters and hunters; hollow grind. **Technical:** BG on Integrals. **Prices:** $1450 to $5200. **Remarks:** First knife sold in 1992. **Mark:** First initial and last name.

VELICK, SAMMY
3457 Maplewood Ave, Los Angeles, CA 90066, Phone: 310-663-6170, metaltamer@gmail.com
Specialties: Working knives and art pieces. **Patterns:** Hunter, utility and fantasy. **Technical:** Stock removal and forges. **Prices:** $100 and up. **Mark:** Last name.

VENSILD, HENRIK
GI Estrup, Randersvei 4, Auning, DENMARK 8963, Phone: +45 86 48 44 48
Specialties: Classic and traditional working and using knives of his design; Scandinavian influence. **Patterns:** Hunters and using knives. **Technical:** Forges Damascus. Hand makes handles, sheaths and blades. **Prices:** $350 to $1000. **Remarks:** Part-time maker; first knife sold in 1967. **Mark:** Initials.

VERONIQUE, LAURENT
Avenue du Capricorne, 53, 1200 Bruxelles, BELGIUM, Phone: 0032-477-48-66-73, whatsonthebench@gmail.com
Specialties: Fixed blades and friction folders. **Patterns:** Bowies, camp knives, ladies' knives and maker's own designs. **Technical:** Maker's own San Mai steel with a Blue Paper Steel edge and pure-nickel-and-O1 outer layers, called "Nickwich" (nickel in sandwich), and damascus, numerical milling embellishments and inlays, and hand-fashioned sheaths. **Prices:** Start at $350. **Remarks:** Part-time maker since 2005, ABS journeyman smith since 2013.

VESTAL, CHARLES
26662 Shortsville Rd., Abingdon, VA 24210, Phone: 276-492-3262, charles@vestalknives.com; Web: www.vestalknives.com
Specialties: Hunters and double ground fighters in traditional designs and own designs. **Technical:** Grinds CPM-154, ATS-134, 154-CM and other steels. **Prices:** $300 to $1000, some higher. **Remarks:** First knife sold in 1995.

VIALLON, HENRI
Les Belins, Thiers, FRANCE 63300, Phone: 04-73-80-24-03, Fax: 04 73-51-02-02
Specialties: Folders and complex Damascus **Patterns:** His draws. **Technical:** Forge. **Prices:** $1000 to $5000. **Mark:** H. Viallon.

VICKERS, DAVID
11620 Kingford Dr., Montgomery, TX 77316, Phone: 936-537-4900, jdvickers@gmail.com
Specialties: Working/using blade knives especially for hunters. His design or to customer specs. **Patterns:** Hunters, skinners, camp/utility. **Technical:** Grinds ATS-34, 440C, and D-2. Uses stag, various woods, and micarta for handle material. Hand-stitched sheaths. **ReMark:** Full-time maker. **Prices:** $125 -$350. **Mark:** VICKERS

VIELE, H J
88 Lexington Ave, Westwood, NJ 07675, Phone: 201-666-2906, h.viele@verizon.net
Specialties: Folding knives of distinctive shapes. **Patterns:** High-tech folders and one-of-a-kind. **Technical:** Grinds ATS-34 and S30V. **Prices:** Start at $575. **Remarks:** Full-time maker; first knife sold in 1973. **Mark:** Japanese design for the god of war.

VILAR, RICARDO AUGUSTO FERREIRA
Rua Alemada Dos Jasmins NO 243, Parque Petropolis, Mairipora, SP, BRAZIL 07600-000, Phone: 011-55-11-44-85-43-46, ricardovilar@ig.com.br.
Specialties: Traditional Brazilian-style working knives of the Sao Paulo state. **Patterns:** Fighters, hunters, utility, and camp knives, welcome customer design. Specialize in the "true" Brazilian camp knife "Soracabana." **Technical:** Forges only with sledge hammer to 100 percent shape in 5160 and 52100 and his own Damascus steels. Makes own sheaths in the "true" traditional "Paulista"-style of the state of Sao Paulo. **ReMark:** Full-time maker. **Prices:** $250 to $600. Uses only natural handle materials. **Mark:** Special designed signature styled name R. Vilar.

VILLA, LUIZ
R. Com. Miguel Calfat 398, Itaim Bibi, SP, BRAZIL 04537-081, Phone: 011-8290649
Specialties: One-of-a-kind straight knives and jewel knives of all designs. **Patterns:** Bowies, hunters, utility/camp knives and jewel knives. **Technical:** Grinds D6, Damascus and 440C; forges 5160. Prefers natural handle material. **Prices:** $70 to $200. **Remarks:** Part-time maker; first knife sold in 1990. **Mark:** Last name and serial number.

VILLAR, RICARDO
Al. dos Jasmins 243, Mairipora, SP, BRAZIL 07600-000, Phone: 011-4851649
Specialties: Straight working knives to customer specs. **Patterns:** Bowies, fighters and utility/camp knives. **Technical:** Grinds D6, ATS-34 and 440C stainless. **Prices:** $80 to $200. **Remarks:** Part-time maker; first knife sold in 1993. **Mark:** Percor over sword and circle.

VILPPOLA, MARKKU
Jaanintie 45, Turku, FINLAND 20540, Phone: +358 (0)50 566 1563, markku@mvforge.fi Web: www.mvforge.fi
Specialties: All kinds of swords and knives. **Technical:** Forges silver steel, CO, 8%, nickel, 1095, A203E, etc. Mokume (sterling silver/brass/copper). Bronze casting (sand casting, lost-wax casting). **Prices:** Starting at $200.

VINING, BILL
9 Penny Lane, Methuen, MA 01844, Phone: 978-688-4729, billv@medawebs.com; Web: www.medawebs.com/knives
Specialties Liner locking folders. Slip joints & lockbacks. **Patterns:** Likes to make patterns of his own design. **Technical:** S30V, 440C, ATS-34. Damascus from various makers. **Prices:** $450 and up. **Remarks:** Part-time maker. **Mark:** VINING or B. Vining.

VISTE, JAMES
EDGEWISE FORGE, 9745 Dequindre, Hamtramck, MI 48212, Phone: 313-587-8899, edgewiseforge@hotmail.com
Mark: EWF touch mark.

VISTNES, TOR
Svelgen, NORWAY N-6930, Phone: 047-57795572
Specialties: Traditional and working knives of his design. **Patterns:** Hunters and utility knives. **Technical:** Grinds Uddeholm Elmax. Handles made of rear burls of different Nordic stabilized woods. **Prices:** $300 to $1100. **Remarks:** Part-time maker; first knife sold in 1988. **Mark:** Etched name and deer head.

VITALE, MACE
925 Rt 80, Guilford, CT 06437, Phone: 203-457-5591, Web: www.laurelrockforge.com
Specialties: Hand forged blades. **Patterns:** Hunters, utility, chef, Bowies and fighters. **Technical:** W2, 1095, 1084, L6. Hand forged and finished. **Prices:** $100 to $1000. **Remarks:** American Bladesmith Society, Journeyman Smith. Full-time maker; first knife sold 2001. **Mark:** MACE.

VOGT, DONALD J
9007 Hogans Bend, Tampa, FL 33647, Phone: 813-973-3245, vogtknives@verizon.net
Specialties: Art knives, folders, automatics. **Technical:** Uses Damascus steels for blade and bolsters, filework, hand carving on blade bolsters and handles. Other materials used: jewels, gold, mother-of-pearl, gold-lip pearl, black-lip pearl, ivory. **Prices:** $4,000 to $10,000. **Remarks:** Part-time maker; first knife sold in 1997. **Mark:** Last name.

VOGT, PATRIK
Kungsvagen 83, Halmstad, SWEDEN 30270, Phone: 46-35-30977
Specialties: Working straight knives. **Patterns:** Bowies, hunters and fighters. **Technical:** Forges carbon steel and own Damascus. **Prices:** From $100. **Remarks:** Not currently making knives. **Mark:** Initials or last name.

VOORHIES, LES
14511 Lk Mazaska Tr, Faribault, MN 55021, Phone: 507-332-0736, lesvor@msn.com; Web: www.lesvoorhiesknives.com
Specialties: Steels. **Patterns:** Liner locks & autos. **Technical:** ATS-34 Damascus. **Prices:** $250 to $1200. **Mark:** L. Voorhies.

VOSS, BEN
2212 Knox Rd. 1600 Rd. E, Victoria, IL 61485-9644, Phone: 309-879-2940
Specialties: Fancy working knives of his design. **Patterns:** Bowies, fighters, hunters, boots and folders. **Technical:** Grinds 440C, ATS-34 and D2. **Prices:** $35 to $1200. **Remarks:** Part-time maker; first knife sold in 1986. **Mark:** Name, city and state.

VOTAW, DAVID P
305 S State St, Pioneer, OH 43554, Phone: 419-737-2774
Specialties: Working knives; period pieces. **Patterns:** Hunters, Bowies, camp knives, buckskinners and tomahawks. **Technical:** Grinds O1 and D2. **Prices:** $100 to $200; some to $500. **Remarks:** Part-time maker; took over for the late W.K. Kneubuhler. Doing business as W-K Knives. **Mark:** WK with V inside anvil.

W

WACHOLZ, DOC
95 Anne Rd, Marble, NC 28905, Phone: 828-557-1543, killdrums@aol.com; web: rackforge.com
Specialties: Forged tactical knives and tomahawks. **Technical:** Use 52100 and 1084 high carbon steel; make own Damascus; design and dew own sheaths. Grind up and down fashion on a 3" wheel. **Prices:** $300 to $800. **Remarks:** Part-time maker; started forging in 1999, with ABS master Charles Ochs. **Mark:** Early knives stamped RACK, newer knives since 2005 stamped WACHOLZ.

WADA, YASUTAKA
2-6-22 Fujinokidai, Nara City, Nara, JAPAN 631-0044, Phone: 0742 46-0689
Specialties: Fancy and embellished one-of-a-kind straight knives of his design. **Patterns:** Bowies, daggers and hunters. **Technical:** Grinds ATS-34. All knives hand-filed and flat grinds. **Prices:** $400 to $2500; some higher. **Remarks:** Part-time maker; first knife sold in 1990. **Mark:** Owl eyes with initial and last name underneath or last name.

WAGAMAN, JOHN K
107 E Railroad St, Selma, NC 27576, Phone: 919-965-9659, Fax: 919-965-9901
Specialties: Fancy working knives. **Patterns:** Bowies, miniatures, hunters, fighters and boots. **Technical:** Grinds D2, 440C, 154CM and commercial Damascus; inlays mother-of-pearl. **Prices:** $110 to $2000. **Remarks:** Part-time maker; first knife sold in 1975. **Mark:** Last name.

WAIDE, RUSTY
Triple C Knives, PO Box 499, Buffalo, MO 65622, Phone: 417-345-7231, Fax: 417-345-1911, wrrccc@yahoo.com
Specialties: Custom-designed hunting knives and cowboy working knives in high-carbon and damascus steels. **Prices:** $150 to $450. **Remarks:** Part-time maker; first knife sold in 2010. **Mark:** Name.

WAITES, RICHARD L
PO Box 188, Broomfield, CO 80038, Phone: 303-324-2905, Fax: 303-465-9971, dickknives@aol.com
Specialties: Working fixed blade knives of all kinds including "paddle blade" skinners. Hand crafted sheaths, some upscale and unusual. **Technical:** Grinds 440C, damascus and D2. **Prices:** $100 to $500. **Remarks:** Part-time maker. First knife sold in 1998. Doing business as R.L. Waites Knives. **Mark:** Oval etch with first and middle initial and last name on top and city and state on bottom. Memberships; Professional Knifemakers Association and Rocky Mountain Blade Collectors Club.

WALKER, BILL
431 Walker Rd, Stevensville, MD 21666, Phone: 410-643-5041

WALKER, DON
2850 Halls Chapel Rd, Burnsville, NC 28714, Phone: 828-675-9716, dlwalkernc@gmail.com

WALKER, JIM
22 Walker Ln, Morrilton, AR 72110, Phone: 501-354-3175, jwalker46@att.net
Specialties: Period pieces and working/using knives of his design and to customer specs. **Patterns:** Bowies, fighters, hunters, camp knives. **Technical:** Forges 5160, O1, L6, 52100, 1084, 1095. **Prices:** Start at $450. **Remarks:** Full-time maker; first knife sold in 1993. **Mark:** Three arrows with last name/MS.

WALKER, MICHAEL L
925-A Paseo del, Pueblo Sur Taos, NM 87571, Phone: 505-751-3409, Fax: 505-751-3417, metalwerkr@msn.com
Specialties: Innovative knife designs and locking systems; titanium and SS furniture and art. **Patterns:** Folders from utility grade to museum quality art; others upon request. **Technical:** State-of-the-art materials: titanium, stainless Damascus, gold, etc. **Prices:** $3500 and above. **Remarks:** Designer/MetalCrafts; full-time professional knifemaker since 1980; four U.S. patents; invented LinerLock® and was awarded registered U.S. trademark no. 1,585,333. **Mark:** Early mark MW, Walker's Lockers by M.L. Walker; current M.L. Walker or Michael Walker.

WALL, GREG
4753 Michie Pebble Hill Rd., Michie, TN 38357, Phone: 662-415-2909, glwall36@hotmail.com, www.wallhandmadeknives.com
Specialties: Working hollow-handle survival knives, Ek-style fighters, drop-point hunters and big 7's models. **Technical:** Stock removal method of blade making, convex and flat grinds, using O1 tool steels and 440C stainless steel. **Prices:** $295 to $395. **Remarks:** First knife made and sold in 1983.

WALLINGFORD JR., CHARLES W
9024 Old Union Rd, Union, KY 41091, Phone: 859-384-4141, Web: www.cwknives.com
Specialties: 18th and 19th century styles, patch knives, rifleman knives. **Technical:** 1084 and 5160 forged blades. **Prices:** $125 to $300. **Mark:** CW.

WARD, CHUCK
PO Box 2272, 1010 E North St, Benton, AR 72018-2272, Phone: 501-778-4329, chuckbop@aol.com
Specialties: Traditional working and using straight knives and folders of his design. **Technical:** Grinds 440C, D2, A2, ATS-34 and O1; uses natural and composite handle materials. **Prices:** $90 to $400, some higher. **Remarks:** Part-time maker; first knife sold in 1990. **Mark:** First initial, last name.

WARD, J J
7501 S R 220, Waverly, OH 45690, Phone: 614-947-5328
Specialties: Traditional and working/using straight knives and folders of his design. **Patterns:** Hunters and locking folders. **Technical:** Grinds ATS-34, 440C and Damascus. Offers handmade sheaths. **Prices:** $125 to $250; some to $500. **Remarks:** Spare-time maker; first knife sold in 1980. **Mark:** Etched name.

WARD, KEN
1125 Lee Roze Ln, Grants Pass, OR 97527, Phone: 541-956-8864
Specialties: Working knives, some to customer specs. **Patterns:** Straight, axes, Bowies, buckskinners and miniatures. **Technical:** Grinds ATS-34, Damascus. **Prices:** $100 to $700. **Remarks:** Part-time maker; first knife sold in 1977. **Mark:** Name.

WARD, RON
PO BOX 21, Rose Hill, VA 24281, Phone: 276-445-4757
Specialties: Classic working and using straight knives, fantasy knives. **Patterns:** Bowies, hunter, fighters, and utility/camp knives. **Technical:** Grinds 440C, 154CM, ATS-34, uses composite and natural handle materials. **Prices:** $50 to $750. **Remarks:** Part-time maker, first knife sold in 1992. Doing business as Ron Ward Blades. **Mark:** RON WARD BLADES.

WARD, TOM
204 Village Rd., Wilmot, NH 03287, Phone: 508-277-3190, tempestcraft@gmail.com; Web: www.tempestcraft.com
Specialties: Axes and pattern welding, multi-billet twist constructions. Open to all commissions. **Technical:** Forges to shape, generally using 15N20, 1095 and 1084 blade steels. **Prices:** $400 for mono-steel hunting/camping knives to $3,000 and up on elaborate pieces. **Remarks:** Full-time maker; first knife made in 2008. **Mark:** An ornate T.

WARD, W C
817 Glenn St, Clinton, TN 37716, Phone: 615-457-3568
Specialties: Working straight knives; period pieces. **Patterns:** Hunters, Bowies, swords and kitchen cutlery. **Technical:** Grinds O1. **Prices:** $85 to $150; some to $500. **Remarks:** Part-time maker; first knife sold in 1969. He styled the Tennessee Knife Maker. **Mark:** TKM.

WARDELL, MICK
20 Clovelly Rd, Bideford, N Devon, ENGLAND EX39 3BU, wardellknives@hotmail.co.uk Web: www.wardellscustomknives.com
Specialties: Spring back folders and a few fixed blades. **Patterns:** Locking and slip-joint folders, Bowies. **Technical:** Grinds stainless Damascus and RWL34. Heat-treats. **Prices:** $300 to $2500. **Remarks:** Full-time maker; first knife sold in 1986. Takes limited Comissions. **Mark:** Wardell.

WARDEN, ROY A
275 Tanglewood Rd, Union, MO 63084, Phone: 314-583-8813, rwarden@yhti.net
Specialties: Complex mosaic designs of "EDM wired figures" and "stack up" patterns and "lazer cut" and "torch cut" and "sawed" patterns combined. **Patterns:** Mostly "all mosaic" folders, automatics, fixed blades. **Technical:** Mosaic Damascus with all tool steel edges. **Prices:** $100 to $1000. **Remarks:** Part-time maker; first knife sold in 1987. **Mark:** WARDEN stamped or initials connected.

WARE, J.D.
Calle 40 #342 x 47 y 49, Colonia Benito Juarez Norte, Merida, Yucatan, MEXICO 97119, jdware@jdwareknives.com; Web: www.jdwareknives.com
Specialties: Coin knives, slip-joint folders, chef's knives and hunting/camping/fishing knives. **Technical:** Practices stock-removal and forging methods of blade making using O1, 440C and D2 blade steels. **Prices:** Start at $200. **Remarks:** Full-time maker; first knife made in 1976. **Mark:** Usually etched "JD Ware, Artesano, Merida Yucatan, Hecho a Mano, Mexico."

WARE, TOMMY
158 Idlewilde, Onalaska, TX 77360, Phone: 936-646-4649
Specialties: Traditional working and using straight knives, folders and automatics of his design and to customer specs. **Patterns:** Hunters, automatics and locking folders. **Technical:** Grinds ATS-34, 440C and D2. Offers engraving and scrimshaw. **Prices:** $425 to $650; some to $1500. **Remarks:** Full-time maker; first knife sold in 1990. Doing business as Wano Knives. **Mark:** Last name inside oval, business name above, city and state below, year on side.

WARREN, AL
1423 Sante Fe Circle, Roseville, CA 95678, Phone: 916-257-5904, Fax: 215-318-2945, al@warrenknives.com; Web: www.warrenknives.com
Specialties: Working straight knives and folders, some fancy. **Patterns:** Hunters, Bowies, fillets, lockback, folders & multi blade. **Technical:** Grinds ATS-34 and S30V.440V. **Prices:** $225 to $2,500.**Remarks:** Full-time maker; first knife sold in 1978. **Mark:** First and middle initials, last name.

WARREN, ALAN AND CARROLL
6605 S.E. 69th Ave., Portland, OR 97206, Phone: 503-788-6863 or 503-926-3559, alanwarrenknives@yahoo.com
Specialties: Mostly one-of-a-kind straight knives, bird & trout knives, skinners, fighters, bowies, daggers, short swords and LinerLock folders (tactical and gent's). My designs or custom. **Technical:** Hollow and flat grinds 154CM, ATS-34, CPM-S30V, O1, 5160 and others. Uses just about all handle materials available. Makes custom-to-fit, hand-tooled and hand stitched leather sheaths, some with skin inlays or hard inlays to match knife handle materials such as G-10, Micarta, ironwood, ivory, stag, etc. **Prices:** $200 to $1,800, some to $3,595. **Remarks:** Full-time maker for nine years; first knife sold in 1998. **Mark:** Name, state, USA.

WARREN, DANIEL
571 Lovejoy Rd, Canton, NC 28716, Phone: 828-648-7351
Specialties: Using knives. **Patterns:** Drop point hunters. **Prices:** $200 to $500. **Mark:** Warren-Bethel NC.

WASHBURN, ARTHUR D
ADW CUSTOM KNIVES, 211 Hinman St / PO Box 625, Pioche, NV 89043, Phone: 775-962-5463, knifeman@lcturbonet.com; Web: www.adwcustomknives.com
Specialties: Locking liner folders. **Patterns:** Slip joint folders (single and multiplied), lock-back folders, some fixed blades. Do own heat-treating; Rockwell test each blade. **Technical:** Carbon and stainless Damascus, some 1084, 1095, AEBL, 12C27, S30V. **Prices:** $200 to $1000 and up. **Remarks:** Sold first knife in 1997. Part-time maker. **Mark:** ADW enclosed in an oval or ADW.

WASHBURN JR., ROBERT LEE
636 75th St., Tuscaloosa, AL 35405, Phone: 435-619-4432, Fax: 435-574-8554, rlwashburn@excite.com; Web: www.washburnknives.net
Specialties: Hand-forged period, Bowies, tactical, boot and hunters. **Patterns:** Bowies, tantos, loot hunters, tactical and folders. **Prices:** $100 to $2500. **Remarks:** All hand forged. 52100 being his favorite steel. **Mark:** Washburn Knives W.

WATANABE, MELVIN
1297 Kika St., Kailua, HI 96734, Phone: 808-261-2842, meltod808@yahoo.com
Specialties: Fancy folding knives. Some hunters. **Patterns:** Liner-locks and hunters. **Technical:** Grinds ATS-34, stainless Damascus. **Prices:** $350 and up. **Remarks:** Part-time maker, first knife sold in 1985. **Mark:** Name and state.

WATANABE, WAYNE
PO Box 3563, Montebello, CA 90640, wwknives@yahoo.com
Specialties: Straight knives in Japanese-styles. One-of-a-kind designs; welcomes customer designs. **Patterns:** Tantos to katanas, Bowies. **Technical:** Flat grinds A2, O1 and ATS-34. Offers hand-rubbed finishes and wrapped handles. **Prices:** Start at $200. **Remarks:** Part-time maker. **Mark:** Name in characters with flower.

WATERS, GLENN
11 Shinakawa Machi, Hirosaki City, JAPAN 036, Phone: 0172-886741, watersglenn@hotmail.com; Web: www.glennwaters.com
Specialties: One-of-a-kind collector-grade highly embellished art knives. Mostly folders with a few fixed blades and up-market tactical flippers. **Patterns:** Locking-liner folders and collectible flippers and fixed art knives. **Technical:** Grinds blades from Damasteel, VG-10, CowryX, ZDP-189, San Mai from ZDP-189 and VG-10, and Super Gold 2 powdered stainless by Takefu. Does own engraving, gold inlaying and stone setting, filework and carving. Gold and Japanese precious metal fabrication. Prefers exotic material, high karat gold, silver, Shyaku Dou, Shibu Ichi Gin, precious gemstones. **Prices:** Upscale. **Remarks:** Designs and makes one-of-a-kind highly embellished art knives, often with fully engraved handles and blades that tell a story. A jeweler by trade for 20 years before starting to make knives in 1993. First knife sold in 1994. **Mark:** On knives before 2010, Glenn Waters maker Japan or Glenn in Japanese. Knives since 2010 uses a new engraved logo that says Glenn in Japanese.

WATSON, BERT
9315 Meade St., Westminster, CO 80031, Phone: 303-587-3064, watsonbd21960@q.com
Specialties: Working/using straight knives of his design and to customer specs. **Patterns:** Hunters, utility/camp knives. **Technical:** Grinds O1, ATS-34, 440C, D2, A2 and others. **Prices:** $150 to $800. **Remarks:** Full-time maker. **Mark:** GTK and/or Bert.

WATSON, BILLY
440 Forge Rd, Deatsville, AL 36022, Phone: 334-365-1482, hilldweller44@att.net
Specialties: Working and using straight knives and folders of his design; period pieces. **Patterns:** Hunters, Bowies and utility/camp knives. **Technical:** Forges and grinds his own Damascus, 1095, 5160 and 52100. **Prices:** $40 to $1500. **Remarks:** Full-time maker; first knife sold in 1970. **Mark:** Last name.

WATSON, DANIEL
350 Jennifer Ln, Driftwood, TX 78619, Phone: 512-847-9679, info@angelsword.com; Web: http://www.angelsword.com
Specialties: One-of-a-kind knives and swords. **Patterns:** Hunters, daggers, swords. **Technical:** Hand-purify and carbonize his own high-carbon steel, pattern-welded Damascus, cable and carbon-induced crystalline Damascus. Teehno-Wootz™ Damascus steel, heat treats including cryogenic processing. European and Japanese tempering. **Prices:** $125 to $25,000. **Remarks:** Full-time maker; first knife sold in 1979. **Mark:** "Angel Sword" on forged pieces; "Bright Knight" for stock removal. Avatar on Techno-Wootz™ Damascus. Bumon on traditional Japanese blades.

WATSON, PETER
66 Kielblock St, La Hoff, NW, SOUTH AFRICA 2570, Phone: 018-84942
Specialties: Traditional working and using straight knives and folders of his design. **Patterns:** Hunters, locking folders and utility/camp knives. **Technical:** Sandvik and 440C. **Prices:** $120 to $250; some to $1500. **Remarks:** Part-time maker; first knife sold in 1989. **Mark:** Buffalo head with name.

WATSON, TOM
1103 Brenau Terrace, Panama City, FL 32405, Phone: 850-785-9209, tom@tomwatsonknives.com; Web: www.tomwatsonknives.com
Specialties: Utility/tactical LinerLocks and flipper folders. **Patterns:** Various patterns. **Technical:** Grinds D2 and CPM-154. **Prices:** $375 and up. **Remarks:** In business since 1978. **Mark:** Name and city.

WATTELET, MICHAEL A
PO Box 649, 125 Front, Minocqua, WI 54548, Phone: 715-356-3069, redtroll@frontier.com
Specialties: Working and using straight knives of his design and to customer specs; fantasy knives. **Patterns:** Daggers, fighters and swords. **Technical:** Grinds 440C and L6; forges and grinds O1. Silversmith. **Prices:** $75 to $1000; some to $5000. **Remarks:** Full-time maker; first knife sold in 1966. Doing business as M and N Arts Ltd. **Mark:** First initial, last name.

WATTS, JOHNATHAN
9440 S. Hwy. 36, Gatesville, TX 76528, Phone: 254-223-9669
Specialties: Traditional folders. **Patterns:** One and two blade folders in various blade shapes. **Technical:** Grinds ATS-34 and Damascus on request. **Prices:** $120 to $400. **Remarks:** Part-time maker; first knife sold in 1997. **Mark:** J Watts.

WATTS, RODNEY
Watts Custom Knives, 1100 Hwy. 71 S, Hot Springs, SD 57747, Phone: 605-890-0645, wattscustomknives@yahoo.com; www.wattscustomknives.com
Specialties: Fixed blades and some folders, most of maker's own designs, some Loveless and Johnson patterns. **Technical:** Stock removal method of blade making, using CPM 154 and ATS-34 steels. **Prices:** $450 to $1,100. **Remarks:** Part-time maker; first knife made in 2007. Won "Best New Maker" award at the 2011 BLADE Show. **Mark:** Watts over Custom Knives.

WEBSTER, BILL
58144 West Clear Lake Rd, Three Rivers, MI 49093, Phone: 269-244-2873, wswebster_5@msn.com Web: www.websterknifeworks.com
Specialties: Working and using straight knives, especially for hunters. His patterns are custom designed. **Patterns:** Hunters, skinners, camp knives, Bowies and daggers. **Technical:** Hand-filed blades made of D2 steel only, unless other steel is requested. Preferred handle material is stabilized and exotic wood and stag. Sheaths are made by Green River Leather in Kentucky. Hand-sewn sheaths by Bill Dehn in Three Rivers, MI. **Prices:** $75 to $500. **Remarks:** Part-time maker, first knife sold in 1978. **Mark:** Originally WEB stamped on blade, at present, Webster Knifeworks Three Rivers, MI laser etched on blade.

WEEKS, RYAN
PO Box 1101, Bountiful, UT 84001, Phone: 801-755-6789, ryan@ryanwknives.com; Web: www.ryanwknives.com
Specialties: Military and Law Enforcement applications as well as hunting and utility designs. **Patterns:** Fighters, bowies, hunters, and custom designs, I use man made as well as natural wood and exotic handle materials. **Technical:** Make via forge and stock removal methods, preferred steel includes high carbon, CPM154 CM and ATS34, Damascus and San Mai. **Prices:** $160 to $750.**Remarks:** Part-time maker; Business name is "Ryan W. Knives." First knife sold in 2009.**Mark:** Encircled "Ryan" beneath the crossed "W" UTAH, USA.

WEEVER, JOHN
1162 Black Hawk Trl., Nemo, TX 76070, Phone: 254-898-9595,

john.weever@gmail.com; Web: WeeverKnives.com

Specialties: Traditional hunters (fixed blade, slip joint, and lockback) and tactical. **Patterns:** See website. **Technical:** Types of steel: S30V, Damascus or customer choice. Handles in mammoth ivory, oosic, horn, sambar, stag, etc. Sheaths in exotic leathers. **Prices:** $400 to $1200. **Remarks:** Stock removal maker full-time; began making knives in 1985. Member of knifemakers guild. **Mark:** Tang stamp: head of charging elephant with ears extended and WEEVER curved over the top.

WEHNER, RUDY

297 William Warren Rd, Collins, MS 39428, Phone: 601-765-4997

Specialties: Reproduction antique Bowies and contemporary Bowies in full and miniature. **Patterns:** Skinners, camp knives, fighters, axes and Bowies. **Technical:** Grinds 440C, ATS-34, 154CM and Damascus. **Prices:** $100 to $500; some to $850. **Remarks:** Full-time maker; first knife sold in 1975. **Mark:** Last name on Bowies and antiques; full name, city and state on skinners.

WEILAND JR., J REESE

PO Box 2337, Riverview, FL 33568, Phone: 813-671-0661, RWPHIL413@verizon.net; Web: www.reeseweilandknives.com

Specialties: Hawk bills; tactical to fancy folders. **Patterns:** Hunters, tantos, Bowies, fantasy knives, spears and some swords. **Technical:** Grinds ATS-34, 154CM, 440C, D2, O1, A2, Damascus. Titanium hardware on locking liners and button locks. **Prices:** $150 to $4000. **Remarks:** Full-time maker, first knife sold in 1978. Knifemakers Guild member since 1988.

WEINAND, GEROME M

14440 Harpers Bridge Rd, Missoula, MT 59808, Phone: 406-543-0845

Specialties: Working straight knives. **Patterns:** Bowies, fishing and camp knives, large special hunters. **Technical:** Grinds O1, 440C, ATS-34, 1084, L6, also stainless Damascus, Aebl and 304; makes all-tool steel Damascus; Dendritic D2 from powdered steel. Heat-treats. **Prices:** $30 to $100; some to $500. **Remarks:** Full-time maker; first knife sold in 1982. **Mark:** Last name.

WEINSTOCK, ROBERT

PO Box 170028, San Francisco, CA 94117-0028, Phone: 415-731-5968, robertweinstock@att.net

Specialties: Folders, slip joins, lockbacks, autos. **Patterns:** Daggers, folders. **Technical:** Grinds A2, O1 and 440C. Chased and hand-carved blades and handles. Also using various Damascus steels from other makers. **Prices:** $3000 to 7000. **Remarks:** Full-time maker; first knife sold in 1994. **Mark:** Last name carved in steel.

WEISS, CHARLES L

PO BOX 1037, Waddell, AZ 85355, Phone: 623-935-0924, weissknife@live.com

Specialties: High-art straight knives and folders; deluxe period pieces. **Patterns:** Daggers, fighters, boots, push knives and miniatures. **Technical:** Grinds 440C, 154CM and ATS-34. **Prices:** $300 to $1200; some to $2000. **Remarks:** Full-time maker; first knife sold in 1975. **Mark:** Name and city.

WELLING, RONALD L

15446 Lake Ave, Grand Haven, MI 49417, Phone: 616-846-2274

Specialties: Scagel knives of his design or to customer specs. **Patterns:** Hunters, camp knives, miniatures, bird, trout, folders, double edged, hatchets, skinners and some art pieces. **Technical:** Forges Damascus 1084 and 1095. Antler, ivory and horn. **Prices:** $250 to $3000. **Remarks:** Full-time maker. ABS Journeyman maker. **Mark:** First initials and or name and last name. City and state. Various scagel kris (1or 2).

WELLING, WILLIAM

Up-armored Knives, 5437 Pinecliff Dr., West Valley, NY 14171, Phone: 716-942-6031, uparmored@frontier.net; Web: www.up-armored.com

Specialties: Innovative tactical fixed blades each uniquely coated in a variety of Up-armored designed patterns and color schemes.Convexed edged bushcraft knives for the weekend camper, backpacker, or survivalist. Leather-and synthetic-suede-lined Kydex sheaths. **Patterns:** Modern samples of time tested designs as well as contemporary developed cutting tools. **Technical:** Stock removal specializing in tested 1095CV and 5160 steels. **Prices:** $200 to $500. **Remarks:** Part-time maker; first knife sold in 2010. **Mark:** Skull rounded up by Up-Armored USA.

WERTH, GEORGE W

5223 Woodstock Rd, Poplar Grove, IL 61065, Phone: 815-544-4408

Specialties: Period pieces, some fancy. **Patterns:** Straight fighters, daggers and Bowies. **Technical:** Forges and grinds O1, 1095 and his Damascus, including mosaic patterns. **Prices:** $200 to $650; some higher. **Remarks:** Full-time maker. Doing business as Fox Valley Forge. **Mark:** Name in logo or initials connected.

WESCOTT, CODY

5330 White Wing Rd, Las Cruces, NM 88012, Phone: 575-382-5008

Specialties: Fancy and presentation grade working knives. **Patterns:** Hunters, locking folders and Bowies. **Technical:** Hollow-grinds D2 and ATS-34; all knives file worked. Offers some engraving. Makes sheaths. **Prices:** $110 to $500; some to $1200. **Remarks:** Full-time maker; first knife sold in 1982. **Mark:** First initial, last name.

WEST, CHARLES A

1315 S Pine St, Centralia, IL 62801, Phone: 618-532-2777

Specialties: Classic, fancy, high tech, period pieces, traditional and working/using straight knives and folders. **Patterns:** Bowies, fighters and locking folders. **Technical:** Grinds ATS-34, O1 and Damascus. Prefers hot blued finishes. **Prices:** $100 to $1000; some to $2000. **Remarks:** Full-time maker; first knife sold in 1963. Doing business as West Custom Knives. **Mark:** Name or name, city and state.

WESTBERG, LARRY

305 S Western Hills Dr, Algona, IA 50511, Phone: 515-295-9276

Specialties: Traditional and working straight knives of his design and in standard patterns. **Patterns:** Bowies, hunters, fillets and folders. **Technical:** Grinds 440C, D2 and 1095. Heat-treats. Uses natural handle materials. **Prices:** $85 to $600; some to $1000. **Remarks:** Part-time maker; first knife sold in 1987. **Mark:** Last name-town and state.

WHEELER, GARY

351 Old Hwy 48, Clarksville, TN 37040, Phone: 931-552-3092, LR22SHTR@charter.net

Specialties: Working to high end fixed blades. **Patterns:** Bowies, Hunters, combat knives, daggers and a few folders. **Technical:** Forges 5160, 1095, 52100 and his own Damascus. **Prices:** $125 to $2000. **Remarks:** Full-time maker since 2001, first knife sold in 1985 collaborates/works at B&W Blade Works. ABS Journeyman Smith 2008. **Mark:** Stamped last name.

WHEELER, NICK

140 Studebaker Rd., Castle Rock, WA 98611, Phone: 360-967-2357, merckman99@yahoo.com

Specialties: Bowies, integrals, fighters, hunters and daggers. **Technical:** Forges W2, W1, 1095, 52100 and 1084. Makes own damascus, from random pattern to complex mosaics. Also grinds stainless and other more modern alloys. Does own heat-treating and leather work. Also commissions leather work from Paul Long. **Prices:** Start at $250. **Remarks:** Full-time maker; ABS member since 2001. Journeyman bladesmith. **Mark:** Last name.

WHEELER, ROBERT

289 S Jefferson, Bradley, IL 60915, Phone: 815-932-5854, b2btaz@brmemc.net

WHETSELL, ALEX

PO Box 215, Haralson, GA 30229, Phone: 770-599-8012, www.KnifeKits.com

Specialties: Knifekits.com, a source for fold locking liner type and straight knife kits. These kits are industry standard for folding knife kits. **Technical:** Many selections of colored G10 carbon fiber and wood handle material for kits, as well as bulk sizes for the custom knifemaker, heat treated folding knife pivots, screws, bushings, etc.

WHIPPLE, WESLEY A

1002 Shoshoni St, Thermopolis, WY 82443, Phone: 307-921-2445, wildernessknife@yahoo.com

Specialties: Working straight knives, some fancy. **Patterns:** Hunters, Bowies, camp knives, fighters. **Technical:** Forges high-carbon steels, Damascus, offers relief carving and silver wire inlay and checkering. **Prices:** $300 to $1400; some higher. **Remarks:** Full-time maker; first knife sold in 1989. A.K.A. Wilderness Knife and Forge. **Mark:** Last name/JS.

WHITE, BRYCE

1415 W Col Glenn Rd, Little Rock, AR 72210, Phone: 501-821-2956

Specialties: Hunters, fighters, makes Damascus, file work, handmade only. **Technical:** L6, 1075, 1095, O1 steels used most. **Patterns:** Will do any pattern or use his own. **Prices:** $200 to $300. Sold first knife in 1995. **Mark:** White.

WHITE, CALEB A.

502 W. River Rd. #88, Hooksett, NH 03106, Phone: 603-340-4716, caleb@calebwhiteknives.com; www.calebwhiteknives.com

Specialties: Hunters, tacticals, dress knives, daggers and utilitarian pieces. **Patterns:** Multiple. **Technical:** Mostly stock removal, preferring high-carbon steels. **Prices:** $275 to $4,100. **Remarks:** Full-time maker. **Mark:** Derivation of maker's last name, replacing the "T" with a symbol loosely based on the Templars' cross and shield.

WHITE, DALE

525 CR 212, Sweetwater, TX 79556, Phone: 325-798-4178, dalew@taylortel.net

Specialties: Working and using knives. **Patterns:** Hunters, skinners, utilities and Bowies. **Technical:** Grinds 440C, offers file work, fancy pins and scrimshaw by Sherry Sellers. **Prices:** From $45 to $300. **Remarks:** Sold first knife in 1975. **Mark:** Full name, city and state.

WHITE, GARRETT

871 Sarijon Rd, Hartwell, GA 30643, Phone: 706-376-5944

Specialties: Gentlemen folders, fancy straight knives. **Patterns:** Locking liners and hunting fixed blades. **Technical:** Grinds 440C, S30V, and stainless Damascus. **Prices:** $150 to $1000. **Remarks:** Part-time maker. **Mark:** Name.

WHITE, LOU

7385 Red Bud Rd NE, Ranger, GA 30734, Phone: 706-334-2273

WHITE, RICHARD T

359 Carver St, Grosse Pointe Farms, MI 48236, Phone: 313-881-4690

WHITE, ROBERT J

RR 1 641 Knox Rd 900 N, Gilson, IL 61436, Phone: 309-289-4487

Specialties: Working knives, some deluxe. **Patterns:** Bird and trout knives, hunters, survival knives and locking folders. **Technical:** Grinds A2, D2 and 440C; commercial Damascus. Heat-treats. **Prices:** $125 to $250; some to $600. **Remarks:** Full-time maker; first knife sold in 1976. **Mark:** Last name in script.

WHITENECT, JODY

Halifax County, Elderbank, NS, CANADA B0N 1K0, Phone: 902-384-2511

Specialties: Fancy and embellished working/using straight knives of his design and to customer specs. **Patterns:** Bowies, fighters and hunters. **Technical:** Forges 1095 and O1; forges and grinds ATS-34. Various filework on blades and bolsters. **Prices:** $200 to $400; some to $800. **Remarks:** Part-time maker; first knife sold in 1996. **Mark:** Longhorn stamp or engraved.

WHITESELL, J. DALE

P.O. Box 455, Stover, MO 65078, Phone: 573-569-0753, dalesknives@yahoo.com; Web: whitesell-knives.webs.com

Specialties: Fixed blade working knives,a nd some collector pieces. **Patterns:** Hunting and skinner knives, camp knives, and kitchen knives. **Technical:** Blades ground from O1, 1095, and 440C in hollow, flat and saber grinds. Wood, bone, deer antler, and G10 are basic handle materials. **Prices:** $100 to $450. **Remarks:** Part-time maker, first knife sold in 2003. Doing business as Dale's Knives. All knives have serial number to indicate steel (since June 2010).**Mark:** Whitesell on the left side of the blade.

WHITLEY, L WAYNE

1675 Carrow Rd, Chocowinity, NC 27817-9495, Phone: 252-946-5648

WHITLEY, WELDON G

4308 N Robin Ave, Odessa, TX 79764, Phone: 432-530-0448, Fax: 432-530-0048, wgwhitley@juno.com

Specialties: Working knives of his design or to customer specs. **Patterns:** Hunters, folders and various double-edged knives. **Technical:** Grinds 440C, 154CM and ATS-34. **Prices:** $150 to $1250. **Mark:** Name, address, road-runner logo.

WHITTAKER, ROBERT E

PO Box 204, Mill Creek, PA 17060

Specialties: Using straight knives. Has a line of knives for buckskinners. **Patterns:** Hunters, skinners and Bowies. **Technical:** Grinds O1, A2 and D2. Offers filework. **Prices:** $35 to $100. **Remarks:** Part-time maker; first knife sold in 1980. **Mark:** Last initial or full initials.

WHITTAKER, WAYNE

2900 Woodland Ct, Metamore, MI 48455, Phone: 810-797-5315, lindorwayne@yahoo.com

Specialties: Liner locks and autos.**Patterns:** Folders. **Technical:** Damascus, mammoth, ivory, and tooth. **Prices:** $500 to $1500. **Remarks:** Full-time maker. **Mark:** Inside of backbar.

WICK, JONATHAN P.

5541 E. Calle Narcisco, Hereford, AZ 85615, Phone: 520-227-5228, vikingwick@aol.com

Specialties: Fixed blades, pocketknives, neck knives, hunters, bowies, fighters, Roman-style daggers with full tangs, stick tangs and some integrals, and leather-lined, textured copper sheaths. **Technical:** Forged blades and own damascus and mosaic damascus, along with shibuichi, mokume, lost wax casting. **Prices:** $250 -$1800 and up. **Remarks:** Full-time maker, ABS member, sold first knife in 2008. **Mark:** J P Wick, also on small blades a JP over a W.

WICKER, DONNIE R

2544 E 40th Ct, Panama City, FL 32405, Phone: 904-785-9158

Specialties: Traditional working and using straight knives of his design or to customer specs. **Patterns:** Hunters, fighters and slip-joint folders. **Technical:** Grinds 440C, ATS-34, D2 and 154CM. Heat-treats and does hardness testing. **Prices:** $90 to $200; some to $400. **Remarks:** Part-time maker; first knife sold in 1975. **Mark:** First and middle initials, last name.

WIGGINS, BILL

105 Kaolin Lane, Canton, NC 28716, Phone: 828-226-2551, wncbill@bellsouth.net Web: www.wigginsknives.com

Specialties: Forged working knives. **Patterns:** Hunters, Bowies, camp knives and utility knives of own design or will work with customer on design. **Technical:** Forges 1084 and 52100 as well as making own Damascus. **Prices:** $250 -$1500. **Remarks:** Part-time maker. First knife sold in 1989. ABS board member. **Mark:** Wiggins

WILBURN, AARON

2521 Hilltop Dr., #364, Redding, CA 96002, Phone: 530-227-2827, wilburnforge@yahoo.com; Web: www.wilburnforge.com

Patterns: Daggers, bowies, fighters, hunters and slip-joint folders. **Technical:** Forges own damascus and works with high-carbon steel. **Prices:** $500 to $5,000. **Remarks:** Full-time maker and ABS master smith. **Mark:** Wilburn Forge.

WILCHER, WENDELL L

RR 6 Box 6573, Palestine, TX 75801, Phone: 903-549-2530

Specialties: Fantasy, miniatures and working/using straight knives and folders of his design and to customer specs. **Patterns:** Fighters, hunters, locking folders. **Technical:** Hand works (hand file and hand sand knives), not grind. **Prices:** $75 to $250; some to $600. **Remarks:** Part-time maker; first knife sold in 1987. **Mark:** Initials, year, serial number.

WILKINS, MITCHELL

15523 Rabon Chapel Rd, Montgomery, TX 77316, Phone: 936-588-2696, mwilkins@consolidated.net

WILLEY, WG

14210 Sugar Hill Rd, Greenwood, DE 19950, Phone: 302-349-4070, Web: www.willeyknives.com

Specialties: Fancy working straight knives. **Patterns:** Small game knives, Bowies and throwing knives. **Technical:** Grinds 440C and 154CM. **Prices:** $350 to $600; some to $1500. **Remarks:** Part-time maker; first knife sold in 1975. Owns retail store. **Mark:** Last name inside map logo.

WILLIAMS, JASON L

PO Box 67, Wyoming, RI 02898, Phone: 401-539-8353, Fax: 401-539-0252

Specialties: Fancy and high tech folders of his design, co-inventor of the Axis Lock. **Patterns:** Fighters, locking folders, automatics and fancy pocket knives. **Technical:** Forges Damascus and other steels by request. Uses exotic handle materials and precious metals. Offers inlaid spines and gemstone thumb knobs. **Prices:** $1000 and up. **Remarks:** Full-time maker; first knife sold in 1989. **Mark:** First and last initials on pivot.

WILLIAMS, MICHAEL

333 Cherrybark Tr., Broken Bow, OK 74728, Phone: 580-420-3051, hforge@pine-net.com

Specialties: Functional, personalized, edged weaponry. Working and collectible art. **Patterns:** Bowies, hunters, camp knives, daggers, others. **Technical:** Forges high carbon steel and own forged Damascus. **Prices:** $500 -$12000. **Remarks:** Full-time ABS Master Smith. **Mark:** Williams MS.

WILLIAMS, ROBERT

15962 State Rt. 267, East Liverpool, OH 43920, Phone: 203-979-0803, wurdmeister@gmail.com; Web: www.customstraightrazors.com

Specialties: Custom straight razors with a philosophy that form must follow function, so shaving performance drives designs and aesthetics. **Technical:** Stock removal and forging, working with 1095, O1 and damascus. Natural handle materials and synthetics, accommodating any and all design requests and can incorporate gold inlays, scrimshaw, hand engraving and jewel setting. All work done in maker's shop, sole-source maker shipping worldwide. **Remarks:** Full-time maker; first straight razor in 2005. **Mark:** Robert Williams -Handmade, USA with a hammer separating the two lines.

WILLIAMS JR., RICHARD

1440 Nancy Circle, Morristown, TN 37814, Phone: 615-581-0059

Specialties: Working and using straight knives of his design or to customer specs. **Patterns:** Hunters, dirks and utility/camp knives. **Technical:** Forges 5160 and uses file steel. Hand-finish is standard; offers filework. **Prices:** $80 to $180; some to $250. **Remarks:** Spare-time maker; first knife sold in 1985. **Mark:** Last initial or full initials.

WILLIAMSON, TONY

Rt 3 Box 503, Siler City, NC 27344, Phone: 919-663-3551

Specialties: Flint knapping: knives made of obsidian flakes and flint with wood, antler or bone for handles. **Patterns:** Skinners, daggers and flake knives. **Technical:** Blades have width/thickness ratio of at least 4 to 1. Hafts with methods available to prehistoric man. **Prices:** $58 to $160. **Remarks:** Student of Errett Callahan. **Mark:** Initials and number code to identify year and number of knives made.

WILLIS, BILL

RT 7 Box 7549, Ava, MO 65608, Phone: 417-683-4326

Specialties: Forged blades, Damascus and carbon steel. **Patterns:** Cable, random or ladder lamented. **Technical:** Professionally heat treated blades. **Prices:** $75 to $600. **Remarks:** Lifetime guarantee on all blades against breakage. All work done by maker; including leather work. **Mark:** WF.

WILLUMSEN, MIKKEL

Nyrnberggade 23, S Copenhagen, DENMARK 2300, Phone: 4531176333, mw@willumsen-cph.com Web: www.wix.com/willumsen/urbantactical

Specialties: Folding knives, fixed blades, and balisongs. Also kitchen knives. **Patterns:** Primarily influenced by design that is function and quality based. Tactical style knives inspired by classical designs mixed with modern tactics. **Technical:** Uses CPM 154, RW 134, S30V, and carbon fiber titanium G10 for handles.**Prices:** Starting at $600.

WILSON, CURTIS M

PO Box 383, Burleson, TX 76097, Phone: 817-295-3732, cwknifeman2026@att.net; Web: www.cwilsonknives.com

Specialties: Traditional working/using knives, fixed blade, folders, slip joint, LinerLock® and lock back knives. Art knives, presentation grade Bowies, folder repair, heat treating services. Sub-zero quench. **Patterns:** Hunters, camp knives, military combat, single and multi-blade folders. Dr's knives large or small or custom design knives. **Technical:** Grinds ATS-34, 440C, D2, S30V, CPM 154, mokume gane, engraves, scrimshaw, sheaths leather of kykex heat treating and file work. **Prices:** $150-750. **Remarks:** Part-time maker since 1984. Sold first knife in 1993. **Mark:** Curtis Wilson in ribbon or Curtis Wilson with hand made in a half moon.

WILSON, JAMES G

PO Box 4024, Estes Park, CO 80517, Phone: 303-586-3944

Specialties: Bronze Age knives; Medieval and Scottish-styles; tomahawks. **Patterns:** Bronze knives, daggers, swords, spears and battle axes; 12-inch steel Misericorde daggers, sgian dubhs, "his and her" skinners, bird and fish knives, capers, boots and daggers. **Technical:** Casts bronze; grinds D2, 440C and ATS-34. **Prices:** $49 to $400; some to $1300. **Remarks:** Part-time maker; first knife sold in 1975. **Mark:** WilsonHawk.

WILSON, MIKE

1416 McDonald Rd, Hayesville, NC 28904, Phone: 828-389-8145

Specialties: Fancy working and using straight knives of his design or to customer specs, folders. **Patterns:** Hunters, Bowies, utility knives, gut hooks, skinners, fighters and miniatures. **Technical:** Hollow grinds 440C, 1095, D2, XHP and CPM-154. Mirror finishes are standard. Offers filework. **Prices:** $130 to $600. **Remarks:** Full-time maker; first knife sold in 1985. **Mark:** Last name.

WILSON, P.R. "REGAN"

805 Janvier Rd., Scott, LA 70583, Phone: 504-427-1293, pat71ss@cox.net; www.acadianawhitetailtaxidermy.com

Specialties: Traditional working knives. **Patterns:**Old-school working knives, trailing points, drop points, hunters, boots, etc. **Technical:** 440C, ATS-34 and 154CM steels, all hollow ground with mirror or satin finishes. **Prices:** Start at $175 with sheath. **Remarks:** Mentored by Jim Barbee; first knife sold in 1988; lessons and guidance offered in maker's shop. **Mark:** Name and location with "W" in center of football-shaped logo.

WILSON, PHILIP C
SEAMOUNT KNIFEWORKS, PO Box 846, Mountain Ranch, CA 95246, Phone: 209-754-1990, seamount@bigplanet.com; Web: www.seamountknifeworks.com
Specialties: Working knives; emphasis on salt water fillet knives and utility hunters of his design. **Patterns:** Fishing knives, hunters, utility knives. **Technical:** Grinds CPM10V, S-90V, CPMS110V, K390, K294, CPM154, M-390, ELMAX. Heat-treats and Rockwell tests all blades. **Prices:** Start at $400. **Remarks:** First knife sold in 1985. Doing business as Sea-Mount Knife Works. **Mark:** Signature.

WILSON, RON
2639 Greenwood Ave, Morro Bay, CA 93442, Phone: 805-772-3381
Specialties: Classic and fantasy straight knives of his design. **Patterns:** Daggers, fighters, swords and axes, mostly all miniatures. **Technical:** Forges and grinds Damascus and various tool steels; grinds meteorite. Uses gold, precious stones and exotic wood. **Prices:** Vary. **Remarks:** Part-time maker; first knives sold in 1995. **Mark:** Stamped first and last initials.

WILSON, RW
PO Box 2012, Weirton, WV 26062, Phone: 304-723-2771, rwknives@comcast.net; Web: www.rwwilsonknives.com
Specialties: Working straight knives; period pieces. **Patterns:** Bowies, tomahawks and patch knives. **Technical:** Grinds 440C; scrimshaws. **Prices:** $85 to $175; some to $1000. **Remarks:** Part-time maker; first knife sold in 1966. Knifemaker supplier. Offers free knife-making lessons. **Mark:** Name in tomahawk.

WILSON, STAN
8931 Pritcher Rd, Lithia, FL 33547, Phone: 727-461-1992, swilson@stanwilsonknives.com; Web: www.stanwilsonknives.com
Specialties: Fancy folders and automatics of his own design. **Patterns:** Locking liner folders, single and dual action autos, daggers. **Technical:** Stock removal, uses Damascus, stainless and high carbon steels, prefers ivory and pearl, Damascus with blued finishes and filework. **Prices:** $400 and up. **Remarks:** Member of Knifemakers Guild and Florida Knifemakers Association. Full-time maker will do custom orders. **Mark:** Name in script.

WILSON, VIC
9130 Willow Branch Dr, Olive Branch, MS 38654, Phone: 901-591-6550, vdubjr55@earthlink.net; Web: www.knivesbyvic.com
Specialties: Classic working and using knives and folders. **Patterns:** Hunters, boning, utility, camp, my patterns or customers. **Technical:** Grinds O1 and D2. Also does own heat treating. Offer file work and decorative liners on folders. Fabricate custom leather sheaths for all knives. **Prices:** $150 to $400. **Remarks:** Part-time maker, first knife sold in 1989. **Mark:** Etched V over W with oval circle around it, name, Memphis, TN.

WINGO, GARY
240 Ogeechee, Ramona, OK 74061, Phone: 918-536-1067, wingg_2000@yahoo.com; Web: www.geocities.com/wingg_2000/gary.html
Specialties: Folder specialist. Steel 440C, D2, others on request. Handle bone-stag, others on request. **Patterns:** Trapper three-blade stockman, four-blade congress, single- and two-blade barlows. **Prices:** 150 to $400. **Mark:** First knife sold 1994. Steer head with Wingo Knives or Straight line Wingo Knives.

WINGO, PERRY
22 55th St, Gulfport, MS 39507, Phone: 228-863-3193
Specialties: Traditional working straight knives. **Patterns:** Hunters, skinners, Bowies and fishing knives. **Technical:** Grinds 440C. **Prices:** $75 to $1000. **Remarks:** Full-time maker; first knife sold in 1988. **Mark:** Last name.

WINKLER, DANIEL
PO Box 2166, Blowing Rock, NC 28605, Phone: 828-295-9156, danielwinkler@bellsouth.net; Web: www.winklerknives.com
Specialties: Forged cutlery styled in the tradition of an era past as well as producing a custom-made stock removal line. **Patterns:** Fixed blades, friction folders, lock back folders, and axes/tomahawks. **Technical:** Forges, grinds, and heat treats carbon steels, specialty steels, and his own Damascus steel. **Prices:** $350 to $4000+. **Remarks:** Full-time maker since 1988. Exclusively offers leatherwork by Karen Shook. ABS Master Smith; Knifemakers Guild voting member. **Mark:** Hand forged: Dwinkler; Stock removal: Winkler Knives

WINN, MARVIN
Maxcutter Custom Knives, 587 Winn Rd., Sunset, LA 70584, Phone: 214-471-7012, maxcutter03@yahoo.com Web: www.maxcutterknives.com
Patterns: Hunting knives, some tactical and some miniatures. **Technical:** 1095, 5160, 154 CM, 12C27, CPM S30V, CPM 154, CTS-XHP and CTS-40CP blade steels, damascus or to customer's designs. Stock removal. **Prices:** $200 to $2,000. **Remarks:** Part-time maker. First knife made in 2002. **Mark:** Name and state.

WINN, TRAVIS A.
558 E 3065 S, Salt Lake City, UT 84106, Phone: 801-467-5957
Specialties: Fancy working knives and knives to customer specs. **Patterns:** Hunters, fighters, boots, Bowies and fancy daggers, some miniatures, tantos and fantasy knives. **Technical:** Grinds D2 and 440C. Embellishes. **Prices:** $125 to $500; some higher. **Remarks:** Part-time maker; first knife sold in 1976. **Mark:** TRAV stylized.

WINSTON, DAVID
1671 Red Holly St, Starkville, MS 39759, Phone: 601-323-1028

Specialties: Fancy and traditional knives of his design and to customer specs. **Patterns:** Bowies, daggers, hunters, boot knives and folders. **Technical:** Grinds 440C, ATS-34 and D2. Offers filework; heat-treats. **Prices:** $40 to $750; some higher. **Remarks:** Part-time maker; first knife sold in 1984. Offers lifetime sharpening for original owner. **Mark:** Last name.

WIRTZ, ACHIM
Mittelstrasse 58, Wuerselen, GERMANY 52146, Phone: 0049-2405-462-486, wootz@web.de
Specialties: Medieval, Scandinavian and Middle East-style knives. **Technical:** Forged blades only, Damascus steel, Wootz, Mokume. **Prices:** Start at $200. **Remarks:** Part-time maker. First knife sold in 1997. **Mark:** Stylized initials.

WISE, DONALD
304 Bexhill Rd, St Leonardo-On-Sea, East Sussex, ENGLAND TN3 8AL
Specialties: Fancy and embellished working straight knives to customer specs. **Patterns:** Hunters, Bowies and daggers. **Technical:** Grinds Sandvik 12C27, D2 D3 and O1. Scrimshaws. **Prices:** $110 to $300; some to $500. **Remarks:** Full-time maker; first knife sold in 1983. **Mark:** KNIFECRAFT.

WOLF, BILL
4618 N 79th Ave, Phoenix, AZ 85033, Phone: 623-910-3147, bwcustomknives143@gmail.com; Web: billwolfcustomknives.com
Specialties: Investment grade knives. **Patterns:** Own designs or customer's. **Technical:** Grinds stainless and all steels. **Prices:** $400 to ? **Remarks:** First knife made in 1988. **Mark:** WOLF

WOLF JR., WILLIAM LYNN
4006 Frank Rd, Lagrange, TX 78945, Phone: 409-247-4626

WOOD, ALAN
Greenfield Villa, Greenhead, Brampton, ENGLAND CA8 7HH, info@alanwoodknives.com; Web: www.alanwoodknives.com
Specialties: High-tech working straight knives of his design. **Patterns:** Hunters, utility/camp and bushcraft knives. **Technical:** Grinds 12C27, RWL-34, stainless Damascus and O1. Blades are cryogenic treated. **Prices:** $200 to $800; some to $1,200. **Remarks:** Full-time maker; first knife sold in 1979. Not currently taking orders. **Mark:** Full name with stag tree logo.

WOOD, OWEN DALE
6492 Garrison St, Arvada, CO 80004-3157, Phone: 303-456-2748, wood.owen@gmail.com; Web: www.owenwoodknives.net
Specialties: Folding knives and daggers. **Patterns:** Own Damascus, specialties in 456 composite blades. **Technical:** Materials: Damascus stainless steel, exotic metals, gold, rare handle materials. **Prices:** $1000 to $9000. **Remarks:** Folding knives in art deco and art noveau themes. Full-time maker from 1981. **Mark:** OWEN WOOD.

WOOD, WEBSTER
22041 Shelton Trail, Atlanta, MI 49709, Phone: 989-785-2996, mainganikan@src-milp.com
Specialties: Works mainly in stainless; art knives, Bowies, hunters and folders. **Remarks:** Full-time maker; first knife sold in 1980. Retired guild member. All engraving done by maker. **Mark:** Initials inside shield and name.

WORLEY, JOEL A., J.S.
PO BOX 64, Maplewood, OH 45340, Phone: 937-638-9518, jaworleyknives@gmail.com
Specialties: Bowies, hunters, fighters, utility/camp knives also period style friction folders. **Patterns:** Classic styles, recurves, his design or customer specified. **Technical:** Most knives are fileworked and include a custom made leather sheath. Forges 5160, W2, Cru forge V, files own Damascus of 1080 and 15N20. **Prices:** $250 and up. **Remarks:** Part-time maker. ABS journeyman smith. First knife sold in 2005. **Mark:** First name, middle initial and last name over a shark incorporating initials.

WRIGHT, KEVIN
671 Leland Valley Rd W, Quilcene, WA 98376-9517, Phone: 360-765-3589, kevinw@ptpc.com
Specialties: Fancy working or collector knives to customer specs. **Patterns:** Hunters, boots, buckskinners, miniatures. **Technical:** Forges and grinds L6, 1095, 440C and his own Damascus. **Prices:** $75 to $500; some to $2000. **Remarks:** Part-time maker; first knife sold in 1978. **Mark:** Last initial in anvil.

WRIGHT, L.T.
130b Warren Ln., Wintersville, OH 43953, Phone: 740-317-1404, lt@ltwrightknives.com; Web: www.ltwrightknives.com
Specialties: Hunting, bushcraft and tactical knives. **Patterns:** Drop-point hunters,spear-point bushcraft and tactical. **Technical:** Grinds A2, D2 and O1. **Remarks:** Full-time maker.

WRIGHT, RICHARD S
PO Box 201, 111 Hilltop Dr, Carolina, RI 02812, Phone: 401-364-3579, rswswitchblades@hotmail.com; Web: www.richardswright.com
Specialties: Bolster release switchblades, tactical automatics. **Patterns:** Folding fighters, gents pocket knives, one-of-a-kind high-grade automatics. **Technical:** Reforges and grinds various makers Damascus. Uses a variety of tool steels. Uses natural handle material such as ivory and pearl, extensive file-work on most knives. **Prices:** $850 and up. **Remarks:** Full-time knifemaker with background as a gunsmith. Made first folder in 1991. **Mark:** RSW on blade, all folders are serial numbered.

WRIGHT, ROBERT A
21 Wiley Bottom Rd, Savannah, GA 31411, Phone: 912-598-8239; Cell: 912-656-

9085, maker@robwrightknives.com; Web: www.RobWrightKnives.com
Specialties: Hunting, skinning, fillet, fighting and tactical knives. **Patterns:** Custom designs by client and/or maker. **Technical:** All types of steel, including CPM-S30V, D2, 440C, O1 tool steel and damascus upon request, as well as exotic wood and other high-quality handle materials. **Prices:** $200 and up depending on cost of steel and other materials. **Remarks:** Full-time maker, member of The Knifemakers' Guild and Georgia Custom Knifemaker's Guild. **Mark:** Etched maple leaf with maker's name: R.A. Wright.

WRIGHT, TIMOTHY
PO Box 3746, Sedona, AZ 86340, Phone: 928-282-4180
Specialties: High-tech folders and working knives. **Patterns:** Interframe locking folders, non-inlaid folders, straight hunters and kitchen knives. **Technical:** Grinds BG-42, AEB-L, K190 and Cowry X; works with new steels. All folders can disassemble and are furnished with tools. **Prices:** $150 to $1800; some to $3000. **Remarks:** Full-time maker; first knife sold in 1975. **Mark:** Last name and type of steel used.

WUERTZ, TRAVIS
2487 E Hwy 287, Casa Grande, AZ 85222, Phone: 520-723-4432

WULF, DERRICK
25 Sleepy Hollow Rd, Essex, VT 05452, Phone: 802-777-8766, dickwulf@yahoo.com Web: www.dicksworkshop.com
Specialties: Makes predominantly forged fixed blade knives using carbon steels and his own Damascus.**Mark:** "WULF".

WYATT, WILLIAM R
Box 237, Rainelle, WV 25962, Phone: 304-438-5494
Specialties: Classic and working knives of all designs. **Patterns:** Hunters and utility knives. **Technical:** Forges and grinds saw blades, files and rasps. Prefers stag handles. **Prices:** $45 to $95; some to $350. **Remarks:** Part-time maker; first knife sold in 1990. **Mark:** Last name in star with knife logo.

WYLIE, TOM
Peak Knives, 2 Maun Close, Sutton-In-Ashfield, Notts, England NG17 5JG, tom@peakknives.com
Specialties: Knives for adventure sports and hunting, mainly fixed blades. **Technical:** Damasteel or European stainless steel used predominantly, handle material to suit purpose, embellished as required. Work can either be all handmade or CNC machined. **Prices:** $450+. **Remarks:** Pro-Am maker. **Mark:** Ogram "tinne" in circle of life, sometimes with addition of maker's name.

Y

YASHINSKI, JOHN L
207 N Platt, PO Box 1284, Red Lodge, MT 59068, Phone: 406-446-3916
Specialties: Indian knife sheaths, beaded, tacked, painted rawhide sheaths, antiqued to look old, old beads and other parts, copies of originals. Write with color copies to be made. **Prices:** $100 to $600. Call to discuss price variations.

YESKOO, RICHARD C
76 Beekman Rd, Summit, NJ 07901

YONEYAMA, CHICCHI K.
5-19-8 Nishikicho, Tachikawa-City, Tokyo, JAPAN 190-0022, Phone: 081-1-9047449370, chicchi.ky1007@gmail.com; Web: https://sites.google.com/site/chicchiyoneyama/
Specialties: Folders, hollow ground, lockback and slip-joint folders with interframe handles. **Patterns:** Pocketknives, desk and daily-carry small folders. **Technical:** Stock-removal method on ATS-34, 440C, V10 and SG2/damascus blade steels. **Prices:** $300 to $1,000 and up. **Remarks:** Full-time maker; first knife sold in 1999. **Mark:** Saber tiger mark with logos/Chicchi K. Yoneyama.

YORK, DAVID C
PO Box 3166, Chino Valley, AZ 86323, Phone: 928-636-1709, dmatj@msn.com
Specialties: Working straight knives and folders. **Patterns:** Prefers small hunters and skinners; locking folders. **Technical:** Grinds D2. **Prices:** $75 to $300; some to $600. **Remarks:** Part-time maker; first knife sold in 1975. **Mark:** Last name.

YOSHIHARA, YOSHINDO
8-17-11 Takasago Katsushi, Tokyo, JAPAN

YOSHIKAZU, KAMADA
540-3 Kaisaki Niuta-cho, Tokushima, JAPAN, Phone: 0886-44-2319

YOSHIO, MAEDA
3-12-11 Chuo-cho tamashima, Kurashiki-city, Okayama, JAPAN, Phone: 086-525-2375

YOUNG, BUD
Box 336, Port Hardy, BC, CANADA V0N 2P0, Phone: 250-949-6478
Specialties: Fixed blade, working knives, some fancy. **Patterns:** Drop-points to skinners. **Technical:** Hollow or flat grind, 5160, 440C, mostly ATS-34, satin finish. Using supplied damascus at times. **Prices:** $150 to $2000 CDN. **Remarks:** Spare-time maker; making knives since 1962; first knife sold in 1985. Not taking orders at this time, sell as produced. **Mark:** Name.

YOUNG, CLIFF
Fuente De La Cibeles No 5, Atascadero, San Miguel De Allende, GJ, MEXICO 37700, Phone: 011-52-415-2-57-11
Specialties: Working knives. **Patterns:** Hunters, fighters and fishing knives. **Technical:**

Grinds all; offers D2, 440C and 154CM. **Prices:** Start at $250. **Remarks:** Part-time maker; first knife sold in 1980. **Mark:** Name.

YOUNG, GEORGE
713 Pinoak Dr, Kokomo, IN 46901, Phone: 765-457-8893
Specialties: Fancy/embellished and traditional straight knives and folders of his design and to customer specs. **Patterns:** Hunters, fillet/camp knives and locking folders. **Technical:** Grinds 440C, CPM440V, and stellite 6K. Fancy ivory, black pearl and stag for handles. Filework: all stellite construction (6K and 25 alloys). Offers engraving. **Prices:** $350 to $750; some $1500 to $3000. **Remarks:** Full-time maker; first knife sold in 1954. Doing business as Young's Knives. **Mark:** Last name integral inside Bowie.

YOUNG, JOHN
483 E. 400 S, Ephraim, UT 84627, Phone: 435-340-1417 or 435-283-4555
Patterns: Fighters, hunters and bowies. **Technical:** Stainless steel blades, including ATS-34, 440C and CTS-40CP. **Prices:** $800 to $5,000. **Remarks:** Full-time maker since 2006; first knife sold in 1997. **Mark:** Name, city and state.

YOUNG, RAYMOND L
CUTLER/BLADESMITH, 2922 Hwy 188E, Mt. Ida, AR 71957, Phone: 870-867-3947
Specialties: Cutler-Bladesmith, sharpening service. **Patterns:** Hunter, skinners, fighters, no guard, no ricasso, chef tools. **Technical:** Edge tempered 1095, 516C, mosiac handles, water buffalo and exotic woods. **Prices:** $100 and up. **Remarks:** Federal contractor since 1995. Surgical steel sharpening. **Mark:** R.

YURCO, MICKEY
PO Box 712, Canfield, OH 44406, Phone: 330-533-4928, shorinki@aol.com
Specialties: Working straight knives. **Patterns:** Hunters, utility knives, Bowies and fighters, push knives, claws and other hideouts. **Technical:** Grinds 440C, ATS-34 and 154CM; likes mirror and satin finishes. **Prices:** $20 to $500. **Remarks:** Part-time maker; first knife sold in 1983. **Mark:** Name, steel, serial number.

Z

ZAFEIRIADIS, KONSTANTINOS
Dionyson Street, Marathon Attiki, GREECE 19005, Phone: 011-30697724-5771 or 011-30697400-6245
Specialties: Fixed blades, one-of-a-kind swords with bronze fittings made using the lost wax method. **Patterns:** Ancient Greek, central Asian, Viking, bowies, hunting knives, fighters, daggers. **Technical:** Forges 5160, O1 and maker's own damascus. **Prices:** $1,100 and up. **Remarks:** Full-time maker; first knife sold in 2010. **Mark:** (backward K) ZK.

ZAHM, KURT
488 Rio Casa, Indialantic, FL 32903, Phone: 407-777-4860
Specialties: Working straight knives of his design or to customer specs. **Patterns:** Daggers, fancy fighters, Bowies, hunters and utility knives. **Technical:** Grinds D2, 440C; likes filework. **Prices:** $75 to $1000. **Remarks:** Part-time maker; first knife sold in 1985. **Mark:** Last name.

ZAKABI, CARL S
PO Box 893161, Mililani Town, HI 96789-0161, Phone: 808-626-2181
Specialties: User-grade straight knives of his design, cord wrapped and bare steel handles exclusively. **Patterns:** Fighters, hunters and utility/camp knives. **Technical:** Grinds 440C and ATS-34. **Prices:** $90 to $400. **Remarks:** Spare-time maker; first knife sold in 1988. Doing business as Zakabi's Knifeworks LLC. **Mark:** Last name and state inside a Hawaiian sharktooth dagger.

ZAKHAROV, GLADISTON
Rua Pernambuca, 175-Rio Comprido (Long River), Jacaret-SP, BRAZIL 12302-070, Brazil, Phone: 55 12 3958 4021, Fax: 55 12 3958 4103, arkhip@terra.com.br; Web: www.arkhip.com.br
Specialties: Using straight knives of his design. **Patterns:** Hunters, kitchen, utility/camp and barbecue knives. **Technical:** Grinds his own "secret steel." **Prices:** $30 to $200. **Remarks:** Full-time maker. **Mark:** Arkhip Special Knives.

ZBORIL, TERRY
5320 CR 130, Caldwell, TX 77836, Phone: 979-535-4157, tzboril@tconline.net
Specialties: ABS Journeyman Smith.

ZEMBKO III, JOHN
140 Wilks Pond Rd, Berlin, CT 06037, Phone: 860-828-3503, johnzembko@hotmail.com
Specialties: Working knives of his design or to customer specs. **Patterns:** Likes to use stabilized high-figured woods. **Technical:** Grinds ATS-34, A2, D2; forges O1, 1095; grinds Damasteel. **Prices:** $50 to $400; some higher. **Remarks:** First knife sold in 1987. **Mark:** Name.

ZEMITIS, JOE
14 Currawong Rd, Cardiff Heights, NSW, AUSTRALIA 2285, Phone: 0249549907, jjvzem@bigpond.com
Specialties: Traditional working straight knives. **Patterns:** Hunters, Bowies, tantos, fighters and camp knives. **Technical:** Grinds O1, D2, W2 and 440C; makes his own Damascus. Embellishes; offers engraving. **Prices:** $150 to $3000. **Remarks:** Full-time maker; first knife sold in 1983. **Mark:** First initial, last name and country, or last name.

ZERMENO, WILLIAM D.
9131 Glenshadow Dr, Houston, TX 77088, Phone: 281-726-2459, will@wdzknives.com Web: www.wdzknives.com
Specialties: Tactical/utility folders and fixed blades. **Patterns:** Frame lock and liner lock

folders the majority of which incorporate flippers and utility fixed blades. **Technical:** Grinds CPM 154, S30V, 3V and stainless Damascus. **Prices:** $250 -$600. **Remarks:** Part-time maker, first knife sold in 2008. Doing business as www.wdzknives.com. **Mark:** WDZ over logo.

ZIEBA, MICHAEL

95 Commercial St., #4, Brooklyn, NY 11222, Phone: 347-335-9944, ziebametal@gmail.com; Web: www.ziebaknives.com or www.brooklynknives.com
  Specialties: High-end kitchen knives under maker's last name, ZIEBA, also tactical knives under HUSSAR name. **Technical:** Uses stainless steels: CPM S30V, CPM S35VN, CPM S60V, CPM D2 and AEB-L, and high-carbon steels: 52100 and Aogami #2. Forges carbon steel in his shop. **Remarks:** Full-time maker. Marks: Feather logo (kitchen knives only with 24k gold as a standard), ZIEBA (kitchen knives and folders) and "H" Hussar (tactical).

ZIMA, MICHAEL F

732 State St, Ft. Morgan, CO 80701, Phone: 970-867-6078, Web: http://www.zimaknives.com
  Specialties: Working and collector quality straight knives and folders. **Patterns:** Hunters, lock backs, LinerLock®, slip joint and automatic folders. **Technical:** Grinds Damascus, 440C, ATS-34 and 154CM. **Prices:** $200 and up. **Remarks:** Full-time maker; first knife sold in 1982. **Mark:** Last name.

ZINKER, BRAD

BZ KNIVES, 1591 NW 17 St, Homestead, FL 33030, Phone: 305-216-0404, bzinker@gmail.com
  Specialties: Fillets, folders and hunters. **Technical:** Uses ATS-34 and stainless Damascus. **Prices:** $200 to $600. **Remarks:** Voting member of Knifemakers Guild and Florida Knifemakers Association. **Mark:** Offset connected initials BZ.

ZIRBES, RICHARD

Neustrasse 15, Niederkail, GERMANY 54526, Phone: 0049 6575 1371, r.zirbes@freenet.de Web: www.zirbes-knives.com www.zirbes-messer.de
  Specialties: Fancy embellished knives with engraving and self-made scrimshaw (scrimshaw made by maker). High-tech working knives and high-tech hunters, boots, fighters and folders. All knives made by hand. **Patterns:** Boots, fighters, folders, hunters. **Technical:** Uses only the best steels for blade material like CPM-T 440V, CPM-T 420V, ATS-34, D2, C440, stainless Damascus or steel according to customer's desire. **Prices:** Working knives and hunters: $200 to $600. Fancy embellished knives with engraving and/or scrimshaw: $800 to $3000. **Remarks:** Part-time maker; first knife sold in 1991. Member of the German Knifemaker Guild. **Mark:** Zirbes or R. Zirbes.

ZOWADA, TIM

4509 E Bear River Rd, Boyne Falls, MI 49713, Phone: 231-881-5056, tim@tzknives.com Web: www.tzknives.com
  Specialties: Working knives and straight razors. **Technical:** Forges O1, L6, his own Damascus and smelted steel "Michi-Gane". **Prices:** $200 to $2500; some to $5000. **Remarks:** Full-time maker; first knife sold in 1980. **Mark:** Gothic, lower case "TZ"

ZSCHERNY, MICHAEL

1840 Rock Island Dr, Ely, IA 52227, Phone: 319-321-5833, zschernyknives@aol.com
  Specialties: Quality folders--slip joints and flipper folders. **Patterns:** Liner-lock and lock-back folders in titanium, working straight knives. **Technical:** Grinds ATS-34 and commercial damascus, prefers natural materials such as pearls and ivory. Uses Timascus, mokume, san mai and carbon fibers. **Prices:** Start at $600. **Remarks:** Full-time maker, first knife sold in 1978. **Mark:** Last name with image of a scorpion.

AK

Barlow, Jana Poirier	Anchorage
Brennan, Judson	Delta Junction
Breuer, Lonnie	Wasilla
Broome, Thomas A	Kenai
Chamberlin, John A	Anchorage
Cornwell, Jeffrey	Anchorage
Desrosiers, Adam	Petersburg
Desrosiers, Haley	Petersburg
Dufour, Arthur J	Anchorage
England, Virgil	Anchorage
Flint, Robert	Anchorage
Gouker, Gary B	Sitka
Harvey, Mel	Nenana
Hibben, Westley G	Anchorage
Hook, Bob	North Pole
Kelsey, Nate	Palmer
Knapp, Mark	Fairbanks
Lance, Bill	Palmer
Lance, Lucas	Wasilla
Malaby, Raymond J	Juneau
Mcfarlin, Eric E	Kodiak
Miller, Nate	Fairbanks
Miller, Terry	Healy
Mirabile, David	Juneau
Moore, Marve	Willow
Parrish Iii, Gordon A	North Pole
Stegall, Keith	Wasilla
Van Cleve, Steve	Sutton

AL

Alverson, Tim (R.V.)	Arab
Batson, James	Huntsville
Baxter, Dale	Trinity
Bell, Tony	Woodland
Bowles, Chris	Reform
Brothers, Dennis L.	Oneonta
Coffman, Danny	Jacksonville
Conn Jr., C T	Attalla
Daniels, Alex	Town Creek
Dark, Robert	Oxford
Daughtery, Tony	Loxley
Deibert, Michael	Trussville
Durham, Kenneth	Cherokee
Elrod, Roger R	Enterprise
Gilbreath, Randall	Dora
Golden, Randy	Montgomery
Grizzard, Jim	Oxford
Hammond, Jim	Birmingham
Heeter, Todd S.	Mobile
Howard, Durvyn M.	Hokes Bluff
Howell, Keith A.	Oxford
Howell, Len	Opelika
Howell, Ted	Wetumpka
Huckabee, Dale	Maylene
Hulsey, Hoyt	Attalla
Mccullough, Jerry	Georgiana
Mcnees, Jonathan	Northport
Militano, Tom	Jacksonville
Morris, C H	Frisco City
Pardue, Melvin M	Repton
Ploppert, Tom	Cullman
Russell, Tom	Jacksonville
Sinyard, Cleston S	Elberta
Smith, Lacy	Jacksonville
Thomas, David E	Lillian
Washburn Jr., Robert Lee	Tuscaloosa
Watson, Billy	Deatsville

AR

Anders, David	Center Ridge
Ardwin, Corey	Bryant
Barnes Jr., Cecil C.	Center Ridge
Brown, Jim	Little Rock
Browning, Steven W	Benton
Bullard, Benoni	Bradford
Bullard, Tom	Flippin
Chambers, Ronny	Beebe
Cook, James R	Nashville
Copeland, Thom	Nashville
Cox, Larry	Murfreesboro
Crawford, Pat And Wes	West Memphis
Crotts, Dan	Elm Springs
Crowell, James L	Mtn. View
Dozier, Bob	Springdale
Duvall, Fred	Benton
Echols, Rodger	Nashville
Edge, Tommy	Cash
Ferguson, Lee	Hindsville
Fisk, Jerry	Nashville
Fitch, John S	Clinton
Flournoy, Joe	El Dorado
Foster, Ronnie E	Morrilton
Foster, Timothy L	El Dorado
Frizzell, Ted	West Fork
Gadberry, Emmet	Hattieville
Greenaway, Don	Fayetteville
Herring, Morris	Dyer
Hutchinson, Alan	Conway
Kirkes, Bill	Little Rock
Koster, Daniel	Bentonville
Krein, Tom	Gentry
Lawrence, Alton	De Queen
Lemoine, David C	Mountain Home
Livesay, Newt	Siloam Springs
Lunn, Gail	Mountain Home
Lunn, Larry A	Mountain Home
Lynch, Tad	Beebe
Maringer, Tom	Springdale
Martin, Bruce E	Prescott
Martin, Hal W	Morrilton
Massey, Roger	Texarkana
Newberry, Allen	Lowell
Newton, Ron	London
Nolte, Barbie	Lowell
Nolte, Steve	Lowell
Olive, Michael E	Leslie
Passmore, Jimmy D	Hoxie
Pearce, Logan	De Queen
Perry, Jim	Hope
Perry, John	Mayflower
Peterson, Lloyd (Pete) C	Clinton
Polk, Clifton	Van Buren
Polk, Rusty	Van Buren
Quattlebaum, Craig	Beebe
Randow, Ralph	Greenbrier
Red, Vernon	Conway
Reeves, J.R.	Texarkana
Rhea, Lin	Prattsville
Richards, Ralph (Bud)	Bauxite
Roberts, T. C. (Terry)	Siloam Springs
Seward, Ben	Austin
Stanley, John	Crossett
Stout, Charles	Gillham
Sweaza, Dennis	Austin
Townsend, Allen Mark	Texarkana
Townsley, Russell	Floral
Upton, Tom	Rogers
Walker, Jim	Morrilton
Ward, Chuck	Benton
White, Bryce	Little Rock
Young, Raymond L	Mt. Ida

AZ

Allan, Todd	Glendale
Ammons, David C	Tucson
Bennett, Glen C	Tucson
Birdwell, Ira Lee	Congress
Boye, David	Dolan Springs
Cheatham, Bill	Laveen
Choate, Milton	Somerton
Clark, R W	Surprise
Dawson, Barry	Prescott Valley
Dawson, Lynn	Prescott Valley
Deubel, Chester J.	Tucson
Dodd, Robert F	Camp Verde
Fuegen, Larry	Prescott
Genovese, Rick	Tonto Basin
Goo, Tai	Tucson
Hancock, Tim	Scottsdale
Harris, John	Quartzsite
Hoel, Steve	Pine
Holder, D'Alton	Wickenburg
Jackson, Laramie	Claysprings
Karp, Bob	Phoenix
Kiley, Mike And Jandy	Chino Valley
Kopp, Todd M	Apache Jct.
Lee, Randy	St. Johns
Mcfall, Ken	Lakeside
Mcfarlin, J W	Lake Havasu City
Miller, Michael	Kingman
Montell, Ty	Thatcher
Mooney, Mike	Queen Creek
Newhall, Tom	Tucson
Purvis, Bob And Ellen	Tucson
Robbins, Bill	Sierra Vista
Rybar Jr., Raymond B	Camp Verde
States, Joshua C	New River
Tamboli, Michael	Glendale
Tyre, Michael A	Wickenburg
Weiss, Charles L	Waddell
Wick, Jonathan P.	Hereford
Wolf, Bill	Phoenix
Wright, Timothy	Sedona
Wuertz, Travis	Casa Grande
York, David C	Chino Valley

CA

Abegg, Arnie	Huntington Beach
Adkins, Richard L	Mission Viejo
Andrade, Don Carlos	Los Osos
Athey, Steve	Riverside
Barnes, Gregory	Altadena
Barnes, Roger	Bay Point
Barron, Brian	San Mateo
Begg, Todd M.	Petaluma
Benson, Don	Escalon
Berger, Max A.	Carmichael
Bolduc, Gary	Corona
Bost, Roger E	Palos Verdes
Boyd, Francis	Berkeley
Breshears, Clint	Manhattan Beach
Brooks, Buzz	Los Angles
Brous, Jason	Buellton
Browne, Rick	Upland
Bruce, Richard L.	Yankee Hill
Butler, Bart	Ramona
Cabrera, Sergio B	Wilmington
Cantrell, Kitty D	Ramona
Caston, Darriel	Folsom
Caswell, Joe	Newbury
Clinco, Marcus	Venice
Coffey, Bill	Clovis
Coleman, John A	Citrus Heights
Colwell, Kevin	Cheshire
Connolly, James	Oroville
Cucchiara, Matt	Fresno
Davis, Charlie	Lakeside
De Maria Jr., Angelo	Carmel Valley
Dion, Greg	Oxnard
Dobratz, Eric	Laguna Hills
Doolittle, Mike	Novato
Driscoll, Mark	La Mesa
Dwyer, Duane	Escondido
Ellis, William Dean	Sanger
Emerson, Ernest R	Harbor City
English, Jim	Jamul
Ernest, Phil (Pj)	Whittier
Essegian, Richard	Fresno
Felix, Alexander	Torrance
Ferguson, Jim	Lakewood
Finney, Garett	Loomis
Forrest, Brian	Descanso
Fraley, D B	Dixon
Fred, Reed Wyle	Sacramento
Freeman, Matt	Fresno
Freer, Ralph	Seal Beach
Fulton, Mickey	Willows
Girtner, Joe	Brea
Guarnera, Anthony R	Quartzhill
Hall, Jeff	Paso Robles
Hardy, Scott	Placerville
Harris, Jay	Redwood City
Helton, Roy	San Diego
Herndon, Wm R "Bill"	Acton

Hink Iii, Les	Stockton
Hoy, Ken	North Fork
Humenick, Roy	Rescue
Jacks, Jim	Covina
Jackson, David	Lemoore
Jensen, John Lewis	Pasadena
Johnson, Randy	Turlock
Kazsuk, David	Anza
Kelly, Dave	Los Angeles
Keyes, Dan	Chino
Kilpatrick, Christian A	Citrus Hieghts
Koster, Steven C	Huntington Beach
Larson, Richard	Turlock
Leland, Steve	Fairfax
Lin, Marcus	Murrieta
Lockett, Sterling	Burbank
Luchini, Bob	Palo Alto
Maccaughtry, Scott F.	Camarillo
Mackie, John	Whittier
Massey, Ron	Joshua Tree
Mata, Leonard	San Diego
Maxwell, Don	Clovis
Mcabee, William	Colfax
Mcclure, Michael	Menlo Park
Mcgrath, Patrick T	Westchester
Melin, Gordon C	La Mirada
Meloy, Sean	Lemon Grove
Montano, Gus A	San Diego
Morgan, Jeff	Santee
Moses, Steven	Santa Ana
Mutz, Jeff	Rancho Cucamonga
Naten, Greg	Bakersfield
Orton, Rich	Covina
Osborne, Donald H	Clovis
Palm, Rik	San Diego
Panchenko, Serge	Citrus Heights
Pendleton, Lloyd	Volcano
Perry, Chris	Fresno
Pfanenstiel, Dan	Modesto
Pitt, David F	Anderson
Quesenberry, Mike	Blairsden
Randall, Patrick	Newbury Park
Rozas, Clark D	Wilmington
Schmitz, Raymond E	Valley Center
Schneider, Herman J.	Apple Valley
Schroen, Karl	Sebastopol
Sharp, David	Hesperia
Sibrian, Aaron	Ventura
Sjostrand, Kevin	Visalia
Slobodian, Scott	San Andreas
Smith, Shawn	Clouis
Sornberger, Jim	Volcano
Stapel, Chuck	Glendale
Steinberg, Al	Laguna Woods
Stimps, Jason M	Orange
Strider, Mick	Escondido
Terrill, Stephen	Springville
Tingle, Dennis P	Jackson
Torres, Henry	Clovis
Vagnino, Michael	Visalia
Velick, Sammy	Los Angeles
Warren, Al	Roseville
Watanabe, Wayne	Montebello
Weinstock, Robert	San Francisco
Wilburn, Aaron	Redding
Wilson, Philip C	Mountain Ranch
Wilson, Ron	Morro Bay

CO

Anderson, Mel	Hotchkiss
Booco, Gordon	Hayden
Brock, Kenneth L	Allenspark
Burrows, Chuck	Durango
Corich, Vance	Morrison
Dannemann, Randy	Hotchkiss
Davis, Don	Loveland
Dennehy, John D	Loveland
Dill, Robert	Loveland
Fairly, Daniel	Bayfield
Fredeen, Graham	Colorado Springs
Fronefield, Daniel	Peyton
Graham, Levi	Greeley

Grebe, Gordon S	Canon City
Hackney, Dana A.	Monument
High, Tom	Alamosa
Hockensmith, Dan	Berthoud
Hughes, Ed	Grand Junction
Hughes, Tony	Littleton
Irie, Michael L	Colorado Springs
Kitsmiller, Jerry	Montrose
Leck, Dal	Hayden
Mcwilliams, Sean	Carbondale
Miller, Hanford J	Lakespur
Miller, M A	Northglenn
Nolen, Steve	Longmont
Ott, Fred	Durango
Owens, John	Nathrop
Rexford, Todd	Woodland Park
Roberts, Chuck	Golden
Rollert, Steve	Keenesburg
Ronzio, N. Jack	Fruita
Sanders, Bill	Mancos
Thompson, Lloyd	Pagosa Springs
Waites, Richard L	Broomfield
Watson, Bert	Westminster
Wilson, James G	Estes Park
Wood, Owen Dale	Arvada
Zima, Michael F	Ft. Morgan
Redd, Bill	Broomfield

CT

Buebendorf, Robert E	Monroe
Chapo, William G	Wilton
Cross, Kevin	Portland
Framski, Walter P	Prospect
Jean, Gerry	Manchester
Loukides, David E	Cheshire
Meyer, Christopher J	Tolland
Plunkett, Richard	West Cornwall
Putnam, Donald S	Wethersfield
Rainville, Richard	Salem
Turecek, Jim	Ansonia
Vitale, Mace	Guilford
Zembko Iii, John	Berlin

DE

Willey, Wg	Greenwood

FL

Adams, Les	Hialeah
Alexander,, Oleg, And Cossack Blades Wellington	
Anders, Jerome	Miramar
Angell, Jon	Hawthorne
Atkinson, Dick	Wausau
Bacon, David R.	Bradenton
Barnes, Gary L.	Defuniak Springs
Barry Iii, James J.	West Palm Beach
Beers, Ray	Lake Wales
Benjamin Jr., George	Kissimmee
Blackwood, Neil	Orlando
Bosworth, Dean	Key Largo
Bradley, John	Pomona Park
Bray Jr., W Lowell	New Port Richey
Brown, Harold E	Arcadia
Butler, John	Havana
Chase, Alex	DeLand
Clark, Jason	O'Brien
D'Andrea, John	Citrus Springs
Davis Jr., Jim	Zephyrhills
Dietzel, Bill	Middleburg
Dintruff, Chuck	Seffner
Dotson, Tracy	Baker
Ellerbe, W B	Geneva
Ellis, Willy B	Tarpon Springs
Enos Iii, Thomas M	Orlando
Ferrara, Thomas	Naples
Fowler, Charles R	Ft McCoy
Franklin, Mike	Clermont
Gamble, Roger	Newberry
Gardner, Robert	West Palm Beach
Ghio, Paolo	Pensacola
Goers, Bruce	Lakeland
Granger, Paul J	Largo

Greene, Steve	Intercession City
Griffin Jr., Howard A	Davie
Grospitch, Ernie	Orlando
Heaney, John D	Haines City
Heitler, Henry	Tampa
Hodge Iii, John	Palatka
Hostetler, Larry	Fort Pierce
Hostetter, Wally	San Mateo
Humphreys, Joel	Lake Placid
Hunter, Richard D	Alachua
Hytovick, Joe "Hy"	Dunnellon
Jernigan, Steve	Milton
Johanning Custom Knives, Tom	Sarasota
Johnson, John R	Plant City
King, Bill	Tampa
Krapp, Denny	Apopka
Levengood, Bill	Tampa
Lewis, Mike	DeBary
Long, Glenn A	Dunnellon
Lovestrand, Schuyler	Vero Beach
Lozier, Don	Ocklawaha
Lyle Iii, Ernest L	Chiefland
Mandt, Joe	St. Petersburg
Mason, Bill	Hobe Sound
Mcdonald, Robert J	Loxahatchee
Miller, Ronald T	Largo
Miller, Steve	Clearwater
Newton, Larry	Jacksonville
Ochs, Charles F	Largo
Owens, Donald	Melbourne
Parker, Cliff	Zephyrhills
Partridge, Jerry D.	DeFuniak Springs
Pattay, Rudy	Citrus Springs
Pendray, Alfred H	Williston
Philippe, D A	The Villages
Piergallini, Daniel E	Plant City
Randall Made Knives,	Orlando
Reed, John M	Port Orange
Renner, Terry	Palmetto
Robinson, Calvin	Pace
Robinson Iii, Rex R	Leesburg
Rodkey, Dan	Hudson
Romeis, Gordon	Fort Myers
Russ, Ron	Williston
Schwarzer, Lora Sue	Crescent City
Schwarzer, Stephen	Crescent City
Smith, Michael J	Brandon
Stapleton, William E	Merritt Island
Steck, Van R	Orange City
Stephan, Daniel	Valrico
Stipes, Dwight	Palm City
Straight, Kenneth J	Largo
Tabor, Tim	Lutz
Turnbull, Ralph A	Spring Hill
Vogt, Donald J	Tampa
Watson, Tom	Panama City
Weiland Jr., J Reese	Riverview
Wicker, Donnie R	Panama City
Wilson, Stan	Lithia
Zahm, Kurt	Indialantic
Zinker, Brad	Homestead

GA

Arrowood, Dale	Sharpsburg
Ashworth, Boyd	Powder Springs
Barker, John	Cumming
Barker, Robert G.	Bishop
Bentley, C L	Albany
Bish, Hal	Jonesboro
Brach, Paul	Cumming
Bradley, Dennis	Blairsville
Buckner, Jimmie H	Putney
Busbie, Jeff	Bloomingdale
Cambron, Henry	Dallas
Chamblin, Joel	Concord
Crockford, Jack	Chamblee
Daniel, Travis E	Thomaston
Davidson, Scott	Alto
Davis, Steve	Powder Springs
Fowler, Stephan	Acworth
Frost, Dewayne	Barnesville
Gaines, Buddy	Commerce

Gatlin, Steve	Leesburg
Glover, Warren D	Cleveland
Greene, David	Covington
Hammond, Hank	Leesburg
Hammond, Ray	Woodstock
Hardy, Douglas E	Franklin
Hensley, Wayne	Conyers
Hewitt, Ronald "Cotton"	Adel
Hinson And Son, R	Columbus
Hoffman, Kevin L	Savannah
Hossom, Jerry	Duluth
Kimsey, Kevin	Cartersville
King, Fred	Cartersville
Knott, Steve	Guyton
Landers, John	Newnan
Lockett, Lowell C.	Canton
Lonewolf, J Aguirre	Demorest
Mathews, Charlie And Harry	Statesboro
Mcgill, John	Blairsville
Mitchell, James A	Columbus
Moncus, Michael Steven	Smithville
Parks, John	Jefferson
Peters, Daniel	Columbus
Poole, Marvin O	Commerce
Powell, Robert Clark	Smarr
Prater, Mike	Flintstone
Price, Timmy	Blairsville
Pridgen Jr., Larry	Fitzgerald
Ragsdale, James D	Ellijay
Roghmans, Mark	LaGrange
Rosenfeld, Bob	Atlanta
Sangster, Joe	Vienna
Sculley, Peter E	Rising Fawn
Snow, Bill	Columbus
Sowell, Bill	Macon
Stafford, Richard	Warner Robins
Thompson, Kenneth	Duluth
Tomey, Kathleen	Macon
Whetsell, Alex	Haralson
White, Garrett	Hartwell
White, Lou	Ranger
Wright, Robert A	Savannah

HI

Evans, Vincent K And Grace	Keaau
Gibo, George	Hilo
Lui, Ronald M	Honolulu
Mann, Tim	Honokaa
Matsuoka, Scot	Mililani
Mayo Jr., Tom	Waialua
Mitsuyuki, Ross	Honolulu
Onion, Kenneth J	Kaneohe
Ouye, Keith	Honolulu
Salter, Gregg	Waikoloa
Watanabe, Melvin	Kailua
Zakabi, Carl S	Mililani Town

IA

Brooker, Dennis	Chariton
Brower, Max	Boone
Clark, Howard F	Runnells
Cockerham, Lloyd	Denham Springs
Helscher, John W	Washington
Lainson, Tony	Council Bluffs
Lewis, Bill	Riverside
Mckiernan, Stan	Lamoni
Miller, James P	Fairbank
Thie, Brian	Burlington
Trindle, Barry	Earlham
Westberg, Larry	Algona
Zscherny, Michael	Ely

ID

Alderman, Robert	Sagle
Bair, Mark	Firth
Bloodworth Custom Knives,	Meridian
Burke, Bill	Boise
Eddy, Hugh E	Caldwell
Farr, Dan	Post Falls
Hawk, Grant And Gavin	Idaho City
Hogan, Thomas R	Boise
Horton, Scot	Buhl

Howe, Tori	Athol
Mann, Michael L	Spirit Lake
Metz, Greg T	Cascade
Patton, Dick And Rob	Nampa
Quarton, Barr	McCall
Reeve, Chris	Boise
Rohn, Fred	Coeur d'Alene
Sawby, Scott	Sandpoint
Sparks, Bernard	Dingle
Steiger, Monte L	Genesee
Tippetts, Colten	Hidden Springs
Towell, Dwight L	Midvale
Trace Rinaldi Custom Blades,	Plummer

IL

Bloomer, Alan T	Maquon
Camerer, Craig	Chesterfield
Cook, Louise	Ozark
Cook, Mike	Ozark
Detmer, Phillip	Breese
Dicristofano, Anthony P	Melrose Park
Eaker, Allen L	Paris
Fiorini, Bill	Grayville
Hall, Scott M.	Geneseo
Hawes, Chuck	Weldon
Heath, William	Bondville
Hill, Rick	Maryville
Knuth, Joseph E	Rockford
Kovar, Eugene	Evergreen Park
Leone, Nick	Pontoon Beach
Markley, Ken	Sparta
Meers, Andrew	Carbondale
Meier, Daryl	Carbondale
Myers, Paul	Wood River
Myers, Steve	Springfield
Nowland, Rick	Waltonville
Pellegrin, Mike	Troy
Pritchard, Ron	Dixon
Roosevelt, Russell	Albion
Rosenbaugh, Ron	Crystal Lake
Rossdeutscher, Robert N	Arlington Heights
Rzewnicki, Gerald	Elizabeth
Schneider, Craig M	Claremont
Smale, Charles J	Waukegan
Smith, John M	Centralia
Todd, Richard C	Chambersburg
Veit, Michael	LaSalle
Voss, Ben	Victoria
Werth, George W	Poplar Grove
West, Charles A	Centralia
Wheeler, Robert	Bradley
White, Robert J	Gilson

IN

Ball, Ken	Mooresville
Barkes, Terry	Edinburgh
Barrett, Rick L. (Toshi Hisa)	Goshen
Bose, Reese	Shelburn
Bose, Tony	Shelburn
Chaffee, Jeff L	Morris
Claiborne, Jeff	Franklin
Cramer, Brent	Wheatland
Crowl, Peter	Waterloo
Curtiss, David	Granger
Damlovac, Sava	Indianapolis
Darby, Jed	Greensburg
Fitzgerald, Dennis M	Fort Wayne
Fraps, John R	Indianapolis
Good, D.R.	Tipton
Harding, Chad	Solsberry
Imel, Billy Mace	New Castle
Johnson, C E Gene	Chesterton
Kain, Charles	Indianapolis
Keeslar, Steven C	Hamilton
Keeton, William L	Laconia
Kinker, Mike	Greensburg
Largin, Ken	Connersville
Mayville, Oscar L	Marengo
Minnick, Jim & Joyce	Middletown
Patton, Phillip	Yoder
Quakenbush, Thomas C	Ft Wayne
Robertson, Leo D	Indianapolis

Seib, Steve	Evansville
Shull, James	Rensselaer
Smock, Timothy E	Marion
Thayer, Danny O	Romney
Young, George	Kokomo

KS

Bradburn, Gary	Wichita
Burrows, Stephen R	Humboldt
Chard, Gordon R	Iola
Craig, Roger L	Topeka
Culver, Steve	Meriden
Darpinian, Dave	Olathe
Dawkins, Dudley L	Topeka
Dick, Dan	Hutchinson
Evans, Phil	Columbus
Hegwald, J L	Humboldt
Herman, Tim	Olathe
Keranen, Paul	Tacumseh
King Jr., Harvey G	Alta Vista
Kraft, Steve	Abilene
Lamb, Curtis J	Ottawa
Magee, Jim	Salina
Petersen, Dan L	Auburn
Stice, Douglas W	Wichita

KY

Addison, Kyle A	Hazel
Baskett, Barbara	Eastview
Baskett, Lee Gene	Eastview
Bybee, Barry J	Cadiz
Carter, Mike	Louisville
Downing, Larry	Bremen
Dunn, Steve	Smiths Grove
Edwards, Mitch	Glasgow
Finch, Ricky D	West Liberty
Fister, Jim	Simpsonville
France, Dan	Cawood
Frederick, Aaron	West Liberty
Greco, John	Greensburg
Hibben, Daryl	LaGrange
Hibben, Gil	LaGrange
Hibben, Joleen	LaGrange
Hoke, Thomas M	LaGrange
Holbrook, H L	Sandy Hook
Keeslar, Joseph F	Almo
Pease, W D	Ewing
Pierce, Harold L	Louisville
Rados, Jerry F	Columbia
Richerson, Ron	Greenburg
Rigney Jr., Willie	Bronston
Smith, John W	West Liberty
Soaper, Max H.	Henderson
Steier, David	Louisville
Vance, David	West Liberty
Wallingford Jr., Charles W	Union

LA

Barker, Reggie	Springhill
Blaum, Roy	Covington
Caldwell, Bill	West Monroe
Calvert Jr., Robert W (Bob)	Rayville
Capdepon, Randy	Carencro
Capdepon, Robert	Carencro
Chauvin, John	Scott
Dake, C M	New Orleans
Dake, Mary H	New Orleans
Durio, Fred	Opelousas
Faucheaux, Howard J	Loreauville
Fontenot, Gerald J	Mamou
Gorenflo, James T (Jt)	Baton Rouge
Graves, Dan	Shreveport
Johnson, Gordon A.	Choudrant
Ki, Shiva	Baton Rouge
Laurent, Kermit	LaPlace
Lemaire, Ryan M.	Abbeville
Leonard, Randy Joe	Sarepta
Mitchell, Max Dean And Ben	Leesville
Phillips, Dennis	Independence
Potier, Timothy F	Oberlin
Primos, Terry	Shreveport
Provenzano, Joseph D	Ponchatoula

Randall Jr., James W — Keithville
Reggio Jr., Sidney J — Sun
Sanders, Michael M — Ponchatoula
Tilton, John — Iowa
Trisler, Kenneth W — Rayville
Wilson, P.R. "Regan" — Scott
Winn, Marvin — Sunset

MA

Banaitis, Romas — Medway
Cooper, Paul — Woburn
Dailey, G E — Seekonk
Dugdale, Daniel J. — Walpole
Gedraitis, Charles J — Holden
Grossman, Stewart — Clinton
Hinman, Theodore — Greenfield
Jarvis, Paul M — Cambridge
Khalsa, Jot Singh — Millis
Klein, Kevin — Boston
Kubasek, John A — Easthampton
Lapen, Charles — W. Brookfield
Little, Larry — Spencer
Martin, Randall J — Bridgewater
Mcluin, Tom — Dracut
Moore, Michael Robert — Lowell
Rebello, Indian George — New Bedford
Rizzi, Russell J — Ashfield
Rua, Gary — Fall River
Saviano, James — Douglas
Siska, Jim — Westfield
Smith, J D — Roxbury
Stuart, Mason — Mansfield
Vining, Bill — Methuen

MD

Bagley, R. Keith — White Plains
Barnes, Aubrey G. — Hagerstown
Cohen, N J (Norm) — Baltimore
Dement, Larry — Prince Fredrick
Fuller, Jack A — New Market
Gossman, Scott — Whiteford
Hart, Bill — Pasadena
Heard, Tom — Waldorf
Hendrickson, E Jay — Frederick
Hendrickson, Shawn — Knoxville
Kreh, Lefty — "Cockeysville"
Mccarley, John — Taneytown
Mcgowan, Frank E — Sykesville
Merchant, Ted — White Hall
Nicholson, R. Kent — Monkton
Nuckels, Stephen J — Hagerstown
Presti, Matt — Union Bridge
Sentz, Mark C — Taneytown
Smit, Glenn — Aberdeen
Sontheimer, G Douglas — Gaithersburg
Spickler, Gregory Noble — Sharpsburg
St. Clair, Thomas K — Monrovia
Walker, Bill — Stevensville

ME

Bohrmann, Bruce — Yarmouth
Breda, Ben — Hope
Ceprano, Peter J. — Auburn
Coombs Jr., Lamont — Bucksport
Gray, Daniel — Brownville
Hillman, Charles — Friendship
Leavitt Jr., Earl F — E. Boothbay
Oyster, Lowell R — Corinth
Sharrigan, Mudd — Wiscasset
Steingass, T.K. — Bucksport

MI

Ackerson, Robin E — Buchanan
Alcorn, Douglas A. — Chesaning
Andrews, Eric — Grand Ledge
Arms, Eric — Tustin
Behnke, William — Kingsley
Booth, Philip W — Ithaca
Carr, Tim — Muskegon
Carroll, Chad — Grant
Casey, Kevin — Hickory Corners

Cashen, Kevin R — Hubbardston
Cook, Mike A — Portland
Cousino, George — Onsted
Cowles, Don — Royal Oak
Doyle, John — Gladwin
Ealy, Delbert — Indian River
Erickson, Walter E. — Atlanta
Gordon, Larry B — Farmington Hills
Gottage, Dante — Clinton Twp.
Gottage, Judy — Clinton Twp.
Haas, Randy — Marlette
Harm, Paul W — Attica
Harrison, Brian — Cedarville
Hartman, Arlan (Lanny) — Baldwin
Hoffman, Jay — Munising
Hughes, Daryle — Nunica
Lankton, Scott — Ann Arbor
Lark, David — Kingsley
Logan, Iron John — Leslie
Marsh, Jeremy — Ada
Mills, Louis G — Ann Arbor
Morris, Michael S. — Yale
Nevling, Mark — Owosso
Noren, Douglas E — Springlake
Parker, Robert Nelson — Royal Oak
Repke, Mike — Bay City
Rose Ii, Doun T. — Fife Lake
Sakmar, Mike — Howell
Sandberg, Ronald B — Brownstown
Tally, Grant — Flat Rock
Van Eizenga, Jerry W — Nunica
Vasquez, Johnny David — Wyandotte
Viste, James — Hamtramck
Webster, Bill — Three Rivers
Welling, Ronald L — Grand Haven
White, Richard T — Grosse Pointe Farms
Whittaker, Wayne — Metamore
Wood, Webster — Atlanta
Zowada, Tim — Boyne Falls

MN

Andersen, Karl B. — Warba
Burns, Robert — Carver
Davis, Joel — Albert Lea
Hagen, Doc — Pelican Rapids
Hansen, Robert W — Cambridge
Hebeisen, Jeff — Hopkins
Johnson, Jerry L — Worthington
Johnson, Keith R. — Bemidji
Johnson, R B — Clearwater
Knipschield, Terry — Rochester
Leblanc, Gary E — Little Falls
Maines, Jay — Wyoming
Mesenbourg, Nick — Inver Grove Heights
Metsala, Anthony — Princeton
Mickley, Tracy — North Mankato
Ritchie, Adam — Bloomington
Rydbom, Jeff — Annandale
Shadley, Eugene W — Grand Rapids
Taber, David E. — Winona
Voorhies, Les — Faribault

MO

Abernathy, Lance — Platte City
Allred, Elvan — St. Charles
Andrews, Russ — Sugar Creek
Betancourt, Antonio L. — St. Louis
Braschler, Craig W. — Zalma
Buxton, Bill — Kaiser
Chinnock, Daniel T. — Union
Cover, Jeff — Potosi
Cover, Raymond A — Mineral Point
Davis, W C — El Dorado Springs
Dippold, Al — Perryville
Duncan, Ron — Cairo
Eaton, Frank L Jr — Farmington
Ehrenberger, Daniel Robert — Mexico
Engle, William — Boonville
Hanson Iii, Don L. — Success
Harrison, Jim (Seamus) — St. Louis
Kinnikin, Todd — Pacific
Knickmeyer, Hank — Cedar Hill

Knickmeyer, Kurt — Cedar Hill
Krause, Jim — Farmington
Lee, Ethan — Sturgeon
Martin, Tony — Arcadia
Mccrackin, Kevin — House Spings
Mccrackin And Son, V J — House Springs
Mosier, David — Independence
Mulkey, Gary — Branson
Muller, Jody — Goodson
Newcomb, Corbin — Moberly
Ramsey, Richard A — Neosho
Rardon, A D — Polo
Rardon, Archie F — Polo
Riepe, Richard A — Harrisonville
Robbins, Howard P — Flemington
Robbins, Landon — Crane
Royer, Kyle — Clever
Scroggs, James A — Warrensburg
Seaton, David D — Rolla
Smith, Jerry W. — Willow Springs
Sonntag, Douglas W — Nixa
Sonntag, Jacob D — St. Robert
Sonntag, Kristopher D — Nixa
Steketee, Craig A — Billings
Stormer, Bob — Dixon
Waide, Rusty — Buffalo
Warden, Roy A — Union
Whitesell, J. Dale — Stover
Willis, Bill — Ava

MS

Black, Scott — Picayune
Boleware, David — Carson
Cohea, John M — Nettleton
Davis, Jesse W — Coldwater
Davison, Todd A. — Kosciusko
Evans, Bruce A — Booneville
Flynt, Robert G — Gulfport
Jones, Jack P. — Ripley
Lamey, Robert M — Biloxi
Lebatard, Paul M — Vancleave
May, Charles — Aberdeen
Mayo Jr., Homer — Biloxi
Nichols, Chad — Blue Springs
Phillips, Donavon — Morton
Pickett, Terrell — Lumberton
Provost, J.C. — Laurel
Roberts, Michael — Clinton
Robinson, Chuck — Picayune
Shiffer, Steve — Leakesville
Smith, J.B. — Perkinston
Taylor, Billy — Petal
Tribble, Skylar — Leakesville
Vandeventer, Terry L — Terry
Vardaman, Robert — Hattiesburg
Wehner, Rudy — Collins
Wilson, Vic — Olive Branch
Wingo, Perry — Gulfport
Winston, David — Starkville

MT

Barnes, Jack — Whitefish
Barnes, Wendell — Clinton
Barth, J.D. — Alberton
Beam, John R. — Kalispell
Beaty, Robert B. — Missoula
Bell, Don — Lincoln
Bizzell, Robert — Butte
Brooks, Steve R — Walkerville
Caffrey, Edward J — Great Falls
Campbell, Doug — McLeod
Carlisle, Jeff — Simms
Christensen, Jon P — Stevensville
Colter, Wade — Colstrip
Conklin, George L — Ft. Benton
Crowder, Robert — Thompson Falls
Curtiss, Steve L — Eureka
Dunkerley, Rick — Lincoln
Eaton, Rick — Broadview
Ellefson, Joel — Manhattan
Fassio, Melvin G — Lolo
Forthofer, Pete — Whitefish

Fritz, Erik L — Forsyth
Gallagher, Barry — Lewistown
Harkins, J A — Conner
Hintz, Gerald M — Helena
Hulett, Steve — West Yellowstone
Kauffman, Dave — Clancy
Kelly, Steven — Bigfork
Mcguane Iv, Thomas F — Bozeman
Mckee, Neil — Stevensville
Moyer, Russ — Havre
Nedved, Dan — Kalispell
Olson, Joe — Great Falls
Parsons, Pete — Helena
Patrick, Willard C — Helena
Peele, Bryan — Thompson Falls
Peterson, Eldon G — Whitefish
Pursley, Aaron — Big Sandy
Rodewald, Gary — Hamilton
Ruana Knife Works, — Bonner
Smith, Josh — Frenchtown
Sweeney, Coltin D — Missoula
Taylor, Shane — Miles City
Thill, Jim — Missoula
Weinand, Gerome M — Missoula
Yashinski, John L — Red Lodge

NC

Baker, Herb — Eden
Barefoot, Joe W. — Wilmington
Best, Ron — Stokes
Bisher, William (Bill) — Denton
Brackett, Jamin — Fallston
Britton, Tim — Winston-Salem
Busfield, John — Roanoke Rapids
Craddock, Mike — Thomasville
Crist, Zoe — Flat Rock
Drew, Gerald — Mill Spring
Gaddy, Gary Lee — Washington
Gahagan, Kyle — Moravian Falls
Gingrich, Justin — Wade
Goode, Brian — Shelby
Greene, Chris — Shelby
Gross, W W — Archdale
Hall, Ken — Waynesville
Hege, John B. — Danbury
Johnson, Tommy — Troy
Livingston, Robert C — Murphy
Maynard, William N. — Fayetteville
Mcghee, E. Scott — Clarkton
Mclurkin, Andrew — Raleigh
Mcnabb, Tommy — Bethania
Mcrae, J Michael — Mint Hill
Nichols, Calvin — Raleigh
Parrish, Robert — Weaverville
Patrick, Chuck — Brasstown
Patrick, Peggy — Brasstown
Randall, Steve — Lincolnton
Rapp, Steven J — Marshall
Santini, Tom — Pikeville
Scholl, Tim — Angier
Simmons, H R — Aurora
Sirois, Darrin — Fayetteville
Sterling, Murray — Mount Airy
Summers, Arthur L — Concord
Sutton, S Russell — New Bern
Vail, Dave — Hampstead
Wacholz, Doc — Marble
Wagaman, John K — Selma
Walker, Don — Burnsville
Warren, Daniel — Canton
Whitley, L Wayne — Chocowinity
Wiggins, Bill — Canton
Williamson, Tony — Siler City
Wilson, Mike — Hayesville
Winkler, Daniel — Blowing Rock

ND

Kommer, Russ — Fargo
Pitman, David — Williston

NE

Archer, Ray And Terri — Omaha

Hielscher, Guy — Alliance
Jokerst, Charles — Omaha
Marlowe, Charles — Omaha
Moore, Jon P — Aurora
Sloan, David — Diller
Suedmeier, Harlan — Nebraska City
Syslo, Chuck — Omaha
Tiensvold, Alan L — Rushville
Tiensvold, Jason — Rushville
Till, Calvin E And Ruth — Chadron

NH

Hudson, C Robbin — Rochester
Jonas, Zachary — Wilmot
Saindon, R Bill — Goshen
Ward, Tom — Wilmot
White, Caleb A. — Hooksett

NJ

Fisher, Lance — Pompton Lakes
Grussenmeyer, Paul G — Cherry Hill
Knowles, Shawn — Great Meadows
Lesswing, Kevin — Bayonne
Licata, Steven — Boonton
Mccallen Jr., Howard H — So Seaside Park
Nadeau, Brian — Stanhope
Pressburger, Ramon — Howell
Sheets, Steven William — Mendham
Slee, Fred — Morganville
Viele, H J — Westwood
Yeskoo, Richard C — Summit

NM

Black, Tom — Albuquerque
Burnley, Lucas — Albuquerque
Chavez, Ramon — Belen
Cherry, Frank J — Albuquerque
Cordova, Joey — Bernalillo
Cordova, Joseph G — Bosque Farms
Cumming, Bob — Cedar Crest
Digangi, Joseph M — Los Ojos
Duran, Jerry T — Albuquerque
Dyess, Eddie — Roswell
Fisher, Jay — Clovis
Garner, George — Albuquerque
Goode, Bear — Navajo Dam
Gunter, Brad — Tijeras
Hartman, Tim — Albuquerque
Hethcoat, Don — Clovis
Kimberley, Richard L. — Santa Fe
Leu, Pohan — Rio Rancho
Lewis, Tom R — Carlsbad
Lynn, Arthur — Galisteo
Macdonald, David — Los Lunas
Meshejian, Mardi — Santa Fe
Reid, Jim — Albuquerque
Rogers, Richard — Magdalena
Schaller, Anthony Brett — Albuquerque
Stalcup, Eddie — Gallup
Stetter, J. C. — Roswell
Swearingen, Kurt — Cedar Crest
Terzuola, Robert — Albuquerque
Trujillo, Albert M B — Bosque Farms
Walker, Michael L — Pueblo Sur Taos
Wescott, Cody — Las Cruces

NV

Barnett, Van — Reno
Beasley, Geneo — Wadsworth
Bingenheimer, Bruce — Spring Creek
Cameron, Ron G — Logandale
Dellana, — Reno
George, Tom — Henderson
Hrisoulas, Jim — Henderson
Kreibich, Donald L. — Reno
Nishiuchi, Melvin S — Las Vegas
Rougeau, Derick — Sparks
Thomas, Devin — Panaca
Washburn, Arthur D — Pioche

NY

Baker, Wild Bill — Boiceville
Castellucio, Rich — Amsterdam
Cimms, Greg — Pleasant Valley
Davis, Barry L — Castleton
Derespina, Richard — Brooklyn
Gregory, Matthew M. — Glenwood
Hobart, Gene — Windsor
Johnson, Mike — Orient
Johnston, Dr. Robt — Rochester
Levin, Jack — Brooklyn
Loos, Henry C — New Hyde Park
Ludwig, Richard O — Maspeth
Lupole, Jamie G — Kirkwood
Manaro, Sal — Holbrook
Maragni, Dan — Georgetown
Mccornock, Craig — Willow
Meerdink, Kurt — Barryville
Miller, Chelsea Grace — Brooklyn
Page, Reginald — Groveland
Rachlin, Leslie S — Elmira
Rappazzo, Richard — Cohoes
Rotella, Richard A — Niagara Falls
Scheid, Maggie — Rochester
Schippnick, Jim — Sanborn
Serafen, Steven E — New Berlin
Skiff, Steven — Broadalbin
Smith, Lenard C — Valley Cottage
Smith, Raymond L — Erin
Summers, Dan — Whitney Pt.
Szilaski, Joseph — Pine Plains
Turner, Kevin — Montrose
Welling, William — West Valley
Zieba, Michael — Brooklyn

OH

Bendik, John — Olmsted Falls
Busse, Jerry — Wauseon
Coffee, Jim — Norton
Collins, Lynn M — Elyria
Coppins, Daniel — Cambridge
Cottrill, James I — Columbus
Crews, Randy — Patriot
Downing, Tom — Cuyahoga Falls
Downs, James F — Powell
Etzler, John — Grafton
Francis, John D — Ft. Loramie
Gittinger, Raymond — Tiffin
Glover, Ron — Cincinnati
Greiner, Richard — Green Springs
Hinderer, Rick — Shreve
Humphrey, Lon — Newark
Imboden Ii, Howard L. — Dayton
Johnson, Wm. C. "Bill" — Enon
Jones, Roger Mudbone — Waverly
Kiefer, Tony — Pataskala
Landis, David E. Sr. — Galion
Longworth, Dave — Felicity
Maienknecht, Stanley — Sardis
Marshall, Rex — Wilmington
Mcdonald, Rich — Hillboro
Mcgroder, Patrick J — Madison
Mercer, Mike — Lebanon
Morgan, Tom — Beloit
Munjas, Bob — Waterford
O'Machearley, Michael — Wilmington
Panak, Paul S — Andover
Potter, Billy — Dublin
Roddy, Roy "Tim" — Hubbard
Rose, Derek W — Gallipolis
Rowe, Fred — Amesville
Salley, John D — Tipp City
Schuchmann, Rick — New Richmond
Sheely, "Butch" Forest — Grand Rapids
Shinosky, Andy — Canfield
Shoemaker, Carroll — Northup
Shoemaker, Scott — Miamisburg
Spinale, Richard — Lorain
Strong, Scott — Beavercreek
Summers, Dennis K — Springfield
Thomas, Kim — Seville

Name	City
Thourot, Michael W	Napoleon
Tindera, George	Brunswick
Trout, George H.	Wilmington
Votaw, David P	Pioneer
Ward, J J	Waverly
Williams, Robert	East Liverpool
Worley, Joel A., J.S.	Maplewood
Wright, L.T.	Wintersville
Yurco, Mickey	Canfield
Stidham, Daniel	Gallipolis

OK

Name	City
Baker, Ray	Sapulpa
Berg, Lee	Ketchum
Carrillo, Dwaine	Moore
Coye, Bill	Tulsa
Crenshaw, Al	Eufaula
Crowder, Gary L	Sallisaw
Damasteel Stainless Damascus,	Norman
Darby, David T	Cookson
Dill, Dave	Bethany
Duff, Bill	Poteau
Dunlap, Jim	Sallisaw
Gepner, Don	Norman
Heimdale, J E	Tulsa
Johns, Rob	Enid
Kennedy Jr., Bill	Yukon
Kirk, Ray	Tahlequah
Lairson Sr., Jerry	Ringold
Martin	
Martin, John Alexander	Okmulgee
Mcclure, Jerry	Norman
Menefee, Ricky Bob	Blawchard
Midgley, Ben	Wister
Miller, Michael E	Chandler
Parsons, Larry	Mustang
Schreiner, Terry	Duncan
Shropshire, Shawn	Piedmont
Spivey, Jefferson	Yukon
Stanford, Perry	Broken Arrow
Tomberlin, Brion R	Norman
Williams, Michael	Broken Bow
Wingo, Gary	Ramona

OR

Name	City
Bell, Gabriel	Coquille
Bell, Michael	Coquille
Bochman, Bruce	Grants Pass
Brandt, Martin W	Springfield
Buchanan, Thad	Powell Butte
Buchanan, Zac	Eugene
Buchner, Bill	Idleyld Park
Busch, Steve	Oakland
Carter, Murray M	Hillsboro
Clark, Nate	Yoncalla
Coon, Raymond C	Damascus
Davis, Terry	Sumpter
Dixon Jr., Ira E	Cave Junction
Emmerling, John	Gearheart
Frank, Heinrich H	Dallas
Goddard, Wayne	Eugene
Harsey, William H	Creswell
Horn, Jess	Eugene
House, Cameron	Salem
Kelley, Gary	Aloha
Lake, Ron	Eugene
Little, Gary M	Broadbent
Magruder, Jason	Klamath Falls
Martin, Gene	Williams
Ochs, Eric	Sherwood
Olson, Darrold E	McMinnville
Pruyn, Peter	Grants Pass
Richard, Raymond	Gresham
Richards, Chuck	Salem
Rider, David M	Eugene
Sarganis, Paul	Jacksonville
Scarrow, Wil	Gold Hill
Schoeningh, Mike	North Powder
Schrader, Robert	Bend
Sevey Custom Knife,	Gold Beach
Sheehy, Thomas J	Portland
Sibert, Shane	Gladstone

Name	City
Smith, Rick	Rogue River
Spake, Jeremy	Portland
Squire, Jack	McMinnville
Stucky, Daniel	Springfield
Tendick, Ben	Eugene
Thompson, Leon	Gaston
Thompson, Tommy	Portland
Tuch, William	Portland
Turner, Mike	Williams
Vallotton, Butch And Arey	Oakland
Vallotton, Rainy D	Umpqua
Vallotton, Shawn	Oakland
Vallotton, Thomas	Oakland
Ward, Ken	Grants Pass
Warren, Alan And Carroll	Portland

PA

Name	City
Anderson, Gary D	Spring Grove
Anderson, Tom	Manchester
Appleby, Robert	Shickshinny
Bennett, Brett C	Reinholds
Besedick, Frank E	Monongahela
Blystone, Ronald L.	Creekside
Candrella, Joe	Warminster
Clark, D E (Lucky)	Johnstown
Corkum, Steve	Littlestown
Darby, Rick	Levittown
Evans, Ronald B	Middleton
Frey Jr., W Frederick	Milton
Godlesky, Bruce F.	Apollo
Goldberg, David	Ft Washington
Gottschalk, Gregory J	Carnegie
Harner Iii, "Butch" Lloyd R.	Littlestown
Heinz, John	Upper Black Eddy
Hudson, Rob	Northumberland
Johnson, John R	New Buffalo
Krammes, Jeremy	Schuylkill Haven
Malloy, Joe	Freeland
Marlowe, Donald	Dover
Mensch, Larry C	Milton
Miller, Rick	Rockwood
Moore, Ted	Elizabethtown
Morett, Donald	Lancaster
Nealy, Bud	Stroudsburg
Neilson, J	Towanda
Ogden, Bill	Avis
AVIS	
Parker, J E	Clarion
Root, Gary	Erie
Rose, Bob	Wagontown
Rupert, Bob	Clinton
Sass, Gary N	Sharpsville
Scimio, Bill	Spruce Creek
Sinclair, J E	Pittsburgh
Steigerwalt, Ken	Orangeville
Stroyan, Eric	Dalton
Takach, Andrew	Elizabeth
Whittaker, Robert E	Mill Creek

RI

Name	City
Dickison, Scott S	Portsmouth
Jacques, Alex	Warwick
Mchenry, William James	Wyoming
Olszewski, Stephen	Coventry
Williams, Jason L	Wyoming
Wright, Richard S	Carolina

SC

Name	City
Beatty, Gordon H.	Seneca
Branton, Robert	Awendaw
Cox, Sam	Gaffney
Denning, Geno	Gaston
Estabrook, Robbie	Conway
Frazier, Jim	Wagener
Gainey, Hal	Greenwood
George, Harry	Aiken
Gregory, Michael	Belton
Hendrix, Jerry	Clinton
Hendrix, Wayne	Allendale
Hucks, Jerry	Moncks Corner
Kay, J Wallace	Liberty
Knight, Jason	Harleyville

Name	City
Kreger, Thomas	Lugoff
Langley, Gene H	Florence
Lutz, Greg	Greenwood
Manley, David W	Central
Miles Jr., C R "Iron Doctor"	Lugoff
Odom Jr., Victor L.	North
O'Quinn, W. Lee	Elgin
Page, Larry	Aiken
Parler, Thomas O	Charleston
Peagler, Russ	Moncks Corner
Perry, Johnny	Inman
Smith, Ralph L	Taylors
Thomas, Rocky	Moncks Corner
Tyser, Ross	Spartanburg

SD

Name	City
Boley, Jamie	Parker
Boysen, Raymond A	Rapid Ciy
Ferrier, Gregory K	Rapid City
Thomsen, Loyd W	Custer
Watts, Rodney	Hot Springs

TN

Name	City
Accawi, Fuad	Oak Ridge
Adams, Jim	Cordova
Bailey, Joseph D.	Nashville
Bartlett, Mark	Lawrenceburg
Blanchard, G R (Gary)	Dandridge
Breed, Kim	Clarksville
Brend, Walter	Etowah
Burris, Patrick R	Athens
Byrd, Wesley L	Evensville
Canter, Ronald E	Jackson
Casteel, Dianna	Monteagle
Casteel, Douglas	Monteagle
Claiborne, Ron	Knox
Clay, Wayne	Pelham
Conley, Bob	Jonesboro
Coogan, Robert	Smithville
Corby, Harold	Johnson City
Elishewitz, Allen	Lenoir City
Ewing, John H	Clinton
Fitz, Andrew A. Sr. And Jr.	Milan
Hale, Lloyd	Pulaski
Harley, Larry W	Bristol
Hughes, Dan	Spencer
Hurst, Jeff	Rutledge
Hutcheson, John	Chattanooga
Johnson, David A	Pleasant Shade
Johnson, Ryan M	Signal Mountain
Kemp, Lawrence	Ooltewah
Levine, Bob	Tullahoma
Mccarty, Harry	Blaine
Mcdonald, W.J. "Jerry"	Germantown
Moulton, Dusty	Loudon
Raley, R. Wayne	Collierville
Ridge, Tim	Crossville
Sampson, Lynn	Jonesborough
Smith, Newman L.	Gatlinburg
Soileau, Damon	Kingsport
Taylor, C. Gray	Fall Branch
Vanderford, Carl G	Columbia
Wall, Greg	Michie
Ward, W C	Clinton
Wheeler, Gary	Clarksville
Williams Jr., Richard	Morristown

TX

Name	City
Alexander, Eugene	Ganado
Allen, Mike "Whiskers"	Malakoff
Aplin, Spencer	Brazoria
Appleton, Ron	Bluff Dale
Ashby, Douglas	Dallas
Baker, Tony	Allen
Barnes, Marlen R.	Atlanta
Barr, Judson C.	Irving
Batts, Keith	Hooks
Blackwell, Zane	Eden
Blum, Kenneth	Brenham
Bradley, Gayle	Weatherford
Bratcher, Brett	Plantersville
Brewer, Craig	Killeen

Name	Location
Broadwell, David	Wichita Falls
Brooks, Michael	Lubbock
Brown, Douglas	Fort Worth
Budell, Michael	Brenham
Bullard, Randall	Canyon
Burden, James	Burkburnett
Buzek, Stanley	Waller
Callahan, F Terry	Boerne
Carey, Peter	Lago Vista
Carpenter, Ronald W	Jasper
Carter, Fred	Wichita Falls
Champion, Robert	Amarillo
Chase, John E	Aledo
Chew, Larry	Weatherford
Childers, David	Montgomery
Churchman, T W (Tim)	Bandera
Cole, James M	Bartonville
Connor, John W	Odessa
Connor, Michael	Winters
Cornett, Brian	McKinney
Costa, Scott	Spicewood
Crain, Jack W	Granbury
Crouch, Bubba	Pleasanton
Crowner, Jeff	Plano
Darcey, Chester L	College Station
De Mesa, John	Lewisville
Dean, Harvey J	Rockdale
Debaud, Jake	Dallas
Delong, Dick	Centerville
Dietz, Howard	New Braunfels
Dominy, Chuck	Colleyville
Dyer, David	Granbury
Eldridge, Allan	Ft. Worth
Epting, Richard	College Station
Eriksen, James Thorlief	Garland
Evans, Carlton	Gainesville
Fant Jr., George	Atlanta
Ferguson, Jim	San Angelo
Fisher, Josh	Murchison
Foster, Al	Magnolia
Foster, Norvell C	Marion
Fritz, Jesse	Slaton
Fry, Jason	Abilene
Fuller, Bruce A	Blanco
Gann, Tommy	Canton
Garner, Larry W	Tyler
George, Les	Corpus Christi
Graham, Gordon	New Boston
Green, Bill	Sachse
Griffin, John	Hockley
Grimes, Mark	Bedford
Guinn, Terry	Eastland
Halfrich, Jerry	San Marcos
Hamlet Jr., Johnny	Clute
Hand, Bill	Spearman
Hawkins, Buddy	Texarkana
Hawkins Jr., Charles R.	San Angelo
Haynes, Jerry	Gunter
Hays, Mark	Austin
Hemperley, Glen	Willis
Hicks, Gary	Tuscola
Hill, Steve E	Spring Branch
Horrigan, John	Burnet
Howell, Jason G	Lake Jackson
Hudson, Robert	Humble
Hughes, Lawrence	Plainview
Hunt, Raymon E.	Irving
Jackson, Charlton R	San Antonio
Jaksik Jr., Michael	Fredericksburg
Jangtanong, Suchat	Dripping Springs
Keller, Bill	San Antonio
Ladd, Jim S	Deer Park
Ladd, Jimmie Lee	Deer Park
Lambert, Jarrell D	Granado
Laplante, Brett	McKinney
Lay, L J	Burkburnett
Lemcke, Jim L	Houston
Lennon, Dale	Alba
Lister Jr., Weldon E	Boerne
Love, Ed	San Antonio
Lovett, Michael	Mound
Luchak, Bob	Channelview
Lucie, James R	Austin
Luckett, Bill	Weatherford
Majors, Charlie	Montgomery
Martin, Michael W	Beckville
Mcconnell Jr., Loyd A	Marble Falls
Merz Iii, Robert L	Katy
Minchew, Ryan	Midland
Mitchell, Wm Dean	Mesquite
Moen, Jerry	Dallas
Moore, James B	Ft. Stockton
Neely, Greg	Bellaire
Oates, Lee	La Porte
O'Brien, Mike J.	San Antonio
Ogletree Jr., Ben R	Livingston
Osborne, Warren	Waxahachie
Ott, Ted	Elgin
Overeynder, T R	Arlington
Ownby, John C	Murphy
Packard, Ronnie	Bonham
Pardue, Joe	Hillister
Patterson, Pat	Barksdale
Payne, Travis	Telephone
Pierce, Randall	Arlington
Pollock, Wallace J	Cedar Park
Polzien, Don	Lubbock
Powers, Walter R.	Lolita
Ralph, Darrel	Forney
Ray, Alan W	Lovelady
Richardson, Percy	Lufkin
Richardson Iii, Percy (Rich)	Lufkin
Richardson Jr., Percy	Pollok
Roberts, Jack	Houston
Rucker, Thomas	Spring
Ruple, William H	Pleasanton
Ruth, Michael G	Texarkana
Ruth, Jr., Michael	Texarkana
Schorsch, Kendall	Jourdanton
Self, Ernie	Dripping Springs
Shipley, Steven A	Richardson
Sloan, Shane	Newcastle
Smart, Steve	McKinney
Snody, Mike	Aransas Pass
Stokes, Ed	Hockley
Stone, Jerry	Lytle
Stout, Johnny	New Braunfels
Swenson, Luke	Lakehills
Theis, Terry	Harper
Thuesen, Ed	Damon
Truncali, Pete	Garland
Turcotte, Larry	Pampa
Van Reenen, Ian	Amarillo
Vickers, David	Montgomery
Ware, Tommy	Onalaska
Watson, Daniel	Driftwood
Watts, Johnathan	Gatesville
Weever, John	Nemo
White, Dale	Sweetwater
Whitley, Weldon G	Odessa
Wilcher, Wendell L	Palestine
Wilkins, Mitchell	Montgomery
Wilson, Curtis M	Burleson
Wolf Jr., William Lynn	Lagrange
Zboril, Terry	Caldwell
Zermeno, William D.	Houston

UT

Name	Location
Allred, Bruce F	Layton
Black, Earl	Salt Lake City
Carter, Shayne	Payson
Ence, Jim	Richfield
Ennis, Ray	Ogden
Erickson, L.M.	Ogden
Hunter, Hyrum	Aurora
Johnson, Steven R	Manti
Jorgensen, Carson	Mt Pleasant
Lang, David	Kearns
Maxfield, Lynn	Layton
Nell, Chad	St. George
Nielson, Jeff V	Monroe
Nunn, Gregory	Castle Valley
Palmer, Taylor	Blanding
Peterson, Chris	Salina
Ramos, Steven	West Jordan
Ricks, Kurt J.	Trenton
Strickland, Dale	Monroe
Szczerbiak, Maciej	St. George
Velarde, Ricardo	Park City
Weeks, Ryan	Bountiful
Winn, Travis A.	Salt Lake City
Young, John	Ephraim
Jenkins, Mitch	Manti
Johnson, Jerry	Spring City

VA

Name	Location
Apelt, Stacy E	Norfolk
Arbuckle, James M	Yorktown
Ball, Butch	Floyd
Ballew, Dale	Bowling Green
Batson, Richard G.	Rixeyville
Beverly Ii, Larry H	Spotsylvania
Catoe, David R	Norfolk
Davidson, Edmund	Goshen
Foster, Burt	Bristol
Goodpasture, Tom	Ashland
Harley, Richard	Bristol
Harris, Cass	Bluemont
Hedrick, Don	Newport News
Hendricks, Samuel J	Maurertown
Holloway, Paul	Norfolk
Jones, Barry M And Phillip G	Danville
Jones, Enoch	Warrenton
Kearney, Jarod	Swoope
Martin, Herb	Richmond
Mccoun, Mark	DeWitt
Metheny, H A "Whitey"	Spotsylvania
Mills, Michael	Colonial Beach
Murski, Ray	Reston
Norfleet, Ross W	Providence Forge
Parks, Blane C	Woodbridge
Pawlowski, John R	Barhamsville
Schlueter, David	Madison Heights
Schwartz, Aaron	Woodbridge
Vanhoy, Ed And Tanya	Abingdon
Vestal, Charles	Abingdon
Ward, Ron	Rose Hill

VT

Name	Location
Bensinger, J. W.	Marshfield
Haggerty, George S	Jacksonville
Kelso, Jim	Worcester
Wulf, Derrick	Essex

WA

Name	Location
Amoureux, A W	Northport
Ber, Dave	San Juan Island
Berglin, Bruce	Mount Vernon
Bromley, Peter	Spokane
Brothers, Robert L	Colville
Brunckhorst, Lyle	Bothell
Bump, Bruce D.	Walla Walla
Butler, John R	Shoreline
Campbell, Dick	Colville
Chamberlain, Jon A	E. Wenatchee
Conti, Jeffrey D	Port Orchard
Conway, John	Kirkland
Crowthers, Mark F	Rolling Bay
D'Angelo, Laurence	Vancouver
Davis, John	Selah
De Wet, Kobus	Yakima
Diaz, Jose	Ellensburg
Diskin, Matt	Freeland
Erickson, Daniel	Snohomish
Ferry, Tom	Auburn
Gray, Bob	Spokane
Gray, Robb	Seattle
Greenfield, G O	Everett
Hansen, Lonnie	Spanaway
House, Gary	Ephrata
Keyes, Geoff P.	Duvall
Leeper, Dan	Olympia
Lisch, David K	Seattle
Norton, Don	Port Townsend
O'Malley, Daniel	Seattle
Padilla, Gary	Bellingham

Pedersen, Ole — Monroe
Podmajersky, Dietrich — Seattle
Rader, Michael — Bothell
Roeder, David — Kennewick
Rogers, Ray — Wauconda
Sanford, Dick — Chehalis
Schempp, Ed — Ephrata
Schempp, Martin — Ephrata
Shoger, Mark O — Kalama
Stegner, Wilbur G — Rochester
Sterling, Thomas J — Coupeville
Straub, Salem F. — Tonasket
Swyhart, Art — Klickitat
Thomas, Bob — Ferndale
Wheeler, Nick — Castle Rock
Wright, Kevin — Quilcene

WI

Boyes, Tom — West Bend
Brandsey, Edward P — Janesville
Bruner, Fred Jr. — Fall Creek
Carr, Joseph E. — Menomonee Falls
Coats, Ken — Stevens Point
Delarosa, Jim — Waterford
Deyong, Clarence — Sturtevant
Franklin, Larry — Stoughton
Haines, Jeff — Mayville
Hoffman, Jess — Shawano
Johnson, Richard — Germantown
Kanter, Michael — New Berlin
Kohls, Jerry — Princeton
Kolitz, Robert — Beaver Dam
Lary, Ed — Mosinee
Lerch, Matthew — Sussex
Maestri, Peter A — Spring Green
Martin, Peter — Waterford
Mikolajczyk, Glen — Caledonia
Millard, Fred G — Richland Center
Nelson, Ken — Racine
Niemuth, Troy — Sheboygan
Ponzio, Doug — Beloit
Rabuck, Jason — Springbrook
Revishvili, Zaza — Madison
Ricke, Dave — West Bend
Rochford, Michael R — Dresser
Roush, Scott — Washburn
Schrap, Robert G — Wauwatosa
Steinbrecher, Mark W — Pleasant Prairie
Wattelet, Michael A — Minocqua

WV

Derr, Herbert — St. Albans
Drost, Jason D — French Creek
Drost, Michael B — French Creek
Elliott, Jerry — Charleston
Groves, Gary — Canvas
Jeffries, Robert W — Red House
Liegey, Kenneth R — Millwood
Maynard, Larry Joe — Crab Orchard
Morris, Eric — Beckley
Pickens, Selbert — Dunbar
Reynolds, Dave — Harrisville
Small, Ed — Keyser
Tokar, Daniel — Shepherdstown
Wilson, Rw — Weirton
Wyatt, William R — Rainelle

WY

Amos, Chris — Riverton
Ankrom, W.E. — Cody
Banks, David L. — Riverton
Barry, Scott — Laramie
Bartlow, John — Sheridan
Deveraux, Butch — Riverton
Draper, Audra — Riverton
Draper, Mike — Riverton
Fowler, Ed A. — Riverton
Friedly, Dennis E — Cody
Kilby, Keith — Cody
Oliver, Todd D — Cheyenne
Rexroat, Kirk — Banner
Reynolds, John C — Gillette

Rodebaugh, James L — Carpenter
Ross, Stephen — Evanston
Spragg, Wayne E — Lovell
Whipple, Wesley A — Thermopolis

ARGENTINA

Ayarragaray, Cristian L. — Parana, Entre Rios
Bertolami, Juan Carlos — Neuquen
Gibert, PedroSan Martin de los Andes, Neuquen
Kehiayan, Alfredo — Maschwitz, Buenos Aires
Rho, Nestor Lorenzo — Junin, Buenos Aires
Santiago, Abud — Buenos Aires

AUSTRALIA

Barnett, Bruce — Mundaring, WA
Bennett, Peter — Engadine, NSW
Brodziak, David — Albany, WA
Crawley, Bruce R — Croydon, VIC
Cross, Robert — Tamworth, NSW
Del Raso, Peter — Mt. Waverly, VIC
Edmonds, Warrick — Adelaide Hills, SA
Fludder, Keith — Tahmoor, NSW
Gerner, Thomas — Walpole, WA
Giljevic, Branko — New South Wales
Green, William (Bill) — View Bank, VIC
Harvey, Max — Western Australia 6149
Hedges, Dee — Bedfordale, WA
Husiak, Myron — Altona, VIC
K B S, Knives — North Castlemaine, VIC
Maisey, Alan — Vincentia, NSW
Mcintyre, Shawn — Hawthornm, E VIC
Phillips, Alistair — Amaroo, ACT
Tasman, Kerley — Pt Kennedy, WA
Zemitis, Joe — Cardiff Heights, NSW

BELGIUM

Dox, Jan — Schoten
Laurent, Veronique — 1200 Bruxelles
Lurquin, Samuel — 7133 Buvrinnes Belgique, Binches
Monteiro, Victor — Maleves Ste Marie
Veronique, Laurent — 1200 Bruxelles

BRAZIL

Bodolay, Antal — Belo Horizonte, MG
Bossaerts, Carl — Ribeirao Preto, SP
Campos, Ivan — Tatui, SP
Dorneles, Luciano Oliverira Nova Petropolis, RS
Gaeta, Angelo — Centro Jau, SP
Garcia, Mario Eiras — Caxingui, SP
Ikoma, Flavio — Presidente Prudente, SP
Lala, Paulo Ricardo P And Lala, Roberto P. Presidente Prudente, SP
Neto Jr., Nelson And De Carvalho, Henrique M. Braganca Paulista, SP
Paulo, Fernandes R — Lencois Paulista, SP
Petean, Francisco And Mauricio — Birigui, SP
Ricardo Romano, Bernardes — Itajuba MG
Sfreddo, Rodrigo Menezes Nova Petropolis, RS
Vilar, Ricardo Augusto Ferreira — Mairipora, SP
Villa, Luiz — Itaim Bibi, SP
Villar, Ricardo — Mairipora, SP
Zakharov, Gladiston — Jacaret-SP

CANADA

Arnold, Joe — London, ON
Beauchamp, Gaetan — Stoneham, QC
Beets, Marty — Williams Lake, BC
Bell, Donald — Bedford, NS
Berg, Lothar — Kitchener ON
Beshara, Brent (Besh) — NL
Boos, Ralph — Edmonton, AB
Bourbeau, Jean Yves — Ile Perrot, QC
Bradford, Garrick — Kitchener, ON
Bucharsky, Emil — Alberta
Burke, Dan — Springdale, NL
Daley, Mark — Waubaushene, Ontario
Dallyn, Kelly — Calgary, AB
De Braga, Jose C. — Trois Rivieres, QC
Debraga, Jovan — Quebec
Deringer, Christoph — Cookshire, QC

Desaulniers, Alain — Cookshire, QC
Diotte, Jeff — LaSalle, ON
Doiron, Donald — Messines, QC
Doucette, R — Brantford, ON
Doussot, Laurent — St. Bruno, QC
Downie, James T — Ontario
Friesen, Dave J — British Columbia
Frigault, Rick — Golden Lake, ON
Ganshorn, Cal — Regina, SK
Garvock, Mark W — Balderson, ON
Gilbert, Chantal — Quebec City, QC
Haslinger, Thomas — British Columbia V1B 3G7
Hayes, Wally — Essex, ON
Hindmarch, Garth — Carlyle, SK
Hofer, Louis — Rose Prairie, BC
Jobin, Jacques — Levis, QC
Kaczor, Tom — Upper London, ON
Lambert, Kirby — Regina, SK
Langley, Mick — Qualicum Beach, BC
Lay, R J (Bob) — Logan Lake, BC
Leber, Heinz — Hudson's Hope, BC
Lemelin, Stephanie — Brossard
Lightfoot, Greg — Kitscoty, AB
Linklater, Steve — Aurora, ON
Loerchner, Wolfgang — Bayfield, ON
Lyttle, Brian — High River, AB
Maneker, Kenneth — Galiano Island, BC
Marchand, Rick — Lunenburg, Nova Scotia
Marzitelli, Peter — Langley, BC
Massey, Al — Mount Uniacke, NS
Mckenzie, David Brian — Campbell River, BC
Miville-Deschenes, Alain — Quebec
Moeller, Harald — Parksville, BC
Moizis, Stan — Delta, British Columbia (BC)
Nease, William — LaSalle, ON
Niro, Frank — Kamloops, B.C.
O'Hare, Sean — Grand Manan, NB
Olson, Rod — Nanton, AB
Painter, Tony — Whitehorse, YT
Patrick, Bob — S. Surrey, BC
Pepiot, Stephan — Winnipeg, MB
Piesner, Dean — Conestogo, ON
Poirier, Rick — New Brunswick E4V 2W7
Rassenti, Peter — Quebec J7P 4C2
Ridley, Rob — Sundre, AB
Ross, Tim — Thunder Bay, ON
Schoenfeld, Matthew A — Galiano Island, BC
St. Amour, Murray — Beachburg, Ontario
Stancer, Chuck — Calgary, AB
Storch, Ed — Mannville, AB
Stuart, Steve — Gores Landing, ON
Sylvester, David — Compton, QC
Tedford, Steven J. — Colborne, ON
Tighe, Brian — St. Catharines, ON
Toner, Roger — Pickering, ON
Vanderkolff, Stephen — Mildmay, ON
Whitenect, Jody — Elderbank, NS
Young, Bud — Port Hardy, BC

CZECH REPUBLIC

Rusnak, Josef — 323 00 Plzen
Sevecek, Pavel — Brodek U Konice
Tesarik, Richard — 614 00 Brno

DENMARK

Andersen, Henrik Lefolii — Fredensborg
Anso, Jens — Sporup
Rafn, Dan C. — Hadsten
Strande, Poul — Dastrup
Vensild, Henrik — Auning
Willumsen, Mikkel — S Copenhagen

ENGLAND

Bailey, I.R. — Colkirk
Barker, Stuart — Wigston, Leicester
Boden, Harry — Derbyshire
Ducker, Brian — Colkirk
Farid, Mehr R — Kent
Harrington, Roger — East Sussex
Nowacki, Stephen R. — Southampton, Hampshire
Orford, Ben — Worcestershire
Price, Darrell Morris — Devon

Stainthorp, Guy	Stroke-on-Trent
Wardell, Mick	N Devon
Wise, Donald	East Sussex
Wood, Alan	Brampton
Wylie, Tom	Sutton-In-Ashfield, Notts

FINLAND

Hankala, Jukka	39580 Riitiala
Palikko, J-T	00190 Helsinki
Ruusuvuori, Anssi	Piikkio
Tuominen, Pekka	Tossavanlahti
Vilppola, Markku	Turku

FRANCE

Bennica, Charles	Moules et Baucels
Chomilier, Alain And Joris	Clermont-Ferrand
Doursin, Gerard	Pernes les Fontaines
Graveline, Pascal And Isabelle	Moelan-sur-Mer
Headrick, Gary	Juan Les Pins
Laroche, Jean-Marc	78160 Marly le Roi
Madrulli, Mme Joelle	Salon De Provence
Regel, Jean-Louis	Saint Leger de Fougeret
Reverdy, Nicole And Pierre	Romans
Thevenot, Jean-Paul	Dijon
Viallon, Henri	Thiers

GERMANY

Becker, Franz	75328 Shomberg
Boehlke, Guenter	56412 Grobholbach
Borger, Wolf	Graben-Neudorf
Dell, Wolfgang	Owen-Teck
Drumm, Armin	Dornstadt
Faust, Joachim	Goldkronach
Fruhmann, Ludwig	Burghausen
Greiss, Jockl	Schenkenzell
Hehn, Richard Karl	Dorrebach
Herbst, Peter	Lauf a.d. Pegn.
Joehnk, Bernd	Kiel
Kressler, D F	D-28832 Achim
Rankl, Christian	Munchen
Rinkes, Siegfried	Markterlbach
Selzam, Frank	Bad Koenigshofen
Steinau, Jurgen	Berlin
Tritz, Jean-Jose	Hamburg
Wirtz, Achim	Wuerselen
Zirbes, Richard	Niederkail

GREECE

Filippou, Ioannis-Minas	Athens
Zafeiriadis, Konstantinos	Marathon Attiki

IRELAND

Moore, Davy	Quin, Co Clare

ISRAEL

Shadmot, Boaz	Arava

ITALY

Ameri, Mauro	Genova
Ballestra, Santino	Ventimiglia
Bertuzzi, Ettore	Bergamo
Bonassi, Franco	Pordenone
Esposito, Emmanuel	Buttigliera Alta TO
Fogarizzu, Boiteddu	Pattada
Frizzi, Leonardo	Firenze
Garau, Marcello	Oristano
Giagu, Salvatore And Deroma Maria Rosaria Pattada (SS)	
Moro, Corrado	Torino
Mura, Denis	Cascina (Pi)
Puddu, Salvatore	(Cagliari) Sardinia
Ramondetti, Sergio	CHIUSA DI PESIO (CN)
Riboni, Claudio	Truccazzano (MI)
Scordia, Paolo	Roma
Simonella, Gianluigi	Maniago
Toich, Nevio	Vincenza
Tschager, Reinhard	Bolzano

JAPAN

Aida, Yoshihito	Tokyo
Ebisu, Hidesaku	Hiroshima
Fujikawa, Shun	Osaka
Fukuta, Tak	Gifu
Hara, Koji	Gifu
Hirayama, Harumi	Saitama
Hiroto, Fujihara	Hiroshima
Isao, Ohbuchi	Fukuoka
Ishihara, Hank	Chiba
Kagawa, Koichi	Kanagawa
Kanki, Iwao	Hyogo
Kansei, Matsuno	Gifu
Kato, Shinichi	Aichi
Katsumaro, Shishido	Hiroshima
Keisuke, Gotoh	Oita
Koyama, Captain Bunshichi	Aichi
Makoto, Kunitomo	Hiroshima
Matsuno, Kansei	Gifu-City
Matsusaki, Takeshi	Nagasaki
Michinaka, Toshiaki	Tottori
Narasada, Mamoru	NAGANO
Ryuichi, Kuki	Saitama
Sakakibara, Masaki	Tokyo
Sugihara, Keidoh	Osaka
Sugiyama, Eddy K	Oita
Takahashi, Masao	Gunma
Tamatsu, Kunihiko	Kochi-ken
Toshifumi, Kuramoto	Fukuoka
Uchida, Chimata	Kumamoto
Wada, Yasutaka	Nara
Waters, Glenn	Hirosaki City
Yoneyama, Chicchi K.	Tokyo
Yoshihara, Yoshindo	Tokyo
Yoshikazu, Kamada	Tokushima
Yoshio, Maeda	Okayama

MEXICO

Scheurer, Alfredo E Faes	Distrito Federal
Sunderland, Richard	Puerto Escondido, OA
Ware, J.D.	Merida, Yucatan
Young, Cliff	San Miguel De Allende, GJ

NAMIBIA

Naude, Louis	Okahandja

NETHERLANDS

Brouwer, Jerry	Alkmaar
Sprokholt, Rob	Gatherwood
Van De Manakker, Thijs	Holland
Van Den Elsen, Gert	Tilburg
Van Eldik, Frans	Loenen
Van Ryswyk, Aad	Vlaardingen

NEW ZEALAND

Bassett, David J.	Auckland
Gunther, Eddie	Auckland
Jansen Van Vuuren, Ludwig	Dunedin
Knapton, Chris C.	Henderson, Aukland
Pennington, C A	Kainga Christchurch
Reddiex, Bill	Palmerston North
Ross, D L	Dunedin
Sandow, Brent Edward	Auckland
Sands, Scott	Christchurch 9
Van Dijk, Richard	Harwood Dunedin

NICARAGUA

Deibert, Michael	Managua
Morales, Ramon	Managua

NORWAY

Bache-Wiig, Tom	Eivindvik
Sellevold, Harald	Bergen
Vistnes, Tor	Svelgen

RUSSIA

Kharlamov, Yuri	Tula

SLOVAKIA

Albert, Stefan	Filakovo 98604
Bojtos, Arpad	98403 Lucenec
Kovacik, Robert	Tomasovce 98401
Mojzis, Julius	98511 Halic
Pulis, Vladimir	96701 Kremnica
Santa, Ladislav "Lasky"	97637 Hrochot

SOUTH AFRICA

Arm-Ko Knives,	Marble Ray, KZN
Baartman, George	Bela-Bela, LP
Bauchop, Robert	Munster, KN
Beukes, Tinus	Vereeniging, GT
Bezuidenhout, Buzz	Malvern, KZN
Boardman, Guy	New Germany, KZN
Brown, Rob E	Port Elizabeth, EC
Burger, Fred	Munster, KZN
Burger, Tiaan	Pretoria, GT
Culhane, Sean K.	Horizon, Roodepoort, 1740
Dickerson, Gavin	Petit, GT
Fellows, Mike	Riversdale 6670
Grey, Piet	Naboomspruit, LP
Harvey, Heather	Belfast, MP
Harvey, Kevin	Belfast, LP
Herbst, Gawie	Akasia, GT
Herbst, Thinus	Akasia, GT
Horn, Des	Onrusrivier, WC
Klaasee, Tinus	George, WC
Kojetin, W	Germiston, GT
Lancaster, C G	Free State
Liebenberg, Andre	Randburg, GT
Mackrill, Stephen	Johannesburg, GT
Mahomedy, A R	Marble Ray, KZN
Mahomedy, Humayd A.R.	Marble Ray, KZN
Oelofse, Tinus	Glenstantia, Pretoria
Owen, David J.A.	Johannesburg
Pienaar, Conrad	Free State
Prinsloo, Theuns	Free State
Rietveld, Bertie	Magaliesburg, GT
Russell, Mick	Port Elizabeth, EC
Schoeman, Corrie	Free State
Schutte, Neill	Bloemfontein
Smith, Stuart	Gauteng
Steyn, Peter	Freestate
Thorburn, Andre E.	Warmbaths, LP
Van Den Berg, Neels	Pretoria, Gauteng
Van Der Westhuizen, Peter	Mossel Bay, SC
Van Heerden, Andre	Pretoria, GT
Watson, Peter	La Hoff, NW

SPAIN

Cecchini, Gustavo T.	Sao Jose Rio Preto
Goshovskyy, Vasyl	Castellon de la Plana

SWEDEN

Bergh, Roger	Bygdea
Billgren, Per	Soderfors
Eklund, Maihkel	Farila
Embretsen, Kaj	Edsbyn
Hedlund, Anders	Brastad
Henningsson, Michael (Gothenburg)	430 83 Vrango
Hogstrom, Anders T	Johanneshov
Johansson, Anders	Grangesberg
Lundstrom, Jan-Ake	Dals-Langed
Lundstrom, Torbjorn (Tobbe)	Are
Nilsson, Jonny Walker	93391 Arvidsjaur
Nordell, Ingemar	FŠrila
Persson, Conny	Loos
Styrefors, Mattias	Boden
Vogt, Patrik	Halmstad

SWITZERLAND

Roulin, Charles	Geneva

UNITED KINGDOM

Hague, Geoff	Quarley, Hampshire
Heasman, H G	Llandudno, N. Wales
Horne, Grace	Sheffield
Maxen, Mick	Hatfield, Herts

URUGUAY

Gonzalez, Leonardo Williams	Maldonado
Symonds, Alberto E	Montevideo

ZIMBABWE

Burger, Pon	Bulawayo

the knifemakers' guild

2015 membership

a   Les Adams, Mike "Whiskers" Allen

b   Robert K. Bagley, Tony Baker, Robert Ball, James J. Barry, III, John Bartlow, Barbara Baskett, Gene Baskett, Michael S. Blue, Arpad Bojtos, Tony Bose, Dennis Bradley, W. Lowell Bray, Jr., Fred Bruner, Jr., John Busfield

c   Harold J. "Kit" Carson, Michael Carter, Dianna Casteel, Douglas Casteel, Daniel Chinnock, Richard Clow, Kenneth R. Coats, George Cousino, Pat Crawford, Kevin Cross, Daniel Cummings

d   George Dailey, Alex K. Daniels, Edmund Davidson, Scott Davidson, John H. Davis, Steve Davis, David Dodds, Tom Downing, James Downs, Will Dutton

e   Jim Elliott, William B. Ellis, James T. Eriksen, Carlton R. Evans

f   Cliff Fendley, Lee Ferguson, Robert G. Flynt, John R. Fraps

g   Steve Gatlin, Warren Glover, Gregory J. Gottschalk

h   Philip (Doc) L. Hagen, Jim Hammond, Rade Hawkins, Earl Jay Hendrickson, Wayne G. Hensley, Gil Hibben, Wesley G. Hibben, Kevin Hoffman, Larry Hostetler, Rob Hudson, Roy Humenic

i   Billy Mace Imel, Michael Irie

j   Brad Johnson, Jerry L. Johnson, Ronald B. Johnson, Steven R. Johnson, William "Bill" C. Johnson, Lonnie L. Jones

k   William L. Keeton, Bill Kennedy, Jr., Bill King, Harvey King, Jeff Knox

l   Tim "Chops" Lambkin, Ed Lary, Paul M. LeBetard, Gary E. LeBlanc, David C. Lemoine, William S. Letcher, Jack Levin, Bob Levine, Ken Linton, Don Lozier, Bill Luckett, Gail Lunn, Ernest Lyle

m   Stephen Mackrill, Riccardo Mainolfi, Joe Malloy, Herbert A. Martin, Charlie B. Mathews, Harry S. Mathews, Ken McFall, Ted Merchant, Robert L. Merz, III, Toshiaki Michinaka, James P. Miller, Stephen C. Miller, Jerry Moen, Kyle Moen, Jeff Morgan, Stephen D. Myers

n   Bud Nealy, Larry Newton, Ross W Norfleet

o   Clifford W. O'Dell, Charles F. Ochs, III, Ben R. Ogletree, Sean O'Hare, Jr., Warren Osborne, T. R. Overeynder, John E. Owens

p   Larry Page, Cliff Parker, Jerry Partridge, John R. Pawlowski, W. D. Pease, Michael Pellegrin, Alfred Pendray, James J. Pengov, Jr., John W. PerMar, John Perry, Daniel Piergallini, Leon Pittman, Otakar Pok, Larry Pridgen, Jr., Joseph R. Prince

r   James D. Ragsdale, Simone Raimondi, Steven Rapp, Carl E. Rechsteiner, Lin Rhea, Joseph Calvin Robinson, Michael Rochford, Gordon Romeis, A.G. Russell

s   Michael A. Sakmar, Joseph A. Sangster, Kenneth Savage, Scott W. Sawby, Juergen Schanz, Mike Schirmer, Mark C. Sentz, Eugene W. Shadley, John I Shore, Jim Siska, Steven C. Skiff, Ralph Smith, James Rodney Sornberger, David Steier, Murray Sterling, Douglas W. Stice, Russ Sutton

t   Leon Thompson, Bobby L. Toole, Reinhard Tschager, Ralph Turnbull

v   Charles Vestal, Donald Vogt

w   George A. Walker, Charles B. Ward, John S. Weever, Wayne Whittaker, Stan Wilson, Daniel Winkler, Marvin Winn

y   George L. Young, Mike Yurco

z   Brad Zinker

abs master smith listing

a   David Anders, Gary D. Anderson, E. R. Russ Andrews II

b   Gary Barnes, Aubrey G. Barnes Sr., James L. Batson, Jimmie H. Buckner, Bruce D. Bump, Bill Burke, Bill Buxton

c   Ed Caffrey, Murray M. Carter, Kevin R. Cashen, Hsiang Lin (Jimmy) Chin, Jon Christensen, Howard F. Clark, Wade Colter, Michael Connor, James R. Cook, Joseph G. Cordova, Jim Crowell, Steve Culver

d   Sava Damlovac, Harvey J. Dean, Christoph Deringer, Adam DesRosiers, Bill Dietzel, Audra L. Draper, Rick Dunkerley, Steve Dunn, Kenneth Durham

e   Dave Ellis

f   Robert Thomas Ferry III, Jerry Fisk, John S. Fitch, Joe Flournoy, Don Fogg—retired, Burt Foster, Ronnie E. Foster, Larry D. Fuegen, Bruce A. Fuller, Jack A. Fuller

g   Tommy Gann, Bert Gaston, Thomas Gerner, Greg Gottschalk

h   Tim Hancock, Don L. Hanson III, Heather Harvey, Kevin Harvey, Wally Hayes, E. Jay Hendrickson, Don Hethcoat, John Horrigan, Gary House, Rob Hudson

j   Jim L. Jackson—retired

k   Joseph F. Keeslar, Keith Kilby, Ray Kirk, Hank Knickmeyer, Jason Knight, Bob Kramer

l   Jerry Lairson Sr.

m   J. Chris Marks, John Alexander Martin, Roger D. Massey, Victor J. McCrackin, Shawn McIntyre, Hanford J. Miller, Wm Dean Mitchell

n   Greg Neely, J. Neilson, Ron Newton, Douglas E. Noren

o   Charles F. Ochs III

p   Alfred Pendray, Dan Petersen Ph.D., Alex Dwight Phillips, Timothy Potier

q   Mike Quesenberry

r   Michael Rader, J. W. Randall, Kirk Rexroat, Linden W. Rhea, James L. Rodebaugh, Kyle Royer, Raymond B. Rybar Jr.

s   James P. Saviano, Stephen C. Schwarzer, Mark C. Sentz, Rodrigo Menezes Sfreddo, J.D. Smith, Josh Smith, Raymond L. Smith, Bill Sowell, Charles Stout, Joseph Szilaski

t   Shane Taylor, Jean-paul Thevenot, Jason Tiensvold, Brion Tomberlin, P. J. Tomes, Henry Torres

v   Michael V. Vagnino Jr., Terry L. Vandeventer

w   James L. Walker, Daniel Warren, Aaron Michael Wilburn, Michael L. Williams, Daniel Winkler

professional knifemaker's association

Mike Allen, Pat Ankrom, Shane Paul Atwood, Eddie J. Baca, D. Scott Barry, John Bartlow, Donald Bell, Tom Black, Justin Bridges, Kenneth L. Brock, Lucas Burnley, Craig Camerer, Tim S. Cameron, Ken Cardwell, David Clark, Vance Corich, Del Corsi, Culpepper & Co., John Easter, Ray W. Ennis, Lee Ferguson, Chuck Fraley, Graham Fredeen, Bob Glassman, Levi Graham, Bob Ham, Alford "Alf" Hanna, James Helm, Wayne Hensley, Gary Hicks, Guy E. Hielscher, Jay Higgins, Mike L. Irie, Mitch Jenkins, Harvey King, Todd Kopp, Jim Krause, Tom Krein, Scott Kuntz, Tim "Chops" Lambkin, James R. Largent, Ken Linton, Arthur Lynn, Jim Magee, Jerry & Sandy McClure, Mardi Meshejian, Clayton Miller, Michael Miller, Tyree

L. Montell, Mike Mooney, Steve Myers, Robert Nash, Fred A. Ott, William Pleins, James L. Poplin, Bill Post, Calvin Powell, Steve Powers, Peter Pruyn, Bill Redd, Jim Reid, Steve Rollert, David Ruana, Dennis "Bud" Ruana, Don Ruana, Walter Scherar, Terry Schreiner, M.L. "Pepper" Seaman, Eugene Solomonik, Eddie F. Stalcup, Craig Steketee, Douglas Stice, Mark Strauss, Kurt Swearingen, James D. Thrash, Ed Thuesen, Albert Trujillo, Pete Truncali, Charles Turnage, Mike Tyre, Dick Waites, James Walton, Al Warren, Rodney Watts, Hans Weinmueller, Harold J. Wheeler, Jacob Wilson, R.W. Wilson, Michael C. Young, Monte Zavatta, Russ Zima, Daniel F. Zvonek

state/regional associations

arizona knife collectors association

Lee Beene, Larry Braasch, Bill Cheatam, Bob Dodd, Gary Fields, Tim Hancock, Bob Haskins, D'Alton Holder, Gerard Hurst, Todd M. Kopp, Mike Mooney, Jim Ort, Brian Quinn, Ray Rybar, Paul Vandine, Jim Yarbrough

australian knifemakers guild inc.

Peter Bald, Bruce Barnett, Alex Bean, Walter Bidgood, Matt Black, Scott Broad, David Brodziak, Matt Brook, Zac Cheong, Stephen Cooper, Peter Del Raso, Michael Fechner, Keith Fludder, John Foxwell, Alfred Frater, Adam Fromholtz, Thomas Gerner, Branko Giljevic, James Gladstone, Peter Gordon, Karim Haddad, Mal Hannan, Jamie Harrington, Rod Harris, Glenn Michael Henke, Robert Herbert, Joe Kiss, Michael Masion, Maurie, McCarthy, Shawn McIntyre, Will Morrison, Garry Odgers, Adam Parker, Terri Parker, Jeff Peck, Alistair Phillips, Fred Rowley, Wayne Saunders, Doug Timbs, Stewart Townsend, Rob Wakelin, Jason Weightman, Ross Yeats, Joe Zemitis

california knifemakers association

Paul Anderson, Stewart Anderson, Elmer Art, Kendell Banks, Harold Bishop, Gary Bolduc, Anton Bosch, Roger Bost, Sean P. Bourke, John Burens, Mike Butcher, Joe Caswell, Jon Chabot, Marcus Clinco, George Cummings, Mike Daly, Capt. J-C Demirdjian, Mike Desensi, Albert M. Dorado Sr., Frank Dunkin, Vern Edler III, Eddie Escobar, Chuck Faulkner, Alex Felix, Jim Ferguson, Marcus Flores, Lowell Ford, Brian Forrest, Randy Freer, Bill Fried, Joe Girtner, John Glueck, Corey Gray, Richard Grimm, Ron Gue, Eva Gulbrandsen, Rich Hale, Tim Harbert, John Harris, Roy Helton, Daniel Hernandez, Wm. R. 'Bill' Herndon, Neal A. Hodges, Jerid Johnson, Lawrence Johnson, David Kazsuk, Paul Kelso, Bernie Kerkvliet, Steve Koster, Tom Lewis, Robert Liguori, John Mackie, Bob McCready, Gordon Melin, Jim Merritt, David Moody, Russ Moody, Gerald Morgan, Jeff Morgan, Tim Musselman, Jeff Mutz, Helen Nauert, Aram Nigoghossian, Bruce Oakley, Rich Orton, John Powers, Robert Reid, E.J. Robison, Valente Rosas, Clark Rozas, H.J. Schneider, Laurence Segel, Mikhail Shindel, Sam Silva, Matt Steeneken, Alexander Strickland, Bill Stroman, Reinhardt Swanson, Tony Swatton, Billy Tinkley, Scott Tolman, William Tracy, Bill Traylor, Tru-grit, Mike Tyre, Wayne Watanabe, Martin Wells, Blaine Whitney, Tim Withers, Trent Wong

canadian knifemakers guild

Gaetan Beauchamp, Charles Bennica, Paul Bold, Paolo Brignone, Mark Daley, Jose deBraga, Christoph Deringer, Alain Desaulniers, Rob Douglas, Jason Duclos, James Emmons, Emmanuel Esposito, Paul-Aime Fortier, Rick Frigault, Aaron Gough, Sharla and Shawn Hansen, Wally Hayes, Gil Hibben, Des Horn, Suchat Jangtanong, Nathan Knowles, Kirby Lambert, Stephanie Lemelin, Matthew Lerch, Steve Linklater, Elizabeth Loerchner, Wolfgang Loerchner, David MacDonald, Mike Mossington, William Nease, Rod Olson, Warren Osborne, Simone Raimondi, Steven Rapp, David Riccardo,

Murray St. Amour, Paul Savage, Eugene Shadley, John W. Smith, Ken Steigerwalt, Jurgen Steinau, Brian Tighe, Libor Tobolak, Stephen Vanderkolff, Craig Wheatley, Murray White

finnish knifemakers guild

Tonu Arrak, Jukka Hankala, Pasi Jaakonaho, Arto Liukko, Jari Liukko, Erik Nylund, Jakob Nylund, Simon Nylund, JT Palikko, J-P Peltonen, Anssi Ruusuvuori, Teuvo Sorvari, Pekka Tuominen, Rauno Vainionpaa, Kay Vikstrom, Markku Vilppola

florida knifemaker's association

James J. Barry III, Terry Betts, Dennis Blaine, Dennis Blankenhem, Dean Bosworth, W. Lowell Bray Jr., Michael Buell, Patrick Burris, Lowell Cobb, John H. Davis, Jim Elliott, Tom M. Enos, Ernie Grospitch, Larry Hostetler, Joe "Hy" Hytovick, Tom Ivey, Mark James, Richard Johnson, Paul S. Kent, George Lambert, William (Bill) Letcher, Ernie Lyle, Steve Miller, James Mustain, Larry Newton, Dan Piergallini, Marvin Powell, Jr., Carlo Raineri, Roland Robidoux, Ann Sheffield/Sheffield Knifemaker's Supply, Jimmie Smith, Martin Snailgrove, Dale Thomas, John Thorsby, Ralph Turnbull, Louis M. Vallet, Voodoo Daggers, Don Vogt, ned Whitner, Stan Wilson, Denny Young, Maggie Young, Brad Zinker

georgia custom knifemakers' guild

Don R. Adams, Doug Adams, Larry Akins, Adam Andreasen, Joel Atkinson, Paul Brach, Dennis Bradley, Bobby Bragg, Steve Brazeale, Aaron Brewer, Marsha Brewer, Jerry Brinegar, James Brooker, Brian Brown, Mike Brown, Robert Busbee, Jeff Busbie, G.H. Caldwell, Henry Cambron, Rob Carper, Paul Chastain, Frank Chikey, Jim Collins, Jerry Costin, Nola Costin, Scott Davidson, Carol W. Dutton, Dan Eastland, Kerrie Edwards, Emory Fennell, Jarrett Fleming, Dylan Fletcher, Stephan Fowler, Jack Frost, Grady Gentles, Warren Glover, Jim Hamer, George Hancox, Rade Hawkins, Rebecca Hensley, Wayne Hensley, Ronald Hewitt, Kevin Hoffman, Jimmy Kirkland, Christopher Linton, Damon Lusky, Charlie Mathews, Harry Mathews, Vince McDowell, Larry McEachern, Russell McNabb, David McNeal, James Mitchell, Ralph Mitchell, Sandy Morrisey, Daniel Moye, Dan Peters, James Poplin, Joan Poythress, Carey Quinn, Jim Ragsdale, Nathan Raptis, Eddie Ray, Carl Rechsteiner, Adam Reese, David Roberts, Andy Roy, Joe Sangster, Jamey Saunders, Craig Schneeberger, Randy Scott, Ken Simmons, Jim Small, Dave Smith, Johnny Smith, Bill Snow, Luke Snyder, Brian Sorensen, Richard Stafford, Derek Stepp, Allen Suris, Cliff Thrower, Don Tommey, Owen Welch, Alex Whetsel, David White, Gerald White, Michael Wiesner, Chris Wilkes, Mike Wilson, Robert A. Wright, Judy Yoon

kansas custom knifemakers association

Roger Ball, James W. "Jim" Bevan, William Bevan, Gary Bradburn, Claude Campbell, Clint Childers, Roger Craig, Jacob Culver, Steve Culver, Mike Curran, Dave Darpinian, Richard Davis, Dan Dick, Ed Day, Laural "Shorty" Ediger, Jacob Ellis, Phil Evans, Andy Garrett,

Jim Glines, Ernie Grospitch, Jim Haller Jr., Jim Haller Sr., Steve Hansen, Billy Helton, Jon Finley, Ross Jagears, Chris Jones, Donald Judd, Carolyn Kaberline, Paul Keranen, Harvey King, Ray Kirk, Doug Klaus, Troy Klaus, Bob Kneisler, Kelly Kneisler, Knives N' Such (Tom and Susie Durham), Tom Lyles, Bill Lyons, Matt Manley, Gilbert Masters, Bruce Miller, Channing "Red" Morford, Joe O'Neill, Dan L. Peterson, Lister Potter, John Sandy, Robert Schornick, M.L. "Pepper" Seaman, Joe Skupa, David Sloane, Eric Showalter, Michael Sparta, Greg Steinert, Douglas Stice, Frank Weiss, Jeff Wells, Kevin Werth, Jim Wharton, Wesley Workman, Roy C. Young III, Tony Zanussi

knife group association of oklahoma

Mike "Whiskers" Allen, Howard Allman, David Anders, Rocky Anderson, Dale Atkerson, Richard Barchenger, Roy Brinsfield, Troy Brown, Tom Buchanan, F. L. Clowdus, Charles Conner, Bill Coye, Gary Crowder, Steve Culver, Marc Cullip, David Darby, Voyne Davis, Dan Dick, Lynn Drury, Bill Duff, Steve Elmenhorst, Beau Erwin, David Etchieson, Harry Fentress, Lee Ferguson, Linda Ferguson, Gary Gloden, Steve Hansen, Paul Happy, Calvin Harkins, Billy Helton, Ed Hites, Tim Johnston, Les Jones, Jim Keen, Bill Kennedy, Stew Killiam, Andy Kirk, Ray Kirk, Nicholas Knack, Jerry Lairson, Sr., Al Lawrence, Ken Linton, Newt Livesay, Ron Lucus, Matt Manley, John Martin, Jerry McClure, Sandy McClure, Jim McGuinn, Gary McNeill, Rick Menefee, Ben Midgley, Michael E. Miller, Roy Miller, Ray Milligan, Gary Mulkey, Allen Newberry, Jerald Nickels, Jerry Parkhurst, Chris Parson, Larry Parsons, Jerry Paul, Paul Piccola, Cliff Polk, Ron Reeves, Lin Rhea, Gary Robertson, Mike Ruth, Dan Schneringer, Terry Schreiner, Allen Shafer, Shawn Shropshire, Randell Sinnett, Clifford Smith, Doug Sonntag, Michel Sparkman, Perry Stanford, Jeremy Steely, Douglas Stice, Mike Stott, Michael Tarango, Don Thompson, Brian Tomberlin, Tom Upton, Chuck Ward, Jesse Webb, Jesse Webb, Rob Weber, Joe Wheeler, Bill Wiggins, Joe Wilkie, Daniel Zvonek

knifemakers' guild of southern africa

Jeff Angelo, John Arnold, George Baartman, Francois Basson, Rob Bauchop, George Beechey, Arno Bernard, Buzz Bezuidenhout, Harucus Blomerus, Chris Booysen, Thinus Bothma, Ian Bottomley, Peet Bronkhorst, Rob Brown, Fred Burger, Sharon Burger, Trevor Burger, William Burger, Brian Coetzee, Rucus Coetzee, Jack Connan, Larry Connelly, Andre de Beer, André de Villiers, Melodie de Witt, Gavin Dickerson, Roy Dunseith, Johan Ellis, Bart Fanoy, Mike Fellows, Werner Fourie, Andrew Frankland, Brian Geyer, Ettoré Gianferrari, Dale Goldschmidt, Stan Gordon, Nick Grabe, John Grey, Piet Grey, Heather Harvey, Kevin Harvey, Dries Hattingh, Gawie Herbst, Thinus Herbst, Greg Hesslewood, Rupert Holtshausen, Des Horn, Oubaas Jordaan, Nkosilathi Jubane, Billy Kojetin, Mark Kretschmer, Andre Lesch, Steven Lewis, Garry Lombard, Steve Lombard, Ken Madden, Abdur-Rasheed Mahomedy, Peter Mason, Shelley Mason, Francois Massyn, Edward Mitchell, George Muller, Günther Muller, Deon Nel, Tom Nelson, Andries Olivier, Christo Oosthuizen, Johan Oosthuysen, Cedric Pannell, Willie Paulsen, Nico Pelzer, Conrad Pienaar, David Pienaar, Jan Potgieter, Lourens Prinsloo, Theuns Prinsloo, Hilton Purvis, Derek Rausch, Chris Reeve, Martin Reeves, Bertie Rietveld, Melinda Rietveld, Dean Riley, John Robertson, Neels Roos, Corrie Schoeman, Neill Schutte, Eddie Scott, Harvey Silk, Mike Skellern, Toi Skellern, Carel Smith, Stuart Smith, Ken Smythe, Graham Sparks, Kosie Steenkamp, Willem Steenkamp, Peter Steyn, Peter Szkolnik, André Thorburn, Hennie Van Brakel, Fanie Van Der Linde, Johan van der Merwe, Van van der Merwe, Lieben Van Der Sandt, Marius Van der Vyver, Louis Van der Walt, Johann Van Deventer, Cor Van Ellinckhuijzen, Andre van Heerden, Ben Venter, Willie Venter, Gert Vermaak, René Vermeulen, Erich Vosloo, Jan Wahl, Desmond, Waldeck, Albie Wantenaar, Henning Wilkinson, John Wilmot, Wollie Wolfaardt, Owen Wood

montana knifemaker's association

Peter C. Albert, Gordon Alcorn, Chet Allinson, Marvin Allinson, Tim & Sharyl Alverson, Bill Amoureux, Wendell Barnes, Jim & Kay Barth, Bob & Marian Beaty, Donald Bell, Brett Bennett, Raymond Bernier, Bruce Bingenheimer, Robert Bizzell, BladeGallery, Chuck Bragg, Frederick Branch, Peter Bromley, Emil Bucharksky, Thomas and Linda Buckner, Bruce & Kay Bump, Chuck and Brenda Bybee, Jim & Kate Carroll, Rocco Chicarilli & Linda McNeese, Clayton Christofferson, Seth Coughlin, Bob Crowder, John Davis, John Doyal, Rich & Jacque Duxbury, Kevin Easley, Arnold Erhardt, Daniel Erickson, Mel & Darlene Fassio, E.V. Ford, Stephen & Kathy Garger, Chris & Jolene Giarde, Robb & Brandis Gray, Dana & Sandy Hackney, Doc & Lil Hagen, Gary & Betsy Hannon, Tedd Harris, Roger & Diane Hatt, Cal Heinrich, Sam & Joy Hensen, Gerald & Pamela Hintz, Tori Howe, Kevin Hutchins, Karl Jermunson, Keith Johnson, Don Kaschmitter, Steven Kelly, Jay Kemble, Dan & Penny Kendrick, Monte Koppes, Sheridan Lee, David Lisch, James Luman, Robert Martin, Neil McKee, Larry McLaughlin, Mac & Nancy McLaughlin, Phillip Moen, Daniel O'Malley, Tim Olds, Joe Olson, Collin Paterson, James Petri, Tim & Becca Pierce, Riley Pitchford, James Poling, Richard Prusz, Greg Rabatin, Jim Raymond, Darren Reeves, Tom Rickard and Cathy Capps, Ryan Robison, Ruana Knifeworks, Dean Schroeder, Rachel Slade, Gordon St. Clair, Terry Steigers, George Stemple, Dan & Judy Stucky, Art & Linda Swyhart, Jim Thill, James & Sharon Thompson, Dennis & Dora VanDyke, Bill & Lori Waldrup, Jonathan & Doris Walther, Michael Wattelet, Gerome & Darlene Weinand, Walter Wengrzynek, Daniel & Donna Westlind, Richard Wheeler, Sheldon & Edna Wickersham, Dave Wilkes, Randy Williams, R.W. Wilson, Mike & Seana Young

new england bladesmiths guild

Rick Barrett, Kevin Cashen, Mike Davis, Don Fogg, Burt Foster, Ric Furrer, Brian Lyttle, Bill McGrath, W.D. Pease, Jake Powning, Jim Siska, Tim Zowada

north carolina custom knifemakers' guild

Joe Aker, Dr. James Batson, Wayne Bernauer, Tom Beverly, William "Bill" Bisher, Jamin Brackett, William P. Brixon, Jr., Mark Carey, Barry Clodfelter, Travis Daniel, David Diggs, Jeffrey W. Foster, Jimmy Freeman, Russell Gardner, Anthony Griffin, Ken Hall, Mark Hall, Ed Halligan, Koji Hara, John B. Hege, Lian Hoffman, Terrill Hoffman, Jesse Houser, B.R. Hughes, Dan Johnson, Tommy Johnson, Barry and Phillip Jones, Frank Joyce, Jake Kirks, Michael Lamb, Dr. Jim Lucie, Robert Luck, Stuart Maynard, Scott McGhee, Arthur McNeil, Carl Mickey Jr., William Morris, Randy Nance, Ron Newton, Victor L. Odom Jr., J.D. Palmer Jr., Howard Peacock, Daniel Pica, James Poplin, Murphy Ragsdale, Steve Randall, Bruce Ryan, Joel Sandifer, Tim Scholl, Andy Sharpe, William Shoaf, Harland Simmons, Jeff Simmons, Darrin Sirois, Gene Smith, Charles E. Staples Jr., Murray Sterling, Arthur Summers, Russell Sutton, Jed Taylor, Bruce Turner, Ed & Tanya Van Hoy, Christopher M. Williams, Michael Wilson, Daniel Winkler.

ohio knifemakers association

Raymond Babcock, Van Barnett, Steve Bottorff, Harold A. Collins, Larry Detty, Tom Downing, Jim Downs, Patty Ferrier, Jeff Flannery, James Fray, Bob Foster, Raymond Guess, Scott Hamrie, Rick Hinderer, Curtis Hurley, Ed Kalfayan, Michael Koval, Judy Koval, Gene Loro, Larry Lunn, Stanley Maienknecht, Dave Marlott, Mike Mercer, David Morton, Patrick McGroder, Charles Pratt, Darrel Ralph, Roy Roddy, Michael Sheppard, Carroll Shoemaker, Clifton Smith, Jerry Smith, John Smith, Art Summers, Jan Summers, Donald Tess, Dale Warther, John Wallingford, Earl Witsaman, Joanne Yurco, Mike Yurco

saskatchewan knifemakers guild

Dennis Allenback, Vern Alton, David Beck, Marty Beets, Dan Bowers, Clarence Broeksma, Irv Brunas, Emil Bucharsky, Jim Clow, Murray Cook, Don Crane, Jonathan Crane, Bob Crowder, Jim Dahlin, Cole Dale, Kim Davis, Kevin Donald, Jordan Doucette, Brian Drayton, Ray Fehler, Cal Ganshorn, Kaila Garchinski, Brandon Gray, Gary Greer, Wayne Hamilton, Kent Hanmer, Diane and Roger Hatt, Robert Hazell, Garth Hindmarch, Rolf Holzkaemper, Chris Johnson, Rod Johnson, Cliff Kaufmann, Donald Kreuger, Nathan Kunkel, Paul Laronge, Bryan Lipp, Jared Longard, Pat Macnamara, Chris

Mathie, Len Meeres, Brian Mercer, Cory Miller, Robert Minnes, Ralph Mitton, Ron Nelson, Morris Nesdole, Ben Parry, Blaine Parry, Greg Penner, John Perron, Gary D. Peterson, Barry Popick, Jim Quickfall, Rob Robson, Pat de la Sablonniere, Robert Sainsbury, Kim Senft, Bob Serban, Carter Smyth, Don Spasoff, Ed Storch, Jim Takenaka, Isaac Tamlin, Tim Vanderwekken, Jay West, Merle Williams

south carolina association of knifemakers

Douglas Bailey, Ken Black, Dick Brainard, Bobby Branton, Richard Bridwell, Dan Cannady, Rodger Casey, Robert L. Davis, Geno Denning, Charlie Douan, Eddy T. Elsmore, Robert D. Estabrook, Lewis A. Fowler, Jim Frazier, Wayne Hendrix, T.J. Hucks, Johnny Johnson, Lonnie Jones, John Keaton, Col. Thomas Kreger, Gene Langley, David Manley, C.R. Miles, Gene Miller, Barry L. Myers, Paul G. Nystrom, Lee O'Quinn, Victor Odom Jr., Larry Page, Johnny L. Perry, James Rabb, Ricky Rankin, Jerry Riddle, Rick Rockwood, John Sarratt, Ralph L. Smith, David Stroud, Rocky Thomas, Justin Walker, Mickey Walker, H. Syd Willis Jr.

photo index

The firms listed here are special in the sense that they make or market special kinds of knives made in facilities they own or control either in the U.S. or overseas. Or they are special because they make knives of unique design or function. The second phone number listed is the fax number.

sporting cutlers

A.G. RUSSELL KNIVES INC
2900 S. 26th St
Rogers, AR 72758-8571
800-255-9034
fax 479-631-8493
ag@agrussell.com; www.agrussell.com
The oldest knife mail-order company, highest quality. Free catalog available. In these catalogs you will find the newest and the best. If you like knives, this catalog is a must

AL MAR KNIVES
PO Box 2295
Tualatin, OR 97062-2295
503-670-9080; fax 503-639-4789
info@almarknives.com;
www.almarknives.com
Featuring our Ultralight™ series of knives. Sere 2000™ Shrike, Sere™, Operator™, Nomad™ and Ultralight series™

ATLANTA CUTLERY CORP.
2147 Gees Mill Rd., Box 839
Conyers, GA 30013
770-922-7500; fax 770-918-2026
custserv@atlantacutlery.com;
www.atlantacutlery.com
Outdoor sporting and hunting knives, mail order

BARK RIVER KNIVES
6911 County Road 426 M.5 Road
Escanaba, MI 49829
906-789-1801
jacquie@barkriverknives.com
www.barkriverknifetool.com
Family-owned business producing bushcraft, hunting, Canadian, deluxe game, professional guide, search & rescue and EDC knives

BEAR & SON CUTLERY, INC.
111 Bear Blvd. SW
Jacksonville, AL 36265
256-435-2227; fax 256-435-9348
www.bearandsoncutlery.com
Bear Jaws®, three sizes of multi-tools, cutlery, hunting and pocketknives in traditional and innovative patterns and designs

BECK'S CUTLERY & SPECIALTIES
51 Highland Trace Ln.
Benson, NC 27504
919-902-9416
beckscutlery@embarqmail.com;
www.beckscutlery.com

BENCHMADE KNIFE CO. INC.
300 Beavercreek Rd
Oregon City, OR 97045
800-800-7427
info@benchmade.com;
www.benchmade.com
Sports, utility, law enforcement, military, gift and semi custom

BERETTA U.S.A. CORP.
17601 Beretta Dr.
Accokeek, MD 20607
301-283-2191
www.berettausa.com
Full range of hunting & specialty knives

BLACKHAWK PRODUCTS GROUP
6160 Commander Pkwy.
Norfolk, VA 23502
757-436-3101; fax 757-436-3088
cs@blackhawk.com
www.blackhawk.com
Leading manufacturer of tactical sheaths and knives

BLADE-TECH INDUSTRIES
5530 184th St. E, Ste. A
Puyallup, WA 98375
253-655-8059; fax 253-655-8066
tim@blade-tech.com
www.blade-tech.com

BLUE GRASS CUTLERY, INC.
20 E Seventh St, PO Box 156
Manchester, OH 45144
937-549-2602; 937-549-2709 or 2603
sales@bluegrasscutlery.com;
www.bluegrasscutlery.com
Manufacturer of Winchester Knives, John Primble Knives and many contract lines

BOKER USA INC
1550 Balsam St.
Lakewood, CO 80214-5917
800-992-6537; 303-462-0668
sales@bokerusa.com; www.bokerusa.com
Wide range of fixed-blade and folding knives for hunting, military, tactical and general use

BROUS BLADES
POB 550
Buellton, CA 93427
805-717-7192
contact@brousblades.com
www.brousblades.com
Custom and semi-custom knives

BROWNING
One Browning Place
Morgan, UT 84050
800-333-3504; Customer Service:
801-876-2711 or 800-333-3288
www.browning.com
Outdoor hunting & shooting products

BUCK KNIVES INC.
660 S Lochsa St
Post Falls, ID 83854-5200
800-326-2825; Fax: 800-733-2825
www.buckknives.com
Sports cutlery

BULLDOG BRAND KNIVES
P.O. Box 23852
Chattanooga, TN 37422
423-894-5102; fax 423-892-9165
Fixed blade and folding knives for hunting and general use

BUSSE COMBAT KNIFE CO.
11651 Co Rd 12
Wauseon, OH 43567
419-923-6471; 419-923-2337
www.bussecombat.com
Simple & very strong straight knife designs for tactical & expedition use

CAMILLUS C/O ACME UNITED CORP.
60 Round Hill Rd.
Fairfield, CT 06824
800-835-2263
orders@shopatron.com
www.camillusknives.com

CANAL STREET CUTLERY
30 Canal St.
Ellenville, NY 12428
845-647-5900
info@canalstreetcutlery.com
www.canalstreetcutlery.com
Manufacturers of pocket and hunting knives finished to heirloom quality

CAS IBERIA
650 Industrial Blvd
Sale Creek, TN 37373
800-635-9366
www.casiberia.com
Extensive variety of fixed-blade and folding knives for hunting, diving, camping, military and general use. Japanese swords and European knives

CASE, W.R. & SONS CUTLERY CO.
50 Owens Way
Bradford, PA 16701
800-523-6350; Fax: 814-368-1736
consumer-relations@wrcase.com
www.wrcase.com
Folding pocket knives

CHRIS REEVE KNIVES
2949 S. Victory View Way
Boise, ID 83709-2946
208-375-0367; Fax: 208-375-0368
crkinfo@chrisreeve.com;
www.chrisreeve.com
Makers of the Sebenza, Umnumzaan and Mnandi folding knives, the legendary Green Beret knife and other military knives

COAST CUTLERY CO
8033 N.E. Holman
Portland, OR 97218
800-426-5858; Fax: 503-234-4422
www.coastportland.com
Variety of fixed-blade and folding knives and multi-tools for hunting, camping and general use

COLD STEEL INC
6060 Nicolle St.
Ventura, CA 93003
800-255-4716 or 805-642-9727
sales@coldsteel.com
www.coldsteel.com
Wide variety of folding lockbacks and fixed-blade hunting, fishing and neck knives, as well as bowies, kukris, tantos, throwing knives, kitchen knives and swords

COLONIAL KNIFE, A DIVISION OF COLONIAL CUTLERY INT.
61 Dewey Ave.
Warwick, RI 02886
401-421-6500; Fax: 401-737-0054
stevep@colonialknifecorp.com
www.colonialknifecorp.com
Collectors edition specialty knives. Special promotions. Old cutler, barion, trappers, military knives. Industrial knives-electrician.

CONDOR™ TOOL & KNIFE
7557 W. Sand Lake Rd., #106
Orlando, FL 32819
407-354-3488; Fax: 407-354-3489
rtj2@att.net; www.condortk.com

CRAWFORD KNIVES, LLC
205 N Center
West Memphis, AR 72301
870-732-2452
www.crawfordknives.com
Folding knives for tactical and general use

CRKT
18348 SW 126th Place
Tualatin, OR 97062
800-891-3100; fax 503-682-9680
info@crkt.com; www.crkt.com
Complete line of sport, work and tactical knives

CUTCO CORPORATION
1116 E. State St.
Olean, NY 14760
716-372-3111
www.cutco.com
Household cutlery / sport knives

DPX GEAR INC.
2321 Kettner Blvd.
San Diego, CA 92101
619-780-2600; fax: 619-780-2605
www.dpxgear.com
Hostile environment survival knives and tools

EMERSON KNIVES, INC.
1234 254th St.
Harbor City, CA 90710
310-539-5633; fax: 310-539-5609
www.emersonknives.com
Hard use tactical knives; folding & fixed blades

ESEE KNIVES
POB 99
Gallant, AL 35972
256-613-0372
www.eseeknives.com
Survival and tactical knives

EXTREMA RATIO
Mauro Chiostri/Maurizio Castrati
Via Tourcoing 40/p
Prato (PO) 59100
ITALY
0039 0576 584639; fax: 0039 0576 584312
info@extremaratio.com
Tactical/military knives and sheaths, blades and sheaths to customers specs

FALLKNIVEN
Granatvägen 8
S-961 43 Boden
SWEDEN
46-(0)-921 544 22; Fax: 46-(0)-921 544 33
info@fallkniven.se; www.fallkniven.com
High quality stainless knives

FAMARS USA
2091 Nooseneck Hill Rd., Ste. 200
Coventry, RI 02816
855-FAMARS1 (326-2771)
www.famarsusa.com
FAMARS has been building guns for over 50 years. Known for innovative design, quality and craftsmanship. New lines of gentleman's knives, tactical fixed blades and folders, hunters and utility pieces.

FOX KNIVES USA
9918 162nd St. Ct. E, Ste. 14
Puyallup, WA 98375
303-263-2468
www.foxknivesusa.com
Designer, manufacturer and distributor of high-quality cutlery

FROST CUTLERY CO
PO Box 22636
Chattanooga, TN 37422
800-251-7768
www.frostcutlery.com
Wide range of fixed-blade and folding knives with a multitude of handle materials

GATCO SHARPENERS/TIMBERLINE
PO Box 600
Getzville, NY 14068
716-646-5700; fax: 716-646-5775
gatco@gatcosharpeners.com;
www.gatcosharpeners.com
Manufacturer of the GATCO brand of knife sharpeners and Timberline brand of knives

GERBER LEGENDARY BLADES
14200 SW 72nd Ave
Portland, OR 97223
503-403-1143; fax: 307-857-4702
www.gerbergear.com
Knives, multi-tools, axes, saws, outdoor products

GINSU/DOUGLAS QUIKUT
118 E. Douglas Rd.
Walnut Ridge, AR 72476
800-982-5233; fax: 870-886-9162
www.douglasquikut.com
Household cutlery

GROHMANN KNIVES
PO Box 40
116 Water St
Pictou, Nova Scotia B0K 1H0
CANADA
888-7KNIVES; Fax: 902-485-5872
www.grohmannknives.com
Fixed-blade belt knives for hunting and fishing, folding pocketknives for hunting and general use. Household cutlery.

H&B FORGE CO.
235 Geisinger Rd
Shiloh, OH 44878
419-895-1856
www.hbforge.com
Special order throwing knives and tomahawks, camp stoves, muzzleloading accroutements

HALLMARK CUTLERY
POB 220
Kodak, TN 37764
866-583-3912; fax: 901-405-0948
www.hallmarkcutlery.com
Traditional folders, tactical folders and fixed blades, multi-tools, shotgun shell knives, Bad Blood, Robert Klaas and Chief brand knives, and Super Premium care products

HISTORIC EDGED WEAPONRY
1021 Saddlebrook Dr
Hendersonville, NC 28739
828-692-0323; fax: 828-692-0600
histwpn@bellsouth.net
Antique knives from around the world; importer of puukko and other knives from Norway, Sweden, Finland and Lapland; also edged weaponry book "Travels for Daggers" by Eiler R. Cook

JOY ENTERPRISES-FURY CUTLERY
Port Commerce Center III
1862 M.L. King Jr. Blvd
Riviera Beach, FL 33404
800-500-3879; fax: 561-863-3277
mail@joyenterprises.com;
www.joyenterprises.com;
www.furycutlery.com
Fury™ Mustang™ extensive variety of fixed-blade and folding knives for hunting, fishing, diving, camping, military and general use; novelty key-ring knives. Muela Sporting Knives. Fury Tactical, Muela of Spain, Mustang Outdoor Adventure

KA-BAR KNIVES INC
200 Homer St
Olean, NY 14760
800-282-0130; fax: 716-790-7188
info@ka-bar.com; www.ka-bar.com
Manufacturer of law enforcement, military, hunting and outdoor knives

KAI USA LTD.
18600 S.W. Teton Ave.
Tualatin, OR 97062
800-325-2891; fax 503-682-7168
info@kai-usa.com
www.kershawknives.com
Manufacturer of high-quality, lifetime-guaranteed knives. Kai USA brands include Kershaw Knives for everyday carrying, hunting, fishing and other outdoor use; Zero Tolerance Knives for professional use; and Shun Cutlery, providing premium-quality kitchen knives

KATZ KNIVES, INC.
10924 Mukilteo Speedway #287
Mukilteo, WA 98275
480-786-9334; fax 460-786-9338
katzkn@aol.com; www.katzknives.com

KELLAM KNIVES WORLDWIDE
P.O. Box 3438
Lantana, FL 33465
800-390-6918
info@kellamknives.com;
www.kellamknives.com
Largest selection of Finnish knives, handmade and production

KLOTZLI (MESSER KLOTZLI)
Hohengasse 3 CH 3400
Burgdorf
SWITZERLAND
41-(34)-422-23 78
info@klotzli.com; www.klotzli.com
High-tech folding knives for tactical and general use

KNIGHTS EDGE LTD.
5696 N. Northwest Highway
Chicago, IL 60646-6136
773-775-3888; fax 773-775-3339
sales@knightsedge.com;
www.knightsedge.com
Medieval weaponry, swords, suits of armor, katanas, daggers

KNIVES OF ALASKA, INC.
Charles or Jody Allen
3100 Airport Dr
Denison, TX 75020
903-786-7366; fax 903-786-7371
info@knivesofalaska.com;
www.knivesofalaska.com
High quality hunting & outdoorsmen's knives

KNIVES PLUS
2467 Interstate 40 West
Amarillo, TX 79109
800-359-6202
www.knivesplus.com
Retail cutlery and cutlery accessories since 1987; free catalog available

LANSKY KNIFE, TOOL & SHARPENERS
POB 800
Buffalo, NY 14231
716-877-7511; fax 716-877-6955
cfire@lansky.com
www.lansky.com
Knives, multi-tools, survival axes, sharpeners

LEATHERMAN TOOL GROUP, INC.
12106 N.E. Ainsworth Cir.
Portland, OR 97220-0595
800-847-8665; fax 503-253-7830
info@leatherman.com;
www.leatherman.com
Multi-tools

LONE STAR WHOLESALE
2401 Interstate 40 W
Amarillo, TX 79109
806-836-9540; fax 806-359-1603
sales@lswtexas.com
www.lswtexas.com
Great prices, dealers only, most major brands

MANTIS KNIVES
520 Cameron St.
Placentia, CA 92870
714-996-9673
gwest@mantis.bz
www.mantisknives.com
Manufacturer of utility, karambit, fixed and folding blades, and Neccessikeys

MARBLE ARMS C/O BLUE RIDGE KNIVES
166 Adwolfe Rd.
Marion, VA 24354-6664
276-783-6143
onestop@blueridgeknives.com
www.blueridgeknives.com

MASTER CUTLERY INC
700 Penhorn Ave
Secaucus, NJ 07094
888-227-7229; fax 888-271-7228
www.mastercutlery.com
Largest variety in the knife industry

MEYERCO USA
4481 Exchange Service Dr.
Dallas, TX 75236
214-467-8949; fax 214-467-9241
www.meyercousa.com
Folding tactical,rescue and speed-assisted pocketknives; fixed-blade hunting and fishing designs; multi-function camping tools and machetes

MICROTECH KNIVES
300 Chestnut Street Ext.
Bradford, PA 16701
814-363-9260; Fax: 814-363-9030
info@microtechknives.com
www.microtechknives.com
Manufacturers of the highest quality production knives

MISSION KNIVES
13771 Newhope St.
Garden Grove, CA 92843
714-638-4692; fax 714-638-4621
info@missionknives.com
www.missionknives.com
Manufacturer of titanium and steel knives and tools with over 20 years in business. Tactical, combat, military, law enforcement, EOD units, survivalist, diving, recreational straight blades, folding blades and mine probes, and more.

MOKI KNIFE COMPANY LTD.
15 Higashisenbo
Seki City GIFU
Pref JAPAN
575-22-4185; fax 575-24-5306
information@moki.co.jp
www.moki.co.jp
Pocketknives, folders, fixed-blade knives and gent's knives

MUSEUM REPLICAS LTD.
P.O. Box 840, 2147 Gees Mill Rd
Conyers, GA 30012
800-883-8838; fax: 770-388-0246
www.museumreplicas.com
Historically accurate and battle-ready swords and daggers

NEMESIS KNIVES, LLC
179 Niblick Rd., #180
Paso Robles, CA 93446
562-594-4740
info@nemesis-knives.com
www.nemesis-knives.com
Semi-custom and production kinves

ONTARIO KNIFE CO.
26 Empire St.
Franklinville, NY 14737
800-222-5233; fax 716-676-5535
knifesales@ontarioknife.com
www.ontarioknife.com
Fixed blades, tactical folders, military and hunting knives, machetes

OUTDOOR EDGE CUTLERY CORP.
9500 W. 49th Ave., #A-100
Wheat Ridge, CO 80033
800-447-3343; 303-530-7667
moreinfo@outdooredge.com;
www.outdooredge.com

PACIFIC SOLUTION MARKETING, INC.
1220 E. Belmont St.
Ontario, CA 91761
Tel: 877-810-4643
Fax: 909-930-5843
sales@pacificsolution.com
www.pacificsolution.com
Wide range of folding pocket knives, hunting knives, tactical knives, novelty knives, medieval armor and weapons as well as hand forged samurai swords and tantos.

PRO-TECH KNIVES LLC
17115 Alburtis Ave.
Artesia, CA 90701-2616
562-860-0678
service@protechknives.com
www.protechknives.com
Manufacturer specializing in automatic knives for police, military and discriminating collectors

QUEEN CUTLERY COMPANY
507 Chestnut St.
Titusville, PA 16354
814-827-3673; fax: 814-827-9693
jmoore@queencutlery.com
www.queencutlery.com
Pocketknives, collectibles, Schatt & Morgan, Robeson, club knives

RANDALL MADE KNIVES
4857 South Orange Blossom Trail
Orlando, FL 32839
407-855-8075; fax 407-855-9054
grandall@randallknives.com;
www.randallknives.com
Handmade fixed-blade knives for hunting, fishing, diving, military and general use

REMINGTON ARMS CO., INC.
870 Remington Drive
Madison, NC 27025-0700
800-243-9700
www.remington.com

RUKO LLC.
PO Box 38
Buffalo, NY 14207-0038
800-611-4433; fax 905-826-1353
info@rukoproducts.com
www.rukoproducts.com

SANTA FE STONEWORKS
3790 Cerrillos Rd.
Santa Fe, NM 87507
800-257-7625
knives@rt66.com
www.santafestoneworks.com
Gemstone handles

SARCO KNIVES LLC
449 Lane Dr
Florence AL 35630
256-766-8099; fax 256-766-7246
www.TriEdgeKnife.com
*Etching and engraving services, club knives, etc.
New knives, antique-collectible knives*

SARGE KNIVES
2720 E. Phillips Rd.
Greer, SC 29650
800-454-7448; fax 864-331-0752
cgaines@sargeknives.com
www.sargeknives.com
*High-quality, affordable pocketknives, hunting,
fishing, camping and tactical. Custom engraving for
promotional knives or personalized gifts*

SOG SPECIALTY KNIVES & TOOLS, INC.
6521 212th St SW
Lynnwood, WA 98036
425-771-6230; fax 425-771-7689
sogsales@sogknives.com
www.sogknives.com
*SOG assisted technology, Arc-Lock, folding knives,
specialized fixed blades, multi-tools*

SPARTAN BLADES, LLC
625 S.E. Service Rd.
Southern Pines, NC 28387
910-757-0035
contact@spartanbladesusa.com
www.spartanbladesusa.com
Tactical, combat, fighter, survival and field knives

SPYDERCO, INC.
820 Spyderco Way
Golden, CO 80403
800-525-7770; fax 303-278-2229
sales@spyderco.com
www.spyderco.com
Knives, sharpeners and accessories

STONE RIVER GEAR
75 Manor Rd.
Red Hook, NY 12571
203-470-2526; fax 866-258-7202
info@stonerivergear.com
www.stonerivergear.com
*Fighters, tactical, survival and military knives,
household cutlery, hunting knives, pocketknives,
folders and utility tools*

SWISS ARMY BRANDS INC.
15 Corporate Dr.
Orangeburg, NY 10962
800-431-2994
customer.service@swissarmy.com
www.swissarmy.com
*Folding multi-blade designs and multi-tools for
hunting, fishing, camping, hiking, golfing and
general use. One of the original brands (Victorinox)
of Swiss Army Knives*

TAYLOR BRANDS LLC
1043 Fordtown Road
Kingsport, TN 37663
800-251-0254; fax 423-247-5371
info@taylorbrandsllc.com
www.taylorbrandsllc.com
*Smith & Wesson Knives, Old Timer, Uncle Henry
and Schrade.*

TIMBERLINE KNIVES
7223 Boston State Rd.
Boston, NY 14075
800-liv-sharp; fax 716-646-5775
www.timberlineknives.com
*High technology production knives for
professionals, sporting, tradesmen and kitchen use*

TRU-BALANCE KNIFE CO. EAST
PO Box 807
Awendaw, SC 29429
843-928-3624
Manufacturing and sale of throwing knives

UNITED CUTLERY
475 U.S. Hwy. 319 S
Moultrie, GA 31768
800-548-0835; fax 229-551-0182
customerservice@unitedcutlery.com
www.unitedcutlery.com
*Wholesale only; pocket, sportsman knives, licensed
movie knives, swords, exclusive brands*

WILLIAM HENRY STUDIO
3200 NE Rivergate St
McMinnville, OR 97128
503-434-9700; Fax: 503-434-9704
www.williamhenry.com
Semi-production, handmade knives

WUU JAU CO. INC
2600 S Kelly Ave
Edmond, OK 73013
405-359-5031; fax 405-340-5965
mail@wuujau.com; www.wuujau.com
*Wide variety of imported fixed-blade and folding
knives for hunting, fishing, camping and general
use. Wholesale to knife dealers only*

XIKAR INC
3305 Terrace, PO Box 025757
Kansas City MO 64111-3637
888-266-1193; fax 917-464-6398
info@xikar.com; www.xikar.com
Gentlemen's cutlery and accessories

importers

A.G. RUSSELL KNIVES INC
2900 S. 26th St.
Rogers, AR 72758-8571
800-255-9034
fax 479-631-8493
ag@agrussell.com; www.agrussell.com
*The oldest knife mail-order company, highest
quality. Free catalog available. In these catalogs you
will find the newest and the best. If you like knives,
this catalog is a must. Celebrating over 40 years in
the industry*

ADAMS INTERNATIONAL KNIFEWORKS
8710 Rosewood Hills
Edwardsville, IL 62025
Importers & foreign cutlers

ATLANTA CUTLERY CORP.
P.O.Box 839
Conyers, Ga 30012
770-922-7500; Fax: 770-918-2026
custserve@atlantacutlery.com;
www.atlantacutlery.com
Exotic knives from around the world

BAILEY'S
PO Box 550
Laytonville, CA 95454
800-322-4539; 707-984-8115
baileys@baileys-online.com;
www.baileys-online.com

BELTRAME, FRANCESCO
Fratelli Beltrame F&C snc Via dei Fabbri
15/B-33085 MANIAGO (PN)
ITALY
39 0427 701859
www.italianstiletto.com

BOKER USA, INC.
1550 Balsam St
Lakewood, CO 80214-5917
800-992-6537; 303-462-0668
sales@bokerusa.com; www.bokerusa.com
Ceramic blades

CAMPOS, IVAN DE ALMEIDA
R. Stelio M. Loureiro, 205
Centro, Tatui
BRAZIL
00-55-15-33056867
www.ivancampos.net

C.A.S. IBERIA
650 Industrial Blvd
Sale Creek, TN 37373
800-635-9366; fax 423-332-7248
mhillian@casiberia.com; www.casiberia.com

CATOCTIN CUTLERY
PO Box 188
Smithsburg, MD 21783

CLASSIC INDUSTRIES
1325 Howard Ave, Suite 408
Burlingame, CA 94010

COAST CUTLERY CO.
8033 N.E. Holman
Portland, OR 97218
800-426-5858
staff@coastcutlery.com;
www.coastcutlery.com

COLUMBIA PRODUCTS CO.
PO Box 1333
Sialkot 51310
PAKISTAN

COLUMBIA PRODUCTS INT'L
PO Box 8243
New York, NY 10116-8243
201-854-3054; Fax: 201-854-7058
nycolumbia@aol.com;
http://www.columbiaproducts.homestead.
com/cat.html
Pocket, hunting knives and swords of all kinds

COMPASS INDUSTRIES, INC.
104 E. 25th St
New York, NY 10010
800-221-9904; Fax: 212-353-0826
jeff@compassindustries.com;
www.compassindustries.com
Imported pocket knives

CONAZ COLTELLERIE
American Office
4179 Cristal Lake Dr.
Deerfield Beach, FL 33064
561-809-9701 or 754-423-3356
Fax: 954-781-3693
susanna@consigliscarperia.com;
www.consigliscarperia.it
*Handicraft workmanship of knives of the ancient
Italian tradition. Historical and collection knives*

CONSOLIDATED CUTLERY CO., INC.
696 NW Sharpe St
Port St. Lucie, FL 34983
772-878-6139

CRAZY CROW TRADING POST
PO Box 847
Pottsboro, TX 75076
800-786-6210; Fax: 903-786-9059
info@crazycrow.com; www.crazycrow.com
Solingen blades, knife making parts & supplies

DER FLEISSIGEN BEAVER
(The Busy Beaver)
Harvey Silk
PO Box 1166
64343 Griesheim
GERMANY
49 61552231; 49 6155 2433
Der.Biber@t-online.de
Retail custom knives. Knife shows in Germany & UK

EXTREMA RATIO
Mauro Chiostri; Mavrizio Castrati
Via Tourcoing 40/p
59100 Prato (PO)
ITALY
0039 0576 58 4639; fax 0039 0576 584312
info@extremaratio.com;
www.extremaratio.com
Tactical & military knives manufacturing

FALLKNIVEN
Granatvagen 8
S-961 43 Boden
SWEDEN
+46 (0) 921 544 22; fax +46 (0) 921 544 33
info@fallkniven.se
www.fallkniven.com
High quality knives

FREDIANI COLTELLI FINLANDESI
Via Lago Maggiore 41
I-21038 Leggiuno
ITALY

**GIESSER MESSERFABRIK GMBH,
JOHANNES**
Raiffeisenstr 15
D-71349 Winnenden
GERMANY
49-7195-1808-29
info@giesser.de; www.giesser.de
Professional butchers and chef's knives

HIMALAYAN IMPORTS
3495 Lakeside Dr
Reno, NV 89509
775-825-2279
unclebill@himalayan-imports.com; www.
himilayan-imports.com

**IVAN DE ALMEIDA CAMPOS-KNIFE
DEALER**
R. Xi De Agosto
107, Centro, Tatui, Sp 18270
BRAZIL
55-15-251-8092; 55-15-251-4896
campos@bitweb.com.br
Custom knives from all Brazilian knifemakers

JOY ENTERPRISES
1862 Martin Luther King Jr. Blvd.
Riviera Beach, FL 33404
561-863-3205; fax 561-863-3277
mail@joyenterprises.com;
www.joyenterprises.com
Fury™, Mustang™, Hawg Knives, Muela

KELLAM KNIVES WORLDWIDE
POB 3438
Lantana, FL 33465
561-588-3185 or 800-390-6918
info@kellamknives.com;
www.kellamknives.com
Knives from Finland; own line of knives

KNIFE IMPORTERS, INC.
11307 Conroy Ln
Manchaca, TX 78652
512-282-6860, Fax: 512-282-7504
Wholesale only

KNIGHTS EDGE LTD.
5696 N Northwest Hwy
Chicago, IL 60646
773-775-3888; fax 773-775-3339
www.knightsedge.com
*Exclusive designers of our Rittersteel, Stagesteel
and Valiant Arms and knightedge lines of weapon*

LEISURE PRODUCTS CORP.
PO Box 1171
Sialkot-51310
PAKISTAN

L. C. RISTINEN
Suomi Shop
17533 Co Hwy 38
Frazee MN 56544
218-538-6633; 218-538-6633
icrist@wcta.net
*Scandinavian cutlery custom antique, books and
reindeer antler*

LINDER, CARL NACHF.
Erholungstr. 10
D-42699 Solingen
GERMANY
212 33 0 856; Fax: 212 33 71 04
info@linder.de; www.linder.de

MARTTIINI KNIVES
PO Box 44 (Marttiinintie 3)
96101 Rovaniemi
FINLAND

MATTHEWS CUTLERY
POB 2768
Moultrie, GA 31776
800-251-0123; fax 877-428-3599
www.matthewscutlery.com
Wholesale of major brands

MESSER KLÖTZLI
PO Box 104
Hohengasse 3, 3400 Burgdorf
SWITZERLAND
0041 (0)34 422 23 78; fax 0041 (0)34 422
76 93; info@klotzli.com; www.klotzli.com

MUSEUM REPLICAS LIMITED
2147 Gees Mill Rd
Conyers, GA 30012
800-883-8838; fax 770-388-0246
mrw@museumreplicas.com
www.museumreplicas.com
*Subsidiary of Atlanta Cutlery. Battle-ready swords
and other historic edged weapons, as well as
clothing, jewelry and accessories.*

NICHOLS CO.
Pomfret Rd
South Pomfret, VT 05067
*Import & distribute knives from EKA (Sweden), Helle
(Norway), Brusletto (Norway), Roselli (Finland). Also
market Zippo products, Snow, Nealley axes and
hatchets and snow & Neally axes*

NORMARK CORP.
Craig Weber
10395 Yellow Circle Dr
Minnetonka, MN 55343

PIELCU
Parque Empresarial Campollano
Avenida 2a Numero 25 (esquina con C/E)
02007 Albacete
SPAIN
+34 967 523 568; fax +34 967 523 569
pielcu@pielcu.com; www.grupopielcu.com
Tactical, outdoor, fantasy and sporting knives

PRODUCTORS AITOR, S.A.
Izelaieta 17
48260 Ermua
SPAIN
943-170850; 943-170001
info@aitor.com
Sporting knives

PROFESSIONAL CUTLERY SERVICES
9712 Washburn Rd
Downey, CA 90241
562-803-8778; 562-803-4261
Wholesale only. Full service distributor of domestic & imported brand name cutlery. Exclusive U.S. importer for both Marto Swords and Battle Ready Valiant Armory edged weapons

SVORD KNIVES
Smith Rd., RD 2
Waiuku, South Auckland
NEW ZEALAND
64 9 2358846; fax 64 9 2356483
www.svord.com

SWISS ARMY BRANDS INC.
15 Corporate Dr.
Orangeburg, NY 10962
800-431-2994 or 914-425-4700
customer.service@swissarmy.com
www.swissarmy.com
Importer and distributor of Victorinox's Swiss Army brand

TAYLOR BRANDS, LLC
1043 Fordtown Road
Kingsport, TN 37663
800-251-0254; fax 423-247-5371
info@taylorbrandsllc.com;
www.taylorbrandsllc.com
Fixed-blade and folding knives for tactical, rescue, hunting and general use. Also provides etching, engraving, scrimshaw services.

UNITED CUTLERY
475 U.S. Hwy. 319 S
Moultrie, GA 31768
800-548-0835 or 229-890-6669; fax 229-551-0182
customerservice@unitedcutlery.com
www.unitedcutlery.com
Harley-Davidson ® Colt ® , Stanley ®, U21 ®, Rigid Knives ®, Outdoor Life ®, Ford ®, hunting, camping, fishing, collectible & fantasy knives

VICTORINOX SWISS ARMY, INC.
7 Victoria Dr.
Monroe, CT 06468
203-929-6391
renee.hourigan@swissarmy.com
www.swissarmy.com
Genuine Swiss Army Knives and Swiss Watches

WORLD CLASS EXHIBITION KNIVES
Cary Desmon
941-504-2279
www.withoutequal.com
Carries an extensive line of Pius Lang knives

ZWILLING J.A. HENCKELS LLC
171 Saw Mill River Rd
Hawthorne, NY 10532
914-747-0300; fax 914-747-1850
info@jahenckels.com;
www.jahenckels.com
Zwilling, Henckels International, Miyabi, Staub, Demeyere kitchen cutlery, scissors, shears, gadgets, cookware, flatware

knifemaking supplies

AFRICAN IMPORT CO.
Alan Zanotti
22 Goodwin Rd
Plymouth, MA 02360
508-746-8552; 508-746-0404
africanimport@aol.com
Ivory

ALABAMA DAMASCUS STEEL
PO Box 54
WELLINGTON, AL 36279
256-310-4619 or 256-282-7988
sales@alabamadamascussteel.com
www.alabamadamascussteel.com
We are a manufacturer of damascus steel billets & blades. We also offer knife supplies. We can custom make any blade design that the customer wants. We can also make custom damascus billets per customer specs.

ALPHA KNIFE SUPPLY
425-868-5880; Fax: 425-898-7715
chuck@alphaknifesupply.com;
www.alphaknifesupply.com
Inventory of knife supplies

AMERICAN SIEPMANN CORP.
65 Pixley Industrial Parkway
Rochester, NY 14624
585-247-1640; Fax: 585-247-1883
www.siepmann.com
CNC blade grinding equipment, grinding wheels, production blade grinding services. Sharpening stones and sharpening equipment

ANKROM EXOTICS
Pat Ankrom
306 1/2 N. 12th
Centerville, IA 52544
641-436-0235
ankromexotics@hotmail.com
www.ankromexotics.com
Stabilized handle material; Exotic burls and hardwoods from around the world; Stabilizing services available

ATLANTA CUTLERY CORP.
P.O.Box 839
Conyers, Ga 30012
770-922-7500; Fax: 770-918-2026
custserve@atlantacutlery.com;
www.atlantacutlery.com

BLADEMAKER, THE
Gary Kelley
17485 SW Phesant Ln
Beaverton, OR 97006
503-649-7867
garykelley@theblademaker.com;
www.theblademaker.com
Period knife and hawk blades for hobbyists & re-enactors and in dendritic D2 steel. "Ferroulithic" steel-stone spear point, blades and arrowheads

BOONE TRADING CO., INC.
PO Box 669
562 Coyote Rd
Brinnon, WA 98320
800-423-1945; Fax: 360-796-4511
bella@boonetrading.com
www.boonetrading.com
Ivory of all types, bone, horns

BORGER, WOLF
Benzstrasse 8
76676 Graben-Neudorf
GERMANY
wolf@messerschmied.de;
www.messerschmied.de

BOYE KNIVES
PO Box 1238
Dolan Springs, AZ 86441-1238
800-853-1617 or 928-272-0903
boye@citlink.net
www.boyeknives.com
Dendritic steel and Dendritic cobalt

BRONK'S KNIFEWORKS
Lyle Brunckhorst
Country Village
23706 7th Ave SE, Suite B

Bothell, WA 98021
425-402-3484
bronks@bronksknifeworks.com;
www.bronksknifeworks.com
Damascus steel

CRAZY CROW TRADING POST
PO Box 847
Pottsboro, TX 75076
800-786-6210; Fax: 903-786-9059
info@crazycrow.com; www.crazycrow.com
Solingen blades, knife making parts & supplies

CULPEPPER & CO.
Joe Culpepper
P.O. Box 690
8285 Georgia Rd.
Otto, NC 28763
828-524-6842; Fax: 828-369-7809
info@culpepperco.com
www.knifehandles.com
www.stingrayproducts.com
www.oldschoolknifeworks.com
Mother of pearl, bone, abalone, stingray, dyed stag, blacklip, ram's horn, mammoth ivory, coral, scrimshaw

CUSTOM FURNACES
PO Box 353
Randvaal, 1873
SOUTH AFRICA
27 16 365-5723; 27 16 365-5738
johnlee@custom.co.za
Furnaces for hardening & tempering of knives

DAMASCUS USA
149 Deans Farm Rd
Tyner, NC 27980-9718
252-333-0349
rob@damascususa.com;
www.damascususa.com
All types of damascus cutlery steel, including 100 percent finished damascus blade blanks

DAN'S WHETSTONE CO., INC.
418 Hilltop Rd
Pearcy, AR 71964
501-767-1616; fax 501-767-9598
questions@danswhetstone.com;
www.danswhetstone.com
Natural abrasive Arkansas stone products

DIAMOND MACHINING TECHNOLOGY, INC. (DMT)
85 Hayes Memorial Dr
Marlborough, MA 01752
800-666-4DMT
dmtcustomercare@dmtsharp.com;
www.dmtsharp.com
Knife and tool sharpener—diamond, ceramic and easy edge guided sharpening kits

DIGEM DIAMOND SUPPLIERS
7303 East Earll Drive
Scottsdale, Arizona 85251
602-620-3999
eglasser@cox.net
#1 international diamond tool provider. Every diamond tool you will ever need 1/16th of an inch to 11'x9'. BURRS, CORE DRILLS, SAW BLADES, MILLING SHAPES, AND WHEELS

DIXIE GUN WORKS, INC.
1412 West Reelfoot Ave.
Union City, TN 38281
731-885-0700; Fax: 731-885-0440
www.dixiegunworks.com
Knife and knifemaking supplies

EZE-LAP DIAMOND PRODUCTS
3572 Arrowhead Dr
Carson City, NV 89706
775-888-9500; Fax: 775-888-9555
sales@eze-lap.com; www.eze-lap.com
Diamond coated sharpening tools

FINE TURNAGE PRODUCTIONS
Charles Turnage
1210 Midnight Drive
San Antonio, TX 78260
210-352-5660
info@fineturnage.com
www.fineturnage.com
Specializing in stabilized mammoth tooth and bone, mammoth ivory, fossil brain coral, meteorite, etc.

FLITZ INTERNATIONAL, LTD.
821 Mohr Ave
Waterford, WI 53185
800-558-8611; Fax: 262-534-2991
info@flitz.com; www.flitz.com
Metal polish, buffing pads, wax

FORTUNE PRODUCTS, INC.
2010A Windy Terrace
Cedar Park, TX 78613
800-742-7797; Fax: 800-600-5373
www.accusharp.com
AccuSharp knife sharpeners

GALLERY HARDWOODS
Larry Davis, Eugene, OR
www.galleryhardwoods.com
Stabilized exotic burls and woods

GILMER WOOD CO.
2211 NW St Helens Rd
Portland, OR 97210
503-274-1271; Fax: 503-274-9839
www.gilmerwood.com

GIRAFFEBONE KNIFE SUPPLY
3052 Isim Rd.
Norman, OK 73026
888-804-0683
sandy@giraffebone.com;
www.giraffebone.com
Exotic handle materials

GLENDO CORPORATION/GRS TOOLS
D.J. Glaser
900 Overlander Rd.
Emporia, KS 66801
620-343-1084; Fax: 620-343-9640
glendo@glendo.com; www.grstools.com
Engraving, equipment, tool sharpener, books/videos

HALPERN TITANIUM INC.
Les and Marianne Halpern
PO Box 214
4 Springfield St
Three Rivers, MA 01080
888-283-8627; Fax: 413-289-2372
info@halperntitanium.com;
www.halperntitanium.com
Titanium, carbon fiber, G-10, fasteners; CNC milling

HAWKINS KNIFE MAKING SUPPLIES
110 Buckeye Rd
Fayetteville, GA 30214
770-964-1023
Sales@hawkinsknifemakingsupplies.com
www.HawkinsKnifeMakingSupplies.com
All styles

HILTARY INDUSTRIES
6060 East Thomas Road
Scottsdale, AZ 85251
Office: 480-945-0700
Fax: 480-945-3333
usgrc@usgrc.biz, eglasser@cox.net
OEM manufacturer, knife and sword importer, appraiser, metal supplier, diamond products, stag, meteorite, reconstituted gems, exotic wood, leather and bone

HOUSE OF TOOLS LTD.
#54-5329 72 Ave. S.E.
Calgary, Alberta
CANADA T2C 4X
403-640-4594; Fax: 403-451-7006
www.houseoftools.net

INDIAN JEWELERS SUPPLY CO.
Mail Order: 601 E Coal Ave
Gallup, NM 87301-6005
2105 San Mateo Blvd NE
Albuquerque, NM 87110-5148
800-545-6540; fax: 888-722-4172
orders@ijsinc.com; www.ijsinc.com
Handle materials, tools, metals

INTERAMCO INC.
5210 Exchange Dr
Flint, MI 48507
810-732-8181; 810-732-6116
solutions@interamco.com
Knife grinding and polishing

JANTZ SUPPLY / KOVAL KNIVES
PO Box 584
309 West Main
Davis, OK 73030
800-351-8900; 580-369-3082
jantz@jantzusa.com
www.knifemaking.com
Pre shaped blades, kit knives, complete knifemaking supply line

JMD INTERNATIONAL
2985 Gordy Pkwy., Unit 405
Marietta, GA 30066
678-969-9147; Fax: 770-640-9852
knifesupplies@gmail.com;
www.knifesupplies.com
Serving the cutlery industry with the finest selection of India stag, buffalo horn, mother-of-pearl and smooth white bone

JOHNSON, R.B.
I.B.S. Int'l. Folder Supplies, Box 11
Clearwater, MN 55320
320-558-6128; 320-558-6128
www.foldingknifesupplies.com
Threaded pivot pins, screws, taps, etc.

JOHNSON WOOD PRODUCTS
34897 Crystal Rd
Strawberry Point, IA 52076
563-933-6504

K&G FINISHING SUPPLIES
1972 Forest Ave
Lakeside, AZ 85929
928-537-8877; fax: 928-537-8066
csinfo@knifeandgun.com;
www.knifeandgun.com
Full service supplies

KOWAK IVORY
Roland and Kathy Quimby
(May-Sept): PO Box 350
Ester, AK 99725
907-479-9335
(Oct-April)
Green Valley, AZ 85662
520-207-6620
sales@kowakivory.com;
www.kowakivory.com
Fossil ivories

LITTLE GIANT POWER HAMMER
Roger Rice
6414 King Rd.
Nebraska City, NE 68410
402-873-6603
www.littlegianthammer.com
Rebuilds hammers and supplies parts

LIVESAY, NEWT
3306 S Dogwood St
Siloam Springs, AR 72761
479-549-3356; 479-549-3357
Combat utility knives, titanium knives, sportsmen knives, custom made orders taken on knives and after market Kydex© sheaths for commercial or custom cutlery

M MILLER ORIGINALS
Michael Miller
3030 E. Calle Cedral
Kingman AZ 86401
928-757-1359
mike@mmilleroriginals.com;
www.mmilleroriginals.com
Supplies stabilized juniper burl blocks and scales, mosaic damascus, damascus

MARKING METHODS, INC.
Sales
301 S. Raymond Ave
Alhambra, CA 91803-1531
626-282-8823; Fax: 626-576-7564
sales@markingmethods.com;
www.markingmethods.com
Knife etching equipment & service

MASECRAFT SUPPLY CO.
254 Amity St
Meriden, CT 06450
800-682-5489; Fax: 203-238-2373
info@masecraftsupply.com;
www.masecraftsupply.com
Natural & specialty synthetic handle materials & more

MEIER STEEL
Daryl Meier
75 Forge Rd
Carbondale, IL 62903
618-549-3234; Fax: 618-549-6239
www.meiersteel.com

NICO, BERNARD
PO Box 5151
Nelspruit 1200
SOUTH AFRICA
011-2713-7440099; 011-2713-7440099
bernardn@iafrica.com

NORRIS, MIKE
Rt 2 Box 242A
Tollesboro, KY 41189
606-798-1217
Damascus steel

NORTHCOAST KNIVES
17407 Puritas Ave
Cleveland, Ohio 44135
www.NorthCoastKnives.com
Tutorials and step-by-step projects. Entry level knifemaking supplies.

OSO FAMOSO
PO Box 654
Ben Lomond, CA 95005
831-336-2343
oso@osofamoso.com;
www.osofamoso.com
Mammoth ivory bark

OZARK CUTLERY SUPPLY
5230 S. MAIN ST.
Joplin, MO 64804
417-782-4998
ozarkcutlery@gmail.com
28 years in the cutlery business, Missouri's oldest cutlery firm

PARAGON INDUSTRIES, L.P.
2011 South Town East Blvd
Mesquite, TX 75149-1122
800-876-4328 or 972-288-7557
info@paragonweb.com;
www.paragonweb.com
Heat treating furnaces for knifemakers

POPLIN, JAMES / POP'S KNIVES & SUPPLIES
1654 S. Smyrna Church Rd.
Washington, GA 30673
706-678-5408
www.popsknifesupplies.com

PUGH, JIM
PO Box 711
917 Carpenter
Azle, TX 76020
817-444-2679; Fax: 817-444-5455
Rosewood and ebony Micarta blocks, rivets for Kydex sheaths, 0-80 screws for folders

RADOS, JERRY
134 Willie Nell Rd.
Columbia, KY 42728
606-303-3334
jerryr@ttlv.net
www.radosknives.com
Damascus steel

REACTIVE METALS STUDIO, INC.
PO Box 890
Clarksdale, AZ 86324
800-876-3434; 928-634-3434; Fax: 928-634-6734
info@reactivemetals.com; www.reactivemetals.com

R. FIELDS ANCIENT IVORY
Donald Fields
790 Tamerlane St
Deltona, FL 32725
386-532-9070
donaldbfields@earthlink.net
Selling ancient ivories; Mammoth, fossil & walrus

RICK FRIGAULT CUSTOM KNIVES
1189 Royal Pines Rd.
Golden Lake, Ontario
CANADA K0J 1X0
613-401-2869
jill@mouseworks.net
www.rfrigaultknives.ca
Selling padded zippered knife pouches with an option to personalize the outside with the marker, purveyor, stores-address, phone number, email web-site or any other information needed. Available in black cordura, mossy oak camo in sizes 4"x2" to 20"x4.5"

RIVERSIDE MACHINE
201 W Stillwell Ave.
DeQueen, AR 71832
870-642-7643; Fax: 870-642-4023
uncleal@riversidemachine.net
www.riversidemachine.net

ROCKY MOUNTAIN KNIVES
George L. Conklin
PO Box 902, 615 Franklin
Ft. Benton, MT 59442
406-622-3268; Fax: 406-622-3410
bbgrus@ttc-cmc.net
Working knives

SAKMAR, MIKE
903 S. Latson Rd. #257
Howell, MI 48843
517-546-6388; Fax: 517-546-6399
sakmarent@yahoo.com
www.sakmarenterprises.com
Mokume bar stock. Retail & wholesale

SANDPAPER, INC. OF ILLINOIS
P.O. Box 2579
Glen Ellyn, IL 60138
630-629-3320; Fax: 630-629-3324
sandinc@aol.com; www.sandpaperinc.com
Abrasive belts, rolls, sheets & discs

SCHMIEDEWERKSTATTE
Markus Balbach e.K.
Heinrich-Worner-Str. 1-3
35789 Weilmunster-Laubuseschbach, Germany
06475-8911 Fax: 912986
Damascus steel

SENTRY SOLUTIONS LTD.
PO Box 214
Wilton, NH 03086
800-546-8049; Fax: 603-654-3003
info@sentrysolutions.com
www.sentrysolutions.com
Knife care products

SHEFFIELD KNIFEMAKERS SUPPLY, INC.
PO Box 741107
Orange City, FL 32774
386-775-6453; fax: 386-774-5754
email@sheffieldsupply.com;
www.sheffieldsupply.com

SHINING WAVE METALS
PO Box 563
Snohomish, WA 98291
425-334-5569
info@shiningwave.com;
www.shiningwave.com
A full line of mokume-gane in precious and non-precious metals for knifemakers, jewelers and other artists

SMITH'S
747 Mid-America Blvd.
Hot Springs, AR 71913-8414
501-321-2244; Fax: 501-321-9232
sales@smithsproducts.com
www.smithsproducts.com

STAMASCUS KNIFEWORKS INC.
Ed VanHoy
24255 N Fork River Rd
Abingdon, VA 24210
276-944-4885; Fax: 276-944-3187
stamascus@centurylink.net
www.stamascusknifeworks.com
Blade steels

POUL STRANDE
Søster Svenstrup Byvej 16
4130 Viby Sjælland
Denmark
45 46 19 43 05; Fax: 45 46 19 53 19
www.poulstrande.com

STOVER, JEFF
PO Box 43
Torrance, CA 90507
310-486-0976
edgedealer@aol.com;
www.edgedealer.com
Fine custom knives, top makers

TEXAS KNIFEMAKERS SUPPLY
10649 Haddington Suite 180
Houston TX 77043
713-461-8632; Fax: 713-461-8221
sales@texasknife.com;
www.texasknife.com
Complete line of knifemaking supplies, equipment, and custom heat treating

TRU-GRIT, INC.
760 E Francis St., Unit N
Ontario, CA 91761
909-923-4116; Fax: 909-923-9932
www.trugrit.com
The latest in Norton and 3/M ceramic grinding belts. Also Super Flex, Trizact, Norax and Micron belts to 3000 grit. All of the popular belt grinders. Buffers and variable speed motors. ATS-34, 440C, BG-42, CPM S-30V, 416 and Damascus steel

TWO FINGER KNIFE, LLC
4574 N. Haroldsen Dr.
Idaho Falls, ID 83401
208-523-7436; Fax: 208-523-7436
twofingerknife@gmail.com
www.twofingerknife.com
USA-forged and hand-ground finished damascus blades, and blades in 5160, 1095, 52100, D2, 440C, ATS 34, ELMAX and other steels. Finishes sword blades, sword-cane blades, damascus bar stock and tomahawk heads. Offers folder kits, custom sheaths, in-house heat treating.

WASHITA MOUNTAIN WHETSTONE CO.
PO Box 20378
Hot Springs, AR 71903-0378
501-525-3914; Fax: 501-525-0816
wmw@hsnp

WEILAND, J. REESE
PO Box 2337
Riverview, FL 33568

813-671-0661
rwphil413@verizon.net
www.reeseweilandknives.com
Folders, straight knives, etc.

WILSON, R.W.
PO Box 2012
113 Kent Way
Weirton, WV 26062
304-723-2771
rwknives@hotmail.com

WOOD CARVERS SUPPLY, INC.
PO Box 7500
Englewood, FL 34295
800-284-6229
teamwcs@yahoo.com
www.woodcarverssupply.com
Over 2,000 unique wood carving tools

WOOD LAB
Michael Balaskovitz
2471 6th St.

Muskegon Hts., MI 49444
616-322-5846
woodlabgroup@gmail.com
www.woodlab.biz
Acrylic stabilizing services and materials

WOOD STABILIZING SPECIALISTS INT'L, LLC
2940 Fayette Ave
Ionia, IA 50645
800-301-9774; 641-435-4746
mike@stabilizedwood.com;
www.stabilizedwood.com
Processor of acrylic impregnated materials

ZOWADA CUSTOM KNIVES
Tim Zowada
4509 E. Bear River Rd
Boyne Falls, MI 49713
231-881-5056
tim@tzknives.com; www.tzknives.com
Damascus, pocket knives, swords, Lower case gothic tz logo

mail order, sales, dealers and purveyors

A.G. RUSSELL KNIVES INC
2900 S. 26th St
Rogers, AR 72758-8571
800-255-9034 or 479-631-0130
fax 479-631-8493
ag@agrussell.com; www.agrussell.com
The oldest knife mail-order company, highest quality. Free catalog available. In these catalogs you will find the newest and the best. If you like knives, this catalog is a must

ARIZONA CUSTOM KNIVES
Julie Maguire
3670 U.S. 1 S, Suite 260-F
St. Augustine, FL 32086
904-826-4178
sharptalk@arizonacustomknives.com;
www.arizonacustomknives.com
Color catalog $5 U.S. / $7 Foreign

ARTKNIVES.COM
Fred Eisen Leather & Art Knives
129 S. Main St.
New Hope, PA 18938
215-862-5988
fredeisen@verizon.net
www.artknives.com
Handmade knives from over 75 makers/high-quality manufacturers, leather sheath maker

ATLANTA CUTLERY CORP.
P.O.Box 839
Conyers, Ga 30012
770-922-7500; Fax: 770-918-2026
custserv@atlantacutlery.com;
www.atlantacutlery.com

BECK'S CUTLERY SPECIALTIES
51 Highland Trace Ln.
Benson, NC 27504
919-902-9416
beckscutlery@embarqmail.com;
www.beckscutlery.com
Knives

BLADE HQ
400 S. 1000 E, Ste. E
Lehi, UT 84043
888-252-3347 or 801-768-0232
questions@bladehq.com
www.bladehq.com
Online destination for knives and gear, specializing in law enforcement and military, including folders, fixed blades, custom knives, asisted-opening folders, automatics, butterfly knives, hunters, machetes, multi-tools, axes, knife cases, paracord, sharpeners, sheaths, lubricants and supplies

BLADEART.COM
14216 S.W. 136 St.
Miami, FL 33186
305-255-9176
sales@bladeart.com
www.bladeart.com
Custom knives, swords and gear

BLADEGALLERY.COM
107 Central Way
Kirkland, WA 98033
425-889-5980 or 877-56BLADE
info@bladegallery.com;
www.bladegallery.com
Bladegallery.com specializes in handmade, one-of-a-kind knives from around the world. We have an emphasis on forged knives and high-end gentlemen's folders

BLADEOPS, LLC
1352 W. 7800 S
West Jordan, UT 84088
888-EZ BLAD (392-5233)
trevor@bladeops.com
www.bladeops.com
Online dealer of all major brands of automatic knives, butterfly knives, spring-assisted folders, throwing knives, manual folders, survival and self-defense knives, sharpeners and paracord

BLUE RIDGE KNIVES
166 Adwolfe Rd
Marion, VA 24354
276-783-6143; fax 276-783-9298
onestop@blueridgeknives.com;
www.blueridgeknives.com
Wholesale distributor of knives

BOB'S TRADING POST
308 N Main St
Hutchinson, KS 67501
620-669-9441
bobstradingpost@cox.net;
www.bobstradingpostinc.com
Tad custom knives with Reichert custom sheaths one at a time, one of a kind

BOONE TRADING CO., INC.
PO Box 669
562 Coyote Rd
Brinnon, WA 98320
800-423-1945; Fax: 360-796-4511
bella@boonetrading.com
www.boonetrading.com
Ivory of all types, bone, horns

CARMEL CUTLERY
Dolores & 6th
PO Box 1346
Carmel, CA 93921
831-624-6699; 831-624-6780
sanford@carmelcutlery.com;
www.carmelcutlery.com
Quality custom and a variety of production pocket knives, swords; kitchen cutlery; personal grooming items

CLASSIC CUTLERY
66 N. Adams St., Ste. 1
Manchester, NH 03104
classiccutlery@earthlink.net
www.classiccutleryusa.com
Private-label zip-up knife cases and all brands of production cutlery and outdoor gear

CUTLERY SHOPPE
3956 E Vantage Pointe Ln
Meridian, ID 83642-7268
800-231-1272; Fax: 208-884-4433
orders@cutleryshoppe.com;
www.cutleryshoppe.com
Discount pricing on top quality brands

CUTTING EDGE, THE
2900 South 26th St
Rogers, AR 72758-8571
800-255-9034; Fax: 479-631-8493
ce_info@cuttingedge.com;

www.cuttingedge.com
After-market knives since 1968. They offer about 1,000 individual knives for sale each month. Subscription by first class mail, in U.S. $20 per year, Canada or Mexico by air mail, $25 per year. All overseas by air mail, $40 per year. The oldest and the most experienced in the business of buying and selling knives. They buy collections of any size, take knives on consignment. Every month there are 4-8 pages in color featuring the work of top makers

DENTON, JOHN W.
703 Hiawassee Estates Dr.
Hiawassee, GA 30546
706-781-8479
jwdenton@windstream.net
www.boblovelessknives.com
Loveless knives

EDGEDEALER.COM
PO BOX 43
TORRANCE, CA 90507
310-532-2166
edgedealer1@yahoo.com
www.edgedealer.com
Antiques

EPICUREAN EDGE
107 Central Way
Kirkland, WA 98033
425-889-5980
info@epicedge.com
www.epicedge.com
Specializing in handmade and one-of-a-kind kitchen knives from around the world

EXQUISITEKNIVES.COM
770 Sycamore Ave., Ste. 122, Box 451
Vista, CA 92083
760-945-7177
mastersmith@cox.net
www.exquisiteknives.com and
www.robertloveless.com
Purveyor of high-end custom knives

FAZALARE INTERNATIONAL ENTERPRISES
PO Box 7062
Thousand Oaks, CA 91359
805-496-2002
ourfaz@aol.com
Handmade multiblades; older Case; Fight'n Rooster; Bulldog brand & Cripple Creek

FROST CUTLERY CO.
PO Box 22636
Chattanooga, TN 37422
800-251-7768
www.frostcutlery.com

GODWIN, INC. G. GEDNEY
PO Box 100
Valley Forge, PA 19481
610-783-0670; Fax: 610-783-6083
sales@gggodwin.com;
www.gggodwin.com
18th century reproductions

GPKNIVES, LLC
2230 Liebler Rd.
Troy, IL 62294
866-667-5965
gpk@gpknives.com
www.gpknives.com
Serving law enforcement, hunters, sportsmen and collectors

GRAZYNA SHAW/QUINTESSENTIAL CUTLERY
POB 11
Clearwater, MN 55320
320-217-9002
gshaw@quintcut.com
www.quintcut.com
Specializing in investment-grade custom knives and early makers

GUILD KNIVES
Donald Guild
320 Paani Place 1A
Paia, HI 96779
808-877-3109
don@guildknives.com;
www.guildknives.com
Purveyor of custom art knives

HOUSE OF BLADES
6451 N.W. Loop 820
Ft. Worth, TX 76135
817-237-7721
sales@houseofblades.com
www.houseofbladestexas.com
Handmades, pocketknives, hunting knives, antique and collector knives, swords, household cutlery and knife-related items.

JENCO SALES, INC. / KNIFE IMPORTERS, INC. / WHITE LIGHTNING
PO Box 1000
11307 Conroy Ln
Manchaca, TX 78652
800-531-5301; fax 800-266-2373
jencosales@sbcglobal.net
Wholesale distributor of domestic and imported cutlery and sharpeners

KELLAM KNIVES WORLDWIDE
POB 3438
Lantana, FL 33465
800-390-6918; 561-588-3185
info@kellamknives.com;
www.kellamknives.com
Largest selection of Finnish knives; own line of folders and fixed blades

KNIFEART.COM
13301 Pompano Dr
Little Rock AR 72211
501-221-1010
connelley@knifeart.com
www.knifeart.com
Large internet seller of custom knives & upscale production knives

KNIFEPURVEYOR.COM LLC
919-295-1283
mdonato@knifepurveyor.com
www.knifepurveyor.com
Owned and operated by Michael A. Donato (full-time knife purveyor since 2002). We buy, sell, trade, and consign fine custom knives. We also specialize in buying and selling valuable collections of fine custom knives. Our goal is to make every transaction a memorable one.

KNIVES PLUS
2467 I 40 West
Amarillo, TX 79109
806-359-6202
salessupport@knivesplus.com
www.knivesplus.com
Retail cutlery and cutlery accessories since 1987

KRIS CUTLERY
2314 Monte Verde Dr
Pinole, CA 94564
510-758-9912 Fax: 510-758-9912
kriscutlery@aol.com; www.kriscutlery.com
Japanese, medieval, Chinese & Philippine

LONE STAR WHOLESALE
2401 Interstate 40 W
Amarillo, TX 79109
806-836-9540; fax 806-359-1603
sales@lswtexas.com
www.lswtexas.com
Nationwide distributor of knives, knife accessories and knife-related tools

MATTHEWS CUTLERY
PO Box 2768
Moultrie, GA 31776
800-251-0123; fax 877-428-3599
www.matthewscutlery.com

MOORE CUTLERY
PO Box 633
Lockport, IL 60441
708-301-4201
www.moorecutlery.com
Owned & operated by Gary Moore since 1991 (a full-time dealer). Purveyor of high quality custom & production knives

MUSEUM REPLICAS LIMITED
2147 Gees Mill Rd
Conyers, GA 30012
800-883-8838
www.museumreplicas.com
Historically accurate and battle ready swords & daggers

NEW GRAHAM KNIVES
560 Virginia Ave.
Bluefield, VA 24605
276-326-1384
mdye@newgraham.com
www.newgraham.com
Wide selection of knives from over 75 manufacturers, knife sharpening and maintenance accessories

NORDIC KNIVES
436 1st St., Ste. 203A
Solvang, CA 93463
805-688-3612; fax 805-688-1635
info@nordicknives.com
www.nordicknives.com
Custom and Randall knives

PARKERS' KNIFE COLLECTOR SERVICE
6715 Heritage Business Court
Chattanooga, TN 37421
423-892-0448; fax 423-892-9165
www.bulldogknives.org
Online and mail order dealer specializing in collectible knives, including Bulldog Knives, Weidmannsheil and Parker Eagle Brand. Parkers' Greatest Knife Show On Earth

PLAZA CUTLERY, INC.
3333 S. Bristol St., Suite 2060
South Coast Plaza
Costa Mesa, CA 92626
866-827-5292; 714-549-3932
dan@plazacutlery.com;
www.plazacutlery.com
Largest selection of knives on the west coast.

Custom makers from beginners to the best. All customs, William Henry, Strider, Reeves, Randalls & others available online, by phone

ROBERTSON'S CUSTOM CUTLERY
4960 Sussex Dr
Evans, GA 30809
706-650-0252; 706-860-1623
customknives@comcast.net
www.robertsoncustomcutlery.com
World class custom knives, custom knife entrepreneur

RUMMELL, HANK
10 Paradise Lane
Warwick, NY 10990
845-769-7273
hank@newyorkcustomknives.com;
www.newyorkcustomknives.com

SCHENK KNIVES
4574 N. Haroldsen Dr.
Idaho Falls, ID 83401
208-523-2026
schenkknives@gmail.com
www.schenkknives.com
High-performance factory custom knives. All models offered in the USA forged from damascus steel, forged 52100 bearting steel and ELMAX stainless steel.

SMOKY MOUNTAIN KNIFE WORKS, INC.
2320 Winfield Dunn Pkwy
PO Box 4430
Sevierville, TN 37864
800-564-8374; 865-453-5871
info@smkw.com; www.smkw.com
The world's largest knife showplace, catalog and website

TRUE NORTH KNIVES
82 Blair Park Rd. #955
Williston, VT 05495
866-748-9985
info@TNKUSA.com
www.TNKUSA.com
Custom and production knife purveyor

VOYLES, BRUCE
PO Box 22007
Chattanooga, TN 37422
423-238-6753
bruce@jbrucevoyles.com;
www.jbrucevoyles.com
Knives, knife auctions

knife services

appraisers

Levine, Bernard, P.O. Box 2404, Eugene, OR, 97402, 541-484-0294, brlevine@ix.netcom.com

Russell, A.G., Knives Inc, 2900 S. 26th St., Rogers, AR 72758-8571, phone 800-255-9034 or 479-631-0130, fax 479-631-8493, ag@agrussell.com, www.agrussell.com

Voyles, J. Bruce, PO Box 22007, Chattanooga, TN 37422, 423-238-6753, bruce@jbrucevoyles.com, www.jbrucevoyles.com

custom grinders

McGowan Manufacturing Company, 4720 N. La Cholla Blvd., #190, Tucson, AZ, 85705, 800-342-4810, 520-219-0884, info@mcgowanmfg.com, www.mcgowanmfg.com, Knife sharpeners, hunting axes

Peele, Bryan, The Elk Rack, 215 Ferry St. P.O. Box 1363, Thompson Falls, MT, 59873

Schlott, Harald, Zingster Str. 26, 13051 Berlin, GERMANY, 049 030 9293346, harald.schlott@T-online.de, Custom grinder, custom handle artisan, display case/box maker, etcher, scrimshander

Wilson, R.W., P.O. Box 2012, Weirton, WV, 26062, 304-723-2771 rwknives@comcast.net, www.rwwilsonknives.com

custom handles

Cooper, Jim, 1221 Cook St, Ramona, CA, 92065-3214, 760-789-1097, (760) 788-7992, jamcooper@aol.com

Burrows, Chuck, dba Wild Rose Trading Co, 102 Timber Ln., Durango, CO, 81303, 970-317-5592, chuck@wrtcleather.com, www.wrtcleather.com

Fields, Donald, 790 Tamerlane St, Deltona, FL, 32725, 386-532-9070, donaldfields@earthlink.net, Selling ancient ivories; mammoth & fossil walrus

Grussenmeyer, Paul G., 310 Kresson Rd, Cherry Hill, NJ, 08034, 856-428-1088, 856-428-8997, pgrussentne@comcast.net, www.pgcarvings.com

Holland, Dennis K., 4908-17th Pl., Lubbock, TX, 79416

Imboden II, Howard L., Hi II Originals, 620 Deauville Dr., Dayton, OH, 45429, 513-439-1536

Kelso, Jim, 577 Collar Hill Rd, Worcester, VT, 05682, 802-229-4254, (802) 229-0595

Marlatt, David, 67622 Oldham Rd., Cambridge, OH, 43725, 740-432-7549

Mead, Dennis, 2250 E. Mercury St., Inverness, FL, 34453-0514

Myers, Ron, 6202 Marglenn Ave., Baltimore, MD, 21206, 410-866-6914

Schlott, Harald, Zingster Str. 26, 13051 Berlin, GERMANY, 049 030 9293346, harald.schlott@T-online.de, Custom grinder, custom handle artisan, display case/box maker, etcher, scrimshander

Snell, Barry A., 4801 96th St. N., St. Petersburg, FL, 33708-3740

Vallotton, A., 621 Fawn Ridge Dr., Oakland, OR, 97462, 541-459-2216

Watson, Silvia, 350 Jennifer Lane, Driftwood, TX, 78619

Wilderness Forge, 315 North 100 East, Kanab, UT, 84741, 435-644-3674, bhatting@xpressweb.com

Williams, Gary, (GARBO), PO Box 210, Glendale, KY, 42740-2010 270-369-6752, scrimbygarbo@gmail.com, www.scrimbygarbo.com

display cases and boxes

Bill's Custom Cases, P O Box 603, Montague, CA, 96064, 541-727-7223, billscustomcases@earthlink.net, www.billscustomcases.com

Culpepper & Company, 8285 Georgia Rd., Otto, NC, 28763 828-524-6842, info@culpepperco.com, www.knifehandles.com

McLean, Lawrence, 12344 Meritage Ct, Rancho Cucamonga, CA, 91739, 714-848-5779, lmclean@charter.net

Miller, Michael K., M&M Kustom Krafts, 28510 Santiam Highway, Sweet Home, OR, 97386

Miller, Robert, P.O. Box 2722, Ormond Beach, FL, 32176

Retichek, Joseph L., W9377 Co. TK. D, Beaver Dam, WI, 53916

Robbins, Wayne, 11520 Inverway, Belvidere, IL, 61008

S&D Enterprises, 20 East Seventh St, Manchester, OH, 45144, 855-876-9693, 937-549-2602, sales@s-denterprises.com, www.s-denterprises.com, Display case/ box maker. Manufacturer of aluminum display, chipboard type displays, wood displays. Silk screening or acid etching for logos on product

Schlott, Harald, Zingster Str. 26, 13051 Berlin, GERMANY, 049 030 9293346, harald.schlott@T-online.de, Custom grinder, custom handle artisan, display case/box maker, etcher, scrimshander

engravers

Adlam, Tim, 1705 Witzel Ave., Oshkosh, WI, 54902, 920-235-4589, www.adlamengraving.com

Alcorn, Gordon, 10573 Kelly Canyon Rd., Bozeman, MT 59715, 406-586-1350, alcorncustom@yahoo.com, www.alcornengraving.com

Alfano, Sam, 45 Catalpa Trace, Covington, LA, 70433, alfano@gmail.com, www.masterengraver.com

Baron, David, Baron Engraving, 62 Spring Hill Rd., Trumbull, CT, 06611, 203-452-0515, sales@baronengraving.com, www.baronengraving.com, Polishing, plating, inlays, artwork

Bates, Billy, 2302 Winthrop Dr. SW, Decatur, AL, 35603, bbrn@aol.com, www.angelfire.com/al/billybates

Blair, Jim, PO Box 64, 59 Mesa Verde, Glenrock, WY, 82637, 307-436-8115, jblairengrav@msn.com, www.jimblairengraving.com

Booysen, Chris, South Africa, +27-73-284-1493, chris@cbknives.com, www.cbknives.com

Churchill, Winston G., RFD Box 29B, Proctorsville, VT 05153, www.wchurchill.com

Collins, Michael, 405-392-2273, info@michaelcollinsart.com, www.michaelcollinsart.com

Cover, Raymond A., 1206 N. Third St., Festus, MO 63010 314-808-2508 cover@sbcglobal.net, http://learningtoengrave.com

DeLorge, Ed, 6734 W Main St, Houma, LA, 70360, 985-223-0206, delorge@

triparish.net, http://www.eddelorge.com/

Dickson, John W., PO Box 49914, Sarasota, FL, 34230, 941-952-1907

Dolbare, Elizabeth, PO Box 502, Dubois, WY, 82513-0502 edolbare@hotmail.com, http://www.scrimshaw-engraving.com/

Downing, Jim, PO Box 4224, Springfield, MO, 65803, 417-865-5953, handlebar@thegunengraver.com, www.thegunengraver.com, engraver and scrimshaw artist

Duarte, Carlos, 108 Church St., Rossville, CA, 95678, 916-782-2617 carlossilver@surewest.net, www.carlossilver.com

Dubber, Michael W., 11 S. Green River Rd., Evansville, IN, 47715, 812-454-0271, m.dubber@firearmsengraving.com, www.firearmsengraving.com

Eaton, Rick, 313 Dailey Rd., Broadview, MT 59015, 406-667-2405, rick@eatonknives.com, www.eatonknives.com

Eklund, Maihkel, Föne Stam V9, S-820 41 Färila, SWEDEN, info@art-knives.com, www.art-knives.com

Eldridge, Allan, 7731 Four Winds Dr., Ft. Worth, TX 76133, 817-370-7778

Ellis, Willy B, Willy B's Customs, 1025 Hamilton Ave., Tarpon Springs, FL, 34689, 727-942-6420, wbflashs@verizon.net, www.willyb.com

Flannery Gun Engraving, Jeff, 11034 Riddles Run Rd., Union, KY, 41091, 859-384-3127, engraving@fuse.net, www.flannerygunengraving.com

Gournet, Geoffroy, 820 Paxinosa Ave., Easton, PA, 18042, 610-559-0710, ggournet@yahoo.com, www.gournetusa.com

Halloran, Tim, 316 Fenceline Dr., Blue Grass, IA 52726 563-260-8464, vivtim@msn.com, http://halloranengraving.com

Hands, Barry Lee, 30608 Fernview Ln., Bigfork, MT 59911, 406-249-4334, barry_hands@yahoo.com, www.barryleehands.com

Holder, Pat, 18910 McNeil Ranch Rd., Wickenburg, AZ 85390, 928-684-2025 dholderknives@commspeed.net, www.dholder.com

Ingle, Ralph W., 151 Callan Dr., Rossville, GA, 30741, 706-858-0641, riengraver@aol.com

Johns, Bill, 1716 8th St, Cody, WY, 82414, 307-587-5090, http://billjohnsengraver.com

Kelso, Jim, 577 Collar Hill Rd, Worcester, VT, 05682, 802-229-4254, jimkelsojournal@gmail.com, www.jimkelso.com

Koevenig, Eugene and Eve, Koevenig's Engraving Service, Rabbit Gulch, Box 55, Hill City, SD, 57745-0055

Kostelnik, Joe and Patty, RD #4, Box 323, Greensburg, PA, 15601

Kudlas, John M., 55280 Silverwolf Dr, Barnes, WI, 54873, 715-795-2031, jkudlas@cheqnet.net, Engraver, scrimshander

Lark, David, 6641 Schneider Rd., Kingsley, MI 49649, Phone: 231-342-1076 dblark58@yahoo.com

Larson, Doug, Dragon's Fire Studio, Percival, IA, Phone: 402-202-3703 (cell) dragonsfirestudio@hotmail.com

Limings Jr., Harry, 5793 Nichels Ln., Johnstown, OH, 43031-9576

Lindsay, Steve, 3714 West Cedar Hill, Kearney, NE, 68845, Phone: 308-236-7885 steve@lindsayengraving.com, www.lindsayengraving.com

Lurth, Mitchell, 1317 7th Ave., Marion, IA 52302, Phone: 319-377-1899 www.lurthengraving.com

Lyttle, Brian, Box 5697, High River AB CANADA, T1V 1M7, Phone: 403-558-3638, brian@lyttleknives.com, www.lyttleknives.com

Lytton, Simon M., 19 Pinewood Gardens, Hemel Hempstead, Hertfordshire HP1 1TN, ENGLAND, 01-442-255542, simonlyttonengraver@virginmedia.com

Markow, Paul, 130 Spinnaker Ridge Dr. SW, B206, Huntsville, AL 35824, 256-513-9790, paul.markow@gmail.com, sites.google.com/site/artistictouch2010/engraving

Mason, Joe, 146 Value Rd, Brandon, MS, 39042, 601-519-8850, masonjoe@bellsouth.net, www.joemasonengraving.com

McCombs, Leo, 1862 White Cemetery Rd., Patriot, OH, 45658

McDonald, Dennis, 8359 Brady St., Peosta, IA, 52068

McLean, Lawrence, 12344 Meritage Ct, Rancho Cucamonga, CA, 91739, 714-848-5779, lmclean@charter.net

Meyer, Chris, 39 Bergen Ave., Wantage, NJ, 07461, 973-875-6299

Minnick, Joyce, 144 N. 7th St., Middletown, IN, 47356, 765-354-4108

Morgan, Tandie, P.O. Box 693, 30700 Hwy. 97, Nucla, CO, 81424

Morton, David A., 1110 W. 21st St., Lorain, OH, 44052

Moulton, Dusty, 135 Hillview Ln, Loudon, TN, 37774, 865-408-9779, dusty@moultonknives.com, www.moultonknives.com

Muller, Jody & Pat, 3359 S. 225th Rd., Goodson, MO, 65663, 417-852-4306/417-752-3260, mullerforge2@hotmail.com, www.mullerforge.com

Nelida, Toniutti, via G. Pasconi 29/c, Maniago 33085 (PN), ITALY

Nilsson, Jonny Walker, Akkavare 16, 93391 Arvidsjaur, SWEDEN, +(46) 702-144207, 0960.13048@telia.com, www.jwnknives.com

Parke, Jeff, 1365 Fort Pierce Dr. #3, St. George, UT 84790, Phone: 435-421-1692 jeffrey_parke@hotmail.com, https://www.facebook.com/jeff.parke1

Patterson, W.H., P.O. Drawer DK, College Station, TX, 77841

Peri, Valerio, Via Meucci 12, Gardone V.T. 25063, ITALY

Pilkington Jr., Scott, P.O. Box 97, Monteagle, TN, 37356, 931-924-3400, scott@pilkguns.com, www.pilkguns.com

Pulisova, Andrea, CSA 230-95, 96701 Kremnica, Slovakia, Phone: 00421 903-340076 vpulis@gmail.com

Rabeno, Martin, Spook Hollow Trading Co, 530 Eagle Pass, Durango, CO, 81301

Raftis, Andrew, 2743 N. Sheffield, Chicago, IL, 60614

Riccardo, David, Riccardo Fine Hand Engraving, Buckley, MI, Phone: 231-269-3028, riccardoengraving@acegroup.cc, www.riccardoengraving.com

Roberts, J.J., 7808 Lake Dr., Manassas, VA, 20111, 703-330-0448, jjrengraver@aol.com

Robidoux, Roland J., DMR Fine Engraving, 25 N. Federal Hwy. Studio 5, Dania, FL, 33004

Rosser, Bob, Hand Engraving, 2809 Crescent Ave Ste 20, Birmingham, AL, 35209, 205-870-4422, brengraver1@gmail.com, www.hand-engravers.com

Rudolph, Gil, 20922 Oak Pass Ave, Tehachapi, CA, 93561, 661-822-4949

Rundell, Joe, 6198 W. Frances Rd., Clio, MI, 48420

Sawby, Marian, 480 Snowberry Ln., Sandpoint, ID 83864, 208-263-4253, http://sawbycustomknives.com/

Schönert, Elke, 18 Lansdowne Pl., Central, Port Elizabeth, SOUTH AFRICA

Shaw, Bruce, P.O. Box 545, Pacific Grove, CA, 93950, 831-646-1937, 831-644-0941, shawdogs@aol.com

Simmons, Rick W., 3323 Creek Manor Dr., Kingwood, TX, 77339, 504-261-8450, exhibitiongrade@gmail.com www.bespokeengraving.com

Slobodian, Barbara, 4101 River Ridge Dr., PO Box 1498, San Andreas, CA 95249, 209-286-1980, fax 209-286-1982, barbara@dancethetide.com. Specializes in Japanese-style engraving.

Small, Jim, 2860 Athens Hwy., Madison, GA 30650, 706-818-1245, smallengrave@aol.com

Smith, Ron, 5869 Straley, Ft. Worth, TX, 76114

Smitty's Engraving, 21320 Pioneer Circle, Harrah, OK, 73045, 405-454-6968, mail@smittys-engraving.us, www.smittys-engraving.us

Soileau, Damon, P.O. Box 7292, Kingsport, TN 37664 423-297-4665, oiseaumetalarts@gmail.com, www.oiseaumetalarts.etsy.com

Spode, Peter, Tresaith Newland, Malvern, Worcestershire WR13 5AY, ENGLAND

Swartley, Robert D., 2800 Pine St., Napa, CA, 94558

Takeuchi, Shigetoshi, 21-14-1-Chome kamimuneoka Shiki shi, 353 Saitama, JAPAN

Theis, Terry, 21452 FM 2093, Harper, TX, 78631, 830-864-4438

Valade, Robert B., 931 3rd Ave., Seaside, OR, 97138, 503-738-7672, (503) 738-7672

Waldrop, Mark, 14562 SE 1st Ave. Rd., Summerfield, FL, 34491

Warenski-Erickson, Julie, 590 East 500 N., Richfield, UT, 84701, 435-627-2504, julie@warenskiknives.com, www.warenskiknives.com

Warren, Kenneth W., P.O. Box 2842, Wenatchee, WA, 98807-2842, 509-663-6123, (509) 663-6123

Whitmore, Jerry, 1740 Churchill Dr., Oakland, OR, 97462

Winn, Travis A., 558 E. 3065 S., Salt Lake City, UT, 84106, 801-467-5957

Zima, Russ, 7291 Ruth Way, Denver, CO, 80221, 303-657-9378, rzima@rzengraving.com, www.rzengraving.com

etchers

Baron Engraving, David Baron, 62 Spring Hill Rd., Trumbull, CT, 06611, 203-452-0515 sales@baronengraving.com, www.baronengraving.com

Fountain Products, 492 Prospect Ave., West Springfield, MA, 01089, 413-781-4651

Hayes, Dolores, P.O. Box 41405, Los Angeles, CA, 90041

Holland, Dennis, 4908 17th Pl., Lubbock, TX, 79416

Kelso, Jim, 577 Collar Hill Rd, Worcester, VT, 05682, 802-229-4254, jimkelsojournal@gmail.com, www.jimkelso.com

Larstein, Francine, Francine Etched Knives, 368 White Rd, Watsonville, CA, 95076, 800-557-1525/831-426-6046, francine@francinetchedknives.com, www.francineetchedknives.com

Lefaucheux, Jean-Victor, Saint-Denis-Le-Ferment, 27140 Gisors, FRANCE

Myers, Ron, 6202 Marglenn Ave., Baltimore, MD, 21206, (acid) etcher

Nilsson, Jonny Walker, Akkavare 16, 93391 Arvidsjaur, SWEDEN, +(46) 702-144207, 0960.13048@telia.com, www.jwnknives.com

Schlott, Harald, Zingster Str. 26, 13051 Berlin, GERMANY, 049 030 9293346, harald.schlott@T-online.de, Custom grinder, custom handle artisan, display case/box maker, etcher, scrimshander
Vallotton, A., Northwest Knife Supply, 621 Fawn Ridge Dr., Oakland, OR, 97462
Watson, Silvia, 350 Jennifer Lane, Driftwood, TX, 78619

heat treaters

Bodycote Inc., 443 E. High St., London, OH 43140 740-852-5000, chris.gattie@bodycote.com, www.bodycote.com
Kazou, Okaysu, 12-2 1 Chome Higashi, Ueno, Taito-Ku, Tokyo, JAPAN, 81-33834-2323, 81-33831-3012
O&W Heat Treat Inc., One Bidwell Rd., South Windsor, CT, 06074, 860-528-9239, (860) 291-9939, owht1@aol.com
Pacific Heat Treating, attn: B.R. Holt, 1238 Birchwood Drive, Sunnyvale, CA, 94089, 408-736-8500, www.pacificheattreating.com
Paul Bos Heat Treating c/o Paul Farner, Buck Knives: 660 S. Lochsa St., Post Falls, ID 83854, 208-262-0500, Ext. 211 / fax 800-733-2825, pfarner@buckknives.com, or contact Paul Bos direct: 928-232-1656, paulbos@buckknives.com
Progressive Heat Treating Co., 2802 Charles City Rd, Richmond, VA, 23231, 804-717-5353, 800-868-5457, sales@pecgears.com
Texas Heat Treating Inc., 155 Texas Ave., Round Rock, TX, 78680, 512-255-5884, buster@texasheattreating.com, www.texasheattreating.com
Texas Knifemakers Supply, 10649 Haddington, Suite 180, Houston, TX, 77043, 713-461-8632, sales@texasknife.com, www.texasknife.com
Tinker Shop, The, 1120 Helen, Deer Park, TX, 77536, 713-479-7286
Valley Metal Treating Inc., 355 S. East End Ave., Pomona, CA, 91766, 909-623-6316, ray@valleymt.net
Wilson, R.W., P.O. Box 2012, Weirton, WV, 26062, 304-723-2771 rwknives@comcast.net, rwwilsonknives.com

leather workers

Abramson, David, 116 Baker Ave, Wharton, NJ, 07885, 973-713-9776, lifter4him1@aol.com, www.liftersleather.com
Burrows, Chuck, dba Wild Rose Trading Co, 102 Timber Ln., Durango, CO 81303, 970-317-5592, wrtc@wrtcleather.com, www.wrtcleather.com
Clements' Custom Leathercraft, Chas, 1741 Dallas St., Aurora, CO 80010, Phone: 303-364-0403, chasclements@comcast.net
Cole, Dave, 620 Poinsetta Dr., Satellite Beach, FL 32937, 321-773-1687, www.dcknivesandleather.blademakers.com. Custom sheath services.
CowCatcher Leatherworks, 2045 Progress Ct., Raleigh, NC 27608, Phone: 919-833-8262 cowcatcher1@ymail.com, www.cowcatcher.us
Cubic, George, GC Custom Leather Co., 10561 E. Deerfield Pl., Tucson, AZ, 85749, 520-760-0695, gcubic@aol.com
Dawkins, Dudley, 221 N. Broadmoor Ave, Topeka, KS, 66606-1254, 785-817-9343, dawkind@reagan.com, ABS member/knifemaker forges straight knives
Evans, Scott V, Edge Works Mfg, 1171 Halltown Rd, Jacksonville, NC, 28546, 910-455-9834, fax 910-346-5660, support@tacticalholsters.com, www.tacticalholsters.com
Genske, Jay, 283 Doty St, Fond du Lac, WI, 54935, 920-921-8019/Cell Phone 920-579-0144, jaygenske@hotmail.com, http://genskeknives.weebly.com, Custom Grinder, Custom Handle Artisan
Green River Leather, 1098 Legion Park Road, PO BOX 190, Greensburg, KY, 42743, Phone: 270-932-2212 fax: 270-299-2471 email: info@greenriverleather.com
John's Custom Leather, John R. Stumpf, 523 S. Liberty St, Blairsville, PA, 15717, 724-459-6802, 724-459-5996, www.jclleather.com
Kravitt, Chris, Treestump Leather, 443 Cave Hill Rd., Waltham, ME, 04605-8706, 207-584-3000, sheathmkr@aol.com, www.treestumpleather.com, Reference: Tree Stump Leather
Layton, Jim, 2710 Gilbert Avenue, Portsmouth, OH, 45662, 740-353-6179
Lee, Sonja and Randy, P.O. Box 1873, 270 N 9th West, St. Johns, AZ, 85936, 928-337-2594, 928-337-5002, randylee.knives@yahoo.com, info@randyleeknives.com, Custom knifemaker; www.randyleeknives.com
Long, Paul, Paul Long Custom Leather, 108 Briarwood Ln. W, Kerrville, TX, 78028, 830-367-5536, PFL@cebridge.net
Lott, Sherry, 1098 Legion Park Road, PO BOX 190, Greensburg, KY, 42743, Phone: 270-932-2212 fax: 270-299-2471 email: info@greenriverleather.

com, sherrylott@alltel.net
Mason, Arne, 258 Wimer St., Ashland, OR, 97520, 541-482-2260, (541) 482-7785, am@arnemason.com, www.arnemason.com
Metheny, H.A. "Whitey", 7750 Waterford Dr., Spotsylvania, VA 22551, 540-582-3228 Cell 540-842-1440, fax 540-582-3095, hametheny@aol.com, http://whitey.methenyknives.com
Morrissey, Martin, 4578 Stephens Rd., Blairsville, GA, 30512
Niedenthal, John Andre, Beadwork & Buckskin, Studio 3955 NW 103 Dr., Coral Springs, FL, 33065-1551, 954-345-0447, a_niedenthal@hotmail.com
Neilson, Tess, 187 Cistern Ln., Towanda, PA 18848, 570-721-0470, mountainhollow@epix.net, www.mountainhollow.net, Doing business as Neilson's Mountain Hollow
Parsons, Larry, 539 S. Pleasant View Dr., Mustang, OK 73064 405-376-9408 l.j.parsons@sbcglobal.net, www.parsonssaddleshop.com
Red's Custom Leather, Ed Todd, 9 Woodlawn Rd., Putnam Valley, NY 10579, 845-528-3783, redscustomleather@redscustomleather.com, www.redscustomleather.com
Rowe, Kenny, Rowe's Leather, 3219 Hwy 29 South, Hope, AR, 71801, 870-777-8216, fax 870-777-0935, rowesleather@yahoo.com, www.rowesleather.com
Schrap, Robert G., Custom Leather Knife Sheaths, 7024 W. Wells St., Wauwatosa, WI, 53213, 414-771-6472, fax 414-479-9765, rschrap@aol.com, www.customsheaths.com
Strahin, Robert, 401 Center St., Elkins, WV, 26241, 304-636-0128, rstrahin@copper.net, *Custom Knife Sheaths
Walker, John, 17 Laber Circle, Little Rock, AR, 72210, 501-455-0239, john.walker@afbic.com

miscellaneous

Robertson, Kathy, Impress by Design, PO Box 1367, Evans, GA, 30809-1367, 706-650-0982, (706) 860-1623, impressbydesign@comcast.net, Advertising/graphic designer
Strahin, Robert, 401 Center St., Elkins, WV, 26241, 304-636-0128, rstrahin@copper.net, *Custom Knife Sheaths

photographers

Alfano, Sam, 36180 Henery Gaines Rd., Pearl River, LA, 70452
Allen, John, Studio One, 3823 Pleasant Valley Blvd., Rockford, IL, 61114
Bilal, Mustafa, Turk's Head Productions, 908 NW 50th St., Seattle, WA, 98107-3634, 206-782-4164, (206) 783-5677, info@turkshead.com, www.turkshead.com, Graphic design, marketing & advertising
Bogaerts, Jan, Regenweg 14, 5757 Pl., Liessel, HOLLAND
Box Photography, Doug, 1804 W Main St, Brenham, TX, 77833-3420
Brown, Tom, 6048 Grants Ferry Rd., Brandon, MS, 39042-8136
Butman, Steve, P.O. Box 5106, Abilene, TX, 79608
Calidonna, Greg, 205 Helmwood Dr., Elizabethtown, KY, 42701
Campbell, Jim, 7935 Ranch Rd., Port Richey, FL, 34668
Cooper, Jim, Sharpbycoop.com Photography, 9 Mathew Court, Norwalk, CT 06851, jcooper@sharpbycoop.com, www.sharpbycoop.com
Courtice, Bill, P.O. Box 1776, Duarte, CA, 91010-4776
Crosby, Doug, RFD 1, Box 1111, Stockton Springs, ME, 04981
Danko, Michael, 3030 Jane Street, Pittsburgh, PA, 15203
Davis, Marshall B., P.O. Box 3048, Austin, TX, 78764
Earley, Don, 1241 Ft. Bragg Rd., Fayetteville, NC, 28305
Ehrlich, Linn M., 1850 N Clark St #1008, Chicago, IL, 60614, 312-209-2107
Etzler, John, 11200 N. Island Rd., Grafton, OH, 44044
Fahrner, Dave, 1623 Arnold St., Pittsburgh, PA, 15205
Faul, Jan W., 903 Girard St. NE, Rr. Washington, DC, 20017
Fedorak, Allan, 28 W. Nicola St., Amloops BC CANADA, V2C 1J6
Fox, Daniel, Lumina Studios, 6773 Industrial Parkway, Cleveland, OH, 44070, 440-734-2118, (440) 734-3542, lumina@en.com, lumina-studios.com
Francesco Pachi, Loc. Pometta 1, 17046 Sassello (SV) ITALY Tel-fax: 0039 019 724581, info@pachi-photo.com, www.pachi-photo.com
Freiberg, Charley, PO Box 42, Elkins, NH, 03233, 603-526-2767, charleyfreiberg@tds.net, charleyfreibergphotography.com
Gardner, Chuck, 116 Quincy Ave., Oak Ridge, TN, 37830
Gawryla, Don, 1105 Greenlawn Dr., Pittsburgh, PA, 15220
Goffe Photographic Associates, 3108 Monte Vista Blvd., NE, Albuquerque, NM, 87106
Hanusin, John, Reames-Hanusin Studio, PO Box 931, Northbrook, IL, 60065 0931, 847-564-2706

Hodge, Tom, 7175 S US Hwy 1 Lot 36, Titusville, FL, 32780-8172, 321-267-7989, egdoht@hotmail.com

Holter, Wayne V., 125 Lakin Ave., Boonsboro, MD, 21713, 301-416-2855, mackwayne@hotmail.com

Hopkins, David W, Hopkins Photography inc, 201 S Jefferson, Iola, KS, 66749, 620-365-7443, nhoppy@netks.net

LaFleur, Gordon, 111 Hirst, Box 1209, Parksville BC CANADA, V0R 270

Lear, Dale, 6544 Cora Mill Rd, Gallipolis, OH, 45631, 740-245-5482, dalelear@yahoo.com, Ebay Sales

LeBlanc, Paul, No. 3 Meadowbrook Cir., Melissa, TX, 75454

Lester, Dean, 2801 Junipero Ave Suite 212, Long Beach, CA, 90806-2140

Leviton, David A., A Studio on the Move, P.O. Box 2871, Silverdale, WA, 98383, 360-697-3452

Long, Gary W., 3556 Miller's Crossroad Rd., Hillsboro, TN, 37342, 931-596-2275

Martin, Cory, 4249 Taylor Harbor #7, Racine, WI 53403, 262-352-5392, info@corymartinimaging.com, www.corymartinimaging.com

McCollum, Tom, P.O. Box 933, Lilburn, GA, 30226

Mitch Lum Website and Photography, 22115 NW Imbrie Dr. #298, Hillsboro, OR 97124, mitch@mitchlum.com, www.mitchlum.com, 206-356-6813

Moake, Jim, 18 Council Ave., Aurora, IL, 60504

Moya Inc., 4212 S. Dixie Hwy., West Palm Beach, FL, 33405

Norman's Studio, 322 S. 2nd St., Vivian, LA, 71082

Owens, William T., Box 99, Williamsburg, WV, 24991

Pachi, Francesco, Loc. Pometta 1, 17046 Sassello (SV) ITALY Tel-fax: 0039 019 724581, info@pachi-photo.com, www.pachi-photo.com

Palmer Studio, 2008 Airport Blvd., Mobile, AL, 36606

Payne, Robert G., P.O. Box 141471, Austin, TX, 78714

Pigott, John, 9095 Woodprint LN, Mason, OH, 45040

Point Seven, 6450 Weatherfield Ct., Unit 2A, Maumee, OH, 43537, 312-420-4647 pointseven@pointsevenstudios.com, www.ericegglyphotography.com

Rob Andrew Photography, Rob Szajkowski, 7960 Silverton Ave., Ste. 125, San Diego, CA 92126, 760-920-6380, robandrewphoto@gmail.com, www.robandrewphoto.com

Professional Medica Concepts, Patricia Mitchell, P.O. Box 0002, Warren, TX, 77664, 409-547-2213, pm0909@wt.net

Rasmussen, Eric L., 1121 Eliason, Brigham City, UT, 84302

Rhoades, Cynthia J., Box 195, Clearmont, WY, 82835

Rice, Tim, PO Box 663, Whitefish, MT, 59937

Richardson, Kerry, 2520 Mimosa St., Santa Rosa, CA, 95405, 707-575-1875, kerry@sonic.net, www.sonic.net/~kerry

Ross, Bill, 28364 S. Western Ave. Suite 464, Rancho Palos Verdes, CA, 90275

Rubicam, Stephen, 14 Atlantic Ave., Boothbay Harbor, ME, 04538-1202

Rush, John D., 2313 Maysel, Bloomington, IL, 61701

Schreiber, Roger, 429 Boren Ave. N., Seattle, WA, 98109

Semmer, Charles, 7885 Cyd Dr., Denver, CO, 80221

Silver Images Photography, 2412 N Keystone, Flagstaff, AZ, 86004

Slobodian, Scott, 4101 River Ridge Dr., P.O. Box 1498, San Andreas, CA, 95249, 209-286-1980, (209) 286-1982, www.slobodianswords.com

Smith, Earl W., 5121 Southminster Rd., Columbus, OH, 43221

Smith, Randall, 1720 Oneco Ave., Winter Park, FL, 32789

Storm Photo, 334 Wall St., Kingston, NY, 12401

Surles, Mark, P.O. Box 147, Falcon, NC, 28342

Third Eye Photos, 140 E. Sixth Ave., Helena, MT, 59601

Thurber, David, P.O. Box 1006, Visalia, CA, 93279

Tighe, Brian, 12-111 Fourth Ave., Ste. 376 Ridley Square, St. Catharines ON CANADA, L2S 3P5, 905-892-2734, www.tigheknives.com

Towell, Steven L., 3720 N.W. 32nd Ave., Camas, WA, 98607, 360-834-9049, sltowell@netscape.net

Verno Studio, Jay, 3030 Jane Street, Pittsburgh, PA, 15203

Ward, Chuck, 1010 E North St, PO Box 2272, Benton, AR, 72018, 501-778-4329, chuckbop@aol.com

Wise, Harriet, 242 Dill Ave., Frederick, MD, 21701

Worley, Holly, Worley Photography, 6360 W David Dr, Littleton, CO, 80128-5708, 303-257-8091, 720-981-2800, hsworley@aol.com, Products, Digital & Film

scrimshanders

Adlam, Tim, 1705 Witzel Ave., Oshkosh, WI, 54902, 920-235-4589, ctimadlam@new.rr.com, www.adlamengraving.com

Alpen, Ralph, 7 Bentley Rd., West Grove, PA, 19390, 610-869-7141

Anderson, Terry Jack, 10076 Birnamwoods Way, Riverton, UT, 84065-9073

Ashworth, Boyd, 1510 Bullard Pl., Powder Springs, GA 30127, 404-583-5652, boydashworthknives@comcast.net, www.boydashworthknives.com

Bailey, Mary W., 3213 Jonesboro Dr., Nashville, TN, 37214, Phone: 615-889-3172 mbscrim@aol.com

Baker, Duane, 2145 Alum Creek Dr., Cambridge Park Apt. #10, Columbus, OH, 43207

Barrows, Miles, 524 Parsons Ave., Chillicothe, OH, 45601

Brady, Sandra, Scrimshaw by Sandra Brady, 9608 Monclova Rd., Monclova, OH 43542, 419-866-0435, 419-261-1582 sandy@sandrabradyart.com, www.sandrabradyart.com

Beauchamp, Gaetan, 125 de la Riviere, Stoneham, QC, G3C 0P6, CANADA, 418-848-1914, fax 418-848-6859, knives@gbeauchamp.ca, www.gbeauchamp.ca

Bellet, Connie, PO Box 151, Palermo, ME, 04354 0151, 207-993-2327, phwhitehawk@gwl.net

Benade, Lynn, 2610 Buckhurst Dr, Beachwood, OH, 44122, 216-464-0777, llbnc17@aol.com

Bonshire, Benita, 1121 Burlington Dr., Muncie, IN, 47302

Boone Trading Co. Inc., P.O. Box 669, Brinnon, WA, 98320, 800-423-1945, bella@boonetrading.com, www.boonetrading.com

Bryan, Bob, 1120 Oak Hill Rd., Carthage, MO, 64836

Burger, Sharon, Glenwood, Durban KZN, South Africa, cell: +27 83 7891675, scribble@iafrica.com, www.sharonburger-scrimshaw.co.za/

Byrne, Mary Gregg, 1018 15th St., Bellingham, WA, 98225-6604

Cable, Jerry, 332 Main St., Mt. Pleasant, PA, 15666

Caudill, Lyle, 7626 Lyons Rd., Georgetown, OH, 45121

Cole, Gary, PO Box 668, Naalehu, HI, 96772, 808-929-9775, 808-929-7371

Collins, Michael, Rt. 3075, Batesville Rd., Woodstock, GA, 30188

Conover, Juanita Rae, P.O. Box 70442, Eugene, OR, 97401, 541-747-1726 or 543-4851, juanitaraeconover@yahoo.com

Courtnage, Elaine, Box 473, Big Sandy, MT, 59520

Cover Jr., Raymond A., 1206 N. 3rd St., Festus, MO, 63010, Phone: 314-808-2508 cover@sbcglobal.net, learningtoengravecom

Cox, J. Andy, 116 Robin Hood Lane, Gaffney, SC, 29340

Dietrich, Roni, Wild Horse Studio, 1257 Cottage Dr, Harrisburg, PA, 17112, 717-469-0587, ronimd@aol

Dolbare, Elizabeth, PO Box 502, Dubois, WY, 82513-0502

Eklund, Maihkel, Föne Stam V9, S-82041 Färila, SWEDEN, +46 6512 4192, info@art-knives.com, www.art-knives.com

Eldridge, Allan, 1424 Kansas Lane, Gallatin, TN, 37066

Ellis, Willy B., Willy B's Customs by William B Ellis, Tarpon Springs, FL, 34689, 727-942-6420, wbflashs@verizon.net, www.willyb.com

Fisk, Dale, Box 252, Council, ID, 83612, dafisk@ctcweb.net

Foster Enterprises, Norvell Foster, P.O. Box 200343, San Antonio, TX, 78220

Fountain Products, 492 Prospect Ave., West Springfield, MA, 01089

Gill, Scott, 925 N. Armstrong St., Kokomo, IN, 46901

Hands, Barry Lee, 30608 Fernview Ln., Bigfork, MT, 59911, 406-249-4334, barry_hands@yahoo.com, www.barryleehands.com

Hargraves Sr., Charles, RR 3 Bancroft, Ontario CANADA, K0L 1C0

Harless, Star, c/o Arrow Forge, P.O. Box 845, Stoneville, NC, 27048-0845

Harrington, Fred A., Summer: 2107 W Frances Rd, Mt Morris MI 48458 8215, Winter: 3725 Citrus, St. James City, FL, 33956, Winter 239-283-0721, Summer 810-686-3008

Hergert, Bob, 12 Geer Circle, Port Orford, OR, 97465, 541-332-3010, hergert@harborside.com, www.scrimshander.com

Hielscher, Vickie, 6550 Otoe Rd, P.O. Box 992, Alliance, NE, 69301, 308-762-4318, g-hielsc@bbcwb.net

High, Tom, 5474 S. 112.8 Rd., Alamosa, CO, 81101, 719-589-2108, rmscrimshaw@gmail.com, www.rockymountainscrimshaw.com, Wildlife Artist

Himmelheber, David R., 11289 40th St. N., Royal Palm Beach, FL, 33411

Holland, Dennis K., 4908-17th Place, Lubbock, TX, 79416

Hutchings, Rick "Hutch", 3007 Coffe Tree Ct, Crestwood, KY, 40014, 502-241-2871, baron1@bellsouth.net

Imboden II, Howard L., 620 Deauville Dr., Dayton, OH, 45429, 937-439-1536, Guards by the "Last Wax Technic"

Johnson, Corinne, W3565 Lockington, Mindora, WI, 54644

Johnston, Kathy, W. 1134 Providence, Spokane, WA, 99205

Karst Stone, Linda, 903 Tanglewood Ln, Kerrville, TX, 78028-2945, 830-896-4678, 830-257-6117, linda@karstone.com, www.karstone.com

Kelso, Jim, 577 Collar Hill Rd, Worcester, VT 05682, 802-229-4254 kelsomaker@gmail.com, www.jimkelso.com

Koevenig, Eugene and Eve, Koevenig's Engraving Service, Rabbit Gulch, Box 55, Hill City, SD, 57745-0055

Kostelnik, Joe and Patty, RD #4, Box 323, Greensburg, PA 15601

Lemen, Pam, 3434 N. Iroquois Ave., Tucson, AZ, 85705

Martin, Diane, 28220 N. Lake Dr., Waterford, WI, 53185

McDonald, René Cosimini-, 14730 61 Court N., Loxahatchee, FL, 33470

McFadden, Berni, 2547 E Dalton Ave, Dalton Gardens, ID, 83815-9631

McGowan, Frank, 12629 Howard Lodge Dr., Winter Add-2023 Robin Ct Sebring FL 33870, Sykesville, MD, 21784, 863-385-1296

McGrath, Gayle, PMB 232 15201 N Cleveland Ave, N Ft Myers, FL, 33903

McLaran, Lou, 603 Powers St., Waco, TX, 76705

McWilliams, Carole, P.O. Box 693, Bayfield, CO, 81122

Mitchell, James, 1026 7th Ave., Columbus, GA, 31901

Moore, James B., 1707 N. Gillis, Stockton, TX, 79735

Ochonicky, Michelle "Mike", Stone Hollow Studio, 31 High Trail, Eureka, MO, 63025, 636-938-9570, www.stonehollowstudio.com

Ochs, Belle, 124 Emerald Lane, Largo, FL, 33771, 727-536-3827, contact@ oxforge.com, www.oxforge.com

Pachi, Mirella, Localita Pometta 1, 17046 Sassello (SV), ITALY, +39 019 72 00 86, www.pachi-photo.com

Parish, Vaughn, 103 Cross St., Monaca, PA, 15061

Peterson, Lou, 514 S. Jackson St., Gardner, IL, 60424

Pienaar, Conrad, 19A Milner Rd., Bloemfontein 9300, SOUTH AFRICA, Phone: 027 514364180 fax: 027 514364180

Poag, James H., RR #1 Box 212A, Grayville, IL, 62844

Polk, Trena, 4625 Webber Creek Rd., Van Buren, AR, 72956

Pulisova, Andrea, CSA 230-95, 96701 Kremnica, Slovakia, Phone: 00421 903-340076 vpulis@gmail.com, www.vpulis.host.sk

Purvis, Hilton, P.O. Box 371, Noordhoek, 7979, SOUTH AFRICA, 27 21 789 1114, hiltonp@telkomsa.net, http://capeknifemakersguild.com/?page_id=416

Ramsey, Richard, 8525 Trout Farm Rd, Neosho, MO, 64850

Ristinen, Lori, 14256 County Hwy 45, Menahga, MN, 56464, 218-538-6608, lori@loriristinen.com, www.loriristinen.com

Roberts, J.J., 7808 Lake Dr., Manassas, VA, 22111, 703-330-0448, jjrengraver@aol.com, www.angelfire.com/va2/engraver

Rudolph, Gil, 20922 Oak Pass Ave, Tehachapi, CA, 93561, 661-822-4949

Rundell, Joe, 6198 W. Frances Rd., Clio, MI, 48420

Satre, Robert, 518 3rd Ave. NW, Weyburn SK CANADA, S4H 1R1

Schlott, Harald, Zingster Str. 26, 13051 Berlin, +49 030 929 33 46, GERMANY, harald.schlott@web.de, www.gravur-kunst-atelier.de

Schulenburg, E.W., 25 North Hill St., Carrollton, GA, 30117

Schwallie, Patricia, 4614 Old Spartanburg Rd. Apt. 47, Taylors, SC, 29687

Selent, Chuck, P.O. Box 1207, Bonners Ferry, ID, 83805

Semich, Alice, 10037 Roanoke Dr., Murfreesboro, TN, 37129

Shostle, Ben, 1121 Burlington, Muncie, IN, 47302

Smith, Peggy, 676 Glades Rd., #3, Gatlinburg, TN, 37738

Smith, Ron, 5869 Straley, Ft. Worth, TX, 76114

Steigerwalt, Jim, RD#3, Sunbury, PA, 17801

Stuart, Stephen, 15815 Acorn Circle, Tavares, FL, 32778, 352-343-8423, (352) 343-8916, inkscratch@aol.com

Talley, Mary Austin, 2499 Countrywood Parkway, Memphis, TN, 38016, matalley@midsouth.rr.com

Thompson, Larry D., 23040 Ave. 197, Strathmore, CA, 93267

Toniutti, Nelida, Via G. Pascoli, 33085 Maniago-PN, ITALY

Trout, Lauria Lovestrand, 1136 19th St. SW, Vero Beach, FL 32962, 772-778-0282, lovestranded@aol.com

Tucker, Steve, 3518 W. Linwood, Turlock, CA, 95380

Tyser, Ross, 1015 Hardee Court, Spartanburg, SC, 29303

Velasquez, Gil, Art of Scrimshaw, 7120 Madera Dr., Goleta, CA, 93117

Williams, Gary, PO Box 210, Glendale, KY, 42740, 270-369-6752, scrimbygarbo@gmail.com, scrimbygarbo.com

Winn, Travis A., 558 E. 3065 S., Salt Lake City, UT 84106, 801-467-5957

Young, Mary, 4826 Storeyland Dr., Alton, IL, 62002

organizations

AMERICAN BLADESMITH SOCIETY

c/o Office Manager, Cindy Sheely; P. O. Box 160, Grand Rapids, Ohio 43522; cindy@americanbladesmith.com; (419) 832-0400; Web: www.americanbladesmith.com

AMERICAN KNIFE & TOOL INSTITUTE

Jan Billeb, Comm. Coordinator, AKTI, 22 Vista View Ln., Cody, WY 82414; 307-587-8296, akti@akti.org; www. akti.org

AMERICAN KNIFE THROWERS ALLIANCE

c/o Bobby Branton; POB 807; Awendaw, SC 29429; akta@ akta-usa.com, www.AKTA-USA.com

ARIZONA KNIFE COLLECTOR'S ASSOCIATION

c/o Mike Mooney, President, 19432 E. Cloud Rd., Quen Creek, AZ 85142; Phone: 480-244-7768, mike@moonblades. com, Web: www.arizonaknifecollectors.org

ART KNIFE COLLECTOR'S ASSOCIATION

c/o Mitch Weiss, Pres.; 2211 Lee Road, Suite 104; Winter Park, FL 32789

BAY AREA KNIFE COLLECTOR'S ASSOCIATION

c/o Larry Hirsch, 5339 Prospect Rd. #129, San Jose, CA 95129, bladeplay@earthlink.net, Web: www.bakcainc.org

ARKANSAS KNIFEMAKERS ASSOCIATION

David Etchieson, 60 Wendy Cove, Conway, AR 72032; Phone: 501-554-2582, arknifeassn@yahoo.com, Web: www. arkansasknifemakers.com

AUSTRALASIAN KNIFE COLLECTORS

PO BOX 149 CHIDLOW 6556 WESTERN AUSTRALIA TEL: (08) 9572 7255; FAX: (08) 9572 7266. International Inquiries: TEL: + 61 8 9572 7255; FAX: + 61 8 9572 7266, akc@knivesaustralia.com.au, www.knivesaustralia.com.au

CALIFORNIA KNIFEMAKERS ASSOCIATION

c/o Clint Breshears, Membership Chairman; 1261 Keats St; Manhattan Beach CA 90266; 310-372-0739; breshears1@ verizon.net
Dedicated to teaching and improving knifemaking

CANADIAN KNIFEMAKERS GUILD

c/o Wolfgang Loerchner; PO Box 255, Bayfield, Ont., CANADA N0M 1G0; 519-565-2196; info@canadianknifemakersguild.com, www. canadianknifemakersguild.com

CUSTOM KNIFE COLLECTORS ASSOCIATION

c/o Kevin Jones, PO Box 5893, Glen Allen, VA 23058-5893; E-mail: customknifecollectorsassociation@yahoo.com; Web: www.customknifecollectorsassociation.com
The purpose of the CKCA is to recognize and promote the artistic significance of handmade knives, to advnace their collection and conservation, and to support the creative expression of those who make them. Open to collectors, makers purveyors, and other collectors. Has members from eight countries. Produced a caledndar which features custom knives either owned or made by CKCA members.

CUTTING EDGE, THE

2900 S. 26th St., Rogers, AR 72758; 479-631-0130; 800-255-9034; ce_info@cuttingedge.com, www.cuttingedge.com
After-market knives since 1968. We offer about 1,000 individual knives each month. The oldest and the most experienced in the business of buying and selling knives. We buy collections of any size, take knives on consignment or we will trade. Web: www.cuttingedge.com

FLORIDA KNIFEMAKERS ASSOCIATION

c/o President John H. Davis, (209) 740-7125; johndavis@ custom-knifemaker.com, floridaknifemakers@gmail.com, Web: www.floridaknifemakers.org

JAPANESE SWORD SOCIETY OF THE U.S.

PO Box 712; Breckenridge, TX 76424, barry@hennick.ca, www.jssus.org

KNIFE COLLECTORS CLUB INC, THE

2900 S. 26th St, Rogers, AR 72758; 479-631-0130; 800-255-9034; ag@agrussell.com; Web: www.agrussell.com/kcc-one-year-membership-usa-/p/KCC/

The oldest and largest association of knife collectors. Issues limited edition knives, both handmade and highest quality production, in very limited numbers. The very earliest was the CM-1, Kentucky Rifle

KNIFEMAKERS' GUILD, THE

c/o Gene Baskett, Knifemakers Guild, 427 Sutzer Creek Rd., La Grange, KY 42732; 270-862-5019; Web: www.knifemakersguild.com

KNIFEMAKERS GUILD OF SOUTHERN AFRICA, THE

c/o Andre Thorburn; PO Box 1748; Bela Bela, Warmbaths, LP, SOUTH AFRICA 0480; +27 82 650 1441 andrethorburn@gmail.com; Web: www.kgsa.co.za

MONTANA KNIFEMAKERS' ASSOCIATION, THE

1439 S. 5th W, Missoula, MT 59801; 406-728-2861; macnancymclaughlin@yahoo.com, Web: www.montanaknifemakers.com

Annual book of custom knife makers' works and directory of knife making supplies; $19.99

NATIONAL KNIFE COLLECTORS ASSOCIATION

PO Box 21070; Chattanooga, TN 37424, 423-667-8199; nkcalisa@hotmail.com; Web: www.nkcalisa.wix.com/nkca-website-2

NEO-TRIBAL METALSMITHS

5920 W. Windy Lou Ln., Tucson, AZ 85742; Phone: 520-744-9777, taigoo@msn.com, Web: www.neo-tribalmetalsmiths.com

NEW ENGLAND CUSTOM KNIFE ASSOCIATION

Vickie Gray, Treasurer, 686 Main Rd, Brownville, ME 04414; Phone: 207-965-2191, Web: www.necka.net

NORTH CAROLINA CUSTOM KNIFEMAKERS GUILD

c/o Tim Scholl, President, 1389 Langdon Rd., Angier, NC 27501, 910-897-2051, tschollknives@live.com, Web: www.ncknifeguild.org

NORTH STAR BLADE COLLECTORS

PO Box 20523, Bloomington, MN 55420; info@nsbc.us, Web: www.nsbc.us

OHIO KNIFEMAKERS ASSOCIATION

c/o Jerry Smith, Anvils and Ink Studios, P.O. Box 151, Barnesville, Ohio 43713; jerry_smith@anvilsandinkstudios.com, Web: www.oocities.org/ohioknives/

OREGON KNIFE COLLECTORS ASSOCIATION

Web: www.oregonknifeclub.org

ROCKY MOUNTAIN BLADE COLLECTORS ASSOCIATION

Mike Moss. Pres., P.O. Box 324, Westminster, CO 80036; rmbladecollectors@gmail.com, Web: www.rmbladecollectors.org

SOUTH CAROLINA ASSOCIATION OF KNIFEMAKERS

c/o Col. Tom Kreger, President, (803) 438-4221; tdkreger@bellsouth.net, Web: www.southcarolinaassociationofknifemakers.org

SOUTHERN CALIFORNIA BLADES KNIFE COLLECTORS CLUB

SC Blades, PO Box 231112, Encinitas, CA 92023-1112; Phone: 619-417-4329, scblades@att.net, Web: www.scblades.org

THE WILLIAM F. MORAN JR. MUSEUM & FOUNDATION

4204 Ballenger Creek Pike, Frederick, MD 21703, info@billmoranmuseum.com, www.williammoranmuseum.com

publications

AUTOMATIC KNIFE RESOURCE

c/o Lantama Cutlery, POB 721, Montauk, NY 11954; 631-668-5995; info@latama.net, Web: www.thenewsletter.com,

Unique compilation and archive for the switchblade/automatic knife fan. Sheldon Levy's Newsletter was first published in 1992, and was a labor of love from its inception and has remained informative and insightful.

BLADE AND BLADE'S COMPLETE KNIFE GUIDE

700 E. State St., Iola, WI 54990-0001; 715-445-4612; Web: www.blademag.com, www.KnifeForums.com, www.ShopBlade.com, facebook.com/blademag

The world's No. 1 knife magazine. The most indepth knife magazine on the market, covering all aspects of the industry, from knifemaking to production knives and handmade pieces. With 13 issues per year, BLADE® boasts twice the distribution of its closest competitor.

CUTLERY NEWS JOURNAL (BLOG)

http://cutlerynewsjournal.wordpress.com

Covers significant happenings from the world of knife collecting, in addition to editorials, trends, events, auctions, shows, cutlery history, and reviews

KNIFE WORLD

PO Box 3395, Knoxville, TN 37927; Phone: 865-397-1955, knifepub@knifeworld.com, www.knifeworld.com

Since 1977, a monthly knife publication covering all types of knives

KNIVES ILLUSTRATED

22840 Savi Ranch Pkwy. #200, Yorba Linda, CA 92887; Phone: 714-200-1963; bmiller@engagedmediainc.com; Web: www.knivesillustrated.com

All encompassing publication focusing on factory knives, new handmades, shows and industry news

THE LEATHER CRAFTERS & SADDLERS JOURNAL

222 Blackburn St., Rhinelander, WI 54501; Phone: 715-362-5393; info@leathercraftersjournal.com, Web: www.leathercraftersjournal.com

Bi-monthly how-to leathercraft magazine